The Rise of Conservation in South Africa

The Rise of Conservation in South Africa

Settlers, Livestock, and the Environment
1770–1950

WILLIAM BEINART

OXFORD
UNIVERSITY PRESS

OXFORD
UNIVERSITY PRESS

Great Clarendon Street, Oxford OX2 6DP

Oxford University Press is a department of the University of Oxford.
It furthers the University's objective of excellence in research, scholarship,
and education by publishing worldwide in

Oxford New York

Auckland Bangkok Buenos Aires Cape Town Chennai
Dar es Salaam Delhi Hong Kong Istanbul Karachi Kolkata
Kuala Lumpur Madrid Melbourne Mexico City Mumbai Nairobi
São Paulo Shanghai Taipei Tokyo Toronto

Oxford is a registered trade mark of Oxford University Press
in the UK and in certain other countries

Published in the United States
by Oxford University Press Inc., New York

First published 2003

First published in paperback 2008

British Library Cataloguing in Publication Data
Data available

Library of Congress Cataloging in Publication Data
Data available
ISBN 978-0-19-926151-2 (Hbk.)   978-0-19-954122-5 (Pbk.)

10 9 8 7 6 5 4 3 2 1

Typeset by Laserwords Private Limited, Chennai, India.
Printed in Great Britain
on acid-free paper by
CPI Antony Rowe, Chippenham, Wiltshire

CONTENTS

LIST OF ILLUSTRATIONS

LIST OF MAPS

LIST OF FIGURES

LIST OF TABLES

PREFACE AND
ACKNOWLEDGEMENTS

Historians must inhabit their imaginations, especially when they write about places in which they no longer live. Distance, in space as well as time, sharpens the sense of landscape. While writing, mostly in an Oxford terraced house, my mind was constantly transposed back to the rural expanses of the Karoo and eastern Cape. My memory of this landscape often works on predictable lines: its stillness; its space; the heady smell of distant rain; roads and fences stretching to the horizon; mountains rearing up from the veld; bleating sheep; pronking springboks; clanking windmills; unlikely Victorian farm-steads with corrugated roofs and wraparound verandahs (stoeps); white-washed thatched homesteads on hilltops with free-range chickens; and earnest conversation about sheep and cattle, veld, and ancestors. Poring over maps took me back to places that I had visited too briefly, and to walks through the veld, in the hopeless quest of learning to distinguish between Karoo bushes or grass types. Romantic images jostle with an acute sense of the harshness of this environment: the shock of eroded dongas; the poverty of farm-workers and African villages; the dryness. Yet in my memory, it is sometimes unbearably attractive.

This book focuses largely on the livestock farming districts of the semi-arid Karoo, or midland Cape, and the eastern Cape grasslands. In pre-colonial times, the midlands were settled by Khoisan peoples who survived by transhumant pastoralism and by hunting and gathering. Population densities were low and political units small. African societies, which had developed more intensive agrarian systems, occupied the wetter eastern districts where rainfall exceeded 500 mm. They were organized into a number of major chiefdoms, the Xhosa, Thembu, Mpondo, and others.

Dutch settler conquest of the midlands was largely complete by 1806, when the British took control of the Cape, and most of the Khoisan popula-tion had been displaced as independent landholders. Africans proved more difficult to dislodge. Their political and demographic weight underpinned a long military resistance through the nineteenth century. Boer and British settlers were eventually able to secure a major portion of Xhosa territory, west of the Kei river, and the margins of Thembuland, around what became Queenstown. But Africans retained substantial settlements, which later became the basis for reserved land in the Transkei and Ciskei.

Settlers also found that the midlands were too dry for large-scale crop production. Together with some wetter districts to their east, the area became
the site of an increasingly intensive commercial pastoral economy in which
sheep took pride of place. For much of the period from about 1830 to 1950,
pastoral production and wool exports were a major motor of the Cape's economy. Cattle remained essential for domestic use, transport, and internal
markets.

Livestock farming was largely dependent on the natural pastures, called
veld both in Afrikaans and English. Surprisingly soon, almost at the outset of
commercial pastoral expansion, some farmers and officials perceived that
livestock were beginning to degrade the veld and erode the soil. In the early
decades of the twentieth century such concerns reached a crescendo and
formed the basis for far-reaching state intervention aimed at conserving natural resources and regulating this part of the South African environment. Soil
erosion, overstocking, pastures, and water supplies stood alongside wildlife
protection as the central preoccupations of South African conservationists.

A major theme of this book is the history of conservationist ideas. It traces
debates about environmental degradation in successive eras of South African
history. Some of the ideas discussed here are similar to those that have been
investigated by historians in their search to understand the origins of modern
Western environmentalism.[1] Those who worked at the Cape were influenced
by these global developments, and new concepts of nature framed their concerns. However, we know that experiences at the peripheries of empire made
considerable impact on the evolution of Western conservationism and, in this
sense, the Cape was a significant small stream in a wider current of thought.[2]
Cape society generated its own vernacular understandings, partly from
indigenous people, and its own local anxieties, as farmers and officials struggled to come to terms with the difficult terrain. The comparative framework

---

[1] Clarence Glacken, *Traces on the Rhodian Shore: Nature and Culture in Western Thought from
Ancient Times to the End of the Eighteenth Century* (University of California Press, Berkeley, 1967);
Roderick Nash, *Wilderness and the American Mind* (Yale University Press, New Haven, 1973);
Donald Worster, *Nature's Economy: A History of Ecological Ideas*, 2nd edn. (Cambridge University
Press, New York, 1994; first published 1977); Max Oelschlager, *The Idea of Wilderness: From Pre-
history to the Age of Ecology* (Yale University Press, New Haven, 1991); Peter Coates, *Nature:
Western Attitudes Since Ancient Times* (Polity Press, Cambridge, 1998).

[2] Richard Grove, *Green Imperialism: Colonial Expansion, Tropical Island Edens and the Origins of
Environmentalism, 1600–1860* (Cambridge University Press, Cambridge, 1995); Tom Griffiths
and Libby Robin (eds.), *Ecology and Empire: Environmental History of Settler Societies* (Keele Univer-
sity Press, Edinburgh, 1997); Thomas R. Dunlap, *Nature and the English Diaspora: Environment and
History in the United States, Canada, Australia, and New Zealand* (Cambridge University Press,
Cambridge, 1999).

is important, but my narrative necessarily navigates, and is sometimes washed up in, these local backwaters.

At another level, this is a collective biography, highlighting individuals —little-known in the historiography—who made key contributions to the understanding of environmental change in the country. Inevitably, the history of science at the Cape looms large in the discussion. Many of those who pursued conservationist ideas were influenced by new scientific perceptions in fields such as botany, geology, forestry, veterinary science, zoology, and water management. My argument is that the development of these and related fields constitute a major but neglected element in the history of knowledge and intellectual life in South Africa.

At the same time, and more hesitantly, this book is intended as a contribution to the analysis of environmental change. While ecological relationships are viewed through the eyes and understandings of particular historical actors, their observations were often sharp. They allow us, perhaps, to say something about the transformations that they were witnessing. Moreover, my aim in some chapters is to write an environmental history that is more than a history of ideas, and in which natural forces are more than just a backdrop to human history. The environmental constraints imposed by the Karoo, its climate, its vegetation, and its indigenous fauna were real enough to those who lived and farmed there. Animals such as jackals and plants such as prickly pear became, in a sense, historical actors.

In examining ideas and policies at the Cape, this book also has something to say about agrarian history. It seems to me essential that an analysis of conservationist concerns—at least of the kind explored here—should be rooted in some discussion of the rural political economy. Agricultural production, environmental understanding, and the attempts to conserve natural resources were intimately linked. Officials and leading farmers were centrally concerned with efficient use of natural resources, in order to assure the future of agriculture. In dealing with these aspects of agricultural policy and environmental regulation, I hope to address neglected features of the Cape and Union states, and also to suggest that historians have not yet come to terms with the character and activities of the Department of Agriculture.

Lastly, I should say something about the unit of study. My main focus is on the area controlled by the Cape government. This gradually expanded in the nineteenth century, as African chiefdoms were annexed, reaching its fullest extent in 1894. Initially ruled by a British Governor, the colony, as in the case of others dominated politically by settlers, achieved a significant degree of self-government: a representative parliament in 1854; and its own responsible ministry after 1872, with a local executive and prime minister. The vote was granted on a non-racial basis to men only, but educational and property qualifications ensured that white, male settlers retained political power. From the late nineteenth century, the parliament increasingly intensified segregation on racial lines. In 1910 the Cape joined the Union of South Africa as a province.

Livestock farming was, of course, not restricted to the Cape. Especially after Union, it is impossible to analyse conservationist thinking and agricultural policy within an exclusively provincial context. The discussion sometimes ranges more broadly in order to follow particular individuals and themes. Concurrently, I have tried to weave in a local history in order to help provide texture and detail. Running through the book are references to Wellwood farm, about 20 kilometres north of Graaff-Reinet town, in an area that was close to the heart of sheep farming. The farm, owned from 1838 to the present by the Rubidge family, was not necessarily typical. But it is of interest as one of the leading merino sheep studs, as a site of investment, innovation, and experiments in conservation, and because its owners kept an archive.

These are wide-ranging aims, and it may be wise to say more about the provenance of my interest and the limits of the approach. The book has had a long genesis. The bulk of my earlier research work focused on the history of African people in the eastern Cape—and especially on the Transkeian region, which was the largest area reserved for African settlement in the country.[3] When I first attempted sustained interviewing in 1976–7, I found that many rural people, as well as local officials, were keenly debating the battered agricultural economy in general and the betterment or rehabilitation schemes in particular.

Betterment schemes, initiated in 1939, entailed the villagization of scattered African settlements, fencing of communal pastures into camps (large paddocks) that could be rotated, and the separation of arable land from residential and grazing land. They probably constituted the most disruptive intervention into rural life since conquest in the nineteenth century. Although unevenly implemented, they sparked opposition in many rural African communities. The policy was still being pursued in the 1970s amidst considerable resentment. Officials, African as well as white, justified it very largely on the basis of conservationist ideas. Through these measures alone, they believed, could the soil and vegetation of the Transkei be saved. Many

[3] William Beinart, *The Political Economy of Pondoland 1860–1930* (Cambridge University Press, Cambridge, 1982); William Beinart and Colin Bundy, *Hidden Struggles in Rural South Africa* (James Currey, London, 1987).

saw what they had done as a benevolent intervention, which would help to secure the basis for African agriculture in the long term.

In the early 1980s I wrote more generally about the origins of the ideas underpinning such state intervention.[4] This book grows directly from three of the central themes laid out there: that the approach evolved in the betterment programmes originated in the regulation of white farmers rather than of Africans; that conservationism had deep roots in southern Africa; and that conservation was designed, in the minds of its protagonists, not to curtail agricultural production but to ensure its viability and efficiency. There seemed to be a good deal of similarity between the conservationist ideas pursued in the United States in the early twentieth-century Progressive era and those in South Africa.

In delving further (although irregularly) into an archaeology of these ideas, my research was taken in new directions. I started out trying to understand interventions into African life, but my analysis here returns to this issue only tangentially, in a penultimate chapter. An enquiry into the origins of betterment has turned partly into an environmental history of the Karoo. The first staging post was a recognition of the influence of South Africa's Drought Investigation Commission (1920–3), appointed to examine why drought losses were becoming so serious.[5] It concentrated on white-owned sheep farms and painted a dire picture of eroding pastures and desert conditions in the making. From there, I followed the commissioners' preoccupation with the influence of predators or vermin (especially jackals) on the Cape's pastoral economy.[6] In their view, jackals caused degradation because they forced farmers to kraal their sheep nightly—which was deeply injurious to the veld. It was a short step to recognize that the jackal problem was being conceptualized within the context of wide-ranging prescriptions for conservationist farming and the improvement of the settler pastoral economy.

So much for the provenance of the book. As to its limitations, it must be said at the outset that it deals very largely with the ideas and actions of officials, together with white, largely English-speaking men, who were

---

[4] William Beinart, 'Soil Erosion, Conservationism and Ideas About Development: A Southern African Exploration', *Journal of Southern African Studies* (*JSAS*), 11 (1984) and 'Agricultural Planning and the Late Colonial Technical Imagination: The Lower Shire Valley in Malawi, 1945–1960', in J. McCracken (ed.), *Malawi: An Alternative Pattern of Development* (Centre for African Studies, University of Edinburgh, 1985).

[5] Union of South Africa, *Final Report of the Drought Investigation Commission*, U.G.49-1923.

[6] William Beinart, 'The Night of the Jackal: Sheep, Pastures and Predators at the Cape', *Past and Present*, 158 (1998), 172–206, first given as a paper at the School of Oriental and African Studies, London, and the University of Cape Town in 1991–2 and published in the *Revue Français d'Histoire d'Outre-mer*, 80: 298 (1993), 105–29.

self-consciously progressive, wealthier farmers or landowning politicians. My justification for this focus is, firstly, that the conservationist approaches central to the book emanated—at least in their more articulated, evolved, and written forms—largely from the anglophone elite. Secondly, while historians have written a great deal about this group's racial attitudes and economic dominance, other aspects of their thinking have been neglected. Thirdly, it is important to understand the ideas of this section of the Cape's ruling class precisely because of their power. They had a disproportionate impact on policy. And the conservationist concerns that some of them espoused were of considerable significance to other communities.

The cost of my approach is the very limited coverage of other social groups and themes that would properly become part of a full and rounded history of the Cape's pastoral economy and society. Although white women did write about the Cape and participated in the formation of ideas about landscape and environment, very few were able to become landowners, politicians, officials, or scientists.[7] Afrikaners are introduced, especially where they were self-defined progressives, and a chapter is devoted to one Afrikaner official. Resistance by some rural Afrikaners to environmental and disease regulation provides a backdrop to this history. But Afrikaans-speakers, a majority of landowners, are somewhat relegated in the narrative. Even more so, black workers on the farms and the African peasantry in the reserves have only a shadowy presence in the book. While Khoisan and African indigenous ideas weave themselves into the earlier chapters, and some reference is made to important developments in African environmental ideas in Chapter 10, my major theme is the rise of conservationist and scientific approaches amongst the white ruling group.

It is my hope that the discussion will nevertheless be of interest to a range of different audiences. To historians of South Africa, and especially historians of the countryside who have written so vividly about agrarian change, this book may be a reminder that we have underestimated the significance of the pastoral economy and society of the Cape. The Karoo was not simply an arid wasteland, to be viewed listlessly from railway windows, or conjured in exile reminiscences as the quintessence of an untouched South African landscape. It was not an underdeveloped backwater, once minerals were discovered. On the contrary, the semi-arid Cape was a crossroads for new species, new agricultural techniques, and new ideas. More capital was probably invested into

---

[7] Michelle Adler, 'Skirting the Edges of Civilization: British Women Travellers and Travel Writers in South Africa, 1797–1899', unpublished Ph.D thesis, University of London (1995); W. Beinart, 'Men, Science, Travel and Nature in the Eighteenth and Nineteenth Century Cape', *Journal of Southern African Studies*, 24 (1998), 775–99; Alan Cohen, 'Mary Elizabeth Barber: South Africa's First Lady Natural Historian', *Archives of Natural History*, 27 (2000), 187–208.

the pastoral farms of the Karoo and eastern Cape than in the diamond mines of Kimberley. The Cape landowners were of significance in shaping not only their own world, but the character of the Cape state as a whole.

To environmental historians, who have launched an exciting new subdiscipline over the last few decades, this exploration may be of comparative interest. Many of the conservationist ideas and scientific interests that were of such importance at the Cape had evolved elsewhere—in Britain, the United States, India, and the settler Commonwealth. The book is also addressed to those in development studies, and to students of environmental ideas in contemporary Africa, who have the patience to read about a world that may initially appear rather distant and foreign to them. The Cape was probably the first colonial state in Africa to develop a sophisticated bureaucracy, with an overarching modernist agenda, and to elaborate many of the functions that became familiar in Africa during the colonial period. The approaches and policies pursued were transferred to neighbouring southern African colonial states and to some extent further afield. Conflicts over developmentalist, conservationist patterns of intervention, so evident during the late colonial period in African countries, were a feature of Cape and later Union politics, amongst both white and black communities.

Much of the recent literature on conservationist interventions in Africa has been critical of the limitations of science, and the clumsiness or incompetence of the state.[8] The Cape experience may open the way for a rather different perspective. The degree of environmental regulation was probably greater, and my argument suggests that it was based on increasingly sophisticated understanding of the local environment. While many rural Afrikaners were initially deeply suspicious of experts and state intervention, significant elements of the settler population were in the vanguard of lobbies for scientific agriculture and conservation. Nor did all Africans oppose environmental and disease regulation at the time.

Those with non-academic interests in South Africa may also enjoy parts of this narrative, precisely because the subject matter is lodged in many families' memories, and touched upon in novels and popular literature. Environmental history facilitates an exploration of the interconnections between nature, people, and animals that are of increasing public interest. Nor should such a focus be construed simply as an imposition of late twentieth-century environmental and academic preoccupations on an earlier era. Environmental problems of the kind described in this book were deeply familiar to rural South African people of all backgrounds at the time.

[8] For a review, W. Beinart, 'African History and Environmental History', *African Affairs*, 99 (2000), 269–302.

Thanks are due to a number of institutions for funding. The British Academy and the University of Bristol assisted with an initial research trip in the late 1980s. My knowledge of the farmlands was greatly enhanced when working on land reform in projects funded by the British Overseas Development Administration and Economic and Social Research Council (1993), and by the Border Rural Committee, East London, South Africa (1994–5). Research momentum was achieved through a British Academy/Leverhulme Trust Senior Research Fellowship (1995–6) and leave from Bristol; this time off was essential and I greatly appreciate the assistance given. A grant from the Nuffield Foundation (2000–1) extended my research on prickly pear. And my current employers, the University of Oxford, funded a final research trip.

The librarians at the Library of Commonwealth and African Studies at Rhodes House, Oxford, have been especially helpful, as have the archivists at the South African government depots in Pretoria, Cape Town, and Umtata. The Rubidge family, Wellwood, Graaff-Reinet, and General H. de V. du Toit, Pretoria, were particularly generous in allowing extended access to their family papers. Other collections are mentioned in the footnotes; thanks to their archivists or keepers, particularly at Kew. Through the years, I have interviewed in a number of districts, in the Karoo, eastern Free State, and in the former Transkei and Ciskei. I am very grateful to the many people have taken time to talk to me, and who have offered hospitality. I have in the end made little direct use of this oral material here, but it has contributed in many ways to my understanding and analysis.

One of the pleasures of working on South African history is the opportunity it has given me for encounters with a wide range of engaged academics, practitioners, and postgraduates. I cannot name them all, but for discussion and debate, which has fed into the book somewhere, or help with materials, thanks to Sean Archer, Karen Brown, Jeff Butler, Jane Carruthers, Peter Coates, Peter Delius, Saul Dubow, Dan Gilfoyle, Richard Grove, Timm Hoffman, Mike Kenyon, Rosalie Kingwill, Vimbai Kwashirai, Deborah Lavin, Shula Marks, JoAnn McGregor, Karen Middleton, Colin Murray, Dawn Nell, Lungisile Ntsebeza, Ravi Rajan, Terence Ranger, Robert Ross, Paul Sephton, Kate Showers, Mottie Tamarkin, Helen Tilley, Lance van Sittert, Gavin Williams, Luvuyo Wotshela. Rebekah Lee worked with skill and patience on the Figures. For every kind of support and help, I am deeply grateful to Troth Wells.

William Beinart

St Antony's College
University of Oxford
2002

NOTE ON MEASUREMENTS

The old measurements for areas of land have largely been retained in the text because they reflect the sources and are often given in round figures; 6,000 morgen (the old Dutch measurement), or 50 acres (the British unit which was used alongside it), would look strange, translated exactly into hectares: 1 morgen = 2.1 acres; 1 hectare = 1.2 morgen = 2.5 acres

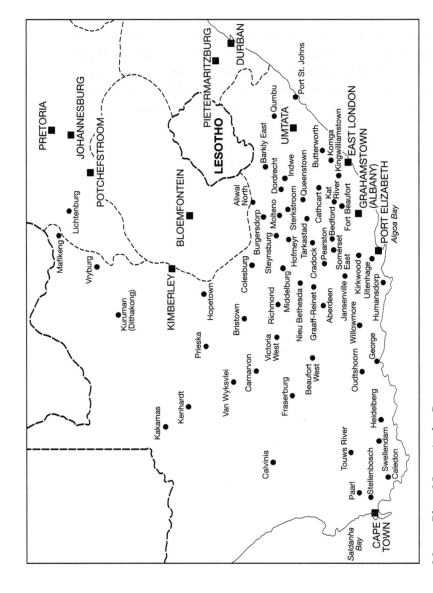

MAP 1. Place-Names in the Cape

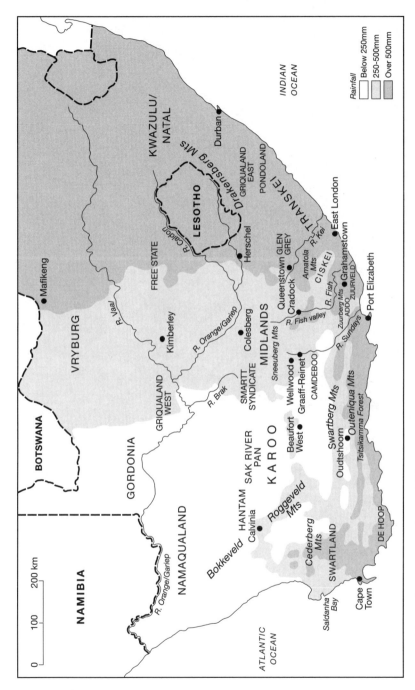

MAP 2. Natural Features, and Rainfall Zones

Livestock Farming and Environmental Regulation at the Cape

Livestock, Conquest, and Environment

The expansion of European economic and political power, as well as settlement, has been one of the overwhelmingly important features of world history over the last 500 years. To speak of the rise of an increasingly interconnected global capitalist system over this long period, however, begs as many questions as it answers. Succeeding phases of European economic growth prompted strikingly different imperatives for expansion, for natural-resource exploitation, and for the social organization of extra-European production. In the eighteenth century, for example, sugar, African slaves, and shipping in the Atlantic world provided one major dynamic of empire. But in the nineteenth century antipodean settlement and trade, especially that resulting from expanding settler pastoral frontiers, was responsible for some of the most dramatic social and environmental transformations.

In pursuit of an understanding of these global interconnections, historians working within the anglophone world have perhaps focused most systematically on Atlantic societies, the slave trade, and the plantation, which also provided key resources for British industrialization. As the formal colonial empires finally crumbled, a compelling theme in the historiography has been a critique of these exploitative systems. The moral as well as economic issues involved in understanding and exposing the history of slavery have correctly been seen as a central historical problem in a decolonizing era.

Plantations concentrated capital, and large numbers of people, in profoundly hierarchical institutions in relatively small areas on tropical islands and littorals. They occupied relatively little space in the new social geography of world production. By contrast, commercial pastoralism, which took root most energetically in the temperate and semi-arid regions of the newly conquered world, was land-hungry but relatively light in its demands for labour. The Spanish empire based in Mexico can be considered a forerunner, followed by settler intrusions in the vast land-masses of southern Latin America, southern Africa, Australasia, and North America.[1]

Meat, especially from cattle, was one early priority to supply shipping routes, or rapidly growing urban centres. Bovine accumulation, dairy production, and internal markets remained the major stimulus to commercial stock rearing in North America.[2] But for well over a century, from the 1830s to the 1930s and beyond, sheep flooded the southern lands. Although mutton (or lamb) became a significant export from New Zealand and South America, wool was probably the key product of these pastoral hinterlands—and certainly the major focus of production in Australia and South Africa.

The growth in antipodean sheep numbers was enormous. From very few at the turn of the nineteenth century, the sheep population of Argentina, Uruguay, South Africa, Australia, and New Zealand reached about 250 million in the 1930s; north America housed about 60 million more.[3] It is true that the total in the Eurasian land-mass was even higher, at about 350 million, but these were old zones of sheep farming. And whereas there were probably about five people to a sheep in Eurasia in the 1930s, and two to a sheep in central/north America, there were perhaps six or seven sheep to a person in the five southern countries. In the Cape, the proportion of livestock to people was even higher.

Wool was a truly colonial commodity: the bulk of Australian and South African produce was exported to Britain and Europe. Although it had long been manufactured, industrial production of woollen yarn enabled far larger quantities of cloth and clothes to be produced. As in the case of other colonial products, including sugar, cocoa, cotton, beaver skins, palm oil, and cod, wool consumption in the nineteenth century was intimately linked to changing consumer tastes.[4] To some degree, wool from farmed sheep replaced furs

[1] Elinor G. K. Mellville, *A Plague of Sheep: Environmental Consequences of the Conquest of Mexico* (New York: Cambridge University Press, 1994). Slaves were used in Mexican wool farming in the sixteenth and seventeenth centuries.

[2] William Cronon, *Nature's Metropolis: Chicago and the Great West* (W. W. Norton, New York, 1991).

[3] Rough numbers, drawn from B. R. Mitchell, *International Historical Statistics*, and Union of South Africa, *Yearbooks*, which often compared South Africa sheep numbers with other countries. M. L. Ryder, *Sheep and Man* (Duckworth, London, 1983).

[4] Sidney W. Mintz, *Sweetness and Power: The Place of Sugar in Modern History* (Penguin, Harmondsworth, 1985); W. G. Clarence-Smith, *Cocoa and Chocolate, 1765–1914* (Routledge, London, 2000); Mark Kurlansky, *Cod: A Biography of the Fish that Changed the World* (Jonathan Cape, London, 1998); Martin Lynn, *Commerce and Economic Change in West Africa: The Palm Oil Trade in the Nineteenth Century* (Cambridge University Press, Cambridge, 1998); Harald A. Innis, *The Fur Trade in Canada: An Introduction to Canadian Economic History* (Yale University Press, New Haven, 1930).

from less renewable wild animals. Growing populations and rising incomes in Europe enabled a greater number of people to purchase a wider range of garments—effectively a wardrobe. Military demand was important. Improved woollen materials could be used for 'a vast variety of new descriptions of goods, light, beautiful, cheap, and adapted both for dress and furniture'.[5]

From the late eighteenth century British wool was increasingly considered too coarse for garments.[6] It was gradually displaced by longer, finer wool from merino sheep, procured first from Spain, the home of that breed. When Spanish production and export was disrupted by the Napoleonic wars, Saxony, where the merino had been introduced in 1765, supplanted it in British markets. Joseph Banks, botanist, farmer, and President of the Royal Society, supervised an experimental merino flock in Britain—without longer-term success.[7] By 1830 26 million pounds of wool, out of the total of around 30 million imported, came from Germany. Within a few decades, by 1860, Germany had in turn been displaced by rocketing colonial production. Wool imports trebled to about 90 million pounds and had crept up to half of British domestic production. By the 1930s British wool output had slipped to about 120 million pounds whereas Australia and South Africa, the two biggest merino wool producers, accounted for nearly ten times that amount. Wool manufacturers were increasingly concentrated in Yorkshire, which had the advantages of specialization, skilled workers, plentiful good water, cheap coal, and easy access to ports. They were now supplying a global market; South Africa became a major importer of British blankets in the nineteenth century.

The mills of Bradford spun their links extraordinarily wide, helping to bind the southern hemisphere to the north. Just as they pulled in tens of thousands of mill-workers, so they also created the opportunity for hundreds of thousands of British people to manage the sheep in far-flung conquered lands. Indigenous communities did sometimes adapt to the new sheep, where they could retain sufficient land to do so: the Navaho in the United States and the Xhosa and Sotho in South Africa are cases in point.[8] In southern Africa alone, of all the southern zones mentioned, there had been a well-developed pre-colonial pastoral economy, although the sheep then in the hands of the Khoikhoi and Africans were fat-tailed varieties with hair rather than wool.

[5] Edward Baines, 'On the Woollen Manufacture of England, with special reference to Leeds Clothing District', *Report of the Proceedings of the British Association for the Advancement of Science, Transactions of the Sections* (1858), 159.

[6] D. T. Jenkins and K. G. Ponting, *The British Wool Textile Industry 1770–1914* (London, 1982).

[7] Patrick O'Brian, *Joseph Banks: A Life* (Harvill, London, 1987).

[8] Colin Bundy, *The Rise and Fall of the South African Peasantry* (Heinemann, London, 1979).

However, Khoikhoi land was appropriated by the early nineteenth century, not least for settler livestock farming, and Africans were not major participants in merino wool production. Whereas they still held up to half the cattle in the Cape by 1930, the great majority of sheep were accumulated on white-owned farms by Afrikaners and British settlers. The descendants of the Khoikhoi—like the gauchos of South America, who included mestizo Native Americans—became a pastoral working class.

Despite the great richness of the recent agrarian historiography on South Africa, and important comparative works such as Denoon's *Settler Capitalism*, the pastoral economy has been relatively neglected.[9] Agrarian historiography has been deeply influenced by the comparative model of the transition from feudalism to capitalism in Europe; historians have focused on crop production, the maize revolution, and tenancy relationships in the more densely populated arable belts such as the highveld. Similarly, the rich comparative work on slavery has helped to focus attention on the well-watered vineyards and wheat-fields of the western Cape—a distinctive zone, almost a social and environmental island.[10]

The highveld was certainly central to agrarian transformation, and a critical site for struggles between white landowners and black tenants. Yet perhaps 60 per cent of South Africa's surface receives rainfall of less than 500 mm a year and some of the rest is mountainous. These areas have been dominated by livestock. It is intriguing that historians of a country with so small a percentage of arable land, compared to Europe and even the United States, should have neglected its pastoral history, or understood it primarily in terms of the pre-colonial frontier or Afrikaner trekboer experience.[11] Compared to

[9] M. Morris, 'The Development of Capitalism in South African Agriculture', *Economy and Society*, 3 (1976); T. Keegan, *Rural Transformations in Industrialising South Africa: The Southern Highveld to 1914* (Macmillan, London, 1987); Helen Bradford, *A Taste of Freedom* (Yale University Press, New Haven, 1987). W. Beinart, P. Delius, and S. Trapido (eds.), *Putting a Plough to the Ground: Accumulation and Dispossession in Rural South Africa, 1850–1930* (Ravan Press, Johannesburg, 1986) both expands the highveld model and develops a critique, and see Colin Bundy 'Vagabond Hollanders and Runaway Englishmen: White Poverty in the Cape before Poor Whiteism', ibid. 101–28 for the agrarian Cape; J. Crush and A. Jeeves (eds.), *White Farms, Black Labour: The State and Agrarian Change in Southern Africa, 1910–1950* (James Currey, Oxford, 1997). For comparative work, Donald Denoon, *Settler Capitalism* (Oxford University Press, Oxford, 1983).

[10] Nigel Worden, *Slavery in Dutch South Africa* (Cambridge University Press, Cambridge, 1985); R. Elphick and H. Giliomee (eds.), *The Shaping of South Africa, 1652–1820* (Maskew Miller/Longman, Cape Town, 1989); N. Worden and C. Crais (eds.), *Breaking the Chains: Slavery and its Legacy in the Nineteenth Century Cape Colony* (Witwatersrand University Press, Johannesburg, 1994).

[11] This is not to suggest an absence of analysis of the economics of the trekboer frontier, first elaborated in S. D. Neumark, *Economic Influences on the South African Frontier, 1652–1836* (Stanford University Press, Stanford, 1957); Susan Newton-King, *Masters and Servants on the Cape Eastern Frontier* (Cambridge University Press, Cambridge, 1999).

the outpouring of material on mining or other aspects of the agrarian economy, livestock farming has attracted a silence that echoes the stillness of the veld. South Africa's commercial pastoral economy seems to have been dwarfed internationally by Australasia and Argentina, or locally by the behemoths of mining and maize.

Of course, in a pre-mechanical age pastoral and arable production were closely intertwined, but this study concentrates largely on livestock farming, which in areas such as the Karoo was a relatively specialized activity. I will argue that we need to reassess the significance of commercial livestock production and that such an exercise may have important implications for an understanding of Cape society. A comparative framework that draws on the experience of other British settler frontiers of conquest and exploitation, such as Australia and the United States, rather than on Europe, helps to elucidate these elements of the South African past.[12] When I began this research in the 1980s, environmental history perspectives provided me with a route by which to reassess agrarian history in general and the pastoral economy in particular.[13] Recent South African agrarian history has tended to neglect the environmental context, and there are strong arguments for reinserting environmental issues, as well as pastoral farming, closer to the heart of South African history.

Perhaps we can learn something from an earlier generation of historians of the settler dominions who were deeply aware of the interface between nature, commodity extraction, and the construction of nation. Harold Innis argued of Canada that 'it is no mere accident that the present Dominion coincides roughly with the fur-trading areas of northern North America'.[14] Hancock's

[12] For other comparative exercises, Howard Lamar and Leonard Thompson (eds.), *The Frontier in History: North America and Southern Africa Compared* (Yale University Press, New Haven, 1981); William Beinart and Peter Coates, *Environment and History: The Taming of Nature in the USA and South Africa* (Routledge, London, 1995).

[13] Books which helped me in thinking about this research include Alfred Crosby, *Ecological Imperialism: The Biological Expansion of Europe, 900–1900* (Cambridge University Press, New York, 1986); Donald Worster, *Dust Bowl: The Southern Plains in the 1930s* (Cambridge University Press, New York, 1979) and *Rivers of Empire: Water, Aridity and the Growth of the American West* (Pantheon, New York, 1985); Thomas R. Dunlap, *Saving America's Wildlife: Ecology and the American Mind, 1850–1990* (Princeton University Press, Princeton, 1988); Joseph Powell, *Environmental Management in Australia* (Oxford University Press, Melbourne, 1976) and *An Historical Geography of Modern Australia: The Restive Fringe* (Cambridge University Press, Cambridge, 1988); Geoffrey Bolton, *Spoils and Spoilers: A History of Australians Shaping their Environment*, 2nd edn. (Allen & Unwin, Sydney, 1992); Mellville, *A Plague of Sheep*; Cronon, *Nature's Metropolis*; Lisa Mighetto, *Wild Animals and American Environmental Ethics* (University of Arizona Press, Tucson, 1991).

[14] Innis, *The Fur Trade of Canada*, 396.

aphorism, that 'wool made Australia a solvent nation, and, in the end, a free one', is often quoted.[15] He was particularly interested in the spatial, technological, and environmental aspects of pastoral expansion by the 'invaders of Australia': 'their mastery of the continent has followed from their triumphs in pastoral and agricultural technique.'[16]

Even before the emergence of wool production, livestock were of great importance to Cape settler society. As in Mexico, 'the expansion of pastoralism enabled the conquest of the indigenous populations and the domination of vast areas of rural space'.[17] We should be cautious in extending this argument directly to South Africa. Settlers found it difficult to expand their territory beyond that previously occupied by the Khoikhoi: the boundaries of the Cape were partly defined by the demographic and political weight of African kingdoms. Unlike the United States, Canada, Australia, Argentina, Uruguay, and New Zealand, the settler population never predominated numerically. Nevertheless, settlers penetrated deep into the interior on the backs of their livestock in the first two centuries of colonization. In turn, they were funnelled in part by the natural environment. Eric Walker, writing in the 1920s, explored one aspect of this interrelationship: how the 'lie of the land dictated . . . movement', as the Boers travelled up the 'least line of resistance' on routes shaped by the physical relief of the country.[18]

P. J. van der Merwe, who published fascinating histories of the trekboers in the 1930s, interpreted the Boers' Great Trek (1836–8) as in part an extension of incremental pastoral spread. Even though he was an Afrikaner nationalist, keen to stress Boer antipathy to British hegemony and the abolition of slavery, van der Merwe developed the most thoroughgoing environmental explanation of the trek. He explored the dynamics of expansion, the perceived shortage of land, and the severity of droughts and locusts in the eastern and midland Cape, where Boers were concentrating by the 1830s (Chapter 2).[19] The limits of settler expansion were also to some degree influenced by environmental constraints. There is some coincidence between the boundaries of the Cape, later South Africa as a whole, and the southern reaches of the desert, malaria, and tsetse belts, so uncongenial to nineteenth-century settler pastoralism.

[15] W. K. Hancock, *Australia* (Ernest Benn, London, 1930), 4.

[16] Ibid. 30–1.   [17] Mellville, *A Plague of Sheep*, p. xi.

[18] Eric Walker, 'Relief and the European Settlement of South Africa', *South African Journal of Science*, 26 (1929), 100–6.

[19] P. J. van der Merwe, *Die Noortwaartse Beweging van die Boere voor die Groot Trek (1770–1842)* (W. P. van Stockum, The Hague, 1937); E. Walker, *The Great Trek* (Adam & Charles Black, London, 1934).

Within the conquered zones, farms were often established at water sources, or near favourable pastures. Small towns grew up around fountains, or along trekking and transport routes, as church and state combined in the attempt to hold settlers within a colonial grasp. To a significant extent, the rhythms of social life at the Cape, well into the twentieth century, were attuned to the relationship with animals. At one level this is a bigger point about the significance of hunting, domestication of animals, and animal power, in the long history of many human societies up to very recent centuries.[20] At another level, it is an argument about the specificity of economic and cultural life in this and perhaps other southern settler-controlled societies. In the Cape, the centrality of animals may have been particularly marked over a long period: it was the only one of the southern hemisphere colonies in which the indigenous population had depended upon domesticated livestock as a major resource; it had an unusually rich and varied wildlife; the indigenous wild animals included predators that plagued livestock owners; and the Cape probably had a higher proportion of its population in the rural areas engaging with livestock, up to the early twentieth century, than any other of the southern settler-dominated zones.

Many African men, and to a certain degree white, woke up to tend animals, spent their days with animals as youths, regularly chased animals for long periods, travelled with horses and oxen, killed and processed animals, and ate them. When John Croumbie Brown, later the Colonial Botanist, visited a house in the Karoo in 1847, he recalled that he was offered tea, and asked for bread.

'Bread', said the farmer, 'we have not seen bread for nearly three years' . . . 'Because of the drought . . . we cannot raise corn'. 'Then what do you eat?' 'Mutton'.

'But what do you eat with the mutton?' 'Mutton'.

'What do you mean?' 'I mean what I say, we eat the fat with the lean, and the lean with the fat and so do the best we can'.[21]

Brown, and others after him, underestimated the extent to which the colonists travelled with seeds, as well as stock, and rapidly established kitchen gardens and orchards wherever water supplies permitted. Yet meat, milk products, fat, and skins were vital in the subsistence and material culture of rural communities, black and white.

[20] R. Lewinsohn, *Animals, Men and Myths: An Informative and Entertaining History of Man and the Animals around Him* (Harper & Bros., New York, 1954); James Serpell, *In the Company of Animals: A Study of Human–Animal Relationships* (Canto, Cambridge, 1996); Harriet Ritvo, *The Animal Estate: The English and Other Creatures in the Victorian Age* (Penguin, Harmondsworth, 1987).

[21] John Croumbie Brown, *Water Supply of South Africa and Facilities for the Storage of It* (Oliver & Boyd, Edinburgh, 1877), 350.

The knowledge, understanding, and folklore of many of the Cape's inhabitants—what may be called, borrowing from Andre Hugo, the Cape vernacular—was shaped by this daily interaction.[22] We could explore the histories of tracking, trekking, hunting, horsemanship, herding, pre-scientific veterinary care, breeding, shearing, hide preparation, the processing and trading of animal products. Working with livestock in turn necessitated knowledge about predators, plants, water, disease, insects, veld, drought, and climate. Despite the brutality of the colonial conquest, many of these areas of knowledge developed initially from the interpenetration of indigenous and settler ideas: travellers and trekboers, for example, learnt a great deal about the behaviour of wild animals from their Khoisan trackers and servants; Africans in turn adopted and mastered introduced skills of horse riding and ox-team management (Chapter 1).[23] Indigenous oral literature and folklore was rich in animal stories, which seeped into and intermingled with settler literature and children's stories.

Aside from wild animals and livestock, Lichtenstein, the early nineteenth-century German traveller, noted the centrality of large, fierce 'Danish' dogs, to settler rural life. He saw ten to fifteen of them at stock farms, fed with animal entrails. 'It is not too much to assert', he commented, 'that without dogs, and such dogs, the country would be absolutely uninhabitable.'[24] They took on leopards and hyenas, scared away jackals, acted as guards, tracked and hunted—sometimes by themselves, and sometimes, in the brutal dispossession of the Khoisan, in pursuit of human as well as animal victims.

Tasks and knowledge related to animal management and the environment were differentiated by race and by gender. Especially in African societies, women were often at one remove from daily interaction with livestock, and generally did not hunt. Custom forbade them from handling cattle; the division of labour assigned them more to the crops and household. Unlike African women, rural English-speaking white women were at least permitted by the mores of their society to ride horses, but they were not usually much involved with livestock. These divisions of labour are in themselves indicative of the perceived importance of hunting and pastoral activities, for men have quintessentially attempted to claim such key resources. Domestic patriarchal power was manifest in control of animals and access to them.

---

[22] A. M. Hugo, *The Cape Vernacular* (University of Cape Town, Cape Town, 1970), inaugural lecture, NS, no. 2.

[23] Beinart, 'Men, Science, Travel and Nature'.

[24] W. H. C. Lichtenstein, *Travels in Southern Africa in the Years 1803, 1804, 1805 and 1806* (van Riebeeck Society, Cape Town, 1928; first published 1812, 1815), ii. 18.

Globally, the settler frontiers of hunting, livestock management, and resource extraction provided powerful symbols both for new nations and settler masculinities: the west and the cowboy in the United States; the pampas and the gaucho in Argentina and Uruguay; the outback, squatter, and shearer in Australia; the canoe teams in Canada, trading beaver skins across the lakes. The legacy of South African pastoral expansion is troubled. It could not easily be projected as part of national culture, even amongst a divided white society. Yet treks, outdoor life, and the ox-wagon remained attractive and powerful symbols for Afrikaner nationalists in the twentieth century.

Counting Sheep

One way of understanding the significance of livestock is to consider the numbers involved and also to look at these in comparative terms. Statistics are problematic because of expanding colonial boundaries, changing perceptions of what needed to be quantified, and difficulties in collection.[25] Nevertheless the Cape figures have considerable historical depth and value; it is also possible to correlate the carefully recorded wool export series with the more uncertain livestock counts.[26] Sheep numbers within colonial boundaries stood at perhaps 1.5 million—mostly the fat-tailed, non-woolled sheep adopted from indigenous Khoisan people—when the British finally took control in 1806.[27] Numbers of woolled merino sheep leapt to about 5 million in 1855 and 10 million in 1875. They increased gradually to a nineteenth-century peak of about 12 million in 1891 and then fell so that by 1904 they were well below the 1875 figure (Fig. I.1). In other words, numbers were relatively static for a thirty-year period from 1875 to 1905.

[25] Dawn Nell, '"For the Public Benefit": Livestock Statistics and Expertise in the Late Nineteenth-Century Cape', in Saul Dubow (ed.), *Science and Society in Southern Africa* (Manchester, Manchester University Press, 2000), 100–15.

[26] I have assembled statistical series from a number of different documents published by the Cape Colonial and Union of South Africa governments, including censuses, agricultural censuses, statistical registers, reports of the Chief Inspector of sheep, and reports of the Department of Agriculture.

[27] P. van Duin and R. Ross, *The Economy of the Cape Colony in the Eighteenth Century* (Leiden, Centre for the History of European Expansion, 1987), calculate close on half-a-million sheep in the official *opgaaf* figures by 1795 but suggest that the true figures were perhaps three times this total. H. B. Thom, *Die Geskiedenis van die Skaapboerdery in Suid-Afrika* (Swets & Zeitlinger, Amsterdam, 1936) 58, 76, concurs about the *opgaaf* and gives 1.25 million in 1806. John Barrow, *Travels into the Interior of Southern Africa* (T. Cadell & W. Davies, London, 1806) vol. 1, records 1.45 million in 1797.

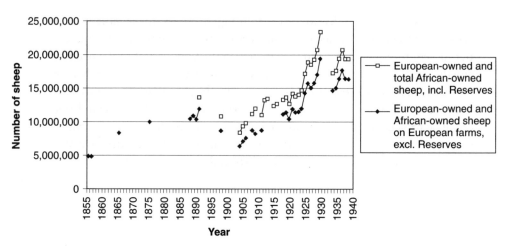

FIG. I.I. Cape Woolled Sheep, 1855–1939

Graaff-Reinet, founded in the 1780s in the heart of the new sheep-rearing districts, had less than fifty dwellings in 1811.[28] By 1860 it was a thriving centre with nearly 5,000 people. Still the largest town in the Karoo, it had been overtaken by the eastern Cape ports and administrative centres. Khoisan country had been turned into colonial districts, each with its small town, its magistrate or civil commissioner, its church, and gaol. In 1865 nearly one-third (58,000) of the total white population of the Cape was recorded in the far-flung rural districts and small towns of the midland and eastern livestock farming districts. (This figures does not include the population of the ports or of Kingwilliamstown and Grahamstown, which partly serviced the rural districts.) The number had doubled by 1904, although it was by then a far smaller proportion of the white population as a whole. The black population of these districts exceeded the white. Considering the dry environment, and the large farms, this was a significant total.

While there is strong awareness of the early boom in sheep farming in the literature, historians see it as supplanted by diamond mining as the engine of the Cape economy from the 1870s.[29] Most have missed the further spectacu-

[28] Robert Ross, 'The Origins of Capitalist Agriculture in the Cape Colony: A Survey', in Beinart et al. (eds.), *Putting a Plough to the Ground*, and Kenneth Smith, *From Frontier to Midlands: A History of the Graaff-Reinet District, 1786–910* (Institute of Social and Economic Research, Grahamstown, 1976).

[29] Alan Mabin, 'The Underdevelopment of the Western Cape, 1850–1900', in W. James and M. Simons (eds.), *The Angry Divide* (David Philip, Cape Town, 1989), 82–93, and 'The Rise and Decline of Port Elizabeth', *International Journal of African Historical Studies*, 19: 2 (1986), 275–303, both drawing on Mabin, 'The Making of Colonial Capitalism: Intensification and Expansion in the

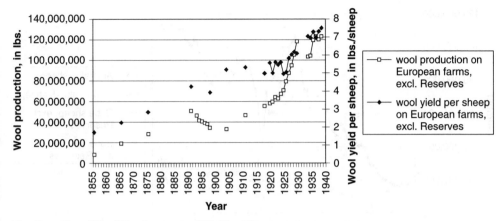

Fig. I.2. Cape Wool Production and Yields, 1855–1939

lar rise in sheep numbers in the early decades of the twentieth century. Numbers of woolled sheep in the Cape nearly trebled to over 23 million in the twenty-five years from 1905 to 1930 (Fig. I.1). Growth in South Africa as a whole, especially the Free State, was even more rapid; numbers reached 44 million woolled sheep in 1930 and nearly 60 million small stock in all. Cattle numbers also swelled, despite devastating diseases such as rinderpest and east coast fever, by two to three times between 1904 and 1930. It is clear that intensification of livestock farming was not merely a nineteenth-century phenomenon. Nor was this just a question of numbers. Wool yields increased steadily, from an average of less than 2 pounds per sheep in the 1850s to over 7 pounds in the 1930s (Fig. I.2).

Australia, the great home of sheep, supported over 100 million in the early 1890s or about eight times the number in the Cape (Fig. I.3).[30] To South African observers, Australia seemed to have many natural advantages, including 'a softer and more succulent pasture' and an absence of predators.[31] But we should be cautious about leaving the comparison there. If we include all small stock, and not only merinos, Australia had closer to five times the Cape

Economic Geography of the Cape Colony', unpublished Ph.D. thesis, Simon Fraser University (1984), presents this sequence, although he is also acutely aware of the expansion of the pastoral economy. Saul Dubow, *Land, Labour and Merchant Capital in the Pre-Industrial Rural Economy of the Cape: The Experience of the Graaff-Reinet District (1852–72)* (Centre for African Studies, University of Cape Town, 1982), also illustrates intensification of sheep farming.

[30] It is intriguing to note that the nineteenth-century peak numbers in both Australia and the Cape were in the early 1890s.

[31] *Agricultural Journal of the Cape of Good Hope*, 1: 21 (9 May 1889), 174: C. J. Watermeyer, 'Notes by a Cape Farmer on a Recent Australian Tour'.

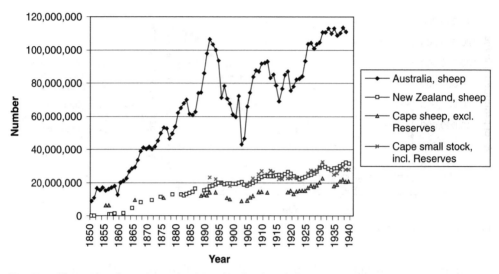

FIG. I.3. Sheep Numbers: Australia, New Zealand, and the Cape, 1850–1939

numbers and it was twelve times the size. Comparisons are difficult, because they would require more systematic analysis of the climate and terrain: Australia had an even higher proportion of arid and semi-arid land. But for its size and climate, the Cape appears to have been heavily stocked by the late nineteenth century.

It is also intriguing to note that sheep numbers languished in Australia for over thirty years from the early 1890s, reaching 100 million again only in the late 1920s (Fig. I.3). Australia was more easily tamed than South Africa, but depressed prices, denuded pastures, weeds, feral animals, and a plague of rabbits set the national flock back.[32] By the 1920s numbers in the Cape had increased to over one-fifth those in Australia. South Africa was by then the second largest producer of merino wool in the world, and the other countries with more woolled sheep, such as the Soviet Union and the United States, were far larger. (Numbers in New Zealand had caught up with those in the Cape, but while that country was only half the size, its rainfall and pastures allowed for far heavier stocking.) Comparative material suggests that, given its nature, the Cape was groaning under the weight of stock at this time.

Consideration of exports also yields surprising results. Wool exports peaked first in 1872 at £3.3 million and then declined, hovering around £2 million annually for the thirty-year period to 1905 (Fig. I.4). Diamonds, discovered in 1867, overtook wool as the major export by value from the Cape

---

[32] Bolton, *Spoils and Spoilers*, 81.

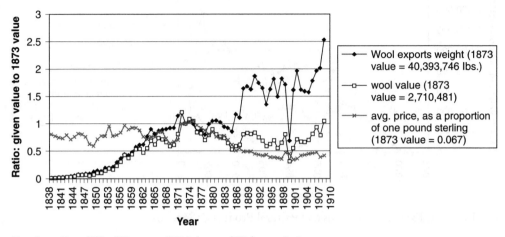

FIG. I.4. Cape Wool Exports, Weights and Values, 1838–1909

around 1880, but wool remained the most important agricultural commodity, bringing in half the value of diamonds on external markets. Moreover, weakness in wool was largely compensated for by diversification and the export of other pastoral products, such as ostrich feathers, mohair from angora goats, horns, cattle hides, and sheep- and goat-skins. The number of farmed ostriches increased from very few to 800,000 between 1865 and 1909, by which time the feathers fetched close on £2 million annually. After the South African War (1899–1902), the Cape also exported live animals to help restock other parts of southern Africa; in 1909 £1.5 million worth of cattle, sheep, horses, and mules was recorded in the export figures. If they are included, the value of pastoral exports as a whole was much the same as diamonds up to about 1905 and then exceeded them (Fig. I.5).[33]

It is important to add that up to 1870, two-thirds of the wool leaving the Cape was washed or scoured, greatly enhancing its value (Fig. I.6). The term 'washing' was used to describe a cleaning process usually done on the farm, while scouring was done in small factories in villages and urban centres. Wool-washing then gradually collapsed as a colonial industry, despite the fact that in 1910 scoured wool still fetched twice the price of unwashed greased wool (Fig. I.7).[34] If wool-washing had survived, the value of wool exports would have been higher throughout this period of relative decline and would

[33] Some figures for pastoral exports are missing in the Cape statistical register. The totals given here in a number of years are therefore understatements. (Cattle hides: 1874, 1878, 1904–9; cattle horns: 1874, 1906–9; live animals: 1874, 1878–83; sheep- and goat-skins: 1904–9.)

[34] Mabin, 'Underdevelopment of the Western Cape' and 'The Making of Colonial Capitalism'.

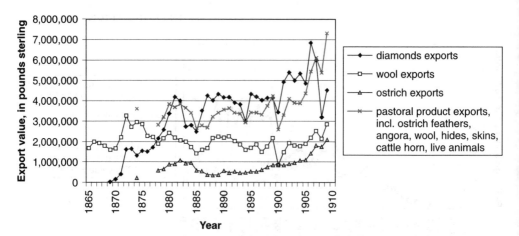

FIG. I.5. Cape Exports: Diamonds and Pastoral Products, 1865–1910

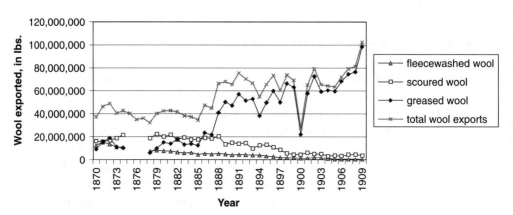

FIG. I.6. Cape Wool Exports by Type, 1870–1909

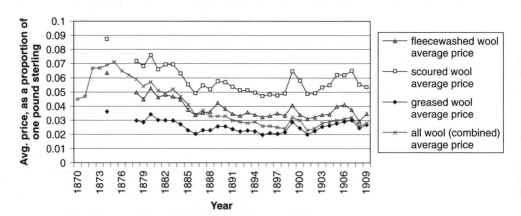

FIG. I.7. Average Price of Wool Exports by Wool Type, 1870–1909

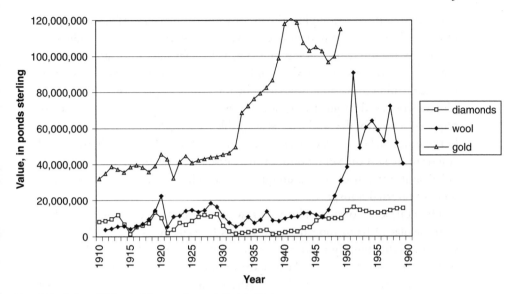

Fɪɢ. I.8. Sales of Wool, Diamonds, and Gold, Union 1910–1959

have continued, even without other pastoral products, to exceed diamonds. The demise of an industry, rather than the hiccup in wool production, reduced the value of wool exports from the 1870s.

The market for ostrich feathers collapsed during the First World War, never to recover; international taste for ostrich meat is relatively recent. But wool exports again increased dramatically, and during the first half of the twentieth century their value was usually second to gold nationally (Fig. I.8). Diamonds excited attention; their sparkle, the crowds of people they attracted, and the compound labour system which they spawned have drawn in historians. In the longer term, and for any other period than the twenty-five years after 1880, exports of animal products from the Cape exceeded in value those of diamonds. The income derived was also far more widely distributed.

Yet another way to emphasize the scale and value of the pastoral economy is to note that, in commercial as well as subsistence economies, livestock can be a multi-purpose asset: animals provided meat, milk, and fat for subsistence and for internal urban markets, as well as transport and draught power. While it is difficult to calculate values of meat production, because so much was consumed locally or marketed informally, figures suggest that per-capita urban consumption increased during the first few decades of the twentieth century, at a time when the cities were growing rapidly. By the late 1930s the value of meat produced in the Cape alone was probably in the region of £6 million annually.

Oxen were the key draught animals for whites and blacks. Africans adopted ploughs during the nineteenth century, so that their arable production became very largely dependent on oxen. White farmers were slow to adopt mechanical traction: there were only roughly 4,000 tractors on 100,000 private farming units in South Africa by the Great Depression of the 1930s. Horses were used largely for personal transport and military purposes. They required scarce fodder, and were susceptible to periodic epizootics of insect-borne horse sickness. Oxen were not as efficient, but they were hardier, and could survive off the veld. South of the tsetse belt and the deserts, they pro-vided southern Africa with a unique continental advantage in the develop-ment of internal transport.

The number of oxen and horses grew quickly up to the 1890s, when they were displaced from long-distance routes by railways and later by motor vehicles. Subsequently there was no precipitous decline because they were still required for draught and transport on farms and in African reserves, as well as carriage to railheads. In the African areas oxen numbers increased through to the 1930s. Neither the Agricultural Censuses, nor compilations such as the official *Union Statistics for Fifty Years*, frequently used in the sec-ondary literature, assign any value to animals in transport. By 1911 750,000 oxen were worth perhaps £5 million and horses about the same; this remained roughly stable to the 1930s.

I have sought to assign approximate financial values to pastoral production, however difficult such an exercise may be, because they help to underline the scale of activities. Export income, together with internal consumption and the value of animals in transport, perhaps totalled around £20 million in 1910 and over £30 million by 1930 in the Cape alone. If dairy products were added, these figures would be considerably enhanced. Aside from commercial dairy production, milk, soured milk (*amasi* in Xhosa), or butter were consumed daily on farms and in African homesteads. Estimates made in the African reserve district of Herschel in the 1920s placed the value of dairy products well above that of meat.[35]

Early capitalism in South Africa has been strongly identified with the mining industry. Undoubtedly, mining as a whole, and particularly gold, was the key motor of growth for the country as a whole from the late nineteenth century. But the figures also point to a striking intensification in pastoral production, which exceeded in value that of diamonds nationally, and grew as quickly as rapidly expanding arable production, at least up to the early 1950s, when wool prices soared during the Korean War. If it were possible to

---

[35] W. M. Macmillan, *Complex South Africa* (Faber & Faber, London, 1930), 155.

calculate investment into pastoral farming over the long term, the argument might be strengthened further.

While investment into the livestock economy was tangentially related to mining and industrialization—for example through markets for meat—the export of wool and other pastoral products was part of a rather different commodity frontier and social complex. The figures suggest that it was an arena of considerable significance locally, and even on a global scale. The arguments advanced here have a bearing both on approaches to South African agrarian history and on understandings of capitalist accumulation more generally.

Science, the State, and Environmental Regulation

This quantitative sketch has important implications for the social and environmental history of the Cape. A central theme of this book is that livestock farming was not simply the subject of waning traditional knowledge but of growing scientific interest. The difficulties of managing the pastoral economy, especially after it became the site of investment and wealth from the mid-nineteenth century, produced a vivid and critical literature. Some of this was contained in government reports and commissions, important vehicles for the expression of colonial intellectual endeavour. Sciences such as botany, geology, veterinary medicine, zoology, forestry, entomology, and ecology increasingly informed and framed debates on improvement and environmental regulation. The growth of natural sciences was not simply attributable to agriculture requirements, but, as in the case of geology, so critical to the mining industry, economic priorities helped to shape the scope of research.

Scientific disciplines were not a single, bounded field of specialized study, especially at this time. Progressive farmers conducted experiments of a kind, invented techniques, professed a scientific approach, and tried to maintain some active interest in broader developments. They gathered information through a range of non-specialist networks or publications from agricultural journals to newspapers. Many of them, as 'practical' men—to use the language of the time—were sceptical of 'theoretical' knowledge. While various scientific fields were being professionalized, the number of practitioners in South Africa was initially small and they often worked with farmers. Scientific ideas were unevenly assimilated and intensely debated, especially when they became absorbed into public policy. Nevertheless, the rhetoric of science, and participation in technological change, helped to define the approach and identity of officials and leading farmers. These areas of white intellectual life have been little explored by historians, except those reviewing the past of their own disciplines.

It would not be possible to include sequential histories of each of these areas of knowledge over the whole of the period covered here. Growing scientific understanding is explored in different fields when these impacted directly upon key environmental debates. For example, botanists are discussed from the 1850s to the 1870s, when they were becoming profoundly aware of vegetation change and denudation (Chapter 2). Even though the number of botanical experts in the country increased greatly in the twentieth century, they feature only sporadically in later chapters. Similarly, vets are the focus of a chapter dealing with the 1870s and 1880s, because they made so great an impact on environmental debates at the time. They believed that animal health and pastoral production were suffering because of the 'decadence' or degradation of the natural veld. Although vets subsequently became central to the Cape and Union Departments of Agriculture, and veterinary services accounted for over half the departmental expenditure up to the 1930s, I do not pursue the history of this important discipline in later chapters.

Underestimation of the significance of the pastoral economy has also led to gaps in understanding of the Cape state. A strong historiography has focused on conquest, land appropriation, merchant capital, enforcement of private property, 'native' administration, and the control of labour. An important strand in the literature dwells on the rise and travails of Cape liberalism, and the relatively non-racial institutions established.[36] The dominant narrative of transition has been from merchant to mining capital, from a heavily contested Victorian Christian incorporationism (now less emphasized as a major influence) to the three-pronged imperatives of labour mobilization, regional conquest, and racial segregation. Our gaze is constantly directed to the titan Cecil Rhodes, Kimberley mining magnate, politician, and Cape Prime Minister from 1890 to 1896, who epitomized such trends.

To be sure, agrarian interests have been allowed a look in, especially in the earlier phases of settler dominance.[37] But insofar as they have been seen as a

---

[36] Bundy, *South African Peasantry*; S. Trapido, ' "The Friends of the Natives": Merchants, Peasants and the Political and Ideological Structure of Liberalism in the Cape, 1854–1910', in S. Marks and A. Atmore (eds.), *Economy and Society in Pre-Industrial South Africa* (Longman, London, 1980); C. Crais, *The Making of the Colonial Order: White Supremacy and Black Resistance in the Eastern Cape, 1770–1865* (Witwatersrand University Press, Johannesburg, 1992); Timothy Keegan, *Colonial South Africa and the Origins of the Racial Order* (Leicester University Press, London, 1996).

[37] Crais, *Colonial Order* and Keegan, *Colonial South Africa*, although both underestimate its later significance.

force in the late nineteenth century, it has largely been in the shape of the western Cape Afrikaner Bond, the survivors of the old Cape Dutch gentry, farming wheat and vines.[38] The influence of self-consciously progressive farmers in the midland and eastern districts, many of whom concentrated on pastoral production, has been underestimated. A significant proportion came from English-speaking backgrounds and some developed environmental concerns.[39] It is not accurate to equate mining and commercial capital with English-speakers and agrarian with Afrikaners in the Cape. This group of anglophone landowners (together with progressive, bilingual Afrikaners) acquired a disproportionate influence over state policy in certain spheres and, conversely, the state extended its functions in regulating the pastoral economy and encouraging more intense, but wise usage of natural resources. Ovine accumulation, land, and knowledge were an important nexus of power.

I have used the term progressive, without repeated resort to inverted commas, to describe this landowning group or class because it is a word they often used themselves. Improving, or modernizing, are sometimes used as alternatives, but they do not capture the language of the time. Those who mobilized in an anglophone party in the 1890s, in support of Rhodes, called it the Progressive Party; it came to power under Jameson between 1904 and 1908. Progressives absorbed some of the economic and political ideas of the eponymous American movement, which was at its height under Theodore Roosevelt's presidency (1900–8). In particular they advocated a regulated capitalism, and conservationism, in which the state had a role. The term was, however, used over a much longer period, and as a point of reference for a wider range of social groups. Educated Africans, often Christian, also called themselves progressives and shared some of the same ethos. White progressives were not, however, liberals in their racial views; most of them also expected the state to extend segregation. The focus on Cape liberalism in the historiography of South Africa has tended to obscure this other, and more dominant, set of ideas.

State intervention in Cape agriculture could be periodized roughly into three phases. (The mobilization and control of an agricultural labour force, which is not analysed in this book, remained a preoccupation throughout.)

[38] The precise role of the Bond in shaping the Cape state is still neglected; see T. R. H. Davenport, *The Afrikaner Bond, 1880–1911* (Oxford University Press, Cape Town, 1966); M. Tamarkin, *Cecil Rhodes and the Cape Afrikaners: The Imperial Colussus and the Colonial Parish Pump* (Frank Cass, London, 1996).

[39] For a comparative approach (which excludes South Africa), Thomas R. Dunlap, *Nature and the English Diaspora: Environment and History in the United States, Canada, Australia, and New Zealand* (Cambridge University Press, Cambridge, 1999).

First, from the outset of British rule in 1806 to the 1870s, conquest, dispossession, the control of land, and establishment of administrative authority were priorities. The infrastructure was laid for capitalist farming. Secondly, from about the 1880s to the 1940s, when the settler agricultural economy was more securely established but environmental problems diagnosed, environmental regulation became a far more central concern to the state both at local and national levels. Thirdly, control of agricultural commodity markets, as well as price subsidization, became an important focus for state policy from the 1930s Depression until the 1980s.

This book concentrates upon the second phase, although it also traces the ideas that informed environmental understanding in an earlier period (Chapters 1–3). I must be cautious about elevating environmental preoccupations in general, simply because they are the subject of this research. But measures to conserve or control access to natural resources have been a condition of accumulation and modernity in many contexts. While we have a detailed picture of tenancy and labour relations in South African agriculture, it is only relatively recently that the conceptual tools and approaches have been developed for historians to consider fully the import of environmental regulation.

There was a long legacy of relatively unsuccessful regulation from the period of Dutch company rule, for example, in attempts to control deforestation and hunting. The sponsorship of a botanical garden, introduction of plants, and expeditions to collect indigenous species proved to be more important. During the nineteenth century new perceptions of environmental change presaged more extensive state intervention. The spread of plant and livestock diseases from the 1870s helped to trigger intense concern. Phylloxera in grapes was one; we should return to the livestock figures in order to contextualize others (Figs. I.1 and I.4).

Wool prices peaked between 1872 and 1875, probably at their highest level, in real terms, since merinos were introduced. Yet Cape farmers were unable to take advantage by increasing their wool exports (Fig. I.9). They identified the problem largely as one of disease, and a Commission of Inquiry, as well as the first state veterinary surgeon, were appointed (Chapter 4). Early incumbents in the post had to confront persistent diseases, and a wave of destructive epizootics such as redwater, rinderpest, and east coast fever. They prescribed far-reaching changes in the methods of livestock farming prevalent at the Cape and were instrumental in elaborating a legislative framework to eradicate disease; veterinary concerns were a major factor in the establishment of a Department of Agriculture in 1887 and its subsequent growth.

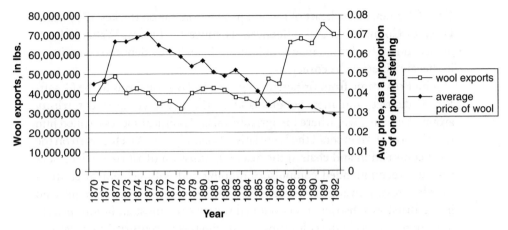

FIG. I.9. Cape Wool Exports and Prices, 1870–1892

   This and related agencies, together with farmer-politicians, aided by
rapidly growing scientific understanding, took on a range of other perceived
pests, from locusts and weeds to jackals. They espoused a clear social and economic agenda that envisaged the end of transhumance and kraaling—both
seen as major causes of disease and environmental degradation. They tried
to conserve and enhance water supplies through far-reaching forestry and
engineering projects. Some of the interlocking agricultural, political, and
official elite perceived disease and environmental problems as being major
causes of agricultural problems in the late nineteenth and early twentieth
centuries.[40] They wrote with surprising frequency about veld degradation,
pastures exhausted by overstocking, and springs drying up. Ideas about many
environmental ills were also contained within the assertion that drought was
getting worse. For them, strategies of environmental control and conservation of natural resources went hand in hand.
   Their influence can be traced in agricultural associations, parliamentary
representation, a range of commissions and select committees, and in legislation. Many individuals were protagonists of improvement and regulation; a
few examples must suffice here. John Molteno, first Cape Prime Minister
under responsible government from 1874, was a sheep farmer near Beaufort
West and one of the largest landowners in the Colony. His government
appointed the first Colonial Veterinary Surgeon and the first Hydraulic
Engineer. Charles Rubidge, possibly the most important sheep-breeder in

---

[40] A number of the most important landowners and officials, English and Afrikaner, also had
military experience.

Graaff-Reinet, at the heart of merino production, sat on the key 1877 Stock Diseases Commission and influenced its concerns; his son Walter, a land-owner and parliamentarian, was ubiquitous in giving evidence to committees in the late nineteenth century.

John Frost came from Britain in 1849, worked first on farms in the Graaff-Reinet district, and then bought land in the newly conquered territory around Queenstown, where his agricultural and political success gained him the position of Member of the Legislative Assembly (MLA). He served on the 1877 commission and chaired the Scab Commission of 1892–4, which suc-cessfully recommended compulsory dipping and enforcement of controls over livestock movement. Thomas Smartt, an Irish physician, bought land in the Britstown district and developed some of the most ambitious private irrigation projects in the colony in the late nineteenth century—again largely for livestock breeding. He was elected as an MLA and became a central figure in the Cape Progressive Party which took power in 1904.

There are similar Afrikaner figures, most rising to power a little later. H. C. van Heerden, sheep farmer from Cradock, was the modernizing Minister of Agriculture under Botha and Smuts in the 1910s. Frederic de Waal, Belgian-born lawyer, who came to South Africa for his health, became a newspaper editor in the dry, lung-friendly Karoo district of Middelburg, and later the long-serving Administrator of the Cape Province. He made jackal eradica-tion a special project. Heinrich du Toit, who cut his agricultural teeth on his father's sheep farm on the borders of Graaff-Reinet and Middelburg, fought for the Transvaal in the South African War and subsequently established himself as perhaps the leading Afrikaner agricultural bureaucrat of the early decades of the twentieth century. He chaired and wrote the Drought Com-mission report (1923), which even today is a striking conservationist docu-ment. There was always significant opposition to such individuals and their projects, so that these issues were at the heart of Cape rural politics for whites and blacks.

We have evidence for environmental problems not only in their comments and descriptions but perhaps also in the decline of sheep numbers in the period between the 1870s and 1905 (Fig. I.1). Before accepting that the difficulties of the livestock economy can be attributed to disease and degra-dation, we should also explore economic questions, and in particular wool prices. Australian output of fine wools was increasingly dominant. The surge in Australian production as well as less favourable terms of trade for primary commodities in the late nineteenth century drove down the wool price (Figs. I.4 and I.7). Cape farmers themselves used this as an explanation for investment in angora goats and ostriches.

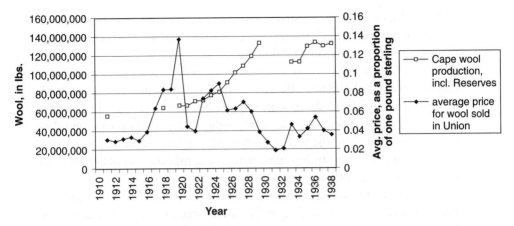

FIG. I.10. Wool Production and Price, 1910–1939

Yet we should be cautious about seeing falling prices as the main cause of stasis. Livestock numbers increased over the long term from 1800 to 1930, despite fluctuations in prices. There are periods between 1860 and 1940 when the relationship between falling prices and numbers (or its inverse) did not hold. For example, from about 1880 to the early 1890s sheep numbers and wool production gradually increased despite plummeting wool prices. This pattern is repeated during the late 1920s (Figs. I.1, I.4, I.9, I.10). In the short term, falling prices can sometimes be correlated with increased sheep numbers and wool output because farmers tried to produce more in order to pay interest on debts and to maintain their standard of living. Similar patterns can be found during the Great Depression of the early 1930s amongst other colonial commodity producers, including West African cocoa farmers.

At other times, however, there does seem to have been a more predictable relationship between wool prices and sheep numbers. The sustained wool price decline, evident from 1875 to 1900, and increase from 1910 to the early 1920s, coincided respectively in a decline and rise in sheep numbers, although this was a somewhat delayed response. In the last couple of decades of the twentieth century falling sheep numbers also coincided with lower wool prices (Fig. 11.1). The relationship is unpredictable, and each episode requires separate explanation. The figures suggest that a short-term price decline was sometimes met by increased production, but a longer-term decline by diversification. Undoubtedly, the alternative opportunities afforded by ostriches and angoras was a factor in shifting patterns of production in the late nineteenth century. Yet these animals did not always displace sheep directly: they were sometimes all kept on the same farms, as each could to some degree exploit different pasture and fodder resources.

There does not seem to be strong evidence that the stasis in sheep numbers during the late nineteenth century was only or primarily due to price. We are thrown back onto environmental explanations—although for the period of the South African War (1899–1902), conflict and seizure of livestock was a major factor. While rainfall affected the quality and abundance of the veld, this was a seasonal and short-term impact. Numbers built up through the nineteenth century despite cycles of drought; they grew faster in the relatively dry decade of the 1920s than in the wetter decade of the 1930s. Disease and environmental constraints must remain a significant part of the explanation for late nineteenth-century problems.

Similarly, the boisterous increase in sheep numbers in the early decades of the twentieth century is unlikely to be simply related to wool prices; rather, key environmental constraints were removed. To summarize, state intervention and private investment in the fields, sequentially, of disease control (Chapter 4), water provision (Chapter 5), predator extermination (Chapter 6), fodder (Chapters 8 and 9), fencing and soil erosion (Chapters 7–11) were probably key factors. Officials could respond quickly to epizootics, they introduced compulsory dipping of sheep and tightened the state's capacity to control animal movements. Cape farmers and farm-workers were responsible in the nineteenth century for innovative intermediate water technology, in the way that they led out fountains into channels, built weirs to divert storm waters, and constructed earth and stone dams. From the 1890s this was supplemented by the introduced technology of deep boring and windmills, and irrigation projects. Settler hunting associations, together with fences and higher rewards for vermin, finally turned the tide against jackals by the 1920s. Fencing enabled livestock to be left out at night, and facilitated the rotation of camps or paddocks. Animals could graze for longer periods, and reach all parts of the huge pastoral farms; less of the natural veld was trampled and more systematic pasture management became feasible. Fodder crops reduced dry-season winter and drought losses.

While state expenditure was not vast, a number of departments were involved and private capital remained of great importance. The largest element in Cape government expenditure by far throughout the period 1880–1910 was on the railways, but increasingly this was in response to demands for a network geared to farming districts, rather than to service the key urban and mining centres in the interior. In this sense, railways epitomized rural modernization. Railways also diminished the need for trekking and ox-wagon transport—identified as major causes of disease. Cecil Rhodes backed a number of these innovations but he did not initiate them (and is largely absent from this discussion).

It is difficult to establish which aspect of intervention was most successful; all were intricately linked in ideology and practice. One test may be offered by comparing livestock numbers on white-owned farms and in the largest African reserve of the Transkeian Territories (Fig. 10.1). Both show a sharp increase during the early decades of the twentieth century. Although there was less investment in the Transkei, especially in stock-breeding, water provision, and fencing, the area was subject to equally rigorous veterinary controls. On this evidence, veterinary measures were probably the most significant contributor to the increase in animal numbers at this time—and the scale of state expenditure suggests that officials were of the same view. But private investment was more varied. Water provision and storage was certainly seen as a priority by many progressive farmers at the time.

John Iliffe has argued that 'Africans have been and are the frontiersmen who have colonised an especially hostile region of the world on behalf of the entire human race . . . It is why they deserve . . . careful study'.[41] Settlers and the state continued that process, far more intensively, on the pastoral farms of the Cape, reshaping the environment and securing higher levels of production; the rest of the world, especially Britain, directly benefited from the produce exported. The human cost was high, in the displacement of the Khoisan and Xhosa, but the strategies equally deserve careful study.

This is not least so because the landowners and officials in the vanguard of agricultural improvement articulated conservationist ideas: they were deeply concerned about the limits of the natural veld. Evidence of severe soil erosion was accumulating in the early twentieth century. And an underlying element in their argument was that prevention was better than cure. Conservationist farming would underpin future agrarian accumulation. But investment and improvement preceded a willingness to limit livestock numbers, which reached their peak around 1930, both on white-owned farms and in African reserves. In the next few years, when drought was severe, small stock numbers declined by about 6 million in the Cape and 14 million nationally (Fig. I.1). They have never been so high again. Key environmental constraints were mastered before an adequate system of regulating livestock owners was put in place.

It should not assumed, however, that scientific officials neglected their conservationist mission. In many respects, the Depression, and subsequent expansion of state functions, spurred them on to more zealous action. In the penultimate chapter I discuss the impact of conservationist ideas on the

[41] John Iliffe, *Africans: The History of a Continent* (Cambridge University Press, Cambridge, 1995), 1.

planning of new systems of livestock management in the African reserve areas of the Ciskei and Transkei during the 1930s and 1940s. It was my attempt to understand such policies that set me on this research project as a whole. Officials found it difficult to devise a strategy of intervention. Although they won some African allies, their mode of operation was shaped by the political context of white domination and segregation. Poverty, African agrarian systems, and communal tenure constrained the scope for planning on the lines that they advocated. Their system of 'betterment', imposed on rural communities, was derived from the model of improvement on white-owned farms; it was often unpopular and was difficult to sustain.

By contrast, in the final chapter, dealing with the longer term, I suggest that regulation on the white-owned farms has been more successful—at least in environmental terms. The scientific basis for environmental regulation, and especially grazing controls, has been strongly disputed in recent years; so has the outcome of such policies. However, I suggest that experts developed considerable understanding of the complex ecologies of the semi-arid districts. They invented many of the ideas and categories available to us in assessing environmental change. State intervention on the white-owned farms was less coercive than in African reserves, and conservationist measures helped to channel subsidies to the farms. Such strategies, together with a range of other factors, may have stabilized livestock numbers and environmental conditions. While the apartheid state was authoritarian, this recognition should not be an argument against the whole legacy of conservation and environmental regulation; the state and experts remain important in devising strategies in this sphere, as in others.

There is no doubt that, economically speaking, the relative significance of the pastoral economy in South Africa declined from the 1950s in relation to crop and fruit production, mining, and especially manufacturing and services. In the late twentieth century depressed prices for pastoral products, insecurity, and theft in both the farmlands and African homelands intensified the decline. However, there were countervailing processes. Private wildlife farming, as well as national and provincial parks, expanded rapidly. There were greater numbers of indigenous wildlife, across a wide range of species, in the Cape at the turn of the twenty-first century than there have been for over 150 years; biodiversity has certainly benefited. Wildlife are farmed to provide venison, hunting, and trophy opportunities, and also for viewing. Indigenous animals are at the heart of a tourist industry that may become one of South Africa's economic mainstays. In this sense, the animal life in some parts of the country is almost coming full circle.

Harold Innis called in the 1930s for recognition of the centrality of the apparently barren Canadian shield—and the early staple products of beaver skin and timber which were wrestled from it—in the nation's history and identity. There was similar advocacy of the value of the veld by conservationists in inter-war South Africa. They emphasized the links between the health of the pastures, of livestock, and of the nation.[42] New developments in environmental history will facilitate an exploration of the role of these interconnections between nature, people, and animals, in the making of distinctive features of the South African economy, society, and identity.

[42] T. D. Hall, 'South African Pastures: Retrospective and Prospective', *South African Journal of Science*, 31 (1934), 59–97, and *Our Veld: A Major National Problem* (Johannesburg, 1942).

1

Scientific Travellers, Colonists, and Africans: Chains of Knowledge and the Cape Vernacular, 1770–1850

Enlightenment Travellers and the Cape Environment:
Sparrman and his Successors, 1770–1820

Anders Sparrman arrived at the Cape from Sweden aged 24 in 1772. He had studied with Linnaeus, the renowned Swedish botanist, qualified as a doctor, and, as a young man, travelled to East Asia.[1] After a sojourn in Cape Town, he spent nearly two years as an assistant naturalist on Captain Cook's *Resolution*, travelling to the Polynesian islands and the Antarctic. He returned in 1775 to make a nine-month journey through the rural Cape collecting botanical and zoological specimens. Sparrman was not the first eighteenth-century scientific traveller to record the Cape environment, nor was he necessarily the most accurate. But his book, *A Voyage to the Cape of Good Hope*, published in English in 1785, was widely read and often cited in subsequent travel texts. It included sharp insights about colonial society, and he evinced considerable sympathy towards the indigenous Khoisan people. Sparrman sought explicitly to discuss the natural world and was amongst the first to record environmental problems.

The western and southern Cape, and parts of the semi-arid Karoo, had been conquered by the time Sparrman arrived; its Khoisan population was devastated by war, displacement, and disease. Recent historical literature on the seventeenth and eighteenth centuries has emphasized the violence of colonial incursions, the imposition of colonial systems of authority and

---

[1] Anders Sparrman, *A Voyage to the Cape of Good Hope Towards the Antarctic Polar Circle Round the World and to the Country of the Hottentots and the Caffres from the Year 1772–1776*, ed. V. S. Forbes (van Riebeeck Society, Cape Town, 1977).

knowledge, along with the growth of a slave-holding society.[2] Undoubtedly
these must remain the major historiographical themes. Yet, especially in the
interior of the country, in the pastoral districts, settlers depended both on the
labour and the environmental knowledge of the indigenous inhabitants
whom they had elbowed aside. Some of the visiting travellers and scientists
who wrote about the Cape during the late eighteenth and early nineteenth
centuries recorded snippets of Khoisan knowledge, on occasion with admiration, and affirmed how useful it could be to them and the colonists.

Scientific travel literature in this period has been characterized as imposing an 'urban, lettered, male authority over the whole of the planet; it elaborated a rationalizing, extractive, dissociative understanding which overlaid
functional, experiential relations among people, plants and animals'.[3] But
we should be cautious about oversimplifying this tradition of writing. Self-
consciously scientific understandings of the Cape environment were in their
infancy and were not initially developed in separation from other forms and
fonts of knowledge. Science itself was a less defined and specialized sphere,
especially in a colonial context. The expanding colony was very varied in
its topography, fauna, and flora; knowledge was built from a multiplicity
of indigenous and colonial agents, each with different languages, modes
of living, and views of nature. The writings of scientific travellers such as
Sparrman and William Burchell, an English naturalist who visited in the
1810s, reflected elements of this diversity. They provide a vivid window on
Cape society at the time.

Up to the early decades of the nineteenth century, a chain of interlinked
knowledge informed ideas about the Cape landscape and natural resources.
From the late seventeenth century Khoikhoi men were employed as herders
on colonial farms; by the mid-eighteenth century most of the surviving
Khoikhoi within colonial boundaries were at least partly dependent on farm
labour.[4] Khoikhoi women became household servants. As masters and servants or patrons and clients on the same farms, using the same space and managing the same animals, settler and Khoisan environmental knowledge was

[2] Richard Elphick, *Khoikhoi and the founding of White South Africa* (Ravan Press: Johannesburg,
1985); Robert Ross, *Cape of Torments: Slavery and Resistance in South Africa* (Routledge, London,
1983); Nigel Worden, *Slavery in Dutch South Africa* (Cambridge University Press, Cambridge,
1985); Susan Newton-King, *Masters and Servants*.

[3] Mary Louise Pratt, *Imperial Eyes: Travel Writing and Transculturation* (Routledge, London,
1992), 38; Carolyn Merchant, *The Death of Nature: Women, Ecology, and the Scientific Revolution*
(Harper & Row, San Francisco, 1990). For a critique see Beinart, 'Men, Science, Travel and
Nature'.

[4] Elphick, *Khoikhoi*.

imbricated in complex, although asymmetrical, ways. Command of labour undoubtedly increased the capacity of colonists to extract knowledge and, literally, created a common language by the late eighteenth century.

European botanists, travellers, and hunters frequently called on frontier farmers, from whom they received accommodation, hospitality, and space to park their wagons. They gleaned information and ideas and in this way tapped into local knowledge. They also visited and spoke to Khoisan and African people, usually through interpreters. Most of all they drew extensively on the experience and knowledge of their Khoisan guides and servants. The latter, in turn, as 'colonial Hottentots', had acquired new skills of language, new techniques of hunting with horses and firearms, and of trekking with ox-wagons which enabled them to facilitate travel and interpret the social and physical geography of the country to outsiders. Burchell, one of the most persistent and successful scientific explorers in the early nineteenth century, noted that he travelled for four years with 'no companion or assistant, nor other attendants than a few Hottentots, the number of whom never exceeded ten'.[5] This loose group of travel auxiliaries, some drawn from the Cape Hottentot Regiment, some in service, and some recruited along the way, were key figures in establishing an amalgam of knowledge and techniques which underpinned ox-wagon travel and expeditions of all kinds in the colony.

Travellers relied on the hierarchical relationships of Cape society, and the subservient role of auxiliaries was not in question. Nevertheless, some travellers developed a camaraderie with their servants during the long and arduous ox-wagon treks, and on horseback hunting expeditions to provision the party. Most had to be cautious about over-exploiting their guides, who could desert, or their Afrikaner hosts, who could deny access to critical resources. Their adventures demanded continuous negotiation rather than simple requisitioning of people and nature.[6]

And so it was with knowledge. Many Boers and Africans had a close familiarity with routes, geography, water, plants, and animals of immediate concern to travellers' progress as well as their botanical and zoological researches. In turn, scientific travellers could offer a comparative experience and intense curiosity that elicited stories and information from local people. Critically, they wrote about their experiences, often including some record of

[5] William J. Burchell, *Travels in the Interior of Southern Africa* (Batchworth Press, London 1953); reprint of 1822–4 edn. vol. i, p. 4.

[6] Janet J. Ewald, 'Strangers in a Strange Land: Travellers and the Construction of Male Genders in Nineteenth Century Africa', unpublished paper to the conference on 'Gendering Men in Africa', Minneapolis, 1990.

what they had been told. Literacy transmitted an accumulated knowledge and in this way vernacular ideas and experiences, admittedly overlaid by their recorders, were diffused back to Europe, to later generations of visitors, to those of the Cape elite who read their publications and, now, to historians.

For the pastoral farmers of the interior, who lived in part from livestock and wildlife, the transfer of local knowledge was of greater importance than for the agriculturalists of the western Cape, more dependent upon introduced crops and imported slave workers. P. J. van der Merwe, the first systematic historian of the trekboers, argued that 'the Khoikhoi presence in the interior undoubtedly contributed much to making the migration into the country possible.'[7] Not all Khoisan knowledge was initially easily available, and witholding it could be a mode of political resistance. As a Dutch source noted in the late seventeenth century: 'they are determined to keep their secret remedies to themselvs [sic].'[8] But some skills, such as hunting strategies, the location of water, use of fire, and grazing practices, were less easy to disguise than medical knowledge. This legacy of syncretic techniques, especially in the sphere of livestock management, became a central issue for the colony in the second half of the nineteenth century.

Hunting of the extraordinarily rich variety of Cape wildlife was one essential skill for survival, although van der Merwe noted that the moment in each succeeding frontier zone when mobile hunting provided a significant contribution to subsistence was relatively short-lived.[9] Hunting was used to clear land, reap income, and provide meat so that slaughter of domestic animals could be avoided. Settlers replicated the local strategy of hunting by waterholes and sometimes relied directly on the skills of the Khoikhoi servants, now hunting with firearms, for a meat supply.[10] Khoisan bows, arrows, and spears became redundant where there was sufficient firepower. So did pitfalls, although these were still reported in the mid-nineteenth century in the Kalahari.[11] Guns and horses (also a colonial introduction) were more

[7] P. J. van der Merwe, *The Migrant Farmer in the History of the Cape Colony 1657–1842*, trans. Roger B. Beck (Ohio University Press, Athens, 1995), 115, first published in Afrikaans (Cape Town, 1938).

[8] William ten Rhyne, 'A Short Account of the Cape of Good Hope and of the Hottentots who Inhabit that Region', in I. Schapera and E. Farrington (eds.), *The Early Cape Hottentots* (Negro University Press, Westport, 1970), 153.

[9] P. J. van der Merwe, *Trek: Studies oor die Mobiliteit van die Pioneersbevolking aan die Kaap* (Nasionale Pers Beperk, Kaapstad, 1945), 17–19.

[10] Carl Peter Thunberg, *Travels at the Cape of Good Hope 1772–1775* ed. V. S. Forbes (van Riebeeck Society, Cape Town, 1986), 94.

[11] M. Wilson and L. Thompson, *The Oxford History of South Africa*, vol. 1 (Clarendon Press, Oxford, 1969), 48; Peter E. Raper and Maurice Boucher (eds.), *Robert Jacob Gordon: Cape Travels, 1777 to 1786* (Brenthurst Press, London, 1986), i. 87.

efficient, and provided more mobility, allowing the hunters to shorten the time in pursuit of injured animals. They were also more suitable for small, isolated groups who were on the move for purposes other than hunting.

Khoikhoi men brought some of their older techniques to the new modes of hunting. They, as also the Sotho and Xhosa, had long trained their oxen for riding, or as pack animals, in order to meet the demands of their pastoral system which put so high a premium on mobility. Oxen were tamed as calves with a pin through their nostrils. Within the boundaries of the colony, where Khoikhoi servants had been prevented, at least in law, from owning horses, Sparrman 'had no small pleasure in seeing . . . some Hottentots riding their oxen. They rode pretty hard over hill and dales.'[12] They could develop suffi-cient speed to run down an eland. Burchell commented that 'the facility and adroitness with which Hottentots manage the [riding] ox, has often excited my admiration. It is made to walk, trot, or gallop, at the will of its master.'[13] Baines's extraordinary drawing (1865) of a 'Namaqua Hottentot on Riding-Ox with his Bushman' was reproduced in the *Oxford History of South Africa* to illustrate clientship.[14] It also illuminates the survival of this skill into the nine-teenth century, and the complexity of cultural and technological interchange: a mounted Namaqua man, clothed and shoed, with musket and powder horn, rides alongside a San man on foot carrying bow, arrows, and a firearm.

Such animal-management skills were transferred to the new sphere of driving the large teams of oxen required to pull wagons. Sparrman marvelled at Cape servants' 'incomparable knack' of keeping the ox-teams going. Lichtenstein, a German physician who visited in the early nineteenth cen-tury, though less sympathetic to the Khoikhoi, affirmed that 'they know best how to keep pace with the oxen, as well as how to dress and tend upon them.'[15] Khoikhoi team leaders seldom used whips, but shouted continuously to named oxen on long wagon treks—a technique which was highly effective in disciplining and encouraging the animals, but wearisome for travellers.

Tracking as well as trekking remained a critical skill in this phase of colon-ization and travel. Khoisan men had required the ability to track not only in finding wildlife but because their techniques of hunting, by arrow or spear, did not immediately kill animals; these had to be followed—sometimes for long distances—once they had been injured. Though firearms hastened the death of many hunted animals, texts testify that arduous searches were still

[12] Sparrman, *Voyage*, i. 227–8; Wilson and Thompson, *Oxford History* i. 71.

[13] Burchell, *Travels in the Interior of Southern Africa*, i., 163.

[14] Wilson and Thompson, *Oxford History*, Pl. I, facing p. 62. The original drawing appears to be entitled 'Namaqua Hottentot on loose horned riding ox and his Bushman', 17 March 1865.

[15] Lichtenstein, *Travels*, i. 17–18.

1. Namaqua Hottentot on Riding-ox with his Bushman

sometimes essential. Travelling parties also found that their oxen and live-stock strayed frequently and had to be tracked down. Following the spoor, as it became called in Dutch, after strays, thefts, or raids, played a large and time-consuming role in the life of pastoral communities of all kinds. Sparrman argued that tracking skills resulted from 'the faculty of observation, and judgement of the Hottentots.'[16] Lichtenstein found this capacity 'really wonderful.'[17] Burchell compared it to complex branches of European

---

[16] Sparrman, *Voyage*, ii. 223.

[17] Lichtenstein, *Travels*, i. 151; Barrow, *Travels*, i. 101. Barrow, a British official, had also read Sparrman, which he considered a 'very extensive and satisfactory account', although sometimes 'credulous enough to repeat many of the absurd stories told of the Hottentots by his predecessor Kolbe, with the addition of others collected from the ignorant boors'. In fact, Sparrman seems rather to have listened to the Khoikhoi guides—and some readers were unsettled by his explicit sympathy with the indigenous inhabitants of the Cape.

knowledge: 'these Africans pay an extraordinary degree of attention to every little circumstance connected with the habits and mode of life of the wild animals.'[18] Tracking required a capacity to read a multitude of symbols imprinted on the earth, almost a form of literacy.

Hunting, especially of larger animals, so greatly facilitated by firearms, created problems in conserving and transporting meat. Sparrman noted that, where possible, hunters tried to drive animals, and especially the large and greatly favoured eland, to a more convenient site for a kill before dispatching them.[19] The Khoikhoi capacity for meat consumption after a hunt made a great impression on him, as did their use of other parts of slaughtered animals, notably fat for smearing their bodies. Once so covered, a British contemporary noted, Khoikhoi people were 'defended from the influence of the air, and may in a manner reckon themselves dressed.'[20] Neither travellers nor Boers seem to have adopted the practice of smearing their whole bodies, although unguents and extracts culled from wild animals certainly played a role in Boer medication. Animal fat of all kinds was widely used for everything from wagon grease to candles. Sparrman was taught how to prepare fat from the heart of an eland for 'dressing victuals with, and for eating on bread.'[21] The fat tails of Cape sheep were also eaten and even exported to Britain as a delicacy.[22]

Conserving meat was a priority after a kill. Here the Khoikhoi technique of cutting it into strips and hanging it to dry, sometimes after salting, was very valuable to the Boers. Sparrman noted that farmers visiting the salt pan at the Zwartkops river (near present day Port Elizabeth) 'shot several heads of game, which they had hung up in large slips and shreds on the bushes, waggons, and poles, in order to dry it in the sun, in the same manner as the Hottentots did the elephant's flesh near *Diep-rivier*, as I mentioned before.'[23] Boer women and children, together with their servants, participated in the meat feast. The term biltong as well as the introduction of vinegar, coriander, pepper, and salpetre to help cure beef, were clearly colonial innovations.

Skins from both wild and domestic animals were rapidly brought into use for riems (leather strips), ropes, clothes, and shoes.[24] Sparrman was uncertain about the origin of the soft, raw leather shoes called velskoen. Khoikhoi

[18] Burchell, *Travels*, ii. 66.   [19] Sparrman, *Voyage*, ii. 161–2.

[20] Lieut. William Paterson, *A Narrative of Four Journeys into the Country of the Hottentots and Caffraria in the Years One Thousand Seven Hundred and Seventy-Seven, Eight, and Nine* (J. Johnson, London, 1789), 14.

[21] Sparrman, *Voyage*, ii. 161.

[22] Geoffrey Jenkins and Eve Palmer, *The Companion Guide to South Africa* (Collins, London, 1978), 265.

[23] Sparrman, *Voyage*, ii. 20–1; Thunberg, *Travels*, 94.   [24] van der Merwe, *Trek*, 143.

people wore them during his visit, and he described how a guide whom he recruited immediately went to make himself a pair before setting out. Sparrman adopted velskoen himself, and was a great advocate for them: he found them comfortable and cool, moulding themselves to the foot, and ideal for the hot, dry weather of the interior—although they were less well suited to the rain and damp of the Cape peninsula. He took a pair home, intending them as a model: 'whatever is useful, whether it come from *Paris* or the country of the *Hottentots*, alike deserves our attention and imitation.'[25]

Sparrman not only noted the use of Khoisan techniques but explicitly advocated, with a clarity startling to the modern reader, the value of indigenous knowledge. In one of a number of outbursts against colonial tyranny and slavery, he listed a range of cures, such as 'peruvian bark' (cinchona, from which Native Americans derived an anti-malarial drug), 'calculated for preserving millions of our species', which were 'learned . . . from those we call savages'. He asked rhetorically whether it would not be far better to learn 'from the fruits of their useful experience' than to slaughter them all.[26]

He learnt from a 'Hottentot-Boshiesman' 'that the root of the da-t'kai, a shrub of the mesembryanthemum kind pretty common here, eaten raw, was, in fact, very well-tasted'.[27] Burchell recorded: 'from the neighbouring hills, Speelman brought home a short fleshy plant, well known to the Hottentots, by the name of *Guaap*, and to botanists by that of *Stapelia pilifera* used for quenching thirst.'[28] Travellers sampled the *uyntjes* or wild onions eaten by the Khoisan; its growth was an indicator of the seasons. They tasted the edible fruits of 'Hottentot figs', a species of mesembryanthemum, and heard that their leaves, laid over a poisoned wound after sucking, had medicinal properties.[29]

Sparrman, often critical of the Boers, felt that 'the African colonists . . . are not near so forward to investigate the virtues of the plants of this country as by encroachments to increase their property.'[30] Here, perhaps, he allowed his prejudices to feed a generalization that his own evidence sometimes contradicted. Both immigrant slaves and frontier farmers did adopt and adapt local medicinal plants and substances.[31] Sparrman's Swedish contemporary Thunberg, also a student of Linnaeus, who visited the Cape at the same time but was more sympathetic to the Dutch colonists, took a different position. The Boers, he noted, without the services of apothecaries,

---

[25] Sparrman, *Voyage*, i. 191; Thunberg, *Travels*, 94. Paterson, *A Narrative*, 18–19. Paterson, who published after Sparrman's English edition, which he noted in his Introduction, seems to take some of this section word for word from Sparrman.

[26] Sparrman, *Voyage*, i. 55.   [27] Ibid. ii. 78–9.   [28] Burchell, *Travels*, i. 173.
[29] Sparrman, *Voyage*, ii. 31.   [30] Ibid. 78–9.   [31] Ibid. i. 82–3.

had prudently thought of trying the indigenous plants of Africa; and among these they had discovered various useful remedies in different diseases. As a botanist and physician, I . . . never lost an opportunity of adding to the slender stock of my knowledge, which often proved serviceable both to myself, and the benevolent and obliging colonists.[32]

Sparrman himself recorded a number of such uses, from *wilde alsies* (*Artemesia afra*) for worms, to an extract of hippopotamus brain as a remedy for convulsions.[33]

Ludwig Pappe, a German physician and botanist (Chapter 2), listed indigenous medicinal plants in the 1830s, and it is interesting that he sometimes distinguished between Boer and Khoikhoi uses. The Khoikhoi, who smeared buchu herbs mixed with fat on their bodies as a cosmetic, also infused it for a drink; it was adopted by the Boers especially as a base for medicinal brandy.[34] Settlers developed an export trade in aloe (*Aloe ferox*) extract for medicine and cosmetics; this was widely used in African societies as a skin ointment.[35] Khoikhoi people in turn incorporated imported species, such as tobacco and dagga (*Cannabis sativa*), into their pharmacopia. Khoikhoi women, acting as midwives for trekboers, mixed a stomach smear of dagga and tobacco with milk, alongside the indigenous buchu, for difficult births.[36]

Although their pastoral system made some impact on the vegetation, and Khoikhoi people gathered many plants, they had not apparently domesticated any. One reason may have been the lack of suitable species at the Cape.[37] Despite the fact that Dutch colonial regimes were alert to the potential of local plants, and had an experimental garden from the seventeenth century, few were found suitable for cultivation as food or medicine. Western Cape agriculture was very largely dependent upon plants introduced from Europe. To a limited degree, settlers adopted crops grown by Xhosa-speaking Africans in the eastern summer rainfall zone, which the trekboers had reached by the middle of the eighteenth century. Sparrman found the African crop sorghum being grown as far west as the Tsitsikamma—in this case for

[32] Thunberg, *Travels*, 160.   [33] Sparrman, *Voyage*, ii. 137, 217.

[34] 'Buchu' seems to have been the name for a number of species, and was used also for pain and lameness: Sparrman, *Voyage*, i. 156; Thunberg, *Travels*, 77.

[35] Sparrman, *Voyage*, ii. 248.

[36] Harriet Deacon, 'Midwives and Medical Men in the Cape Colony Before 1860', *Journal of African History*, 39: 2 (1998), 289; David Gordon, 'From Rituals of Rapture to Dependence: The Political Economy of Khoikhoi Narcotic Consumption, *c*.1487–1870', *South African Historical Journal*, 35 (1996), 70.

[37] Jared Diamond, *Guns, Germs and Steel: A Short History of Everybody for the Last 13,000 years* (Vintage, London, 1998).

cattle feed.[38] Maize, introduced from the Americas, became ubiquitous in both Xhosa and settler plots. Cape species proved most popular internationally for garden and greenhouse flowers; by the nineteenth century, pelargonium cultivars (geraniums) graced houses and balconies throughout Europe.

Sparrman's text is full of stories, based on Khoikhoi experience of animals, which came to be part of the common Cape vernacular folklore. Knowledge of the routes, lairs, and watering holes of wild animals were important in shaping hunting expeditions. His guides knew where to find honey in trees because they could see where ratels ('honey badgers') had gnawed at the trunks. He was clearly fascinated when they taught him about the honeyguide bird, which also led alert humans to honey.[39] The nightly campfire, at the heart of all travel at the Cape, derived partly from Khoikhoi understanding of animal behaviour. As Sparrman noted, 'fires and fire-brands are universally reckoned . . . to be a great preservative and defence against lions and other wild beasts'.[40] Fire was, of course, more generally necessary for cooking and warmth, a prerequisite for human life.

Sparsity of water sources profoundly shaped many aspects of Cape life, not least travel itself. The routes into the interior worked along fountains and streams, like discontinuous rivers. Sparrman admired his servants' capacity to find water, although they themselves suggested that it was often the cattle that scented it first at a great distance.[41] It was not necessarily difficult to detect streams in the semi-arid interior. When Lichtenstein described the view from the Roggeveld mountains, eastward across the Great Karoo he saw

a parched and arid plain, stretching out to such an extent that the vast hills by which it is terminated are almost lost in the distance. The beds of numberless little rivers cross, like veins, in a thousand directions, this enormous space; the course of them might in some places be clearly distinguished by the dark green of the mimosas [*Acacia karoo*] which spread along their banks.[42]

A British traveller affirmed that 'if a running stream lies in his route, he will see it afar off, and will be able to trace its course by the . . . thick shrubbery extending along both its banks'.[43] But a change in vegetation, though likely evidence of water, was no guarantee that it would be found in usable quantity. Guides were sometimes essential in locating aars, or geological faults, where water often reached the surface.

---

[38] Sparrman, *Voyage*, ii. 19.   [39] Ibid. 144.   [40] Ibid. 40.
[41] Ibid. 14, 19.   [42] Lichtenstein, *Travels*, i. 138.
[43] John Howison, *European Colonies in Various Parts of the World Viewed in their Social, Moral, and Physical Condition* (Richard Bentley, London, 1834), i. 204–5.

The vital needs of domesticated animals taught all their owners something about water resources and veld. Some cattle were descended from breeds that had traversed the semi-arid districts under Khoikhoi management for centuries; they were, in a sense, excellent dowsers and good botanists. Their herders could direct them, but animals, moving long distances, had to decide which plants to eat. When the first professional veterinary surgeons discussed the nutritional needs of livestock, they took it for granted that livestock instinctively sought a balanced diet (Chapter 4). Animals' predeliction for particular vegetation could create problems for travellers. A mid-nineteenth-century geologist described how his oxen sought out the highly palatable 'Bushman grass' (stipagrostis): 'they will go twenty miles in a night to get back to it . . . and lose themselves.'[44] He spent a good deal of his time searching for strays.

Khoisan people brought such skills, and their accumulated experience as pastoralists, to the colonial agricultural economy. In the Sneeuberg, north of Graaff-Reinet village, where Boer expansion was temporarily delayed by Bushman raids, 'it was quickly observed that certain Bushmen were excellent and skilled shepherds who knew where the best grazing was to be had beyond the limits of the farmer's boundary'.[45] Farmers initially used Khoisan clients to take care of their herds in dry seasons and found the cattle much improved on return. Khoisan livestock keepers, Elphick argued, had long been susceptible to ecological cycles and there were periods, after droughts or political conflicts, when some clans were deprived temporarily of livestock.[46] On the eighteenth-century frontier, some shepherds took payment in animals and were able to build up their own flocks for as long as they could find land on which to do so.

San herders 'watched over the farmers' livestock by day and at night kept the fires burning around the stock pens in order to keep away wild animals'.[47] In 1799, shortly after the south-eastern Tarka area had been colonized, 'seventy Bosjeman' lived on the farm of Johannes P. van der Waldt, credited as one of the first Boers to reach an accommodation with them. As shepherds they went 'to the fields armed with a Bow and quiver of poisoned arrows', protecting the flocks from theft and 'the Lion, the Wolf, the tyger, or

---

[44] Wylie, *Appendix* (Case of Good Hope, *Appendix* to *The Report of the Geological Surveyor presented to Parliament in June 1859* (Government Prints Cape Town, 1860)), 26. F. P. van Oudtshoorn, *Gids tot Grasse van Suid-Afrika* (Briza publikasies, Pretoria, 1994), describes two species of 'Bushman grass', abundant in the Karoo and northern Cape, which are particularly valuable as fodder.

[45] C. Garth Sampson, 'Acquisition of European Livestock by the Seacow River Bushmen between AD 1770–1890', *South African Field Archaeology*, 4 (1995), 33. Thanks to Sean Archer for this reference.

[46] Elphick, *Khoikhoi*.   [47] van der Merwe, *Migrant Farmer*, 115.

Jackall'.[48] Burchell noted the 'incredible' facility of Khoikhoi herders for distinguishing individual sheep.[49] Howison, after commenting on their 'natural
genius for tending and managing cattle', marvelled at the fact that shepherds
could drive 'several thousand sheep two or three hundred miles without
losing one of them', through the most inhospitable country.[50]

For travellers in the Cape interior, the rhythms of life were not least determined, as they were for its local people, by animals and their needs. The veld
was not only of import because endless vistas of the Karoo, fringed by mountain ranges, dominated the landscape, but because it was the lifeblood of the
animals. Many travellers commented on the veld and few omitted to inform
their readers that 'Karoo' was derived from the Khoikhoi word for dry, or
'horridly parched up and arid'. Speaking of the western Cape, Sparrman
noted that

the warmer part of the year, there hardly falls a drop of rain. The ground is as dry
and bare of grass as a high road; and the shrubs on it are, to all appearance at least,
dried up . . . The earth . . . seems languishing with drought and thirst . . . The sun
scorches the traveller up with its reflected rays, and the ground almost burns him
through the soles of his shoes.[51]

Descriptions of aridity and drought became commonplace in travellers' texts
and, like animal stories, successive authors drew on one another to solidify
this characterization of the Cape.

By the time of Sparrman's visit, travellers were well aware that the winter
rainfall of the western region gave way to summer rain towards the east: the
dividing line went roughly north-east from around Port Elizabeth, cutting
the Karoo in two. They also reported on more localized climatic variety. The
independent Khoikhoi had followed the dictates of veld and rainfall, moving
their whole settlements at different times of the year. Although some trekboers did initially replicate this pattern, living in tents and wagons for long
periods, settlement in most frontier districts soon became more stable. The
'majority of colonists were not trekkers, but settlers who, having acquired a
desirable farm, often kept it for life'—or at least till they heard of better
land further into the interior.[52] Nevertheless, within this framework of

---

[48] Edna and Frank Bradlow (eds.), *William Somerville's Narrative of his Journeys to the Eastern
Cape Frontier and to Lattakoe 1799–1802* (van Riebeeck Society, Cape Town, 1979), 26. 'Tiger' was
used for leopard and 'wolf' for hyena; Wilson and Thompson, *Oxford History*, 71.

[49] Burchell, *Travels*, i. 172.   [50] Howison, *European Colonies*, 242.

[51] Sparrman, *Voyage*, i. 234–5.

[52] Susan Newton-King, 'The Enemy Within: The Struggle for Ascendency on the Cape
Eastern Frontier, 1760–1800', unpublished Ph.D. thesis, University of London (1992), 45, 80.

increasingly strong property rights, farmers in particular areas often did have to move their animals. Afrikaner stockowners are better described as practising transhumance than nomadism, either sending animals away or moving between two or three fixed points during the year.

By the early nineteenth century many different patterns of transhumance had evolved, depending on local society, climate, terrain, and vegetation. In the western, winter-rainfall zone, Khoikhoi herders had moved in and out of the coastal strip around Saldanha Bay. Travellers reported that some coastal pastures contained nutrients that were a prophylaxis against the deficiency disease in cattle called *lamziekte* by Boers (Chapter 4).[53] The Khoikhoi left this area during the dry summers for inland pastures along permanent rivers in the Swartland. Boer stockowners learnt to send their cattle to this strip of coast when the disease threatened, and by the early nineteenth century the owners of west-coast farms were able to charge for the hire of their pastures.[54]

Sparrman reported on the colonial distinction between sweet and sour veld, which also shaped patterns of transhumance. Sourveld, he understood, tended to be predominant in higher, cooler, or wetter areas. It had more perennial species, a thicker sward, and grasses with tougher blades. But it was deficient in some respects, so that cattle grazing on it tended to chew leather, bones, and horns. Sparrman thought this was because of its 'acid quality' which could be transmitted to the animal's stomach. At this time Boers were moving into the summer-rainfall coastal sourveld area of Xhosa and Khoikhoi settlement, east of Algoa Bay, that became the heavily contested Zuurveld. Even in this rich grazing zone, the Xhosa chiefdoms found the sourveld best after the rains in the spring and summer (roughly October to April) when it was green and soft. During the dryer winter (April to September)—when the grass became rank and tough and lost its nutritional value—they tried to move to sweeter pastures in river valleys or further inland.[55]

Sweetveld tended to predominate in lower areas, with apparently sandier soil, such as the Karoo flats. By the 1770s Sparrman could report with confidence that

for the purpose of feeding sheep, the Carrow [Karoo] is considered as the best land, and the *Zuurvelden* the least, if at all, fit. For cattle it [sourveld] has been found to answer better, when they could be removed off and on from one of these kinds of

[53] Andrew B. Smith, *Pastoralism in Africa: Origins and Development Ecology* (Witwatersrand University Press, Johannesburg, 1992), 193–5.

[54] Lichtenstein, *Travels*, i. 59–60.

[55] J. B. Peires, *The House of Phalo: A History of the Xhosa People in the Days of their Independence* (Ravan Press, Johannesburg, 1981), 8–11.

land to the other. The constant and unequivocal experience of the colonists, with regard to this point, agrees with the result of the practice of the Hottentots.[56]

Sparrman was struck by the fact that sheep did not 'fare ill' on Karoo bushes even in the dry months. Increasing concentration on sheep rather than cattle in the interior, even before woolled Merino varieties were adopted, reflected the trekboer attempts to come to terms with the difficult terrain.

Lichtenstein in particular grasped the range of transhumant practices. In the winter-rainfall western mountains of the Roggeveld and Bokkeveld, farmers with properties in higher zones migrated down to their *legplaats* on the Karoo flats in the winter, from around June to October, to escape the damp cold. Animals could be saved from the frost, which diminished the nutritional value of veld, and the disease of the mountains.[57] Firewood was more plentiful on the flats and ganna (salsola species) could be found to mix with sheep fat for soap; antelope were abundant for hunting. Too dry for permanent settlement, the Karoo blossomed into a 'glorious meadow' when rain fell and the refreshed plants were 'a remedy, if [stock] were diseased, which speedily restores them to health'.[58] This sense of the nutritional and healing powers of Karoo shrubs remained strong throughout the nineteenth century. It was a maxim amongst farmers that, even if their sheep did not move long distances, 'the oftener their place of feeding is changed, the better they thrive'; bad pasture and drought was seen to have an immediate impact in the manifestation of disease, especially *brandsiekte* (scab), a scourge of sheep everywhere.[59]

Towards the eastern boundaries of the colony, in the summer-rainfall area, some farmers in the high, cold, Sneeuberg area, north of Graaff-Reinet town, where it 'sometimes snow[ed] to a man's length in depth', took their sheep down to the warm, dry plains of the Camdeboo, south of the settlement. When the indigenous people had been displaced, they also moved seasonally to the north (now Middelburg and Richmond districts). Similarly, those in the Karoo flats might seek pastures on the mountains in the summer. Robert Jacob Gordon, commander of the Cape garrison, explorer, and scientific authority, heard in the 1770s that horses were sent to the Sneeuberg from the lowland Camdeboo flats to avoid horse-sickness.[60]

The Sneeuberg uplands were bereft of trees, except for stunted 'mimosa' (*Acacia karoo*) in sheltered kloofs. Dung and even the viscera of sheep

[56] Sparrman, *Voyage*, i. 238.
[57] van der Merwe, *Trek*, 130 ff.; Bradlow, *William Somerville's Narrative*, 206.
[58] Lichtenstein, *Travels*, i. 122.   [59] Ibid. 130; Paterson, *Narrative of Four Journeys*, 47.
[60] Raper and Boucher (eds.), *Gordon*, i. 81.

sometimes had to be used as fuel. The mountains and hilltops, however, had an unusually dense grass cover, mostly sourveld in type, that was especially valuable, in a summer-rainfall area, after the spring rains. Water could also be found at this time. Although Gordon concurred that usually 'sheep prefer shrubs and cattle grass', the grassy Sneeuberg was an exception. It was already recognized as an excellent summer grazing ground for sheep when he visited in 1777, barely twenty years after it was first colonized.[61] Others confirmed that it 'may be considered the best nursery for sheep in the whole colony', with average animal weights considerably higher than elsewhere.[62] Dr Mackrill, who started the government farm at Somerset (East) in 1814, travelled to the Sneeuberg in 1816 to purchase top quality stock. He found 'no sickness among them, and all animals Man and Beast enjoy AN UNINTER-RUPTED STATE OF HIGH HEALTH'.[63] (He also noted that dung used as cooking fuel imbued the 'mutton chop a la caca' with a distinctive flavour.)

Mackrill felt that 'a more productive Grass Land is not to be found upon earth'. European farmers with such a resource might have made hay for the winter. Nevertheless, the cold was so intense on the mountain farms that shelter as well as fodder would have been necessary for livestock in the winter months, and few Boers could contemplate the investment required to house thousands of sheep. Moreover, even in this area it was believed that sheep did better if moved for substantial periods to lowland, Karoo veld when there was enough water.

Trekboer transhumance in search of water and pastures could be the first step towards permanent migration into a new frontier district. In the early decades of the nineteenth century farmers moved into the north-eastern Cape between the Sneeuberg and Gariep (Orange) river. The area was particularly susceptible at this period to droughts, locust plagues, and large herds of migratory springboks, all of which made serious inroads into the pastures.[64] Andries Stockenstrom, magistrate of Graaff-Reinet, wrote of 'Springbucks, called Trek Bokken . . . in such droves that all numerical description must appear exaggerated'.[65] Locusts tended to swarm, as in 1824, when drought was broken, compounding the difficulty of recovery. In 1826 Robert Moffat, missionary amongst the Tswana, north of Cape's boundary at Dithakong, despaired that 'all other earthly powers, from the fiercest lion to a marshalled army are nothing compared with these diminutive insects'.[66]

[61] Ibid. 83.   [62] Barrow, *Travels*, i. 204.

[63] Margaret Kannemeyer, 'Dr. Mackrill's Notebook', *Africana Notes and News*, 8: 2 (1951), quoted in James Walton, *Homesteads and Villages of South Africa* (J. L. van Schaik, Pretoria, 1952), 57–9.

[64] van der Merwe, *Noortwaartse Beweging*, esp. chap. 6.   [65] Quoted in ibid. 181.

[66] Quoted in ibid. 197.

Trekboers could at best try to protect their gardens with smoke, as Africans did, or trample voracious voetgangers (hoppers) with their herds and flocks.[67]

It was not only trekboers who had to adapt to the pastures and seasons. The commercial wagon traffic from Cape Town to Graaff-Reinet was also seasonal, restricted to the wetter months when there was water and pasture for the oxen in the Karoo tracts which they had to cross.[68] In very dry years, such as 1818, trans-Karoo wagon traffic came to a standstill. The opening of Port Elizabeth and East London soon afterwards largely supplanted this long and arduous route for the transport of goods, although stock still had to be driven overland to market. An element of seasonality arose around the East London wagon traffic too. Farmers and transport riders liked to get their oxen down to the moist coastal grazing in the dry winter months, when the grass of the interior had far more limited feeding value.

Lichtenstein enjoyed the idea that even he, as a scientist in a large, official touring party, was to some degree subject to the general restless movement of South Africa:

We were indeed becoming perfect nomades, sharing the lot of most of the inhabitants of southern Africa, whom nature disposes, or compels, to stated changes of habitation. The colonists are driven by the snow from the mountains down to the Karoo; the Caffre hordes forsake their valleys when food for their cattle begins to fail, and seek others where grass is more abundant; the Bosjeman is fixed to no single spot of his barren soil, but every night reposes his weary head in a different place from the former; the numerous flocks of light footed deer, the clouds of locusts, the immeasurable trains of wandering caterpillars, these, all instructed by nature, press forward from spot to spot, searching the necessary means by which that nature is to be supported.[69]

Lichtenstein felt, like Sparrman, that the veld was categorized too simply as sweet and sour, or healthy and unhealthy, and that vegetation and diseases, then seen as 'wholly enigmatical', should be scientifically researched.[70] Both probably underestimated the knowledge of at least some stockowners and their servants. Even though systematic botanical classification to which these travelling scientists aspired was lacking, it is striking, in retrospect, how many plants were named, and how often travellers reported these vernacular names, together with specific plant properties. The seemingly careless admixture of local languages used for plant names by Boers and Khoikhoi

[67] Barrow, *Travels*, i. 213, 355.

[68] George Thompson, *Travels and Adventures in Southern Africa* vol. 1 (van Riebeeck Society, Cape Town, 1967), 43. Thompson, who was relatively sympathetic to the Khoi, had read Sparrman and Burchell, amongst others.

[69] Lichtenstein, *Travels*, i. 414.   [70] Ibid. 441–2.

guides is evidence in itself of intense cultural interchange. Some were drawn from Khoikhoi words, like ganna, buchu, karee, or nenta (a poisonous plant); some, like palmiet, rooigras, uyentjies, vygies, or spekboom from Dutch; some, like aloe, were internationally used botanical names.[71]

Most of the scientific travellers commented on the use of fire in pasture management, evident since the very first reports on the Khoikhoi. Van Riebeeck found fire so troublesome and dangerous in the earliest years of settlement that he and his successors tried to control it. Similarly, fire was essential in Xhosa pasture management, especially of sourveld grasses. These were burnt when they became dry and rank in the winter, so that space was made, and ash fertilizer provided, for the fresh shoots when the spring rains fell around October. The use of fire to burn old grass soon became a central technique of Afrikaner stockowners wherever grass was more abundant than shrubs. This applied in coastal and upland sourveld, and in the mixed grassveld of the eastern districts. Travelling down the eastern end of the Langkloof (towards present-day Humansdorp), Sparrman thought his wagon was in danger, so fierce were the flames set by a farmer 'for the purposes of destroying the dry plants, grass, and bushes that grew on his land'.[72]

As in the case of many African stock-keepers, the Khoikhoi deployed livestock loaning systems in order to distribute animals, lighten the impact of large herds, and cement social relationships of clientage or interdependence.[73] Whether by emulation or necessity, similar practices evolved on the Dutch frontier. Sparrman described how he was encouraged by a woman to settle with the Boers in Agterbruintjieshoogte (near present Somerset East): 'here are people enough, who will send you that part of their cattle to keep which they cannot conveniently look after themselves, on conditions that you shall have the young ones produced by them for your trouble.'[74] A similar arrangement operated in the early nineteenth century for Dutch East India Company servants and soldiers who married into Boer families.[75]

Settlers initially adopted or captured Khoikhoi livestock, although the cattle in particular were gradually interbred with introduced stock. Local livestock were adapted to the pastures and to the threat of predators, so dangerous in the Cape. Predators often attempt to separate weaker animals from a herd or flock, which is facilitated if the prey scatter when frightened. Cape sheep, unlike some introduced varieties, were 'strong runners' and

---

[71] There seems to be no obvious pattern in the retention of Khoikhoi names, except perhaps in the case of shrubs which were particularly important to them.

[72] Sparrman, *Voyage*, ii. 241.   [73] Elphick, *Khoikhoi*, 62.

[74] Sparrman, *Voyage*, ii. 133; Smith, *From Frontier to Midlands*.

[75] Newton-King, 'The Enemy Within', 37.

'usually bunch[ed] together when in danger'.[76] Cattle at the Cape also appear to have developed an instinct for self-preservation. When threatened by predators in their kraals, 'all collected in a body with their horns towards the door and formed a crescent'.[77]

Khoikhoi pastoral systems, going back perhaps two thousand years, were deeply influenced in other ways by the threat of predators.[78] In order to protect animals and minimize theft and straying, all livestock were returned nightly to the settlement from their pastures. The Khoikhoi guarded cattle within a circle of huts; small kraals were made for calves and lambs to protect them against jackals.[79] Africans throughout the wetter parts of southern Africa operated a similar system of nightly kraaling. Predators were, in a sense, ready for colonists' sheep and, in the unfenced pastures of the colony, this necessitated adoption of African systems. In the interior Boer hunters and pastoralists built tak-kraals of thorn bushes; stone or timber structures followed more permanent settlements.[80] The system of kraaling in itself drew the indigenous inhabitants into the colonial pastoral economy, because it was relatively labour intensive and required full-time shepherds to drive the animals to and from the pastures on a daily basis.

By the early nineteenth century the Khoisan communities within the colonial boundaries had been conquered, decimated, and largely incorporated as a servile class. Yet their knowledge and to some degree their language were absorbed into the dominant colonial culture and survived in many facets of the pastoral economy. Despite smallpox, they remained perhaps one-third of the population within colonial boundaries in the early nineteenth century, before the African communities of the eastern Cape were conquered. The Khoikhoi were not bearers of a static culture. As Robert Ross has argued, some communities on mission stations may have developed more orthodox Christian religious expression and village settlements, than some of those, identified as Boers, who drew on the old Khoikhoi pastoral techniques. Ross borrowed the term 'creolisation' to describe this uneven intermingling of settler and indigenous practices.[81]

Creolization, along with hybridity, has been frequently invoked in analyses of colonial cultures and languages, including that of the Cape slave

[76] N. J. van der Merwe, 'The Jackal', *Flora and Fauna*, 4 (1953), 17.

[77] Elphick, *Khoikhoi*, 59.   [78] Ibid. 59.

[79] Smith, *Pastoralism in Africa*, 203.   [80] van der Merwe, *Trek*, 19.

[81] Robert Ross, 'The Anthropology of the Germanic-speaking Peoples of Southern Africa', unpublished paper presented to the conference on 'History and Anthropology in Southern Africa', University of Manchester (1980), 9, drawing on Sidney W. Mintz and Richard Price, *An Anthropological Approach to the Afro-American Past: A Caribbean Perspective* (Philadelphia, 1976).

population.[82] 'Creole space' has been used to describe the Kat river mission and village settlements of 'colonial Hottentots'.[83] However, the term has Caribbean, Latin American, and West African connotations that sit uneasily in the South African context. It might also suggest a balance of cultural influence between settlers and indigenous people. While it is possible to argue that vestiges of Khoikhoi culture remained far more pervasive than their sudden loss of land and power might indicate, this was not an even exchange.

Van der Merwe saw the process of adaption by settlers as a 'verafrikaansing' of practices and culture. He seems to have implied that settlers became 'of Africa' and adapted to the African environment, rather than that they were Africanized.[84] More appropriate might be the idea of a 'Cape Vernacular' coined by the classicist Andre Hugo in the 1970s to describe the colonial culture that emerged from the chains of slavery and conquest.[85] Hugo was more concerned with the amalgam of settler with slave than with Khoikhoi. He adopted the term vernacular from the word for a Roman household slave, often closely attached to a slave-owning family. He played also on its English meaning in the sense of home-grown or local language, culture, or architecture. As a liberal Afrikaner academic, uneasy about apartheid, he was invoking his classical knowledge to challenge Afrikaner self-perception as exclusively European and different from Coloured people:

Have we ever paused to ask ourselves what the full significance is of the circumstance that generation after generation of our Afrikaans ancestors were nurtured at the breasts of Indian, Hottentot and negro women, and received a good part of their early education from slave and Hottentot men who, ignorant of classical traditions, acted unwittingly as their trusted and beloved 'pedagogues'? What strange lore was imbibed, to be passed on to future generations? What stories were learnt? And the language they learnt from the lips of those slaves—was it not the *Lingua vernacula*, the Cape Dutch of the slaves, the Cape vernacular? Truly, our forebears may be said to have imbibed the vernacular language together with the vernacular milk.[86]

Sparrman himself recorded that in the interior, 'where they have no other servants than Hottentos [*sic*], the children of the Christians frequently learn the Hottentot language more easily, and before they do the Dutch'.[87]

---

[82] Robert C.-H. Shell, 'The Tower of Babel: The Slave Trade and Creolization at the Cape, 1652–1834', in Elizabeth A. Eldredge and Fred Morton, *Slavery in South Africa: Captive Labor on the Dutch Frontier* (Westview Press, Boulder, 1994).

[83] P. R. Anderson, 'The Human Clay: An Essay in the Spatial History of the Cape Eastern Frontier 1811–35', unpublished M. Litt. thesis, University of Oxford (1992), 93.

[84] van der Merwe, *Trek*, 87–98.   [85] Hugo, *The Cape Vernacular*.

[86] Ibid. 18.   [87] Sparrman, *Voyage*, i. 219.

Although the Cape vernacular was a culture of conquest, the frontier settlers not only adapted to their local environment, but also learnt how to do so from the people they displaced. This process deeply influenced the colonial pastoral economy.

British Settlers: Colonial Imposition and Adaption, 1820–1860

Khoisan knowledge was less influential for the western Cape arable and slave-holding farmers or the nineteenth-century British settlers. The English-speaking immigrants, clustered in the newly colonized eastern Cape districts from 1820, initially looked back home to the powerful, confident metropolitan culture from which they came. They could also remain more closely linked to their European roots than most Dutch settlers because of their literacy, the improvement of communications in the nineteenth century, and the global reach of the empire that spawned them. Unlike the French Huguenots, they kept their language; this has been of critical importance in South Africa's history.

During the nineteenth century British officials and a significant number of settlers became committed protagonists of bureaucratic government and scientific agriculture. This placed them at odds with locally evolved rural modes of living and pastoral practices. Yet even British settlers, and especially those who survived as farmers, had to make some adaptions to the local environment. Some developed identities that took account of their locality as colonial nationalists, as eastern Cape separatists, or in expressing the distinctiveness of their Britishness in a colonial territory. Even those who advocated intensive agriculture, and were deeply influenced by British ideas of property and improvement, recognized that their technology and methods would need to take account of local resources and constraints. In this sense, they also developed a vernacular culture.

Some attempt was made in the 1820 Albany settlement to replicate 'the England of enclosure, of country squires and cottage agriculture', with small fields, valley-based homes, and mixed farming.[88] A Cape Town merchant who travelled to the eastern districts at this time celebrated one of the wealthiest and most successful early settler homesteads: 'the hedges and ditches, and walled fences, presented home-looking pictures of neatness and industry, very different from the rude and slovenly premises of the back-country boers.'[89] The women in one settler party were each given a British acorn, 'in

---

[88] Anderson, 'The Human Clay', 49.   [89] Thompson, *Travels and Adventures*, i. 20.

2. Albany Farmhouse, 1820s

hopes that the British Oak would rear its head and remain for ages in com-
memoration of the event of the landing'.[90] Over the next few decades, the cultural disposition and economic ambitions of some British settlers encouraged
them to 'recreate home'.[91] As one wrote: 'in the "artificial" Country you live
in you are delighted with "Nature" where you can find it—We are directly
the reverse, we have so much of the latter that we are enchanted at the least
appearance of . . . a bank or hedge.'[92] Improvement of land was seen not only
as potentially profitable, but as a moral and religious good, bringing civilization and order, and justifying, in some eyes, appropriation of resources from
indigenous people and Boers.[93]

British officials and settlers, like their Dutch predecessors, gave some of
their towns and farms new names, from Grahamstown and Kingwilliamstown, to Port Elizabeth and East London. Clifton Crais sees not so much a
re-creation of Britain, as a new landscape of British power, 'centred on the
opposition of colonial (rationally organized) space and African (sensual and
inferior) space'.[94] Settlers built 'substantial manor houses', some initially
fortified. Although his analysis allows that British buildings increasingly

[90] The Dutch, of course, had planted oaks in the western Cape (Chap. 2).
[91] Jill Payne, 'Re-Creating Home: British Colonialism, Culture and the Zuurveld Environment
in the Nineteenth Century', unpublished MA thesis, Rhodes University (1998).
[92] Ibid. 33.   [93] Drayton, *Nature's Government*.
[94] Crais, *Making of the Colonial Order*, 133.

'opened to a less threatening and more anglicised landscape of pastures, fields and gardens tended by workers', Crais essentially argues that the architecture exuded and expressed power, and reshaped the landscape.[95] Space was carefully segregated and controlled within different rooms and different zones around the farmhouse.

Given the tendency in older South African historiography to contrast the harshness of Boer frontier society with a more liberal, bureaucratic British presence, it is worth emphasizing that British conquest could also be brutal—and it was generally more successful.[96] Settlers were prepared to fight, along with colonial forces, sometimes mercilessly, for the land they had carved out from Xhosa territory. Yet such understandings of conquest and the imposition of military, social, and spatial control should not preclude consideration of an important sub-text in the social history of British settlement. From the start, there was some appreciation that the Cape environment was essentially different. At least amongst settler authors, echoing earlier travellers, wildness and aridity could be an object of admiration as well as unease.

British settlers found themselves adopting some of the words and practices that the Dutch had developed. Even before the 1820 settlement, anglicized Dutch words such as inspan and vlei were coming into travellers' texts. *The Chronicle of Jeremiah Goldswain* demonstrates the breadth of early borrowing—often of those terms linked to farming or the environment like veld, kraal, kaross, krantz, trek, and skei.[97] (Cape oxen were thought to understand only Afrikaans commands.[98]) Established Dutch and African vernacular names for wild animals, for plant species, and for livestock diseases were also used. The mixing of people from all over Britain tended quite quickly to produce a common and distinctive English-speaking culture which sought some of its cement in the specifically South African context.[99]

A number of early British settlers first built 'thatched shelters more or less after the native fashion', or 'hartebeest' huts in the manner of trekboers.[100]

[95] Ibid. 136.

[96] Ben McLennan, *A Proper Degree of Terror: John Graham and the Cape's Eastern Frontier* (Ravan Press, Johannesburg, 1986); J. B. Peires, *The Dead Will Arise: Nongqawuse and the Great Xhosa Cattle-Killing Movement of 1856–7* (Ravan Press, Johannesburg, 1989).

[97] L. F. Casson, *The Dialect of Jeremiah Goldswain, Albany Settler* (Oxford University Press, Cape Town, 1955), Inaugural Lecture, University of Cape Town Lecture Series, no. 7; Una Long (ed.), *The Chronicle of Jeremiah Goldswain, Albany Settler of 1820*, 2 vols. (van Riebeeck Society, Cape Town, 1946, 1949); Guy Butler (ed.), *The 1820 Settlers: An Illustrated Commentary* (Human & Rousseau, Cape Town, 1974), 76.

[98] Butler, *1820 Settlers*, 135.   [99] Ibid.

[100] Ronald Lewcock, *Early Nineteenth Century Architecture in South Africa: A Study in the Interaction of Two Cultures, 1795–1837* (A. A. Balkema, Cape Town, 1963), 133—more correctly *hardbieshuisies* (reed houses).

Thomas Pringle records constructing a Xhosa-style beehive hut 'in the mode practised by the natives'. Dr Mackrill wrote, when describing the well-developed Boer farm of Andries Pretorius in Graaff-Reinet in 1816, that the floors were still made of cow dung in African style: 'literally to make a House in Africa clean you have only to beshit all over with manure.'[101] Pringle and others 'received instruction' from Khoikhoi employees about plastering with sand and cow dung, and flooring with soil from anthills. He scooped out, in local fashion, an anthill, and plastered it inside, for an oven.[102] Wattle-and-daub techniques (known also in Britain) were used for huts and some settlers rebuilt trekboer homes which had been damaged or deserted during the wars of the previous two decades.

Mission stations in the 1820s sometimes combined a mix of square and round buildings.[103] Xhosa-speaking servants and tenants living on the farms and premises of their employers built their own huts in the styles that they knew, sometimes alongside settler structures. As eminent a personage as the recently arrived archdeacon of Grahamstown could tolerate a 'Kafir hut' in his garden in mid-century.[104] Adaptions of the round hut later became a more established style for settlers themselves with the invention of the rondavel, which became part of a broader national architectural vernacular. The 'Cape Dutch' architectural style was adopted and developed by British as much as Dutch settlers. Many key examples are from the period after Dutch rule: 'nowhere else in the world did historical accident bring together the Dutch and British colonial traditions so abruptly or so completely.'[105] The buildings and settlements that resulted from British occupation were not simply an imposition of new styles and new conceptions of space.

In Albany, some British settlers found they had Dutch-speaking neighbours, who had survived the early battles with the Xhosa for the Zuurveld. An interchange of skills, as well as social and sexual intercourse, soon followed. The Bowkers, one of the biggest and wealthiest of British families, received help from a neighbour, Piet Oosthuizen, and two sons married daughters of his.[106] Bertram Bowker recalled how, as a youth, he visited an Afrikaner family. 'I paid him L2.5. to allow me to help him make a wagon. They were right good people. I stayed one month with them. We made a pair of wheels

---

[101] Walton, *Homesteads and Villages*, 57.

[102] Thomas Pringle, *Narrative of a Residence in South Africa*, vol. 1 (Empire Book Association, Brentwood, Essex, 1986), 39; first published 1834.

[103] Butler, *1820 Settlers*, 311, picture of Buntingville.

[104] Peires, *The Dead Will Arise*, illustration facing p. 160.

[105] Lewcock, *Early Nineteenth Century Architecture*.

[106] I. Mitford-Barberton, *Comdt. Holden Bowker: An 1820 settler Book Including Unpublished Records of the Frontier Wars* (Human & Rousseau, Cape Town, 1970), 12–24.

and then spent the rest of the month in hunting, shooting and larking with the girls.'[107]

Pringle was unusually sympathetic to the colonized people of the Cape, and also, fifty years after Sparrman, deeply aware of cultural interchange and its value. His sketch of a campfire during his party's trek up to what became the Glen Lynden settlement vividly portrays a microcosm of Cape society: Boers with their 'roers' [muskets]; immigrants 'conversing in broad Scotch ... on the comparative merits of long and shorthorned cattle'; 'young men and servant lads ... standing around the Hottentots ... practising with them a lesson of mutual tuition in their respective dialects'; and 'a Bushman ... mimicking' everyone.[108]

British settlers were forced to experiment. The story that one settler planted a whole maize cob, with its kernels, is more likely a metaphor for the initial strangeness of the terrain, than an often repeated mistake.[109] Memories of the British incapacity to drive sheep or their innocent purchase of kapaters, castrated goats, as breeding stock, are in the same vein.[110] Although the initial agricultural close settlement schemes were not a success, it is striking how quickly many understood the problems they faced and began to adapt to them. Settlers' wheat was attacked by rust, probably imported with the seed, which thrived in the damper coastal districts. Within a couple of seasons some had switched to maize, already acclimatized in the summer-rainfall districts of the eastern Cape by Africans and Boers. Pringle described how the Scots settlers at Glen Lynden soon adopted the whole range of established colonial plants directly from neighbouring Boers. Except for the potatoes, most of the seeds that they brought from Europe failed, and were replaced with 'colonial seed' and 'slips, grafts and cuttings' of less familiar plants such as peach, apricot, almond, lemon, fig, and vines, with gardens 'encircled by hedges of quince and pomegranate'.[111]

Some British settlers were alert to the potential of indigenous plants as well as acclimatized imported food species. Miles Bowker 'did little in this colony but make gardens'; these included local aloes and succulents.[112] Two of his children, Mary and James Henry, became collectors and champions of indigenous plants (Chapter 2).[113] William Atherstone, a leading physician in Grahamstown, recorded the use of medicinal plants as remedies by both Khoikhoi and Boers. He also noted British settlers experimenting with one of them called 'Kow Goed' (chewing material):

[107] Ibid. 60.   [108] Pringle, *Narrative*, i. 20–1; Butler, *1820 Settlers*, 301.
[109] Payne, 'Re-creating Home', 72.   [110] Butler, *1820 Settlers*, 136.
[111] Pringle, *Narrative*, i. 38.   [112] Mitford-Barberton, *Holden Bowker*, 44.
[113] Beinart, 'Men, Science'.

Walter Biggar used it for a narcotic and pleasing intoxicant against the evil effects of opium . . . It is used for severe cases of diarrhoea in children and by all the Boers for Insomnia—one leaf for an adult, a half for a child. Dr. Mears at Prince Albert chewed a leaf and fell asleep and Dr. Lawrence at George also tried it.[114]

British settlers acquired their animals largely from Boers and Africans. Before they could afford horses, some used Xhosa oxen in the manner of Africans as pack-animals and even in mounted races.[115] Finding themselves in the sourveld summer-rainfall coastal area, they were quick to adopt the African and Boer techniques of managing the pastures. Within a season of their arrival, one wrote: 'in winter we tried the Savages' method of burning . . . The first rain after burning instantaneously brings up the grass & all looks as inviting as ever.'[116] And like the Boers, British settlers soon demanded African workers, with their established skills, some of whose land they now occupied.

If the failure of early attempts at arable production were partly due to inexperience, it also resulted from the difficulty of the Zuurveld environment.[117] Floods in 1823 literally swept some homesteads away. The rapidity of bush clearance in valley bottoms probably helped to create channels for flood-water.[118] It soon became plain that there were more remunerative opportunities in the growing urban settlements or in barter across the frontier with Africans. For some, however, arable failure invited a switch to pastoral farming which, in itself, encouraged a shift to higher ground.[119]

British settlers were in the forefront of sheep farming and wool production. Robert Jacob Gordon had first attempted to introduce wool-bearing merinos into the Cape in the late eighteenth century, an initiative followed up in the brief Dutch interregnum of 1803–6. The government farm at Groote Pos in the western Cape kept a flock.[120] But when the British took control in 1806 fewer than 14,000 woolled sheep were enumerated in the Colony—less than 2 per cent of the total in settler hands.[121] Many Boers were reluctant to abandon fat-tailed sheep, so well adapted to the terrain and climate, and so hardy in the face of water shortage, predators, and constant trekking.

---

[114] Nerina Mathie, *Man of Many Facets: Atherstone, Dr. W. G. 1814–1898, Pseudo-Autobiography* (Grocott & Sherry, Grahamstown, 1998), ii. 474. This is a three-volume compilation based on Atherstone's diaries and written in the mode of an autobiography. The extracts are not necessarily verbatim quotes from the diaries, but the author sticks closely to this source.

[115] Butler, *1820 Settlers*, 140.   [116] Payne, 'Re-Creating Home', 58.

[117] Crais, *Making of the Colonial Order*, 88–9.   [118] Butler, *1820 Settlers*, 153.

[119] Anderson, 'The Human Clay'.

[120] H. B. Thom (ed.), *Willem Stephanus van Ryneveld se Aanmerkingen over de Vebetering van het Vee aan de Kaap de Goede Hoop, 1804* (van Riebeeck Society, Cape Town, 1942).

[121] Thom, *Skaapboerdery*, 76.

Farming sheep for wool implied a more commoditized approach that prioritized export rather than multi-purpose local consumption of fat, skins, and meat. Wool production signalled a range of transformations in pastoral and transport systems. While mutton sheep could be driven to market, wool required wagon transport to the coastal entrepôts of Port Elizabeth and East London.

Woolled sheep were pioneered in the Albany district, near the coast, initially with some success, despite earlier perceptions that this area was unsuitable for small stock. The problems of acclimatizing this new breed to the Cape in itself drew British settlers into a closer engagement with the local environment. They had to learn more about the capacities of animals and pastures, as well as the threats to them. Miles Bowker, who had farmed merinos before he came to South Africa, was amongst the first settlers to purchase them from Groote Pos in 1823. The flocks established on settler farms in the 1820s and 1830s became the nucleus of the Cape's most valuable nineteenth-century product and soon spilled over onto the land of Boers and Africans. In the half-century up to 1855, sheep numbers in the colony increased at least fourfold to 6.5 million; of these three-quarters were now woolled. Despite what seem to have been low average annual yields of about 2 pounds per sheep, wool exports increased from half a million pounds (worth £27,000) in 1838 to 12 million pounds (worth £634,000) in 1855. Prices were particularly high in the 1850s (Fig. 1.4).

It was not least on the backs of merino sheep that British settlers moved to the interior, as Burchell had advised in his *Hints on Emigration*.[122] In the 1830s they purchased land cheaply from departing trekboers and those who went on the Great Trek. A British landed presence was carved out in what became the districts of Fort Beaufort, Adelaide, Bedford, and Somerset East immediately to the north and north-west of Grahamstown, as well as further afield in Cradock, Graaff-Reinet, and beyond. Some were greatly aided by the profits that had accrued from trading operations, not least the supply of troops in the colonial war of 1835.[123] Amongst them were families who had failed as agriculturalists in lower Albany. Although some land was purchased in the interior by absentee individuals and merchant firms, many actually moved onto their farms. This migration into the interior has received far less attention in the historiography of British settlers than their initial travails in Albany.

[122] William J. Burchell, *Hints on Emigration to the Cape of Good Hope* (J. Hatchard & Son, London, 1819), 43.

[123] Crais, *Making of the Colonial Order*, 133–5; Keegan, *Colonial South Africa*, 158–61. For later links between trading and agricultural capital, Beinart et al. (eds.), *Putting a Plough to the Ground*.

Once they moved into the semi-arid interior, British settlers were subject to many of the same environmental constraints as their predecessors. The large farms could not easily be enclosed. The *Grahamstown Journal* in 1832 published criticism of the 'trekboer propensity for "chasing thundershowers in the wilderness"'. It was nevertheless difficult for British farmers to live by the creed that 'nothing is more essential to perfect civilization than a fixed residence'.[124] Those who went into trade often had to master the skills of the ox-wagon trek. As F. W. Reitz, one of the leading Afrikaner farmers in the colony, noted, British settlers soon stopped ridiculing 'the idea of stock farms six thousand acres in extent being necessary for the support of a single family'.[125] Some purchased a great deal more.

Two examples can be found in the Collett and Rubidge families, both of whom left diaries. James Collett arrived at the Cape in 1821, a little after the main party of settlers, as an employee, and did not receive a land grant.[126] He had a reasonable education, and in 1823 he moved to Grahamstown and found some success in trading, not least with the Khoikhoi at the Kat river settlement. In 1826 he purchased a significant landholding, vacated by an unsuccessful settler party, close to the coast in Albany and moved there with his family in 1832. The farm had good sourveld grazing for cattle, but was less suitable for sheep, and all animals were susceptible to diseases—probably tick-borne, although their cause was not known at the time.

By 1831 he had accumulated sufficient capital to start puchasing land on the Koonap river, near Fort Beaufort, 150 kilometres from the coast, where the pasture was sweeter. He did so specifically in order to expand his merino holdings, for which he developed a 'passionate fondness'.[127] Some of Miles Bowker's sons moved to the same area. In 1834 the Collett family took occupation of a substantial double-storey house on their main Koonap farm, Olifantbeen. Afrikaners were particularly mobile at this time, and Collett bought farms largely from them, usually of a few thousand morgen. He sold and swapped as well as bought land, and by 1840 he had about 5,000 merinos on a contiguous block of farms that was probably close to 20,000 morgen (*c.*17,000 hectares).[128] This was a large farm even at that time, especially in what was considered a prime location for merinos.

---

[124] Anderson, 'The Human Clay', 104; quoting from an article in the *Grahamstown Journal* (27 July 1832), reproduced in van der Merwe, *Noordwaartse Beweging*, 285.

[125] F. W. Reitz, 'Irrigation', *Cape Monthly Magazine*, 1 (1857), 135.

[126] Joan Collett, *A Time to Plant: Biography of James Lydford Collett, Settler* (Joan Collett, Katkop, Cradock, 1990). This biography uses the diary of James Collett, kept almost daily from 1835 to 1875, as well as family letters and photographs.

[127] Ibid. 38.

[128] Ibid. 76—area calculated roughly from the map of farms provided. Some of his land was hired.

The Koonap was close to the front line during the war against the Xhosa in 1835, and continued to be vulnerable to conflict and stock theft. Relatives had moved further north-west, and in 1841 Collett sold up precipitately and started anew on farms purchased north of Cradock. Based at Groenfontein, his land here both had better arable potential than the Koonap and—with its mix of karoo bush and sweetveld grass—was seen as ideal sheep territory. With the help of his sons and employees, grain production was so successful that Collett built a mill and negotiated a contract to supply the colonial forces with oat hay, used as fodder for horses. By 1850 he ran about 6,000 sheep on his main farms and possibly 9,000 overall.[129] His merino ram flock of 150–300, used and sold for breeding, was a lucrative additional source of income. Of his 500 oxen, over 100 were trained for wagon transport. Agricultural success brought political influence. Collett was elected as a member of the Cape's first legislative assembly in 1854. He was a supporter of Godlonton, a passionate advocate of the settler interest and eastern Cape separatism, but he withdrew from parliament in the next year.[130]

In 1857, at the height of his farming success, when wool prices were buoyant, Collett sold his home farm Groenfontein for £6,000. He found it too isolated from his main block of farms, and at 57 was looking to provide for his sons, for whom, as was also the custom amongst Afrikaners, he had set aside sheep.[131] He diversified again, back into commerce, by purchasing a shop in Cradock. This was one step too far, and after nearly forty years of accumulation he became relatively impoverished in the 1860s, dragged down by the commercial depression and the difficulties of his sons.

Collett's drive to maximize his farming operations is striking. He had limited commitment to particular farming sites and moved through three— the Albany coast, Koonap, and the Upper Fish river in Cradock—though clearly the last was the most stable. This was not a completely new ethos in farming; purchase of land to optimize location had been an element in Afrikaner strategies and there were frequent sales of farms in frontier districts both before and after the British occupation.[132] Even in the more established agrarian districts of the western Cape in the nineteenth century, frequent

---

[129] Collett, *A Time to Plant* does not give exact figures. In the 1850s numbers seem to have fluctuated from 5,000–6,000, with additional sheep set aside for his sons.

[130] B. A. le Cordeur, 'Robert Godlonton as Architect of Frontier Opinion, 1850–1857', *Archives Year Book for S. A. History* (Cape Town, 1959).

[131] One reason why Miles Bowker had emigrated to the Cape was to secure land for his many sons, which would have been impossible in Britain. In this sense, the strategies of some British families came to resemble that of the Boers. See van der Merwe, *Trek*, 103.

[132] Ibid. 106 ff.

bankruptcies and failures, alongside relatively easy credit networks, contributed to a high turnover of individual farms, if not of farming families.[133]
Collett's passage through three different farming areas over thirty years, in
each of which he invested heavily, was partly, like the mobility of frontier
Boers, related to the search for new and better pastures, but his rapidly accumulated capital gave him considerably more power and his decisions had a
harder commercial edge.

The first Rubidge at the Cape, a former naval officer, arrived in 1821.
Unlike Collett, he was sufficiently wealthy to buy land near Grahamstown;
he named the farm Gletwyn after the family home in Wales. In 1838,
together with members of the Southey and Powell families, he purchased a
large farm in Graaff-Reinet district, 200 kilometres to the north-west, in a
semi-arid zone with half the rainfall of Grahamstown.[134] The low price of
land in Graaff-Reinet, and the potential for merino farming, influenced his
decision to move. Graaff-Reinet's Karoo shrubs were well known as excellent
sheep fodder, and the sourveld on elevated areas provided an alternative seasonal pasture in spring. Rubidge family tradition records that the departing
Boer sold because of droughts in Graaff-Reinet in the 1830s, the unreliability
of the water supply, and the attraction of better-grassed areas in the interior.
He did not join the Great Trek, but moved to the north-eastern Cape.

The land purchased was divided between the three families, who were
already linked by marriage. Rubidge's eldest son, Charles (b. 1818) received
12,000 morgen (c.10,000 ha), and in 1840 settled on part of this, which had an
established Boer homestead, outbuildings, fields, and, critically, a fountain
(spring). But the homestead was far from the main road, on a difficult route.
A shearing shed was established on a section of the farm nearer to town, with
a seasonal vlei (shallow lake or pool), because it was conveniently situated for
wagon transport. Renamed Wellwood, it became the site for the handsome
new farmhouse (which still stands) in the early 1850s.

---

[133] Wayne Dooling, 'Agricultural Transformations in the Western Districts of the Cape
Colony, c.1838–1900', unpublished D.Phil. thesis, University of Cambridge (1997).

[134] Rubidge papers, Wellwood Farm, Graaff-Reinet: 'Extracts and Notes from Wellwood
Diary, 1845 to 1892', in a book titled 'Correspondence on Mangin Brown Case'. The Rubidge
diaries, covering the period from about 1850 to the present, are perhaps the best-preserved farming journals in the midland Cape. A number of stock books, summaries of family history, cuttings,
and files also survive on the farm, and there is a small collection (MSB 406) at the South African
Public Library, Cape Town. See also Richard Rubidge, *The Merino on Wellwood: Four Generations*
(Richard Rubidge, Graaff-Reinet, 1979). Smith, *Frontier to Midlands*, 53, dates the transaction to
August 1837. The land mentioned there, two farms of 15,000 acres, does not include the whole of
the purchase of the three families. The sum mentioned of £375 is also less than that of £1,500
recorded in family histories.

Charles Rubidge won great success as a sheep farmer. He was more of a specialist, with very limited arable land, than Collett, and although he did speculate in stock, he had few ambitions in trade. With a smaller farm, in a drier area, his livestock numbers did not rival those of Collett. He had received the land from his father with only a small mortgage, and perhaps his relative financial security allowed for a more cautious approach. His strategy was to invest in improving his sheep and existing land rather than to purchase new farms. He bought pedigree French Rambouillet rams, imported by Mosenthals and other merchants, and by the 1850s, his sheep were yielding an average of 5–6 pounds of wool each, well above the colonial average.[135]

Benefiting from the sustained high wool price in the 1850s, Charles Rubidge visited France himself to purchase rams in 1861. He became one of the leading colonial breeders, selling stud stock throughout the eastern and midland Cape. Calculating his assets on the eve of his trip to Europe, he arrived at a total of £23,895: about half was the value of his land and house; a quarter his livestock; and the rest largely in equipment, possessions, and promissory notes of debts owed to him by a range of farmers, both Boer and British.[136] The existing credit networks in the rural Cape often relied on such personal interconnection.[137] Landowners also often stood surety for debts, which in Collett's case had compounded his financial problems. Charles Rubidge died on Wellwood in 1889.

Successful wool production and investment in water (Chapter 2) sustained more intensive settlement in the semi-arid interior than had been possible by Khoikhoi or Boers up to the 1820s. But merino sheep farmers, British as well as Boer, were still primarily dependent on the natural veld for their grazing resources. Collett's acquisitiveness was designed not only to provide more grazing for his sheep, but different types of veld and a range of water sources. He observed the condition of the veld continuously and moved animals around to avoid overgrazing. 'Tracked today with my ewe flock and lamb troop to the river [—] a timely removal', he noted one day in 1838; 'the whole of my flocks had been grazed at home for about one month and has fed it bare'.[138]

At his Koonap farms, his sheep were particularly susceptible to what he called kielsiekt or geelsick, which seemed to be worse after rain, or rainy seasons, and in grassy areas (Chapter 4). He moved his sheep, as the Khoikhoi and Boers had done, when they became ill even if he did not at that stage

---

[135] Rubidge diaries, 15 Apr. 1852, based on calculations by Sidney Rubidge more than a century later and noted in the diary.

[136] Rubidge papers, Assets of C. Rubidge, 1861–Jan. 31.

[137] Dooling, 'Agricultural Transformations'.   [138] Collett, *A Time to Plant*, 71.

understand the cause of disease. Whether from observation, or on the advice of his shepherds, he believed that kielsiekt seemed less prevalent 'on stoney land', and when sheep were moved there 'the disease suddenly became arrested'.[139] In Graaff-Reinet, Charles Rubidge also moved his stock to mountain pasture when 'gielsiekte' broke out after rains in the lowlands. While some British landowners in Graaff-Reinet regularly took their animals up into the Sneeuberg grasslands in the summer, this form of medium-distance transhumance declined and Rubidge prided himself on avoiding it. Generally his animals remained within the boundaries of Wellwood. The farm was about two-thirds Karoo flats, dominated by shrubs and some sweet-veld grass, and one-third mountain sourveld, so that he had a range of grazing resources close at hand.

For the British settlers, as for their predecessors, it was 'highly necessary to secure the herds and flocks at night, in folds or kraals fenced round generally with a strong hedge of "mimosa" or other thorny bushes'.[140] Both the Collett and Rubidge diaries report regular attacks by predators, as well as continuous attempts to hunt them and poison them with strychnine.[141] In the Koonap, Collett experienced the greatest problems in the 1830s from wild dogs; he also recorded leopards (called tigers), hyenas, and jackals.[142] By the mid-nineteenth century in Graaff-Reinet, when the Rubidge diaries begin, losses from wild dogs and leopards were occasionally mentioned, but it was mainly jackals that threatened the sheep (Chapter 5).[143]

On these large farms sheep were not generally all brought back daily to the central homestead. They were divided into a number of flocks, each based at kraals dispersed around the farm, which to some degree minimized their concentration. The outlying Rubidge kraals were named after the shepherds in charge of them—'Ruiters' or 'Old Platjes'. In the mid-nineteenth century most kraals, especially those that may not have been intended as permanent, were still made by 'dragging bushes' of the ubiquitous, thorny *Acacia karoo*.[144]

[139]   Ibid. 71. One of the farms he bought on the Koonap, Leeuwfontein, later became the government's first centre for research into tickborne diseases (Chap. 4); Rubidge diaries, Oct. 1853.

[140]   Pringle, *Narrative*, i. 48; Thompson, *Travels and Adventures*, i. 28.

[141]   Collett, *A Time to Plant*, 72, 89, 102.

[142]   Leopard were called 'tyger' by the Dutch settlers, after the similar animal in the East, and this was adopted by British immigrants. As a result a number of Cape place-names include tiger (an animal never found or introduced in South Africa) but few leopard; Sparrman, *Voyage*, ii. 192–3. In the early decades of the nineteenth century most British writers were switching to the zoologically accepted word leopard; C. J. Skead, *Historical Mammal Incidence in the Cape Province: The Western and Northern Cape*, vol. 1 (Cape Provincial Council, Cape Town, 1980).

[143]   Rubidge diaries, 2 Apr. 1852, 20 May 1852, 11 July 1852, 3 Jan. 1853, 21 Feb. 1853, 16 Nov. 1854.

[144]   Ibid. 17 May 1853.

At the Koonap, where wood was plentiful, Collett also used some moveable wooden hurdles, widespread in Australia. Wood had been used in the original Zuurveld British settlement for fencing; where this took the form of chopped bush, hedgerows took root and gave the area a more British look.[145]

In inland areas such as the Sneeuberg, and most of the districts to the north and east of it, where temperatures were more extreme, trees fewer, and wood for construction scarce, stone kraals were built. They were noted on Graaff-Reinet farms, such as Andries Pretorius's Letts Kraal, as early as the 1810s.[146] Stone walls were also used to enclose gardens, vleis, and small fields. From the 1820s they were often constructed by specialist teams of migrant, Sotho-speaking 'Mantatee' workers. The name Mantatees derived from the Tlokoa chieftainess Manthathisi, who established a powerful polity in the Caledon river valley in the early 1820s, but was probably applied to a range of refugees and migrants escaping the turmoil on the highveld at that time. Some sought refuge in the Cape: in Graaff-Reinet; in Somerset East, where a group attempted to forge an independent existence; and as apprentices to British settlers in Albany.[147] Some migrated from mission stations established in the eastern Free State, and further groups moved down as farm-workers after the defeat of Sekonyela by Moshoeshoe in 1853. Partly stone-built homesteads, kraals, and defensive walls had long been used by Africans on the highveld and Mantatee workers brought their skills with them. Their walls were of dry-packed stone, not dissimilar to those in Britain, but based on established vernacular techniques. They, along with the Mfengu, were perhaps the first African migrant workers in South Africa.[148]

In the 1840s Collett commissioned walls around his fields in Cradock; on one farm, four miles were constructed.[149] 'Mantatees' also built stone cottages for workers, although for his own farmhouses Collett, as in the case of most landowners, employed British workers. On the Rubidge farm, Wellwood, 'Mantatees commenced building stone kraals' in 1851, and in 1853 Rubidge 'hired 4 Mantatees to build wall around 5 acres of ground'. He paid partly in livestock.[150] Prickly pear hedges were also used to enclose one section of the garden, the fruit on the inside being reserved for the family and that on the outside for servants. In the 1850s larger stone-wall enclosures were built to serve as small paddocks near the house.

[145] Payne, 'Re-creating Home', 63.   [146] Walton, *Homesteads and Villages*, 57.
[147] Crais, *Making of the Colonial Order*, 77.
[148] Peter Delius, *The Land Belongs to Us* (Heinemann, London, 1982), notes Pedi migrants from the Transvaal in the Eastern Cape by the 1830s, but the Mantatees preceded them.
[149] Collett, *A Time to Plant*, 87, 89.
[150] Rubidge, *The Merino*, 8; Rubidge diaries, 16 Mar. 1853, 31 May 1853.

Thus, even where new techniques and spatial controls were being introduced, settler farmers relied partly on local materials and adapted indigenous skills. There was no shortage of stones in the Karoo. The purpose of the stone walls was not strictly speaking to enclose land. The great bulk even of these model farms, into which unusually large amounts of capital were being invested, remained unfenced at this period; they were simply too large. Up to the 1870s walls were built to keep animals in restricted spaces near the homestead, and to keep animals out of gardens, rather than to enclose the bulk of veld, or to mark the boundaries of a property.

Charles Rubidge named his farm Wellwood, in English, after the nearby kloof of *Acacia karoo* and in recognition that water supplies initially came from a well rather than fountain. The family remained staunch royalists, celebrating Queen Victoria's birthday with an annual springbok hunt, well known locally, which symbolized the links between hunting and empire.[151] But they and their neighbours adopted many colonial words and usages. They retained the names Patrysfontein and Bloemhof for sections of the original purchase. This combination of renamed English properties and older Afrikaans names was not unusual amongst settler farmers: Collett anglicized the name of his Koonap home farm to Elephant's Fountain, but continued to use Groenfontein, and other Dutch names, for his Cradock properties.

The Rubidge's new house on Wellwood was in Cape Dutch style, with gables and stoep. They made biltong from the springbok they shot, like their Boer predecessors. They planted well-acclimatized fruit trees such as quince and pomegranate for hedging, oranges—which lined the streets of Graaff-Reinet town—as well as figs, peaches, watermelons, and vines. The latter at least were obtained from their neighbour van der Berg. Although many settlers introduced new trees by mid-century, they generally forsook British species, which struggled in the harsh climate of the interior: rather, they planted eucalypts from Australia, pines from Europe, and pepper trees. Rubidge also planted indigenous acacia, which was used for grazing, firewood, and rough timber, as he thought there were too few on the farm.[152]

Charles Rubidge married (1840) within his class, but out of the immediate British settler community. His wife, Louisa Liesching, was granddaughter of a German doctor who had settled in Cape Town in 1787; two of Liesching's

---

[151] John MacKenzie, *The Empire of Nature: Hunting, Conservation and British Imperialism* (Manchester University Press, Manchester, 1988).

[152] Rubidge, *Merino*, 8, from diaries, 19 Oct. 1853. In wetter areas, and along stream banks, many planted poplars.

(anglicized) sons moved to Graaff-Reinet and became major landowners in the late 1830s. F. A. G. Liesching bought Letts Kraal from the trekker leader Andries Pretorius; naturally well favoured, it became another of the model farms of the district.[153] The marriage took place in the Dutch Reformed Church. During the nineteenth century there was considerable intermarriage between British and Boer landowning families in the district. Charles Rubidge's diary in the 1850s describes extensive contacts with the surrounding Afrikaner farmers, as well as with African workers; his list of debtors, assembled in 1861, included Afrikaans names. To one of the Bowkers, who perhaps valued their metropolitan connections more intensely, the young Rubidges seemed to have been 'brought up amongst Boors!'[154]

In the confident vein of mid-century British colonialism, settlers not only came to terms with existing Cape ways, but sometimes consciously attempted to generate a local British identity under the imperial umbrella. Henry Hall, the military engineer, mapmaker, and author of probably the first South African geography textbook, took this approach in discussing the 'strange jumble' of place-names in the Cape.[155] His activities required the formal naming of places in order to represent them in a fixed, colonial, spatial logic. Writing in 1858, he was anxious not to impose an insensitive British 'geographical nomenclature'. Especially in the western Cape, the intensity of Dutch naming had overwhelmed Khoikhoi terms, and he could see this process continuing. The Gariep river, for example, was the Khoikhoi name used by settlers and travellers until the early nineteenth century.[156] Gordon called it the Orange in the late eighteenth century, after the Dutch royal house rather than the river's eponymous muddy colour, and the new name began to stick when trekkers moved north in numbers. The Orange was adopted in government documents and maps. The old name did survive a little longer for its tributaries, such as the Ky Gariep and Nu Gariep, but the former was by the 1850s generally called the Vaal. Like Sparrman in the 1770s and Burchell—who apologized to his readers for using Dutch place-names—Hall was concerned that this process of change did not become overwhelming.[157]

[153] Patricia McMagh, *The Three Lieschings and their Contribution to Medical History at the Cape 1800–1843* (Privately published, 1987).

[154] Albany Museum, Grahamstown, Mary Barber papers, John Mitford Bowker to Mary Barber, 26 June 1846.

[155] H. Hall, 'Modern Geographical Nomenclature, From a Colonial Point of View', *Cape Monthly Magazine*, 3 (1858), 359–68.

[156] Ibid. 367; Thompson, *Travels and Adventures*, uses Orange and Gariep interchangeably in the 1820s; William Cornwallis Harris, *The Wild Sports of Southern Africa* (Struik, Cape Town, 1963), 229, reprint of 5th edn.

[157] Sparrman, *Voyage*, ii. 26, 31, 65, 148; Burchell, *Travels*, i. 202.

The many Khoikhoi place-names still used in Namaqualand could be confusing, Hall confessed, with their 'formidable phalanx of x', q' and k's'. In some cases, he was relieved 'that . . . plain Batavian has superseded the unpronouncable jargon of the ancient "Quaequae"'. But he accepted that 'our map must remain a jumble'. If more sensitivity had been shown in the past, 'Calvinia would not have been where Hantam ought to have been, nor would George have superseded Outeniqua, nor that barbarous compound Swellendam the old kraal of Hessaquas'. A significant number of geographical features did retain Khoikhoi names, even if 'the orthography [was] corrupted by the defective ear, ignorance, or carelessness of the original discoverers'.[158] This included rivers (kamma) and mountains such as the Gamka, Kraggakamma, Kammanassie, Kariega, Kasouga, Outeniqua, Tsitsikamma, and Kouga, and zones such as the Camdeboo (also named after a river) and the Gouph. Because districts and even towns were occasionally named after natural features, old words survived to describe new places such as the villages of Leeu-Gamka, Dwyka, Coega, and Karreedouw. On balance Hall expressed regret at the loss of so many 'aboriginal names', and suggested that some British names be abandoned.

Lichtenstein had commented in the early nineteenth century on the repetitive character of Dutch place-naming, especially of their farms—often described by the character of their springs such as Brakfontein (brack), Palmietfontein (palm rush), or Rietfontein (reed). He had advocated, following a suggestion from the Batavian government, that Cape place-names be rationalized and their variety increased to avoid confusion.[159] One traveller found 'Modder-Fonteyn (muddy fountain) . . . an appellation so common in the Colony, that I have visited, I believe, above a dozen places of that name'.[160] Terms like Zwart (black), Zeekoe (hippo), and Baviaan (baboon) were repeatedly used without 'that nice and accurate discrimination which seizes the distinctive and peculiar features alone, and embodies them in the name'.

Hall differed. He found an exciting variety in the 'expressive nomenclature' used, for example, as part of compounds describing high ground—berg, rand, heuvel, hoogte, kop, kopje, ruggens, and krantz.[161] His argument in favour of retaining 'the strange jumble' of Khoikhoi, Dutch, Xhosa, and British was a plea for a form of Cape vernacular. As the most significant mid-nineteenth-century mapmaker, his approach effectively triumphed. Hall had the confidence to celebrate the variety of Cape names because they were

---

[158] Hall, 'Geographical Nomenclature', 360.
[159] Lichtenstein, *Travels*, i. 93.
[160] Thompson, *Travels and Adventures*, 46.
[161] Hall, 'Geographical Nomeclature', 365.

being put on his map and translated into his form of knowledge. Colonists could not, of course, stop the colonized using older names. Many parts of the eastern Cape, including new towns, retained African names in common usage that did not appear on maps (although they were sometimes used in the African press). But despite considerable anglicization, even the official Cape colonial geography remained less dominated by anglophone naming than could have been the case.

'Geographical nomenclature' reflected the character of British South African colonial intrusion in a number of respects: it could be coercive and insensitive; it retained a strong sense of home; empire was celebrated in the prominence given to royalty, aristocracy, governors, and their wives. Yet even where the British settlers established a strong presence and cultural weight, such as in Albany and the new towns, they did not achieve a demographic preponderance. In many respects both the colonial government and British settlers had to come to terms with the complexity of established societies, with their way of doing things, and with the farming environment. The historiography of the early phases of some settler colonial societies now emphasizes such processes.[162] Compared to much of the Americas, Australia, and New Zealand, the pace of transformation in South Africa was relatively slow. While the very mobility of Cape society facilitated conceptualization of the geography of the colony as a whole, it was far less easy to remould it socially or spatially.

[162] William Cronon, *Changes in the Land: Indians, Colonists, and the Ecology of New England* (Hill & Wang, New York, 1983); Richard White, *The Middle Ground: Indians, Empires and Republics in the Great Lakes Region, 1650–1815* (Cambridge University Press, New York, 1991).

2

Defining the Problems: Colonial Science and the Origins of Conservation at the Cape, 1770–1860

Botany, Vegetation, and Overgrazing

Veld, forests, water, and wild animals were critical natural resources for Khoisan and African people, as well as the landowners who were increasingly the backbone of the colonial economy. Colonial regimes were alive to the dangers of overexploitation. At the Cape, attempts at regulation—along European lines—began soon after Company rule was established. Comments and debates about environmental degradation are evident surprisingly early in the history of European settlement. They arose from the emerging understandings of the environment, from the experience of farmers, and from international scientific advances that framed environmental problems in new ways.

Botany, which along with zoology was one of the strongest spheres of scientific knowledge about the eighteenth- and early nineteenth-century Cape, began to identify the richness of the Cape flora, and, very hesitantly, threats to that natural wealth. Developments in geology are another useful point of entry in exploring how environmental change was being formulated and discussed at the time. Commentators also borrowed some of the language of global debates about desiccation, and combined these with everyday concerns about overgrazing, fire, fuelwood, and water. New knowledge helped to fill out the idea of 'veld', with its multiple connotations of plant life, soil, nature, and landscape. The state of the veld became an increasingly central concern as merino sheep numbers expanded rapidly from the 1830s and wool became the Cape's major export. Scientific ideas were closely linked to mid-Victorian colonial notions of progress, agricultural improvement, and economic growth. It is important to stress that conservation, even at this stage, often implied wise usage of natural resources rather than protection.

The Cape was not insignificant as a laboratory for the growing science of botany, when an attempt was being made in the eighteenth century to classify species on a world scale. Colonial empires were already geared towards trade and cultivation of valuable exotic crops. Although many such plant transfers were made informally by individuals, the Dutch East India Company became involved in systematic, state-sponsored activities, including afforestation and the establishment of botanical gardens. The Dutch, Richard Grove argues, combined their highly interventionist ideas about managing domestic envir-onments with strong networks of international botanical knowledge.[1] Gardens, largely used for commercial cultivation, were also a site for 'the study and improvement of botany, in which the most rare and useful plants from every quarter of the world are arranged in the most excellent order'.[2]

While Cape pastoralism initially drew heavily on local breeds of sheep and cattle, as well as natural veld and transhumant techniques, agriculture depended from the start almost entirely on a wide range of introduced species: from wheat and vines, to fruit and vegetables. The settlement at Cape Town was from its very earliest years short of timber, because local supplies were so limited, and transport from distant forests so expensive.[3] Systematic planting of European oaks, ash, and alder began in the 1670s. Dutch officials, such as the governors Simon and Willem van der Stel, were ardent planters with broad botanical interests. It is difficult to understand colonization with-out analysing the opportunities for, and constraints on, introduced species of plants and animals. Botanical knowledge was, in this way, intimately bound up with colonial expansion.

The Cape became a significant reference point for the growth of European botanical knowledge because of its location on the shipping routes to the East, and especially because of the extraordinary variety, new to European science, of its flora and fauna. European collectors vied for the bounty of its flowering plants, alive or dead.[4] Botanical and zoological exploration was an important driving force for a succession of scientific visitors.[5] Linnaeus, the

[1] Grove, *Green Imperialism*, 127.   [2] Ibid. 196.

[3] A. Appel, 'Die Geskiedenis van Houtvoorsiening aan die Kaap, 1652–1795', unpublished MA dissertation, University of Stellenbosch (1966). Thanks to Robert Ross for the reference.

[4] P. MacOwan, 'Personalia of Botanical Collectors at the Cape', *Transactions of the South African Philosophical Society* (1886), p. xxxi.

[5] Popular literature includes John Hutchinson, *A Botanist in Southern Africa* (P. R. Gawthorn, London, 1946); Conrad Lighton, *Sisters of the South* (Hodder & Stoughton, London, 1952); Vernon Forbes, *Pioneer Travels in South Africa* (Struik, Cape Town, 1965); Peter Raby, *Bright Paradise: Victorian Scientific Travellers* (Chatto & Windus, London, 1996). Biographies in the *Dictionary of South African Biography* (*DSAB*) are numerous and helpful; in themselves they suggest the importance of botany in South Africa.

most successful protagonist of a global system of classification, worked in Holland with Dutch botanists who had accumulated Cape specimens. Ryk van Tulbagh, Cape Governor from 1751 to 1771, was particularly interested in botany and patron of the Company garden, which collected a wide range of species.[6] Company officials such as Robert Gordon, who played host to visiting scientists, provided a focus for natural-history activity. In addition to his explorations, he probably introduced the Norfolk pine, recently found by Cook in the Pacific, which became ubiquitous in coastal Cape gardens.[7] Thunberg and Sparrman, both pupils of Linnaeus, were sent out as part of this global endeavour.[8] Thunberg's record of 3,100 species formed a classificatory basis for later botanists.[9] Burchell's four year trip (1811–15) yielded 63,000 natural-history specimens and extensive geographical notes.

Enlightenment scientific enterprise was clearly concerned to classify nature and discover economic uses for plant and animal species. But it included other elements. Questions were raised about the 'arrogance of humanity' and its capacity to destroy nature.[10] Writers found an aesthetic value in nature, and a balance or wholeness.[11] Nor should enlightenment scientific thinking be divorced from romantic ideas about nature that flourished in the early decades of the nineteenth century. If one set of scientific images was mechanistic, another, especially in the natural sciences, could be lyrical.[12] All of these ideas are reflected in texts on the Cape.

Comments about the impact of colonization on the environment focused especially on the pastoral economy, which was so central to settler livelihoods. By the mid-eighteenth century, observers noted the 'disappearance of grass and the springing up of small bushy plants in its stead'.[13] P. J. van der Merwe, historian of the trekboers, sensitized by the report of the Drought Investigation Commission of 1923 (Chapter 7), cited evidence from eighteenth-century sources on what he called 'die tradisie van roofbou' (tradition of agricultural rapacity).[14] Magistrates cited overgrazing as an argument

---

[6] MacOwan, 'Personalia', p. xxxiv.   [7] Lighton, *Sisters of the South*, 53, 168.

[8] Thunberg, *Travels*, 29.   [9] MacOwan, 'Personalia', p. xxxvii; *DSAB* i. 793.

[10] Keith Thomas, *Man and the Natural World: Changing Attitudes in England 1500–1800* (Penguin, Harmondsworth, 1985), 167–9.

[11] Gilbert F. LaFreniere, 'Rousseau and the European Roots of Environmentalism', *Environmental History Review* (1990), 41–72; Worster, *Nature's Economy*.

[12] Jonathan Bate, *Romantic Ecology: Wordsworth and the Environmental Tradition* (Routledge, London, 1991), makes this link between Romantic poetry, scientific understanding, and the origins of conservation.

[13] T. D. Hall, 'South African Pastures', 66; Newton-King, 'The Enemy Within', 189–90.

[14] van der Merwe, *Trek*, 71 ff. The images of farmers robbing, mining, or raping the earth were frequently used in the inter-war years of the twentieth century.

against further settlement in Stellenbosch and Drakenstein by the mid-eighteenth century. In Swellendam they spoke of the 'verswachen der velds' or weakening of pastures. It was not least for this reason that farmers sent animals to grazing farms in the interior, and that some farmers moved themselves. Van der Merwe saw this tendency to overexploit the veld for immediate advantage as a major feature of early settler pastoralism.

Many later authors drew on Sparrman, who developed a sustained discussion of the problem which was one of the first in print. It is worth quoting him at length, because so much of what he noted was later repeated by others:

In direct contradiction to the custom and example of the original inhabitants the Hottentots, the colonists turn their cattle out constantly into the same fields, and that too in a much greater quantity than used to graze there in the time of the Hottentots; and they keep not only a number sufficient for their own use, but likewise enough to supply the more plentiful tables of the numerous inhabitants of Cape Town, as well as for the victualling of the ships in their passage to and from the East-Indies . . . In consequence of the fields being thus continually grazed off, and the great increase of the cattle feeding on them, the grasses and herbs which these animals most covet are prevented continually more and more from thriving and taking root; while, on the contrary, the *rhinoceros bush*, which the cattle always pass by and leave untouched, is suffered to take root free and unmolested, and encroach on the place of others . . . [T]his punishment for their sins (as they call the rhinoceros bush) together with several other dry, barren shrubs and bushes is found in greater abundance than anywhere else near their farms.[15]

Elsewhere he talked of land as 'fresh', because it was not yet 'grazed off': 'beyond a shadow of doubt,' he confidently asserted, 'such places as before abounded in grass are now fallen off considerably, so that it is feared that they must in a short time be given up.'[16] Sparrman mused that 'future ages may see this part of Africa entirely changed and different from what it is at present'.[17]

Sparrman highlighted what became called overstocking, overgrazing, and vegetation change. He distinguished between settler and Khoikhoi pastoral methods, despite the similarities between them. He thought that the Khoikhoi, who moved their dwellings and livestock more frequently, were more sensitive to such degradation. For this reason, he suggested, the cattle of the Khoikhoi were larger and better-fed than those of the settlers— although on this point his critic, Robert Gordon, the commander of the Cape garrison in the 1770s, strenuously disagreed.

Sparrman also suggested that wildlife, using both browse and veld, grazed in a more balanced way than cattle, which concentrated on grass and thus

[15] Sparrman, *Voyage*, i. 239.   [16] Ibid. ii. 130.   [17] Ibid. i. 241.

facilitated the spread of unpalatable bushes.[18] Despite his avarice for samples and willingness to shoot for the pot, Sparrman was aware that Cape wildlife as well as pasture was imperilled because of profligate shooting.[19] The Dutch East India Company had already passed proclamations trying to curb excessive destruction of valuable wild animals. Sparrman advocated wildlife preservation for more complex reasons. By browsing and spreading their dung, more antelopes might improve the veld and help to extirpate the unwanted bush.

To this end, Sparrman suggested that colonists should attempt to domesticate local wild species, in the same way as the Swedes had tamed the reindeer and the elk: 'the animals which occur only in Africa are, in my opinion, as much designed for the plants peculiar to this climate, as the plants are for the animals.'[20] Farming of local species might both add to the store of resources for human use and prevent settlers from 'laying waste their country, and rendering it a desert'. A Cape Town merchant had, apparently with some success, included a quagga (a lesser striped zebra) alongside horses in his carriage team. Gordon also advocated such domestications, especially of the eland, which was easy to hunt, provided a much-favoured meat, and could possibly be used for milk and draught.[21] Vernon Forbes, editor of Sparrman's text, noted that this was perhaps the first proposal for game farming in the country; he was struck more generally by Sparrman's digressions on the 'the cumulative effects of man's destructive hand upon the environment'.[22]

Although he indulged in speculation and presented his ideas in fragments through the text, Sparrman clearly held a sophisticated view of balance in nature. Predators, he felt,

serve[d], in conjunction with mankind, to keep in a just equilibrium the increase of the animal kingdom; so that it may not exceed the supplies afforded it by the vegetable part of creation, and by this means prevent the necessary renewal of the latter by seeds, etc. and thus, by desolating it and laying it waste, in the end impoverish and destroy themselves.[23]

Similar understandings became one of the foundation stones of modern environmentalism.[24] Sparrman thought that hyenas, though deeply unpopular with settlers, had great value in clearing up areas that would otherwise be

---

[18] Hall, 'South African Pastures', 75.   [19] Sparrman, *Voyage*, ii. 60.
[20] Ibid. i. 240; Skead, *Historical Mammal Incidence*, i. 364–7.
[21] Raper and Boucher (eds.), *Gordon*, i. 83 ff.   [22] Sparrman, *Voyage*, i. Foreword, 3.
[23] Ibid. 170.
[24] Aldo Leopold, *A Sand County Almanac* (Oxford University Press, New York, 1949); Susan Flader, *Thinking Like a Mountain: Aldo Leopold and the Evolution of an Ecological Attitude Toward Deer, Wolves and Forests* (University of Missouri Press, Columbia, 1974).

'hideous and disfigured with carcases and skeletons'; this was why bones were seldom to be seen on the veld.

Sparrman also recorded discussion on the complex interactions between locusts and grass cover, suggesting that here too there was some balance in nature. Locusts, he heard, as well as 'white ants' (termites), were eaten in large quantities by the Khoikhoi, who welcomed their appearance despite their impact on the pastures. In addition to roasting the mature insects, the Khoikhoi made soup of the females in egg. Nor was the useful place of locusts in nature simply restricted to the fortuitous food supply they offered. They played a role in natural regeneration. In locust plagues, as after fire, so widely used both by colonists and Khoikhoi, 'the ground is . . . stripped quite bare; but merely in order that it may shortly afterwards appear in a much more beautiful dress, being, in this case, decked with many kinds of annual grasses, herbs, and superb lilies, which had been choked up before by shrubs and perennial plants'.[25] He envisaged that similar processes could restore veld invaded by bush.

It is clear that in some respects Sparrman was reflecting more general perceptions held at the Cape. For example, a few years later the Dutch visitor, Swellengrebel, noted that within seven or eight years of the Boer occupation of the Camdeboo, the Karoo plain south of Graaff-Reinet, 'the luxuriance of the grass . . . [had] already started to deteriorate markedly', and that the veld would soon 'become wholly deteriorated just like that which lies nearer the Cape'.[26] Swellengrebel blamed lack of markets for livestock, the 'indolence' of Cape farmers, and their tendency to expand in new areas rather than invest in their land: 'unimproved [wild] veld, without any management, cannot sustain so many livestock', he noted.[27] This in turn necessitated transhumance or sending of livestock to 'some remote farm', and 'a wide dispersion of farms' with concomitant danger that the colonists would 'fall back into barbarism' and violence, unconstrained by law.[28]

By building an environmental dimension into their critiques of Cape settler pastoralism, both Sparrman and Swellengrebel anticipated a range of later conservationist comments. Sparrman may have been amongst the last to praise Khoikhoi methods of lighter stocking and rapid transhumance. Swellengrebel's comments were more congruent with the Company argument for more intensive farming and closer settlement. It was this strand of

---

[25] Sparrman, *Voyage*, i. 330–1.   [26] Newton-King, 'The Enemy Within', 98–101.
[27] G. J. Schutte (ed.), *Briefwisseling van Hendrik Swellengrebel Jr oor Kaapse Sake 1778–1792* (van Riebeeck Society, Cape Town, 1982), 166, 355.
[28] Ibid. 350.

official and specialist thinking, which inveighed against transhumance or nomadism, whether by settlers or Africans, that became dominant.

Governor de Mist's report during the short Dutch administration of 1803–6 epitomized this view.[29] His Commission focused largely on the introduction of merino sheep and European Friesland cattle, rather than on systems of pasturage.[30] But the commissioners heard about the veld in established settler districts being 'old'. One of their main informants, John van Reenen, whose family were amongst the wealthiest western Cape farmers, was already experimenting with systems of horse farming which did not involve nightly kraaling—animals were left to run on the open veld in the Hantam area.[31] De Mist advocated a system of grazing within walled paddocks, rotated in turn, as part of his plan for the intensification of settlement and control of 'half-wild Europeans'.[32] His prescriptions were later infused with a range of new supporting arguments and became a clarion-call for improvers for much of the next two centuries.

This social undertone to remarks about environmental degradation was evident in a number of contexts. William Somerville, a British physician and official, commented in the 1790s on a Griqua settlement, with large herds and flocks, which he encountered in the interior near the Gariep river. 'The water is not super abundant,' Somerville wrote, 'and however fertile the soil may be it is now so overstocked that every blade of grass is consumed.'[33] His own party's oxen could not find grazing. Far better for all concerned, Somerville mused, if people such as the Griqua could be persuaded to remain within the colony, where they made 'the most intelligent and faithful servants', rather than indulge 'habits of idleness' and wasteful farming practices on the frontier.

Stockenstrom, landdrost of Graaff-Reinet in the 1810s and 1820s, for whom the political and social consequences of trekboer expansion were a major preoccupation, thought that the Boers kept too many animals for their farms, and argued that some should be forced into other modes of living. His attempts to control the dispersal of the settler population were deeply unpopular. He was reluctant to allow new British settlers into his district because pasturage was too short—a decision which won him yet more opponents.[34]

[29] Kathleen M. Jeffreys (trans.), *The Memorandum of Commissary J. A. de Mist containing recommendations for the form and administration of the government at the Cape of Good Hope 1802* (van Riebeeck Society, Cape Town, 1920), 197–9, 208.

[30] H. B. Thom (ed.), *Willem Stephanus van Reyneveld se Aanmerkingen over de Verbetering van het Vee aan de Kaap de Goede Hoop 1804* (Van Riebeeck Society, Cape Town, 1942).

[31] Lichtenstein, *Travels*, i. 111 ff.   [32] *Memorandum of Commissary J. A. de Mist*, 199.

[33] Bradlow (eds.), *William Somerville's Narrative*, 100, and see 24.

[34] van der Merwe, *Noordwaarts Beweging*, 210; *DSAB* i. 775.

For him, also, environmental problems, including longer-term decline in vegetation, were closely related to the transhumant life of trekboers.

Even before the language of romanticism became well established in literary descriptions in the early nineteenth century, authors could rejoice in the beauty of the Cape. Gordon, often prosaic and matter-of-fact, with a strong devotion to accuracy in reporting, visited the farm Vrede, south of Graaff-Reinet town, soon after it had been settled; he recorded 'the most beautiful and finest region one can visualize, being full of lush grass and trees, mainly thorn-trees or mimosa'.[35] By no means all travellers found the tangled, thorn-decked *Acacia karoo* thickets so attractive.

Burchell also brought a romantic turn of phrase to his writing. He spent five years on the island of St Helena, partly as government botanist, before he moved to the Cape, and wrote lyrically of the island scenery: of 'sublime' views and a 'luxuriance of the verdure' which caused 'a delightful feeling strangely mixed with sensations of fear and wonderment'.[36] In his published work he was less forthcoming than Sparrman about environmental change. He explained, but did not criticize, the much-emulated 'Bushman' practice of burning 'old withered grass' to attract game or renew pastures.[37] He commented on the wide distribution of rhinoceros bush, but not its spread. However, he did note the problem of drifting sands on the Cape flats.[38] As a botanical collector, he worried that frequent fires on the slopes of 'Devil's Mountain' above Cape Town would destroy its range of 'curious and beautiful plants'.[39] Anxious about the paucity of grazing for his oxen around a farm in the Roggeveld, he wrote with feeling that 'the sheep of the place consumed, like locusts, every blade of grass and leafy twig within a moderate compass'.[40] He was also an advocate of tree planting.[41]

On occasions when Burchell's vision of nature was made explicit, he presented a view of complex interaction similar to Sparrman's:

In this arid country, where every juicy vegetable would soon be eaten up by the wild animals, the great creating power, with all-provident wisdom, has given to such plants either an acrid or poisonous juice, or sharp thorns, to preserve the species

[35] Raper and Boucher (eds.), *Gordon*, i. 77.

[36] Grove, *Green Imperialism*, 350–1; Richard Grove, 'Scotland in South Africa: John Croumbie Brown and the Roots of Settler Environmentalism', in Griffiths and Robin (eds.), *Ecology and Empire*.

[37] Burchell, *Travels*, i. 39, 101–2, 419; Thunberg, *Travels*, i. 83.

[38] Grove, *Green Imperialism*, 354.   [39] Burchell, *Travels*, i. 38–9.

[40] Ibid. 172. The comparison between sheep and locusts was later made famous by John Muir ('hooved locusts'). Burchell described sheep 'moving in a compact body, like an army invading the country'.

[41] Burchell, *Hints on Emigration*, 43.

from annihilation, in those regions, where, for good and wise purposes, they have been placed. The harmony which pervades every part of the universe, is not less wonderful and beautiful in the distribution of animals and vegetables over the face of the globe, than in the planetary system . . . In the wide system of created objects, nothing is wanting, nothing is superfluous . . . Each has its peculiar part to perform, conducive ultimately to the well-being of all. Nothing more bespeaks a littleness of mind, and a narrowness of ideas, than the admiring of a production of Nature, *merely* for its magnitude, or the despising of one, merely for its minuteness: nothing more erroneous than to regard as useless, all that does not visibly tend to the benefit of *man*.[42]

Although there was not a wide Cape readership for travel texts published in Europe, they were known to a few settlers and officials with a literary or scientific bent. Local collectors assisted visiting scientists and some exported indigenous seeds and bulbs. Burchell was struck by the extent to which local plants were grown in Cape Town gardens—including gardenia, strelitzia, amaryllis, erythrina, and aloes—along with imported European and Asian species.[43] In the first half of the nineteenth century scientific endeavour increasingly found a local base, especially amongst physicians. One new network of knowledge rested on German immigrants in Cape Town. Medical training in Germany, as in Scotland, included the natural sciences; pharmacy was still firmly linked to botany.[44] Dr F. L. Liesching, who arrived in 1787, practised both as doctor and apothecary and started a herb garden.[45]

Carl Ludwig, who came to Cape Town in 1806, initially worked as an assistant to Liesching.[46] Later a successful businessman, he became a major collector of plants and birds. While the old Company garden was neglected under British rule, he founded his own 'famous garden', Ludwigsburg, in Kloof Street in the 1830s. It became a significant site of botanical interchange and an important port of call for visitors. Baron von Ludwig, as he became, was credited with 1,660 introductions. He sent a number of collections of Cape plants back to Europe and was a participant in early scientific associations, such as the South African Literary and Scientific Institution, the South African Public Library, and Cape of Good Hope Agricultural Society.

The German apothecary P. H. Pohlmann, who ran a pharmacy in Strand Street, Cape Town, hosted Burchell during his visit, climbed Table Mountain with him, and accompanied him on botanical expeditions. Carl Drege, one of

---

[42] Burchell, *Travels*, i. 161.   [43] Ibid. 22.   [44] Grove, *Green Imperialism*.

[45] McMagh, *The Three Lieschings*; Edmund H. Burrows, *A History of Medicine in South Africa* (A. A. Balkema, Cape Town, 1958), 76.

[46] Frank R. Bradlow, 'Baron von Ludwig and the Ludwig's-burg Gardens', *Quarterly Bulletin of the South African Library*, 18: 2 (Dec. 1963), 82–93; *DSAB* i. 856.

the most successful plant collectors, worked for Pohlmann. He amassed thousands of local species in the 1820s and 1830s, which found their way as live plants, seeds, and pressed specimens to the herbaria of Europe. Burchell had made detailed notes, which remained largely unpublished, on the location and habitat of the species he found. Drege, a German-trained horticulturalist, was especially significant in linking the geography, climate, and flora of particular areas.[47] He was clearly influenced by Alexander von Humboldt and others to chart 'the native stations of plants' or phytogeography. This approach provided a far clearer basis for understanding regional variety, the distribution of species, and also botanical change.

These developments found their way into local publications through the work of William Harvey and Ludwig Pappe. Harvey came to the Cape with his brother, the new Colonial Treasurer, in 1835 and replaced him in the post when he fell ill. Already an ardent botanizer, and a regular correspondent with W. J. Hooker (then still in Glasgow, but soon to become Director of Kew), he sought out both Pringle and Burchell in England.[48] In Cape Town Harvey was in close touch with von Ludwig, spent much time at his garden, and named the *Tulbaghia ludwigiana* after him.[49] He kept guinea fowl, ostriches, and a secretary bird—fashionable in Cape Town gardens because it caught frogs, slugs, and snakes. Before work, he collected plants on the mountain: 'there is no greater pleasure,' he wrote, 'than that of seeing and gathering a plant in its natural situation and observing all about it where it grows'.[50]

Harvey helped to create a wide network of correspondents in the colony and beyond. He worked to define the extraordinary variety and generally narrow geographical range of Cape plants: ericas, and rushes (restionaceae) in the south-west; grasses, aloes, and euphorbia in the east; the rare stapelia in the east and north. When visiting Paarl for the first time, he noted: 'I was greatly struck with the difference in the commonest shrubs, though the distance is but thirty-five miles.'[51] His major contribution at this phase was a short book on South African plants, published locally in 1838 and intended

[47] *DSAB* i. 25. Some of his work was published in Germany in the 1830s; it was first published in English in the *Cape Monthly Magazine*, 7 (1873): Ernst Meyer, 'On the Geographical Distribution of Plants in South Africa', translated, with notes, by H. Bolus.

[48] For Kew, see Lucille Brockway, *Science and Colonial Expansion: The Role of the British Royal Botanic Garden* (Academic Press, New York, 1979); Drayton, *Nature's Government*.

[49] Kew Archives, Director's Letters, vol. 58, W. H. Harvey to W. J. Hooker, 2 Nov. 1835, 5 June 1836.

[50] Ibid., Harvey to Hooker, 23 Mar. 1836.

[51] *Memoir of W. H. Harvey, M.D.. F.R.S., etc. etc. Late Professor of Botany, Trinity College, Dublin,* no author (Bell & Daldy, London, 1869), 104.

'to cultivate a taste for botany generally in the colony'.[52] He left in that year, but back in Ireland, with a collection of 4,000 South African species, he eventually became Curator of the herbarium (1844–56), and later Professor of Botany (1856–66), at Trinity College, Dublin. He then launched a definitive and comprehensive record of the *Flora Capensis*; the first volume was published in 1859.

Ludwig Pappe arrived in 1831 to establish a medical practice in Cape Town. Born in Germany and qualified from Leipzig, he saw botany as his leading interest.[53] He also worked in von Ludwig's garden, formed close links with visiting botanists such as Harvey, published a list of Cape plants in 1833–34, and became a foundation member of the Literary and Scientific Institution. He helped to preserve and develop von Ludwig's collection, and continued to chart the extraordinary range of plants at the Cape.[54] A definitive publication of Cape plants remained a priority for him, and he sent materials to Kew, and to Harvey for the *Flora Capensis*.[55] But, as Richard Grove has argued, Pappe was important not only as a botanist who stayed, but because of his understanding of environmental change.

In 1847 Pappe published a small volume on the medicinal use of plants. He usually noted whether berries or fruit of a species was edible and sometimes mentioned Khoikhoi names and uses. In dealing with 'rhinosterboschjes', for example, he described their bitter, resinous taste, their use as a tonic for dyspepsia and, in powdered form, as a treatment for diarrhoea in children.[56] His *Silva Capensis* was a similar work, largely a list of trees, prepared initially to accompany a Cape display at the Paris Universal Exhibition of 1855 and extended for the London International Show of 1862 (at which the Cape was not, in the event, represented). By no means exhaustive, it recorded botanical names, common names, economic uses of plants for timber or fruit,

[52] William Henry Harvey, *The Genera of South African Plants arranged according to the Natural System* (Juta, Cape Town, 1868), 11 (2nd edn. of the 1838 volume, ed. J. D. Hooker); *Memoir of W. H. Harvey*, 96.

[53] *DSAB* ii. 532–4; Burrows, *History of Medicine*, 141–2; Richard Grove, 'Early Themes in African Conservation: The Cape in the Nineteenth Century', in D. Anderson and R. Grove (eds.), *Conservation in Africa: People, Policies and Practices* (Cambridge University Press, Cambridge, 1987), 21–39; Richard Grove, 'Scottish Missionaries, Evangelical Discourses and the Origins of Conservation Thinking in Southern Africa 1820–1900', *JSAS*, 15: 2 (1989), 163–87.

[54] P. J. Venter, 'An Early Botanist and Conservationist at the Cape: The Reverend John Croumbie Brown, Ll.D., F.R.G.S., F.L.S.', *Archives Year Book for South African History* (1952), ii. 279–93.

[55] Cape of Good Hope, *Report of the Colonial Botanist for 1859*, G.37-1860; Kew, Director's Letters, vol. 60, L. Pappe to W. J. Hooker, 19 Apr. 1859.

[56] L. Pappe, *Florae Capensis Medicae Prodromus; or, an Enumeration of South African Plants used as Remedies by the Colonists of the Cape of Good Hope*, 2nd edn. (W. Brittain, Cape Town, 1857), 25.

and occasional anecdotes. For example, he explained that sneezewood, a hardwood used for joinery and posts, was so called because its sawdust caused violent sneezing; and he noted that the incidence of the wild plum, used for yokes and poles, was 'considered as a criterion of excellent pasturage for wool-bearing flocks'.[57] Both of these works, as also his notes on ferns, were designed for a local, non-specialist audience.

In the 1840s Pappe became absorbed in attempts to resurrect the neglected botanical gardens in Cape Town, and offered himself as its curator.[58] When Governor Harry Smith reopened them in 1848, Pappe wrote that 'part of this ground will be devoted exclusively to the cultivation of South African plants, and it will be possible by these means, not only to appreciate the richness of our vegetation, but to make them known throughout the world'.[59] He called for the appointment of an official Colonial Botanist—and became the first incumbent in 1858.[60] In this position he travelled around the colony twice (with a copy of Burchell), collecting plants and identifying areas for new agricultural enterprises.[61] Some of his work was practical: suggesting methods to combat the destructive mildew that infected Cape vineyards, and to stabilize the sands of the Cape flats.

Drawing on the findings of Drege and Harvey, and the ideas of von Humboldt on phytogeography, Pappe was deeply aware not only of the variety of Cape flora but their possible uniqueness:

nowhere else upon the whole surface of the earth do we meet with a country exhibiting in the same manner such a combination of orders or families of plants, so dissimilar to each other and usually so widely separated by different latitudes. Hence the richness of the South African flora, which, while it includes representatives both of the tropical and cold temperate zones within a limited space, displays that almost incredible variety of indigenous vegetation for which it is so justly renowned.[62]

Thunberg had recorded over 3,000 species in the 1770s. In the 1830s Harvey had recorded 1,086 genera and 8,500 species, while Drege had named 1,008 genera and 7,092 species. Ernst Meyer, who wrote about Drege's collections,

---

[57] Ludwig Pappe, *Silva Capensis or A Description of South African Forest Trees and Arborescent Shrubs used for Technical and Economic Purposes*, 2nd edn. (W. Brittain, London and Cape Town, 1862), 5.

[58] Kew, Director's Letters, vol. 59, Pappe to Hooker, 20 June 1846.

[59] Ibid., Pappe to Hooker, 13 May 1848.   [60] Ibid., Pappe to Hooker, 28 Jan. 1857.

[61] Cape of Good Hope, *Report of the Colonial Botanist on an Official Tour through certain of the Western Districts*, G.41-1859; *Report of the Colonial Botanist for 1861*, G.34-1862.

[62] *Cape Monthly Magazine*, 8 (1860), 237–49: The Colonial Botanist, 'Botanical Geography and the Distribution of South African Plants'.

estimated that there might be as many as 12,000 plant species in South Africa: 'in this vast number of different forms, Southern Africa far excels all other known regions.'[63] In view of the rate of discovery, and the fact that so many species were confined to narrow geographical limits, Pappe reckoned that South Africa might have 18,000 plant species.[64]

For Pappe these numbers served to underline the richness of Cape flora. Moreover, he knew that relatively few were 'social' species, growing together in large numbers, and relatively few very widely distributed; the palmiet rush (*Juncus serratus*), after which many fountains and farms were named, was an exception. Few indigenous plants seemed to be aggressive colonizers, although the rhinoceros bush (*Elytropappus rhinoceratis*) and *Acacia karoo* could be. This made it more likely that rapid environmental change in any one area could result in the loss of species. There was already some awareness of the extinction of animals such as the blaaubok and the quagga, as well as the extreme rarity of the bontebok and Cape mountain zebra, which were saved at this time by the action of individual farmers.[65] Pappe transferred this concern to plants. To an extraordinary extent, the Cape flora had been mapped. He propagated a sense of their uniqueness and variety in articles written for the *Cape Monthly Magazine*, which were picked up in more widely circulated guides and geography books by the late 1850s and early 1860s.[66]

Pappe articulated an urgent concern for the preservation of this unique plant kingdom. His travels enabled him to see a wide range of landscapes at first hand, and to talk to farmers and local officials about veld and plants. He witnessed the results of burning, used by farmers to clear vegetation and remove tough, sour grass so that the pastures could be rejuvenated by early rains. Whereas late eighteenth-century travellers had accepted widespread burning of vegetation as necessary for pastoral farming, 'fire abolitionism', expressed in strongly moral tones, was now taking root (Chapter 3).[67] In both the second edition of *Silva Capensis* and his reports as Colonial Botanist, Pappe found his voice as a conservationist and condemned the 'wanton destruction of vegetation by fire':

[63] *Cape Monthly Magazine*, 7 (1873), 198.

[64] This was in line with Drege's much earlier suggestion of 16,000 to 20,000: *Cape Monthly Magazine*, 8 (1874), 53. In introducing the second edition of Harvey, *Genera of South African Plants*, 6, J. D. Hooker estimated more conservatively 1,209 genera and 8,777 species.

[65] Skead, *Historical Mammal Incidence*, i. 547–8.

[66] Henry Hall, *Manual of South African Geography* (Saul Solomon and Co., Cape Town, 1859); A. Wilmot, *A Historical and Descriptive Account of the Colony of the Cape of Good Hope* (F. Algar, London, and de Villiers, Noble and Co., Cape Town, 1863), 59–60.

[67] Stephen J. Pyne, 'Frontiers of Fire', in Griffiths and Robin (eds.), *Ecology and Empire*, 19–34.

The most awful consequences must necessarily attend such outrageous conduct, and I ascribe the excessive drought with which these districts have been visited of late, in no small measure to the annihilation of the bushes and trees in the ravines of their mountains, it being universally known that woods and forests attract and increase moisture, produce rain, and give rise to springs and running streams, while tracts deprived of vegetation, become strongly-heated, dreary and dry.[68]

Comparing such acts to arson, he asked for stronger measures by which to 'denounce and convict the perpetrators'.

Elements of an degradationist critique had been formulated at the Cape by 1860. Visiting scientific travellers such as Sparrman, frequently referred to by later authors, had been important in identifying some key issues such as overgrazing, exhaustion of pasturage, and vegetation change. It is clear that he was in part reporting ideas already being articulated at the Cape. By the mid-nineteenth century these concerns had been taken up and given further definition by local botanical specialists. A concern for the balance of nature, and the loss of species was linked to a critique of Cape pastoral practices. Although this formal botanical knowledge was unavailable to all but the most educated and interested of colonists, a sense of the special botanical character of this unique region was beginning to be popularized. In the eyes of a few experts, at least, fire was being identified as a major threat to the vegetation.

Drought, Desiccation, and Geological Denudation

Pasture exhaustion and vegetation change were recognized before the end of the eighteenth century and seen as a cause of trekking. Drought, P. J. van der Merwe concluded from his immersion in the sources, was also frequently noted in the first few decades of the nineteenth century. Farmers perceived that good years were becoming less frequent and that rainfall was declining.[69] Lichtenstein heard this in the Roggeveld and Hantam very early in the nineteenth century; 'old people' reminisced that

half a century back the superabundance of water in the district was such that in the middle of the summer the nearest neighbours could not get to each other, on account of the rivers being overflowed, and of the deep morasses in the valleys. There seldom at that period passed a week, even in the hottest months, that violent thunderstorms did not bring with them a profuse supply of rain: on the

[68] G.41-1859, 3; Cape of Good Hope, *Report of the Colonial Botanist for 1861*, G.34-1862.
[69] van der Merwe, *Noordwaartse Beweging*, 186.

contrary, whole summers had of late years passed without the intervention of a single storm.[70]

By the 1820s similar complaints emanated from the midlands. Howison, of the East Indian Company, was certainly struck by the natural 'desolation' of the interior, with its 'ranges of mountains denuded of soil, and traversed by deep furrows—their summits carved into fantastic shapes by the action of the elements'.[71] Although he recognized its beauty, he thought South Africa, compared to other settler colonies, seemed 'to be a worn-out and emaciated country . . . like an animal body in which the circulation has ceased from disease or exhaustion'.[72] But he distinguished between longer-term and recent change. What he heard from farmers were tales of increasing drought:

It is very certain that in many parts of the interior of the country the springs and rivulets are drying up and the annual rains become more scanty and irregular. The traveller often meets with houses and farms that have been deserted by their owners on account of a permanent failure in the supply of water which they once enjoyed.[73]

The area around the town of Beaufort West, he heard, established in 1818 because of its well-watered location and 'luxuriant' pastures, had by 1830 become dry and barren. Albany settlers had the same perception of their area and anticipated that they might have to move.

Influenced by Annales history and ecological explanations, van der Merwe attributed both the gradual trekboer movement to the north, and also the Great Trek itself, not least to the interrelationship between people, livestock, and natural resources. It is an important argument that has not been sufficiently rehearsed in later literature preoccupied with the political causes of the Trek.[74] The areas north of the Sneeuberg, which trekboers began to occupy in the early nineteenth century, had fewer permanent fountains, forcing them into frequent, nervous movements. When rains fell in a particular area, farmers descended on it with their stock, rapidly exhausting the veld. Those who arrived first could choose the best land and, critically, the best water sources; those who followed sometimes condemned themselves to seasonal trekking in order to find water. With more stockowners chasing the same water sources, supplies were quickly exhausted and perceived to be

[70] Lichtenstein, *Travels*, i. 123–4, 150. He was writing soon after a serious drought which, on the east coast, has been associated with the rise of the Zulu kingdom.

[71] Howison, *European Colonies*, i. 189.   [72] Ibid. 190.

[73] Ibid. 210, quoted by van der Merwe.

[74] van der Merwe, *Noortwaartse Beweging*, 176–204 and 294 ff., where he tries to undermine arguments that preliminary treks were primarily about asserting the right to hold slaves.

declining. By the 1820s Boers were crossing the Gariep into what became the Free State; by the 1830s over one thousand were based there. Water supplies were more secure and the veld was better for cattle. They moved across the country, van der Merwe suggested in a vivid metaphor, like water taking the easiest path over uneven ground.[75]

The fact that 1835–7 proved to be particularly difficult years, environmentally speaking, was a further factor in precipitating major movements northwards. Contemporary sources made this connection. In 1839 Jacobus Boshoff, formerly a clerk in Graaff-Reinet, who later became the second President of the Orange Free State, wrote to the *Grahamstown Journal* to explain the trek. In addition to the political issues, he noted that too many animals were kept by farmers in the northern Cape, which is why they moved seasonally into the interior. 'In addition thereto the seasons for the last eight or ten years became gradually worse and worse', he noted; 'springs and large pools dried up everywhere, so that the farmers in many instances were compelled to migrate, from want of water'.[76]

While some visitors to the interior of Cape, unaccustomed to its aridity and periodic droughts, could judge it, initially, as degraded, much of the discourse of desiccation came from local people who had lived there a long time. Most travellers soon came to evaluate the landscape in its own terms and could distinguish between the generally arid appearance and the perception of decline. Van der Merwe was struck that a century later, in the 1930s, when he was researching, this belief that droughts were getting worse was just as strong amongst Afrikaner farmers, and that each generation seemed to notice the phenomenon; this made him sceptical about idealization of the good times.[77] He was inclined to follow the interpretation of the Drought Commission report of 1923, that fountains dried up because of denudation and human-induced degradation.

Boer experiences, and reports upon these, were one fertile source of desiccationist ideas, and they had developed well before British or scientific perceptions were brought to bear. As Grove has illustrated, Robert Moffat, the Scottish missionary amongst the Tswana, bemoaned the desiccation around Dithakong in the northern Cape in the 1820s—at the same time that travellers were recording similar reports from Afrikaners. The Tswana themselves recalled an era of 'incessant showers which clothed the very rocks with

---

[75] van der Merwe, *Trek*, 100.

[76] van der Merwe, *Noordwaartse Beweging*, 188, quoting letter by J. Boshoff to editor of the *Grahamstown Journal*, 17 Feb.1839; reproduced in full in John Bird, *The Annals of Natal 1495 to 1845* (P. Davis & Sons, Pietermaritzburg, 1888), i. 505.

[77] van der Merwe, *Noortwaartse Beweging*, 190.

verdure . . . They boasted of the Kuruman and other rivers with their impassable torrents, in which the hippopotami played, [and] the lowing herds walking to their necks in grass, filling their *mukakas* with milk, making every heart to sing for joy'.[78] Severe droughts in much of southern Africa in 1823 may have influenced Tswana perceptions of recent desiccation. Moffat drew also on biblical motifs, welding religious and natural explanations. He blamed the Tswana themselves, both for their state of sin, and as 'a nation of levellers . . . cutting down every species of timber'. Clearly, desiccationist ideas could have African, Boer, and Scottish roots.

David Livingstone, Moffat's son-in-law, developed this idea of 'the general desiccation of the country'; his writings were read and reviewed at the Cape.[79] As evidence, he cited dry riverbeds as well as 'eyes', or fountain mouths, that were now without water. Echoing Sparrman, he commented that the arid northern Cape had formerly been 'covered with a coating of grass', but that this had disappeared, along with the antelopes which fed on it, after Boer occupation. Antelopes, he suggested, had been partly responsible for regenerating grass by eating and excreting seed; with their demise, Karoo shrubs such as mesembryanthemums spread. Intriguingly, Livingstone thought that Boers encouraged this process because they perceived that the new shrubby vegetation was better for sheep and goats:

A few waggon-loads of mesembryanthemum-plants, in seed, are brought to a farm covered with a scanty crop of coarse grass, and placed on a spot to which the sheep have access in the evenings. As they eat a little every night, the seeds are dropped over the grazing grounds, in this simple way, with a regularity which could not be matched except at the cost of an immense amount of labour. The place becomes in the course of a few years a sheep farm, as the animals thrive on such herbage.[80]

It was 'a clever imitation of one process in nature by Cape farmers'. The *Cape Monthly Magazine*, reviewing his book, commented that sheep farmers believed that once an area was 'fully stocked and eaten down, it will answer well as a sheep country'.[81]

Not everyone accepted desiccationist ideas, and vegetation change was also welcomed elsewhere in the world. In America's New England, for example, commentators hoped that forest destruction would contribute to a dryer and

[78] Grove, 'Scottish Missionaries', 169–9.

[79] David Livingstone, *Travels and Researches in South Africa* (Amalgamated Press, London, 1905), 87–9, first published 1857.

[80] Ibid. 88–9.

[81] *Cape Monthly Magazine*, 3 (1858), 322: FWR, 'A Country Farmer: Agricultural Notes and Queries on Dr. Livingstone's Researches', was, however, sceptical about Livingstone's story of the Boers planting mesembryanthemums.

warmer climate.[82] Yet the idea of degradation was already being fixed in reports on the Cape. Andrew Wylie, the Colonial Geologist from 1855 to 1859, saw, on a Roggeveld farm, 'ground, for a long way round the homestead, trampled brown and bare by the troops of long-tailed Cape sheep'.[83] Travelling north of Fraserburg, in the dry Zak river valley, he was told that the grass was 'not now so abundant as formerly, and has totally disappeared in some places, owing probably to its having been scorched by drought or eaten off by cattle before it has shed its seed'.[84] Even the bones and horns of springbok were to be seen on the veld.[85] Desiccation was viewed by some as a universal phenomenon in the tropics, hastened by irrigation, deforestation, burning, and European settlement.[86]

Henry Hall, the military engineer and mapmaker (Chapter 1), absorbed these ideas and reproduced them in a standard text on which others drew. His *Manual of South African Geography* (1859) was written at the request of the Colonial Secretary for senior school education and civil service exams. Recent writing on the history of geography tends to emphasize its close links with imperialism—although the subject did not become a major componenent of the Cape school syllabus in the nineteenth century.[87] Hall's book inculcated British values not least by summarizing knowledge about this colonial territory in a convenient and portable form. The Cape was conceptualized as a whole, analysed as discrete natural and social units, and its potential assessed. He included sections on social geography, farming, and African peoples. Although he eschewed any detailed treatment of indigenous botanical features, he did outline the variety of Cape plants and especially the natural history of the key mammal species, partly with a preservationist's eye on their possible extinction.[88] He spoke of fountains drying up and getting weaker in Namaqualand and the Karoo as part of a long-term decline.[89]

In discussion of desiccation and degradation, a number of authors juxtaposed geological time-scales with shorter-term human impacts. Such geological ideas were themselves fresh and were drawn into Cape debates, especially by a group of eastern Cape intellectuals. Dr. W. G. Atherstone provided a particular focus for scientific enterprise. Born in England in 1814, he

<hr/>

[82] Glacken, *Traces on the Rhodian Shore*, 658 ff.   [83] Wylie, *Appendix*, 12.
[84] Ibid. 19.   [85] Ibid. 20.
[86] J. S. Wilson, 'On the general and gradual desiccation of the Earth and the Atmosphere', *Report of the Proceedings of the British Association for the Advancement of Science* (1858), 155–6 and 'On the increasing desiccation of inner Southern Africa', ibid. (1864), 150.
[87] Harold M. Wesso, 'The Colonization of Geographic Thought: The South African Experience', in Anne Godlewska and Neil Smith (eds.), *Geography and Empire* (Blackwell, Oxford, 1994), 318.
[88] Hall, *Manual of South African Geography*, 116.   [89] Ibid. 97 ff.

came with his family to the Cape in 1820.[90] Trained by his father, the district surgeon of Albany, he qualified in 1839 after a few years of formal study in Dublin, London, and Heidelberg. He returned to launch a successful medical career in Grahamstown: he is well known as the first physician in South Africa to have used anaesthetics—for which he constructed his own apparatus.

Atherstone became a polymath involved in musical, artistic, literary, and scientific activities. He contributed to Hall's 1857 map of South Africa and conducted early ostrich-hatching experiments. 'In his unbounded enthusiasm for knowledge', he devoted a good deal of his time to veterinary science, zoology, and ornithology.[91] From 1847 he sent botanical specimens to Sir William Hooker at Kew and Harvey in Dublin; he arranged 'pic-nic excursions' and camping holidays with his wife, daughters, and friends to collect them. Atherstone argued successfully for a botanical garden in Grahamstown, as well as the renewal of the Cape Town institution.[92] After taking Pappe for a botanical walk at the reservoir near Grahamstown in 1861, he wrote down from memory the botanical names of over sixty plants which they had seen.[93] His own large collection of plant specimens was later presented to the Albany museum.[94] Harvey's *Flora Capensis*, he thought:

will be productive of great *moral* good I feel convinced from the character of many who have requested me to order it . . . A love of science is incompatible with indulgence in any of the animal . . . propensities and in a country where intellectual amusements are very scarce . . . botany cannot be too highly appreciated by the isolated farmer or the nomadic carrier who lives in his bullock-wagon. To my astonishment men of this class ask me for the 'flora'. If you induce the carrier and the sheep farmer to reflect and study nature you prevent a corresponding amount of crime proportional to the idleness and ennui otherwise endured by them.[95]

Atherstone was in close touch with western Cape networks and was consulted on a range of official issues. When an 1860 government select committee was appointed to examine the worrying spread of the 'spiny burr-weed' (*Xanthium spinosum*), he was the main source of information for the eastern Cape.[96] The plant originated in southern Europe and had already colonized temperate zones in North and South America, and Australia. It was

[90] Burrows, *History of Medicine*, 168–73; *DSAB* i. 25–7.   [91] *DSAB* i. 26.
[92] Kew, Director's letters, vol. 59, W. G. Atherstone to Sir W. J. Hooker, 20 Apr.1848 and 17 Oct.1848.
[93] Mathie, *Atherstone*, ii. 488–491.
[94] Kew, Director's letters, vol. 59, Atherstone to Hooker, 8 Mar.1847 and subsequent letters.
[95] Ibid., vol. 60, Atherstone to Hooker, 18 Oct. 1860.
[96] Cape of Good Hope, *Report of the Select Committee on the Plant Xanthium Spinosum*, A.15-1860.

first noted in 1849, but Pappe found that it did not invade the western Cape. Atherstone saw the plant near Grahamstown in 1858 and found it to be spreading quickly along roads. The danger of burrweed was that the spines on its seed case easily hooked into wool and were very difficult to extract. It could be spread by sheep in this manner and threatened the colony's leading export. His intervention helped to secure noxious-weeds legislation against it.

For all Atherstone's botanical research, geology was perhaps his major extra-medical interest, and his significance in this field was recognized by the fact that the first diamond discovered in South Africa was brought to him in 1867 for definitive identification. He and others were strongly influenced in their geological pursuits by Andrew Geddes Bain, 1820 settler, frontier hunter, soldier, and engineer who became a convert to geological exploration after reading Charles Lyell's, *Principles of Geology* in 1837.[97] Bain's main profession as a road-builder—responsible for the construction of some of the earliest, breathtaking Cape mountain passes—provided him with a perfect opportunity to work systematically in the field.[98] From 1838 he discovered a string of fossils. After exhibiting them in Grahamstown in 1844, when he formed his strong link with Atherstone, he sent them to the Geological Society in London. Bain also wrote preliminary accounts of the 'Geology of the Eastern Province', and later of the Cape as a whole, which gained him considerable recognition.[99] His work, together with renewed interest in the Namaqualand copper deposits, resulted in the appointment of geologist Andrew Wylie, from Ireland, in 1855 as one of the first specialist scientific officers in the colony.

Lyell and others had emphasized the importance of geological change over time, and had anticipated Darwin by illustrating the long history of the formation of the earth's surface and the changing fossil remains associated with different ages. Bain developed such ideas with reference to South Africa. It was Bain who formulated the theory that the Karoo plains had been a 'mighty', ancient freshwater lake, 'more than double the extent of all the Canadian lakes put together'.[100] He had found small bivalve shells near the

[97] Margaret Lister (ed.), *Journal of Andrews Geddes Bain: Trader, Explorer, Soldier, Road Engineer and Geologist* (van Riebeeck Society, Cape Town, 1949); *DSAB* i. 35–8; cf. William Smith, the canal-building geologist in England: Simon Winchester, *The Map that Changed the World: A Tale of Rocks, Ruin and Redemption* (Vintage, London, 2001).

[98] A. W. Rogers, 'The Pioneers in South African Geology and Their Work', *Transactions of the Geological Society of South Africa*, 39 (1937), annexure.

[99] Lister, *Journals of Andrew Geddes Bain*, 217–37.

[100] Rogers, 'Pioneers', 30, quoting a letter from Bain to Prof. Richard Owen in 1848.

3. Geological Denudation of the Karoo

tops of mountains, as well as fossils of vertebrates—the 'Saurians' that he thought inhabited the lake. The landscape of the Karoo had then been shaped by upwards geological movement of the lake bed, and its draining. The interior mountains, he argued with their *'perfectly horizontal'* strata, together with the plains between them, could only have been caused by lifting followed by 'denudation on a stupendous scale' because of the 'erosive power of water'.[101]

Bain recognized that his ideas were far from 'faultless' and despaired that 'the want of proper books' was 'a great drawback to the progress of science here'.[102] Wylie, amongst others, soon challenged his theory of a great lake. But his approach remained influential through the nineteenth century, and helped to provide a basis for research and a language for discussion that permeated beyond small geological circles. The idea of denudation by water flows was particularly important in this respect. A later geologist confirmed that 'one feature upon which all observers are agreed is the enormous amount of denudation that has taken place in this southern portion of the continent, wearing away the higher plateaux, leaving flat-topped hills still covered by caps of trap-rock, indicating the original level of the country'.[103] Geological insights, along with botanical, fed into new ways of describing and analysing the Cape environment.

Bain's enthusiasms were taken up by Atherstone and his friend Richard Rubidge (b. 1819), younger brother of the sheep farmer Charles (Chapter 1).[104] When the rest of his family moved to Graaff-Reinet district around 1838, Richard stayed in Grahamstown to train in medicine with Atherstone. After qualifying in Britain, he practised in Graaff-Reinet for a few years before moving to Port Elizabeth in 1850. He played a key role in establishing the provincial hospital, the public library, and a natural-history society. Rubidge was a keen plant collector and lectured on botany to schools in Port Elizabeth. But his major interest, as one of the few colonial 'lovers of science',

---

[101] Bain, 'Geology of the Eastern Province', in Lister, *Journals of Andrew Geddes Bain*, 228.

[102] Ibid. 233.

[103] Hugh Exton, 'Inaugural Address by the President', *Transactions of the Geological Society of South Africa*, 1: 1 (1896), 5. Wylie, *Appendix*, 28, 39, also uses the idea of geological denudation in specific contexts.

[104] Burrows, *History of Medicine*, 152; Rubidge Papers, Wellwood farm, Graaff-Reinet: notes made by Sidney Rubidge for enquiry by *DSAB*.

was also in geology and fossils.[105] In 1851 his fossils were exhibited at the British Association in Ipswich and some went to the British Museum. He visited Namaqualand with Atherstone for a geological survey in 1854. His own major interest was in metamorphism or rock formations.[106] He had a particularly strong technical understanding and published in British as well as local journals.

Rubidge and his colleagues did not see geology as simply about charting rock formations and the history of great lakes. Wylie's work as the first Government Geologist (1855–9) was largely concerned with evaluating mineral discoveries. Geology, Rubidge argued, would uncover other 'hidden treasures of the earth' and open the doors to many new routes of colonial development through agriculture.[107] Bain had begun to make links between the nature of rocks, soil, and pastures. Describing the 'beautifully verdant, fertile and healthy' area around the Winterberg (north of Bedford), he noted that it was not highly valued for grazing as the grass was sour:

I have found all sandstone countries, *sour* with delightfully sweet water; whereas, when the Argillaceous rocks prevail the grass is *sweet* and the water brackish. I know not whether this observation has been made in Europe, but so much am I convinced of its correctness here, that if I were about to purchase a cattle or sheep farm I should give that place the preference whose waters were brackish![108]

Many sheep farmers would have agreed.

Rubidge affirmed that 'careful analysis of rocks of different formations and of the soil derived from them, enables us to predict what crops will grow and what will not on a particular part, and to suggest the means of supplying the deficient elements, so that poor and barren soils may be rendered highly productive'. Together with new developments in agricultural chemistry and soil science, geology could underpin colonial wealth and counteract Malthusian dangers of overpopulation. Rubidge evinced a powerful commitment to Victorian ideas of science and progress. But his concern with colonial development was tempered by the application of his scientific understanding to the other side of that coin: the dangers of overexploitation. Geology, like botany, took dedicated observers into the field and gave them the eyes to see other processes taking place in the Cape environment.

[105] R. N. Rubidge, 'Section of the Zuurberg', *Eastern Cape Monthly Magazine*, 2 (1857–8), 187–96; 'On the Relationship of Certain Geological Formations in this Colony', ibid. 541–4. He was probably also the author of the uncredited 'Oeconomic Geology of the Colony', ibid. 372–9, although this may have been from the hand of Atherstone.

[106] Rogers, 'Pioneers in South African Geology', 67.

[107] Anon. (Rubidge?), 'Oeconomic Geology of the Colony', 372.

[108] Bain, 'Geology of the Eastern Province', in Lister, *Journals of Andrew Geddes Bain*, 227.

Rubidge's contribution to this debate was informed by the writing on longer-term processes of historical denudation and desiccation, by understandings of botanical and geological change, and not least by his observations of sheep farming. His essay entitled 'Evils of Over-pasturage' was published in 1857 in the *Eastern Province Monthly Magazine*.[109] The monthly magazine format was well established in the anglophone world as a vehicle for a wide range of general but erudite articles on literature, science, travel, nature, and politics. The *Eastern Province Monthly Magazine*, launched in 1856 in Grahamstown, and the *Cape Monthly Magazine*, begun in Cape Town in 1857, were for a few years the main vehicles for literary and scientific writing in the colony outside of newspapers.[110] Editors explicitly fostered a local, colonial intellectual milieu, and Atherstone's network provided important contributors.

Richard Rubidge continued to visit his family in Graaff-Reinet and he collected some of his fossil specimens in the environs of Wellwood, his brother's farm. It is instructive to look at sheep-holdings on the farm during these years. High wool prices in the 1850s encouraged heavier stocking. Figures suggest that the total number of sheep grew from less than 4 million around 1840 to nearly 10 million by 1865, of which more than 8 million were woolled. Wool exports increased nearly fourfold, from about 6 million pounds in 1850 to 23 million pounds in 1860. Holdings on Wellwood, for which there are reasonably good figures, reflected this more general pattern. Although numbers on the 12,000-morgen farm fluctuated during each year because of lambing, deaths, and sales, the annual average showed an increase from a low of 2,874 sheep in 1853 to 4,865 in 1860.[111] About 300 goats and 100 cattle were also kept. This level of stocking must have had an impact, and it is no coincidence that soil-erosion control measures were first taken on the farm in 1862 when imported agaves (*Agave americana*—confusingly called aloes in the Cape) were planted.[112]

As in the case of Spain, Rubidge argued, the Cape was 'fast being ruined by its large flocks of Merinos'. It is worth quoting his argument in full,

---

[109] R. N. Rubidge, 'Evils of Over-pasturage', *Eastern Cape Monthly Magazine*, 2 (1857–8), 155–9.

[110] A. M. Lewin Robinson (ed.), *Selected Articles from the Cape Monthly Magazine (New Series 1870–76)* (van Riebeeck Society, Cape Town, 1978). The Eastern Province publication lasted only for a couple of years; the western Cape version survived until 1861 and was revived for a longer run in 1870.

[111] Rubidge papers, Wellwood, stock books of Charles Rubidge. The stock books are uneven in their quality but quarterly totals were recorded for the years 1848–60; averages of the four figures have been used. There may have been changes in the amount of land available. In January 1861 an audit gave 4,350 sheep and 300 goats.

[112] Rubidge, *Merino*, 12.

because it so clearly summarized what was to become a general discourse about degradation:

Sheep, it is well known, crop the grass close; and in dry and sandy soils pull it up by the roots—thus laying the soil bare, and exposing it to be washed away by the heavy rains. Moreover, sheep tread much in the same tracks, and thus form little paths which serve as drains to convey the water away rapidly from the surface into the brooks, which, swollen into temporary rivers, wash away the sedges that impeded their course. The consequences of this too rapid drainage of the bared soil are, that little water sinks in to nourish the roots of the grasses and useful plants, and less soaks through the soil to replenish the springs,—so that in many overworked farms some of the springs no longer yield so much water as they formerly did, while others have entirely failed. The destruction of the grass and small bushes, and the quick drainage prevent the retention of the water on the surface, and its slow but continuous evaporation, thus probably diminishing the quantity of rain which falls. The rivers, as well as the smaller streams undergo a change. In former times, the sedges and long grass which grew on the sides of the small tributaries of the Zeekoe and Sunday's River afforded cover to the rhinoceros, the hippopotamus, and the buffalo,—whereas now a spring-buck could scarce hide himself . . . [The] Sunday's and Fish Rivers, which now flow in such deep channels, formerly ran almost level with their banks, which were fringed by a luxuriant growth of sedge and palmiet.[113]

Rubidge also discussed the spread of rhenosterbos and the decline in palatable plants. He wondered if the 'longer pastured districts' had not reach their maximum capacity. The solution, he argued, was to rest farms, giving seeds time to generate, and to cultivate pastures in order to 'obliterate the paths made by the sheep'. He quoted both Pappe and Humboldt on the virtues of afforestation, whether poplars by rivers or firs on the mountains. He was especially keen on dams, 'not the small ponds collected to afford water to a few hundred sheep, or to irrigate a few acres of garden . . . but the stoppage of the gorge of large rivers'.[114] He cited Wheatlands farm in the Camdeboo, by then in the hands of the Parkes family, as a model of what could be done with water and manure: they and others had shown that Karoo soils were excellent.

If the Government Geologist concentrated on soils rather than minerals, and the Cape authorities emulated Lord Clarendon in Ireland by arranging demonstrations for farmers, then, Rubidge argued, it would compete with Australia:

let England understand that the Karoo plains of South Africa, the lonely haunt of the Ostrich and the Quagga, which have afforded the poets a type of the most

---

[113] Rubidge, 'Evils of Over-pasturage'.   [114] Ibid. 157.

dreary and desolate wilderness, have a soil and climate which, with the aid of industry and skill, will render them highly productive,—that all they want to convert them to smiling corn-fields and vineyards are the strong arms and stout hearts which are now wasted with famine and wearied with hopeless drudgery in the mother country.

In this and a later article, Rubidge explicitly made the links between denudation, gulley formation, conservation of veld and water, tree planting, and irrigation.[115] In 1866 he 'passed over the bare plains between the Milk River and Graaffreinnet [sic] just after a heavy shower of rain'. He saw great torrents of water 'rushing uselessly and destructively to the sea . . . carrying along . . . some of the most fertile soil of the country'. That water could 'convert [a] wilderness into a smiling garden'.

Irrigation and Trees

Richard Rubidge was by no means the only person to write on water supply, dams, and their potential both for storage and conservation. Settlement had everywhere depended on streams and fountains that determined the location of farms, and were their lifeblood. By the mid-eighteenth century, half of the new farm names registered in the Cape referred to a water source.[116] The absence of water, or drought, was often invoked to explain trekboer dependence on meat. Gordon spoke of venison used like bread; Burchell of trekboers with large flocks who ate three meals of mutton a day.[117] Howison recorded inland Boers living 'exclusively upon animal food . . . When they slaughter an ox, which they seldom do, the greater part of its flesh is smokedried, and forms what they call *bill-tong*; and this they occasionally eat along with fresh meat, as a substitute for bread and vegetables'. Van der Merwe's reading of the early sources led him to the same conclusion about trekboers on the arid northern frontier.[118]

A rich literature on African peasantries has emphasized their adoption of new plants and techniques in the nineteenth century. Boer frontier cultivation has also been underestimated. Both villages and farmsteads had systems

---

[115] Dr. Rubidge, 'Irrigation and Tree-planting', in Roderick Noble (ed.), *The Cape and Its People and Other Essays* (J. C. Juta, Cape Town, 1869), 343–56.

[116] Leonard Guelke and Robert Shell, 'Landscapes of Conquest: Frontier Water Alienation and Khoikhoi Strategies of Survival', *JSAS* 18: 4 (1992).

[117] Newton-King, 'Enemy Within', 195; Burchell, *Travels*, i. 171.

[118] van der Merwe, *Migrant Farmer*, 176 ff., though he also suggests that British sources underestimated trekboer success in cultivation; Brown, *Water Supply*, 350.

of diverting water through channels from streams and fountains so that it could be used for household consumption and irrigation. Many trekboers travelled with seed as well as stock and rapidly set up gardens and fields with what was becoming a typical range of Cape produce. Travellers noticed cultivated land in the interior because it provided such striking oases of verdure in the semi-arid terrain.

Sparrman had an eye for gardens.[119] Land then freshly appropriated near the outer reaches of settlement boasted 'orchards and kitchen-gardens recently laid out, and some of them cut through with water furrows'.[120] Elsewhere in the Karoo, he rejoiced in 'fields of corn, kitchen gardens, and vineyards, verdant and flourishing in the highest degree, while the wild plants around them die, or languish with drought'; water was 'brought down at pleasure from the nearest mountains'.[121] In 1777 Gordon visited a farm in the Camdeboo with a garden 'full of flowers, vegetables and fruit trees'; he saw irrigated vineyards and wheatlands.[122] Manure was plentiful, though not always used; as typical perhaps was the 'cattle boor, who had left a memorable monument of his residence in a prodigious dunghill just in front of the house'.[123] These piles were reported through the nineteenth century. Prickly pears (*opuntia*) from meso-America also found their way to the Cape and probably reached the eastern frontier by the 1770s. Their leaves were used for stock food and their fruits for human consumption (Chapter 8). They did not require irrigation.

In the 1810s Burchell stayed on a farm in the Agter Sneeuberg, north-east of Graaff-Reinet, where he was given not only mutton and milk, but a 'salad of cucumbers'. He saw maize, dagga, cabbages, pumpkins, lettuce, and tobacco in the garden.[124] Thomas Pringle described the variety of a Boer garden in the Tarka valley in the early 1820s, an area from which many later trekked to the interior. 'A small mountain-rill' helped to feed 20 acres of wheat and drove a mill.[125] When the Pringles established themselves at Glen Lynden in 1821, they too cut irrigation trenches and obtained apple, pear, peach, apricot, almond, walnut, plum, lemons, figs, vines, quince, and pomegranate from their neighbours.[126] In the Hantam (Calvinia), a visitor thought that the farm of François Lubbe, with its huge variety of fruit and vegetables, 'the richest and most beautiful . . . that I looked upon during the whole of my stay in Africa'.[127] Travellers in the 1820s reported Boers growing

[119] Sparrman, *Voyage*, i. 105.   [120] Ibid. ii. 129.   [121] Ibid. i. 236.
[122] Raper and Boucher, *Gordon*, i. 97–9.   [123] Thompson, *Travels and Adventures*, 37.
[124] Butler, *The 1820 Settlers*, 74.   [125] Pringle, *Narrative*, i. 47.   [126] Ibid. i. 37–8.
[127] Adolphe Delegorgue, *Travels in Southern Africa*, vol. 1 (University of Natal Press, Pietermaritzburg, 1990), 32. First published 1847.

sufficient to sell to the small towns.[128] Graaff-Reinet town itself included a large number of intensively cultivated smallholdings irrigated by furrow systems from two dams on the Sundays river.[129] Before they were destroyed by disease, oranges and lemons lined its roads. Wine and brandy production was significant; fruit jams and preserves were an important part of the diet.[130] Women participated especially in the processing of fruit.

Major irrigation projects were developed from furrow systems. By 1834 the Kat river settlers of Khoikhoi origin had cut 40,000 feet of canals to form one of the most intensively developed irrigation systems in the colony.[131] They led river water in channels above alluvial fields, with a system of sluices to control its flow. Similar arrangements had been developed at Enon Moravian mission on the slopes of the Zuurberg near Port Elizabeth. The irrigation works powered a mill and watered 'Hottentot gardens' which included oranges and peaches.[132]

Boers in the northern Cape 'opened' old, dry springs, marked by rushes and a reddish grass, by cutting away the ground or rock around them and leading away canals.[133] Livingstone thought that some of these fountains had closed because the vegetation attracted sand and silt, thus covering the 'eye'. Springs were similarly opened in the north-eastern Cape around Hopetown, by cutting into limestone banks.[134] A description of the process in 1847 mentions a party with crowbars, pickaxes, and sledgehammers breaking open an ironstone dyke.[135] In the longer term, the opening of fountain eyes in order to facilitate a faster flow probably contributed to their drying up.

Channeling rivers, streams, and fountains effectively limited farmers to locations where a relatively constant and visible supply of water was available. Burchell commented in 1819 on the reluctance of frontier Boers to dig wells, a difficult and risky strategy with the tools at hand in the areas they occupied.[136] Likely spots could be identified and aars (dykes), along which water flowed underground, close to the surface, were usually marked by karee-doorn and similar bushes 'almost as legible as footpaths'; Africans could

---

[128] Thompson, *Travels and Adventures*, part 1, 37.

[129] For a detailed discussion of water politics in Graaff-Reinet, see Smith, *From Frontier to Midlands*.

[130] Thompson, *Travels and Adventures*, 42.

[131] Crais, *White Supremacy*, 82; Stephen Kay, *Travels and Researches in Kaffraria* (Harper Bros., New York, 1834), 413.

[132] Brown, *Water Supply*, 473.   [133] Livingstone, *Travels and Researches*, 100.

[134] Wylie, *Appendix*, 33.

[135] D. E. Neville, 'European Impacts on the Seacow River Valley and its Hunter-Gatherer Inhabitants, AD 1770–1900', unpublished MA thesis, University of Cape Town (1997).

[136] Burchell, *Hints on Emigration*, 43.

detect them by 'the burrowing of the king ant-eater (aardvark), the meerkat, or even the fieldmouse'.[137] But in the first half of the nineteenth century they could seldom go deep enough, the water was often brak, and the technology for raising water was limited. There were, nevertheless some successes, and Livingstone was convinced that the bowl-shaped Karoo valleys had over a long period trapped water that would be accessible through deep wells.

An alternative was to build dams. Farmers in arid areas were already using what became called the saaidam (sewing dam) system, where flood-water in flat natural vleis or depressions was retained by building small earth walls, and the seed planted in the wet soil. Such vlei or dambo agriculture was prac-tised in African chiefdoms, including the Tswana. Low earth dams were also used by Africans to trap fish after rivers flooded their banks.

Dam construction had begun in the early nineteenth century, in order to store water from springs.[138] Although shallow pools were exposed to the 'action of the sun', earth and stone dams proved to be the most effective new strategy of water provision in the early decades of the nineteenth century. Grahamstown secured its water supply in this way; the town had been built on a site from which a farmer had trekked annually to find water at the Fish river, and a dam proved essential to sustain the new urban settlement. Robert Moffat began a dam at Dithakong in the dry interior in the 1820s.[139] In the area north of the Sneeuberg, through which trekboers moved so quickly in the early nineteenth century, denser and more permanent settlement in districts such as Burgersdorp and Colesberg was partly dependent on dam construction from the 1830s. A return of landed property in Hopetown dis-trict in 1859 recorded one or more dams on half the farms; others had springs, or diverted river water from the Gariep.[140] Water supplies clearly enhanced the value of the land.

Farm dams were now planned to catch large volumes of erratic rainwater, rather than continuous streams of fountain water.[141] This was the key develop-ment in the northern districts, so that by the 1850s they were 'covered with valuable farms and afford[ed] some of the best sheep-walks in the country'.[142]

---

[137] Noble, Descriptive Handbook, 138.   [138] Barrow, Travels, ii. 281.

[139] Grove, 'Scottish Missionaries', 172; Nancy Jacobs, 'The Flowing Eye: Water Management in the Upper Kuruman Valley, South Africa, c.1800–1962', Journal of African History, 37: 2 (1996), 237–60; K. Shillington, 'Irrigation, Agriculture and the State: The Harts Valley in Historical Perspective', in Beinart et al. (eds.), Putting a Plough to the Ground, 311–35.

[140] Cape of Good Hope, G.1-1860, 40–1; Cape of Good Hope, Blue Book, 1861, JJ.25, Hope Town.

[141] Cape of Good Hope, Report and Proceedings of the Committee of the Legislative Council on Irrigation, July 1862, C.3-1862, 9, evidence J. F. Ziervogel, Member of the House of Assembly for Graaff-Reinet.

[142] Hall, Manual, 129; van der Merwe, Noordwaartse Beweging, 337.

A similar process had opened the interior of the arid north-west to settlement from the 1840s; trekvelden formerly usable for only a few months after rain became the site of 'comfortable homesteads surrounded by trees and gardens'.[143] New water-sources were not a guarantee of security. In Burgersdorp, large farm dams, 'some from half a mile to a mile in circumference', were dry in the 1859–60 drought.[144] But earth and stone dam construction was a highly successful locally generated intermediate technology. Similar dams remain ubiquitous on farms in South Africa, and their potential has still not been fully realized in areas of African occupation.

Ambitious dam-construction was one reason why newly arrived English-speakers were able to intensify production so rapidly in long-settled districts, such as Graaff-Reinet. The Hobson family claimed to be the first English farmers to dam water in Jansenville, in 1840; they saw themselves 'laughed at for . . . stone-breaking, dam making, and vaderland-skaap propensities'.[145] Within twenty-five years all their neighbours had dams. In the early years of settlement, some Graaff-Reinet farmers had both summer farms in the Sneeuberg and winter farms on the flats.[146] When water could be provided on a more permanent basis, transhumance to the Sneeuberg was gradually curtailed.[147]

In the Camdeboo, on the route between Graaff-Reinet and Somerset East, near present-day Pearston, Gerrit Coetzee built a dam in the early 1840s at a spot where he noted that pools collected naturally. After 'the first rain the dam was filled, and he could reside constantly on the spot with his flock'.[148] Bought by an English-speaking farmer in 1864, it was developed by its later owners, the Palmers, into Cranemere, one of the model farms of the Camdeboo. When J. L. Botha built a dam 27 feet high and 600 yards across in the same district in the early 1860s, it was opened with a volley of firearms.[149]

The ideal sites for dams were across natural watercourses with banks and exposed rock that could provide purchase for the walls and a route for the overflow. At the best sites, only one wall was necessary. But dams could also be made by scooping out soil on more level lands. Charles Rubidge, at

---

[143] J. Noble, *Descriptive Handbook of the Cape Colony: Its Conditions and Resources* (J. C. Juta, Cape Town, 1875), 130, 136 ff.

[144] Cape of Good Hope, *Blue Book, 1861*, JJ.26, Albert.

[145] Brown, *Water Supply*, 482. 'Vaderlandskap' refers to adherence to the practices of the European homeland.

[146] Noble, *Descriptive Handbook*, 148.

[147] Smith, *From Frontier to Midlands*, 44; Noble, *Descriptive Handbook*, 149.

[148] C.3-1862, 10. Eve Palmer, *The Plains of the Camdeboo* (Fontana, London, 1974), 19, first published in 1966, expands on the subsequent history of farm.

[149] Brown, *Water Supply*, 526.

Wellwood, embarked on a major series of such dams from the late 1840s. There was no reliable fountain near the new farmhouse site, so that water development was essential. Lacking a natural river or physical barrier around which to work, the construction team had to build on sloping land with walls on three sides. For every bucket of water to be stored, family tradition recalls, a bucket of earth had to be dug out. Water was led in by artificial channels.

Building on this scale, with basic technology, was highly labour intensive. Earth was dug up onto shaped ox-hides and dragged by teams of oxen. Income from wool allowed farmers to employ workers on a far larger scale, including specialist British contractors and Mantatees. Dams in Graaff-Reinet district facilitated more intensive use of former state land, driving off African tenants.[150] Erven (plots) in town with water rights were four times the value of those without; dry erven were only valuable in the centre of town for commercial premises. Water rights could be leased for up to £200 a year.[151]

Dam building in the Karoo, except for a few municipal projects, was generally a private concern and had a restricted purpose—to provide water for livestock, gardens, and small fields. Although there were some early forays into irrigated fodder, this was not generally considered economic.[152] Larger-scale, state-funded irrigation projects were, however, being hazarded. Amongst the most powerful advocates of state intervention in irrigation by mid-century was F. W. Reitz, farmer and politician in Swellendam.[153] After four years studying agriculture in Scotland, and visiting irrigation projects in Italy, Reitz had invested heavily in his farm Rhenosterfontein on the Breede river. He founded the first agricultural association in the colony (1832), attempted to start an agricultural journal, and was elected an MLA in the first representative government.

Reitz was concerned that large-scale irrigation, using rivers, might be considered too 'theoretical'—a frequently deployed term of Cape derision.[154] Inspired by Italian and Indian examples, Reitz, like Rubidge, saw irrigation as opening the tap to a flow of wealth and increased revenue: 'we had no reason to complain of want of fresh water, as long as a drop of it was allowed to run into the ocean.' He advocated that Cape students be sent for education in hydraulic engineering. The idea of damming the Gariep river, and leading its

---

[150] S. Dubow, *Land, Labour and Merchant Capital: The Experience of the Graaff-Reinet District in the Pre-Industrial Rural Economy of the Cape, 1852–1872*, Centre for African Studies, University of Cape Town, Communications, no. 6 (1982).

[151] C.3-1862.

[152] Palmer, *Plains of the Camdeboo*, C.3-1862, Evidence, J. F. Ziervogel, MLA, Graaff-Reinet.

[153] *DSAB* ii. 575–7; he was father of F. W. Reitz, later President of the Free State.

[154] F. W. Reitz, 'Irrigation', *Cape Monthly Magazine*, 1 (1857), 135–42.

water into the Fish river valley, eventually realized in the 1970s, had already been canvassed.[155] Some put their hope in 're-converting the Karoo into an inland lake'.[156]

Aside from lack of state revenue and commitment, one stumbling-block to major projects was the colonial law, which entrenched strong riparian rights to water, and did not encourage joint enterprise. In particular, it was difficult for one farmer to run water over another's land. Irrigation was largely restricted to those who could dam a water-course or lead water directly from a river on their own land.[157] Farmers downstream also feared that they would lose out if too many weirs were built up river, and litigation over water frequently came to the Cape courts.

Although wells were relatively rare, pumps were tried for lifting water. The large, Dutch-style windmills used for grain in the western Cape were not replicated in the interior. An imported American wind-pump proved to be insufficiently robust, and could not cater for changes in windspeed. Steam power was difficult to generate because of lack of fuel and the limited scale required by most farmers. Unsuccessful attempts were made in the 1850s to develop a wood and metal wind-pump. Wylie, the geologist, was a protagonist of a vernacular intermediate technology, suggesting that 'in the museum now building there should be a special department devoted to the collection of all such machines or implements as are specially adapted to the wants of the colony'. He hoped this would 'drive out an idea which seems to have got a strong hold of the colonial mind,—that people must either go on in the steps of their forefathers, or rush at once into English ways . . . perfectly unsuited to this country'.[158] He left too quickly, after four years, to see his project through.

The Cape could be a difficult place for modernizers. But improving farmers as well as officials saw water supplies as essential to production and prosperity. These concerns were brought before the government in the 1862 Select Committee on Irrigation.[159] Chaired by J. C. Molteno, later to be first Prime Minister of the Colony, it considered construction of large dams, their economic impact, the settlement that might result, and financing through government loans and foreign capital. It was widely believed that the Karoo soils were rich, if only a reliable water supply could be obtained.[160] The committee argued that there were 'immense tracts of land, consisting of the most productive soil, lying in an almost useless state for want of water'. The

---

[155] C.3-1862, 19.
[156] William Atmore, 'Irrigation—What Hinders It?', *Cape Monthly Magazine*, 2 (1857), 136.
[157] Ibid.   [158] Wylie, *Appendix*, 23.   [159] C.3-1862.   [160] Reitz, 'Irrigation', 137.

government had its eye on self-sufficiency in grain should the Colony's population increase significantly.

The 1862 Committee also debated afforestion. By the 1850s clear links were being made in writings by Richard Rubidge and Ludwig Pappe between denudation, loss of vegetation, and threats to the colony's water supply. There was a long history of piecemeal attempts to control forests, as well as to plant trees, in the Dutch period.[161] Initially the motives were to ensure wood supplies, and it is difficult to overestimate the centrality of trees to pre-industrial societies.[162] As early as the seventeenth century, the Dutch began systematic planting of oaks, ash, and alder on Company land, and settlers were supplied with saplings for their farms. For a time there was a requirement that recipients of land grants plant 100 oaks annually. Although this was not enforced by the Company, which had little control once the settlers moved beyond the Hottentots Holland, free burghers and trekboers took a wide range of useful species with them as they moved out from the peninsula.[163] Oak, initially introduced for carpentry supplies, grew too quickly and unevenly for this purpose at the Cape, but by the early eighteenth century plantings were being made along the streets of new settlements, such as Stellenbosch and Drakenstein, for shade and aesthetic purposes.

From van Riebeeck's time, attempts were made to control the cutting of indigenous timber, notably valuable yellowwoods, and a number of Company officials in the eighteenth century recorded their concern about destruction of trees. By the 1770s Swellengrebel thought that the best trees had been cut from the great Outeniqua forests of the south coast.[164] It had become clear by this time that the colony was as sparse in dense forest as it was rich in botanical variety; aside from pockets around the Cape peninsula, the main forest areas were on the south coast, the Cedarberg range, and beyond the eastern border, around the Katberg and Amatola mountains and on the east coast.

Many of the major forested areas remained Crown lands.[165] After a brief attempt to protect the south coast forests for naval supplies between 1811 and 1820, cutting was subsequently permitted by licence.[166] By mid-century Crown forests totalled an estimated 110,000 morgen, though some were still

---

[161] J. C. Brown, *Management of Crown Forests at the Cape of Good Hope under the Old Regime and under the New* (Edinburgh, Oliver & Boyd, 1887); T. R. Sim, *The Forests and Forest Flora of the Colony of the Cape of Good Hope* (Taylor & Henderson, Aberdeen, 1907).

[162] Appel, 'Die Geskiedenis van Houtvoorsiening'.   [163] Ibid. 129 ff.   [164] Ibid. 172.

[165] Cape of Good Hope, *Report of the Select Committee on Forests Bill*, A.6-1888, 2-3.

[166] Report by Capt. Jones, of the Royal Navy, on the southern Cape forests in 1812, in Brown, *Management*.

being alienated.[167] In 1854 a more controlled system of licensing in the remaining Crown forests was instituted and new officials appointed. But as the first conservator, Harrison, noted of the south coast forests: 'I have received them in a most crippled state.'[168] The licence system was sufficiently liberal to make little impact on conservation. Some thought that it created an incentive for the government to exploit the forests.[169]

The conservator succeeded in passing Act 18 of 1859, 'For more effectually preventing the unlawful cutting down or otherwise destroying the Forests and Herbage in this Colony'.[170] In effect, it applied only to Crown land, because authority to cut on private land could be obtained by 'leave and licence' from the owner. It had wider application in the case of fire, where anyone who was responsible for damaging vegetation not on their property could be in contravention of the Act. Dealing in timber illegally cut in Crown lands was also an offence. Although it did contribute to stabilizing a few major forest reserves, the 1859 Act proved very difficult to implement. In the words of T. R. Sim, a professional forester at the turn of the century, 'it was . . . lightly handled for many years'.[171] An 1868 commission, which considered closing the Crown forests completely, agreed that the number of rangers were insufficient to maintain even existing, limited state control.[172] An 1880s committee expressed similar dismay about lack of enforcement.[173]

While forest protection proved difficult, and forestry was limited, tree-planting linked to agriculture became widespread by the mid-nineteenth century. In addition to European deciduous species established by the Dutch, Huguenots brought with them pines, which were gradually disseminated from the late eighteenth century.[174] From the early decades of the nineteenth century eucalypts from Australia, especially the Blue Gum (*Eucalyptus globula*), became ubiquitous.[175] Wattles probably arrived in Natal in the 1830s; hakea and Port Jackson, the acacia species named after the site of the first sheep imports to Australia, were used to stabilize the sand on the Cape flats in the 1840s and 1850s.[176] As Julius Mosenthal, the Port Elizabeth merchant, who also imported pedigree merino sheep and angora goats, noted in 1860:

[167] Sim, *Forests*, 79.
[168] Cape of Good Hope, *Report of the Conservator of Crown Forests, Uitenhage, 1861*, G.10-1862.
[169] Sim, *Forests*, 80.   [170] Cape of Good Hope, Statutes, Act 18-1859 (July 1859).
[171] Sim, *Forests*, 81.
[172] Cape of Good Hope, *Report of a Commission to Inquire into matters connected with the Working, etc., of the Crown Forests*, G.28-1868.
[173] A.6-1888, 3.   [174] Lighton, *Sisters of the South*, 53, 168.
[175] Kew, Director's Letters, vol. 190, 1059/60, Peter MacOwan to J. D. Hooker, 16 Nov. 1867.
[176] *Cape Monthly Magazine*, 1 (1857), 25, and 2 (1857), 12, 417.

'we live on acclimatized products.'[177] The *Eastern Province Monthly Magazine* ran a series of tree autobiographies in the late 1850s to familiarize its readers with different species. Tree-planting landowners were held up as models.[178]

There was a distinct shift in the focus of debates about the value of trees. They were linked more firmly not only to timber supplies, but also to water provision and agricultural production. Trees, it was suggested, would soften drought, especially on the 'parched plains' of the interior by waylaying the winds that drove rain from the veld.[179] Correspondents quoted the 'well-known and oft-told fact, that the presence of trees increases the moisture, and of course the herbage'. Trees could replace dung as fuel, liberating it for manure on the lands. 'The question of rendering this country well wooded', one article concluded, 'is perhaps, the most important the colonists have to deal with.'

The botanical gardens in Cape Town and Grahamstown exchanged plant species with a wide variety of other centres—from Mumbai to Rio de Janeiro, as well as England.[180] The Grahamstown garden dispersed a wide range of imported timber and ornamental trees around the eastern and central Cape—over 10,000 annually by the 1870s.[181] John Croumbie Brown, who travelled through parts of the colony in 1863, claimed that '[e]verywhere . . . have I seen at farm-steads blue gums growing with greater or less luxuriance'.[182] In the late 1860s Peter MacOwan, schoolteacher and botanist in Grahamstown, reported that the blue gum was the commonest tree and gave visual relief in the 'huge undulating treeless landscape'.[183] They were in fact already going out of fashion because their spreading roots devoured moisture and their leaf litter killed off other vegetation. Increasingly, he reported 'pines are all the rage', and 'the planting mania is spreading, thank God'. A new garden was established in Graaff-Reinet in the 1870s, where the heat, drought, and temperature variations made tree-growing far more difficult. Some pines (*Pinus pinea, pinaster, longifolia,* and *insignis*) survived, as did a few eucalypts and pepper trees from Latin America. Cypresses also 'seemed quite oblivious of the drought and excessive heat', and were supplied to the Jewish cemetery in the town.[184]

[177] Ibid. 7 (1860), 299.   [178] Ibid. 11 (1862), 378.

[179] Ibid. 6 (1859), 351: 'On Agricultural Prospects: How to Grow Trees', 348–55.

[180] Cape of Good Hope, *Report of the Botanical Garden, Cape Town for 1861,* G.33-1862.

[181] Cape of Good Hope, *Report of the Botanical Garden, Grahamstown, 1861,* G.24-1862.

[182] G.23-1864, 16.

[183] Kew, Director's Letters, vol. 190, 1059/60, Peter MacOwan to J. D. Hooker, 16 Nov. 1867.

[184] Cape of Good Hope, *Report of Botanic Garden Grahamstown for the year 1875,* G.27-1876; *Report of the Botanic Garden, Graaff-Reinet for the year 1875,* G.44-1876; *Report of the Botanic Garden, Graaff-Reinet, for the Year 1876,* G.46-1877.

Forestry conservation, and tree-planting, had been initiated both by the state and private landowners in order to provide a future timber supply. By the 1850s expanding tree cover was being more firmly linked to combating desiccation and improving rainfall. The Irrigation Committee and the Colonial Botanist felt secure enough to make firm recommendations in this regard. More broadly, a limited number of experts, officials, and farmers had by the early 1860s formulated a wide-ranging analysis of environmental degradation. Despite the weakness of the Cape state in respect of controlling settlers, and its slim revenue base, it was perceived to have some role to play in environmental regulation. Improvement in this regard required invest-ment, afforestation, irrigation, and more careful livestock management. Such ideas were firmly associated with views of progress, civilization, and enhanced production. Agrarian accumulation and colonial development were becoming linked to environmental regulation and conservation of resources. These ideas were even more forcefully put by John Croumbie Brown, who was appointed as Colonial Botanist following Pappe's death in 1862.

3

Fire, Vegetation Change, and Pastures, 1860–1880

Fire, Veld, and God: John Croumbie Brown at the Cape

Debates about environmental degradation were well established in colonial circles at the Cape by the early 1860s. They stemmed from the practical dilemmas of a pre-industrial society: the experience of transhumance, drought, or firewood shortage. They arose specifically from problems in competition for and use of natural resources, especially the grazing lands of the colony. Colonists, drawing on indigenous knowledge, had developed complex naming systems and modes of recognition for these resources. Many had opinions on the value of bushes and grass and on the impact of drought and fire. More explicitly, scientific classification drew on, and fed back into, such realms of environmental knowledge. By the mid-nineteenth century scientific endeavour was increasingly finding a local base. Environmental debates had become associated with attempts to intensify settlement and agriculture, as part of the broader priority of colonial development.

John Croumbie Brown became Colonial Botanist in 1862.[1] Following missionary work in Russia, he had visited South Africa from 1844 to 1848 for the London Missionary Society.[2] Even then he was interested in environmental issues, and when he had completed his missionary task in 1847 he toured the colony, including a journey through the Karoo. There, he later recalled, he witnessed privations due to aridity. Bones of oxen were strewn along the road; missionaries in Namaqualand could not get grain. Everywhere there were lamentations about drought and the loss of stock. 'At Colesberg cabbage was sold at a penny the leaf; and there was shown to me a bundle of fodder, which I grasped with my forefinger and thumb, which was kept as a memorial

---

[1] Venter, 'An Early Botanist'; Grove, 'Early Themes', 'Scottish Missionaries', and 'Scotland in South Africa'.

[2] J. C. Brown, *Hydrology of South Africa* (Henry S. King and Co., London, 1875), 8.

specimen of what had been sold for *half-a-crown* each.'³ Yet he was told of the Karoo bursting into flower after rain; and 'seeing the deluges of water rushing in torrents to the sea, I was often ready to cry out, Wherefore is this waste?'

Brown returned to Scotland in 1848 and continued his calling as a Presbyterian minister. But the arid Cape was seared into his memory. He studied botany, including South African flora, and taught the subject at the University of Aberdeen from 1853. He was thus well-prepared to take the position of Colonial Botanist—through the good offices of Saul Solomon, the liberal politician and publisher—when it became vacant. His reports from 1863 to 1866 were far fuller than the brief notes left by Pappe. When his contract was terminated in 1866, and he returned to Scotland, he continued to read about the Cape and correspond with his contacts.⁴ This material found its way into three books, published between 1875 and 1887, which, to a greater extent than any previous attempt, synthesized the existing material on environmental questions in South Africa.⁵

Brown's writing could be verbose and florid. He often published his own letters and memoranda in full, and sometimes included letters from correspondents with opposing points of view or long quotations from other works. He did this consciously, to a degree, as a mode of argument: 'it may be unusual to insert in a professional report lengthened quotations from published works,' he argued, but 'an intense desire to carry home conviction must plead my excuse for the course I have followed.'⁶ He clearly hoped that in this way his work would be accessible and educational.

Brown's skill was as a synthesizer rather than a field scientist. He was deeply familiar with a wide range of work on natural history, devoured the literature on the Cape, and acknowledged his sources, including some of the travellers discussed above, Pappe, Hall, Atherstone, Rubidge, the *Monthly Magazines*, and relevant government inquiries such as the 1862 Irrigation Committee. It is for these very reasons that his reports and books are valuable, and the termination of his contract, whatever its results for the colony at the time, undoubtedly deprived historians of what could have been a major collation of material on environmental history.

³ Ibid. 11.
⁴ Brown's surviving private papers at the South African Library, Cape Town (MSC 5), do not contain copies of this correspondence. They are largely a collection of cuttings and published articles as well as manuscripts for his books.
⁵ Brown, *Hydrology*; J. C. Brown, *Water Supply*. For lists of Brown's publications see Venter, 'An Early Botanist', 292, and Grove, 'Scotland in South Africa', 151, n. 4.
⁶ Cape of Good Hope, *Report of the Colonial Botanist for the Year 1863*, G.23-1864, 9.

A short biography by Venter, and articles by Grove, respectively place Brown in the context of Cape politics and of international scientific developments. Brown was influenced by discussions on phytogeography and desiccation, forestry and irrigation.[7] He was also interested in geology and physical geography, which formed a major part of his books on *Hydrology* (1875) and *Water Supplies* (1877). New evolutionary thinking, following Wallace and Darwin, found its way into his writing. While recognition of vegetation change certainly preceded the Darwinian revolution, ideas about competition between species added a further dimension to its analysis. Brown was an eclectic polymath of the natural sciences. His central ideas explicitly linked more intense and rational use of natural resources with their conservation. His work provides a fascinating window on the state of scientific thought at the time, and, like Sparrman before him, he was frequently quoted by later authors.

Brown was prompted by Harvey in Dublin, who contacted him before his departure from Scotland, to 'diffuse a taste for botany as much as possible, and to induce persons in the country districts to communicate the interesting plants of their neighbourhood'.[8] Following Harvey's example, he set up networks of information throughout the colony, specifically seeking the support of women as well as men, and of missionaries who were settled beyond colonial boundaries. He travelled for three months at the end of 1863, 'with a view to acquiring a general idea of the physical geography of the Colony, its capabilities and its production'.[9] He gave frequent lectures, and found that there was considerable curiosity, but limited knowledge, about the naming, classification, and properties of plants.

Ambitious for botany, for himself, and for colonial development, Brown proposed a range of schemes to remedy this situation. Aside from a reissue of Harvey's 1838 book, requested by 'Dr Rubidge and other friends', he planned to establish decentralized herbariums, label the species in the Cape Town gardens, plant more indigenous species there, and publish a catalogue.[10] Such strategies would fulfil the dual role of education and conservation:

many species might be preserved for futurity, that are at present fast disappearing from their native wilds. Their conservation would enable the director to furnish foreign applicants more readily, and at less expense than long, tedious, uncertain,

---

[7] Grove, *Green Imperialism*; Peter J. Bowler, *The Fontana History of the Environmental Sciences* (Fontana, London, 1992).

[8] G.23-1864, 3; Venter, 'An Early Botanist', 283.

[9] Cape of Good Hope, *Report of the Colonial Botanist for the year 1864*, G.24-1865, 3.

[10] G.23-1864, 33; James McGibbon, *Catalogue of Fruit Bearing Trees and Plants in the Collection of the Botanic Garden* (Saul Solomon, Cape Town, 1864).

and expensive journeys could produce, many species being extremely confined to their native localities.[11]

Much of his work involved advising on economic botany, on the potential for new commercial species, and on the problems being experienced with the old.

The first section of Brown's first report was devoted to forestry and desiccation. He agreed that there were indications that South Africa had at one time been less arid. He was convinced that this was 'not a mere fancy' or a belief that former days were always better. But he was convinced that desiccation resulted from human action, especially the 'disastrous consequences following the destruction of bush and herbage by fire'.[12]

Brown was not certain that there was any simple relationship between vegetation cover and rainfall. It seemed clear that warmer air could hold more moisture; clouds would form, and rain might fall, when such air was driven upwards into layers of cooler air or across cooler surfaces. He illustrated the point by explaining the tablecloth cloud formation on Table Mountain. It formed when warm air was driven from the south upwards over the colder mountain top. The moisture then evaporated again when it sunk down into a layer of warmer air, at a lower altitude, on the north-facing slope above the city; this produced the clean edge.

It seemed logical that this process would apply in other contexts. In the open veld, for example, the temperature of soil 'exposed to the direct rays of the sun' was higher than soil in the shade. Soil temperatures would be higher 'in a barren, sterile, stony district'.[13] 'Abundant vegetation' was the most likely factor to cool the soil.[14] Hot wind blowing over cooler land would result in a decline in the amount of water that could be held as vapour, and thus moisture was more likely to precipitate, in the shape of dew, mist, or rain, on vegetation.

Although he quoted sources that linked deforestation to diminished rainfall, Brown recognized that this might not follow directly in all cases. What he did argue with greater certainty was that hotter soil would also result in increased evaporation of moisture into the air. While he noted that many factors, including soil types and topography, could affect the precise rate at which moisture was lost, the basic relationship between vegetation cover, evaporation, and the capacity of the soil to hold water was significant:

At present, I rest satisfied with stating that what is done by forests on a large scale is done on a smaller scale by the bush, herbage, and grass of the veldt. If they do not attract rain, they at least retain moisture; and the destruction of them allows that moisture to be carried off.

[11] G.24-1865, 71.   [12] G.23-1864, 5.   [13] Ibid. 15.   [14] Ibid. 6.

To this he added the argument, but with less conviction, that certain soils with high mineral content of 'potash and common salt' tended to absorb and attract water and that this property was enhanced by 'decayed or decaying vegetative matter'.[15] Quoting Scottish research, he later developed this idea to argue that soil overexposed to light underwent changes that diminished its capacity to retain moisture. Moreover, he suggested that humus in soil, like certain salts, absorbed water from the atmosphere even in the absence of dew or rain, and that, possibly, organic matter was destroyed more rapidly in soil exposed to direct sunlight. In sum, a lack of decomposing vegetable matter dried out the soil.

Brown did not invent these ideas, but was probably the first to outline them in print in the Cape, and he repeated them forcefully in writing and lectures. It is interesting that he focused initially on temperature as the major factor affecting moisture in the soil, and hence desiccation. In many later analyses it was the role of vegetation in providing a physical barrier to soften the impact of heavy rainfall, to prevent run-off, and to facilitate the absorption of moisture into the soil, that was more strongly stressed.

For Brown, the root of all of these problems was fire. Around Cape Town, the blackened stubble left by mountain fires clearly offended him; he was also concerned about the vulnerability of new forest plantations.[16] Following Pappe (Chapter 2), he applied the language of Victorian morality to deforestation by fire, which left mountains 'naked and bare'. Moffat had used the word 'extermination' in connection with the Tswana practice of burning dry grass and shrubs, which he was sure contributed to 'the long succession of dry seasons'.[17]

Despite his hostility to fire, Brown had some understanding of its significance and drew on a variety of sources to illustrate its use in settler as well as African agriculture. He noted that, well before settlers arrived, Portuguese mariners had called South Africa *Terra de fume*.[18] Descriptions of Africans firing their lands, especially on the east coast, were commonplace in the literature. Brown quoted a letter from Alfred White, a trader on the Pondoland coast at Port St John's, who noted that Africans in the vicinity 'maintain, and do so probably with reason, that the soil on which trees have grown is the best land for their gardens, and, therefore, every bush and tree disappears from around their place of residence'.[19] To clear it they used fire, which fertilized the land. White felt that even in his experience between 1850 and 1865, areas of forest had disappeared and 'scarcely a patch of bush was to be seen from the road to Maritzburg'.

---

[15] Ibid. 15.   [16] Brown, *Hydrology*, 171.   [17] G.23-1864, 8.
[18] Brown, *Hydrology*, 167.   [19] Ibid. 170.

It was obvious to Brown that burning was not simply an old African or Boer strategy but had become an important part of English-speaking commercial farming practice. This in particular upset him, and confirmed that 'the history of civilized man in his colonization of new countries has been in every age substantially this—he has found the country a wilderness; he has cut down trees, and he has left it a desert'.[20] He decried the colonial conviction, held even by the most 'intelligent, enterprising, and energetic' English-speaking farmers, that veld should be burnt to support livestock.[21] In a rhetorical way, Brown wondered if he, as a 'theorist' without any financial stake, had a right to express so strong an opinion. He justified himself on the basis of his 'knowledge of facts embodied in science'.

Brown pursued the theme of burning in debate with F. Tudhope of Grahamstown, who had set out systematically some of the benefits to be derived from the practice.[22] Dry, inedible grass had to be removed for fresh growth, and ash was a good fertilizer, rapidly absorbed after rain. Burning was a quick and economical way of producing fresh green pastures. Some farmers maintained that coarse grass was not only inedible but drowned out the sweeter, more favoured species unless fired. Grazing requirements had changed with the widespread introduction of merino sheep, which thrived on shorter, sweeter grass. Livingstone had observed that springbok also preferred the short and sappy grass springing up after a shower had freshened burnt vegetation—*jonge brand*, in colonial parlance.[23] Many farmers believed that veld was best for sheep when heavily burnt and 'eaten down'. This applied especially in the more grassy, sourveld areas of the coastal and eastern districts—areas where English-speaking landowners were most heavily concentrated.

But Brown asked if it was all gain. Whole plant species could be 'utterly destroyed by the conflagration'. No one knew whether the plants that sprouted after burning were more valuable that those lost. Burning was like exhausting capital. Natural resources such as trees had a direct and calculable economic value, in his view. Fire 'swept the young trees off by hundreds of thousands' and lost farmers thousands of pounds-worth of vegetation in order to bring them a short-term improvement in profits. Pulling together this argument in his book on *Hydrology*, Brown quoted a Dutch Reformed

[20] G.23-1864.   [21] G.24-1865, 105–6.

[22] Ibid. 103, 'Letter to F. Tudhope, Esq., Grahamstown, on the question whether good or evil preponderates in the results obtained by burning the Veldt . . .', 16 Dec. 1864.

[23] *Cape Monthly Magazine*, 4 (1858), 322: FWR: 'Agricultural Notes and Queries on Dr. Livingstone's Researches'.

minister at Somerset East, who lamented the annual burning of the mountains above the town:

it was covered with high grass and thousands of beautiful bulbous flowering plants and shrubs, and its whole face and off-shoots adorned with Yellow-wood or other valuable trees; now these are all gone; not a Yellow wood or other tree worth anything left, and only a useless growth of bushes occupy their place, and the consequence is that a stream that supplied my garden and some others, runs now only after rain.[24]

Brown's analysis of the spread of unpalatable species such as rhenoster bush also placed more emphasis on fire.[25] The 'prevalent opinion' that he heard was that this 'evil', resinous bush was spread by sheep. He differed. The seed, he noted, was attached to down-like material—hence the term pappus in the Latin botanical name. This facilitated its spread by wind, in much the same way as a dandelion or thistle. If it lodged in a well-grassed spot it was unlikely to take root. But if it reached uncovered soil, denuded by 'the short-sighted policy of burning the veldt', it would 'grapple firmly to the ground'. Fire 'specially prepared' the soil for the seed.[26] Droughts and burning probably also destroyed the competitors of this 'invader', which thereby got a great advantage over the 'down-trodden descendants of the previous occupants'. 'There is going on everywhere', Brown argued, 'what Darwin has described as the struggle for life.'

Tudhope also cited how the 'grand and magnificent' burning of the veld near Grahamstown reservoir had been followed by copious rain. Brown agreed that in certain circumstances this was possible. Volcanic eruptions or extensive conflagrations, such as an artillery battle during the Crimean War, did appear to cause rain.[27] This could be explained by hot air rising rapidly from such events and, if conditions were suitable, forming clouds in the cooler layers above. But Brown maintained that this was a localized and temporary effect which did not improve rainfall overall; burnt veld dried the soil in the longer term.

A Caledon farmer argued that burning helped to contain disease, notably lamziekte, or paralysis, in cattle. Lamziekte (Chapters 1 and 4) was thought to be related to certain areas of sourveld, especially in drought years.[28] In the western Cape stockowners knew that they could prevent it by moving cattle

---

[24] Brown, *Hydrology*, 175.   [25] G.23-1864, 29; Hall, 'South African Pastures', 66.
[26] G.23-1864, 30; the argument is repeated in G.24-1865, 106.   [27] G.23-1864, 7.
[28] Hall, 'South African Pastures', 82–3 discusses travellers comments on lamziekte from the late eighteenth century.

between different veld types. Fire provided an alternative solution: after two or three burns, he argued, cattle losses from lamziekte declined rapidly and sheep also thrived.

Brown found this evidence more difficult to counter. Generally he felt that 'the instinct of animals leads them to eat only that which is good for food, excepting where semi-starvation compels them'.[29] Lamziekte was therefore likely to be due to an insufficiency of healthy food; this could surely be procured by a less destructive process than burning. In an attempt to find a telling metaphor, Brown quoted the Charles Lamb story 'A Dissertation on Roast Pig', in which people discovered this delicacy by burning down houses. Burning might help prevent lamziekte, but only, in his view, at an unacceptable cost. He advocated a 'higher style of agriculture', with better fodder provision for animals, which would also increase overall humidity.[30]

Colonists advocated controlled burning in order to prevent an 'American style' prairie fire that would destroy crops, houses, and even flocks of sheep.[31] Africans also burnt around their homesteads, to create a firebelt. Such uncontrolled conflagrations were not infrequent at the Cape. Shortly after this debate, in December 1865, a rampant veld fire travelled over 100 Kilometres from the Zuurberg to reach Cradock and Adelaide districts. In the words of one of Brown's correspondents: 'it was awful . . . For miles the country is denuded of copse and forest, even the rushes about the rivulets, vleys, and rivers are seared and scorched . . . roast venison could be discovered everywhere.'[32] Following a major fire in February 1869, which spread over 200 kilometres from Swellendam to Uitenhage, a correspondent wrote that bridges, houses, gardens, orchards, and forests, were 'all gone'. Livestock and people died.

The Conservator of Forests in the southern Cape thought that attempts to curtail and prohibit burning in the legislation of 1859 led to the disastrous fire of 1865. He had burnt annually around the forests, but 'science then said I was wrong, and burning was prohibited'.[33] Foresters tended to have a limited view of what constituted valuable timber, and felt that the dense 'fyn bosch', which Brown so valued, was 'useless alike to man and beast'.[34] Brown had no difficulty with the strategy of a *brand pad* or firebelts around houses and valuable forests. This was a legitimate use of fire in his eyes, but he insisted

---

[29] G.24-1865, 108. Such ideas had been expressed in systematic form in the Cape: *Eastern Province Monthly Magazine* (1858), 580, speech by W. Edmunds.

[30] G.24-1865, 109. [31] Ibid. [32] Brown, *Hydrology*, 17. [33] Ibid. 178.

[34] Cape of Good Hope, *Report of a Commission to Inquire into matters connected with the Working, etc., of the Crown forests*, G.28-1868.

that most fires resulted from those specifically kindled to destroy the bush and grass.

What is really objected to, and must be suppressed by rigorous law, is the universal incendiarism that obtains throughout the Colony at certain seasons, when every ragged herd, instigated thereto, assumes the patriot and claims the privilege of devastating by fire, right and left, the country in every direction, reckless of consequences.

Harrison, the Conservator of Forests, similarly blamed Africans and squatters for initiating the 1865 conflagration.[35] But Brown was not simply appealing to colonists by blaming African shepherds; his argument was with farmers who ordered the setting of fires—and then sometimes blamed servants. Even accidents were sometimes more like carelessness: 'some picnic party or some outspanning travellers have left their fire burning . . . or some smoker . . . thrown upon the ground a lighted match or half-burned cigar.'

Brown would have agreed with Stephen Pyne's recent adage that 'nomadism and expansion have always favoured fire; enclosure and high-yield farming have always restricted it'.[36] Control of fire, he was certain, was essential for improvement and cultivation, and for the escape from an economy based simply on extensive ranching of cattle and sheep. In a fascinating evolutionary model, he posited that just as the exhaustion of game led to the diplacement of hunting by pastoralism, so the exhaustion of pasturage would lead to extended arable activity, and eventually a 'manufacturing nation'.[37]

Farmers also asked: if degradation was taking place, how could they be producing more? 'The only thing that would induce farmers to think seriously whether they are doing right or wrong by burning the veld', one wrote, 'would be to prove to them that their farms are yearly carrying less and less live-stock per morgen.' This Brown could not do in the 1860s, although he and Rubidge predicted such an outcome. By the 1870s a significant number of people at the Cape became convinced that there was, at least in some areas, just such a 'decadence' in sheep farming, and had figures, they felt, to prove it (Chapter 4). Fire was not, however, then cited as a major cause.

Brown was not simply imposing expectations of green Cape pastures drawn from romantic visions or his memories of Scotland. To a significant extent he reflected and interpreted what he was hearing and reading. Farmers were not united in their views, and some, especially in the Karoo districts, agreed with him. Although many had accumulated experience in pasture

[35] Brown, *Hydrology*, 178.
[36] Melville, *A Plague of Sheep*, 88, quoting Pyne, *Fire in America*.   [37] G.24-1865, 112.

management, farmers of all kinds were facing new conditions. Merino numbers were spiralling. English-speaking immigrants were moving out to the
semi-arid districts, and human population densities were thickening. In the
1865 census one-third of the settler population of the Cape was counted in
the rural districts and small towns of the main midland and eastern stock-
rearing zone. African communities were also adopting new breeds of livestock on more constricted areas of land. New problems, together with scientific
prescriptions, produced uncertainty about the state of pastures and how to
manage them.

A sense of these debates is manifest in the evidence from farmers to the
1877 Stock Diseases Commission (Chapter 4), appointed to examine the
decline in sheep numbers in key Cape districts. A number of witnesses were
directly confronted by commissioners with the view that the veld had been
mismanaged, had deteriorated—and that this was an important cause of disease. The commissioners included Charles Rubidge, who clearly shared some
of his brother's views. Farmers' responses were uneven, even within the same
district: while some were defensive, many agreed with aspects of the critique.

Justifications of burning followed much the same lines as outlined in
Brown's 1860s reports, but other emphases were added. 'By burning', one
argued, 'you destroy vermin, ticks, etc.'[38] While J. W. Bowker in Albany
agreed that veld was deteriorating and some of the most palatable grasses
were being displaced by rhenoster bush, he nevertheless found that the best
way to improve the veld was to rest it and then burn it, sometimes more than
once. This had helped to restore grass.[39] By contrast, John Webb, a percept-
ive farmer in the same coastal district, noted that burning of veld destroyed
smaller birds and wildlife that may have been useful in controlling vermin,
including ticks. He was also sceptical of the idea that burning in itself
destroyed ticks, and agreed that grass was sometimes deprived of the chance
to seed.[40] But he still argued, on balance, that it was worth burning veld in
Albany, 'because stock improve faster on the burnt grass, sheep in some
places would die on the old grass if not burnt, [and] the ewes would lose their
lambs if the grass was not burnt to obtain a supply of young grass'.[41]

A number of farmers appreciated that there were complex and subtle links
between burning, grazing intensity, and changes in the veld. J. Bezuidenhout
of Fort Beaufort, where diseases were becoming particularly acute, was
highly committed to burning, but argued that overstocking had led to a
dimunition in grass so that proper burning was difficult. This resulted in a

[38] G.3-1877, 31.   [39] Ibid. 118.   [40] Ibid. 34.
[41] Ibid. 111. Evidence J. Webb, Albany.

lack of fresh grass and also an increase in ticks which, he suggested, thrived on older grass. 'I am sure the sheep do better if the veldt is burnt', he argued, but when stock numbers became so high as to shorten the grass and prevent effective burning, 'the sheep do badly at once'.

He also distinguished between the results of burning at different times of year: 'if grass is burnt when the soil is dry, it destroys the roots, but it does no harm if the ground is wet.'[42] In the summer-rainfall zone, this meant avoiding the height of the dry winter season, when the grass burnt best. Brown had argued further that if burning was too early, grass seeds were destroyed and reproduction reduced; seeds, he thought, with more 'nitrogenous and oleaginous' material, remained nutritious for longer than the dry blades. This was one of his major concerns about burning. The alternative was to burn late, when the spring rains began in October, but this was generally seen as too late to benefit the new grass. Some farmers clearly burnt at inappropriate times.

Witnesses suggested that burning controlled weeds, both directly by fire and indirectly because it destroyed manure. In some districts weeds were thought to flourish if the veld became 'too rich' from manure. This was a controversial view, because many believed that manure enhanced soil and veld. A few witnesses recorded that *Acacia karoo*, locally called mimosa, spread where the veld was not burned regularly.[43] This may have had foundation, especially under conditions of heavy grazing.[44] Recent experiments suggest that acacia seedlings of less than a year succumb to fire, but plants established for longer sprout again after burning. Acacia, like rhenoster bush, tends to colonize where competition from grass sward is reduced by grazing. While acacia was a valuable fodder for browsing goats, it was less favoured by sheep.

By the 1860s and 1870s dryer Karoo farms were not seen to benefit from burning, except in patches where there was thick grass cover, because rainfall was too unpredictable to ensure quick recovery; fire could also destroy valuable Karoo bushes which took many years to recover. Fire abolitionism amongst farmers was strongest in these Karoo districts. S. J. Hobson, who farmed in a mixed grass and Karoo bush area in Cradock, 'would not allow it on any account'.[45] Bertram Bowker, in the dry Fish river valley section of northern Albany, agreed that it was better to 'feed down' than fire veld.[46]

---

[42] Ibid. 128–9.

[43] Ibid. 133. Evidence G. Stokes. See also evidence R. J. Dick, Kingwilliamstown, 141–3.

[44] R. D. Barnes, D. L. Filer, and S. J. Milton, *Acacia karoo: Monograph and Annotated Bibliography* (Oxford Forestry Institute, Oxford, 1996), 21.

[45] G.3-1877, 77.

[46] Ibid. 111; R. A. Dyer, *The Vegetation of the Divisions of Albany and Bathurst*, Botanical Survey of South Africa, memoir no. 17 (Government Printer, Pretoria, 1937).

While most farmers in the grassier southern and eastern districts were advocates of burning, there were dissidents even amongst them. John Gardiner, in the sourveld, coastal section of Albany, felt that burning encouraged sour species and destroyed manure.[47] This view is now widely held with respect to the Transkeian grasslands, where unpalatable ngongoni (aristida) is believed to have spread. For him, heavier stocking would be the best solution. Frederick Halse, an ambitious accumulator in the grassland district of Sterkstroom, also advocated leaving manure on the ground. When asked if he approved of burning, he was adamant: 'No, it is the ruin of the country, it makes the grass hard and sour, the sweeter grass is destroyed by the fire, and the tougher coarser grasses gain the ascendancy. I have been going in for tree planting, but the grass fires destroy a great number of my trees.'[48]

Farmers were not all firebrands, but the fact that so many burnt the pastures rendered all land vulnerable. Those who did not favour fire could seldom escape it for very long. Many areas had combustible vegetation, and there were few natural barriers in the rural Cape, such as large rivers or forests, or even wide, maintained roads. As in the case of livestock diseases, fire was no respector of boundaries.

For Brown, the solution lay not only in the curtailment of burning but also in the resting of pastures and especially afforestation. In the first instance, this would stop further destruction of established forests because fresh tree-belts could provide a protective barrier. Without protection, each successive fire penetrated further into the remaining woodland especially where it was cut. Secondly, in the longer term, vegetation would increase humidity. He favoured indigenous trees, especially where they could be shown to have economic value as well.[49] Aside from larger forest or timber trees, he approved of karee and acacia planting by farmers in Graaff-Reinet because of their value as fuel and browse for livestock.[50] He thought that acacia also served as shelter for more valuable fodder plants, notably salt bushes like *ganna* (salsola species).

Indigenous plantations were little pursued by the state or farmers, because they proved difficult to establish and most species were slow-growing. Brown recognized that Cape trees tended to be unadaptable, and he allowed that exotic species would probably have to take precedence if planting was to take place on the scale required.[51] There were few places where trees of some kind would not grow, but some farmers told him that they did not plant because

---

[47] G.3-1877, 53. Evidence John Gardiner.   [48] Ibid. 55. Evidence F. Halse.
[49] G.23-1864, 16.   [50] G.1-1866, 94, 95.
[51] G.23-1864, 10, 16; G.1-1866, *Report of the Colonial Botanist for the Year 1865*, 2.

they feared fire and goats. To this he retorted: would not another animal be more profitable than goats if the cost of keeping them was to curtail tree planting? Moreover, failing to plant because of fear of fire was in effect paying a licence fee to burn—a tax which, if it was levied directly, would be found 'burdensome in the extreme'.[52] In this latter argument, again, Brown was seeing both forests and smaller stands of trees as a critical economic resource with a direct, calculable value.

By the time he published *Hydrology* (1875), Brown agreed with Richard Rubidge that sheep increased the incidence of run-off, especially when sudden deluges broke droughts, such as in 1862–3.[53] Uncontrolled 'torrents' featured strongly in Brown's sense of environmental degradation. As in the case of fire, there was not only an immediate loss in the waste of water, but a destruction of capital because floods, such as those in 1867 and 1874, destroyed bridges, roads, and houses.[54] Brown's solution to floods, just as to desiccation, was to stop burning and start afforestation. 'Rain falling on a metallic roof rushes off,' he explained, 'while the same rain falling on a thatched roof trickles down in drops; from the bared ground the rain runs off in streamlets long before it runs off in a similar way from the grass-field or the thicket.' He accepted Bain's explanation of the major geological causes of desiccation over the longer term: the elevation and then erosion of the central plateau. But he saw the more immediate cause as human folly, subject to correction and intervention.[55] Forest plantations, along the French model, would convert 'the lion to the lamb' and cost less than the damage done by floods.

Brown drew on the well-established idea that Karoo soil was rich to paint it 'as the hope of the Colony', in which was 'stored up resources which are inexhaustible'.[56] He consistently advocated extending agriculture of all kinds: 'at some time or another in the future many of these plains are to be covered with waving corn.'[57] The lack of water could be remedied by arboriculture and dam building. Very large dams, financed by the state, might allow water to percolate over a wide area and refresh springs. He drew from Henry Hall's *Geography* the improving example of Grahamstown's dam, that had produced a regular water supply for 5,000 people.[58]

---

[52] G.23-1864, 17.   [53] Brown, *Hydrology*, 211–12.

[54] Ibid. 244; Cape of Good Hope, *Blue Book, 1874*, JJ.19 ff. Brown received Cape government material and quoted such sources.

[55] J. C. Brown, *Reboisement in France* (H. King, London, 1876); the Preface was quoted at length in *Hydrology*.

[56] G.24-1865, 8–9.   [57] Ibid. 10–11.   [58] Ibid. 14.

Brown remained deeply religious and sought to justify his analysis and strategies in theological as well as practical, economic terms. Here he had directly to confront a rather different religious tradition, though ironically both to some degree stemmed from a Calvinist root. Sparrman had noted, a century before, that environmental ills such as the spread of rhenoster bush were seen by some Boers as a punishment by God (Chapter 1). The sternest Dutch Reformed ministers of that time argued, on the basis of the Old Testament, that storms and plagues such as drought, locusts, and caterpillars, which beset Cape farmers, could be God's retribution for sin.

British conquest, commercial development, constitutional change, and expanding wool production had transformed Cape politics and ideologies by the mid-nineteenth century. Explicitly progressive ideas were articulated by a powerful, vocal lobby, many but by no means all English-speaking settlers. They espoused more universal, rationalist values, a free press, freer markets, as well as education, technical development, and investment. L. H. Meurant, Dutch-speaking progressive editor of the *Cradock News*, in the heart of sheep territory, sketched what progress meant in the agricultural sphere in 1861:

the advantage of getting 14 per ct. per annum for their money by purchasing shares in the 'Cradock Union' and other Banks . . . —the benefits arising from Agricultural Societies—planting trees—making Dams,—buying Cawoods's American pumps . . . the pleasure and comfort which they will be sure to derive by improving their homesteads,—having a nice little flower-garden.[59]

They challenged the older Afrikaner landowning classes as well as frontier conservatism and the Dutch Reformed Church. These ideas threatened to undermine older systems of credit, inheritance, and the transmission of landed property amongst Afrikaners in the 1860s.[60]

Du Plessis has argued that conservatism was reformulated in the religious sphere by men such as van der Lingen, the Dutch Reformed minister at Paarl. Many rural people still saw providence as fate, which was difficult to counteract by human intervention, and justified relative inaction. This view was reinforced by poverty or by the failure to profit from investment in the land in the harsh environment of the Cape. Van der Lingen's theology tried both to come to terms with new progressive ideas and to reinforce the bonds of a religious and church community amongst Afrikaners. He set himself not only against 'fallacies and lies under the name of "liberalism"', but also against

[59] Jean du Plessis, 'Colonial Progress and Countryside Conservatism: An Essay on the Legacy of Van der Lingen', unpublished MA dissertation, University of Stellenbosch (1988), 61, quoting the *Cradock News*, 8 Jan. 1861.

[60] Dooling, 'Agricultural Transformations'.

specific innovations where they seemed to undermine church authority.[61] He was opposed to trains running on Sunday, to the delinking of church from state, and to the English press.[62]

Van der Lingen also opposed fire insurance for the church in Paarl, on the grounds that its survival would depend better on God's providence and that the premiums would enrich the very financial and merchant groups against whom he railed. From the 1830s, when fire and life assurance companies were founded, an increasing number of Cape buildings were insured and this had a major impact on architectural styles. Imported Welsh slate and 'rolled zinc' roofs, which were favoured by insurers, displaced the older shingle and thatch. (Corrugated metal roofs, lined by gutters, also proved useful for the collection of water.) For conservatives, insurance epitomized planning for the future, a collective effort to guard against acts of God.[63] Even if this type of religious discourse sometimes operated at a rhetorical level, without precluding specific measures of improvement or insurance, it was invoked by both sides as a brake on innovation and investment.

Brown's theology worked in an opposite direction. While the judgement of God could be manifest in environmental disaster, he was equally sure that God's will was best followed by planning, improvement in agriculture, development of natural resources, and economic growth. His ideas are recorded in a letter to a Dutch Reformed minister, the Revd Stegman of Adelaide, who had requested help in controlling the spread of the rhenoster bush. First, Brown reasoned, it was sinful to neglect God's gifts:

The heaven, even the heavens are the Lord's, but the earth has He given to the children of men. But he has given it to them to be used. He has done with this as with every other gift, wealth and strength, physical, intellectual, and spiritual: Use it and it is yours, and the more you use it within certain limits the more will it improve; but let it lie waste and you will lose the benefit.[64]

Secondly, it was God's own way, revealed in the Old Testament, to improve the earth with vineyards, fields, and orchards, and to turn 'the wilderness into a standing water and dry ground into water-springs'.[65] Humans had the

[61] du Plessis, 'Colonial Progress', 152.

[62] Andre du Toit, 'The Cape Afrikaners' Failed Liberal Moment 1850–1870', in J. Butler, R. Elphick, and D. Welsh (eds.), *Democratic Liberalism in South Africa* (Wesleyan University Press, Middletown, 1987), 35–63.

[63] du Plessis, 'Colonial Progress', 145.

[64] G.23-1864, 30–1: letter to the Revd W. Stegmann, Adelaide, on the spread of the Rhenoster bush, 13 Jan. 1864.

[65] Brown, *Hydrology*, 213.

capacity to understand this, and it was incumbent upon them to take up where God left off.

Thirdly, although Brown did have a concept of providential government and punishment, he argued that this would come into play if people failed to carry God's baton and improve the earth. In this context, Brown argued, it was those who left matters to providence, or took the easiest course, who would suffer: he that 'burns the veldt as an improvident means of saving himself trouble . . . may read his sin in his punishment.' For those who transgressed 'the Lord "turneth rivers into a wilderness, and the water-springs into dry ground; a fruitful land into barrenness" '.[66]

European Protestantism was a religious form that had been comfortable with capitalism and self-improvement. Elements of Brown's complex and self-serving combination of creationism, religiosity, capitalism, natural history, evolutionary thought, conservationism, and advocacy of hard work were commonplace amongst anglophone Cape settlers. Yet it was easy for outsiders such as Brown to tread on the toes of Cape communities, even when they were more sympathetic to his prophecies. He was a bombastic presence, 'critical of the established ways of the locals and perpetually trying to intercept and alter them'.[67] His use of religion, and regular preaching, to communicate and justify his views was all the more challenging.[68] To repeatedly accuse the colonists of 'wickedness', of being sinners deserving punishment, for burning their veld was strong language in the context of the time.[69] As the evidence to the 1877 Commission reveals, most farmers with grassland continued to burn.

Botanical Successors and Understandings of Vegetation Change

Fire was only one feature of debates about natural resources in the rural Cape during the 1860s and 1870s. The commercial pastoral economy was of great value to the colony, and some of its most influential landowners and politicians were deeply committed to this sector. A number of them sensed more general threats to the veld on which the future of pastoral accumulation depended. The questions they faced were: whether the pastures were changing; how should they change; and how could they be improved? Their understanding of these issues, influenced both by everyday experiences and by emerging scientific perceptions, was becoming more sophisticated in these

---

[66] Ibid.   [67] du Plessis, 'Colonial Progress', 46.
[68] Venter, 'An Early Botanist', 285.   [69] G.23-1864, 31.

decades. Often working together, experts and farmers identified more securely what they thought were both the best and the worst plant species for grazing.

Brown's position was discontinued in 1866. To a degree, he precipitated his dismissal by presenting a petition to parliament for an increase in salary and allowances.[70] He had to meet the costs of travel and equipment; he had no facilities for experimental work, or clerical assistance. His timing was not of the best. The Cape was hardly the most generous of employers, financial constraints were tight in the 1860s depression, and the post had been 'precarious' from the outset.[71] Brown had clearly provoked opposition. He pestered the government for funds, he was outspoken on religious matters, preached an uncomfortable message during his tours, and alienated some farmers. The tone of his writings suggests both an intensity of purpose and an insensitivity to his audience.

Although he worked with botanical networks at the Cape, some were uneasy about his apparent lack of classificatory knowledge. Peter MacOwan, the science teacher in Grahamstown, was concerned that the post was being terminated 'by our parliamentary retrenchers' and lamented that the colony now thought itself 'too poor for science'.[72] But he remarked to J. D. Hooker at Kew that 'Dr Brown does not collect even', and complained that Brown made no useful response when he was sent a plant to identify.[73] MacOwan was keen to increase resources available in the eastern rather than western districts. A close associate of his, the amateur botanist and businessman Henry Bolus of Graaff-Reinet, also complained that Brown did too little scientific work and 'wasted public funds in the publication of voluminous reports . . . of a trifling character'.[74] Intriguingly, one of Brown's critics claimed that the Cape already knew about its environmental problems: 'every man in the Colony, unscientific as well as scientific, was . . . well aware . . . that forests attracted rain and that bush, herbage and grass, retain moisture.'[75]

These critics were somewhat unfair. Brown's work was not without value in the strictly botanical sense: he received many plants; sent specimens to Dublin to Harvey for detailed description and recording; and rearranged part of Pappe's collection. In his final report, he collated a list of 460 indigenous

[70] Cape of Good Hope, *Report of the Colonial Botanist for the Year 1866*, G.38-1866.
[71] Cape Archives, Colonial Secretary, CO 4145, 79, John C. Brown to Colonial Secretary, 12 Feb. 1867 and note on letter.
[72] Kew, Director's Letters, vol. 190, 1055, MacOwan to Hooker, 12 Dec. 1866.
[73] Ibid., vol. [1]90, 1053, MacOwan to Hooker, 1 Dec. 1866.
[74] Venter, 'An Early Botanist', 285.
[75] Ibid. 288, quoting article from the *Cape Farmers Magazine*, Nov. 1864.

tree species, far larger than Pappe's.[76] Some at least of his tours and talks were received with enthusiasm, and he recalled all-day meetings with large groups of farmers, including visits to vineyards and dams to discuss practical issues. Brown devoted much of the rest of his life to writing on environmental topics—often with reference to the Cape.

At this stage, however, the Cape government had a very limited commitment to environmental regulation. The Botanical Gardens had their own officers. There was little legislation to enforce, which might have called into being a specialist botanical or agricultural bureaucracy. The 1822 Act controlling hunting was little implemented; the 1859 Forest Act, which addressed burning, was the responsibility of Forest Conservators and civil commissioners. Enforcement of the Act (1864) to eradicate burrweed was devolved to Divisional Councils and local officials. They were empowered, in cases of non-compliance, to undertake the work themselves and charge the costs to the farmer. It was certainly a measure that went far further than most at the time; the principle of compulsory regulation was strongly contested in later years. But the Colonial Botanist was not involved; he had been given only a research and educational, not a regulatory, role.

The absence of an office did not, however, destroy the networks which had developed around Brown, Harvey in Dublin, the Hookers at Kew, and Atherstone in Grahamstown. Britain's natural-history craze to some degree rippled out to the colonies. The archives at Kew, where many Cape letters survive, give a sense of the variety of correspondents. For example, David Arnot, the lawyer in Colesberg—who played a key role in the dispute over the diamond fields—was a friend of Atherstone's and a keen collector who corresponded with Harvey, Hooker, and Brown. He mobilized a group of his 'farming lady-friends' to collect plants for exchange. The Griqua, for whom he acted as agent, were also drawn in: 'The Chief Waterboer and sons have taken a great liking to making collections of botanical specimens—and they have promised to furnish me with a fine assortment.' Arnot sent Brown a collection of various sheep pasture bushes. Dr Gill, District Surgeon at Somerset East, had studied botany with William Hooker at Glasgow. He left money when he died to the local college for research and teaching in science. Sir Henry Barkly, Governor in the 1870s, and his wife also maintained a strong botanical interest.

In pursuit of a better understanding of the distribution of species, Brown encouraged correspondents such as J. H. Davis, who farmed in the far north of the Colony at Colesberg, D. W. Hopley in Burgersdorp, and Alfred Ella to

---

[76] G.38-1866, Appendix, list of South African trees with local names.

record grasses more systematically. Ella came from Australia to Cradock in 1849 and then moved to the newly conquered Queenstown district in 1854, where he set up business as a wool-washer and farmer.[77] In his role as secretary of the Divisional Council, he met and was enthused by Brown. Initially Ella had focused on finding a new, dry-season, winter fodder grass for the district, but he, along with other correspondents, developed an enduring interest in indigenous species. His experiments in the 1860s and 1870s with various English fescue grass species all failed.[78] He supplied Brown with specimens, conducted his own experiments, and gave important evidence to the 1877 Stock Diseases Commission.

Mary Elizabeth Barber, daughter of Miles and Anna Bowker, was one of the few women in nineteenth-century South Africa able to realize her scientific ambitions.[79] Her family was part of Atherstone's circle and she married Frederick Barber, Atherstone's cousin and a chemist, who came to farm in South Africa. They settled on Highlands, near Grahamstown, in 1848 and, together with her Bowker kin, she began collecting and drawing plants. She initiated a long correspondence with Harvey in Dublin and became one of his principle suppliers, helping to name and classify species. Living in a 'paradise for the naturalist', she extended her interests to zoology, entomology, and lepidoptery, and was in touch with many of the key scientists at the Cape. Barber expressed her own concerns about the impact of sheep, for example, in trampling a rare species of wingless grasshopper and, along with the plant collectors, threatening the rare and beautiful stapelia genus.[80] She was also an early protagonist of 'useful' insect-eating birds.

Within this network, Peter MacOwan and Dr John Shaw were perhaps most influential in shaping interpretations of environmental change. The son of a Methodist minister, MacOwan studied at the University of London and taught chemistry before migrating to South Africa, aged 32, in 1862.[81] Assailed by bronchial infection, caught in a Huddersfield laboratory, he was one of a number of health migrants to the Cape who were to play an important role in scientific and political spheres. He worked first at Shaw College, the Methodist school in Grahamstown, and met Atherstone and Barber. MacOwan built up his own herbarium of eastern Cape plants, was one of Brown's main correspondents, and supplied specimens to the Cape Town gardens.[82]

---

[77] G.3-1877, 175, 'Some Observations on the Pasture Grasses of the Division of Queen's Town, by Alfred N. Ella of Melton, near Queen's Town'.

[78] G.3-1877, 175.   [79] Beinart, 'Men, Science'; Cohen, 'Mary Elizabeth Barber'.

[80] Kew, Director's Letters, vol. 190, M. E. Barber to Hooker, 9 Mar. 1866.

[81] *DSAB* ii. 423–4.

[82] Kew, Director's Letters, vol. 190, MacOwan to Hooker, 3 Feb. 1866. Whether or not due to the Cape climate, he survived to the age of 79.

In the mid-1860s MacOwan co-ordinated information on plant locations, and arranged plant exchanges, in the eastern Cape.[83] In 1867 he accompanied Atherstone on an expedition to the Fish river valley, 'he for patients, I for plants', and they sent euphorbia specimens back to Hooker.[84] The most active and professional of his collaborators was Bolus, in Graaff-Reinet, until he left for Cape Town in 1874.[85] To Hooker, MacOwan lamented a lack of local expertise: 'we sadly want—a second Dr Harvey.'[86] Arguing that the eastern Cape was a more important centre for research, MacOwan hoped that Hooker might use his influence to have Pappe's herbarium transferred to the new Albany Museum in Grahamstown, and to have himself appointed as keeper.[87] In the event, this was not to happen.

In 1869 MacOwan was appointed science master at Gill College in Somerset East, and began to publish on Cape plants, economic botany, veld management, and the history of botanical exploration.[88] Through his long sojourn in the eastern Cape, MacOwan was able to develop a familiarity with local vegetation, especially around Grahamstown and Somerset East, that shorter-term visitors such as Brown could not. For much of the late nineteenth century he was probably the best-informed person on Cape plants, particularly those with agricultural or pastoral significance; in a different sphere, he slowly gained the authority of a second Harvey. He was rewarded in 1880 with the appointment as Professor of Botany at the South African College, and Curator of the Cape Town botanical gardens.

To a greater extent than any previous expert, MacOwan was able both to learn from the settler population and to translate scientific ideas and botanical knowledge into terms that they could understand. He worked with local farmers, especially James Leonard in Somerset East, to understand species favoured by animals. He wrote extensively for the *Agricultural Journal of the Cape of Good Hope*, launched in 1889. Where Brown was verbose and general, MacOwan was often terse and specific. He seems to have imbibed some of the caution of the Cape, and was deeply conscious of the political constraints on modernization and scientific approaches. His writing sometimes reflected a dry, schoolmasterly humour, bordering on the sarcastic.

[83]   Ibid., MacOwan to Hooker, 30 July 1866.

[84]   Ibid., MacOwan to Hooker, 16 Apr. 1867.

[85]   *DSAB* i. 89. Bolus had been enthused by Francis Guthrie, who came to South Africa in 1861 to teach mathematics at Graaff-Reinet and gave public lectures there on Botany. He became Professor of Mathematics at the South African College in 1878 (*DSAB* ii. 279).

[86]   Kew, Director's Letters, vol. 190, MacOwan to Hooker, 30 July 1866.

[87]   Ibid., MacOwan to Hooker, 12 Dec. 1866 and 16 Apr. 1867.

[88]   MacOwan, 'Personalia'.

John Shaw, a geologist trained in Glasgow, arrived at the Cape in 1867 to become headmaster of the school in Colesberg; he also bought land there. Like many Victorian scientists, he had wide interests including a sub-specialization in mosses. He was welcomed by MacOwan when he stopped in Grahamstown on his way to Colesberg, and they went in search of mosses together in nearby kloofs. MacOwan and his network took pity on Shaw, in that 'his station, Colesberg . . . being all Karroo and stones', was 'about as un-muscological a locality as could be found'.[89] They sent him 500 specimens to classify so that he could at least do analytical work.

Shaw made contact with his well-established fellow Scotsman Roderick Noble, Professor of Physical Sciences at the South African College. Both Roderick Noble, in his teaching and lecturing, and his brother John, Clerk of the House of Assembly from 1865, who took over editing the *Cape Monthly Magazine*, were important conduits in popularizing scientific ideas.[90] Shaw wrote both on mosses and on Darwinism for Noble's compilation *The Cape and its People* (1869). Richard Rubidge's last, posthumous, piece was published in the same collection, which included four chapters on environmental themes. Shaw wrote geological articles, including one of the earliest on the diamond deposits in Kimberley, for the first issue of the revived *Cape Monthly* (1870).[91] He succeeded Noble as Professor in 1874 and became College Principal in 1876—this was the leading educational institution in the colony. In 1878 he published a school text on geography.[92]

Shaw was strongly influenced by Darwin. On the one hand, he discerned a 'deadly struggle' for life in nature: 'everywhere there is a warfare, remorseless, uncompromising, impartial, in which the weak go to the wall.'[93] On the other, he had a well-developed sense of the interdependence of species. The struggle, he accepted, 'causes a balance of opposing forms of life . . . By it peace comes out of incessant warfare; order out of the grappling of foe with

---

[89] Kew, Director's Letters, vol. 190, MacOwan to Hooker, 16 Nov. 1867.

[90] *DSAB* ii. 518.

[91] John Shaw, 'The Geology of the Diamondiferous Tracts of South Africa', *Cape Monthly Magazine*, 1 (1870); and 2 (1871). He also wrote on the geology of the Vaal for the *Grahamstown Journal* in 1869 and the *South African Magazine*; Rogers, 'Pioneers in South African Geology', 97.

[92] John Shaw, *The Geography of South Africa: Physical and Political* (Darter Brothers & Walton, Cape Town, 1878).

[93] Dr John Shaw, 'The Struggle for Existence in Nature, and its Relations to Speculations in Natural Theology', in R. Noble (ed.), *The Cape and Its People*, 66. He took his title from Charles Darwin, *On the Origin of Species by Means of Natural Selection, or the Preservation of Favoured Races in the Struggle for Life* (first published 1859), chap. 3, 'The Struggle for Existence'. Shaw was quickly identified by Noble, Atherstone, and Rubidge as one of the 'principle thinker and writers' of the Cape.

foe'.[94] He thought that the great diversity of species in South Africa must have resulted from similar plants within the same genera competing for similar food; the same applied to animals.[95]

These ideas made Shaw highly receptive to an analysis of environmental change. In the case of South Africa, new competitors in the shape of merino sheep had arrived, along with 'civilization by man', and as a result the antelopes were 'vanishing as before the march of a plague'.[96] Drawing again on Darwin, he was deeply aware of invasive plant species. He cited Darwin's example of the English clover in New Zealand, North American water-weed in Cambridge rivers, and *Xanthium spinosum* at the Cape. Extermination of one species, it followed, such as birds in the vineyards of France, could result in rapid expansion of their prey, thus altering 'the balance of natural life which formerly existed'.[97] 'Man everywhere is a disturbing agent, introducing and destroying as he lists, and therefore even modifying the combinations of organisms, and paralyzing the balance of Nature, wherever he goes.'

During the 1860s and 1870s understandings of botanical change became more sophisticated and precise, although there was still a great deal of uncertainty about the nature of particular species involved, especially when it came to grass. Attempts were made to define the relationship between sourveld and sweetveld; to assess the effects of heavy grazing; and to identify both the best and the least palatable plant species. As noted above, sheep farmers, especially in the coastal and eastern sourveld areas, where there was more grass, usually saw shorter grass as most suitable for sheep. Even those who were uneasy about burning believed that grass was best kept 'fully stocked and eaten down'.[98]

Ella noted in a memorandum to the 1877 Stock Diseases Commission that when Queenstown was first appropriated by colonists in 1853–4 the grass was considered 'too luxuriant and heavy'. Through drought (especially in 1862) and heavy grazing it 'improved' so that 'sweet grass . . . displaced some of the stronger sorts of heavy pasture called by farmers *sour grass*'.[99] Farmers from Dordrecht, bordering the Transkei, which was a rich grass district, felt it had been improved by heavy grazing and the spread of karoo bushes.[100] A Kingwilliamstown farmer agreed: '30 years ago, when I knew Peelton, it was long rank sour grass, now it is good sheep veldt.'[101] At Fort Beaufort there were advocates of overstocking: 'the healthiest part of my farm is the part that

[94] Ibid. 73.   [95] Ibid. 69.   [96] Ibid. 71.   [97] Ibid. 74.

[98] *Cape Monthly Magazine*, 4 (1858), 322: FWR, 'Agricultural Notes and Queries on Dr. Livingstone's Researches'.

[99] G.3-1877, 175, Ella, 'Some Observations'.   [100] Ibid. 44. Evidence E. L. Wipener (*sic*).

[101] Ibid. 144. Evidence, J. Landrey, Hangman's Bush, Kingwilliamstown.

has been constantly grazed for the last 26 years.'[102] Brown was told that even in dryer Karoo districts heavy rain produced herbage too 'rich and luxuriant'. These were the conditions that were thought to cause *giel ziekte*.[103] Sheep could 'die off to a frightful extent, though to all appearance healthy and fat'; grass could drown out the best shrubs.

Yet some sheep farmers also perceived dangers in vegetation change, and this view of degrading pastures was taken up by the small, interconnected group of botanists. The problem was how to know when grazing was at its best, and which types of change could be considered undesirable. On the basis of his correspondence with farmers, Brown refined ideas about what would become called selective grazing. His analysis, in an 1864 letter to Ella and Hopley, was republished as an appendix to the Stock Diseases Commission report in 1877. He argued that livestock consumed their preferred grasses and diminished their chances of seeding. 'In the struggle for life', seeds from less palatable grasses and plants took possession.[104] For Brown there was one obvious remedy. It was necessary to identify the best pasturage grasses of the Colony and cultivate them. Sheep farming and wool production would otherwise decline, 'and be thought of only as a thing of the past'. Poisonous plants were also sent to Brown for identification, notably nenta (see Chapter 4) and dronk gras. He wondered if the prevalence of poisoning was also due to 'an undersupply of nutritious and wholesome food'.[105]

Brown's Colesberg correspondent, J. H. Davis, had a clear sense of denudation. He thought that the sweetveld grazing there was generally better than in the southern Karoo, because of looser soil and flatter land that retained moisture better. But in much the same way as Rubidge, he saw sheep as destroying this advantage. Not only was erosion of soil being caused by torrents in streams and rivers, but also by a less obvious process: 'where these plains are inclined even at a low angle, the light top soil does get washed away, leaving the hard earth below exposed at the surface; and wherever this takes place the grass disappears and the heath with other short scrubby plants spring up.' Grass roots were exposed and gradually disappeared, to leave farms bare, 'even in the most favourable seasons'.[106] He was describing in the 1860s what later became called sheet erosion, or soil washing.

Within a year or two of arriving in Colesberg, Shaw had absorbed this critique and developed the Darwinian interpretation offered by Brown. He pictured an overall transition from a 'feral state' where land was 'covered with

[102] Ibid., 135.
[103] Ibid., Evidence A. Vigne, Cradock, 74; A. Nel, Somerset Eeast, 80; F. Botha, Cradock, 60.
[104] Ibid. 177.   [105] Ibid. 186.   [106] G.24-1865, 84.

grass and a meagre sprinkling of bushes', to a 'bush veldt', and subsequently to bare land where sheep were 'overstocked' (see Chapter 11).[107] The only survivor was the bitter bush *Chrysocoma tenuifolia*. In later years this was often cited as a marker of denudation, and it seems to have been first regularly noticed in written reports at this time. This plant was dominant on 'a *vley* upon which I look as I write . . . once covered with beautiful and luxurious grass'. The bitterbos was highly suited to 'ascendency and conquest'; it could withstand drought and as a compositae was well-adapted to scattering large quantities of seed.

Shaw's views offered too sharp a sequence, and he could not have known from personal observation what vegetation his vlei had supported in the past. But he expanded on his ideas in the early 1870s, as he familiarized himself with his surroundings and read the old sources.[108] He was one of the first to capture, in succint form, the idea of a spreading Karoo. Shaw had a clear perception of the regional botanical divisions, and the differences between western, eastern, southern, and midland Cape characteristics. The midlands, the main sheep country, he argued, was once 'in the time of Burchell and other old botanical travellers, covered with luxuriant prairie-like grass':[109]

Since sheep have been introduced, the grass has fast disappeared, the ground (by the hurried march of the sheep for food amongst a scattered bush) has become beaten and hardened, and the seasonable rains which do come are accordingly allowed to run off the surface without soaking into the ground to the extent formerly the case. The country is thus drying up, the fountains becoming smaller and smaller, and the prospect is very clear that the midland regions will turn into a semi-desert. Indeed the plants of the singular regions known as the Karoo . . . favoured little by rain . . . are travelling northwards rapidly and occupying this now similar dry tract of country. The herbage is essentially a Karoo one already. It contains most prominently Karoo plants, such as the *Chrysocomas* and the *Elytropappi*.

Karoo bush was moving as far as Griqualand West and the Vaal.

Shaw extended the idea that overgrazing allowed poisonous herbs—'some Asclepiads, poisonous Tripteres, and the intoxicating Melicae (the "dronk" grass of the Dutch colonists)'—to spread; so much so that transport riders could not stop in some areas for fear of their animals being disabled. Chrysocoma, he thought, originated in the south-western Karoo, but had travelled eastwards to become the most prevalent small bush of the southern

---

[107] Shaw, 'The Struggle for Existence', 75.

[108] John Shaw, 'On the Changes going on in the Vegetation of South Africa through the introduction of the Merino Sheep', *Journal of the Linnean Society*, Botanical 14 (1875), 202–8; thanks to Richard Grove for the reference.

[109] Shaw, 'Vegetation', 204.

midlands. Sheep ate it out of desperation, and 'the mutton, from the beginning of the year to the end, tastes and smells of it'.[110] The legislation against burrweed was a drop in the ocean compared to more general botanical change and the 'evil of overstocking', which were far less easy to legislate against. The spread of Karoo plants in itself 'added their energies' to the displacement of the 'proper' flora. Farmers called the result bitter veld.

Like Sparrman, Shaw wondered about the effects of millions of antelopes and locusts on the veld in pre-colonial times. He concluded that they were less harmful in that they were migratory, while sheep became 'persistent occupiers'.[111] Not only that, but sheep had to walk so far during each day to find food and water that they 'cause more destruction by treading down than even by eating'.[112] This hardened the ground and increased the run-off. Water could no longer soak into the earth to replenish fountains. His solutions replicated those of Brown and others in the 1860s. 'Colossal dams' would be needed to prevent 'poverty and death to an incalculable extent amongst our flocks in South Africa.'[113]

Atherstone, visiting Colesberg on a trip to the Transvaal, found it unsurprising that Shaw should write about desiccation there, with its 'baked Karoo clay soil, browner rocks, black fetid ditch . . . and where famine peeped through the boulders'. 'Living in such a place,' Atherstone mused 'where only Karroo Boer and rabbit would choose to live', 'what else could he write on'.[114] But Shaw's analysis was echoed in the report of the Civil Commissioner for Colesberg and in John Noble's writing.[115] In 1875 the latter published a *Descriptive Handbook of the Cape Colony*.[116] He saw himself as extending and developing Hall's *Geography*. He singled out Colesberg, and to a lesser extent Richmond, as areas of degradation although the former was still one of the best wool-producing districts in the colony.[117]

MacOwan added his weight to the consensus that the most dangerous and rapid spreader, where land was overstocked, was the *Chrysocoma tenuifolia*, the bitter karoo bosje: 'untouched by the sheep except under pressure of the direct necessity, it blossoms and scatters its seed without let or hindrance, till

[110] Ibid. 207. Chrysocoma is now widely regarded as an invader, but is unlikely to have been so restricted in its origins.

[111] Ibid. 206.   [112] Ibid.   [113] Ibid. 208.   [114] Mathie, *Atherstone*, i. 120.

[115] Cape of Good Hope, *Blue Book, 1875*, reports of the Civil Commissioner for Colesberg, JJ.28.

[116] Noble, *Descriptive Handbook*, 159, 259, 260; John Noble, *The Cape and South Africa* (Longmans Green & Co. London, 1878) effectively a second edition, has less detailed descriptive material on individual districts; John Noble, *South Africa, Past and Present: A Short History of European Settlements at the Cape* (Longman & Co., London, 1877).

[117] Noble, *Descriptive Handbook*, 157–9.

in many places it forms over fifty per cent. of the natural produce.' Chrysocoma could produce biliousness, and semi-fluid, tar-like faeces, 'and the animal pines away'.[118] Like the rhenoster bush, spreading around Grahamstown, it was very difficult to eradicate and seldom worth the expenditure.

He detected other dangerous spreaders, such as thorny *Mesembryanthemum spinosum* and *Lycium asparagus*, which could not be browsed and hence became pests. When dry in winter, the wild asparagus branchlets broke off and stuck in wool, and especially in the hair of angoras. MacOwan suggested that the special legislation devoted to the burrweed had led to underestimation of more destructive plants. He agreed that indigenous poisonous plants such as nenta and tulp-bloem were gaining ground, because of overgrazing and a failure by farmers to eradicate them:

The conclusion I have come to, after some years' observation of the pasturage of the colony in the districts of Albany and Somerset, is that a decided deterioration is in progress, arising partly from over-stocking, partly from unintelligent use of pasturage, and partly from the neglect of precautionary measures of reserve, renewal, and repair. The evil is not so great but that improvement may be expected from any and every well-directed effort, and it by no means yet calls for legislative interference. The great thing to be desired is that the *farniente* custom of considering the veld as an inexhaustible balance put to the farmer's credit by Providence, and capable of reckless use, should give place to a wise provision and economy; in short, that the pasturage be held to be inconvertible capital, demanding as much sharpness of observation and appliance, as much quickness to detect deterioration and skill to devise a remedy, as is requisite in manipulating convertible capital on the money market.[119]

Renewal would require scientific methods such as fallows, eradicating weeds, and sowing selected indigenous grass seeds; then 'the paddock and meadow will be the rule, the hungry veld the exception'.[120]

Although there were many everyday Dutch names for indigenous grasses, it is clear from Brown's reports that neither he, nor the most alert and concerned farmers, could classify them botanically with any confidence, nor clarify their characteristics. MacOwan addressed the issue of valuable grass plants 'with much diffidence, for the widest variations of opinion prevails upon the comparative value of these food-plants'. 'Roode zaad gras' was widely seen as the most valuable species; Brown identified it incorrectly as *Tristachia leucothrix*. Hopley and Ella thought haas gras and schaap gras were also good sweet pasture. Brown was sent the highly palatable breede blaauw zaad gras which he called an eragrostis species.

[118] G.3-1877, 197.   [119] Ibid. 199.   [120] Ibid. 196.

Brown thought that roode zaad gras might be mistaken for *Anthisteria cili-ata*, the Australian kangaroo grass. Ella, using Australian botanical descriptions and lithographs from Victoria, decided that this Australian grass was in fact the same as the 'prevailing red grass of the Queen's Town District'.[121] He also noted that, as in Australia, 'it soon disappears before overstocking'. MacOwan then confirmed this botanical naming of the 'bluish Rooi Gras' as *Anthistiria ciliata Retz.* Their botanical classification was different from that used in the earlier travel literature, and also from that which became accepted later for rooigras—*Themeda triandra.* What they all could agree on was the quality of this species. 'It may be affirmed pretty certainly', MacOwan wrote, 'to be the best native grass for permanent pasture, to remain nutritive longer and under more severe conditions than any other of social growth, and to be not easily killed by drought or by the ravages of locusts.'[122] The identification of rooigras and its role has been central to understandings of South African pastures.[123]

MacOwan also tried to expand on 'the interminable quarrel as to *zoet gras* and *zuur gras*'. He rejected the idea that sweet and sour in this context had much to do with acidity, and tried to understand them as variable terms referring very largely to the rapidity with which cell tissue hardened. Grasses, including some aristida species, which became fibrous very quickly, were named sour, as were districts where they were dominant. Sweetveld contained a greater predominance of grass, such as rooigras, which remained less fibrous through the dry season, but this species could also occur, he conjectured, in sourveld. In some circumstances, drought or other conditions could render a species that was usually associated with sweetveld sour, because the cell walls hardened more quickly.

Evidence available to MacOwan suggested that *Pentzia virgata*, as it was called then, seemed to be the most favoured Karoo shrub; it reproduced itself rapidly both by seed and by branches touching the soil and taking root. A sample had been sent of this schaap bos to Brown as an example of one of the 'best we have'. It retained its nutritious properties during the dry, frosty, winter months, when the grasses became 'worthless'.[124] Hooker at Kew advocated it as one of the most valuable fodder crops for arid climates in general.[125] This was probably what is now called *Pentzia incana*, or ankerkaroo, so named because its branches anchor in the soil and start new growth.[126] Ankerkaroo is

[121] Ibid. 208.   [122] Ibid. 196.
[123] E.g. D. Meredith (ed.), *The Grasses and Pastures of South Africa* (Central News Agency, Cape Town, 1955).
[124] G.3-1877, 184.   [125] Noble, *Descriptive Handbook*, 131.
[126] P. M. le Roux et al., *Bossieveld*, 126.

now thought of as having variable nutritive value, but is of particular importance because of its abundance. Other pentzia species were possibly sometimes mistaken for it, and some are now considered unpalatable invaders.

MacOwan thought that *Pentzia virgata* could be an excellent defence
against *sluits* (small, denuded run-off channels) caused by overgrazing—a
'truly South African curse'—because of its rooting capacity.[127] He named
Diplopappus filifolius (draai-bosje), which also seeded profusely, and some
mesembryanthemums as essential brak grazing. In the southern districts,
spekboom (*Portulacaria afra*) was undoubtedly the most valuable resource: 'I
have witnessed from year to year the gradual disappearance of large thickets
of this tree by ruthless feeding . . . but have never heard of any person starting a few cuttings to replace the trunks worn down by cattle.'[128]

In giving evidence to the parliamentary committee that sat in 1882 to discuss the appointment of a Minister of Agriculture, MacOwan articulated a
deep concern about environmental degradation. For him, conservation had
become 'of national importance'.[129] His priorities were very much drawn
from Brown: 'the reboisement of the country, the reforming of the surface
denuded of soil by torrents, the storage of water, etc.'[130] But he took a sceptical position about the role of the state. First, it would be necessary to co-
ordinate the activities of existing officials—the Hydraulic Engineer, Colonial
Geologist, Superintendent of Forests, Veterinary Surgeon, and Botanist. He
argued in turn against model farms, against agricultural colleges, and even
against agricultural societies: 'shows are a pleasant holiday for farmers, but
the practical results are small.' He was perturbed about the prospects of a
political appointment to the Department of Agriculture. 'You cannot make
the people scientific by Act of Parliament', MacOwan argued, and 'I object to
the government going about as hawkers of scientific knowledge'. 'The farmers', he added, 'are not very prone to take the advice of theoretical strangers.
They ridicule the idea of experts from Europe being able to show them anything, and maintain that they are practically failures.'[131] It was only when
MacOwan was pushed to confront the example of the American and
Canadian agricultural colleges that he admitted that there could be effective
transmission of knowledge and expertise.

It is striking that by the 1870s, less than a half-century after intensive wool
production began, many features of vegetation change and soil erosion had
been identified at the Cape: gulley erosion; sheet erosion; changing species;

[127] G.3-1877, 193.   [128] Ibid. 194.
[129] Cape of Good Hope, *Report of the Select Committee appointed by the Legislative Council to
Consider and Report upon the Appointment of a Minister of Agriculture*, C.2-1882, 11.
[130] C.2-1882, 6.   [131] Ibid. 2.

the spreading Karoo; tramping of soil. These all became well established in debates on degradation and conservation in the twentieth century. It was difficult even for experts to identify the best species amongst the hundreds of veld grasses and shrubs. While they certainly held strong opinions about overgrazing, they had as yet little practical advice as to how to enrich the pastures. It was not primarily the indigenous grass or Karoo bush species that subsequently found favour as cultivated pastures. The growth of ostrich production put a premium on fodder, and lucerne seemed to provide the best solution (Chapter 5). By intent and happenstance, prickly pear became both a boon and a curse in some districts (Chapter 8). But key recommendations about managing the veld had been suggested; they were developed and urgently advocated from the late 1870s as a response to animal diseases.

4

Vets, Viruses, and Environmentalism in the 1870s and 1880s

Kraaling and Environmental Explanations of Disease

Kraaling of cattle and sheep at night in order to safeguard them from predators and theft was central to livestock farming in South Africa. Millions of animals had to be driven, often long distances, to and from the pastures every day. By the 1870s there were increasingly frequent comments about the environmental problems caused by this practice. Those with botanical and geological interests had played the major role in elaborating and defining environmental ills at the Cape. In the late nineteenth century veterinary scientists became the key protagonists of reform in livestock management. Vets left behind them a large volume of literature, often in government publications—a testament to the importance of animal disease to the state. The first two Colonial Veterinary Surgeons made close links between the health of animals, agricultural productivity, and environmental conditions.

This chapter explores the early veterinary contribution to the critique and transformation of Cape pastoral practices. These developments had important implications for the physical, as well as the social, landscape of the colony. Consideration of veterinary prescriptions also reveals fascinating examples of conflict, in a colonial context, between scientific and local knowledge. In this case the conflict was between colonial scientists and some settler farmers. Their different ways of conceiving how to cope with a harsh and unpredictable environment, and of diagnosing the many ills that beset farm animals in the colony, evokes later clashes of perception between colonial officials and African people. But evidence from the late nineteenth-century Cape should also caution us against drawing simple lines of division between scientific specialists on the one hand, and traditionalists with 'local knowledge' on the other. Settler farmers were unified neither socially nor in their approach to stock management. As has been illustrated, many of the most ardent improvers, who helped set the modernizing political and technical agenda of the colonial state, came from their ranks.

Specialists also learned a great deal from those on the land. Ultimately, the vets' approach was framed by metropolitan scientific knowledge.[1] Nevertheless, in a moving metropolis, they were to a significant degree part of an interactive process of research and policy formation.[2] Moreover, scientific and technical ideas were by no means stable and predictable. The two first government vets, William Branford and Duncan Hutcheon, tended towards different interpretations of disease which reflected the rapidly changing science of the time. Most historians of colonial encounters have now been educated out of a static view of indigenous people or local tradition; it is just as important to complicate notions of 'modern' and 'scientific'.

By the 1870s, after a few decades of rapid growth, perceptions of the health of the pastoral economy became uncertain. There were good reasons for these doubts, in that a ceiling in wool production appeared to have been reached. In 1872 international prices for wool went through the roof and the value of wool shipped rose by 50 per cent (Table 4.1). Income from wool exports in this year, at £3.3 million, was not again exceeded before Union in 1910. While prices remained high, peaking in 1875, farmers could not take advantage of these extremely favourable market conditions by increasing production. Wool-export volumes declined from their 1871–2 peaks despite the fact that the area under sheep was still expanding, along with the colony's conquests and boundaries, and Free State supplies were increasing.

The colonial census of 1875 clarified concerns that were already growing about the state of sheep farming. Although the total number of woolled sheep in the colony had grown modestly over ten years, from 8.4 million to nearly 10 million (Table 4.1), not all districts shared in this expansion. Between 1865 and 1875 the major increases in sheep numbers were registered in two areas where merinos were relatively recent introductions: first, the more arid northern Cape, where vast stretches of Crown lands were being thrown open to settlement; and secondly, in the rich grasslands of the recently colonized border districts, on the eastern and north-eastern frontier, abutting the Transkeian African chiefdoms, with 500 mm. of rain and above annually. By contrast, falling numbers were recorded in some of the best-established sheep-farming districts in the eastern Cape, including areas

[1] R. MacLeod and M. Lewis (eds.), *Disease, Medicine and Empire: Perspectives on Western Medicine and the Experience of European Expansion* (London, 1988); R. Macleod, 'On Visiting the "Moving Metropolis": Reflections on the Architecture of Imperial Science', *Historical Records of Australian Science*, 5 (1982), 1–16; M. Vaughan, *Curing Their Ills: Colonial Power and African Illness* (Polity, Cambridge, 1991); R. Packard, *White Plague, Black Labour: Tuberculosis and the Political Economy of Health and Disease in South Africa* (James Currey, London, 1989).

[2] Jan Todd, *Colonial Technology: Science and the Transfer of Innovation to Australia* (Cambridge University Press, Cambridge, 1995).

TABLE 4.1. Wool Exports, Prices and Sheep Numbers, Cape Only, 1865–1885

Year	Weight of wool exports (lbs.)	Value (£)	£/lb.	Numbers (woolled)	Numbers (other)
1865	32,767,679	1,680,826	.051	8,370,000	1,466,000
1866	35,229,289	1,994,054	.057		
1867	36,026,614	1,927,628	.057		
1868	36,466,310	1,806,459	.049		
1869	37,220,540	1,602,528	.043		
1870	37,283,291	1,669,518	.045		
1871	46,279,639	2,191,233	.047		
1872	48,822,562	3,275,150	.067		
1873	40,393,746	2,710,481	.067		
1874	42,620,481	2,948,571	.069		
1875	40,339,674	2,855,899	.071	9,986,000	990,000
1876	34,861,339	2,278,942	.065		
1877	36,020,571	2,232,755	.062		
1878	32,127,167	1,888,928	.059		
1879	40,087,593	2,156,609	.054		
1880	42,469,362	2,429,382	.057		
1881	42,770,244	2,181,937	.051		
1882	41,689,119	2,062,180	.049		
1883	38,029,495	1,992,745	.052		
1884	37,270,615	1,745,193	.047		
1885	34,432,562	1,426,108	.041		

settled by progressive and successful English-speaking farmers, such as Albany and Fort Beaufort. Holdings around Graaff-Reinet and Cradock were static.

Drought in 1873, followed by unusually cold weather, rains, locusts, and floods, could partly explain sheep losses.[3] But the Cape climate was always unpredictable. It was clear to farmers that their animals were victims of disease, rather than just the weather. The perception that diseases were spreading prompted the colonial government to appoint its first Colonial Veterinary Surgeon in 1876. Developments in the Cape state, and in the veterinary profession more generally, cleared the way for this innovative step that had far-reaching consequences. Increasing state revenues from both diamonds and pastoral exports allowed the government to be more ambitious

[3] Cape of Good Hope, *Blue Book 1874*, JJ.19 ff.; Brown, *Hydrology*.

in its bureaucratic expansion in the 1870s. There were already specialist scientific posts in the Cape civil service. District Surgeons combined their responsibilities with private practice; the Colonial Botanist (temporarily), a few forestry officers, surveyors, and geologists were other cases in point. The Cape's transition to responsible government in 1874 brought an elected ministry, under Molteno, which was more alert to the priorities of its propertied, articulate, and organized constituents. Molteno had chaired the 1862 Irrigation Committee. His sheep holdings in Beaufort West, reported at 35,000 in 1875, were possibly the biggest in the colony.[4] A Colonial Hydraulic Engineer was also appointed to develop water supplies (Chapter 5).

The Veterinary Surgeon was perhaps the first official appointed to deal specifically with agricultural questions. (Attempts to cope with the vine disease phylloxera was another major stimulus towards the foundation of an agricultural bureaucracy.) Although British military vets had served in South Africa, few if any vets were based in the Cape, and at least one attempt to set up a private practice had failed.[5] Livestock owners, white and black, doctored their own livestock. Flocks and herds were large, losses to drought, disease, and predators were frequent, and individual animals were not generally seen as of sufficient value to merit the costs of professionals. A few rural physicians did, however, take great interest in the diagnostic challenges offered by animals, and seem positively to have relished the relative freedom which animal post-mortems offered. Medicine was then a less specialized field, and comparative medicine, as it is now called, which included work with animals, was at the cutting edge of science in the 1870s, in the hands of Pasteur and Koch.[6]

Major advances were being made in Britain and Europe in identifying the causes of disease, animal as well as human. The Royal College of Veterinary Surgeons received its charter in 1844, and in 1848 a professional register listed 1,500 names. Training was available at the London Veterinary School and in Edinburgh; veterinary journals recorded advances in the field. The value of pedigree and working animals, especially horses and cattle, created scope for an expanding profession. At the same time, the mid-Victorian British state had taken on increasing responsibilities for managing diseases. Cattle plague (rinderpest) in 1865 proved to be a turning-point both for the status of veterinary science and for government involvement in preventing

---

⁴ Noble, *Descriptive Handbook*, 133.

⁵ Cape Archives, Colonial Secretary, CO 4110, M116, M122 and CO 4143, 131, G. A. Martin to Colonial Secretary, 16 May 1866.

⁶ Lise Wilkinson, *Animals and Disease: An Introduction to the History of Comparative Medicine* (Cambridge University Press, Cambridge, 1992).

animal epizootics.[7] Leading vets, such as James Simonds, had argued powerfully and, after the loss of about half-a-million cattle, successfully for stringent controls over imports and stock movements.

William Catton Branford, who qualified in London in 1857, and became
Professor at the Royal (Dick) Veterinary College, Edinburgh in 1869, was
appointed as Cape Colonial Veterinary Surgeon in 1876. One of his first
tasks was to sit on the Stock Diseases Commission.[8] He was the first in a long
line of specialists, which included the famous German scientist Robert Koch,
to be imported by southern African governments in order to deal with the
devastating epizootics and intractable endemic diseases that afflicted the
region.[9] Branford's three published reports, together with that of the 1877
Commission, provide a startling record of a pastoral economy under pressure. Branford was, to put it bluntly, horrified by what he saw. In his view,
the flocks and herds were seething with disease. Like Brown, he was self-
confident in his role as the outside expert, outspoken, even opinionated; he
lost few opportunities of expressing his views and presenting remedies.

The farmers amongst whom Branford worked had long categorized the
diseases which they encountered by Dutch names which described their
symptoms or the parts affected: for example, brandziekte (fire/burning disease, or scab), lamziekte (lame sickness), dunsiekte (emaciation), stijfziekte
(stiffness or paralysis), longsiekte (lungsickness or pleuropneumonia),
meltziekte (spleensickness or anthrax), geilsiekte or gielsiekte (rich lands or
grass sickness) and hartwater (water on the heart). The names themselves
reflected a concept of medicine widespread amongst rural Afrikaners, but not
them alone, that diseases were definable by their symptoms and to some
extent curable by treating those symptoms. Afrikaner boeremiddels (home
remedies), many of them culled from indigenous plants and some from
Khoikhoi knowledge, were legion (Chapter 1). Many of these names for diseases had been adopted and partly anglicized by the English-speaking farmers.

Branford saw one of his tasks as imposing an enlightenment order on this
naming system, trying to identify which diseases were known to Victorian
veterinary science. Scab, which followed woolled sheep around the world,

---

[7] Iain Pattison, *The British Veterinary Profession 1791–1948* (J. A. Allen, London, 1983); J. F.
Smithcors, *The American Veterinary Profession: Its Background and Development* (Iowa State University Press, Iowa, 1963).

[8] G.3-1877, Cape of Good Hope, *Report of the Commission Appointed to Inquire into and Report
upon Diseases in Cattle and Sheep in this Colony.* The Commission began its sessions in Sept. 1876, a
few months after Branford arrived at the Cape.

[9] Paul F. Cranefield, *Science and Empire: East Coast Fever in Rhodesia and the Transvaal* (Cambridge University Press, Cambridge, 1991).

and lungsickness, a major cattle killer, were well known in Europe and had already been identified at the Cape. Lungsickness had devastated colonial and African herds in the 1850s and 1860s. Nevertheless, some Afrikaner farmers held that the local brandziekte was distinctive. Many also perceived other diseases as specific to the Cape or their locality. Branford wanted 'to remove an impression which has taken possession of the minds of some of the colonists, viz., that the diseases to which cattle and sheep are liable in the Cape Colony are widely different to diseases which are met with in the British Isles, or even in Europe'.[10] If he could establish this, he felt, the relevance of advances in European veterinary science, and the application of scientific solutions, would be plain.

Farmers were not entirely wrong. While the Cape was highly susceptible to introduced diseases precisely because so many new types of stock had been imported, there were nevertheless many ill-understood and apparently local maladies. Poisonous plants were also seen to claim a significant number of animals. For some Cape farmers, especially Dutch-speakers, the idea that their animal diseases were the same as the British ones became linked with threats of intervention by outside experts. Claims about the geographically specific nature of diseases were linked to a defence of their cherished beliefs about stock-keeping—especially seasonal transhumance.

Legislation had been passed for the isolation of infected cattle during the Cape's lungsickness epidemic in the 1860s. The lines were being drawn in the battle over scab control. Most of the Australian colonies, increasingly seen as a model by Cape officials and progressive sheep farmers, had effectively confronted scab by stringent legislation governing stock movements, together with dressing (washing) or dipping with chemicals. In 1874 the Cape government passed a Scab Act that, although it was not compulsory, envisaged similar controls. Farmers resented interference that might curtail seasonal movements of animals, and many refused to accept that scab was passed between sheep. By emphasizing the uniqueness of Cape animal diseases, they could convince themselves that Branford was another interfering British official who did not understand their country.

Branford was not, however, isolated. He found strong support for some of his ideas among the network of politicians, officials, and improving farmers, including Molteno, which had steered through the Scab Act and his appointment.[11] The Stock Disease commissioners, such as Charles Rubidge (Chapter 1), John Frost (Introduction), J. B. Hellier, William Hockley, and

---

[10] Cape of Good Hope, *Report of Colonial Veterinary Surgeon for the Years 1878–79*, G.54-1879, 1.

[11] Ibid. 9. A similar post was created in Natal at this time.

Arthur Douglass, were drawn largely from this overlapping agrarian and political elite. Frost went on to become a minister in Rhodes's government and chaired the politically sensitive Scab Commission in the 1890s. Hellier served as a municipal and state official, published a short-lived paper called *The Farm*, and edited the *Agricultural Journal* in the 1890s. Douglass, born in England (1843), came to the Cape as a surveyor in 1864 but made his name as an ostrich farmer near Grahamstown. With Atherstone, he developed an effective system of incubating ostrich eggs, which allowed for systematic mass breeding. He was subsequently elected as MLA for Grahamstown in 1884. This group had a broad commitment to pastoral reform, but as investors in increasingly expensive stud animals, they also had a particular interest in reducing the risks of disease. The Commission drew on the knowledge of local scientists such as MacOwan, and medical practitioners.[12] Most witnesses to the 1877 Commission were asked directly whether they supported compulsory measures for scab eradication and were left in no doubt as to the commissioners' view.

Branford, who had participated in implementing rinderpest controls in Britain, brought with him both confidence in scientific ideas and a belief in the state's role: diseases had to be addressed at a colony-wide level or the threat of reinfection would remain.[13] Although he held strong scientific opinions, he studied before Pasteur and Koch had developed their germ theories and practised before these had been widely accepted. Following the dominant ideas of that time, he tended to seek the explanation for disease primarily in environmental conditions, rather than in microscopic bacteria and viruses.[14] Improving the health of people and animals alike, at the height of the Victorian era of urban social reform, involved not least attempts to clean up and regulate the environment. This did not preclude a recognition of the role of contagion and infection in specific diseases such as rinderpest and lungsickness. But in his brief, intense encounter with the animals of the Cape, he came to the conclusion that contagious diseases and even external parasites such as scab, serious though they were, did not consitute the major problem.

After conducting a number of post-mortems on sheep, Branford became convinced that internal parasites were more dangerous, although by

---

[12] G.3-1877, evidence Dr Berry, Queenstown, 18; Dr Bekker, Grahamstown, 125; Dr Watkins, Alice, 137.

[13] *The Veterinarian*, 38 (1865), 915; 42 (Aug. 1869), 624. Estate papers at the Cape Archives MOOC 6/9/296, 1516.

[14] Pattison, *British Veterinary Profession*, suggests that while Simonds in London rapidly assimilated and propagated Pasteur's ideas in the 1860s, the main Edinburgh veterinary teaching institution was initially divided.

weakening animals these also made them more susceptible to other diseases. Many of the sheep that he examined were infested with worms or fluke. He had little hesitation in arguing that these were the primary cause of losses in the colony. Sheep in Fort Beaufort district, where mortality rates had been amongst the highest, nurtured three or four different kinds of worm in liver, stomach, and intestine; they were 'literally eaten up alive by parasites'.[15] Tapeworms were especially prevalent in the intestines of younger animals and destroyed many lambs. Roundworms, or nematodes, were widespread; Branford had made a special study of these.[16] Perhaps the most destructive parasite was a small red-and-white spiral or wireworm (*Strongylus contortus*), sometimes compared to a needle, found in huge numbers in the fourth stomach of sheep. It had been identified scientifically in 1858 by Simonds.[17]

Many farmers called the disease that had killed so many sheep in grassland districts heartwater. It was so named because the sheep suffering from the condition, after developing dropsical swellings under the throat, were found to have large amounts of fluid in their hearts. 'Upon opening the sheep,' George Judd of Queenstown explained to the Commission, 'there is little or no blood in the body, heart bag [is] very full of water, the heart when opened discharges a great quantity of clear fluid, and a small quantity of very dark clotted blood.'[18] An Afrikaner who had farmed for twenty-eight years in Dordrecht, which he considered 'the healthiest part of the country' until about 1870, lost all but 600 of his 4,000-strong flock. He found not only the heart affected but 'the fat is watery, and would not fry out'.[19] Another noted that if you hung a sheep, dead from heartwater, 'nearly a bucketful of water runs out'.[20] In many sheep, knotted, contorted intestines were evident.

Although farmers did their own dissections and post-mortems, it was difficult for them to identify symptoms systematically. Some also gave the name heartwater to slightly different symptoms. In these cases the colour of the liquid was yellow; it did not drip when exposed to the atmosphere but formed a jelly. They noted that this heartwater, which some believed was gielsiekte, or related to it, could affect apparently healthy sheep. These 'would go out of the kraal fat and well, and come home in the evening with their heads drooping and bodies soft and flabby, next morning they would all be dead'.[21]

---

[15] G.8-1877, *Report of the Colonial Veterinary Surgeon on Sheep and Cattle Diseases in the Colony*, 17.

[16] Ibid. 20.

[17] *Agricultural Journal of the Cape of Good Hope* (27 July 1893), 284, 'Diseases of Animals: The Discovery of Wire-worm', taken from the *Journal of the Royal Agricultural Society*, 24 (1863).

[18] G.3-1877, 4.   [19] Ibid. 40.   [20] Ibid. 42.

[21] Ibid., evidence W. Ayliff, MLA, 120.

A number of farmers, especially in the districts immediately north and north-east of Queenstown, also connected the disease of heartwater with the infestation of the sheep's liver by fluke. A few in the coastal district of Albany made a direct connection between gielsiekte, heartwater, and ticks, especially the bonte (variegated or tortoiseshell) tick.[22] They believed that this tick—possibly imported from Zululand or the Transkei—had spread in the eastern Cape since the 1850s, and a few could give the commissioners information on its natural history.

Branford was aware that ticks could harm stock and that they may have been spreading; he questioned farmers about the link between extensive burning of veld and the decline of tick-eating birds. But there was very little scientific understanding at this time of maladies conveyed by parasites and their vectors in the warmer regions of the world. On the evidence he heard, he was convinced that heartwater was due to worms, especially the wire-worm. Farmers had not generally appreciated this, he felt, because even those who dissected were by no means all able to navigate as far as the small fourth stomach, stronghold of the wireworm; they significantly underestimated the degree of infestation. One farmer mentioned, perhaps teasing the anatomically obsessed commissioners, that he 'did not know a sheep had four stomachs'.[23] Branford did admit that the form of yellow heartwater encountered in the coastal districts, which attacked flocks in good condition, was probably unrelated to these internal parasites. Heartwater from worms, he believed, was the wasting disease, where swellings appeared under the throat.

The life-cycle of the liver-fluke, well known to Branford, depended upon wet, marshy land. It was rarely found in the dry Karoo but became a major scourge of better-watered grassland districts to the east. Evidence to the Commission clearly suggested that fluke was relatively new in the area and it could be devastating; the number of sheep on a 'beautiful grass veldt' farm in the Stormberg had been reduced from 6,000 to 700 in five years.[24] Infestation could often be directly linked to stock drinking in vleis, and was worse in rainy seasons. Once the fluke was established in the liver, it was very difficult to eradicate with the medicines then available. Branford therefore recommended preventative action, by regular dosing with salt. As important, the fluke could be controlled by fencing vleis and marshes to control access or by draining them. Fencing was expensive. But farmers did have another incentive to drain vleis: these were often the richest land for crops. Heavier and more efficient American ploughs which came into use at the time facilitated

---

[22] Ibid., pp. xiii, 30–1, 108. Atherstone noted this in 1860: Mathie, *Atherstone*, ii. 484.

[23] G.3-1877, evidence G. Stokes, 133–4.   [24] Ibid., p. xiv.

their cultivation. Draining was seen as the best solution for fluke, and in this sense veterinary recommendations contributed to what was later seen as an environmentally destructive practice.

The approach to worms was different. Branford, the commissioners, and some farmers were convinced that the prevalence of worms was linked to overstocking, the deterioration of pastures, and the system of kraaling. They took up and developed the critique of Cape sheep farming which had gained considerable currency. One way in which the commissioners sought to demonstrate degradation was by asking questions about the weight of sheep. While a few demurred, witnesses who gave evidence on this point suggested a significant fall of about 10 pounds per head on average since the early 1860s, to around 40 pounds.[25] Overstocking, Branford argued, meant that sheep had to 'work harder for a living' and suffered in the competition for food.[26]

The term 'overstocking' was frequently used in this nineteenth-century context, and similar comments had been made about Australian pastures, where sheep farming seemed so much more advanced to observers from the Cape.[27] By the 1870s some farmers worked with a clear notion of how much stock a particular type of veld could 'carry', and were able to specify this in respect of their own farms and districts. Overstocking was now firmly linked by the commissioners to soil erosion: 'the gradual washing out of the sluits and gulleys' and the 'denudation of the soil which has been very much accelerated since the occupation of the land by sheep'.[28]

Branford expanded on the idea of uneven or selective grazing patterns which Brown and his botanical successors had formulated—and which they saw as responsible for the spread of unpalatable species. The process, he argued, not only impaired nutrition but had a specific relationship to worms and health. It was widely understood that animals required an intake of saline substances for their health. Afrikaner farmers generally had some knowledge of the 'brak' plants or brakveld that served this function, and tried to ensure that these formed part of their sheeps' diet. Their abundance in the Karoo, and relative scarcity in some of the grassland districts to the south and east, was one reason why the semi-arid zones were seen as particularly good for small stock. The commissioners argued that saline bushes helped to keep

[25] Ibid. 12.   [26] G.8-1877, 10–11.

[27] The 1877 Commission specifically drew on: Department of Lands and Agriculture, Victoria, *Second Annual Report of the Secretary for Agriculture* (Melbourne, 1874); W. H. L. Ranken, *The Dominion of Australia: An Account of its Foundations* (London, Chapman & Hall, 1874); and Anthony Trollope, *Australia and New Zealand* (London, Chapman & Hall, 1873). For summaries of the Australian experience, see Bolton, *Spoils and Spoilers*; Mellville, *A Plague of Sheep*.

[28] G.3-1877, p. xiii.

internal parasites in check and were the first to be overgrazed. As stock increased and 'these bushes which act as medicines' disappeared, the parasites 'gained the ascendency'.[29] In Australia, salt bush (atriplex species) had been strongly associated with the control of sheep parasites.[30]

It was widely believed that animals had an instinctive sense of the nutrients they required. The vet and witnesses talked of animals developing cravings for particular substances, such as brakgrond (saline ground) or bones (for phosphates), lacking in their diet. The fact that sheep licked brakgrond, which tended to contain salts in very limited quantities, confirmed to Branford that the pasturage was inadequate and deteriorating. He was dubious of its value: animals ingested large quantities of soil which lodged in their intestines, causing painful death. Post-mortems of such animals revealed sand so 'firmly cemented together' that it prevented excretion.[31]

Branford was appalled that people who saw themselves as stockmen, whether Afrikaner or English, could be so callous about their animals. Some farmers did use salt, along with brak bushes, as a preventative and cure for internal parasites. But many admitted that they gave these supplements irregularly. For Branford, salt supplements and dosing were an essential part of systematic stock farming, not an optional ingredient to be administered when the farmer chose or when the sheep showed a craving. Supplements, however, were not an alternative to restoring healthy veld and a pastoral system that allowed valuable plants to recover.

Branford saw the most deeply rooted problem as 'the abominably injurious system of KRAALING'.[32] He drew together the arguments against kraaling in powerful language which suggested a moral imperative to this element of improvement. At the core of his argument was the health risk. Kraaling facilitated the spread of disease of all kinds by bringing animals into huddled contact every night. Scab acari and worms could transfer themselves with little effort; contagious diseases found a perfect environment. Many farmers exacerbated the infectious milieu by allowing the accretion of 'faecal and excrementitious material' in the kraals, so that sheep would literally stand

[29] G.3-1877.

[30] Victoria, *Second Annual Report of the Secretary of Agriculture*. Here fluke was seen as the major problem, and overstocking was associated not so much with desiccation, but with 'trampling' which made 'the surface soil impervious'. Overstocking thus led to an increase in rank 'water-grasses' and and swampy areas which harboured fluke (pp. 150–5). See also *The Veterinarian* (1872), 543; and (1873), 698.

[31] G.54-1879, 6.

[32] G.8-1877, 10. Noble, *Descriptive Handbook*, 259, summarized the environmental arguments against kraaling before the Commission; Noble, *Cape and South Africa*, 159 ff.

4. Sheep Kraal, Karoo, Late Nineteenth Century

knee-deep in dung, especially when it was wet, for 'a night's misery'.[33] If they lay down, manure and mud coated their fleeces. 'How in the name of goodness can health be expected in animals exposed to such influences', Branford expostulated.[34] He revealed his strongly environmental concept of disease transmission by emphasizing that kraals generated 'gaseous matters, and miasma', impure air which affected the blood and tissues.[35] The laws governing control of epidemics, 'so far as they were known', were all being broken.

Direct threats to health, Branford argued, were compounded by less obvious effects on environment and nutrition. By concentrating manure near the farmstead, kraaling deprived the veld of fertilizing material. Admittedly some manure was used for gardens and crops. But this did not help the pastures. The seeds of bushes favoured by sheep were deposited in the kraals rather than on the veld. Perhaps worst of all, the daily trek to and from pastures weakened sheep and destroyed vegetation around the farmhouse and along the routes. The commissioners invoked that evocative word 'tramping' to

[33] G.8-1877, 10.   [34] Ibid. 11.   [35] Ibid.

describe the process: '[t]his system has been carried on to such an extent that farms on which sheep increased rapidly for many years are now almost useless.'[36] Tramping as much as burning denied grasses the opportunity to ripen and shed their seed.

Arguments against kraaling were accepted by improving farmers, who at least tried to disperse kraals around their property. Shepherds did sometimes leave animals out overnight where conditions permitted it. But the commissioners advocated more radical changes: fenced paddocks in which the animals could stay out at nights.[37] Such recommendations had been made at the Cape since the early nineteenth century (Chapter 2). Clearly the British experience of enclosure and rotation was an important reference point; Australian graziers were also fencing rapidly. The 'gradual decadence of some of the best grasses and herbs' was attributed not only to tramping, but also to the failure to rest portions of veld, and farmers' inability to keep their neighbours out.[38]

In fenced paddocks sheep would walk less, graze more evenly, deposit manure and seeds, grow fatter, and yield more wool. The seeds of valuable plants most eaten by the sheep would not only be deposited where they belonged, but, if sections of pasture were rested, would germinate and restore the balance of the veld. 'By this means,' the commissioners affirmed, 'farmers will be able to keep a larger number of sheep on a given quantity of ground, than under the present system.'[39] They recognized that there were dangers in even higher levels of stocking, given that 'overstocking' had 'been carried out to a large extent', especially because of cyclical natural calamities such as droughts and locust plagues. They had little advice to offer on the control of predators which, along with the expense of fencing—and uneasiness about its implications—remained the major reason for kraaling (Chapter 6). But they had no doubt that the key to resolving disease, degradation, and the 'decadence' of sheep farming lay in fenced paddocks.

'To those whose farms are "sheep-sick",' Branford argued, 'I would say, sub-divide, under-stock, and without delay sow.' Most diseases, and particularly worms, could be combated 'by a supply of good sound digestible food, with careful changes of such to the stock, and occasional ordinary use of salt, sulphur and iron compounds'. Farmers had to end the 'present happy-go-lucky, take-your-chance, easy style of living', together with the expectation that 'a panacea [was] to be found in a single dose of medicine forced down the animal's throat'.[40] Healthy flocks required careful management and improved veld.

[36] G.3-1877, p. xxi.   [37] Ranken, *Dominion of Australia*, 80 ff.
[38] G.3-1877, p. xxi.   [39] Ibid., p. xxii.   [40] G.54-1879, 14.

Branford admitted to the limits of knowledge at the time. By the time of his final report he had also acquired a more sophisticated historical sense of Cape pastoral farming, and saw the possibility of cycles of environmental decline followed by partial recovery. This might apply to the pastures of the Albany area, which he had diagnosed as played out, if they were rested: 'the bank of nature' might again 'honour . . . the cheque of her avaricious customers'.[41] He developed a closer knowledge of the physical and economic constraints faced by Cape farmers, recognizing, for example, the difficulties in fencing and forage production in a semi-arid, often mountainous terrain. Like others, Branford hoped that the intensive methods required for ostrich production (and the profits they yielded) might provide the springboard for more general improvement.

Branford's term of office ended, towards the end of 1879, in a bitter wrangle with the government over payment.[42] He stayed on in Cape Town for at least a year after his appointment ended, in an attempt to get the money which he believed was owed to him, and mounted an unsuccessful petition to parliament. Found guilty of fraud in a humiliating court case over a public lottery for a racehorse which he owned, he was struck from the Royal College of Veterinary Surgeons register in 1880.[43] Branford clearly made enemies—like Brown, partly because of his outspoken views as a British expert.

Nevertheless, some of his policy recommendations were followed. A new Contagious Diseases Act, for which he had pressed, was passed in 1881.[44] This gave the government additional powers to restrict the movement of animals in order to combat epizootics. He had also strongly advocated the establishment of an experimental farm so that the particular problems of disease in the eastern Cape could be examined. This materialized quickly at Leeuwfontein, once owned by John Collett, near Fort Beaufort in 1880. Previously considered one of the best sheep farms in the area, it was almost cleared by heartwater. Along with Groot Constantia, the wine farm near Cape Town, it was then the only experimental farm in the colony.[45]

Clearly some of Branford's prescriptions worked, particularly in the prevention of worms and fluke; clearly also, farmers' existing remedies were inadequate. J. A. Burgher, an Afrikaner MLC, perhaps exaggerated in

[41] Ibid. 11.

[42] Cape Archives, Colonial Secretary's Papers, CO 4197, B52, Branford to Colonial Sec., 4 July 1878; CO 4203, B44, B46, B50, B52; CO 4208, B34.

[43] In 1890 he appealed successfully against his conviction. P. J. Posthumus, *Past Veterinarians in South Africa*, vol. 1, A–L, 20 and *The Veterinary Record* (5 Apr. 1890), 543.

[44] Act 2-1881, partly modelled on the revised British legislation of 1878.

[45] There had been government farms early in the century at Groote Post in the western Cape and Somerset East in the eastern Cape.

recalling that 'the advice given by him was so valuable, that it was followed by all the farmers, and in a very short time the fluke disappeared'.[46] But the environmental thinking espoused by Branford and the commissioners reinforced and developed a powerful interpretation of degradation and improvement.

Germ Theory, Veterinary Control, and Transhumance

Veterinary issues remained significant in colonial politics for the next two decades. As the vets gained further knowledge and authority, they were able to translate their approach into public policy. This began to have far-reaching effects on the pastoral economy and social practices, particularly transhumance. The politicization of scientific knowledge grew precisely in relation to the determination by the state, and improving farmers, to act upon it. Yet in the longer term, veterinary views of disease and its control gradually dominated public debate.

Branford was replaced in 1880 by Duncan Hutcheon (b. 1842), who qualified in Edinburgh in 1871 and subsequently worked in Scotland. Hutcheon was immediately landed in a punishing programme of disease fire-fighting, travel, talks, experiments, and post-mortems that demanded huge commitment and energy. For most of the 1880s he was the sole qualified government specialist. Like Branford, he saw his annual reports as a means of publicizing his work and ideas, so that he devoted considerable effort to them. They contain detailed and fluent accounts of his experiences, revealing an acute Victorian rationality and a detective's mind for epidemiological material in this unique southern laboratory.

Hutcheon could also be critical of farmers. In his first attempt to implement the Contagious Diseases Act, to control lungsickness amongst valuable angora goats in 1881, he ordered the slaughter of infected animals. The result was a rash of farmers' meetings 'characterizing [the Act] as being only a futile wrestling against Providence, and likely to prove ruinous to the country'.[47] He did not hide his disdain for those Afrikaner farmers who thought 'that the beginning of the end ha[d] come' because the government ordered the slaughter of 6,000 animals to control the disease.[48]

Hutcheon was, however, more cautious about advocating radical changes in farming and tended to be more diplomatic than Branford and Brown

[46] C.2-1882, evidence, The Hon. J. A. Burgher, MLC, 42.
[47] G.25-1882, *Report of the Colonial Veterinary Surgeon for the period from March 16th 1881 to February 28th 1882*, 42.
[48] Ibid. 42.

before him. His strict Calvinist upbringing gave him a deep knowledge of the Bible, deployed less to castigate farmers than as 'a valuable supplement to a courteous demeanour' in gaining farmers' respect.[49] He survived through the highly politicized 1890s as Chief Veterinary Surgeon over a much expanded service, and subsequently became Director of Agriculture at the Cape.

Hutcheon believed that Branford was incorrect in some of his diagnoses and prescriptions, and this also made him a little more cautious. He had clearly been swept up in the exciting discoveries of germ theory that were gaining widespread acceptance in the veterinary and medical world. It is important not to exaggerate the discontinuities with his predecessor; practitioners often brought an eclectic variety of approaches to different diseases. But whereas Branford's first instincts were to concentrate on worms, pastures, and the muck and miasma of the sheep kraal, Hutcheon first looked for invisible 'viruses' or 'poisons'. He thought that expanding knowledge of contagious diseases was most likely to fill gaps in understanding.[50] The diseases that initially confronted him, notably lungsickness and heartwater, reinforced his position—although in the latter case mistakenly. In addition to immediate slaughter of infected animals, he strongly advocated inoculation.[51]

Hutcheon's first headquarters was at Leeuwfontein experimental farm and, when time was available, he began a series of tests to determine the causes of heartwater. Starting from Branford's conviction that it was linked to internal parasites and a lack of saline ingredients in the veld, he divided a newly introduced flock into two and tried to feed one with supplements. Noting a high infestation of wireworm, he dosed the sheep with salt, saltpetre, and sulphur. This cleared the worms but made little impact on the death rate from heartwater. The symptoms of worm infestation—slow wasting with external swellings—also seemed to differ from the disease he saw. As coastal farmers had argued during the 1877 inquiry, this heartwater, where the liquid was more yellow, affected apparently healthy sheep. It became increasingly clear to him through 1881 that there were two distinct sets of symptoms called heartwater. One was caused by internal parasites. The type he was investigating, the major killer in the coastal districts, was related neither to worms nor malnutrition.

While some farmers had agreed that there was a link between this disease and pasture degradation in 1877, a number in the coastal districts expressed

---

[49] Robert Wallace, *Farming Industries of Cape Colony* (P. S. King & Son, London, 1896), p. vii. Wallace, a fellow Scot, travelled with Hutcheon who was a voracious reader; on the road 'he would tell a humorous story, sing a Scottish ditty, or quote at length from the Bible, Huxley or Herbert Spencer (two of his favourite authors)'.

[50] G.25-1882, 42.   [51] G.52-1881, *Report of the Colonial Veterinary Surgeon for 1880*.

scepticism. Hutcheon was impressed with an article, in the *Grahamstown Journal* in 1881, which pointed out that some denuded farms in the dry Fish river valley were free of heartwater, whereas sheep died on others where pasturage seemed excellent and cattle thrived.[52] The disease seemed to be worse amongst sheep which had grazed in kloofs (steep-sided valleys or ravines); some believed that a shade-loving plant was the cause. Although Hutcheon accepted that other features of the microclimate of kloofs, such as higher levels of moisture, might be a factor, he rejected the explanation that heartwater was caused by a plant.

Like Branford, Hutcheon ignored suggestions from a few leading farmers, such as Jonathan Webb of Albany, that heartwater had followed the spread of the bonte tick, on the grounds that the disease was apparently absent from some tick-infested areas.[53] He came to the conclusion that heartwater was a 'blood disease' caused by a specific virus.[54] It seemed sufficiently similar to anthrax for him—excited by Pasteur's experiments in this field—to import vaccine from France.[55] After two failures at inoculation on the flock at Leeuwfontein, he concluded that heartwater was likely to be distinct. He felt sure, however, that the disease was also 'specific', with a definite incubation period and regular pattern of occurence—and that it was possibly retained in the soil. Anthrax was not a major disease in the Cape, unlike in Australia, possibly because of the prevalence of scavengers that rapidly cleared up the carcasses of dead animals.[56]

Hutcheon was now disturbed that heartwater was 'always . . . associated in men's minds with overstocking'—a legacy of Branford's view.[57] In his report for 1884 he tried to dispel this idea.[58] He was sensitive about Leeuwfontein, where he had now been in charge since 1880 and still had not solved the heartwater mystery. There had been public criticism of model farms during the troubled discussion about the founding of a Department of Agriculture.[59] He was keen to emphasize that the farm's pastures and stock were in excellent condition except for this 'peculiar disease'. The disease, he argued, manifested itself on different types of veld along the coast as far as Natal, as well as inland in some grassland districts. It had 'no connection whatever with exhaustion of the soil' but with some more 'subtle and intangible . . . poison'

[52] G.25-1882, 64.   [53] G.3-1877, 108.   [54] G.25-1882, 66.

[55] A.88-1882, *Supplementary Report by the Colonial Veterinary Surgeon 18.5.1882*.

[56] For anthrax in Australia, Todd, *Colonial Technology*.

[57] G.45-1884, *Report of the Colonial Veterinary Surgeon, 1883*, 78.

[58] G.31-1885, *Report of the Colonial Veterinary Surgeon for the Year 1884*, 42.

[59] C.2-1882, 7, 8, 15. An MLC suggested that the farm had been mismanaged and had failed. He cited Branford's arguments about pasture problems in support of his views.

transmitted by animals themselves.[60] Sheep brought onto Leeuwfontein that survived heartwater were, he maintained, in better condition than most.

This point gave Hutcheon his cue for a more far-reaching criticism of easy assumptions about overstocking. In respect of the coastal and grassland districts, he tended to side with farmers who believed that heavy stocking improved the veld by helping to convert sourveld to more nutritious sweetveld; sheep also deposited phosphates in their comparatively rich dung. If farmers stocked heavily in the wet summer and provided fodder during the leaner winter months, there might be overall gains in the condition of the veld. In sum, Hutcheon did not believe that veld degradation was a general problem in the grassland districts nor a particular cause of heartwater. While he was an enthusiastic advocate of fencing and paddocks, he did not see them as a specific cure for this disease. He did not, however, deny the possibility of overstocking, especially in semi-arid Karoo districts.

The disease nenta in goats was called after a Khoikhoi word associated also with a plant. Potentially lethal when eaten by goats, but less so for sheep, this grew especially on shady, south-facing slopes.[61] The problem for Hutcheon was that he was shown up to ten different plants believed to cause the disease. Thunberg recorded in the eighteenth century that nenta was identified by Khoikhoi informants as a species of the genus zygophyllum—a small bush with yellow or cream flowers.[62] Brown classified the plant thought to cause the symptoms as *Lessertia annularis*, a legume with a pod curved like the new moon.[63] In 1883 MacOwan affirmed this view: 'I have satisfied myself by examination of the contents of the stomach of animals dying from the peculiar disease referred to, that it is the direct cause of the mischief.'[64] Some farmers related the disease to overgrazing, and thought that poisonous veld was less damaging after rain. As noted, poisonous plants were seen to spread in denuded veld—and nenta is still strongly associated with overgrazing.

Hutcheon, however, saw the disease on farms with little of this plant and looked more closely at other species growing on the shady side of ridges in Graaff-Reinet. Working with a farmer who experienced a serious outbreak, he tried to narrow down the causes and find a possible cure. Nenta seemed to be worse if goats became overheated through exercise. For this reason, Hutcheon was sure that kraaling intensified the symptoms: 'if farms were fenced and wild animals destroyed, so that goats could graze at leisure, and be

---

[60] G.31-1885, 44.   [61] G.64-1883, 8; G.31-1885, 29 ff.

[62] Thunberg, *Travels*, 248.   [63] G.3-1877, 185–6.

[64] G.31-1885, 29. Lessertia species are a type of legume, some of which are highly nutritious for small stock.

relieved from the journeys to and from the kraals, the percentage of deaths from this disease would be very small.'[65] In view of the conflicting evidence, he even suggested that everyone might be wrong about the cause of the disease. Noting its similarity to cerebro-spinal meningitis in humans, he felt it might be the result of a virus.

From the mid-1880s Hutcheon's attention was distracted from investigations into these diseases as he became increasingly absorbed in scab eradication campaigns. But in 1890 the recently appointed vet J. F. Soga made a further attempt to isolate the nenta plant by experiment.[66] Jotello Soga, son of Tiyo Soga, the first African presbyterian minister, and his Scottish wife, had trained in Edinburgh and was one of two additional vets appointed in 1889. He was then probably the most senior black official in Cape government service. Despite the fact that he was Xhosa-speaking, Soga found that the Khoikhoi and Xhosa shepherds whom he interviewed were unable to identify any specific plant as the cause. They seemed to apply the term nenta to a range of 'herbal poisons'.[67] Soga did succeed in isolating one plant that produced the nenta symptoms regularly. MacOwan, when he received it for identification, found it to be the *Cotyledon ventricosa*, a type of crassula; he was greatly surprised, because he thought that these succulents did not in general have such toxic properties.[68]

Hutcheon was not intent upon dismissing environmental explanations for all diseases, as is evident from his assessment of nenta. His views gradually became more open on this score and his encounter with stijfziekte (stiffness) and lamziekte (lameness) amongst cattle in the northern Cape is a case in point.[69] In 1884 Hutcheon was called to Colesberg, Kimberley, and Griqualand West to investigate these diseases. Verbal evidence suggested that stijfziekte manifested itself especially in young cattle, in the later part of the winter, before the rains, when grasses were rank and had shed their seeds. Animals suffered stiffness in their forelegs, which prevented them from walking to find food; they died from starvation. Suckling calves were unaffected, nor were mature cattle very susceptible. Farmers distinguished this from lamziekte, where animals suffered paralysis in their hindquarters. They would then lie down, and even if food and drink was brought to them would die within four to eight days. Animals subject to this condition suffered from hard, dry faeces, congested intestines, and impacted rectums.

[65] Ibid. 31.

[66] J. F. Soga, 'Disease "Nenta" in Goats', *Agricultural Journal of the Cape of Good Hope* (29 Jan. 1891), 140.

[67] Thunberg's identification is still recognized as a toxic plant.

[68] Soga, 'Disease "Nenta"'.   [69] G.31-1885, 1.

Explanations of these two afflictions were held up by Hutcheon as further examples of the inadequacy of local knowledge:

There is a very strong opinion amongst the farmers generally, that 'Lam Ziekte' is caused by some poisonous herb or herbs which the cattle pick up in the veld, and in support of this opinion they will tell you that if they allow their cattle to feed on a certain portion of their veld, some of the cattle will manifest the symptoms of the disease directly.[70]

Farmers also noted that animals could recover quickly if moved. Trans-humance in the western Cape had been partly geared to avoid a similar dis-ease (Chapter 1). Hutcheon tested, without success, a number of plants thought to cause the disease. His observations led him in other directions. In Griqualand West cattle displayed a 'craving for bones and all kinds of animal matter', to the extent that they became carnivorous: 'they actually devoured young lambs, eating up greedily every vestige of the carcasses.'[71]

This suggested to Hutcheon that the cattle were suffering from a phos-phate deficiency and other deficiency diseases. The prevalence of serious lamziekte seemed to tie in clearly with a seasonal pattern of dearth, and with periods of drought such as the early 1880s:

At Douglas I met a Mr Wright, who . . . informed me that an old Griqua, whose age was estimated at nearly one hundred years, told him that this disease 'lamziekte' had prevailed as an epizootic over the whole territory of Griqualand West, three times during his life-time, each time carrying off nearly the whole of their cattle, and each visitation of the disease was during an exceptional drought.[72]

For Hutcheon, the answer was clear: most farmers could not understand the evidence of malnutrition when it presented itself. There was probably phos-phate deficiency in the soil of parts of the northern Cape; alternatively, plants could not absorb the phosphates in the soil at certain times of year. Similar deficiencies had been noted in the Ghaap range of the central Karoo and in some sourveld districts—where cattle were prone to the same behaviour. Digestive problems experienced with the disease were, he argued, the result of dry food and the inability of weakened animals to reach water. Suckling calves were immune because they received a balanced diet in milk.

In this case Hutcheon developed a clear environmental explanation of dis-ease. His solutions were also straightforward. Rather than transhumance, animals needed phosphates in the shape of bonemeal, widely used in the United States. 'There is a vast amount of wealth in the shape of valuable phosphates, given to the aasvogels [vultures]', he argued, 'and other

<hr>

[70] Ibid. 10.   [71] Ibid. 1.   [72] Ibid. 4.

unremunerative consumers . . . which might easily be collected.'[73] Fodder, such as maize stalks, or cut grass in dryer districts would also help. In fact his explanation was later revised by Arnold Theiler, Director of Veterinary Research in the Transvaal and Union. After a long period of investigation Theiler concluded that stijfziekte and lamziekte were names applied to a number of discrete diseases. Farmers were correct in that one type was linked to a poisonous plant. Another resulted from deficiencies in certain pastures, which induced a craving for bones and animal remains. In turn, bacteria ingested from rotting animal matter, rather than phosphate deficiency itself, caused the symptoms of the disease.[74] Nevertheless, Hutcheon's recommendations were influential in shaping farmers' strategies.

In 1882–3 Hutcheon was called on to deal with an outbreak of redwater among cattle that, along with scab in sheep, led him to develop a highly critical approach to trekking or transhumance. He did not know the cause of redwater, and he did not attribute it primarily to environmental change. His emphasis was more on the need for veterinary controls that had significant implications for pastoral practices and environmental management.

One major early confrontation over transhumance took place, before disease became an issue, in the western and northern districts. Here there had been a regular pattern of movement by Boer stockowners between the higher, cold mountain areas (the Hantam, Roggeveld, and Bokkeveld) and the state-owned 'trekvelden' in the arid Karoo, used for winter grazing on a partially communal basis (Chapter 1). 'Baster' and Khoikhoi groups also used these state lands. In the 1860s the Cape government surveyed and rented or sold sections of the trekvelden. The parcels of land alienated were centred on water sources such as vleis and fountains, which were then removed from more general seasonal access.

Officials supporting the policy explicitly argued that the government should derive some income from the large tracts of Crown land that had been available for minimal payments. Civil commissioners in the 1860s reported that common access to the trekvelden produced 'constant bickerings'. Long-term leases or private property would resolve such conflicts. Moreover, officials believed that such restrictions would stimulate investment in water provision, obviating the need to migrate.[75] In justifying the policy against

---

[73] Ibid. 13.

[74] Hutcheon himself realized by the 1890s that these names probably applied to more than one disease. *Agricultural Journal of the Union of South Africa*, 1: 1 (1911), 10–28; *Agricultural Journal*, 3: 4 (1912), 463–78, 639–50; 4: 1 (1912), 1–56: Dr. A Theiler, 'Facts and Theories about Stijfziekte and Lamziekte'. Union of South Africa, *Department of Agriculture, Report with Appendices for the Year Ended 1919*, U.G.40-1919, 15.

[75] Cape of Good Hope, *Blue Book, 1859*, JJ.3–4, Report of the Civil Commissioner, Calvinia.

critics, John X. Merriman later noted that 'as the colony has advanced, the country has been taken up, and people have had to pay for what they formerly used for nothing'.[76] In commenting on the resulting social problems, Cecil Rhodes asked: 'Don't you think that a great deal of the distress is caused by men acquiring land who should rather be servants than masters?'[77]

By the 1870s officials were convinced that the policy was successful; sheep numbers in these arid districts increased rapidly. The costs for farmers who had depended on seasonal movement were seen to be offset by an overall increase in production, colonial wealth, and government revenues. The critique of transhumance dwelt initially on these classical Victorian motifs of improvement, investment, and the benefits of settled agriculture. To these motifs botanists and progressive farmers had added concerns about tramping and vegetation change. The vets extended the argument to the role of trekking in spreading disease.

Transhumance was not a uniform practice; the reasons for moving animals varied between areas and changed over time. In the recently colonized inland border districts of the eastern Cape, such as Queenstown, some farmers, including English-speakers, trekked to the wetter coastal districts during the cold dry winters when their grass was rank and unpalatable; pasture as much as water was the key factor. This pattern of stock movement became increasingly bound up, by the 1860s and 1870s, with the expanding ox-wagon trade to the Free State, Kimberley, and the Transvaal and also with the carriage of wool. By the 1870s around 40 million pounds of wool was usually exported annually (Table 4.1), much of it moved long distances overland to the eastern Cape ports. This probably required over ten thousand wagon journeys of greatly differing lengths, some taking weeks, and requiring at least sixteen oxen each. Perhaps half the wool trade, and a great deal of other business from the Transkei and Free State, came to East London. Railways only made a significant impact in displacing long-distance wagon carriage from the late 1880s.

Problems in sheep farming persuaded a number of farmers, and especially their sons, to turn their attention to transport riding, or kurveying. The number of oxen recorded in the Cape censuses rose from 249,000 to 422,000 between 1865 and 1875. The bulk of the increase was in the eastern Cape— either in districts where sheep had been lost, or on the main transport corridor from East London via Queenstown to Aliwal North. Although they were slow, oxen were cheaper than horses, and did not require special fodder. The very dependence of the ox-wagon trade on the veld created new resource

---

[76] A.20-1883, Cape of Good Hope, *Report of the Select Committee on Calvinia Distress*, 17.
[77] A.20-1883, 13.

problems. Transport riders tried to time their trips to East London to coincide with the dry winter months, when grazing was at a premium in the interior but higher rainfall kept the coastal grass softer.[78]

Redwater had appeared in the 1870s and returned in a virulent form in 1882 around Kingwilliamstown and East London. Hutcheon was convinced that the disease 'was spread mostly by means of transport'.[79] He attempted to impose the 1881 Contagious Diseases Act in order to prohibit the movement of animals in and out of proclaimed zones of infection.[80] He also advocated that farmers—especially those along transport corridors—should fence their farms to prevent access by passing animals in search of grazing.

Hutcheon's measures had serious implications for the patterns of trekking and transport in the Border districts. While these were now in step with a commercial economy, any movement of stock was potentially hazardous in spreading disease. Hutcheon was again faced by an outcry. As a result the government appointed the Redwater Commission in 1882.[81] Economic arguments lay at the heart of opposition to the imposition of restrictions. William Snyman, farmer and chairman of the Komgha Afrikaner Bond, captured the essence of the problem: 'people must travel in this country and must outspan.'[82] As H. A. Brown of Cathcart argued, 'I make my living with the oxen'. Farmers and kurveyors (a number were both) would lose both income and animals if they had to keep them inland in winter without expensive fodder.[83] For them, redwater deaths, in any case unpredictable, were a reasonable risk. Farmers had long lived with livestock diseases.

Confusion about the nature of redwater made it difficult for Hutcheon to win the argument. The disease was thought to have come from the United States, where it was known as Texas or Spanish fever. Endemic in Texas, it had spread to other southern states and even the midwest, partly because of the huge traffic in cattle between the southern prairies and Chicago meat markets.[84] Redwater had been associated with ticks, but veterinary and specialist opinion in the United States—where the profession was far more developed than in South Africa—remained sceptical about this link. Branford had attributed it to 'impoverished pastures' and burning.[85] William Snyman told

[78] G.3-1877, 21, evidence T. Wiggle, Klipplaat/Whittlesea.

[79] G.64-1883, 62.   [80] Act 2-1881, clause 5.

[81] G.85-1883, Cape of Good Hope, *Commission of Inquiry into the Disease Among Cattle known as Redwater*.

[82] Ibid. 182–3.   [83] Ibid. 152–3.

[84] Smithcors, *The American Veterinary Profession*, 436 ff.

[85] Cape Archives, CO 4193, B4, Colonial Veterinary Surgeon to Colonial Secretary, 9 Jan. 1877.

the 1883 Commission: 'I think that Redwater is just as unintelligible as Heartwater in sheep [and] it will be sure to come in the course of time.'[86] Hutcheon was sure that it was a predictable, infectious disease, either transmitted directly between animals or through food, water, or excretion. It was most virulent in hotter, wetter districts and seasons.

Although Hutcheon was unsuccessful in his attempts to develop a vaccine, farmers did have some success in 'salting' oxen by inserting infectious matter under their skins, usually on the tail. Animals that survived such inoculation could traverse infected areas without risk. This reinforced the hand of transport riders who wished to keep routes open. Even John Frost, MLA for Queenstown, and generally an ardent progressive in favour of stringent controls over sheep movement for scab control, had doubts about control of trekking in this case. Supporting his constituents, he noted that cattle were 'at their very best' on the coast in the dry winter when they languished inland: 'men will run enormous risks in order to bring their bullocks out to ride transport.'

Hutcheon failed to impose the Contagious Diseases Act in 1883. He criticized farmers who simply wanted a cure for their immediate problems without any concerted effort and discipline. 'I entirely differ from this view,' he argued, 'and consider that it is not only a misconception of the true aim of medical science, but it is also a grave error in theology. The commission which man received was, "To replenish the earth and subdue it".' If disease was to be controlled and calamities avoided it was essential for 'scientific men' like himself 'to discover the forces in Nature with which man has to contend, by patient enquiry', and act upon this information across a broad front.[87] It seemed to Hutcheon that enough was known about redwater to justify tight regulations around all infected areas. Instead, 'the Colony settled down in perfect contentment, preferring, as was loudly expressed, to *have* the disease rather than submit to the restrictions'.[88]

For a couple of years redwater was largely restricted to the coastal districts. In 1885, during a wet summer, the disease spread inland as far as Queenstown. Farmers themselves became worried as the foci of infection multiplied, and more stringent measures were accepted. Stock from the Transkeian districts, which, being close to the coast, were seriously affected, were denied entry to the colony. Farmers along the main transport routes fenced more quickly in order to separate their cattle from passing teams. Hutcheon was now sceptical that he could control the disease, and half

---

[86] G.85-1883, 182–3.   [87] G.45-1884, 39.
[88] G.26-1886, *Report of the Colonial Veterinary Surgeon for the Year 1885*, 32.

wished that farmers should stew in their own infectious juices. In 1891 the disease spread as far as Aliwal North and Barkly East, where redwater had not been reported before.[89] Only the onset of winter drought and frost contained it.

In 1892 Hutcheon reported on experiments in Texas that conclusively demonstrated the link between redwater and ticks.[90] Newly aware of the significance of ticks as vectors, the vets soon became convinced that heartwater in sheep was also a tick-borne disease, as had been suggested in 1877. The Cape Department of Agriculture was now securely established and research was no longer dependent on a few overstretched vets. Charles Lounsbury, who arrived in 1895 from the United States as Government Entomologist, made detailed investigations into 'the life history and habits of the notorious bont tick' that spread heartwater.[91]

Conflicts over the state's attempts to control livestock movements came to a head over scab in sheep. While the affliction did not kill directly, it debilitated animals and greatly reduced wool yield and quality. The 1877 commissioners were sure that scab was as important as worms, more so, in retarding production. Vets knew the cause of scab to be tiny mites or acari, scarcely visible to the naked eye, which burrowed into the sheep's skin causing encrusted sores and loss of wool. This was widely accepted amongst the anglophone farmers, together with some Afrikaners. Scab had followed sheep globally, and there was a copious literature on its treatment. Natal introduced the first scab legislation in 1865, and Cape farmers had experimented over some decades with dipping or washing their animals in tobacco and chemical solutions. Yet treatment was of limited value as long as diseased animals could be moved at will.

Movement of livestock was of such importance to many sheep farmers, especially Afrikaners in the dryer northern and western Karoo districts, that agreement could not be reached in the Cape parliament on compulsory controls. Scab Acts were frequently discussed, but the measures passed in 1874 and 1886 were permissive. In the latter case, farmers in a specific district had to agree to implementation before the legislation was proclaimed. Farmers' associations in twenty-six districts, largely in the midland and eastern Cape, were enthusiastic about such restrictions, as many were attempting to keep their flocks 'clean'. They could find a sufficient majority to override the

---

[89] *Agricultural Journal* (24 Mar. 1891), 194, and (7 May 1891), 201.

[90] Ibid. (10 Mar. 1892), 202 seems to be the first report in the Cape. See ibid. (19 Apr. 1894) for a systematic account of the research.

[91] Ibid. (23 Nov. 1897): Charles P. Lounsbury, 'The Bont Tick', 728–42, quote from p. 729.

opposition of others. The implication of the law was that flocks could only be moved to and from proclaimed districts if a scab inspector had certified them as clean. Disease regulation created a bureaucracy and increasing surveillance that were anathema to opponents of the Act.

Some Afrikaners, and not only uneducated livestock owners in remote districts, disputed the very cause of the disease. Many associated it closely with drought and degraded veld, because animals became more susceptible when in poor condition. The word poverty was often applied in relation to unhealthy sheep at this time. Transhumance to better pasture was thus closely linked in their minds with combating scab, rather than spreading it. J. A. van Zyl, MLA for Barkly, stated categorically to an 1884 Select Committee that 'drought . . . is the cause of scab'.[92] If scab was caused in this way, by environmental conditions, it followed that the disease was not infectious. Some believed it to be 'spontaneous', in that it seemed to appear in the absence of any contact with scabby flocks. Spokesmen such as D. P. van der Heever, MLC for the northern Cape district of Albert, who emerged as a key mobilizer against scab controls, added the explanation that sheep suffering from hunger ate 'obnoxious herbs, which affect the blood, causing heat in the system, and thus bringing out scab'.[93] He felt that it was impossible for farmers, especially poorer farmers, to keep their flocks clean, not least because of the cost of dipping and the unpredictability of the disease. If movement was restricted to flocks clear of scab, those who most needed to move their sheep would be prohibited from doing so.

Hutcheon was convinced of the priority of scab controls, and this absorbed an increasing amount of his time from the mid-1880s. Fuelled by his powerful belief in science, he took his microscope on the road, demonstrating specimens of acari, religiously taken from local sheep, to curious but suspicious Afrikaners at country hotels and farms.[94] For Hutcheon, the microscope had the power of explanation—though he by no means convinced all of his audiences. In this context, the Scab Disease Commission, which took exhaustive evidence over eighteen months (1892–4), in preparation for colony-wide compulsory legislation, 'became an educating medium' as well as an inquiry.[95] Initially under the chairmanship of John Frost, until he was appointed Minister for Agriculture, it took pains to provide full interpretation of questions and answers, in Dutch where necessary. Its published report and

[92] A.5-1884, *Report of the Select Committee on the Scab Bill*, 38.   [93] Ibid. 59.

[94] G.14-1887, *Report by the Colonial Veterinary Surgeon for the Year 1886* (G.14-1887).

[95] G.1-1894, 2; a detailed discussion of the disputes over scab is to be published by Mottie Tamarkin, provisionally entitled 'Volk and Flock—Ecology, Culture, Identity, and Politics among Cape Sheep Farmers in the Late Nineteenth Century'.

evidence (736 pages and appendices) must have been one of the longest ever issued as a Cape parliamentary paper.

What the commissioners heard was by no means always encouraging. Dipping, they were told, 'hurts the sheep more than the scab', and it was 'against the nature of a sheep to be made wet by dipping'.[96] Some said they had insufficient water for dipping. F. J. van Zyl of Dordrecht averred that he would prefer to sell off everything he possessed rather than be instructed on how to farm by a young sheep inspector.[97] Even some English-speakers who believed that scab was caused by acari, and that infected sheep could spread the mites, inveighed against restrictions on movement and the powers of officials. An Afrikaner near Cathcart summed up the feelings of many: 'my greatest objection is that we cannot move our sheep about, and this is ruinous to the sheep farmers.'

An 1894 Act instituting compulsory scab control was passed by Rhodes's government, with qualified support from leaders of the Afrikaner Bond, who were then his political allies. The Bond was close to splitting over scab control in the mid-1890s, and was perhaps saved from this fate partly by the Jameson Raid in 1896. Although there proved to be many loopholes in the legislation, it reinforced the slow changes that were manifest in pastoral practice—most notably the gradual shift away from transhumance. The Union government, after 1910, pursued a similar strategy with strong commitment. Barney Enslin, the Boer war general who became Chief Inspector of Sheep, saw the movement of small stock as a 'burning issue', both because the main trek routes were 'prolific sources of scab' and because of 'destruction of the veld'.[98]

Restrictions on movement controlled the spread of disease, but dipping proved to be the most effective means of eradicating both scab and tick-borne diseases. It took considerable experimentation before a completely effective dip against redwater was found.[99] Compulsory dipping of cattle for east coast fever, which Lounsbury also played a major role in identifying as a tick-borne disease, finally brought redwater under control in the early decades of the twentieth century.[100] Dipping of sheep for scab was not, initially, very effective against heartwater, but in the longer term it probably had more impact on livestock diseases than any other measure.

[96] G.1-1894, 392: evidence J. D. Naude, Barkly East.   [97] Ibid. 406.
[98] See Department of Agriculture reports for the 1910s, e.g. U.G.2-1915, *Union of South Africa, Report of the Department of Agriculture, 1913–14*, 64, 83.
[99] *Agricultural Journal* (9 June 1898), 696 ff.; Smithcors, *American Veterinary Profession*, 449–50.
[100] Cranefield, *Science and Empire*.

The first two Colonial Veterinary Surgeons at the Cape tried, in a context where professional knowledge was very limited, to develop diagnoses, preventative measures, and treatments for an extraordinary range of animal diseases. Both learnt a great deal from farmers and, more indirectly—largely through farmers—from African and former Khoikhoi farmworkers. Both, however, tried to systematize this information in the light of their British professional training and in a way that was sometimes at odds with local knowledge.

Although Branford and Hutcheon experienced opposition, the expanding veterinary service had a powerful platform for their views within the government and amongst improving farmers.[101] Their links were initially more with English-speakers and relatively anglicized members of the Afrikaner elite. But there is no doubt that their views were widely influential. Hutcheon wrote numerous articles for the *Agricultural Journal*, launched soon after the Department of Agriculture in 1889, which had a circulation of about 6,000— probably more than all but a few of the largest urban daily newspapers. Soga and other vets worked in African districts and the veterinary legislation was increasingly applied throughout the Cape. The service was greatly extended to over twenty professionals in 1897 to cope with the rinderpest epizootic, and eventual success with inoculation reinforced veterinary authority.[102]

Branford, drawing on existing discourse at the Cape, was sensitive to environmental explanations and conservationist solutions. While he was clearly wrong about the causes of particular animal diseases, there are many echoes in subsequent decades of the formulations which he and the 1877 Commission developed. His approach was holistic, although it was also highly interventionist. Hutcheon's strong conviction about the validity of germ theory led him to look more discretely at each disease. In making his career at the Cape, he was able to observe and investigate over a longer period. While he did not rule out environmental causes, he was more cautious about the general links between disease and veld degradation. His approach suggested different methods of treatment, leading to experiments—at first largely unsuccessful—with vaccines. Occasionally his expectation that viruses caused disease led him to underestimate the importance of ecological factors, especially insect vectors. The major breakthroughs at the Cape in the late nineteenth century came as much from an expanded understanding of tick-borne diseases as of viruses.

---

[101] *Agricultural Journal, passim.*

[102] For the expansion of the Veterinary Service, see Dan Gilfoyle, 'Veterinary Science and Public Policy at the Cape Colony, 1877–1910', unpublished D.Phil. thesis, University of Oxford (2002).

Yet Hutcheon's overall perception of the imperatives of improvement were not greatly different from those of Branford. His experiences with redwater and scab led to an increasing impatience with transhumance, trekking with oxen, and kraaling. He was certain that these practices spread disease and undermined any possibility of control. Investigations into lamziekte convinced him of the need for more careful grazing management as well as fodder supplements. In discussing diseases of sheep, he argued that 'farms must be fenced—a portion of veld reserved for winter-grazing—and shelter, with some artificially preserved food, provided for ewes and lambs'.[103] And he made clear links between good pasture and good health. The legislative measures and administrative interventions which he became skilled in framing during twenty-seven years of government service gave a significant momentum to the transformation of livestock farming. Universal dipping and control over stock movements was a formidable administrative and political task in a dispersed and socially fractured colonial society.

These veterinary prescriptions and interventions, implying changes in both the physical and social landscape of rural districts, are reminiscent of late nineteenth-century medical concerns about sanitation and contagion, which hardened the trend towards urban segregation in the Cape.[104] Animal diseases did not provoke quite the same type of social neuroses. And there is little suggestion in the writings of the vets during the 1870s and 1880s that fears about stock disease led to segregationist demands. Insofar as black-owned stock were mentioned in the 1877 Commission, their condition was usually viewed neutrally or with some favour. One farmer in the Border area wryly suggested that African sheep thrived because, being less susceptible to theft, their owners did not have to kraal them so frequently.[105] But ideas about sanitation and animal health were prominent in justifying other forms of spatial reorganization and separation: notably attempts to separate the sheep from the kraals; and, as a corollary, the fencing of farms and of paddocks or camps within them.

In this sense arguments about animal health were a significant, although by no means the only, factor in the tightening of the Cape's still fluid internal boundaries. As social and environmental changes subtly reinforced each other, farm boundaries became more definitively expressed. The movements of people and animals were curtailed, or redirected. At a later stage, the issue

---

[103] G.45-1884, 79.

[104] M. Swanson, ' "The Sanitation Syndrome": Bubonic Plague and Urban Native Policy in the Cape Colony, 1900–1909', *Journal of African History*, 18 (1977); Harriet Deacon, 'Racial Segregation and Medical Discourse in Nineteenth-Century Cape Town', *JSAS* 22: 2(1996).

[105] G.3-1877, 149, evidence B. Bowker; see also 145, evidence J. Landrey.

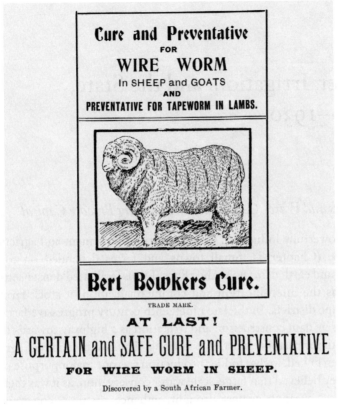

5. Wireworm Cure, 1908

of animal diseases came into play more centrally in attempts to regulate tenancy, as well as define boundaries between white and black.

The early vets saw improved pasturage as essential both for increasing numbers and restoring the health of the flocks and herds. And they considered that well-managed flocks could contribute to the maintenance of healthy veld. Treatment of individual animals was not generally considered economically justified, and they concentrated on general prophylactic measures with some success. Whereas many farmers found disease a barrier in building up stock numbers in the late nineteenth century, this constraint increasingly fell away in the early decades of the twentieth century. It is an irony that the impact of veterinary interventions in the longer term was to contribute to overstocking and soil erosion.

5

Water, Irrigation, and the State, 1880–1930

Farmers and Water Conservation: Applying Private Capital

Water powerfully influenced patterns of rural settlement and agriculture in the Cape (Chapter 2). Small towns and farms depended on fountains, streams, and earth dams up to the 1870s. Dams facilitated denser settlement, as well as the intensification and commercialization of stock farming, in many Cape districts. In the late nineteenth century progressive farmers and officials saw dam construction and irrigation as a highway towards development both for pastoral and arable farming. The two branches of agriculture were often linked, in that fodder production was one major purpose of irrigation. They believed that large-scale water conservation, as it was then called, would be a weapon against drought, enhance pastures, constrain transhumance, expand exports, and ensure that meat markets were fully supplied. In their minds, wise usage of water was closely linked to the conservation of watersheds, of vegetation, and afforestation.

By the early twentieth century, however, the state's technical imagination had hardly materialized in major projects—especially when compared to the United States and other parts of the British empire. Worster has challenged perceptions of the American west as a highly individualist, frontier society by pointing to the scale of corporate investment in water provision. His model of a hydraulic society, if it is indeed valid for the western United States, could not easily be applied to South Africa at this time.[1] The vast majority of investment had been by private landowners on their own land or for local use by bodies such as municipalities and missions. It was only in the 1920s that big dams came on stream, and even then they made little immediate impact on the extent of irrigated land.

[1] Donald Worster, *Rivers of Empire: Water, Aridity, and the Growth of the American West* (Pantheon Books, New York, 1985); for a critique Donald J. Pisani, *To Reclaim a Divided West: Water, Law, and Public Policy, 1848–1902* (University of New Mexico Press, Albuquerque, 1992).

This chapter sketches private water development on Cape farms, especially in the Karoo, and analyses the early years of state involvement. Many factors were at work in restricting corporate irrigation. One was the lack of suitable terrain for big dams. In 1929, at the end of the period discussed here, the Director of Irrigation in the Union emphasized this environmental point: 'the essential trouble is that our mountains are not high enough to hold perpetual snow and our plains are not low enough to . . . build up extensive alluvial flats.'[2] Water came off most watersheds too quickly, there were few ideal dam sites, and the valleys they could serve were too narrow, or infertile. This proved to be the major reason for the lack of dams on the largest river in the country, the Gariep, until the 1960s, when water could be led by tunnel to alluvial flats hundreds of kilometres away in the midlands.

The lack of corporate projects also reflected the absence of a sophisticated state bureaucracy, the costs relative to the markets available, and suspicion of state control. Cape law enshrined particularly strong rights for landowners over the water on their property. On the one hand, this gave individual farmers more incentive to invest; on the other, it made joint action difficult. Moreover, the first two Directors of the colony's irrigation service, established in 1903, backed individual enterprise on large commercial farms. Although irrigation did become bound up with attempts to attract British immigrants in closer settlement schemes, and to address the Afrikaner poor-white problem, such developments gained momentum largely after Union.

The Cape government did not entirely neglect irrigation. In 1875 John Gamble was appointed as Hydraulic Engineer. An Irrigation Act of 1877, piloted through the legislature by John X. Merriman, Commissioner of Crown Lands and Public Works, provided for combined action by farmers to construct water storage works. In addition to Gamble's expertise, farmers were offered favourable interest rates on loans from the state.[3] Although the Act stimulated some works, and within ten years £54,000 had been advanced, the bigger project of facilitating irrigation districts proved largely abortive.

Most farmers were uneasy about taking major loans. Under the legislation, irrigation repayments would take precedence over other debts. Fears were articulated that dams would silt up before the twenty-four-year span for interest payments was complete.[4] Some Afrikaners linked this legislation

---

[2] Union of South Africa, *Report of the Director of Irrigation for the Period 1st April 1928 to 31st March 1929*, U.G.9-1930.

[3] Merriman also served as chair of the *Select Committee appointed to Consider and Report on the Irrigation Act*, A.8-1879.

[4] Cape of Good Hope, *Preliminary Report and Proceedings of the Irrigation Commission (Part I)*, G.80-1883, p. vi.

with other forms of state intervention, taxation, progressivism, and the entry of 'vreemde menschen' (strangers) into their settlements.[5] Yet it was not simply farmers' caution that undermined the Act. The bureaucratic processes proved painfully slow.[6] Gamble's office turned down some applicants because they were seen as having insufficient security, or were tenants rather than owners of land. Applicants from the dry, largely Afrikaner, northern Cape district of Calvinia were refused on the grounds that they were too indebted already or that they were 'holders of unproductive farms'.[7]

On its side, the government soon realized that even a system of loans would inevitably entail considerable costs. When Gamble left state employ after a decade, security on some loans was found to be insufficient and they could not be fully redeemed from insolvent farmers.[8] Municipal water schemes, such as the highly contested project to increase supplies in Graaff-Reinet, had also run into financial difficulties.[9] The two major projects established under the Act were both in the western Cape, where landholdings were smaller and shared action more essential in fruit and wine districts. In 1893 the Act was extended to allow applications from individual farmers, and the rate of engagement increased.

Some leading progressive farmers argued that state involvement was essential. John Parkes at Wheatlands, in the Camdeboo, was one of the most successful livestock farmers in the midlands and built a weir on the Melk river for irrigated vines in the 1860s. By the time he gave evidence to the Irrigation Commission set up in 1883, he found that the water supply was too irregular and the channels were silting. While he agreed that it was essential for farmers to build small earth dams for stock, big state projects were needed: 'no dam should be constructed unless it was of such extent as to be a national work, similar to those in India.'[10] J. A. de Wet, MLA for Somerset East, suggested that farmers would be happier paying the government for water than taking on the responsiblity for works themselves.[11]

However, where the government did take the initiative, at van Wyk's Vley in the arid Carnarvon district, long troubled by drought distress, major problems were experienced: the rainfall was too low to fill the dam adequately; the dam was too shallow, so that evaporation rates were high; and the irrigator's

---

[5] Nell, 'Farmers, the State, and Livestock Enumeration', 61, 64.

[6] Cape of Good Hope, Report of the Hydraulic Engineer for the Year 1881, G.20-1882.

[7] Nell, 'Farmers, the State, and Livestock Enumeration', 59, quoting Gamble.

[8] Cape of Good Hope, Report of the Chief Inspector of Public Works for 1886, G.31-1887.

[9] Smith, From Frontier to Midlands, ch. 8: 'The Politics of Water'.   [10] G.80-1883, 42.

[11] Ibid. 136: evidence S. Stackard; see also evidence J. A. de Wet and A. Essex.

arch-enemy, salinization, plagued the project from the start.[12] Robert Wallace, Professor of Agriculture and Rural Economy at the University of Edinburgh, who reported on the Cape in 1896, considered it a 'white elephant'.[13] The diversion of the Carnarvon river into the dam in 1888 increased flow a little, and a small irrigation colony was established in the longer term. A municipal scheme in Beaufort West was more successful in irrigating one-morgen smallholdings, but siltation was so rapid that the municipality could not repay its debt to the government.

Even Cecil Rhodes was unable to persuade the Cape government to undertake major works in his parliamentary constituency to dam the Harts river in the 1880s. The London Missionary Society, with the support of a Christian Tswana chief, Jantjie Mothibi, had co-ordinated the construction of an amibitious dam in the 1850s but it was bypassed in a flood within a couple of years.[14] Gamble, together with Kimberley's resident engineer, proposed a new scheme in 1882 and Rhodes saw it as an opportunity to increase both food supplies to Kimberley and local employment. The government, however, was cautious about the project, partly because it implied removing Tswana settlements in the Harts valley.

By and large, landowners in the livestock farming areas continued to make provision for themselves. Small earth dams for livestock were relatively inexpensive to construct. Although doubts about the returns on investment into irrigation were consistently aired at this time, a significant number of farmers committed themselves to major water storage or distribution works with increasing enthusiasm. Amongst the leading English-speaking progressive farmers, Parkes was in a minority even in 1883. He would surely have articulated a different position if he had seen his farm in 1910, when 700 acres of the 24,000 morgen were irrigated for cultivation, helping to sustain 900 ostriches, 5,000 merinos, and 5,000 angoras as well as 13 acres of vines.[15] It was one of the largest operations in the colony.

Undoubtedly the key economic factor stimulating irrigation was the burgeoning trade in ostrich feathers. Ostrich numbers increased from 22,000 in 1875 to 260,000 in 1899 and 726,000 in 1911. Feather exports rose from an inconsequential amount, largely from wild ostriches, in 1860 to 793,000 pounds, worth £2.1 million, in 1909 (Fig. I. 4). Their export value had nearly caught up with wool, which weighed one hundred times more for the same

---

[12] Cape of Good Hope, *Reports upon the Reservoir and Irrigable Lands at van Wyks Vley, by Garwood Alston, G. L. S., Bailiff of the Estate, and Professor P. D. Hahn, Ph.D.*, G.49-1888.

[13] Wallace, *Farming Industries*, 426.

[14] Shillington, 'Irrigation, Agriculture and the State'.   [15] Playne, *Cape Colony*, 374.

value. Higher costs of production were offset by high prices and low transport costs.

Ostriches were difficult to herd and hence to farm on an extensive basis.
Certainly they benefited from periods on the natural veld, and many farmers
did put them out. But it was more efficient to enclose flocks in a paddock and
provide them with fodder. Lucerne proved most effective, with prickly pear
as a supplement. Lucerne in turn necessitated irrigation, which was a major
reason why Oudtshoorn, well watered from streams running down from the
Swartberg mountains, became the major centre of ostrich production. In
wetter districts such as Albany, Uitenhage, and Somerset East, three of the
largest ostrich-producing areas, irrigation was not so essential. Ostrich feathers matured best in a crisp, dry atmosphere, so that this combination of
irrigated fodder and semi-arid terrain was the optimum. Many farms further
inland, in the midlands, also had their ostrich pens, with patches of lucerne
where this was possible.

Lucerne, originally a Middle Eastern domesticate, spread widely through
Europe as a cultivated fodder crop and became of great importance in the
intensification of agriculture in the early modern era.[16] It was cultivated
around Grahamstown and Graaff-Reinet by the early 1860s, and from there
it was taken to Oudtshoorn. Lucerne gave a higher yield and protein content
than grain crops grown for fodder. Once established, it was a perennial crop,
so that annual sowings were unnecessary. The soil in Oudtshoorn proved
especially suitable; one planting could last for longer than the seven years
advocated by crop experts. Soil fertility was enhanced by the decaying roots
of this legume and by the dung of the grazing animals. Over the longer term,
fertilized in this way, it was found that the plants tended to produce more leaf
and less seed. Lucerne could also be harvested for hay. A 'miracle crop' for the
Cape, its only disadvantage was that it required a great deal of water.[17]

In their water projects from the 1870s farmers used a variety of techniques,
often more than one, depending upon the physical opportunities and capital
available. The most ambitious built larger storage dams. Construction technology improved in the later decades of the nineteenth century: the dried,
moulded cattle hides on which earth was piled in the early years were
replaced by wooden scraping boxes, and then wheeled scrapers—though
these still had to be pulled by oxen or equines. As an intermediate solution,
those with riparian properties constructed less expensive weirs in order to
divert floods onto their lands. On the flat pans of the north-west, they

[16] Mauro Ambrosoli, *The Wild and the Sown: Botany and Agriculture in Western Europe, 1350–
1850* (Cambridge University Press, Cambridge, 1997).
[17] Wallace, *Farming Industries*, 110 ff.

extended historic saaidams. Where wood was available for fuel, some developed river pumping systems and, by the 1890s, they increasingly sunk boreholes.

Charles Rubidge developed his works on Wellwood, employing contractors to build and maintain five earth-and-stone dams.[18] Lacking a natural stream from which to fill them, Rubidge had an 'arm' or furrow, a few kilometres long, dug at the base of, and parallel to, a long escarpment. Water washing down the slope could collect in the arm and flow into the dams. W. C. Scully, the Cape official and writer, recalled his visits to Wellwood in the 1870s when he was assistant magistrate at Graaff-Reinet. Even though the works were then not complete, he wrote of 'the large mansion which seemed to exude hospitality from every pore', 'embowered in trees' on a 'waterless plain', and the 'ingenious' system of dams whereby 'the torrents, instead of being allowed to hurtle down, laden with valuable alluvium to the all-absorbing oceans were conserved for man's use'.[19] As an old man Rubidge described the works briefly to the Irrigation Commission in 1883, and declared that 'if the whole Colony had been as much improved as my farm, we should have been ten times as rich as we now are'.[20]

In 1888 Charles's son, Richard (the new proprietor), put a small number of breeding fish in the largest dam. Nine years later, when herons were found eating them in a drought, the lake was dragged with a tennis net, hundreds of fish were caught, and redistributed to better filled dams. This ensured a fish supply for many years afterwards.[21] Regular meals of carp were not unusual on the more developed Karoo farms. A photograph from the 1890s shows a rowing boat—an unlikely recreational pursuit in this semi-arid zone.[22]

The major function of the Rubidge dams was to provide a water source for livestock and for increasingly ambitious crop and fodder production. Stud rams were given a higher proportion of fodder, including lucerne, than other sheep. Although sheep remained the mainstay of the farm, ostriches were introduced in the 1870s. Dams watered the orange grove, planted in the 1860s, the flower and kitchen garden, including almond and mango trees (Chapter 9). With a rainfall of only 13 inches, Richard Rubidge grew barley, wheat, oats, maize, and lucerne. At their most extensive, the irrigated fields on this fountainless farm covered over 100 acres (about 40 ha), although they were not all used at one time. A report in 1910 perhaps exaggerated in

[18] Rubidge papers, Wellwood diaries, *passim*.
[19] Ibid., typescript extract from reminiscences by William Charles Scully.
[20] G.80-1883, 28.
[21] Rubidge papers, Wellwood farm, 'Extracts and Notes from Wellwood diary, 1845 to 1892', by Richard Rubidge.
[22] Ibid., photographs. The arrival of a boat is recorded on 18 July 1874.

suggesting that 'it is calculated that 90 per cent of the Cape Colonial flocks registered in the South African Stud Book originated from the Wellwood flock'.[23] Nevertheless, Wellwood was a key merino stud, and the capacity to produce prize rams on this scale depended partly on supplementary water supplies.

Perhaps the most ambitious private irrigation project was undertaken by James Somers Kirkwood in the lower section of the Sundays river valley, directly north of Port Elizabeth.[24] Here the river, which came down through the Karoo districts of Graaff-Reinet and Jansenville, entered a relatively flat area of rich alluvial soil south of the Zuurberg range. Ever since settlers had been given land grants in the area in 1815, they had led water through channels from the river to their lands; the Moravian mission at Enon had also irrigated, although its earth dams could not withstand the flood waters. Kirkwood, a successful auctioneer and businessman in Port Elizabeth, bought a farm in the valley in 1877 and tried unsuccessfully to persuade his neighbours to join him in a scheme that would take advantage of the new Irrigation Act.

Instead, he pursued the project alone, and by 1883 had bought over 35,000 morgen (c.30,000 ha). His holdings were larger than the vast majority in the semi-arid pastoral districts, and perhaps 20 per cent consisted of potentially irrigable land, compared with less than 1 per cent on a Karoo farm such as Wellwood. It is extraordinary that purchasers like Kirkwood could accumulate so much land so quickly—especially in this well-watered area. Most was sold by Afrikaners who had gone to the diamond fields, or into kurveying, as a result of stock diseases, debt, and the 1880s recession. In a private land-holding system, poorer landowners could at least realize cash from their land—a benefit denied to tenants, or Africans who migrated from customary tenure districts.

This was not intended primarily as a livestock venture, although animals were kept on the Zuurberg slopes. By 1886 Kirkwood had constructed two weirs, built extensive canals, planted large areas of grain, fruit, and vegetables, and had over twenty white tenants and a larger number of African. Kirkwood's project, a magnet for boosterish journalists, was widely reported in the 1880s—'the boldest farming enterprise that has ever been attempted in South Africa'.[25] Gamble, the hydraulic engineer, was attracted to the potential of the valley and acted as an advisor. Kirkwood sat on the Irrigation Committee of 1883. Despite the scheme's location near Port Elizabeth

---

[23] Playne, *Cape Colony*, 370.

[24] Jane M. Meiring, *Sundays River Valley: Its History and Settlement* (A. A. Balkema, Cape Town, 1959).

[25] Ibid. 37–8.

markets, with a railway nearby, the public launch of Kirkwood's Sundays River Land and Irrigation Company in 1884 coincided with acute recession, and he was not able to attract further funding. Financially overextended, he was declared insolvent in 1887, and died in 1889. Various of the properties were sold, largely to English-speakers. The weirs and canals continued to be used on a small scale, but the government refused requests to take over the works and develop them.

The Halse family accumulated a 17,500-morgen estate, which they named Carnarvon, in the wetter Sterkstroom district, close to the Transkei border. They constructed three large dams by the 1880s and named the biggest Colossal.[26] Dryland crops were unreliable in their area, because of hard frosts and the limited growing season. The dams, initially with a capacity of about 300 million gallons, enabled them to maximize in good years. Walter Halse, writer of the family diary, recorded his opinion in 1897 that: 'agriculture without irrigation is a fraud.'[27] Edward Halse's reputation as a dam builder was such that Rhodes contracted him to construct one on his Zimbabwean estate, north-east of Bulawayo. The brothers launched an agricultural settlement scheme for indigent immigrants from Britain in 1888.[28] It was not a success; in the language of impatient landlords, they condemned the settlers as a 'worthless set of lazy blackguards'.[29] But they switched to local tenants and a reporter for the *Agricultural Journal* who visited in 1904 found eighteen white and twenty-two African families, cultivating about 50 acres each, some of it irrigated. The owners claimed that they had planted 1 million fruit and timber trees and ran extensive herds of cattle and sheep.

Walter Halse had moved to Vryburg district in the northern Cape in the 1890s, a new frontier of capitalist agriculture, where he specialized in cattle. He secured an even larger territory, carved out of the land of the southern Tswana, of 50,000 morgen, developed a new water-management system, and bought a herd of pedigree black poll Angus cattle from de Beers.[30] Walter Rubidge, eldest son of Charles, who had initially bought his own farm in Aberdeen district, south of Graaff-Reinet, also moved north for a period.

Edward Halse stayed on at Carnarvon to supervise 'gigantic and successful farming operations'. By 1910 there were four dams, storing 400 million gallons, and 2,000 acres under cultivation, with potatoes as the major commercial crop, supplemented by strawberries, grain, and fodder. The waterworks supplied not only the farm and the tenants, but Sterkstroom

---

[26] Cory Library, Rhodes University, MS 17508, Halse Farm diary; interviews Robin Halse and Sean Bryan, Dec. 1995; *Agricultural Journal*, 24: 1 (1 Jan. 1904), 24–8.

[27] Halse diary, 24 Oct. 1897.   [28] Ibid., July/Aug. 1888.   [29] Ibid., 29 Dec. 1888.

[30] Playne, *Cape Colony*, 431–3; Halse papers, cuttings, undated.

village and the railways as well, providing an annual income of about £750.[31] Edward Halse became a gentleman farmer; Carnarvon, like Wellwood, was a much-visited model farm. A keen hunter, he nurtured game birds and spring-bok for himself and visiting dignatories such as Sprigg, the Prime Minister, and Frost.[32] His epitaph, engraved on his tombstone in 1919 in the small family graveyard near the farmhouse, was 'He Planted Trees'.[33] One of the keys to the family's success was private mobilization of capital and skill in water management.

Thomas Smartt, an Irish-born medical practioner, established himself at Britstown, a small centre in the northern Cape, where he could tend passing traffic on the route to Kimberley. He 'fell violently in love with what has been so often described as the "barren Karoo"'.[34] He purchased his first farm in 1884, formed the Smartt Syndicate in 1895, and amassed holdings of 56,000 morgen in arid Britstown and nearly 50,000 more elsewhere.[35] In an area where zaaidams had previously been used, the Syndicate embarked on a major set of irrigation works in the Ongers river valley. The scheme, 'one of the boldest of its kind ever attempted', attracted close involvement by the newly established Colonial Irrigation Service in the first decade of the twentieth century. Smartt's stud merino sheep were advertized alongside his Great Houwater dam as triumphs of modern agriculture: 600–800 acres were irrigated annually; and nearly 1,400 ostriches were kept, one of the largest flocks in the country. He benefited from the new provisions under the Irrigation Act allowing loans to individuals rather than groups. Smartt had become a leading Cape politician, and minister in Jameson's Progressive government (1904–8). His enterprise depended partly upon capital raised from financiers, and Rhodes's old networks, including the Rhodes Trust, recently established in Oxford.

More than one of Smartt's dam walls was washed away, and in 1907 he initiated a major new project, built on a concrete core. Its first engineer, Reenen van Reenen, had recently returned from training in the United States, where he was strongly influenced by the conservation and reclamation policies of Theodore Roosevelt's presidency (Chapter 8). The dam was planned to store about 22,000 million gallons or more than fifty times the

---

[31] Interview, Robin Halse, Carnarvon farm, Dec. 1995.

[32] Halse papers, unattributed cuttings, July 1910 and 1 Aug. 1913.

[33] Halse farm visit, Dec. 1995.

[34] *DSAB* i. 725; *Agricultural Journal*, 36: 3 (Mar. 1910): F. D. MacDermott, 'Agricultural Enterprise in the Arid Sections: The Smartt Syndicate Farms in the Britstown District', 307–22.

[35] Cape Archives, MSB 473, 3 (20), Smartt papers, Mr Mugglestone to Mr F Hirschhorn, 23 May 1936. Thanks to Karen Brown for this photocopy.

6. Dam-Building by the Smartt Syndicate

combined capacity of the Halses'.[36] The Syndicate hoped to irrigate 20,000 acres in this arid district. Siltation and evaporation limited their amibitions to about one-quarter of that area; nevertheless, it was probably the largest private project undertaken in the Cape by that time. A rebuilt dam (1964) on the site has a plaque which is also an epitaph of sorts: 'In memory of the Rt Honourable Sir Thomas William Smartt, PC, KCMG 1858–1929: to whose vision and energy the creation of this reservoir and estate is due. He loved South Africa.'[37]

Optimism about the future of the semi-arid Cape attracted investment in land and storage dams by a number of others who made their money elsewhere. Mining magnate Abe Bailey purchased in Colesberg, and Robert Struben, from the Dutch-Scottish mining family in Pretoria, in Middelburg.[38] But the bulk of investment was undertaken by established farmers who adopted less capital-intensive techniques. The most widespread strategy

[36] Playne, *Cape Colony*, 678–80.   [37] Visit to Smartt Syndicate dam, near Britstown, 2000.
[38] *Agricultural Journal*, 34: 5 (May 1909), 546–549: 'Water Conservation in the Midlands'; Joan Southey, *Footprints in the Karoo: A Story of Farming Life* (Jonathan Ball, Johannesburg, 1990), 153.

in the Karoo was to capture and distribute flood-waters by constructing weirs across natural watercourses. John Parkes had adopted this technique at Wheatlands. In 1871 William Southey purchased a farm straddling the Brak river (a tributary of the Fish) in Middelburg district to the east of the town. His brother Charles, the Civil Commissioner in Middelburg, joined him first as partner and then as a neighbour.[39] The Southey farms were located in a flat valley where waters draining from higher land in Steynsburg district accumulated in vleis.

Some farmers were concerned that vleis were silting up. One factor may have been the demise of wildlife. Parkes informed Gamble in 1883: 'on my place, I have hands who tell me that 30 or 40 years ago there were large sea-cow [hippopotamus] holes, to which no bottom could be found, but which are now all filled up.'[40] The use of vleis as wallows by large numbers of hippos had helped to maintain their capacity. Near Addo, the only place in the Cape where elephants survived, an elephant wallow was used as the basis for a dam. Large herds of antelope probably deepened muddy depressions which held water and fed the springs.[41]

Undoubtedly, the major cause of silting was denudation. Yet some farmers saw silt as a potential boon. William Southey soon recognized that the sluits running off his vleis were wasting both water and soil. Influenced by ideas about desiccation, Southey first tried to stop sluits and then constructed weirs of stone and masonry, which were intended to prevent torrents, and flood large areas of veld during wet seasons.[42] Canals led from the weirs helped to transfer water to the pastures. Initially the flood-water and silt killed bushes, but within a few years rich grasses spread. Although his major aim was to improve the veld for livestock, Southey also irrigated lucerne and crops. Like others, he believed that trapping water strengthened the fountains on his land and, he claimed, for twenty miles down the Brak river valley.[43]

Weirs and flood irrigation systems were built along the whole length of the Great Fish and Sundays rivers, two of the main systems draining the eastern Karoo. Herbert Collett inherited land from the large family holdings around the junction of the Great Brak and Fish rivers, north of Cradock and just south of the Southeys (Chapter 1).[44] He purchased his key farm,

[39] Southey, *Footprints in the Karoo*, 93.   [40] G.80-1883, 44.

[41] *Agricultural Journal of the Union of South Africa*, 4: 4 (Oct. 1913), 694: R. B. Chase, 'Is South Africa Drying Up'.

[42] *Agricultural Journal*, 25: 2 (1 Aug. 1904), 187–91: Mr Southey, 'Flooding the Veld: A Remedy for the Ravages of Sluits'.

[43] Ibid. 188.

[44] Playne, *Cape Colony*, 605; Guy Butler, *Karoo Morning: An Autobiography 1918–35* (David Philip, Cape Town, 1983), 78–80.

Saltpansdrift, between the two rivers in 1881 and extended his holdings to 9,000 morgen by 1910.[45] The railway reached this area in 1883 and greatly facilitated diversification. Up to 1914 his major income was from ostriches, about 600 of them. He bred remounts for the army during the South African War, and retained 150 horses as well as 400 dairy cattle. To maintain these numbers he invested heavily in flood irrigation for lucerne, rebuilding the weir system started by his grandfather.

Herbert Collett bought a gas suction engine; it was fed by charcoal made by clearing bush for lands, thus 'killing two birds with one stone'.[46] This strategy, adopted from the 1880s, was restricted to the largest river valleys such as the Fish and Gariep; even there, uneven flow proved a major problem.[47] In the early twentieth century O. E. G. Evans, the leading breeder of ostriches in Bedford district, similarly used charcoal fuel, made from local acacia thorn bush, to power pumps which lifted water from the Fish river in order to irrigate lucerne.[48] Evans calculated that he could run 3–5 ostriches on an acre of lucerne and make £7–10 annually on the feathers of one bird. His turnover of about £5,000 a year on feathers alone was sufficient to justify expenditure on a pumping system. He also sold ostriches for breeding, and a secure fodder supply was essential for these high-value animals.

In the north-western Cape the saaidam system, or basin irrigation, was expanded. Farmers used *oogmaat* (measurement by eye) to assess the level of the low earth walls, built around vleis, in order to stop floodwaters from draining.[49] The broad flats of Fraserburg, Carnarvon, and the Sak river, north of Calvinia, with its extensive pans or *vloers*, were especially suitable.[50] Floodwater captured in this way could sustain a wheat crop even when rainfall was as low as a few inches per year.[51] Timing was of the essence. As in weir construction, here too silt brought down in the floods was seen to fertilize the soil and reduce the brak, or natural salts. Fish were also caught in the saaidams.

Carel van Zyl, a proponent from Carnarvon, argued in 1914 that if the government's van Wyk's Vlei scheme had made use of the system, instead of a storage dam, the land would not have become 'comparatively useless brakish

---

[45] Collett, *A Time to Plant*, 217.   [46] Playne, *Cape Colony*, 605.

[47] *Agricultural Journal*, (28 July 1892): letter H. Dugmore Ibid. 7: 6 (June 1914): Arthur G. Long, 'Irrigation in the North-West Cape', 853.

[48] Ibid. 34: 5 (May 1909), 528–33: 'Irrigation by Pumping on the Fish River'; Playne, *Cape Colony*, 53: 'Ostrich Farming', by Oscar E. G. Evans.

[49] Lawrence G. Green, *Karoo* (Howard Timmins, Cape Town, 1955), ch. 19, 'Forget the Dry Years', 223–8.

[50] *Agricultural Journal*, 7: 4 (Apr. 1914), 493–5: Carel J. v. Zyl, 'Irrigation by "Zaaidams"'.

[51] Pretoria Archives, Department of Agriculture (PTA LDB) 34, DL 61: Arthur Stead, 'The Zaaidam System of Growing Wheat', undated (1916).

soil'.[52] 'We all know', he argued, 'that it is extremely difficult to irrigate land correctly from a dam or fountain': fresh flood-water and silt could obviate such problems. But saaidams were also vulnerable to salinization. Andrew Bain, magistrate at Calvinia, and descendant of road-builder and geologist Andrew Geddes Bain, bought a farm in the early twentieth century called Twee Riviere, on the Sak.[53] The Afrikaner owners had already built saaidams. Bain's son Donald sold the farm to a consortium, the Zak River Estates, and stayed on as manager of 100,000 morgen. By 1911 160 miles of low earth walls trapped sufficient water to grow 16,000 bags of wheat. Subsequently, the company struck problems with rust in the wheat and brak in the irrigated soil. Despite calling in expert advice, no solution was found. Bain left in 1925, and the company was wound up in the 1930s.

Bain's experience was consistent with scientific opinion on the system. Arthur Stead, an agricultural chemist who investigated saaidams in 1916, noted examples where they caused brak because salts percolated upwards into the standing water from the subsoil.[54] Larger saaidams were likely to result in this kind of problem because the timing of the outlet could not allow for different types of soil and depths of water. Stead argued that such dams should be shallow and small, and if possible constructed around uniform soil types. In this way water could be kept at a more uniform level, reducing the dangers of stagnant pools that facilitated salinity. Early success, followed by failure, he suggested, may have been caused by the initial floods freeing the surface soil of brak, but later heavy flooding causing new chemicals to percolate up from the subsoil.

Boring for underground water supplies presented different problems. Here the capital required for the machines was beyond that available to the great bulk of farmers, who would use them only a few times. Finding water deep underground was also a more risky and difficult undertaking than opening up fountains or locating suitable formations for weirs and earth dams. Wells had been sunk successfully to tap shallow underground water where surface indications were promising. By the time of the 1891 census nearly 5,000 were counted in the colony, but they provided limited quantities of water. Experience in France, the United States, and in Kimberley left little doubt that underground water supplies could be found. (Boreholes were initially called Artesian wells, after a district in France where precursors had been pioneered.) Confidence in underground supplies was supported by the belief that the Karoo was once a freshwater lake.

---

[52] v. Zyl, 'Irrigation by "Zaaidams"', 494.   [53] Green, *Karoo*, 225–8.
[54] PTA LDB 34, DL 61: Arthur Stead, 'The Zaaidam System'.

Gamble introduced government drilling machines in the late 1870s.[55] In the recession years of the early 1880s there was limited demand for this service; farmers were unhappy about being charged whether or not the borehole was successful. Both the equipment and the foreman returned to England.[56] 'I cannot understand', he lamented, 'why wind-engines are not more frequently used.'[57] Thomas Bain, drilling for coal in Fraserburg in 1889, found instead water, which rose to the surface without pumping. Borings of over 200 feet in the Zwartruggens area, south of Graaff-Reinet, met with sucess.[58] By 1891 617 'Artesian wells' were recorded—mostly in the northern and midland districts such as Fraserburg, Middelburg, and Hope Town. Boreholes could penetrate to underground water sources inaccessible in other ways. Their water was more likely to be pure, and to last longer than shallow wells. Government services were resumed and their success celebrated in newspapers and the *Agricultural Journal*.

As in the case of other new technologies, borehole drilling and windmills were regarded with considerable suspicion. By no means every borehole worked; water was sometimes too brak, too limited for irrigation, or inconveniently sited.[59] Drilling foremen were accused of emptying dams by boreholes.[60] On their side, drilling teams found that they could be misled by farmers. In the northern Cape they were told that water 'could always be struck by what are known as "Aars", viz., a well defined line of bushes called "water bushes"'.[61] A divining rod was 'also . . . invoked, but that popular medium proved itself again to be a base deceiver, indicating water where none existed notwithstanding that all other features were favourable to it'.[62] The more obvious and better-known surface indicators were poor evidence for supplies deep underground. Nevertheless, drilling teams met with considerable success. Boreholes were particularly important in parts of the northern Cape with porous soils, because of the lack of suitable sites for dams.

It is striking how quickly new skills of detection were developed. When the drilling service was reviewed in 1903, after 4,000 boreholes had been sunk,

---

[55] Sean Archer, 'Technology and Ecology in the Karoo: A Century of Windmills, Wire and Changing Farming Practice', *JSAS* 26: 4 (2000).

[56] Cape of Good Hope, *Report of the Hydraulic Engineer for 1883*, G.33-1884, 16.

[57] *Agricultural Journal* (28 July 1892): letter H. Dugmore.

[58] Ibid. 1: 16 (26 Jan. 1889), 142–3.

[59] Ibid. (26 Nov. 1896): Harry Saunders, Inspector of Water Drills, 'Irrigation. Results of Boring for Water with Government Water Drills', 624–6, 650–1.

[60] Ibid. 625.

[61] Ibid. 35: 4 (Oct. 1909): F. E. Kanthack, 'Bechuanaland from the Irrigation Standpoint', 409.

[62] Ibid. 410.

roughly 80 per cent were reported as successful.[63] Although government services were gradually withdrawn in the recession that followed, private companies replaced them. The 1911 census recorded 7,513 boreholes in the Cape. Farmers tended to pump water into dams, rather than the concrete storage tanks that became more usual later.

Many of those who had invested in dams also pursued this new technology. For Charles Southey in Middelburg, boreholes seemed to work in direct proportion to his success in trapping water by weirs. By 1910 he had three windmills and one petrol engine producing 360,000 gallons a day. The Rubidges on Wellwood sunk their first boreholes in the 1890s. A. T. Parkes on Wheatlands sunk five by 1910 and built concrete water stores. Montagu Gadd (Chapter 8), on Springfield farm, close to Charles Southey and to the railway line through Middelburg, filled a cement reservoir of 100,000 gallons from two boreholes. Although he was not amongst the largest landowners, he was typical of the progressive elite that had emerged on the semi-arid Cape farms. Aside from merinos, he ran a horse stud, and raced successfully in Johannesburg; he reintroduced wildlife, including springbok, blesbok, and wildebeest; and he experimented in crossing horses with zebra in order to find a locally adapted animal which might be immune from horsesickness.[64]

C. G. Lee, at Klipfontein in Jansenville, specialized in angora goats, and his flock of 5,500 continued one of the key studs in the colony. Cape angora breeders, using lines that were crossed with local goats, had to be particularly inventive because, after 1880, it became increasingly difficult to obtain imported animals.[65] Fodder was especially important for angora lambing; Lee's weir and storage dam, filled by the Doorn river, fed 40 morgen of fields. As President of the Agricultural Union of the Cape Colony in 1908, Lee placed water provision high on his list of priorities:

It is . . . apparent at a glance that the great need of a large proportion of agricultural South Africa is the study of the best means of conserving water in order to guard against the devastating effects of ever-recurring droughts. In conserving water for irrigation purposes and the utilisation of floods lies the great source of wealth for this country. There is some nervousness about large irrigation works, where great bodies of water could be impounded for use during the dry seasons. But this nervousness is gradually disappearing as individuals are succeeding in constructing very large works of their own, which are enabling them to increase their activities a thousand fold. And surely what can be accomplished by individuals should not be beyond the strength of the community. The works now cheerfully undertaken and

---

[63] The 1904 census recorded only 2,168 Artesian wells, and 8,662 other wells. This is less than the number recorded by the government drilling service.

[64] Playne, *Cape Colony*, 608.   [65] Ibid. 339–41.

successfully accomplished in this country by individual effort in the shape of water conservation would have staggered the imagination twenty years ago.[66]

Lee was also convinced that they were sitting on 'some of the richest soil in the world'. Everyone was exhorted to stop water running wastefully to the sea. A common metaphor from the time, taken from Swift's *Gulliver's Travels*, praised men who 'made two blades of grass grow where but one grew before'. These 'hard-working, energetic men', Lee opined, 'will be hailed as the saviours of the State'.[67]

In May 1909 the first South African Irrigation Congress was held at Robertson, a fruit-growing district in the western Cape, which also housed a large ostrich population. One of only two Irrigation Boards under the 1878 Act had been formed on the Breede river in the district. While ostriches provided one impetus for irrigation, the vineyards, recovering from phylloxera, and fruit farms also produced high-value products. Merriman, as Cape Prime Minister and sponsor of the first Act, greeted nearly 100 delegates.[68] Whereas the rhetoric praised private landowners for improving the condition of their land and the colony, organized agricultural lobbies were now convinced of the need for public funding.

Returns were made in the censuses of land under irrigation. It is striking that as much as 146,000 morgen was recorded in 1891. By 1911, at the height of the ostrich boom, this area had almost doubled to 282,000 morgen.[69] Certainly the most ambitious and substantial works were built on the land of relatively few well-capitalized landowners; the examples elaborated above were chosen partly to illustrate the scale of their operations. But the evidence suggests that water storage works were common on livestock farms, and rough calculations from the figures tends to bear this out.

Irrigation was geographically widespread. Oudtshoorn, the heart of ostrich production, returned 24,000 morgen or 8.5 per cent of the total irrigated land. (It held 110,000 ostriches, 15 per cent of the total.) The relatively high-rainfall fruit-farming districts of Worcester (18,500 morgen of irrigated land) and Robertson (13,000 morgen) followed. But the semi-arid, stock-farming, midland Karoo districts of Graaff-Reinet (10,000 morgen), Middelburg (8,800 morgen), and Cradock (7,600 morgen) were not far behind. Calvinia, in the arid northern Cape, returned over 8,000 morgen.

---

[66] *Agricultural Journal*, 33: (July 1908), 80: C. G. Lee, 'The President's Address'.

[67] Ibid. 34: 5 (May 1909), 528–33: 'Irrigation by Pumping on the Fish River', and ibid. 546–9, 'Water Conservation in the Midlands'.

[68] Ibid. 504; (June 1909), 6, 614.

[69] Figures from Cape censuses; the 1904 figure was 196,400 morgen.

Between 1904 and 1911, land under irrigation in Oudtshoorn had stabilized and some of the most rapid increases were in the midland districts.

There were no major state irrigation schemes, and with a few exceptions the largest areas irrigated on individual farms were about 200 morgen. Some of the best-capitalized sheep and angora farmers, such as Rubidge and Lee, irrigated less than 50 morgen. Taking a generous 40 morgen as an average, then over 7,000 private farming units, probably more, had significant irrigated areas. A rough calculation such as this suggests that, of the predominantly white-owned private farms, close on a third had irrigated land. (In 1918, when the first Union agricultural census was conducted, 31,000 farming units were enumerated in the Cape, at an average of 1,845 morgen.)[70]

Returns were also made for the sources of water used on irrigated land. These may be less accurate, in that it would have been difficult for farmers to calculate the proportion of water used from different sources. Moreover, fountain water was sometimes stored in dams. Nevertheless it is interesting to note that the figures show the percentage of land irrigated from perennial fountains and streams decreased from 60 to 50 percent between 1891 and 1911. The area irrigated from flood-water and dams increased.

Census returns on dams bear out the argument that investment in water provision was widespread geographically and distributed across a signficant number of farms. (Some of the small dams were for watering livestock, so that their numbers do not bear a direct relationship to irrigated land.) In 1911 23,960 dams were recorded in the colony. Karoo districts headed the list: Cradock (1,124), Graaff-Reinet (820), Albert (in the northeastern Cape, 818), and Middelburg (705). There were certainly more dams than farms in these districts, although we know that some farming units had more than one dam.

These numbers exclude fountains, which, along with rivers, were the original source of water for most farms, and boreholes. In 1911 a total of 12,800 fountains were recorded in the Cape, considerably fewer than the total number of dams; they were widely distributed through the colony. If these figures are correct, then they are evidence of the extent to which new water supplies had facilitated the multiplication of farming sites. Boreholes, at one-third the number of dams, were growing in importance (7,513). Again, the highest numbers were found largely in the semi-arid livestock farming districts: Cradock (455), Colesberg (428), and Middelburg (385).

Dam construction was essential for more intensive agriculture and a key sign of progress. While the boom in ostrich feathers stimulated investment

---

[70] This excludes land in African reserve districts. Farm size differed hugely between the wetter, western Cape districts and the dryer interior. The average for South Africa as a whole was less than 1,200 morgen.

into larger works, water from dams and other sources was used for a wide range of purposes, not least for the growing number of livestock. For those who invested heavily in stud animals, adequate water and fodder supplies for drought years and dry seasons was a priority. By 1911 livestock numbers had surpassed their nineteenth-century peak. Water conservation undoubtedly played some role, alongside the control of livestock diseases.

Although the state made some limited subsidy for dam building and especially borehole drilling, this aspect of agricultural intensification and conservation was essentially the result of private investment. This point is worth reiterating, in view of the general emphasis in the historiography on the state's role in agricultural development. It is difficult to calculate the scale of investment, but this would be easy to underestimate, given the highly dispersed nature of works. Although such investment could be risky, and upkeep of dams and water channels demanding, farmers perceived it as both essential and profitable. As officials had hoped, new water supplies reduced the need for transhumance.

Irrigation and the State: Thinking in Continents

The enthusiasm for irrigation and improved water provision emanated from politicians and officials as well as farmers. Even if the 1878 Irrigation Act had not been a success, Gamble had acted as an advisor to farmers and the borehole-drilling service had been widely used. The Cape Supreme Court played an increasingly critical role in developing the case law on water rights in such a way that private landowners could invest with reasonable security. In 1903 a Department of Irrigation was established, and in the next few decades the Cape and Union states became deeply involved in the planning and construction of large dams. It is an irony that the expansion of state involvement was accompanied by a reduction in the area of land irrigated in the Cape, as farmers moved out of ostrich breeding and focused again on sheep.

There was no shortage of irrigationist rhetoric from the very inception of the Department of Agriculture in 1887. Abraham Fischer, Professor of Agricultural Chemistry at Stellenbosch and first head of the Department, advertised this in his inaugural address:

if these two ways of improving our agriculture, viz.: the making of dams and the planting of trees, were to be carried out in the better parts of the Karroo, it would soon become the Eldorado of South African agriculture. I am fully convinced that in future our agriculture, viticulture perhaps excluded to a certain extent, will be in the most flourishing condition on the other side of the Drakenstein mountains, in the Karroo, however sceptical those farmers may be, who live in the shade of the Rhenoster bush.[71]

From the 1890s, and especially after the turn of the century, a new optimism and urgency pervaded writings by officials on irrigation. The issue was discussed regularly in the *Agricultural Journal*, and more firmly linked, as a public enterprise, not only to agricultural production but to denudation, tree cover, and soil conservation.[72] Following the extension of the Irrigation Act to private individuals in 1893, a further committee sat in 1896. It focused on the legal difficulties inhibiting combination for irrigation and the strict terms by which the government required the first mortgage on applicants' land.

Part of the problem in contemplating major work was the lack of research. Even high-profile projects such as Smartt's suffered many setbacks. His first dam, completed in 1888, was washed away almost immediately by a flood; another lasted from 1897 to 1899.[73] In the debate generated by the 1896 Committee and a proposed project in Steynsburg, a Graaff-Reinet correspondent argued that a great deal more understanding was needed on the precise nature of run-off in any catchment. Run-off tended to be far greater for a given precipitation from the 'stony hills of the Karoo' than in the grasslands of the eastern and north-eastern districts.[74] Together with the unpredictable storm rainfall, this made Karoo dams particularly vulnerable. The effects of wind, heat, depth, and altitude on evaporation rates in dams were also little researched. Gamble believed that Conservancy Boards were needed to plan systematically how water could be conserved in each river catchment.

As in other spheres, the colonial government called on outside specialists to develop an overarching strategy. W. H. Hall, Hydraulic Engineer to California State, reported in 1896, and Sir W. Willcocks, who worked in India and then Egypt—where he played a major role in the Aswan dam—in 1902. Experts, largely with Indian experience, served in the new Irrigation Departments, launched in the Cape and the Transvaal as part of reconstruction following the South African War. South African prospects were beginning to be conceived in the context of recent spectacular achievements in the control of water in the Punjab, in Egypt, and the American West.

---

[71] Cape of Good Hope, *Memorandum upon the Condition of Agriculture in the Cape Colony, and Suggestions for its Improvement; with the Inaugural Address Delivered at the Stellenbosch College on June, 20th, 1884 by Professor A. Fischer*, G.46-1885, 7–8.

[72] *Agricultural Journal*, 1: 29 (3 Oct. 1889).

[73] Mugglestone, 'Short History on the Smartt Syndicate'.

[74] *Agricultural Journal* (29 Oct. 1896): W. Roe, 'Irrigation', 574–5; see also 7 Jan. 1897.

Hall advised against a state-sponsored boom that might lead to overinvestment without intensive research into river flows, catchment areas, soils, and not least markets. He observed 'the strange fact that the two peoples of the world who colonize arid regions in America and South Africa, namely the English and the Dutch, come from lands where interest has generally been shown in how to get rid of the water, not how to get it, and prize its use'.[75] But Willcocks advocated fuller state control of, and investment in, water resources. Private enterprise required returns too quickly; 'agricultural development is slow but it is permanent and knows of no exhaustion'.[76]

As in progressive America, conservation was linked to national efficiency. The *Agricultural Journal* commented in 1897 on the Cape's continuing need to import food: 'while farmers are listlessly smoking on their stoeps, and landowners are allowing magnificent ground to lie fallow, the country is paying out hundreds of thousands of pounds annually that might well go to increase the wealth and the prosperity of South Africa.'[77] The Transvaal's new Irrigation Engineer yet again bewailed the 'millions of gallons . . . running to waste into the sea'.[78] Failing to invest was like hoarding money; irrigation promised huge increases in the value of land and production. In the first decade of the twentieth century there was growing concern that mineral wealth might run out, and that the colony would be thrown back on its agricultural resources. In this context, water conservation for agriculture was a national issue.

Ideas about desiccation, degradation of veld, and soil erosion could be one stimulus for private landowners, such as the Southeys, to invest in water control.[79] Environmental degradation was directly implicated, alongside disease, as a reason for the decline in the Cape's livestock numbers. Officials laid great stress on the urgency of water management as part of broader attempts to conserve natural resources; to some of them, this was inseparable from colonial development. Agriculture would be impossible without water conservation, and the state had to play a role as arbiter where overexploitation threatened conservation. Such views were strongly articulated by F. E. Kanthack, appointed Director of Irrigation at the Cape in 1906, who became

[75] Ibid 13: 5 (1 Sept. 1898): Address by W. Roe to the Zwart Ruggens Farmers' Association, 282.

[76] W. Willcocks, *Report on Irrigation in South Africa* (Johannesburg, 1901), 8. Willcocks worked for 12 years in India and 18 years in Egypt.

[77] *Agricultural Journal*, 10: 1 (1897), 25.

[78] Ibid. 24: 1 (1 Jan. 1904): C. Dimond H. Braine, 'The Possibilities of Irrigation in South Africa', 48–58; *Transvaal Agricultural Journal*, 5: 18 (Jan. 1907): C. D. H. Braine, 'Farm Irrigation in the Transvaal', 354–61.

[79] Southey, *Footprints in the Karoo*; Southey, 'Flooding the Veld'.

the most influential official in this sphere. He had worked since 1899 in the Public Works Department in the Punjab, on one of the most ambitious irrigation projects in the British empire.[80] (Gordon, his predecessor from 1903 to 1906, and Braine, the Transvaal's Irrigation Engineer, were also recruited from India.) As Director of Irrigation in the new Union government until 1921, Kanthack oversaw the formation of this sub-department (under the Ministry of Lands). From his subsequent bases at the University of Cape Town and in private practice in Johannesburg, he consulted widely on water engineering throughout the subcontinent.[81]

Kanthack brought with him a conviction about the role of the state and was deeply aware of developments in irrigation and forestry in the United States, France, and Germany. He approached his task with the reforming zeal typical of government officers in this progressive era. He wrote extensively about his ideas, and was particularly interested in the broader links between conservation and irrigation. Initially, he underestimated the extent of water development on Cape farms: 'It must be clearly understood', he remarked soon after arriving, 'that a handful of progressive ostrich farmers making great fortunes for themselves does not constitute development.'[82]

Nevertheless, compared to some of those who anticipated immeasurable wealth in watering the Karoo, Kanthack was, from the first years of his career in South Africa, acutely aware of the limits to irrigation development, imposed by rainfall, drainage patterns, and soil. Much of the Karoo uplands, he argued, had soil too shallow and stony to merit irrigation, except flood irrigation to improve the veld. When people pressed him to make real the long-held dream of leading waters from the Gariep, he reminded them that 'water runs down, and not uphill'.[83] After an extensive survey of potential dam sites in the far northern Cape districts of Kuruman and Gordonia in 1909, he came to the conclusion that there was neither sufficient water nor suitable soils. Where dams had been built, water seeped away because of the porosity of the soil.[84]

Kanthack worked initially with Willcocks's figure that about 3 million acres could be perennially irrigated in South Africa as a whole, and that

[80] Kanthack rose from Assistant Engineer, 2nd grade (1899–1901) to Undersecretary, Punjab Irrigation Branch, Public Works Department (1905).

[81] Francis Edgar Kanthack, *The Principles of Irrigation Engineering with Special Reference to South Africa* (Longmans, Green & Co., London, 1924).

[82] F. E. Kanthack, 'Irrigation Development in the Cape Colony: Past, Present and Future', *Agricultural Journal of the Cape of Good Hope*, 24: 6, (1909), 645–57.

[83] Ibid. 651.

[84] *Agricultural Journal of the Cape of Good Hope*, 35: 4 (1909): F. E. Kanthack, 'Bechuanaland from the Irrigation Standpoint: A Reconnaisance Survey', 420.

perhaps half-a-million acres were already under some form of irrigation.[85] (The 1911 census showed this latter figure was probably an underestimate: it recorded nearly 600,000 acres under irrigation in the Cape, and close on a million in the country as a whole.) He soon realized that achieving anything like this area would be difficult because, he calculated, the costs of irrigation in South Africa were possibly five times those in the Punjab. Despite his experience with smallholder production in India, he was not initially a protagonist of irrigation settlement schemes for poor whites, whom he found lacked ambition and were 'too slothful':

When survey parties are engaged in studying the irrigation possibilities of backward districts, the work is viewed by many with undisguised hostility, by others with indifference or with ridicule. Any excuse is good enough to bring up against a scheme. We have been told that God made the rivers so that the water should run in them and hence should not be taken out by artificial means, and also many other quaint objections of a similar nature.[86]

Kanthack's priorities were to secure general environmental conservation, and to facilitate irrigation by progressive farmers with property. He was immediately alerted to the 'evils' of sluits and desiccation, and his writings leave no doubt as to his fundamental concern about 'appalling' erosion, impenetrable soil surfaces, increasingly rapid run-off, and 'drying up of vleis'.[87] At the Smartt Syndicate estate he found a new donga (gulley), 300 feet wide and 18–20 feet deep, 'running through a large chain of what used to be magnificent vleis'. Such destruction was a 'most terrible example of the evil effects of kraaling', and of a country 'gradually tramped out by stock'.[88] He judged the same process to have taken place on Grootfontein farm, Middelburg. Used as a remount depot for the British military authorities in the South African War (1899–1902), it was purchased by the state for the Karoo's experimental farm and agricultural college in 1911. On a visit in 1914, Kanthack was shown a sluit that had expanded from ten feet wide and four feet deep to 100 feet wide and 20 feet deep in fifteen years.[89]

To those who suggested that soil erosion should be explained largely by a geological understanding of the rise of the interior plateau and subsequent drainage patterns, Kanthack responded:

The point I wish to make is that when the white man first came to South Africa the country was in a very different state to what it is in now, and from a practical point

---

[85] The Drought Commission of 1923 arrived at a similar figure for irrigable potential, despite new technology and the huge increase in state investment.

[86] Kanthack, 'Irrigation Development', 646–7.   [87] S.C.2-1914, 49, 51.

[88] Ibid. 50.   [89] Ibid. 50.

of view we are only concerned with this historical period. There is no evidence that the country has moved up or down since the white man has been in it.

He bewailed 'man's . . . utterly selfish and unreasonable claim to absolute individual freedom to do as he will with the resources of Nature . . . by burning, felling, lopping, barking, over-grazing, or other maltreatment of the forests'.[90] Like others at the time, he envisaged that large parts of the country would become uninhabitable.

Kanthack emphasized the link between conservation, agricultural progress, irrigation, control of water, and protection of watersheds.[91] He shared the widespread official conviction in favour of large-scale afforestation. While foresters prioritized timber needs of the country to replace imports, Kanthack, like Brown, focused on the relationship between forests and water conservation.[92] In a speech to the 1908 South African Association for the Advancement of Science, published as the 'Destruction of Mountain Vegetation: Its Effects upon the Agricultural Conditions in the Valleys', he took his lead from progressive America. There the 'efforts to stay the progress of destruction' were remarkable for their 'boldness and the immensity of their scope'.[93] This involved forest reserves, reclamation, irrigation, and fire control.

'We must learn to clothe the word "Forest" with a far wider meaning than is customary,' Kanthack argued, 'to stand for the veld generally.'[94] In the Cape, he identified the coastal ranges as the most urgent problem. Whatever the effect of vegetation on overall rainfall, he was convinced that wooded hillsides, especially those at right angles to prevailing sea winds, induced precipitation by cooling the winds. Vegetation acted as the most effective reservoir for springs; evaporation, run-off, and 'erosive floods' would decline if a dense vegetation and leaf litter was restored.

In a geological time-span, Kanthack recognized, rich valley soils had been deposited by erosion from inland Karoo watersheds: along the Breede river, around Worcester, around Oudtshoorn and Ladismith, and in the Sundays river valley.[95] But it was not appropriate to encourage this process in the Cape, in the hope of artificially creating new valleys of fertile alluvium. The

[90] *Agricultural Journal*, 33: 2 (1908): F. E. Kanthack, 'The Destruction of Mountain Vegetation: Its Effects upon the Agricultural Conditions in the Valleys', 194.

[91] Grove, *Green Imperialism*.

[92] Harald Witt, 'Trees, Forests and Plantations: An Economic, Social and Environmental Study of Tree-Growing in Natal, 1890–1960', unpublished Ph. D. thesis, University of Natal (1998).

[93] Kanthack, 'The Destruction of Mountain Vegetation', 195.

[94] Ibid. 196.   [95] Ibid. 202.

soil then being washed off tended to be poor, infertile grit from Table Mountain sandstones, and it could bury fertile valley soils. Oudtshoorn was a case in point. When rain broke a drought in 1909–10, 'dirty torrents came down from the mountains' and 'much useless silt was deposited on the lands'.[96]

Kanthack despaired of burning for 'trifling and often purely transitory advantage', and was harsh in his judgement of 'the mental condition of a community which allows such a state of things'.[97] While he agreed that it was impossible to plant forest everywhere, even a 'passive forest policy of enclosing and protection', of preventing fires, grazing, and cutting on sensitive mountain slopes, would go a long way to re-create strong, clear, perennial streams and initiate 'reclothing of the mountains'. Only in this way would the torrents be controlled and a regular water flow, conducive to irrigation, be achieved.

By the early 1910s Kanthack had pressurized the Lands Department (under which Irrigation fell) into accepting that no more land in mountainous areas, forming the main watersheds of the country, would be alienated without reference to him.[98] He and some of the key foresters debated this issue in their evidence to the 1914 Senate Committee on Drought and Soil Erosion (Chapter 8). Storr Lister, the Chief Forester of the Union until 1913, also with experience in India, demarcated 400,000 morgen on the Swartberg and Langeberg coastal ranges to protect the water supply. Lister had reservations about such strategies, not least the problem of enforcement. Fencing such reserves was difficult, even though the process had started in the Cape near African settlements.

Charles Legat, Lister's successor in 1914, noted that many Crown lands were still leased for grazing, some to Africans. Lessees fired the range either for hunting or to renew pastures; regular fire made it difficult for young trees to re-establish themselves. But attempts to regulate African grazing in the forest reserves of the Eastern Cape brought foresters into conflict both with Africans and the Native Affairs Department: 'we are constantly getting into hot water, as they claim the forests as their own.'[99] From the Forestry Department's point of view, the expense of fencing or policing mountain ranges in the Karoo or southern Cape, which had little value as timber forests, seemed difficult to justify. In some areas, such as the Amatola range in the eastern Cape, foresters actually advocated grazing access to mountain pastures because the grasses, which became long and rank in winter, could drown out other species and become a fire hazard.

[96] Ibid. 202.   [97] Ibid. 203.   [98] S.C.2-1914, 13, 52.   [99] Ibid. 19.

Although the foresters had somewhat different concerns to Kanthack, they concurred in broad terms about a strategy of watershed protection. They agreed that farmers who 'deliberately destroy the vegetation and "tame" the country, as they call it', had to be curtailed.[100] Carlson, Conservator of Forests in the Free State, who had previously worked in the Cape and Transkei, supported Kanthack in his arguments for far-reaching intervention, with water flow, as much as timber requirements, in mind.[101] In an address to the South African Irrigation Congress in Oudtshoorn in 1913, he argued that forests were more effective than grass in checking run-off. Trees broke the fall of water and conducted it gently to the ground. Humus absorbed up to four times its own weight in water, and forest soils were usually more porous than those in grasslands, which were only partly protected against sun. This more than compensated for the rain lost by failing to reach the ground, or moisture evaporated from the leaves, or lost in transpiration.

Carlson's main concern became protection of the Gariep river catchment. The great bulk (97 per cent) of the 1.6 million acres then reserved as forest in South Africa was in wetter areas on the coast or on the seaward-facing shadows of mountains where indigenous forest and new plantations predominated. There was hardly any protection or afforestation in the Gariep, Vaal, and Caledon river catchments and hence, he argued, particularly uneven water flows in these major rivers. The fact that indigenous forests were absent on the western slopes of the Drakensberg, and the highveld, with their extremes of temperature, did not preclude the growth of exotics, such as American pines, with a wider environmental range than indigenous species.[102]

Carlson counted on multiple benefits from afforestation of this vast watershed: a substantial revenue from timber; replacement of the £1 million of wood imported; an end to the use of dung for fuel, so that organic matter could be returned to the veld; and Aliwal North's river-driven electricity turbine, and its street-lights, would function more regularly. Forests would counter erosion and depopulation in Lesotho and help in the 'continuous warfare against the formation of little sluits on the veld'.[103] His primary aim was to create a natural store of water equal to many inches of rainfall that would underpin conservation and irrigation. 'Our mountain watersheds are the roots of the tree, our rivers its stem, our arable lands its branches and

---

[100] Ibid. 14.

[101] *Agricultural Journal*, 5: 2 (Feb. 1913): K. A. Carlson, 'Forestry in Relation to Irrigation in South Africa. A Practical Proposition', 220–34; S.C.2-1914, Appendix E, p. xxvii.

[102] *Agricultural Journal*, 5: 2 (Feb. 1913): K. A. Carlson, 'Forestry in the Free State', 242–9.

[103] Carlson, 'Forestry in Relation to Irrigation', 226–9.

leaves, and the crops we reap its fruits.'[104] South Africa had to develop policy for the longer term, for the next generation, and 'to think in continents'.[105]

In the minds of engineers, irrigation required not only large-scale conceptions of environmental control, but also technical expertise. Many farmers felt that they knew better what would work under local conditions at the Cape, and had planned their own works with teams of migrant workers or specialist dam contractors. One South African engineer recognized that 'the farmers have shown remarkable aptitude in making the most of local circumstances, and frequently exhibit what may be termed an inborn engineering instinct. They have, often unaided by scientific knowledge, carried out works in a sound businesslike manner and at low cost.'[106] In this sense, Cape water systems were an innovative intermediate technology.

Yet engineers increasingly emphasized the limits of local knowledge. Gamble despaired of the inability of some Cape farmers to understand the significance of velocity as well as aperture in water flow; they spoke commonly of 'an inch' of water, meaning the amount that would pass through an inch pipe in a certain period.[107] In the long-running dispute over development of the Graaff-Reinet town water supplies, it was clear that some Afrikaner smallholders were deeply suspicious of techniques that hid water and its flow from direct vision and surveillance.[108] They felt that they were bound to lose access through such means. Guy Butler's story of the poor 'wood fishermen' in Cradock suggests a similar potential disadvantage of water control. When the floods came down, they threw ropes with grapples to catch timber that would be stored or sold for firewood.[109]

Just as in disputes over livestock diseases, farmers questioned the role of experts: 'it has frequently been stated', an engineer noted, 'that Farmers know more about the Construction of Dams than Civil Engineers.' If it was suggested to farmers that major schemes had been successful elsewhere, they responded: 'Oh! that's in India; this is Africa.' An impatient engineer bemoaned the way that 'these so called "practical men" . . . condemn wholesale all that they have not seen, do not know and cannot understand'.[110] The 1914 Committee attempted to resolve this problem by both commending itself as composed of practical men, and advocating scientific methods as practical.

---

[104] Ibid. 234.   [105] Ibid. 229.
[106] *Agricultural Journal*, 7: 1 (1914): A. M. A. Struben, 'Irrigation Engineering (American Practice)', 171.
[107] G.24-1879.   [108] Smith, *Frontier to Midlands*.
[109] Butler, *Karoo Morning*, 112–3.   [110] Braine, 'Possibilities of Irrigation', 54.

Engineers could cite many mishaps and mistakes. While the opening up of springs, by digging or breaking rock around them, may have increased flow in the short term, Gamble believed that this was at considerable cost in the longer term.[111] In Touws River, Willcocks noted, the discharge declined quickly and the cuttings had to be refilled.[112] Both smaller earth dams for stock and privately built irrigation dams were often breached because of faulty construction or miscalculation of flood-water flows. A major problem in farm dams, Kanthack later concluded, was inadequate spillways.[113] Braine considered it wrong to plant trees on dams—a common practice. If earth dams were risky, masonry construction required even more specialist knowledge. 'Primitive' methods, Braine expostulated, were a success despite their faults: 'it is useless to ridicule science. It is the basis of all prosperity, progress and civilisation.'[114]

Engineers argued that systems of flood irrigation by constructing weirs and 'leading' water through canals were often unreliable and wasteful. Floodwaters could destroy construction works, circumvent weirs, and change the course of drainage channels. Small errors in the gradient of channels could produce flows of great velocity during storm rainfall. Engineers generally preferred storage dams and sluices, controlled outlets, and opportunity for soil to drain. Experts also criticized farmers for their use of water. Fields were over-watered after floods, causing hard-baked ground; water was led to 'radically wrong' places—such as around the trunks of fruit trees.[115]

On visiting William Southey's farm, Manor Holme, in 1902, which had one of the best-developed flood irrigation systems in the Karoo, Willcocks found that extensive silt had collected around the weirs and was blocking the heads of the canals; water therefore washed over the works and threatened to create new sluits.[116] Like the Rubidges in Graaff-Reinet, Southey used rows of *Agave americana* to prevent soil washing (Chapter 9). The spiky leaves also discouraged livestock. Southey's techniques, by channelling all the water onto the veld, did not allow for passing on water, via a spillway, down river. In 1906 his brother, Charles Southey, brought a successful legal action against him for hoarding water.

Willcocks commented in 1902 that 'the farm, as it stands, is a monument of skill and courageous enterprise, but an irrigation engineer with experience of basin irrigation as practised in Egypt, should be able to double and treble

[111] Cape of Good Hope, *Report of the Hydraulic Engineer for the Year 1885*, G.27-1886, 9.
[112] Willcocks, *Irrigation*, 8.   [113] Kanthack, *Principles of Irrigation*, 102.
[114] Braine, 'Possibilities of Irrigation'.
[115] Braine, 'Farm Irrigation in the Transvaal', 354–5.   [116] Willcocks, *Irrigation*, 26.

the value of the estate at a moderate expenditure'.[117] Oral tradition has it that a leading engineer (probably Willcocks) told the owner: 'Well, Mr Southey, it's all very nice indeed but you know you are only doing what the Egyptians have been doing for the last thousand years!'[118] Cosmopolitan officials who had worked in other parts of the empire could express an uncomfortable scepticism about the achievements of self-regarding, English-speaking South Africans who commanded the high ground of progress in their own society.

Oudtshoorn, which had the most intensive weir irrigation works in the colony, became Kanthack's prototype of irrigational folly, typical of the 'extreme individualism which is such a marked characteristic of the South African colonist'. Strong riparian rights made it very difficult to apportion water between owners and created intense conflict between them. In his opinion, there were too many irrigation works, improperly built, liable to be damaged in flood, and to cause erosion. As farmers situated upstream increased the effectiveness of their weirs and canals, so the lower farms were starved of water. Most Cape towns and villages with open-furrow water systems regulated flow by specifying a time-period for which sluices to any property could be opened. This was not possible on large farms using irregular flood systems. Willcocks suggested that the Cape government follow the example of 'the Moors in Spain' by public fixing of the height of weirs, width of sluices, and level of canals so that the lower proprietors were guaranteed some water. These strategies presupposed co-operation, legal mechanisms for enforcement, the measurement of water flows, and thorough planning.

The 1896 Irrigation Committee recommended that irrigation boards, envisaged but hardly realized under the 1878 Act, should have the power to raise local rates and to allocate water. All flood-water should be regarded as the property of the state, rather than of private owners. Willcocks agreed that it was critical for South Africa to recognize itself as arid, to legislate accordingly, and declare rivers as part of the public domain. Italy had done so under Cavour, he argued, and 'modern Italy owes much of its prosperity to this wise and strong legislation'.[119]

The Cape's new Irrigation Department began detailed surveys of water resources, including underground water, and framed legislation in 1906; a similar Act was passed in the Transvaal in 1908. One of Kanthack's preoccupations was to continue the revision of the water laws; he took major

[117] Ibid. 27.
[118] Southey, *Footprints in the Karoo*, 93. The engineer 'designed the Aswan Dam'.
[119] Willcocks, *Irrigation*, 5–6.

responsibility for the national Irrigation and Conservation of Waters Act of 1912.[120] This tried to get around the rights of riparian owners by dividing surface water into private and public. Landowners would continue to have rights to springs and other surface water on their land, provided it did not form part of a 'public stream', in a 'known and defined channel', which was capable of being used for irrigation even if it was sometimes dry. Courts would decide any disputed case.

Having extended the scope of 'public' water, the law was primarily concerned with regulating it. Water use was categorized as primary for domestic purposes and animals; secondary for irrigation; and tertiary for power and industry. Riparian owners retained rights for primary use. The Act also tried to distinguish between normal flows of water and surplus water, to be calculated for each river by the courts. Normal flow could be used by riparian owners for irrigation by direct means such as channels or pumps, but not dammed. Provision was made for lower owners to get access to normal flows, by ensuring the return of water to public streams by upper proprietors. Irrigation had to be 'good and economical'.

The 1912 Act was geared towards large-scale storage systems and underlined the newly established authority of experts, the bureaucracy, and the courts. The Water Court, established in the Cape in 1906, would adjudicate between owners; applications could be made to it for a share of water. This was an administrative and executive body, rather than just a judicial court, which could also decide on any construction of new works. It could authorize submerging of land (with compensation). Critically, the court could give rights to non-riparian owners to lead water over land belonging to others. Such servitudes had begun to be developed in case law by the Cape courts. One implication of this change was that if a substantial dam was to be constructed, riparian owners upstream could be restricted in their use of water. Regulation on this scale was complex, and the Water Court was constituted as an itinerant specialist body, staffed with judges and registrars who did no other work.

Kanthack had initially been critical of 'the big state scheme', which had been pursued under Milner in the reconstruction Transvaal, as advised by Willcocks.[121] His preferred policy at Union was for state financial and engineering assistance to existing farmers, either as individuals or through relatively small-scale Irrigation Boards, with three or more riparian owners.

---

[120] Kanthack, *Principles of Irrigation*, 277–88; Union of South Africa, *Report of the Director of Irrigation 1st April 1918 to 31st March 1919*, U.G.28-1920.

[121] Jeremy Krikler, *Revolution from Above, Rebellion from Below: The Agrarian Transvaal at the Turn of the Century* (Clarendon Press, Oxford, 1993), 78–9.

Within a decade Kanthack's department registered plans for eighty-seven Boards, with loans for £3.4 million covering 137,800 hectares. However, both engineering and political pressures began to change the Department's strategy. Kanthack became concerned about the standards and location of some smaller dams.[122] His preoccuption with large-scale watershed conservation also implied ambitious planning. And the collapse of the ostrich industry, as well as a serious drought in 1913, lent urgency to new approaches. Flood irrigation had been adequate for lucerne; more complex systems, which could feed a wider range of high-value crops, were now essential.

If Milner's anglicization policy failed in its immediate objectives, irrigation remained central to the thinking of those who wished to promote British settlement in South Africa. Smartt, who had strongly supported irrigation development as a minister in Jameson's government (1904–8), drew leading imperial figures into his Britstown syndicate. It included Sir Lewis Michell, former Chairman of the Standard Bank, and De Beers, also a minister in Jameson's cabinet, biographer of Rhodes, and a director of the British South Africa Company. Colonel Byron, aide-de-camp to Lord Roberts in the South Africa War, was subsequently involved in the Westminster estates settlement near Tweespruit, in the Free State, where considerable success was achieved in putting British tenants on relatively large farms.[123] He became chair of the Commission into Land Settlement in 1911, senator in the Union parliament, member of the 1914 Select Committee on Droughts, and later managing director of the Sundays river irrigation scheme.[124] To those who 'thought in continents' about immigration as well as irrigation, British settlement would utilize 'the many millions of acres untended, uncultivated and going to waste in South Africa'. This would both help to relieve Britain of surplus population, and help whites achieve a majority in South Africa. In such arguments, 'irrigation, and irrigation alone' could 'redeem South Africa, the home of the happy idle native races, content to live a precarious existence, from becoming a barren widlerness'.[125]

By the 1910s the promise of state subsidy for irrigation was seen as equally important by Afrikaner politicians. The Kakamas irrigation settlement in the northern Cape, initiated by the Dutch Reformed Church, had strong religious underpinnings. Situated in the heart of old transhumant, trekboer communities, it aimed to resocialize and stabilize poor whites, as well as

[122] Union of South Africa, *Select Committee on Irrigation Projects*, S.C.9-1919.

[123] Colin Murray, *Black Mountain: Land, Class and Power in the Eastern Orange Free State 1880s–1980s* (Edinburgh University Press, Edinburgh, 1992).

[124] Meiring, *Sundays River Valley*, 116; S.C.2-1914.

[125] *Agricultural Journal*, 6: 3 (Sept. 1913), 522–5: F. C. Holland, 'Irrigation in South Africa'.

invest in production. The Revd Marchand, the Dutch Reformed minister most absorbed in the project, agreed with the English advocates of closer settlement that South Africa's land was too dominated by extensive livestock farming. Intensive irrigated settlement, focusing for example on fruit, poultry, and pigs, would provide for the 'small man'.[126] Paarl district provided a model: people had long complained that farms were 'getting too small', but despite the fact that they 'cut them up and cut them up' land prices and production had increased.[127] Marchand also favoured state afforestation schemes as means of creating employment and discipline for 'a class who usually lead dead isolated lives'.[128]

There was widespread concern about the fate of impoverished Afrikaners pouring into the city, and a widespread belief about the social benefits of staying on the land. Despite his earlier perceptions of poor whites, by 1919 Kanthack judged Kakamas as a reasonable success. Although there were problems with white 'squatters', and a tendency by settlers to use the scheme as a base for transport riding and education, intensive production was evident. Kakamas then catered for 371 settlers, some farming up to 8 morgen of high-value crops such as lucerne, oranges, and vines, and making up to £900 a year.[129] Kanthack's department took a leading role in the major irrigation project at Hartebeestpoort, near Pretoria, designed partly for Afrikaner settlement.

Sir Percy Fitzpatrick—political colleague of Rhodes and Jameson, mining magnate, and author—spent ten years from 1913 in attempting to resurrect a major irrigation project in the Sundays river valley.[130] In the southern part of the valley the Addo Land and Irrigation Company had planted fruit in 1908 and began to meet success with citrus. Fitzpatrick, who had been born in the eastern Cape, bought over 8,000 morgen near Addo for £41,800, formed the Cape Sundays River Settlements Company, and acquired existing works together with 2,000 acres of irrigable land. He committed himself to citrus as a core crop, with the support of the Department of Agriculture. Port Elizabeth provided a major market and port nearby, and exports to Europe had already begun, taking advantage of South Africa's reverse season.

Citrus production, however, required a sustained, stable water supply. The droughts of 1913–14 underlined the problems of seasonal flood irrigation. A flood in 1916 reinforced the argument; large volumes of water, perhaps enough to 'irrigate the entire valley of 50,000 acres for three years', were

---

[126] Union of South Africa, *Report of the Select Committee on Drought Distress Relief*, S.C.3-1916, evidence, Revd B. P. J. Marchand.
[127] Ibid. 39.   [128] Ibid. 42.   [129] U.G.28-1920, 134.
[130] Meiring, *Sundays River Valley*.

lost.[131] It was plain to Fitzpatrick and Kanthack alike that a successful scheme would require a major storage dam. In 1917 an Irrigation Board was formed, and the Department became more centrally involved. Kanthack was convinced that the lower Sundays river valley, long seen as an ideal irrigation site, could sustain a big dam with a complex water regime. The scheme was related to another dam project on the river, above Graaff-Reinet, at van Reynevelds poort, designed to provide water for the town and smallholdings, stabilize the river flow for the lower dam, and reduce silt. Kanthack's department was moving towards the planning of whole catchments.

The new dam was located in an isolated spot in Jansenville district. Land had to be purchased, a road built, and the materials carried by donkey and wagon—which also necessitated large forage supplies. Even in the 1910s motor transport was not seen as sufficiently economical or reliable. Fitzpatrick's company began to clear new land with steam ploughs in 1917, and land sales began. Around 100 elephants that had survived in the Addo bush were shot so that they would not trouble farmers. The remainder, less than twenty, survived precariously until they were protected from 1930 in a small National Park. But in its enthusiasm and concern to reap income, Fitzpatrick's company encouraged immigration and settlement too early. Difficulties of construction and access meant that the dam was completed only in 1922.

Kanthack had warned prospective British settlers that they needed £2,000 in capital and enough money to tide them over four years. Even this proved optimistic. Early settlers survived by farming chickens and lucerne; a number had to live and work in Port Elizabeth and Uitenhage. Without rents, the company itself hit financial difficulties; De Beers, one of the shareholders, effectively saved it by purchasing £50,000 worth of its land in 1920. Fitzpatrick visited California again in that year and remained convinced that his scheme had advantages in climate, soil, and in a relatively low price of land. But it was proving difficult to realize his Californian dream. Although the dam did fill in 1923, subsequent drought exacerbated legal wrangling over access to water. Mounting financial demands on the Department of Irrigation led the state to take over the scheme in 1925. The government subsidy for what was, after Hartebeestpoort, the second biggest dam in the country at the time amounted to £560,000.

Willcocks, however, was correct about the long term. Those settlers who survived formed an irrigation board and, working closely with officials, established an effective regime. Citrus required a regular pattern of watering, and

<hr />

[131] Ibid. 68.

it had to take precedence because of the value of the trees. With Mosenthals, the Port Elizabeth merchant house, as their agents, the new Sundays River Cooperative sold oranges and grapefruit successfully under the Three Ring brand until 1936; subsequently, the name Outspan was registered for all choice-grade fruit. By the 1950s much of the valley was under citrus. The surplus was sufficient for large quantities of low-grade oranges to be fed to the elephants in Addo National Park—under spotlights so that visitors could see them at night.[132]

Simultaneously, the Department of Irrigation pursued a major project in the Fish river valley, which had been the site of extensive flood irrigation systems in the late nineteenth and early twentieth centuries. Grassridge dam, on the Groot Brak, near the old Collett properties, which cost the state £173,000, was completed in 1923 and filled with far less trouble than the Sundays river dam. Lake Arthur, near Cradock, was built more quickly than any other large dam in the country at the time; 200 whites and 1,680 Africans were employed. When completed, for £550,000 in 1925, it became the second biggest dam in the country and had the widest wall, at 1,640 feet. The midland Cape was recipient of major state investment at this time.

Enthused by the achievement, some anticipated a transformation from extensive stock farms, 'in the possession of a few men who were lords of all they surveyed over thousands of morgen of land', to closer settlement.[133] Deciduous fruit production, especially apricots at the southern end of the scheme, did expand and attract new settlers. Golden Valley estates invested in a dehydration plant for export dried fruit.[134] But to a greater extent than the Sundays river scheme, Fish river farmers remained integrated into the live-stock economy around them. Existing landowners subdivided their newly irrigable land. Lucerne, long established by the lords of the valley, remained the major crop grown for sale. 'You see green, green, green and green every-where', a reporter enthused in 1925.[135] The scheme was 'a lucerne paradise' because of the lime in the soil; the reliability of the water supply allowed more frequent cropping.[136]

As transhumance became increasingly difficult because of disease regula-tions, and as the number of livestock (excepting ostriches) rose nationally,

[132] Ibid. 89.

[133] *Eastern Province Herald*, 1 Oct. 1925: 'Up and Down the Valley of Surprise; Perennial Rivers in the Making'. Thanks to Jeff Butler for these references.

[134] W. A. Muller, *Middleton en sy Mense* (Swartkops Seesout Beperk, Port Elizabeth, 1988).

[135] *Eastern Province Herald*, 5 Oct. 1925: 'The Miracle of the Great Karroo; Where Lies the Commissariat of the North West'.

[136] Ibid. 'The Call of the Great Fish River Valley; Lands for Men of the Right Type'.

there was increasing demand for fodder supplies. Dried lucerne was railed all over the country. At the far north of the scheme, just below the Grassridge dam, Herbert Collett was a beneficiary. With the demise of the ostrich feather market, he invested back into 4,000 sheep and, situated adjacent to the line of rail, extended commerical lucerne production on 1,000 morgen.[137] Other established English-speaking landowners, such as Gray Barber at Halesowen, irrigated even larger areas of lucerne, cultivated with steam ploughs.

Between these two huge properties, in the area just north of Cradock, a closer settlement project was established on farms of 35 morgen of irrigable land and 300 morgen of natural veld.[138] Local landowners were keen to avoid a poor-white settlement, and the 1820 Settlers' Association in Grahamstown assisted with recruitment in England. Settlers were advised that they would require £3,000 worth of capital. H. A. W. Bladen was their ideal. Cambridge-educated, he had joined the Indian Civil Service and became tutor to a princely family before moving to the Fish river valley.[139] He concentrated on apples and walnuts, intercropped with lucerne, as well as vegetables.[140] But drought and late frosts constrained fruit production so that they relied increasingly on market gardening. When Guy Butler visited as a boy, around 1930, 'there was a kind of holy poverty there'—a decaying gentility sur-rounded by home produce.[141] Bladen stayed on and became an enthusiastic commentator on agriculture, and an expert on local bird life. As in the Sundays river valley, many other British settlers left. Water supplies proved unreliable, and the rates, which took precedence over other payments, were an inescapable burden. Even on irrigation schemes, it was difficult to survive in the rural Karoo without access to the livestock economy.

Big dams brought large amounts of state capital into the semi-arid Karoo. In limited areas, they facilitated more intensive commercial production of citrus, apricots, and lucerne. But there was never enough water to unlock the supposed riches of the Karoo soil on the scale dreamed of at the turn of the century. Big dams did little to facilitate dense settlement. Nor, ironically, did state schemes increase the overall area of irrigated land in the medium term. If census figures are accurate, the 282,000 morgen of land irrigated in the Cape in 1911 declined to 224,000 in 1930. Many farmers reduced fodder production when the market for ostrich feathers collapsed. Peak figures for

[137] Collett, *A Time to Plant*. [138] *Eastern Province Herald*, 3 Oct. 1925.

[139] Butler, *Karoo Morning*, 106.

[140] *Eastern Province Herald*, 30 Sept. 1925: 'Fruit Trees in the Thousands in the Golden Valley; Only Concentrated Block of its Kind in the World'.

[141] Butler, *Karoo Morning*, 107.

angora goats were also reached around 1911, at 3.3 million; numbers subsequently halved to about 1.6 million by 1930. Only in 1946, when the area irrigated reached about 300,000 morgen, was the 1911 figure exceeded.[142] By this time state expenditure nationally had reached £30 million.

Karoo farmers increasingly turned back to woolled merino sheep; numbers recorded in the Cape doubled from about 11 million in 1911 to a peak of 23 million in 1930 (see Introduction). While lucerne and other fodder crops were always useful for sheep farmers, they were less of a priority except in small quantities for stud animals. For some farmers, the costs of maintaining large-scale dams and irrigation works were no longer justified. Dam construction by private farmers was inhibited by law as well as economics, in that the Water Courts tried to ensure adequate flow to the major state dams. Moreover, droughts in the 1910s and 1920s may have discouraged reliance on irrigation, and soil erosion, which almost certainly intensified as livestock numbers increased, exacerbated the problem of siltation in dams.

Most important, other strategies of water and fodder provision were pursued. A decline in irrigated areas did not imply an overall decline in investment in water. Small earth dams for livestock, and boreholes, became the preferred modes of provision, well-suited for dispersed water sources in fenced paddocks. Boreholes were less dependent on unpredictable rainfall, and less water was lost from evaporation, especially if cement tanks were built for storage. The Cape did not become a hydraulic society after the model of the United States, but it did, in its dryer rural reaches, become a borehole society. Clanking metal windmills became a symbol of the farms and small towns of the Karoo.

Following Union, subsidized drilling by government teams accounted for about 600 holes a year in the 1910s, 800 in the 1920s, and even more in the 1930s.[143] By 1926, when borehole numbers were first recorded in the Agricultural Census, the Cape figure had trebled to 22,083 since 1911. The value of windmill imports rose five times between 1909 and 1929.[144] By 1936 36,191 boreholes were enumerated and in 1946, 50,655. Free State numbers increased at a similar rate. The expansion of sheep farming was at least partly dependent upon these new water sources.

In analyses of South African agriculture, intensification of production and technological innovation is often seen as associated with arable production

---

[142] Figures are irregular in the censuses. The figure given in the first agricultural census 1918 is about the same as in 1911. Figures for 1921, 1930 and 1937 are much lower, but there is a rogue figure of 307,000 morgen in 1926.

[143] Figures drawn from annual *Reports of the Director of Irrigation*.

[144] Archer, 'Technology and Ecology in the Karoo'.

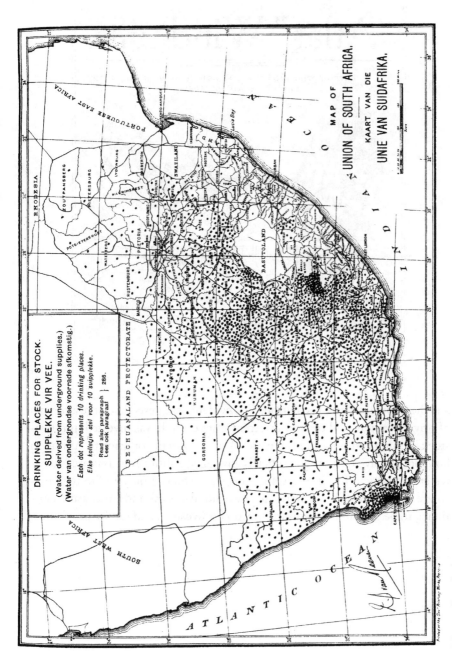

MAP 3. Boreholes, 1923

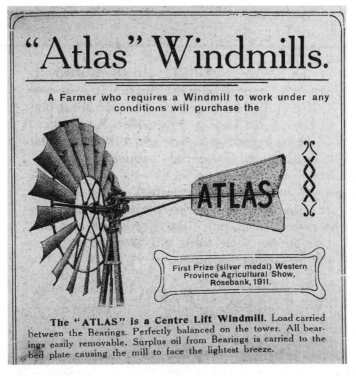

7. Windmill, 1911

and the highveld maize revolution. The evidence suggests that large amounts of private capital, and to a lesser extent state capital, was invested into livestock farming and associated activities. Water was a major priority. Although both progressive farmers and officials envisaged a shift towards more intensive arable agriculture in the Cape, this was achieved only in limited areas where rich valley soils were irrigated by major dams. By and large, water continued to be used in the semi-arid Karoo for livestock and fodder provision.

The Night of the Jackal:
Sheep, Pastures, and Predators,
1890–1930

Predators: The Cunning Jackal

Debates about improvements in the Cape pastoral economy were bedevilled
by the shadowy presence of predators, and especially jackals, on farm boundaries. Jackals stalked the countryside and the imagination of farmers. It was
the losses they caused, and the perceived losses they might cause, which were
so often cited as a major reason for the kraaling system. Jackals were the
enemy of farmers because they killed sheep. They became a particular concern for progressives and conservationists because they inhibited the changes
in livestock farming that were being advocated with ever-stronger conviction. For different reasons, jackals also became a target of the poor.

   The Drought Commission report of 1923, perhaps the most influential
conservationist publication on South Africa, which took sheep farming as its
central point of reference, quintessentially expressed deep concerns about
jackals.[1] This chapter attempts to explain why predators became such a problem in the previous few decades and how the state and farmers attempted to
deal with the 'pirate of the veld'. Analysis of the jackal question in Cape society and politics requires some understanding of the 'history' of this animal, as
well as discussion of conflicts over the control of natural forces, and the management of natural resources, in the colony.[2] To these ends, it is important to
explore how ecological influences actively shape human society, and illustrate
how nature can bite back. This chapter touches on some of these dilemmas
for environmental history, and also on the unpredictable outcomes of human
intervention.

   [1] U.G.49-1923.
   [2] Jane Carruthers, 'Towards an Environmental History of Southern Africa: Some Perspectives',
South African Historical Journal, 23 (1990), 184–95.

Many wild animals succumbed during the colonization of southern Africa. Wildlife eradication has largely been seen as part of the saga of predatory imperial and settler hunting.[3] Less has been said about the impact of settler agriculture, and of changing African peasant economies. Wild animals could be eradicated not only for food, sport, and items of trade but because they competed for grazing. A startling example is the last great migration of springboks in the Cape in 1896. A vast herd, 'as beautiful as it was wondrous', was pushed out of Namaqualand by drought into better-watered pasturages: 'the Boers mounted a huge hunting operation to prevent them damaging the veld and hundreds of thousands were shot.'[4]

The degree to which various species were affected by the settler pastoral economy depended not least on their range.[5] Hunting and game-protection laws, which reached back to the Dutch period at the Cape and were reformulated in the 1820s, were often ignored. Two of the best-known colonial extinctions, of the quagga and bluebuck, took place in the Cape in the early nineteenth century. While neither was particularly favoured for meat, both were restricted to relatively small ecological ranges along the main routes of settler expansion in the southern Cape and Karoo. From the mid-nineteenth century some individual farmers recognized that further exterminations might take place and protected vulnerable species, such as the bontebok and mountain zebra, on private farms. Most species survived because of their wider range, and because they found niches within the new colonial social geography in areas of mountain, dense vegetation, or desert. Some, such as springboks, were kept on farms, not least because they were favoured for hunting.

The Cape probably had a wider range of predators than any other of the southern lands opened up to stock farming in the nineteenth century. Their variety was in turn linked to the climatic and ecological range that sustained an extraordinary diversity of antelope and small mammal species. In the early years of settler colonization, a number of these predators adapted their

---

[3] Mackenzie, *The Empire of Nature*; Jane Carruthers, 'Game Protection in the Transvaal', unpublished Ph.D. thesis, University of Cape Town (1988); Harriet Ritvo, *The Animal Estate: The English and Other Creatures in the Victorian Age* (Penguin, Harmondsworth, 1990); W. Beinart, 'Review Article: Empire, Hunting and Ecological Change in Southern and Central Africa', *Past and Present*, 128 (1990).

[4] Mackenzie, *Empire of Nature*, 116, quoting S. C. Cronwright-Schreiner, *The Migratory Springbucks of South Africa (the Trekbokke)* (T. Fisher Unwin, London, 1925).

[5] C. Skead, *Historical Mammal Incidence*, vol. 2, *The Eastern Half of the Cape Province, including the Ciskei, Transkei and East Griqualand* (Cape Provincial Council, Cape Town, 1987); L. C. Rookemaker, *The Zoological Exploration of Southern Africa 1650–1790* (A. A. Balkema, Rotterdam, 1989).

survival strategies to the livestock economy. As mentioned, the Cape was the only new settler stock-farming zone where indigenous pastoralism had been well established. Unlike Australia, New Zealand, Argentina, and Uruguay, for example, predators had already bridged the divide between wild game and domesticated livestock as a source of food supply. In a sense, the Cape's predators were ready for colonial livestock from the start.

The conditions created by the colonial intrusion were not initially as unfavourable to predators as to grazing species. Opportunities were created in that antelopes were displaced by livestock and the quantity of meat on the colony's pastures increased. Lions attacked colonial stock from van Riebeeck's time: they 'seemed almost to storm the fort to get at the sheep which are kept inside at night'.[6] Robben Island was favoured as an early grazing ground because it was free from predators. Lions, it seems, took a particular liking to introduced horses, which shared characteristics with the wild equines, quagga and zebra, formerly significant as their prey. Accounts describing encounters with lions abound in the hunting and travel literature; they have heavy symbolic loading and must be treated with care. To confront the king of beasts in the wild, more so to experience a close shave, or lose so vital a resource as a horse, both elevated the storyteller and sold books.[7] But such large carnivores, which could threaten human as well as animal life, were vulnerable precisely because they were seen as so dangerous.

Lions also preferred the plains, hunted by day, often near water-sources, and required fresh meat regularly. They were too conspicuous to survive for long—even if they did, as reported, learn to stop roaring in the vicinity of people and traffic.[8] They were usually one of the first species to be shot out in any area of settlement, and had disappeared from the Cape by the mid-nineteenth century. Had their range, by chance, been restricted to the area south of the Gariep, they might have become extinct in South Africa. Some sources suggest that there was a distinct Cape sub-species of lion with heavier mane and darker colouring, and that this may have been exterminated.[9]

Hyenas, called wolves by the Dutch, were mentioned along with lions as the most dangerous animals in the early years of colonization. They too adapted to livestock and could scavenge on the bones and skins of dead

---

[6] Skead, *Historical Mammal Incidence*, i. 150. Skead was not correct to suggest that this was the origins of kraaling in South Africa.

[7] An example which probably influenced others was Pringle, *Narrative*, i. 107. There is no particular reason to doubt his account, in which a lion 'killed my favourite riding horse'. Skead, *Historical Mammal Incidence*, ii. 532.

[8] *Cape Monthly Magazine*, 2 (1871): 'Notes in Natural History' by 'a traveller' (H.E.).

[9] Skead, *Historical Mammal Incidence*, ii. 989–1003. He notes that the colouring and size of lions can differ considerably depending on the habitat, and doubts that there was a separate sub-species.

animals. Unlike lions, hyenas often fed at night. But they too succumbed because they were especially susceptible to traps. Their predeliction for carrion, and apparent lack of suspicion about closed spaces, worked against them. The wolwehok (hyena trap), roughly constructed from stone or wood, was a feature of early frontier farms. Meat, sometimes poisoned, was laid within it and a trap-door designed to shut when the bait was disturbed.

Leopards (initially called tigers) tended to live in secreted locations such as rocky outcrops or krantzes and gorges where tree or bush cover was abundant. They hunted at night, over a limited range, and were less frequently observed. Probably for this reason leopards, although vigorously pursued, survived in the wild when the lion could not. Moreover, their habitat was less immediately attractive to stock farmers, and some of their favoured prey, such as baboons and small antelope, also inhabited these niches. Smaller wild cat species, especially the caracal, often called a lynx or rooikat, frequently attacked farm animals near to their lairs, but were relatively successful in secreting themselves in habitats similar to the leopard's. They survived better than leopards into the twentieth century and remained a problem for small stock farmers at its end; the expanding flocks were easy meat for them.

Stealthier wild felines had an advantage, and the same was true of dogs. The African wild dog (*Lycaon pictus*)—with a blotched coat of brown, white, and black—hunted in packs that were able to tackle a wide range of animals, including the largest antelope. They could chase for long periods, weakening their prey by biting at its hindquarters, a strategy graphically described in some of the older natural-history books on South Africa. Modern zoologists suggest that the wild dog has 'a mostly undeserved reputation as a voracious and indiscriminate killer of game and livestock'.[10] But the wild dog is now amongst the most threatened mammal species, and conservationists have to fight hard for its reputation. There is considerable evidence going back to the seventeenth and eighteenth century to suggest that they were 'a great menace to sheep'.[11] The hunter Cumming recorded in the 1850s that 'the devastation occasioned by these dogs among the flocks of the Dutch Boers is inconceivable'.[12] 'The voracious dogs,' he wrote, 'not contented with killing as many as they can eat, follow resolutely on, tearing and mangling all that come within their reach' in their 'sanguinary massacre'. Cumming had a strong eye for the spectacular, but he was not alone in describing such

[10] J. R. Ginsburg and D. W. Macdonald, *Foxes, Wolves, Jackals, and Dogs: An Action Plan for the Conservation of Canids* (IUCN, Switzerland, 1990), 19.

[11] Skead, *Historical Mammal Incidence*, i. 62–3; Thunberg, *Travels*, 186.

[12] R. G. Cumming, *Five Years' Adventures in the Far Interior of South Africa* (John Murray, London, 1856) revised edn., 104.

behaviour. Others noted that the dogs would 'rip, tear and slaughter five or six times as many victims as they actually devour', or kill sheep for 'pure mischief and devilry'.[13]

Stevenson-Hamilton, first warden of the Kruger National Park, painted a more sympathetic portrait, which is careful to avoid imputing motives to animals, and is clearly based on his own observation.[14] Wild dogs behaved in a similar manner when attacking a herd of impala, their favoured prey in the Transvaal. They preferred shock tactics, killing all they could immediately, and chasing others which they anticipated would flee. Sheep, especially merinos, which tended to scatter when attacked, must have been particularly vulnerable to such a strategy of predation. Wild dogs, unlike jackals, had 'contempt of any but fresh meat', and tended to avoid carrion.[15] They did not usually return to meat or secrete it for further meals. While these natural patterns of behaviour made them difficult to trap, wild dogs had to hunt frequently.

These latter traits may help to explain why they failed to survive. Wild dogs were coursers, not stalkers, usually hunting at dawn or dusk, and were easily seen and shot. Cumming noted that 'they are of a bold and daring disposition, and do not entertain much fear of man, evincing less concern than any other carnivorous animal with which I am acquainted'.[16] Stevenson-Hamilton also noted their 'great indifference to Man's presence, and a reluctance to retire before him'—though he attributed this to a lack of familiarity.[17] While it is difficult to speculate about animal behaviour in the past, there do seem to have been limits to the wild dogs' adaptability. They required extensive ranges—a point stressed by conservationists in order to defend enlarged boundaries for game reserves. They were also susceptible to diseases spread by domestic dogs, especially distemper.[18] By the late nineteenth century they had ceased to be a problem for stock farmers except in the most thinly populated regions of the arid north and north-west; here, even cattle farmers experienced attacks up to the 1920s.[19] They became extinct in South Africa outside of the Kruger National Park.[20]

[13] H. A. Bryden, *Wildlife in South Africa* (G. G. Harrap, London, 1936), 14.

[14] James Stevenson-Hamilton, *Wild Life in South Africa*, 2nd edn. (Cassell, London, 1950), 224–240.

[15] Ibid. 231.   [16] Cumming, *Five Years' Adventure*, 103.

[17] Stevenson-Hamilton, *Wild Life*, 233.

[18] Ginsberg and Macdonald, *Foxes, Wolves*, 19; Stevenson-Hamilton, *Wild Life*, 22, 236–7.

[19] Cape Archives, Provincial Secretary (CA PAS) 3/109, VC8, Evidence to the Vermin Extermination Commission, 1924, 245–7: Evidence Thomas Smith and J. J. Keeley, Mafikeng.

[20] Stevenson-Hamilton, *Wild Life*, notes that wild dogs were shot in the Park for the first three decades of the century, in order to assist the recovery of antelope numbers, but suggests that disease was more significant in their demise.

There were two kinds of jackal in southern Africa as well as a number of species sometimes called jackals.[21] The side-striped jackal (*Canis adustus*) prefers the edges of moister savannahs and more densely wooded areas in central Africa; it was rare in the main sheep zone of South Africa. Within the country, it was largely found in present-day Mpumalanga. The most important sheep predator was the black-backed jackal (*Canis mesomelas*), widespread in southern and eastern Africa, especially in open savannah and semi-arid zones. It was named after the wide saddle of silvery, black hair on its back. For the rest, it is reddish-brown in colour and sometimes called rooijakkals by Afrikaners. The Tswana made striking striped hats and cloaks from its skin.[22] It is a smaller animal than the wild dog, and not particularly big even by jackal standards. But it was able to adapt to changing circumstances better than any other of the wild dogs or cats.

Jackals were not animals sought by hunters, nor are they much mentioned in nineteenth-century hunting literature. Bryden's compilation of game in 1899 does not cite the jackal in 600 pages.[23] However, a good deal was published on jackals around the turn of the century, as natural-history texts displaced hunting sagas. Government committees scrutinized their behaviour; farmers and officials debated strategies of elimination in the *Agricultural Journal*. These agree that jackals were omnivorous. They would eat carrion, bones, small mammals of all kinds—anything that they could catch without too much risk—insects, and reptiles, as well as some vegetation, especially berries and grass. This view is confirmed by more recent scientific studies: a jackal is 'able to exist as a predator on small game, a scavenger, an insect or rodent eater, or a sheep-killer.'[24] One jackal stomach cut open for scientific research contained 1,400 termites. On the west coast of Namibia, jackals survive on marine resources and seabirds.[25]

Jackals can clearly adapt to the predominant food supply, and probably did so more effectively than other predators. The question must be raised as to

[21] Mark Bekoff, 'Social Behavior and Ecology of the African Canidae: A Review', in M. W. Fox (ed.), *The Wild Canids: Their Systematics, Behavioral Ecology and Evolution* (Van Nostrand Reinhold, New York, 1975).

[22] Thompson, *Travels and Adventures*, 86: the kaross worn by the chief he drew was that of a striped wild cat. Cumming, *Five Years' Adventures*, 188; Sol T. Plaatje, *Mhudi* (Heinemann, London, 1978), 27–8.

[23] H. A. Bryden, *Great and Small Game of Africa: An Account of the Distribution, Habits, and Natural History of the Sporting Mammals, with Personal Hunting Experiences* (R. Ward, London, 1899).

[24] D. T. Rowe-Rowe, 'Food of the Black-backed Jackal in Nature Conservation and Farming Areas in Natal', *East African Wildlife Journal*, 14 (1976), 345–8.

[25] G. Avery, D. M. Avery, S. Braine, and R. Loutit, 'Prey of the Coastal Black-backed Jackal *Canis mesomelas* (Mammalia: Canidae) in the Skeleton Coast Park, Namibia', *Journal of Zoology*, 213 (1987), 81–94.

how that adaption took place and whether, as in the case of wild dogs, there were limits to this process. Historical study of animal behaviour, which attempts to go beyond human perceptions of animals, raises particular problems. Although Konrad Lorenz, a founder and popularizer of ethology, insists that 'without supernatural assistance, our fellow creatures can tell us the most beautiful stories', nevertheless animals cannot easily speak for themselves, and changing behaviour must be adduced from external manifestations recorded often incidentally in a wide variety of sources and settings.[26]

There are some fascinating attempts in the older natural histories to offer a history of jackal behaviour and consumption. Natural historians of the early twentieth century, such as F. W. Fitzsimons, Director of the Port Elizabeth Museum, were also less cautious than modern zoologists in using stories and reports from farmers. His discussion in *The Natural History of South African Mammals* (1919) is striking for its literary skill and speculative ambition, which most recent classificatory books lack.[27] He was also clearly influenced by the ecological ideas that were beginning to gain acceptance at the time. Observations of the jackal, he suggested, indicated that when carrion was plentiful, this dominated their diet. Like vultures, they were 'Nature's Sanitary Corps'. They contributed towards the control of disease by clearing up corpses of all kinds very quickly. Jackals coexisted with the big cats in a particular zone and scavenged on lion kills. Mature jackals did mark their territory, but they could become partly migratory—at least for some of the year. They followed large herds of antelope, feeding on weak animals that had fallen behind, or males maimed in fights for superiority.[28]

Fitzsimons argued that the jackal's diet had shrunk with colonization. As herds of antelope were shot out by hunters and farmers blazing their way through the countryside, jackals adapted their behaviour to follow them, attracted by this new source of carrion and the smell of cooking meat. It is in this role that they were sometimes mentioned in the hunting sagas, their characteristic howl piercing the African nights; the call, Fitzsimons noted, 'begins with a mournful wail, and ends with what might be construed into a cynical laugh'.[29] Jackals were not known to attack humans, but they became a

---

[26] Konrad Lorentz, *King Solomon's Ring* (Pan Books, London, 1957), 15.

[27] F. W. Fitzsimons, *The Natural History of South African Mammals*, 4 vols. (Longmans, Green, London, 1919–20), ii. 92 ff. Cf. W. Sclater, *The Mammals of South Africa*, 2 vols. (R. H. Porter, London, 1900–1). Both relied on correspondents rather than observation. One acknowledged source was a Karoo farmer: S. Bonnin Hobson, 'Jackals: Their History, Habits and Depradations', *Agricultural Journal*, 15: 5 (31 Aug. 1899), 351.

[28] Hugo and Jane van Lawick-Goodall, *Innocent Killers* (Collins, London, 1970), 134 ff. N. J. van der Merwe, 'The Jackal', 16, finds no record in South Africa of jackals trailing migratory herds.

[29] Fitzsimons, *South African Mammals*, ii. 104.

pest, 'growling over the garbage cast on the dunghills of a frontier outpost'.[30] Like American coyotes, they developed a taste for leather goods purloined at night. It was only when both carrion and game diminished, Fitzsimons suggested, that they began to depend more heavily on small stock.

A detailed study of changing jackal behaviour, published by N. J. van der Merwe some years later, developed and amended the argument that sheep-killing resulted largely from the decline in other foods available to jackals.[31] He suggested that veld-burning, which destroyed many small mammals, was as harmful as hunting. An increase in the number of domestic dogs, partly to control predators, also resulted in more competition for small animals. Jackal predations tended to be worst in droughts, when other food sources diminished and sheep were weak; in some cases jackals may have been blamed for killing animals already dead from disease or thirst. Fitzsimons, and especially van der Merwe, were approaching the issue as conservationists. Although both accepted that it was essential to exterminate jackals in sheep-rearing areas, nevertheless they suggested environmentally sensitive responses to minimize predation on sheep. Less burning would encourage more small animals and birds; this would benefit the veld, farmers, sheep, and jackals.

Van der Merwe was particularly interested in the similarities between the jackal and the coyote in the United States. He considered that both, while previously important in helping to maintain the natural balance, had lost their usefulness 'with the coming of civilization'.[32] The coyote benefited because of the demise of its enemies, the cougar and golden eagle, and its competitor the wolf. Deforestation, in particular, favoured coyotes against wolves; coyotes thrived on the increase of carrion such as dead horses and wildlife along trade and shooting routes.[33] The range of the coyote seems to have expanded in the second half of the nineteenth century. Similarly, the jackal's competitors and its predators, such as wild dogs, pythons, hyenas, eagles, and large cats, had declined in number: 'man made large areas safe for the jackal.'[34]

Both Fitzsimons and van der Merwe probably saw too clear a sequence in these changes. They tended to assume that jackals preferred wild prey and had somewhat reluctant recourse to livestock as their options narrowed. Such

---

[30]   Hall, *Geography*, 116.   [31]   van der Merwe, 'The Jackal'.

[32]   N. J. van der Merwe, 'The Coyote and the Black-backed Jackal: A Comparison of Certain Similar Characteristics', *Fauna and Flora*, 3 (1953), 45–51.

[33]   H. T. Gier, 'Ecology and Behavior of the Coyote (*Canis latrans*)', in Fox (ed.), *The Wild Canids*, 247 ff. Marc Bekoff and Michael C. Watts, 'Social Ecology and Behaviour of Coyotes', *Advances in the Study of Behavior*, 16 (1986).

[34]   van der Merwe, 'Coyote and Jackal', 47.

ideas are echoed in recent general books claiming that 'only certain individuals take to stock-killing'.[35] It is unlikely, however, that there was a simple inverse relationship between natural food sources and predation on stock. Khoikhoi pastoral systems, going back two thousand years, were deeply influenced by the threat of jackals, even though wildlife was then plentiful.[36] Jackals were eating fat-tailed sheep before colonists arrived, and their population dynamics must already have been attuned to the availability of domesticated species.

Van der Merwe somewhat contradicted himself in accepting that, once the adaption had been made, 'sheepkilling was much easier and the meat perhaps more appetising that that of animals of the veld'.[37] Merinos may have been easier to catch because they tended to scatter when attacked. In this way 'depraved tastes' developed, even when wild prey was available, and jackals may have migrated to sheep areas.[38] This did not mean that jackals ate solely lamb. Van der Merwe's correspondents noted that when black-backed jackals were destroyed on a farm, the number of small antelope and birds, as well as dassies, hares, and other small mammals, tended to increase quickly. Whatever the case, the growth in stock numbers and reduction in other food sources in the nineteenth and early twentieth centuries must have altered the overall balance in the jackal's diet.

Jackal adaptability was facilitated by a number of behavioural features that distinguished them from other predators and were emphasized by the changing nature of their habitat. Their reproductive cycle seems to have been, or became, closely attuned to that of sheep. They would take mature sheep, but predation tended to peak at lambing. In some areas this came in spring, a little after the favoured jackal-breeding season from August to October. Lambs were thus available at a time of peak jackal demand. Unlike wild dogs, jackals tended to hunt alone or in pairs, except when a bitch was teaching its young (usually around five or six) this skill.[39] Although they were occasionally reported to run down their quarry, they were stalkers rather than coursers, using stealth rather than speed. Moreover, most sources are agreed that whereas in the wild jackals were active both diurnally and nocturnally, when they were near people they became very largely creatures of the night. They seemed to be blessed with sensitive smell, hearing, and taste.

In these respects, jackals differed from wild dogs. But they also had a significant advantage over the big cats. They ate a wider range of foods. And

---

[35] Chris and Tilde Stuart, *Field Guide to the Mammals of Southern Africa* (London, 1988), 124.
[36] Elphick, *Khoikhoi and the Founding of White South Africa*, 59; Smith, *Pastoralism in Africa*, 203.
[37] van der Merwe, 'The Jackal', 17.   [38] Ibid. 14.
[39] Fitzsimons, *South African Mammals*, ii. 105; van der Merwe, 'The Jackal', 18.

while caracals and leopards were stealthy and dangerous night hunters, their range was more restricted to the zones immediately around their rocky lairs. Jackals made their base in a wider variety of habitats, and had a considerably broader range of hunting operations—at least up to 25 kilometres away from their main territory (or their lair when they had pups).[40] A Department of Agriculture survey in the early 1920s reported that jackals could travel for long periods at 'a dog-trot, five to six miles an hour' at night for at least 25 miles (42 kms) and possibly more.[41] In a later Transvaal experiment, tagged jackals of six months old were found an average of 55 kilometres, and some over 100 kilometres, from their place of release.[42] Even where farmers succeeded in controlling jackals in their immediate areas, any under-used land could provide a haven for them from which they could rapidly migrate.

Migration was partly related to food supplies, and jackals could follow flocks of transhumant farmers just as they had followed migratory antelopes. Migration was also probably a continuous feature of the jackals' reproductive cycle. Jackal pairs maintained long-term bonds and could also incorporate some of their offspring, both male and female, in sharing the tasks of protection and provisioning. This increased the chances of survival for all. But once they could fend for themselves, and were no longer needed as 'helpers', young jackals were 'driven off or led away by their parents'.[43]

Jackals seem to have been overshadowed as predators by big cats, hyenas, and wild dogs in newer areas of white settlement until about the middle of the nineteenth century.[44] Records of rewards paid for skins are one indication of the impact of various predators. The jackal was not prioritized in the early nineteenth century; the bounty on their head in 1814 was 1 rixdaler, along with wild cats, compared with 25 rixdalers for leopards and 20 for hyenas.[45] By the 1840s, when merinos were established, new rewards offered £3 for a hyena, £2 for a leopard, 6 shillings for a jackal and 1 shilling for a wild cat. In the late nineteenth century the gap had closed: wild dog skins fetched 15 shillings, leopards 10 shillings, jackals and caracals 7 shillings, and baboons 2s. 6d.[46]

[40] Union of South Africa, Province of the Cape of Good Hope, *First and Second Reports of the Vermin Extermination Commission*, C.P.3-1924.

[41] A. Roberts, 'Life-history of the Jackal', *Journal of the Department of Agriculture*, 5: 3 (1922), 238.

[42] J. du P. Bothma, 'Notes on Movement by the Black-backed Jackal and the Aardwolf in the Western Transvaal', *Zoologica Africana*, 6: 2 (1971), 205-7.

[43] Patricia D. Moehlman, 'Jackal Helpers and Pup Survival', *Nature*, 277 (1979), 382-3. Her research was done in the Serengeti.

[44] Sparrman, *Voyage*, ii. 141.   [45] Thom, *Geskiedenis van die Skaapboerdery*, 70-2.

[46] Cape of Good Hope, *Report of the Select Committee on the Destruction of Vermin*, A.9-1899, appendices.

Because of their adaptability and success in the interstices of the colonial pastoral economy, it is likely that jackal numbers actually increased along with sheep. We should probably dismiss the idea that jackals were sparing sheep eaters and that only a limited percentage ate sheep—at least in the early twentieth-century Cape. Amongst the first detailed studies of jackal diets were those in the Transvaal between 1965 and 1971. The contents of over 400 stomachs, mostly killed in eradication programmes, were analysed.[47] Of jackals killed in game reserves, only 6 per cent had sheep remains in their stomachs, but of those killed in farming districts 27 per cent. A study in Natal at about the same time found 35 per cent of stomachs from jackals killed on farms carried sheep remains.[48] These two reports, which showed that between a quarter and a third of jackals ate sheep, were based on research conducted in areas with fewer sheep than the turn-of-the-century Cape, and where jackals' access to sheep was more difficult because of fencing and vermin programmes. An inquiry in 1979 reported that jackals accounted for around 0.07 per cent of sheep annually in the Transvaal and Natal, compared with at least 5 per cent, or hundreds of thousands, at the Cape in the early twentieth century.[49] It is highly probable that a much greater percentage of jackals ate sheep in the Cape.

The jackal's stealthy behaviour encouraged almost everyone, including the most serious of natural historians, to see it as a 'cowardly, treacherous and secretive' animal.[50] Zoological writing in the early twentieth century had not yet jettisoned such anthropomorphic language, nor the attribution of human designs to animals. Settler discourse about jackals, aside from reflecting hard experience, drew on indigenous ideas and European traditions. The jackal often played the role of 'a person full of tricks and cunning' in San, Khoikhoi, and African folk tales.[51] The word 'jackal' was used amongst Dutch settlers to denote a liar by the early eighteenth century.[52] Its reputation for 'cunning' was soon learnt by British settlers in the eastern Cape.[53] Printed English and

[47] J. du P. Bothma, 'Food of Canis Mesomelis in South Africa', Zoologica Africana, 6: 2 (1971), 195–203.

[48] Rowe-Rowe, 'Food of the Black-backed Jackal'.

[49] Oranje-Vrystaat, 'Verslag van die Kommissie van Ondersoek na Ongediertebestryding en Ronloperhonde in die Oranje-Vrystaat 1979', unpublished (Provincial Council, Bloemfontein), 8–10.

[50] Fitzsimons, South African Mammals, ii. 93; cf. Sclater, Mammals of South Africa, 94, who emphasizes cowardliness.

[51] Frank Brownlee, 'Dove and Jackal—Collected from the Xhosa', in S. Gray (ed.), The Penguin Book of South African Stories (Penguin, Harmondsworth, 1985), 14; W. H. I. Bleek, Reynard the Fox in Africa: Or Hottentot Fables and Tales (Trubner, London, 1864); G. R. van Weilligh, Dierestories (J. L. van Schaik, Pretoria, 1980), first published 1906. Rookmaker, Zoological Exploration, 80.

[52] Skead, Mammal Incidence, i. 55.   [53] Pringle, Narrative, 48.

Afrikaans versions of indigenous stories were available by the late nineteenth century.

Both Afrikaner and English stories were influenced by the experience and mythology of foxes: the jackal was frequently compared with the fox, and Bleek entitled his collection of Khoisan folk tales *Reynard the Fox in Africa*. Jackals were also, both in documents and in fiction, conjured as male, despite the fact 'that the bitch is generally recognised as the more active hunter, especially if there are cubs'.[54] It is true that the masculine gender was often used to refer to species, including humans, as a whole. But in fictional stories the female jackal tends to be at home with the cubs. Maleness was clearly a more convenient gender for accommodating the qualities of trickery and treachery ascribed to the jackal.

Stories about the cunning (*slim* in Afrikaans) jackal, some no doubt true, abounded. They could dodge poison and traps; they could recognize and refuse food touched by human hand, or smelling of oil and metal. They knew how to mislead chasing dogs by crossing water, or by running round and round bushes before taking off in a new direction. They would signal submission to dogs, or feign death or injury, only to launch off if the hounds hestitated; female jackals would even try to induce dogs to mate with them. Jackals reputedly developed ploys to attract curious sheep by rolling on their backs. They could climb fences or burrow under them, and once the gap was known it was remembered.

A farmer told the Chief Forester 'that the wily jackal has a trick of rendering himself invisible to the human eye and that he whisks his brush as he moves along so as to obliterate his spoor!'[55] Fitzsimon thought they had learnt to take ostrich eggs from nests and crack them by knocking them together or against a wall. As in the case of sheep predation, it is likely that this was a far older pattern of behaviour. 'Every farmer and every farmhand can tell of some sagacious feat of the jackhal,' P. J. du Toit, later Secretary of Agriculture, wrote in 1904, 'and if conversation round a cup of coffee is in danger of exhaustion, it can at once be revived by raising the jackal question.'[56]

Jackals were represented as almost human opponents. Words such as 'robber', *vrijbuiter* (freebooter or privateer), and 'pirate' were applied to them, signifying the link between property and the control over nature. Similar

---

[54] van der Merwe, 'The Jackal', 19.

[55] Cape Archives, Department of Forestry (CA FCE) 3/1/57, 590, Storr Lister to Under Secretary for Agriculture, 5 June 1905.

[56] CA PAS 3/113 V4, typescript of article by P. J. du Toit, 'South African Jackhals' (1904), who also noted that 'its highly developed sense of self-preservation invests our enemy with so much interest and importance that some apply to him a title of respect'; *Agricultural Journal*, 25: 5 (1904).

sentiments had been used in respect of the San on the peripheries of the colony. Jackals served as a metaphor for malign powers or for ecological and social relationships that farmers could not control. Because of their reputation they may have been blamed more than they deserved for stock losses—in particular, for killing rather than scavenging sheep that had died from disease or drought. Predator losses and stock theft may have been confused, and both jackals and stock thieves may have been blamed when the carelessness of farmers or shepherds (or hungry domestic dogs) were the problem.[57] A recent survey in the eastern Cape suggested that farmers tend to be particularly, and perhaps unjustifiably, hostile to predators when their overall economic position is vulnerable.[58] But there is no doubt that jackals took many lambs and sheep. They tended to kill by biting from underneath the throat, and farmers felt sure that they could distinguish the tell-tale marks.[59]

Methods of Extermination: Trapping, Poisoning, and Hunting

Jackals were hunted by the Khoikhoi, Africans, and settlers in order to protect their flocks. The Khoikhoi had eaten them; some African people made use of their pelts. Although there was an occasional market for skins, settlers killed jackals primarily as vermin. Vermin were broadly defined to include all animals that preyed on stock or were conceived as inimical to the agrarian economy. The term used in Afrikaans, *ongedierte*, expressed accurately the idea of a non-animal or de-animalized creature, which could be treated differently. Jackals were exempt from the restrictions on hunting elaborated during the nineteenth century and consolidated in the Cape's Game Law Amendment Act of 1886. As noted, bounties were sporadically offered to encourage more systematic slaughter.

It was difficult to spot and shoot jackals in the day, so that other strategies of attack were preferred. African hunters had long worked on foot, with dogs. Afrikaners as well as Africans used horses and firearms. The Cape Governor in the 1820s, Lord Charles Somerset, was a devotee of the burgeoning English sport of fox hunting and transposed it to South Africa; he was

---

[57] On stock theft and carelessness, see W. Beinart, 'Settler Accumulation in East Griqualand from the Demise of the Griqua to the Natives Land Act', in Beinart et al. (eds.), *Putting a Plough to the Ground*.

[58] Eureta Janse van Rensburg, 'Problem Animals—Problem People', *Endangered Wildlife*, 7 (1991).

[59] Jackals also maimed escaping sheep by biting them in the rear, in a way more typical of dogs, and here there could have been confusion.

followed by officers of the Indian army who stopped at the Cape on their return home.[60] Frederick Carrington imported new hounds and spread the gospel of the hunt when he became Colonel of the Bechuanaland Police in the 1880s.[61] The Mafikeng hunt ran twice or three times a week throughout the year. New packs were started in Rhodesia, Johannesburg, and in Cape farming districts. Late nineteenth-century hunting, as described by Bryden, who participated in such meets, had become less formal than its English progenitor. Nevertheless he waxed lyrical about the jackal as a quarry. It had a 'beautiful action, smooth, subtle and gliding, stride for stride the exact counterpart of that of his cousin of England': 'a fox of foxes' which could run ahead of the hounds for up to an hour and a half, 'afford excellent sport', and 'die gallantly in the open'.[62]

Sports hunting was not initially the most common or effective means of controlling jackals. In the rough terrain of the Cape, mostly innocent of fences, jackals were difficult to corner. At this time more individual strategies involving traps, poison, and attempts to catch jackals in their lairs were favoured. Lairs or burrows became a major target, especially during the main jackal-breeding season in spring (August to October), also an important lambing season, when jackals were most active as predators. This was one arena where the battle of wits was fought out.

Jackals usually raised their litters in burrows, taken over and adapted from meerkats, aardvarks, or dug in termite mounds. It was not difficult for experienced trackers to spot these, in that debris would be left near the entrance when cubs were in the den. This did not mean that they were easy targets. Adults did not live long with cubs in the den, and if they saw that the lair was spotted, bitches were known to move their cubs some distance at night.[63] Jackals were thought to be expert at defending burrows against fox terriers sent down to hound them out. Sometimes they shared burrows with porcupines, which helped in defence. Parts of the burrows, it was thought, were disguised from dogs by the use of side tunnels blocked temporarily with earth. Adults regurgitated food so that cubs were not exposed when feeding. As a last resort, farmers occasionally used dynamite to blow the burrows up.

The other major strategies for extermination were traps and poison. Walled, enclosed traps built for hyenas were seldom effective for suspicious jackals, even though, like the hyena, they were attracted to rotting meat. It

---

[60] *Cape Monthly Magazine*, 7 (1860), 286.

[61] H. A. Bryden, *Nature and Sport in South Africa* (London, 1897), ch. 10, 'Fox Hunting in Bechuanaland'.

[62] Ibid. 111 ff.; cf. Fitzsimons and Sclater, who stress its cowardliness.

[63] Roberts, 'Life-history of the Jackal', 241.

may be that this differential susceptibility helped to fuel notions of the intelligence gap between 'dom [stupid] wolf' and 'slim [cunning] jakkals', which permeated Khoisan and Afrikaner literature.[64] Sprung traps with metal jaws were more effective for jackals. These were laid in the veld, sometimes with bait, and if possible disguised on known jackal routes. Trapping and hunting could be complementary. 'If dogs are kept,' W. Cloete from Upper Albany advised in 1895, 'let them kill as many of the trapped jackals as convenient as it makes them very keen on jackals in the veld.'[65]

By the late nineteenth century poison, especially odourless strychnine, was the favoured method of attack. The Rubidge family in Graaff-Reinet used poison for jackals and 'tigers' in the early 1850s, if not before, and laid it systematically on and around their farm for the next seventy years.[66] Poisoning clubs were established in the 1880s, and the *Agricultural Journal* (launched 1889) became an important vehicle for spreading and co-ordinating the campaign. In the same year state bounties were renewed in the shape of small rewards for tails, and strychnine was subsidized. At the annual Congresses of the Wild Animal Poisoning Clubs, held in the 1890s, demands for predator control were formulated and technical problems in the use of poison shared. George Palmer, the Secretary, was a leading midland farmer and parliamentarian, based at Cranemere in Pearston district, in the heart of the Camdeboo.[67] In the midlands at least, the clubs were largely, though not exclusively, English-speaking.

Poisoning campaigns had been reasonably successful against the dingo in Australia, whose predations had similarly necessitated 'yarding' (kraaling) sheep at night in some areas. In Australia, to a greater extent than South Africa, the labour costs involved in shepherding were a factor in stimulating dingo eradication, fencing, and paddocking.[68] 'The absence of all destructive wild animals', a leading Graaff-Reinet farmer noted on visiting Victoria in 1889, 'except the dingoe, a kind of wild dog, in some parts, is a very great advantage Australia possesses over the Cape.'[69] Various Australian colonies had used bounties for dingoes, for feral domestic dogs, and for the introduced

---

[64] von Wielligh, *Dierestories*, 42: 'the hyena never learnt from experience—it remained from beginning to end a "domkop" [numbskull].' The literary relationship was elaborated in the popular Afrikaans strip cartoons written and illustrated by T. O. Honiball from 1942 to 1969.

[65] *Agricultural Journal*, 8: 11 (30 May 1895), 283: W. Cloete, letter.

[66] Rubidge diary, 20 May 1852, 11 July 1852, 3 Jan. 1853, 21 Feb. 1853, 26 Nov. 1854, and *passim*. Cape of Good Hope, A.2-1904, *Report of the Select Committee on the Destruction of Vermin*, Evidence Walter Rubidge.

[67] Palmer, *Plains of the Camdeboo*.   [68] Ranken, *The Dominion of Australia*.

[69] *Agricultural Journal*, 1: 21 (9 May 1889): C. J. Watermeyer, Colonies Plaats, 'Notes by a Cape Farmer on a Recent Australian Tour', 176.

English fox.[70] South Africa was at least saved the introduction of exotic foxes; they would probably not have competed successfully with jackals. Similarly, introduced rabbits—a scourge in Australia—made little impact at the Cape, probably because of the prevalence of predators.

During the 1890s Cape bounties increased to a flat rate of 7 shillings per jackal or caracal tail. The poisoning clubs, which charged membership fees, sometimes added a few shillings to the reward in their area, and put bounties on animals that did not feature on the government's list.[71] The total paid out rose quickly, from little over £1,000 a year in the early 1890s to £28,000 in 1898/9.[72] Jackals were the predominant species killed in more arid areas of the northern Cape. In the midlands, baboons (at 2s. 6d.), caracals, wild cats, and monkeys were also killed in large numbers. In 1898–9 over 50,000 rewards were paid out for jackal tails, nearly 10.000 in Vryburg district alone. The campaign faltered during the South African War (1899–1902), but rewards were hiked to 10 shillings for jackals in 1903 and significant payouts resumed.

With this level of state expenditure, scrutiny was inevitable. In 1899 and 1904 the Cape parliament appointed select committees to investigate the operation of the reward system. The 1899 Committee was particularly concerned about rumours of fraudulent claims. Tails only were required as proofs, and some magistrates—or the junior officials assigned by them to supervise the system—were seen to be careless. Manufactured tails of 'skin sewn up' were presented; 'it was cleverly done'.[73] Tails of other animals such as the meerkat were substituted. A few officials were tardy in the unpleasant task of destroying the putrid evidence; rotten tails were occasionally purloined, recycled, and presented for reward more than once. There was a whiff of corruption at a few magistrates' offices.

The largest sums were paid out in the four huge northern Cape districts of Gordonia, Kenhardt, Kuruman, and Vryburg. These areas were being more intensively farmed for the first time, by a new breed of commercial farmer, and it is unsurprising that eradication was energetic. Traders and hunters also brought skins across the border from the Free State, German South West Africa, and especially Bechuanaland.[74] Although, as one witness pointed out,

[70] Bolton, *Spoils and Spoilers.*

[71] Cape of Good Hope, A.9-1899, *Report of the Select Commitee on the Destruction of Vermin,* Appendix.

[72] A.2-1904, Appendix.

[73] A.9-1899, 8, evidence P. Weyer, President, Jansenville Poisoning Club.

[74] For similar complaints in the 1920s, see PAS 3/109, VC8, Minutes of evidence to Vermin Extermination Commission (1924), 281: Evidence, J. W. van Coppenhagen, secretary, Gordonia Divisional Council, Upington.

it was to the benefit of Cape farmers that mobile predators be eradicated in neighbouring territories, not least because the Cape might take them over in the future, the committee felt this was an abuse of the system. In Vryburg, all four of the biggest claimants, who received over £200 each in twelve months, were black. (Farm-workers, though partly paid in kind, would receive less than a tenth of this annually in cash.) 'Jan', the most successful of them, claimed for 5 leopard skins, 32 wild dog, 62 red cat, 17 baboon, and 655 jackal tails in a year. The identity of the major beneficiaries, whether non-Cape traders or black hunters, clearly made some parliamentarians uneasy.

Both committees probably saw fraud as more serious than the evidence presented to them indicated. The 1899 Committee advocated that jackal scalps, with their distinctive ears, should accompany tails for all claims. The 1904 Committee was still disturbed that there might be trade in proofs: both unscrupulous farmers and Jewish storeowners stood accused.[75] It was suggested in evidence that high rewards might encourage 'farming' of jackals. While both committees recommended that the bounty be maintained at a high level, the concerns aired about the bounty system were sufficient for cash-strapped governments to lower or abolish rewards temporarily, both during the South African War and in the severe recession of 1906–8.

Despite massive destruction, the committees heard evidence 'that the jackal plague [was] spreading, and that jackals are now found in many parts of the Colony where they were formerly unknown'.[76] During these investigations, and again in the 1920s, a variety of problems were identified as facilitating their spread, aside from the remarkable capacities of jackals themselves. One central issue was the unevenness of control over the colony as a whole. Jackals were primarily a problem for small stock farmers; they seldom attacked cattle, even calves, although they were attracted to newly born animals and would eat the afterbirth. Sheep farmers in or near districts where cattle predominated, such as Albany, Kingwilliamstown, and Uitenhage, as well as the far northern Cape, complained that their neighbours were not so committed to eradication. In some cases crop farmers actually saw a benefit in harbouring jackals, because they controlled the hare population that damaged crops. Sheep farmers preferred to destroy the jackal and 'have the hare'.[77]

Similarly, under-used farms, or those rented out to African tenants (largely in the eastern Cape), were seen to provide safe breeding grounds for jackals. Owner-occupiers felt that they had many reasons to fulminate against

[75] A.2-1904, 35.   [76] A.9-1899, p. iv.
[77] A.2-1904, 75, evidence William Thomas, MLA.

absentee landowners: they drove up the price of land, bottled up labour by renting to Africans, and allowed the spread of prickly pear (Chapter 8).[78] The idea of a land tax, raised at this time in order to curb speculative holdings, was also discussed as a contribution to predator control. Farms infested with prickly pear were judged to 'serve as breeding places for Jackals, to the annoyance of the neighbours'.[79]

State-owned or Crown lands, and in particular the forest reserves of the eastern Cape, which had expanded in the late nineteenth century, presented a further problem. Hunting in forests was restricted to a limited number of permit-holders. Although permits were specifically granted to hunt vermin, foresters were concerned that protected species, of which there were an increasing number under the 1886 Game Law Amendment Act, would be killed under the guise of jackal extermination. In 1893 the Wild Animals Poisoning Congress specifically requested that the Forestry Department embark upon its own programme of control. Palmer, the President, who was responsible for the distribution of government-sponsored strychnine, advised them how to poison.[80]

Individual foresters were allowed to keep the rewards for the animals that they killed, thus increasing their incentive. However, the Forestry Department's increasingly energetic poisoning provoked opposition from African communities at Gwiligwili and Isidenge, who lived nearby the Amatola forests: they complained that the poison killed cattle. Forestry officials suggested in response that the protest arose because poisoned bait was eaten by dogs taken on illegal hunts.[81] When farmers' representatives reiterated their concern about forests as breeding grounds for predators in 1904, Storr Lister was less defensive, suggesting that some farmers were unsupportive of the enterprise of state forestry as a whole. Plantations in particular, he argued, were not suitable habitats and had few traces of jackal spoors. Some of his foresters were less dismissive, suggesting that the number of predators might have grown along with protected wildlife.

Twenty years later the Vermin Extermination Commission again argued that reserves for forests, game (though these were on a limited scale in the Cape), and Crown land exacerbated the problem of vermin control. 'The jackal finds a place of refuge in those regions and . . . he multiplies there

[78] Beinart, 'Settler Accumulation in East Griqualand'.
[79] Cape Archives, Cape Town municipality (CA 4/CT) 4/1/59, 153/28, Report of the Second Annual Congress of Delegates Representing the Circle Committees, Queenstown, 3 Nov. 1919, 15.
[80] CA FCE 3/1/57, file 594, G. Palmer to J. Storr Lister, Conservator of Forests, Kingwilliamstown, 10 Nov. 1893.
[81] CA FCE 3/1/57, 595, E. S. Dwyer, District Forest Officer to Conservator of Forests, Kingwilliamstown, 1 Jan. 1895 and following correspondence.

undisturbed, continually contaminating other parts where the work of extermination has already been brought to a far advanced stage.'[82] The dense Addo bush, with its herd of elephants, had long been a sore point for local farmers. Elephants trespassed onto farmland, and in 1919, a drought year, most had been shot out by a professional hunter employed by the Provincial Council. This diminished the elephant problem but not that of predators. An experiment in using large wolfhounds for jackal hunting in Addo had to be abandoned in 1920. With the elephants so diminished in number, the bush had become too dense for dogs and hunters to penetrate. The Kalahari Game Reserve in the far north of the colony presented similar problems on Gordonia farms.[83]

By contrast, the areas occupied by Africans in the eastern Cape were generally free from jackals. Though highly adaptable, jackals appear to have been less attracted to the hilly, wetter, east coast zones, where the bulk of the African population resided and where small stock numbers were relatively low. The density of African settlement, intensity of land use, and enthusiastic daily hunting by African men and youths helped to control jackal numbers. 'The native is a sportsman,' Walter Rubidge explained, 'and he hunts a good deal and exterminates them.'[84] African hunters within the reserves were not hampered to the same extent by private property.

Dogs, which abounded in most African settlements, helped to keep predators at bay. Many farmers felt that African-owned dogs were also effective at taking sheep and antelope on farms. Dog taxes were imposed by some Divisional Councils to contain such threats, and were deeply resented by farmworkers and tenants. But in East Griqualand, at least, the Farmers Congress stopped short of passing a motion for a dog tax at the turn of the century. Magistrates were concerned about the political implications of such a measure in an area that had only recently been occupied by whites, where Africans were in a large majority and where an unsuccessful rebellion was still fresh in their minds.[85] Farmers agreed that the benefits of a high concentration of dogs in keeping the jackal population under control outweighed the disadvantages.[86]

Not all working farmers destroyed jackals assiduously. In evidence to the committees, given largely by parliamentarians and progressive farmers, such neglect was usually explained by 'laziness' and the legacy of trekboer life. Undoubtedly, for those in unfenced, arid areas with huge farms, eradication

[82] *Vermin Extermination Commission*, 8.

[83] CA PAS 3/109, VC8, Minutes of evidence to Vermin Extermination Commission (1924), 285: Evidence, Dirk Albertus Kotze, Upington.

[84] A.2-1904, 7, evidence Walter Rubidge.   [85] Beinart and Bundy, *Hidden Struggles*.

[86] Beinart, 'Settler Accumulation in East Griqualand', 290.

seemed a daunting task. Up to the early twentieth century, when veterinary controls began to bite, many still went on trek for parts of the year, or kept farms in two zones which were used at different times. It was very difficult for them to police all this land simultaneously. Northern Cape farmers also experienced ecological costs from eradication. On the peripheries of the Kalahari, jackals were seen to control mice that devoured the roots of plants: 'I know a certain farm . . . near Kenhardt', one witness claimed, where 'the whole veld for six miles had been utterly destroyed by the mice.'[87] Pastures only improved after the severe drought of 1903–4, when both mice and many sheep succumbed.[88]

Jackal depredations could be uneven, not only seasonally, but over time. Sheep-killing was seen as more serious during drought years, when jackals had less to eat and weakened sheep were easy targets. Walter Rubidge, eldest son of Charles, who farmed on his own account in Aberdeen from about 1872 to 1898, estimated that he had lost 10 per cent of his 7,000 sheep and goats to jackals during the drought of 1895. By way of explanation, he added: 'you know how difficult it is to get sheep and goats in of a night which are in poor condition.'[89] Farmers trekked more often for longer distances during drought, and trailing animals could be picked off by jackals. At such times, the cry for action seemed more urgent. It is unsurprising that bounties were increased during drought years such as 1895–6, 1903–4, and 1916; similarly, the losses from drought in 1919–20, which initiated the Drought Investigation Commission, again focused attention on jackals.

Longer-term constraints on jackal eradication were compounded by short-term setbacks. The South African War was a good one for jackals. The bounty on their heads was reduced in the Cape, and large numbers of livestock were on the move or killed. In the Free State, particularly, farms were left less protected as men went to war and women were sent to camps; perhaps three-quarters of the small stock were lost.[90] Carrion was left on the veld after battles, along transport routes, and around the dispersed military encampments. Many of the poisoning clubs which had proliferated in the 1890s faltered in the politically fraught atmosphere, where English- and Afrikaans-speakers as well as loyalist and rebel Afrikaners came into conflict. Although soldiers with their bobberies (dog packs), and black transport auxiliaries hunted in the war, their target was more often game than jackals.[91]

[87] A.9-1899, 17.   [88] CA PAS 3/113 V4, du Toit, 'South African Jackhals' (1904).

[89] A.2-1904, 2, evidence Walter Rubidge.

[90] Figures for the Free State from the census of 1890 and a count of 1903.

[91] W. Nasson, 'Moving Lord Kitchener: Black Military Transport and Supply Work in the South African War, 1899–1902, with particular reference to the Cape Colony', JSAS 11: 1 (1984), 30.

Perhaps the greatest setback, however, was the increasing ineffectiveness of poisoning. Farmers had always experienced some problems in getting jackals to take poison. While strychnine was odourless, and hence ideal in baits, it had a strong bitter flavour that had to be concealed until swallowed. Jackals' sensitive taste helped them to detect poisoned meat, and they were able to regurgitate food very quickly. Regurgitation was an important strategy for jackals, and some other canids such as coyotes; it allowed them to feed cubs well away from the exposed sites of kills. (Big cats do not do this.) Again, a deeply set trait proved useful to jackals as humans reshaped ecological relationships around them. Crystals of strychnine, rather than solutions, were used in poison because they dissolved slowly and imparted less of a taste to meat. For this reason, poisoned jackals would not usually die near the point that they took the bait. Sometimes their corpses were found near water, as strychnine induced a powerful thirst. Sometimes they were not found at all.

Successful poisoning was a much-discussed art. Palmer, President of the poisoning clubs, was clearly a skilled administrator with a fine understanding of the jackal's susceptibility. He set out his ideas when advising the Department of Forestry in 1893, and these instructions were repeated in subsequent forestry circulars:

A dead kid or lamb is a very good bait but the best thing of all is anything that has been killed by the wild animal himself and not totally devoured as he is sure to return to finish it within 48 hours . . . and by poisoning it you are sure to fetch him. But if possible you ought not to touch the carcase with your hand—just cut a slit in with the point of your knife and stick the poison in as many animals have a strong objection to the smell of a human being.[92]

Farmers tried to think through the behaviour patterns of jackals in devising better strategies. Jackal routes were observed. The use of 'pills', or pieces of fat 'rolled tightly around the poison until about the size of a hen's egg', became more general in the late nineteenth century.[93] The fat was best when taken from a recently killed sheep's stomach, 'half warm'; washing made its smell, texture, and taste less palatable. Pills also diminished the risk of poison being shaken loose: Fitzsimons thought that 'the jackal invariably shakes meat before swallowing it'.[94]

Farmers were convinced that jackals were able to smell human and equine scent, even oil and metal, around traps and bait. Some advocated that the

---

[92] CA FCE 3/1/57, 594, Palmer to Storr Lister, 10 Nov. 1893.

[93] *Agricultural Journal*, 9: 17 (20 Aug. 1896) W. Guard Hobson, 'How to Destroy Jackals'.

[94] CA PAS 3/109, VC5, F. W. Fitzsimons, Director, Port Elizabeth Museum, to K. B. Powell, Secretary, Vermin Extermination Commission, 18 Feb. 1924.

hands should be steeped in the contents of a dead sheep's stomach before bait was touched. By the early twentieth century bait and pills were being singed.[95] This helped to remove the smell of humans and attracted the jackals. Tswana herdsmen used dried, ground sheep brains in jackal traps, and it was later found that the bladder of a dead jackal, hung for three days, a sheep's rectum, or a hard-boiled egg were good lures.[96] Concoctions for disguising the smell of people and taste of poison in baits and traps became a Karoo speciality and joke.[97]

Poisoning worked to a degree, but despite ever more 'cute dodges' it was by no means foolproof, and many felt that it was becoming less effective by the early twentieth century. Three main issues were raised. It was frequently claimed that poison distributed by the government was not always of the highest quality, and some jackals survived it.[98] Quicker-acting poisons were discussed, but arsenic—used for baboons—had too strong a smell, and prussic acid had to be administered as a liquid in a vial, which might be shaken loose or pass through the jackal's digestive system.[99] Government chemists suggested that the problem had more to do with the way that strychnine was laid, and the high expectations of farmers who wanted instantaneous, visible deaths. Walter Rubidge agreed that careless poisoning with insufficient continuity, was a major part of the problem. Incorrectly placed bait, or unsuitably large pieces of meat, raised the suspicions of jackals and facilitated regurgitation.[100]

It was not only careless poisoning that undermined the strategy; jackals themselves seemed to be learning. Many years later van der Merwe expressed clearly a perception which was already forming at the turn of the century: 'a black-backed jackal, having once picked up poison and having got rid of it by vomiting, will never, if it survives, eat poisoned bait again.'[101] In reassessing earlier eradication from the vantage-point of the 1950s, van der Merwe saw it as in some senses counter-productive. Half-hearted and sporadic assaults had the effect of 'killing the old jackals, the diseased, the weaklings, the stupid or the young jackals'. The healthy, he concluded, were less often destroyed: 'these true to nature, will breed wary, strong and healthy jackals and the

[95]   du Toit, 'South African Jackhals'; *Agricultural Journal*, 33 (1908), 388, 'How to Administer Poison to Jackals', and 36 (1910), 370 'Poisoning Jackals—Yet Another Cute Dodge'.

[96]   van der Merwe, 'The Jackal', 49, 70.

[97]   Palmer, *Plains of the Camdeboo*, 160, describes a mixture of 'high meat, bad sardines, donkey fat, glycerine and jackal entrails, to be buried in a container for several weeks before using'.

[98]   A.2-1899, 83, evidence Izaak Jacobus van Zyl, MLC.

[99]   CA PAS 3/109, VC5, F. W. FitzSimons, Director, Port Elizabeth Museum, to K. B. Powell, Secretary, Vermin Extermination Commission, 18 Feb. 1924.

[100]   A.2-1904, 18, evidence Walter Rubidge.   [101]   van der Merwe, 'The Jackal', 7.

litters will usually be large. It boils down to this: that in South Africa we have bred a vigorous jackal.'[102] His perception of the emergence of a 'super-jackal' in some ways parallels the view of a learning jackal at the turn of the century.[103] Ethologists would accept that some canids have a considerable capacity for learning and transmitting behaviour patterns to the next generation.

Uncertainty about the effectiveness of poisoning was compounded for a minority by the question of its environmental costs. By the 1890s concerns about the destruction of 'useful species' by indiscriminate poisoning and other means were raised in the *Agricultural Journal*. E. R. Bradfield, farmer and mine manager in Indwe, who became a frequent commentator on environmental issues, argued that by killing raptors 'the balance of nature seems to have been disturbed'; mice and finches, which were very difficult to control by poisoning, proliferated.[104] Dr Arthur Vanes, MLA for Uitenhage, noted that 'valuable animals, such as dogs, vultures, and hawks, have been destroyed by poison. It is a remedy that cuts both ways.' A Karoo farmer criticized careless poisoning that killed 'valuable birds and smaller animals which are the farmers' best friends'.[105] The loss of farm dogs was frequently mentioned; a story was reported to the *Agricultural Journal* that shepherds applying emetics to poisoned dogs had themselves been poisoned.

Debate also developed about which of the species called jackals were damaging flocks. Rewards were claimed and given for the silver jackal (Cape fox or *Vulpes chama*), the maanhaar jackal (aardwolf or *Proteles cristatus*), and the draaijakkals (Delalande's fox or *Otocyon megalotis*) as well as the black-backed jackal. Farmers clearly had differing perceptions and experiences, some asserting that these were useful animals, others vehement that all 'jackals' attacked lambs when the occasion presented. The aardwolf was placed on the vermin list in 1894 and a reward of 6 shillings offered. Most agreed that it lived largely on termites, beetles, locusts, or carrion and was hardly adapted for predation.[106] P. J. du Toit of the Agriculture Department affirmed later that 'an old Bushman' in Kenhardt who 'exhibited an intimate knowledge of the habits of all varieties of jackhal . . . informed the writer that he had opened many Maanhaar jackhals and had never found the stomach contain any food but ants'.[107]

[102] Ibid. 6–7.
[103] Konrad Lorenz, *Evolution and Modification of Behaviour* (Methuen, London, 1966); Mighetto, *Wild Animals*, for popular ideas in the early twentieth-century United States.
[104] *Agricultural Journal*, 9: 14 (9 July 1896), 369.
[105] Ibid. (20 Aug. 1896) W. Guard Hobson, 'How to Destroy Jackals'.
[106] Ibid. (1 Nov. 1894), 533: W. Hammond-Tooke, 'Maanhaar Jakhals, or Aard Wolf'.
[107] CA PAS 3/113 V4, du Toit, 'South African Jackhals'.

In contrast, Palmer reported that careful observation convinced the poisoning clubs that the maanhaar could be a predator. Not only was evidence found of lamb bones in aardwolf burrows—which might merely have proved that they fed on mutton carrion—but farmers claimed to have seen them kill and abduct lambs and to have found fresh meat in their stomachs. Like diseased sheep, dead predators were the subject of post-mortems. Palmer argued that maanhaar jackals might also have undergone a change in diet in the midlands, while the prevalence of their natural food supply in the northern Cape made such adaptions unnecessary.[108] In the early 1920s, however, during the next great extermination campaign, the maanhaar and Cape silver fox were removed from the list of vermin.

In view of the setbacks in vermin control and uncertainty about the effects of poison, three rather different positions were put to the 1904 Committee. Some within the Afrikaner community articulated opposition to any major role for the state in eradication. The political roots of their position stemmed partly from the bruising encounters with an interventionist and still British-dominated state in battles over scab and in the South African War. As Hermanus van Zyl MLC argued: 'My idea is that the farmer should be left alone to look after himself. Every enlightened farmer knows that unless he takes steps to destroy the vermin his stock will suffer.'[109] The bounty system appeared to them at best a 'sporting and money-making affair' for organized Englishmen.[110] Alternatively, they suspected that poor whites and blacks might actually encourage jackals that they could 'farm'. Examples were given where shepherds supposedly watched jackals growing up and killed them only when they were mature, to be sure of the reward. Johannes Schoeman, MLA for the intensively farmed district of Oudtshoorn, where jackals could damage valuable ostrich nests, was nevertheless adamant that farmers should be responsible for vermin control themselves. 'You see there are a great many loafers, who, instead of going to work, go and try and get jackals' tails; they may catch a jackal, but they steal from your neighbour.'[111] Putting more money into the system, according to this logic, would only fuel more corruption.

A second body of opinion, expressed powerfully by men such as Charles Lee, MLA for Uitenhage, who became President of the Poisoning Clubs

---

[108] *Agricultural Journal* (1 Nov. 1894), 533: W. Hammond-Tooke, 'Maanhaar Jakhals, or Aard Wolf'.

[109] A.2-1904, 90.   [110] A.2-1904, 89.

[111] A.2-1899, 25, evidence Johannes Hendrik Schoeman, MLA, Oudtshoorn. It was also suggested, in contradiction to most other evidence, but in an argument popular in South Africa at the time, that farm servants would catch fewer jackals if rewards were increased; their demand for cash was so small that extra income would act as a disincentive.

Congress and of the Cape Agricultural Union, took the opposite view. Whatever success had been achieved in eradication resulted primarily from state subsidies. Some clubs recognized this explicitly by paying more for proofs than the government reward: they would not have done so if it was not effective. Pursuing this logic, he and others felt that if the government doubled its rewards to 20 shillings, they would soon be recompensed by the complete eradication of jackals. He was keen on channelling the reward system through a revived network of clubs. Successful eradication was a social good that depended upon a general mobilization of both farmers and farm-workers. From Lee's perspective, it was 'essential' that 'the low class of white and the natives' participate.[112] Wherever possible, they should be able to claim personally, or through responsible clubs who paid them the full amount.

Progressive farmers seem to have allowed their servants to keep the bulk of the rewards, and some even topped these up. Walter Rubidge affirmed, with the customary slippage in farmers' discourse about who actually performed labour: 'Personally . . . I have always given my natives the benefit of any jackals that I kill.'[113] The revived bounty system of the 1910s and 1920s also provided a temporarily lucrative source of income for the poor in sheep-farming districts: 'in the mountains and wooded regions, shepherds and bywoners [went] to a lot of trouble to exterminate the red cat for reward.'[114] This was one of the few government subsidies to agriculture available directly to the poor.

An alternative view, which was not an argument against state intervention, was propounded by Walter Rubidge and other leading midland farmers such as Arthur Parkes of Wheatlands and G. H. Maasdorp, MLA for Graaff-Reinet, a member of the 1904 Committee. They maintained that the government should go back to the root of the problem, as it had been formulated by the 1877 Stock Diseases Commission. Jackals were so destructive not simply because they took lambs and ostrich eggs, but because they made it essential to kraal. Aside from the higher losses in droughts, Rubidge calculated a fall-off in lambing from 90 to 65 per cent in his thirty years of farming, 'owing to our farms having deteriorated through the kraaling system'.[115] On a colony-wide basis, he calculated, this had enormous financial implications, over £1.5 million a year. Government subsidy should therefore be put into fencing rather than bounties.

[112] A.2-1904, 34–5, evidence Charles Lee, and 68, evidence Alfred Warren, Toise River.
[113] A.2-1904, 8, evidence Walter Rubidge.
[114] C.P.3-1924, 7, 12. In Graaff-Reinet district the vermin club later employed professional jackal-catchers for cash and farmers kept the bounty: interview, Walter Kingwill, Graaff-Reinet, 1993.
[115] A.2-1904, 3.

As has been illustrated, the idea of fenced paddocks or camps had long been advocated to improve both veld and the condition of sheep. The benefits of fencing, however, were limited as long as predators abounded; while barriers could keep sheep in, they could not easily keep jackals out. Predators thus delayed fencing, because many farmers had to kraal and herd their sheep and goats in any case.[116] The problem was how to make fencing jackal-proof. It could be done. Michael van Breda, a leading western Cape farmer, had a four-and-a-half foot high dry-stone wall built around 7,000 morgen of his land in Caledon in the 1850s. The enclosure was then cleared regularly by 'a pack of foxhounds under efficient discipline', especially during lambing season.[117] After the first year, when twenty-four jackals were caught, the annual kill dwindled rapidly to two or three. But few farmers could afford such measures.

Wire fences offered new opportunities. When John Frost gave evidence to the Select Committee on Fencing and Enclosing of Lands in 1889, he had 50–60 miles of wire fencing on his farm in Queenstown. Stone walls had cost him £100 per mile, wire half that.[118] However, unless the wire strands were very close together, thus increasing the cost of the fence, jackals could still get in and out. It was difficult to keep strands tightly stretched on the extensive farms of the Cape, with uneven terrain, which could be swept by fire or flood. Some of the early wire fences built for ostriches needed fewer strands and were ineffective against jackals; barbed wire could maim these valuable birds.

The development of vermin-proof fences in the 1890s was thus a critical technical innovation (borrowed from England and Australia). A system of 'netting' the first three foot, more or less, of the fence with wire mesh was found to be reasonably effective and publicized through the *Agricultural Journal*.[119] Jackals could not get through netting, they would not usually attempt a wire fence of four foot or more. Farmers later built verandas or overhangs to discourage any particularly ambitious jumping jackals. As long as the base of the fence was kept flush with the ground, and the netting connected to a taut wire, jackals could not usually get under. Stones were sometimes stacked where uneven ground left gaps. The costs of netting quickly declined as machines for its manufacture became available.

---

[116] *Agricultural Journal*, 3: 20 (29 Jan. 1891) 136: A. C. MacDonald, Agricultural Assistant Grahamstown, 'Fencing'.

[117] *Cape Monthly Magazine*, 5 (1859), 294 ff.

[118] Cape of Good Hope, A.10-1889, *Report of the Select Committee on Fencing and Enclosing of Lands*, 10.

[119] *Agricultural Journal*, 9: 15 (23 July 1896), 386–8: A. C. MacDonald, Agricultural Assistant, Grahamstown, 'Vermin-Proof Fences'.

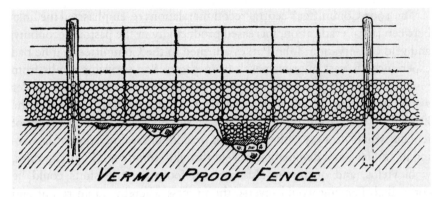

8. Vermin-Proof Fence

The value of netting was not only that sheep could be left out at night once the camp was cleared: a vermin-proof fence greatly facilitated the process of eradication because jackals were restricted to a limited zone. Hunting on horseback with dogs became far more effective once the quarry was to a degree caged. In the longer term, Rubidge argued, it was only by fencing individual farms, and eventually the colony as a whole, that vermin control could be achieved. It would therefore be better to put government money into subsidizing jackal-proof fencing than into bounties.

Many farmers supported some subsidy on fencing, but were sceptical about its immediate benefits against jackals. Jackals were so clever that they would find a way even through netting. One way in which they did so was to exploit tunnels burrowed by aardvarks under fences. 'Die ertvark', a Middelburg farmer noted in 1924, 'neem al die voordeel van die net weg' (The aardvark removes all the advantages of netting).[120] For that reason it too was hunted in some districts, despite the knowledge that a surfeit of termites, its prey, could damage vegetation.

The 1904 Committee agreed that fencing was the 'ultimate hope', but essentially took a compromise position, advising that rewards remain at 10 shillings per jackal and accepting that the system was better than nothing. £11,000 and £18,000 was paid out and tens of thousands of jackals killed for the next two years.[121] Subsequently, deep economic depression, coupled with doubts about the effectiveness of the system, resulted in bounties being reduced to 3 shillings in 1907 and abolished in 1908. A number of Divisional councils, however, continued to pay rewards themselves.

[120] CA PAS 1/109, VC8, Minutes of Evidence to the Vermin Extermination Commission (1924), 187: evidence J. J. van Heerden, Middelburg.
[121] *Vermin Extermination Commission*, 4.

The 1904 Committee's central recommendations re-emphasized the links between jackal eradication, increased productivity in the pastoral economy, and veld conservation. John Parkes affirmed to the Committee that he had experienced a 'vast improvement', from 500 to 800 surviving lambs from his 1,000 ewes, since putting them in a jackal-proof camp, as well as better wool. The argument informed subsequent vermin campaigns as well as the Drought Commission report of 1923. Jackal eradication and jackal-proof fencing would 'do away with the ruinous practice of kraaling', diminish 'driving to and fro', and denudation of veld through 'tramping'. Lambing rates, wool yields, and quality would increase; footpaths and sluits could be controlled. Fencing would reverse the process whereby 'rapid runoff and imperfect penetration . . . of rainwater' led to 'dimunition of underground water and drying up of springs'. It would arrest the 'slow but sure, and already perceptible desiccation of the Karoo districts'.[122]

The Night of the Jackal

After the cessation of systematic state intervention in 1908, eradication campaigns were pursued unevenly, although sometimes highly successfully, by farmers and local government. This was especially so in the western Cape and in the grassland districts of the eastern Cape and Border, where farms were smaller. In the western Cape, Anders Ohlsson, the Swedish brewing magnate in Cape Town, bought a block of land of over 70,000 acres (c.30,000 ha.) from eighteen different owners between the coast and Breede river in Heidelberg district.[123] He created a model farm, the Potteberg estates, not only removing the former owners and many bywoners, but also the vermin: 'every farmhand or shepherd is supplied with a certain number of traps, and is paid at the end of every month for the vermin destroyed, as well as for snakes of every species.'[124] A pack of dogs, specially bred by crossing fox-hounds, lurchers, and Borzois, cleaned up much of the rest so that sheep, exotic deer, and antelope, including the still threatened bontebok, could flourish. Birds were encouraged for hunting.

In the eastern Cape district of Molteno, a collaborative effort by farmers, who found poison ineffective, resulted in energetic jackal-hunt clubs. Using

---

[122] A.2-1904, Report.

[123] *Agricultural Journal*, 33: 6, (1908): Chas. Marais, 'The Potteberg Farms in the Heidelberg District: Mr. Anders Ohlsson's Great Enterprise', 731–41; *DSAB* ii. 523–4. Some of this land has since been absorbed in the Cape's De Hoop Nature Reserve.

[124] 'The Potteberg Farms', 739.

a combination of foxhounds, fox terriers, and crossed greyhounds, mounted men with rifles had great success. By the 1910s vermin counts had been reduced sufficiently for kraaling to be abandoned in much of the district. In 1924 a farmer affirmed: 'My plaas is nie jakhals proef omheind nie, net gewone kampe. My vee loop vry dag en nag.' (My farm is not fenced with jackal-proof fencing, just ordinary camps, but my stock run free day and night.)[125] Caracals were also largely exterminated in the district. The words 'run free, day and night' were often used by Cape farmers in celebration of their deliverance.

In view of such gains, and the gradual spread of fencing, the Provincial Council of the Cape, which took over responsibility for vermin control and other aspects of environmental regulation after Union in 1910, redirected its attention to hunting. In 1914 subsidies were announced of up to £7.10s for a pack of five or more dogs. Hunting clubs, which replaced poisoning clubs, helped to bind a new social identity amongst those who dominated the farm-lands. To a greater extent than the poisoning movement, Afrikaners as well English-speakers joined clubs that 'awakened the "sporting" spirit of the people'.[126] In Queenstown, adjacent to Molteno, the jackal club, formed in 1914, killed 115 jackals on twelve farms in its first year and the number then decreased yearly; 'the stock have run free night and day for the last ten years'.[127] In Cradock, the hunt club killed over 2,300 jackals between 1910 and 1924.[128]

Hunting was not so successful everywhere. In the mountainous districts of the midlands, for example, farmers struggled to make an impact with dogs.[129] Fencing and poison seemed indispensible. Even in the relatively flat lands of the Camdeboo in Pearston district, dog clubs were a failure. Foxhounds could not be used in areas where the ground was too hard and vegetation too stubbly; bred for the soft grass of Britain, 'their feet could not stand the veld'.[130] Molteno and Queenstown were grassier districts. Well imbued with

[125] CA PAS 3/109, VC8, Evidence to the Vermin Extermination Commission (1924), 150: Charl Petrus Marais, Molteno district.

[126] C.P.3-1924, *Vermin Extermination Commission*, 6. CA 4/CT 4/1/59, 153/28, Proceedings of the Second Annual Congress of Delegates Representing the Circle Committees, Queenstown, 3 Nov. 1919, p. 3.

[127] CA PAS 3/109, VC8, Evidence to the Vermin Extermination Commission (1924), 155: J. K. Maclean, Queenstown.

[128] CA PAS 3/121, V 49, J. E. Vosloo to the Provincial Secretary, 21 Dec. 1925.

[129] CA 4/CT 4/1/59, 153/12, Reports, Returns and Resolutions for the Consideration of the Fifth Annual Congress of Delegates Representing the Circle Committees and Divisional Councils, Somerset Strand, 5 Mar. 1923, p. 17.

[130] CA PAS 1/109, VC8, Evidence to the Vermin Extermination Commission (1924), 107: PEG. Hobson, Pearston.

the 'killing spirit', foxhounds tended to go for game, and sometimes also sheep, unless they were very carefully trained. In Pearston, the local poisoning club, one of the oldest and most successful, remained the most effective organization.

In the northern Cape valuable horses, as well as dogs, could suffer from the long chases in high temperatures over hard, uneven ground. Nevertheless, some of the most successful hunt clubs worked in this unpromising area. In Prieska district, with farms averaging 7,000–8,000 morgen or about 6,000 hectares, considerably larger than in the midlands, a high level of organization was achieved amongst Afrikaner farmers. Successful hunting packs were, in a sense, a new technology, alongside jackal-proof fencing. Farmers tried to overcome the disadvantages of particular breeds by crossing them: greyhound (*windhond*) was included for speed and foxhound or terriers for hunting skills. Pure-bred fox-terriers were, however, useful for raiding lairs, and greyhounds were sometimes used for giving chase.

By the mid-1910s the techniques necessary for a further push against vermin were in place. The new Union Department of Agriculture embarked on a more interventionist and far-reaching attempt to control disease and modernize farming. The links between veld conservation, paddocking, and jackal eradication, summarized by the 1904 Committee, were well established. Select Committees on Drought in 1914 and on Drought Relief in 1916 expanded and reiterated concerns about desiccation and degradation (Chapter 8). Enslin, Chief Inspector of Sheep, was determined to eradicate scab. Winning the war against scab necessitated, in his eyes, winning the war against jackals in order to end kraaling. A Fencing Act in 1912 (amended in 1922) provided loans and mechanisms to facilitate joint action by neighbours.

The techniques and conviction were there: only administrative muscle was lacking. Success depended on co-ordinating organized agriculture, the farmers' hunt clubs, and the local state. Sir Frederic de Waal, Administrator of the Cape from 1911 to 1925, made vermin control a special concern. Born in Holland (1853), educated in Belgium, trained as a lawyer and banker, he hardly seemed a likely candidate to espouse so rural and quintessentially South African a concern. He arrived in the rural Cape in 1880 as yet another young man with chest problems; the perceived healing powers of the Karoo drew him there, as they did a number of Europeans.[131] He established himself as a businessman and newspaper editor in Middelburg, at the heart of sheep territory, and became a leading moderate member of the Afrikaner Bond. As MLA for Colesberg from 1898 to 1910, he was clearly attuned to his rural

[131] *DSAB* ii. 189–90.

constituency; as Colonial Secretary under Merriman (1908–10) and Provincial Administrator he was an organized and committed modernizer with considerable power.

The Cape Province Agricultural Association, then under the presidency of a Cradock farmer, organized a meeting on the Jackal Question to precede its 1916 annual congress in Kimberley. The Administrator gave the keynote address. Flanked by the national Minister of Agriculture, H. C. van Heerden, also a midland sheep farmer, he declared that next to education, vermin was the central issue faced by his administration. De Waal's rousing speech, shot through with rural metaphors, was punctuated by enthusiastic applause. Known as a rather autocratic official, he demonstrated that he also had the common touch. De Waal argued that 'they had fought that pest for 28 years in about as incompetent a way as was possible'.[132] The Cape parliament and Provincial Council had spent about £147,000 on jackal eradication from 1890. But frequently, after a short phase of high bounties, the amount paid had been reduced to a level at which people were not prepared to catch jackals in large numbers. This gave the jackal 'not only breathing time, but breeding time'.

By 1916 it was estimated that from 7.5 to 10 per cent of the 15 million woolled sheep in the Cape were killed each year by vermin. Predation seemed to be increasing, in direct relation to the number of sheep. The value of sheep lost now exceeded that calculated by Walter Rubidge in 1904; they were worth £1 million not including the wool, nor the losses attributable to reduced productivity and tramping of veld.[133] The Vermin Extermination Commission in 1924 also tried to calculate these amounts for the late 1910s. It placed losses at around 7 per cent, or 1.4 million sheep annually, similar to the number slaughtered at the Johannesburg and Cape Town abattoirs. To this direct loss of over £1 million a year, they added indirect losses of £5 million annually in the Cape alone.[134]

De Waal projected the task as a national campaign, akin to the war effort in which South Africa was then engaged. There should be no 'armistice' for jackals; they had to fight a continuous campaign. Jackal extermination should be a shared crusade; the congress itself 'proved conclusively . . . that the English-speaking man and the Dutch-speaking man, where they had a unity of interest, could work together.'[135] 'Let them keep politics out of the jackal question', de Waal continued, because jackals 'were non-political chaps' who would 'eat lamb impartially whether it belonged to Unionist, Nationalist or

[132] CA 4/CT 4/1/59, 152/1(b), cutting from *The Diamond Fields Advertiser*, 13 Sept. 1916.
[133] Ibid.   [134] C.P.3-1924, *Vermin Extermination Commission*, 5.
[135] CA 4/CT 4/1/59, 152/1(b), cutting from *The Diamond Fields Advertiser*, 13 Sept. 1916.

SAP man'.[136] There were limits to de Waal's sense of inclusivity. He identified the problem constituency as farmers who were 'not progressing' and
Afrikaners associated with the rebellion in the western Transvaal and northern Cape. They were the sort of people who were also still likely to have
scabby sheep. As in the case of scab, there had to be compulsion—a route the
Free State Provincial Council was pursuing. Jackal clubs had to have power to
go onto the land of the 'nix-nux' farmers who contributed nothing to eradication. Warming to his theme, de Waal struck a chord with his male audience:

Well, I've been under compulsion all my life . . . When I was a child I was under the
compulsion of my schoolmaster and my father. When I was a young man I was
under the compulsion, as I am still to-day of public opinion. When I got married—
(laughter)—I came under control—(renewed laughter)—and I am all the better for
it. (Applause.) Control is an excellent thing.

The principles of predator control enunciated by de Waal were compulsion and continuity of effort, which had been lacking beforehand. He wanted
a 'merciless campaign of extermination' against the 'freebooters'.[137] The
Provincial Council approved a 10 shillings bounty, with the possibility of an
increase as the number of jackals declined to make it worthwhile for people to
continue killing them. A renewed campaign had been launched to destroy
vermin in Crown forests by poison; Coloured trappers were employed in
some areas. In 1919, with wool prices rising, de Waal reaffirmed his view that
'they would get their money back a hundred fold if they got rid of the jackals'.[138] As 'father' of the movement, he helped to frame and support a succession of ordinances that tightened the powers of the state.[139] De Waal was
prepared to take on the urban interests and western Cape crop farmers within
his own party who argued that special expenditure was unwarranted, and
repeated the accusation of jackal farming. A certain humour attended a number of debates, but for him this was a deadly serious business, fundamental
to economic development and the general protection of property rights. The
jackal was 'as much a thief in the country as the man who broke into the
merchant's store in the town'.[140]

[136] CA 4/CT 4/1/59, 153/28, Proceedings of the Second Annual Congress of Delegates
Representing the Circle Committees, Queenstown, 3 Nov. 1919, p. 4.
[137] CA 4/CT 4/1/59, 152/28, Verrichtingen van Het Derde Jaarkongres voor he Uitroien van
Ongedierte, Oudtshoorn, 9 Nov. 1920, p. 4. (English version not available.)
[138] CA 4/CT 4/1/59, 153/28, Proceedings of the Second Annual Congress of Delegates
Representing the Circle Committees, 3, 5.
[139] CA PAS 4/CT, 4/1/59, 153/1(a), Proceedings of the Vermin Extermination Congress held
at Kimberley, 27 Mar. 1922.
[140] CA 4/CT 4/1/59, 153/1(a), *Cape Times*, 7 Mar. 1923, reporting Fifth Annual Congress of
Vermin Extermination Conference, The Strand.

De Waal believed strongly that farmers and local political authorities should be mobilized to take control of eradication themselves. He specifically contrasted this with the approach in the United States, where the government, engaging in a major campaign against the coyote at much the same time, employed specialist hunters and trappers.[141] Certainly skilled assistants and farm-workers could be employed, but the responsibility was to be local. Under the 1917 Vermin Extermination Ordinance, the province was divided into seventeen circles under committees composed of local provincial councillors and divisional council appointees.[142] Circle Committee representatives came together in the Vermin Extermination Congress, which met annually for six years.[143]

The Circle Committees defined the duties of vermin clubs, framed regulations for laying poison, and supervised hunting with dogs and the reward system: 20 shillings for 'Tiger, Leopard or Wild Dog', 15 shillings for lynx or red cat, 10 shillings for jackals, 2 shillings for baboons, and 3d. for grey squirrels. Rewards had to be paid by the Divisional Council, which could claim back two-thirds of the expenditure from the province, rising to three-quarters in the north-western and northern Cape circles.[144] In 1920 the 'wolf' (15s.), eagle or lammervanger (5s.), wild cats (2s. 6d.), and misseljaar cats (2s.), joined the list, while baboon and squirrel rewards were increased. The campaign did not herald a totally unbridled slaughter. The aardwolf was exempted, and in 1923 Jansenville farmers succeeded in removing smaller wild cats from the list in order to control mice and rats. They invoked 'the balance of nature', and the threat of bubonic plague.[145] Circle Committee no. 4 (Vanrijnsdorp) tried unsuccessfully to have eagles removed. Attempts to put otters, badgers, ratels, springhares, and mongoose onto the vermin list all failed.

Some Divisional Councils paid very much more for jackals than the government bounty of 10 shillings—as much as £5 in the case of Bredasdorp. They felt that this kept the district almost 'clean' of jackals, and argued that a very high bounty was a necessary incentive. Here the council itself maintained four packs of foxhounds. Hound-pack subsidies rose to £30 a year. The province continued to supply poison at cost to clubs and landowners,

---

[141] Dunlap, *Saving America's Wildlife*; Mighetto, *Wild Animals and American Environmental Ethics*.

[142] Province of the Cape of Good Hope, Ordinance 9 of 1917 to Provide for the Extermination of Stock-Destroying Carnivora and Animals and Birds injurious to Agriculture and Horticulture, promulgated 7th September, 1917.

[143] CA 4/CT 4/1/59, 152/1(b): minutes but not verbatim records survive in this series.

[144] Vermin Extermination (Amendment) Ordinance, no. 10 of 1920, 7 May 1920.

[145] CA 4/CT 4/1/59, 153/12, Reports, Returns and Resolutions for the Consideration of the Fifth Annual Congress of Delegates Representing the Circle Committees and Divisional Councils, Somerset Strand, 5 Mar. 1923, p. 17.

although the amount distributed gradually declined.[146] Listed vermin were prohibited as pets or breeding animals, except in zoos or for scientific purposes.

Critically, the Circle Committees could authorize vermin clubs to enter private property, even without the consent of the owner, if they had 'reasonable grounds to believe that vermin may be breeding'. This was an important provision in extending the power of the state over the land of individuals, similar to the veterinary regulations. In 1918 the Ordinance was tightened to allow clubs to claim payment for animals killed on land they had to enter forcibly.[147] In 1920 punitive measures were introduced; owners on whose land the clubs had to act without permission would have to pay five times the amount of the reward to the club.[148] A landowner could also be instructed to destroy vermin.

With this more organized assault, the night of the jackal finally arrived. When rewards were lower, from 1914 to 1917, at 5 shillings for jackals and red cats and 1 shilling for baboons, the number of jackal pelts brought in averaged less than 10,000 a year (Table 6.1).[149] Over the next six years 282,134 jackal pelts, nearly 50,000 a year, were brought in, together with many other species. The slaughter was greatest in the large northern and north-western Cape districts, and in the midlands.

These figures do not necessarily represent all the animals killed. Reporting was not always complete. And by no means all skins of slaughtered animals were brought in to councils; some went direct to traders. In the First World War years the price of pelts rose considerably, especially of silver jackal (*Vulpes chama*), leopard, and caracal. Tens of thousands of skins were sold direct to Cape Town and Port Elizabeth merchants. After the war there was less incentive to sell, except in the case of leopard skins, which could fetch up to 80 shillings. These were used for tourist sales, curiosities, and regimental regalia. There was some market for skins amongst Africans, to make karosses. Black-backed jackal skins were not in great demand; to the extent that they sold, winter skins were greatly preferred to the thinner summer ones. Skins of animals killed by poisoning—though they were difficult to detect—were of less value, because the fur fell out far sooner after curing.[150]

---

[146] CA PAS 3/109, VRCG/1, Statement of Expenditure, Destruction of Vermin for the Financial Year 1916/1917: CA PAS 3/108 VCi/1, Provincial Secretary to Secretary, Vermin Extermination Commission, 2 Oct. 1923.

[147] Vermin Extermination (Amendment) Ordinance, no. 10 of 1918, 17 May 1918.

[148] Vermin Extermination (Amendment) Ordinance, no. 10 of 1920, 7 May 1920.

[149] CA PAS 4/1/59, 153/1.

[150] CA PAS 3/109, VC5, E. R. McIlwraith to Secretary, Vermin Commission, 28 Sept. 1923.

TABLE 6.1. Vermin Rewards Granted: Major Species

Year	Jackal	Caracal	Leopard	Wildcat	Eagle	Baboons	Total value (£)
1914	2,501	123	—	—	—	219	667
1915	11,970	807	5	—	—	1,223	3,258
1916	8,652	473	—	—	—	2,071	2,576
1917	12,532	660	3	—	—	2,302	3,853
1918	21,637	1,551	33	501	6	2,685	13,097
1919	58,670	5,700	108	98	—	10,524	20,840
1920	47,641	3,808	127	5,044	352	18,240	31,346
1921	48,849	3,668	139	18,058	962	17,004	28,767
1922	47,845	3,653	128	31,262	782	17,931	35,604
1923	57,492	4,963	—	—	—	—	48,427
TOTAL	317,787	25,406	543	54,963	2,102	72,199	188,435

Source: C.P.3-1924, 6. Rewards were also granted for small numbers of misseljaar cats, squirrels, hyenas, and wild dogs.

One of the major reasons for the appointment of the provincial Vermin Extermination Commission in 1923–4 was not simply to examine the progress of the campaign, but to assess ways in which the authorities, which had been burning all proofs, could raise revenue from their sale. As the reward exceeded the market value of the skin of most species, they had to be careful not to release jackal pelts that could be bought for a few shillings and recycled as rewards. The Commission advocated a clearly marked perforation ('P') as a way of preventing such corruption. Indeed, the renewed drive against vermin attracted less criticism for corruption.[151] Skins still came in from Bechuanaland where no reward was paid (but they were taken in lieu of hut tax.)[152] Heads and tails had now to be presented, and the body pelt was sometimes sold off to traders; for this reason full pelts were later demanded for reward. Perhaps the major complaint was that some farmers financed their private dog packs and avoided dog taxes under the guise of starting hunt clubs.

The strength and continuity of the progressive farming lobby was clear in these congresses. In 1919 the Congress of Circle Committees decided to form a caucus to argue for uniform action at the Scab Congress of 1920. This

[151] CA PAS 3/118, V24, cutting from *Cape Times*, 24 Apr. 1924.

[152] CA PAS 3/108, VC1/1, Sub-Inspector, Bechd. Police to Government Secretary, Mafeking, 30 Jan. 1923.

included Walter Rubidge, who was again farming in Graaff-Reinet, near to the old family property at Wellwood; Montagu Gadd, who had flexed his muscles in progressive farming politics; and G. A. Kolbe. The latter two shortly afterwards became the non-official members of the Drought Investigation Commission (Chapter 8). Its report (1923) affirmed that jackal eradication was one of the highest priorities for the modernization of farming and conservation of resources. It went even further than de Waal in declaring the jackal 'a dangerous menace to the State'.[153]

The Circle Committees and hunt clubs were intended as cross-cutting organizations which would not be hamstrung by political divisions or the competing financial priorities of Divisional Councils. They were not everywhere a success. In some districts, such as Cradock, Graaff-Reinet, Sterkstroom, Victoria West, and Vryburg, Circle Committees were popular and clubs were numerous. In others committees met infrequently.[154] Some hunt clubs were reluctant to force their way onto land, because this upset local social relations; the legal situation as to who would be liable for any damages was not entirely clear.[155] The Drought Commission found that, 'in so far as the law allows trespass in the pursuit of a jackal, it is practically a dead letter'.[156] One farmer who laid poison on a neighbour's land, because infestation by prickly pear made hunting impossible, was threatened with legal action for causing the death of dogs.[157] The 1923 Vermin Congress at the Strand and the 1924 Vermin Extermination Commission advocated successfully that direct control be taken by government and Divisional Councils.[158]

By this time the balance seemed to have swung against predators.[159] The Vermin Extermination Commission found that districts with stock losses as high as 12 per cent per year before the big drive now experienced negligible problems; it suggested that jackals were being pushed towards the borders of the colony.[160] But sustained control was not easily achieved. While bounty payments declined in 1924–5, indicating fewer killings, they then remained

[153] U.G.49-1923, 20.

[154] CA 4/CT 4/1/59, 153/12, Reports, Returns and Resolutions for the Consideration of the Fifth Annual Congress of Delegates Representing the Circle Committees.

[155] CA 4/CT 4/1/59, 153/28, Report of the First Annual Congress of Delegates Representing the Circle Committees, Cape town, 8 Oct. 1018.

[156] U.G.49-1923, 19.

[157] CA 4/CT 4/1/59, 153/28, Report of the Second Annual Congress of Delegates Representing the Circle Committees, 15.

[158] CA 4/CT 4/1/59, 153/12, Proceedings of the Fifth Annual Cape Province Vermin Extermination Congress.

[159] CA 4/CT 4/1/59, 153/28, Proceedings of the Sixth Annual Cape Province Vermin Extermination Congress, City Hall, Cape Town, 26–28th July, 1924, p. 4.

[160] Figures drawn from *Vermin Extermination Committee*.

fairly stable in the second half of that decade at about £25,000 a year.[161] After a sharp decline in the depression years, where the Provincial Council cut rewards, averages again climbed to over £25,000 annually in the late 1930s. A modus vivendi was reached, rather than complete extermination; these figures suggest that jackal numbers may have stabilized. In the 1950s the journalist and popular historian Lawrence Green wrote of jackals as a major presence in his book *Karoo*. He recorded the feats of Broken Toe, a jackal with a distinctive spoor that attracted publicity for its capacity to kill sheep, escape capture, and generate folklore. Jackals had been driven out of core sheep districts but survived elsewhere, and he quoted an estimate that 200,000 sheep still succumbed to them annually.[162]

Such numbers were, nevertheless, very much less than the estimates made in the 1910s. By 1953 van der Merwe considered the jackal to have been effectively reduced in most Karoo districts, and the major problem had shifted to the Free State. There, sustained bounties and the establishment of the Oranjejag hunting organization under the Provincial Council resulted in sheep losses being reduced to perhaps 6,000 a year in the 1970s; despite systematic hunting, less than 500 jackals were then being killed per year.[163] Percentage losses in the Transvaal and Natal were estimated at a hundred times less than in the Cape sixty years before. The scale of losses and of jackal numbers had become relatively inconsequential. In the late twentieth century, however, jackal and caracal numbers in the Cape seem to have increased.[164] Less intensive sheep farming, the spread of state nature reserves, private game farms, as well as changing attitudes to predators were probably all factors in their recovery. At a 1993 conference on 'problem animals', one paper was entitled 'How I Learned to Farm with Jackals'. In this case, the author did not mean farming them for the bounty.

Ultimately, state determination, coupled with more sophisticated techniques of poisoning and hunting, showed that predator control was feasible. Unlike in colonial Zimbabwe and in northern Natal, where wildlife of all kinds was cleared to combat tsetse, the government did not itself stage hunting drives, but relied on the response to rewards.[165] Fencing was of major

---

[161] These figures are obtained from the annual Cape of Good Hope, *Records of the Provincial Council*. Figures are provided for the total sums paid out by Divisional Councils and by the Provincial Council in each year, the latter being roughly 60–70% of the total. Printed figures were not recorded for the number of proofs brought in.

[162] Green, *Karoo*, 165 ff.

[163] Oranje-Vrystaat, 'Verslag van die Kommissie van Ondersoek na Ongediertebestryding', 8–10.

[164] This is based on interviews with a limited number of farmers.

[165] Roben Mutwira, 'A Question of Condoning Game Slaughter: Southern Rhodesian Wildlife Policy (1890–1953)', *JSAS* 15: 2 (1989), 250–62.

importance in imposing control, in preventing return by jackals, and in making horse and dog hunts more effective. The expansion of fencing inhibited the jackals' mobility.

Predators had deeply influenced settler pastoral systems; kraaling had become a necessity, as it was for many African stock-keepers. In the decades straddling the late nineteenth and early twentieth centuries, jackals seem to have adapted themselves with particular success to the colonial agrarian economy. Both their inherited characteristics and their capacity to modify behaviour gave them considerable advantages over other predators. In this sense, it was not only the general ecological context of Cape pastoralism, but the 'history' of an animal which influenced the pattern of agrarian change. Giving animals a history, as well as a natural history, must be part of the inclusion of nature in historical explanation.

Most sheep farmers wanted to get rid of jackals—folk demons, if occasional anti-heroes—in order to diminish losses. In the nineteenth century they had neither the organization nor the techniques for systematic eradication. In the early twentieth century progressive farmers and officials put a specific construction on the linkages between predators, production, disease, and veld conservation. This helped to shape an organized approach to predator extermination that attracted significant amounts of public funding and political support. Poorer farmers and traditionalists did not necessarily support the new styles of ranching, the ending of transhumance, and the coercive aspects of eradication policy, but most could agree on the scourge of the jackal. Jackal bounties provided a valuable source of income for some African and coloured farm-workers, as well as for poor whites and bywoners; some became specialist vermin hunters and trappers.

Jackal eradication did, however, intersect with the increasing dominance of well-capitalized farmers. Fencing, together with paddocking, had the effect of reducing scope for bywoners and diminishing the need for shepherds. It is difficult to specify the precise impact of these innovations, because they coincided with the Great Depression and other changes. But a witness to the Commission of Enquiry into Coloured People (1937) noted of the southern Cape: 'There is less work than in the past. Before, say thirty years ago, they worked the whole year as shepherds, but with fencing most have had to move to villages. Now they work for four months a year for farmers. Subsistence is therefore precarious, especially in June there is little work.' Ultimately it may have been in the interests of employees in the sheep-farming districts to keep the jackal population high and the fence strands wide. The number of owner-occupier farmers, however, did not decrease; the peak was reached around the early 1950s.

Sheep numbers increased rapidly in the 1910s and 1920s; jackal eradication, together with fencing, was a significant factor, alongside veterinary controls and water provision, in this process. The number of woolled sheep in the
Cape climbed from 13.3 million in 1918 to 18.6 million in 1927, a period
which coincided exactly with the jackal campaign, although it also marked
major successes in scab eradication. Sheep numbers subsequently peaked at
23 million, although the continued growth in the late 1920s was probably
largely a result of falling prices.

Both the Drought Commission of 1923 and Vermin Extermination
Commission of 1924 were convinced that lambing and survival rates, carrying capacities and wool yields, would increase quickly following jackal eradication and fencing. The evidence of I. P. van Heerden, MLA for Cradock,
was typical. He began to enclose his 6,600 morgen (5,640 ha) farm in 1912
and completed most of the netting during the First World War.[166] Eleven
internal camps had been fenced by 1924. He then increased the number of
sheep from 4,000 to 7,000 and claimed that wool yields had risen by 2 pounds
per sheep. (Such stocking numbers would now be considered very heavy.) A
survey by the local Farmers Association found that sheep in paddocks or
camps matured more quickly, and were larger and fatter, than those which
were herded and kraaled.

At Wellwood, farmed by Sidney Rubidge, grandson of Charles, from 1913,
fencing proceeded gradually from the 1870s so there was a less dramatic
change (Chapter 9). Jackal-proof perimeter fencing around the 6,700 morgen (5,740 ha) farm was completed around 1920. In the same year the last
jackal was killed on the farm—and no further were reported until 1946. In the
early 1920s Sidney Rubidge did try to push stock numbers up, but lack of
water and grazing resources on this difficult farm constrained his efforts.
Numbers increased from about 1,900 merinos in 1919 to 2,700 in 1925.
Wool yields, already twice the average at about 10.5 pounds per sheep, rose
only slightly, reaching a peak of 12.3 pounds in 1925. Sidney Rubidge noted
in his diary in 1926 that internal fencing allowed him to utilize the pastures
more thoroughly, in that sheep took themselves to the furthest reaches of the
camps. Shepherded animals were less likely fan out so widely. Yet he also
wondered whether he had not taken too large a risk.

His doubts proved justified in the short term. In 1926–7 drought decimated his sheep. It was only in the 1930s, when new water and fodder resources
became available, that stock numbers on Wellwood expanded more rapidly.
The evidence suggests that some farmers were fatally tempted by their new

---

[166] C.P.3-1924, *Vermin Extermination Commission*, 16.

freedom to overstock, thus cancelling out the benefits of potentially improved pastures. The victories over scab, predators, and drought were to some extent achieved before a controlled grazing system had been put in place. Certainly, the pressure on the veld remained such that losses in the early 1930s, when serious drought and locusts returned, were devastating. Perhaps as many as 15 million sheep were lost nationally and 6 million in the Cape. South African sheep numbers were never as high again. Jackals may have played some role in keeping sheep numbers and farmers in control— and it seems that they took mainly the weak.

Naturalists such as Fitzsimons and van der Merwe, who fully supported the extermination of jackals, were nevertheless concerned about its impact. They agreed with those farmers who argued that poison killed 'useful' animals such as snake-eating secretary birds and termite-eating aardvarks; predator eradication could also increase potentially infectious carrion on the veld. Sidney Rubidge made this connection directly: 'What a terrible revenge Nature returns for our having exterminated the jackall,' he noted in 1932; 'this blowfly pest now more than takes the place of jackalls and excludes any advantages and profit in running sheep on free range.'[167] Blowflies seemed to reproduce on carrion and then infest sheep. Chemical remedies provided a solution.

Conservationist interventions not only spelt the demise of wild animals, such as the jackal and caracal, but in doing so contributed to quite the opposite effect than was intended and made some contribution to South Africa's equivalent of the American Dust Bowl in the early 1930s. Conservationist ideas could lead their protagonists into difficult and contradictory terrain. In the longer term, however, it will be argued (Chapter 11) that predator control, fencing, rotational grazing, regulatory legislation, and reduced numbers did eventually bring more stability to livestock farming.

[167] Rubidge diary, 3 Feb. 1932.

7

Drought, Conservation, and Nationalism: The Career of H. S. du Toit, 1890–1930

Dry-farming and Water Conservation

In the early decades of the twentieth century the term drought implied more than a periodic lack of rain. Drought was associated with the perception, frequently articulated, that the country was 'drying up', in the sense that rainfall was declining overall. This in turn became bound up with the idea that surface water was declining, and that denudation was causing rainfall to run off rather than sink into the ground. Drought in this broader sense was manifested in gulleying (dongas) and soil erosion.

The 1914 Senate Select Committee report, which gave these issues a national airing after Union, was entitled 'Droughts, Rainfall and Soil Erosion'. Similarly, the 1923 Drought Investigation Commission was less concerned with rainfall and more with the results of drought in the shape of soil erosion, denudation, and the loss of livestock. Drought was also discussed as intimately bound up with its perceived social consequences, in particular poor-whiteism. Hence a 1916 inquiry into rural poverty, with a focus on the north-west Cape, was called the Drought Distress Commission. Undoubtedly, drought was one factor in exacerbating rural poverty amongst white and black. However, modes of explanation in agricultural circles at the time sometimes laid exaggerated emphasis on environmental or natural causes in shaping poverty.

The Drought Investigation Commission in South Africa (1920–3) produced reports that distilled many of the key arguments developed over the previous half-century about the necessity for a transformation of pastoral farming in South Africa. It provided an eloquent critique of existing farming practices and focused especially on the of exhaustion of the country's natural resources. The final report offered a blueprint for improvement that remained important in summarizing and fixing conservationist discourse and policy, within the country and beyond, for many years. The Commission was chaired and the report primarily written by Heinrich Sebastian du Toit, a senior official in the Department of Agriculture. Du Toit was an ambitious and highly committed agricultural bureaucrat, who courted publicity and was probably the best-known member of the Department at the time.

This chapter is structured around du Toit's career. He was not the originator of the ideas that he espoused so forcefully in the Drought Commission report. But discussion of his experience and approach helps to enlarge the arguments of this book and open up fascinating avenues of enquiry. First, du Toit's early focus was on arable rather than pastoral farming, and his interests illustrate the significance of conservationism in that sphere. Water conservation was important to du Toit from the start of his official career; he was especially interested in techniques, other than irrigation, developed in the United States. Secondly, while du Toit was brought up in the midland Cape, his career was Transvaal-based, and this chapter more explicitly incorporates a national focus. After Union in 1910, the Department of Agriculture in Pretoria increasingly shaped policies that affected the country as whole, including the Cape. Thirdly, although he was not trained at university level, du Toit's concerns and rhetoric reveal the significance of self-consciously scientific approaches in the development of agriculture in early twentieth century. As a corollary, the importance of the Department of Agriculture as a site for scientific and experimental work in diverse fields is illustrated (Chapter 8).

Fourthly, although it has been argued that most key protagonists of conservationist ideas were anglophone Cape farmers and officials, it is clear that such approaches were not restricted to them. Some of the Afrikaner Bond leadership shared these views, and the party was deeply split over agricultural progressivism. Afrikaners were in a majority in the South African Party (SAP), under the former South African War generals Louis Botha and Jan Smuts, which took power after Union and intensified state intervention. Smuts, in particular, was deeply informed about botany and the natural world. Individuals such as Barney Enslin, the Chief Inspector of Sheep, H. C. van Heerden, Minister of Agriculture, and Frederic de Waal, Administrator of the Cape, played a major role in implementing environmental regulation. J. D. Schonken, a Free State physician, published a wide-ranging analysis in Afrikaans entitled *Dorre Suid-Afrika* in 1921.[1] (He acknowledged John

---

[1] J. D. Schonken, *Dorre Suid-Afrika* (Nasionale Pers, Bloemfontein, 1921?). No date is given, but the Preface is dated 1921. Rural problems also featured in Afrikaner fiction, such as C. M. van den Heever, *Droogte* (J. L. van Schaik, Pretoria, 1939).

Croumbie Brown as the first to investigate these issues in detail.) By focusing on du Toit, the Afrikaner role in conservationist strategies can be further explored.

Agricultural development became associated in rhetoric and policy with attempts to forge a unified and modern white nation. As in the case of so much modernizing, developmentalist discourse, the precise construct of nation to which it was attached could differ considerably in the hands of different (and even sometimes the same) protagonists. In the early decades of the twentieth century opportunities for Afrikaners to train in scientific disciplines, initially overseas, then increasingly in South Africa, were opening, and a number were absorbed into the Department of Agriculture. Afrikaner agricultural bureaucrats were not necessarily ethnic nationalists. Some came from wealthier and partly anglicized Cape families, or associated themselves with Botha, Smuts, and a pan-South African white identity. Africans were not excluded from all modernizing initiatives, although intensifying segregation dictated that agricultural interventions and ideas of nationality took on racial shape (Chapter 10).

Du Toit was strongly aware that, as an official, he should act as even-handedly as possible, and he had extensive contact with English-speaking landowners and organizations. He worked for his first sixteen years as a bureaucrat, from 1908 to 1924, within a department where most of his seniors were English-speaking, and under SAP ministers. He actively opposed the 1915 Afrikaner rebellion. Yet the formation of the Nationalist Party by General Hertzog in 1914, who split with Botha and Smuts and took power in 1924, provided an attractive alternative to Afrikaner intellectuals. There was an increasing undercurrent of harder, more exclusive Afrikaner nationalism in du Toit's approach. For him, one key to Afrikaner national development was to spread the message of scientific farming to the mass of white, Afrikaner landowners, many of whom he felt were being bypassed by the Department's research and publicity. He fought to launch an extension service in the country, and along with the authorship of the Drought Commission report, he probably saw this as the pinnacle of his achievement because it brought Afrikaners into the modernizing project. As in the case of the Kruger National Park, conservationist discourse and initiatives in agriculture could be constructed as a national task, in which forward-looking Afrikaners should also be incorporated.[2]

[2] Jane Carruthers, *The Kruger National Park: A Social and Political History* (Natal University Press, Pietermaritzburg, 1995), and 'Nationhood and National Parks: Comparative Examples from the Post-Imperial Experience', in Griffiths and Robin (eds.), *Ecology and Empire*.

Heinrich du Toit was born in 1874 in Middelburg district, at the heart of the Cape's sheep-farming zone. He schooled irregularly, and from the age of 13 to 18 largely worked on his father's farm in the Sneeuberg.[3] In 1892 he attended the English-language Graaff-Reinet College; his reports show him to have been a diligent pupil. Like many of the educated Cape Afrikaner elite in the late nineteenth century, he was at home in both English and Dutch/Afrikaans; much of his correspondence was in English, which he wrote with flair. Du Toit stayed in Graaff-Reinet long enough to pass only a couple of Matric subjects (Agricultural Chemistry and Physiology), because he was offered a teaching post in the Transvaal at the end of 1894. As the *Huisgenoot* magazine later put it: 'the northern republics, where Afrikaners were developing on their own lines, attracted the young blood.'[4] He taught for about three years, and in 1897 was one of only two candidates who passed an examination for entry as an officer into the Transvaal Artillery. He worked as a trainer at the Artillery college and saw active service in the 1898 war against Mphephu in the northern Transvaal. Du Toit achieved the rank of second lieutenant and earned £300 a year. He was able to buy a small farm just north of Pretoria, on which he had a house built; he was a committed tree planter.[5]

Du Toit fought throughout the South African War, returning to the field after receiving serious injuries in 1899. A key figure in the South African Republic's artillery, he led a rearguard action in the northern Transvaal and won renown for blowing up his gun rather than allowing it to fall into British hands. General Louis Botha promoted him to the rank of major in 1901. Du Toit was a 'bittereinder'; he did not surrender in the field, but he was a member of the Boer delegation which signed the Treaty of Vereeniging. Deeply resentful about British control of South Africa, he travelled widely with restless energy between 1902 and 1907. In 1902 du Toit left for the United States, where there had been quite widespread support for the Boer cause. In one source he mentioned that he had initially intended to purchase horses and cattle in Argentina for his own farming operations, but was then called to the United States by F. W. Reitz, former Transvaal Secretary of State, for a support-raising tour.

[3] H. S. du Toit papers, Pretoria (du T), unnumbered scrapbook, 'Examinations passed. Work performed', typescript, *c.*1924. About 30 archive boxes are kept by du Toit's son, a retired army general, at his home in Pretoria. References below refer to box and document numbers. Du Toit's lack of formal education dogged his civil service career. He compiled this and similar documents in his battle to improve his position and pay.

[4] *Die Huisgenoot*, 7: 82 (Feb. 1923), 411. Original: 'die Republieke in die noorde, waar die Afrikaner besig was om op sy eie wyse te ontwikkel, het die jong bloed getrek.'

[5] du T., 280, 27, cutting from *Peoria Herald*, 15 Nov. 1902.

In later years du Toit also recalled that his visit had been planned in order to further the development of Boer agriculture. Certainly, there was a great deal of discussion about agricultural improvement at the time in the Reconstruction Transvaal. Milner's government financed agricultural tours by Boer prisoners-of-war to Australia, New Zealand, and Canada.[6] In the United States du Toit met a representative of the Avery agricultural machinery company of Peoria, Illinois, which he then visited 'to study the methods used in the manufacture of agricultural machinery and to learn thoroughly the manner of operating the different machines'.[7] There are, however, indications that when he first left he was keeping his options open. Before leaving, he applied to the American consul in Pretoria for a commission in the US army and was recommended as a 'fearless and capable officer'.[8] Later that year he signed a declaration of intent to become a US citizen.

Du Toit clearly enjoyed his visit. He had good introductions through Reitz and from Americans who had fought with the Boers.[9] In New York he was received by the American Scouts and 'thousands and ten thousands of other people who came to see a Boer'.[10] He travelled to Mexico where he met the President, saw the Panama Canal, went on to San Francisco, and returned overland, speaking widely about his war experiences. Du Toit told a reporter that he admired Americans and especially rural Americans. He clearly identified with Theodore Roosevelt (whom he also met) and the muscular, go-ahead, organized, can-do ethos of his progressivism. He liked the emphasis on anti-imperialism and a certain vision of freedom: 'men are free to move and act as they please like his own country before it became a part of the British empire.' Conversely, some Americans were attracted to the image of the Boer—especially this 'splendid specimen of manhood'—as a gallant, masculine, outdoors, independent, mounted military hero. After a shorter visit in 1907, du Toit wrote to his family: 'van Amerika heb ik soveel liefde genoten dat het my zwaar was weg te gaan' (I enjoyed so much affection in America that it was difficult for me to leave).[11]

Between these two visits du Toit travelled through Europe, visiting agricultural institutions. He went as far as Russia—another source of pro-Boer sympathy—where he met Tolstoy. If his discussion with the estate-proud giant of Russian literature had been largely about agriculture, it was later recalled, through the haze of Afrikaner nationalist sentiment in the 1930s, to have included other themes. Tolstoy apparently said: 'Don't lose hope, I still

[6] Krikler, *Revolution from Above.*   [7] du T., 280, 27, *Peoria Herald*, 15 Nov. 1902.
[8] du T., scrapbook, 12 Aug. 1902 and 3 Nov. 1902.   [9] du T., 263, 43.
[10] du T., 263, 38, 'Henri' du Toit, Compassberg to Raoul Martin, Paris, 27 Feb. 1905.
[11] du T., Mar. 1907, letter from on board ship to A. G. du Toit, his father.

see a great future for the Boers; they will be a great nation.' In 1905 du Toit wrote: 'I could not stay in S. Africa to see the enemy in possession of our state and camp.'[12] He disdained his twelve days in the 'miserable little island of "John Bull"'.[13] Missing the irony that France had expelled his Huguenot ancestors, he emphasized his affinity with that country. France, du Toit thought, was 'the land of the *Free* and the *Brave*'.[14] In Paris, even without French, he found: 'Just say: "Je suis Boer" then the whole world was right.'

Du Toit nevertheless committed himself to South Africa and became the agent for Avery in the country, adopting the cable address 'Progress'.[15] He was involved in agricultural experiments on his father's farm, Compassberg, on the northern slopes of the Sneeuberg, near the highest peak in the Cape.[16] The farm became well known in later years, under different ownership, as a site for Acocks's investigations into grasses and pasture management (Chapter 11). In 1907 he established himself in the western Cape, operating a borehole drilling and agricultural machinery business.[17] At this point, General Botha, newly in power in the Transvaal, asked him to sacrifice it for 'land and volk'. Botha was keen to put Afrikaners into the civil service; there was a personal connection from the war, and one of du Toit's brothers was working as a manager on Botha's farm. Du Toit started at the end of 1908 as Superintendent of the Dryland Experimental farm at Lichtenburg, in the western Transvaal. Arable 'dry-farming' became his obsession for the next decade.

'Dry-farming', in this context, meant not simply dryland farming of rain-fed (as opposed to irrigated) crops, but particular techniques of cultivation in areas where the rainfall was usually inadequate for a reliable crop. Arable farming in South Africa was generally considered feasible, without irrigation, in areas that received over 20" (500 mm) of rainfall. Dry-farming promised a reliable crop, at low cost, on large areas of land that received even less. Types of dry-farming had a long history in different parts of the world; du Toit had learnt something about them in his travels.[18] The Lichtenburg experimental station was largely the project of William MacDonald, a Scot who had worked initially as farm manager at Lovedale school, the leading educational

---

[12] du T., 263, 38, 'Henri' du Toit, Compassberg to Raoul Martin, Paris, 27 Feb. 1905.

[13] In a later note on his 1902/3 trip, du Toit mentions that he visited Scotland with a view to passing a university entrance exam.

[14] du T., 263, 38, 'Henri' du Toit, Compassberg to Raoul Martin, Paris, 27 Feb. 1905.

[15] du T., 280, 22, card du Toit and De Jager Handelaars (in Dutch).

[16] Heinrich S. du Toit, *Dry-Farming* (Het Westen, Potchefstroom, 1913), 53.

[17] du T., 263, 1, notebook with a few entries for 1908.

[18] *Agricultural Journal*, 14: 11 (25 May 1899), 696: 'Conservation of Soil Moisture.'

institution for Africans in the Cape. MacDonald moved to the Transvaal during Reconstruction and served both as Dryland Agronomist in the Transvaal
Department of Agriculture and as editor of the *Transvaal Agricultural Journal*.
Launched in 1902, along the lines of the well-established Cape publication,
the journal provided MacDonald with an excellent platform for his ideas.

MacDonald had also studied agriculture in the United States and worked
on a state experimental farm in Minnesota. In 1906, during six months' leave
of absence from the Transvaal, he made a further extended tour and wrote
lengthy, well-illustrated articles on his experiences.[19] He saw the American
agricultural colleges as a model and enthused about the demonstration
'gospel train' which spread the message of improvement in tours through
the Midwest.[20] Undoubtedly the subject that excited MacDonald most was
dry-farming.[21] The key to success seemed to lie in techniques of conserving
soil moisture and of breeding drought-resistant seeds. These drew on Jethro
Tull's maxim that 'tillage is manure'. There were three key steps. First, the
land had to be ploughed very deeply, so that rainfall could penetrate the soil
and be stored—as in a natural reservoir. Secondly, as soon as possible after
rainfall, the ploughed field had to be harrowed to form a 'soil mulch' or
'ground-blanket'. The idea was that water could be held in the soil more
effectively when the upper layer was loose because this retarded capillary
action whereby water would reach the surface and evaporate. This operation
was to be repeated after every rainfall. Frequent harrowing also prevented
weed growth, and thus loss of water through transpiration: weeds, du Toit
wrote, 'are moisture and plant-food robbers'.[22]

Thirdly, these long, clean fallows after ploughing had to be maintained for
more than one rainy season before crops were planted. Successful crops could
be grown every second year in this way with as little as ten inches of rainfall
annually. Du Toit compared dry-farming systems to irrigation, except that
water was conserved in soil rather than dams. Research in soil science

[19] *Transvaal Agricultural Journal*, 5: 18 (1907): William MacDonald, 'Agriculture in America',
305–39 and subsequent articles; *The Conquest of the Desert* (T. W. Laurie, London, 1913).

[20] MacDonald, 'Agriculture in America', 312–5.

[21] Summary from MacDonald's writings above; *Transvaal Agricultural Journal*, 8: 29, (Oct.
1909): W. MacDonald, 'The Principles of Dry-Farming', 100–10; ibid. 9: 33 (Oct. 1910), Heinrich
S. du Toit, 'Dry-Farming', 73–8; ibid. 8: 31 (Apr. 1910): 'The Dry-Farming Section', 484–92.
Agricultural Journal, 33: 4 (Oct. 1908), W. F. Sutherst, 'The Conservation of Soil Moisture',
511–13; ibid. 35: 1 (July 1909), O. A. Oosthuisen, MLA, 'Dry Land Farming, Water Storage and
Irrigation in America, Compared with South African Conditions', 10–23; ibid. 36: 3 (Mar. 1910):
R. W. Thornton, 'Dry Land Farming: Experiments at Klipboschlaagte Experiment Station,
Robertson', 286–93.

[22] du Toit, 'Dry-Farming', 77.

suggested that harrowing, in addition to storing rainfall and destroying weeds, promoted the circulation of warm air and bacteria. Du Toit believed that frequent harrowing promoted nitrification, provided a better base for roots, and quickened decomposition of mineral elements in the soil. There were many different variations on these techniques, but by and large they were facilitated by agricultural machinery.

With an eye for the telling phrase, which was later also du Toit's stock-in-trade as a popularizer of improvement, MacDonald illustrated how the 'Mormon Voortrekkers' had made the desert bloom in Utah through such techniques.[23] Nebraska had been a particularly important site for honing dry-farming techniques in the 1890s.[24] MacDonald proposed a series of dry-farming experiments in the Transvaal. Working with white farmers, he had already found that wheat yields increased markedly if these principles were followed. He sold his ideas not only as a means of increasing production, but of facilitating the elusive goal of closer settlement. 'The Homestead Act of 1862 in the United States of America,' he argued, 'which gave 160 acres of dry-land freehold to every settler—has done more than anything else to build up a mighty and prosperous nation.'[25]

Botha, Minister of Agriculture as well as Prime Minister in the Transvaal, supported the project and specified that the main station should be in the neglected south-western Transvaal. Further sites were opened: at Groenkloof, near Pretoria, MacDonald 'cut out an American homestead of 160 acres for demonstration purposes'.[26] A Cape MLA who visited the United States (as well as Egypt and India) in 1908 was less optimistic that such techniques could be widely adopted in the Karoo, because the soils were generally less suitable, the subsoil too shallow except in alluvial pockets, and gradients too steep.[27]

MacDonald had opened up the bureaucratic space in which du Toit could flourish. How far du Toit had developed his ideas independently as a result of his travels is not clear, but they followed along much the same lines. For the first few years in the western Transvaal he was deeply involved in turning a difficult piece of land, formerly partly occupied by bywoners and African

---

[23] MacDonald, 'Agriculture in America', 319.

[24] *Agricultural Journal*, 14: 11 (25 May 1899): 'Conservation of Soil Moisture'.

[25] PTA LDB 33, DL 10/3, William MacDonald to Minister of Agriculture, Pretoria, 17 Aug. 1908. Du Toit, *Dry-Farming*, notes that earlier experimental stations were started in the Free State and the northern Cape.

[26] PTA LDB 32, DL 9/6, William MacDonald to F. S. Malan, Minister of Education, 14 Oct. 1910.

[27] Oosthuisen, 'Dry Land Farming', 13.

tenants, into a fenced, model farm for scientific experiment. He also married a local woman, and bought and developed his own farm in the area—planting 28,000 timber and 500 fruit trees.[28] Although the American example was important, 'reclaiming their so-called deserts without the aid of irrigation', du Toit's experiments at Lichtenburg began to reveal variations in equipment and timing appropriate for South African conditions.[29]

They met with considerable success. MacDonald became Secretary of the International Dry-farming Congress. Agricultural machinery dealers were enthusiastic about the system. MacLarens, the South African agents of the British Fowler steam plough company, pursued these techniques on sections of the intensively farmed Vereeniging Estates owned by the businessman Sammy Marks.[30] William McLaren was the first recipient of the South African 'Jethro Tull medal' for dry-farming in 1911.[31] Marks awarded annual cash prizes in the 'Senator Marks Dry-Farming Competition': most of the winners were Afrikaners. Annual dry-farming Congresses were launched with the support of senior Transvaal politicians. The publicity was full of portentous language: the slogan for the first (1910) dry-farming congress at Klerksdorp was 'The Destiny of South Africa is on the Dry-Lands'. An optimistic diagram promised that 160 million acres through the heart of the semi-arid Karoo and Botswana would be 'the wheat and maize belt of to-morrow'.[32]

It is clear from his cuttings that du Toit, an able and humorous speaker, soon became considerably more than an experimental farm manager. He was the 'heart and soul of the Congress' in Pretoria in 1911.[33] In April 1911 the railway arrived in Lichtenburg and he invited an array of Transvaal notables, both English and Afrikaner, to an opening ceremony which gave further opportunity for publicity. There were many visitors to his experimental farm and his work was reported in the local and national press, from the western Transvaal south to Graaff-Reinet. In 1912–13 he toured the Cape twice to promote dry-farming techniques in the semi-arid areas. In his official work he had clearly overcome his antipathy towards English-speakers, and one of his brothers had worked for Sir Thomas Cullinan as a farm manager.

The superintendent of the de Beers farms, Kimberley, wrote: 'your services have proved of very great value to the country and I feel sure that we all

[28] du T., persoonlike leer, unnumbered, du Toit to P. J. du Toit, 28 Mar. 1915.

[29] *Transvaal Agricultural Journal*, 9: 33 (Oct. 1910): Heinrich S. du Toit, 'Dry-Farming', 73–8.

[30] S. Trapido, 'Putting a Plough to the Ground: A History of Tenant Production on the Vereeniging Estates, 1896–1920', in Beinart et al. (eds.), *Putting a Plough to the Ground*.

[31] du Toit, *Dry-Farming*, 23.   [32] *Transvaal Agricultural Journal*, 8: 31 (Apr. 1910), 485.

[33] du T., 261, 1–41, newspaper cuttings on Dryland station, 1910–12.

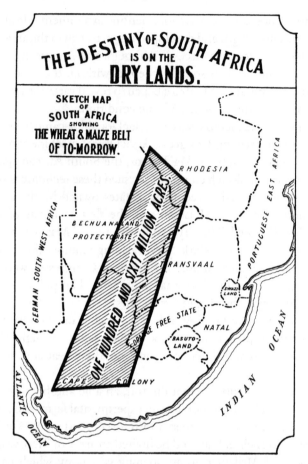

9. 'The Destiny of South Africa is on the Dry Lands'

came away feeling convinced that thousands and thousands of acres of land in the Cape Colony that are now lying idle could be dealt with under the same system as you showed and explained to us.'[34] Another enthusiastic correspondent wrote: 'I feel convinced that this new method is going to revolutionise South Africa.'[35] A magazine praised him for his influence on 'backveld Boers', and published a poem by a Whittlesea (Cape) farmer, in English, dedicated to du Toit and titled 'The Destiny of South Africa is out in the Dry Lands':[36]

[34] PTA LDB 33, DL 10/3, W. W. Fynn to du Toit, 25 Oct. 1911.
[35] Ibid., Thomas Lanham to du Toit, 21 Oct. 1911.
[36] du T. 262, unnumbered file, persoonlik, cutting 17 May 1911, no source given but matches the layout of the newly launched *Farmers' Weekly*.

Methinks I hear thee now in homely Dutch explain
How we should set about to safe the gift of rain,
By ploughing deep the soil and cultivating well,
And harrow, harrow, harrow whether sick or well,
To keep each golden shower to feed the golden grain.

In 1911 du Toit gave evidence to the Senate Select Committee on Closer Land Settlement. Following MacDonald, he believed that dry-farming would enable farmers to survive on far less land, perhaps 160 acres for crops and 20 for gardens and orchards—about 75 ha in all. 'Our Great National Object,' he wrote, 'i.e. to get a larger white population on the land, can never be fully attained until the great importance of dry-farming is fully realised.'[37] There was a racial element in his thinking. As he told the fourth Dry-farming Congress in Johannesburg in 1913, it was their duty to make land more fruitful and 'eindelike een "Land voor Blanken" van te maken'.[38] Up to 1915 he employed largely white men on the experimental farm although he did allow Africans to graze cattle there.[39]

In 1913 du Toit published a short book on dry-farming with *Het Westen* newspaper printers in Potchefstroom. His object was to 'show the world that the hitherto waste "veld" is capable of producing more than wild grasses and bushes'.[40] It was purposely written in what he called 'South African Dutch', perhaps one of the first Afrikaans technical books. Later that year, following requests by English-speaking farmers, he translated it himself. The book is a mixture of basic agronomy, a history of dry-farming, and du Toit's personal experiences. The illustrations are instructive. They include the author, his father, various luminaries who could be associated with the dry-farming movement, from General Botha to William MacDonald, wonderful crops, modern steam ploughs, and machines.

The rhetoric of science suffused the text. Du Toit called on farmers to experiment, study local conditions, and analyse failure: 'always look upon your farm as your own private laboratory.'[41] Every farmer was to be a self-made scientist, like himself. If 'man' could conquer tuberculosis, make stingless bees and thornless cactus, then hazards such as hail and frost would

---

[37] du Toit, *Dry-Farming*, 71.

[38] '. . . ultimately make "a land for whites"'. PTA LDB 34, DL 61, speech at Dryland congress, 1913.

[39] du Toit's personal farming activities—his farm was partly rented out—became for a brief period a point of some unease with the Department. For background on the area, Charles van Onselen, *The Seed is Mine: The Life of Kas Maine, A South African Sharecropper 1894–1985* (James Currey, Oxford, 1997).

[40] du Toit, *Dry-Farming*, 73.   [41] Ibid. 75.

'ultimately be made harmless' and deserts conquered with dry-farming and drought-resistant plants. Farmers should 'stand together and conquer the South African non-irrigable lands'.[42] He ended the book with a picture of 'the future plough (The Author's Prophecy)', in which an aeroplane pulled four ploughs across a field. Du Toit combined imagination and machinery in his view of progress; there was an element of the showman in his speeches and writing.

By 1913 nearly half his time was 'generally taken up in travelling, lecturing, demonstrating, inspecting and directing experiments on other Government and Co-operative dry-land stations'. He wrote while 'out-spanned on the veld, staying in hotels, or boarding-houses or waiting for trains on railway stations'. In 1914 the Dry-farming Congress bought him a motorcar to facilitate his travels around the country, which the Department allowed him to pursue. Du Toit was not modest in his self-assessment. He claimed—'and numbers of farmers will fully endorse the statement'—that the techniques he promoted greatly helped in maintaining crop production through the severe droughts of the early 1910s.[43] They made 'the ordinary farmer think' and stimulated 'new interest in plant life, soils and climatic conditions'.[44] In later years he suggested that the 'introduction of dry-farming methods were responsible not only for an enormous increase in production in South Africa, but also for better and more scientific farming methods generally [and] for the more economic use of water'.[45] Products of the soil, he argued, constituted 'the real wealth and controlling resources of any nation'.[46]

Undoubtedly there were successes in dry-farming, but from the start there were critics. A letter to *Het Westen* in 1909, which du Toit kept, argued that indebted Afrikaner farmers, with few machines and limited ox-draught, would find it difficult to follow his advice about deep ploughing and frequent harrowing.[47] A Graaff-Reinet farmer urged caution, because constant harrowing of light soil might make it susceptible to wind erosion or 'blowing'.[48] An experimental station at Vryburg in the northern Cape operated unsuccessfully for seven years, not least because of this problem. Rains there were too irregular, temperatures and evaporation too high. An official recorded:

[42] Ibid. 67.

[43] PTA LDB 33 DL10/3, du Toit to F. B. Smith, Secretary for Agriculture (Sec. Ag.), 14 Apr. 1915.

[44] Ibid., du Toit to Sec. Ag., 13 Mar. 1916.

[45] du T., unnumbered, persoonlike leer, du Toit to Acting Secretary for Agriculture, 25 Sept. 1922.

[46] du T., 263, notebook, 1908–9, quote from Hugh Pendexter. Du Toit occasionally wrote down quotes which he used in speeches.

[47] du T., 262, unnumbered file, persoonlik, cutting from *Het Westen*, 5 Nov. 1909.

[48] Ibid., cutting from *The Illustrated Star*, 24 Aug. 1912.

we had such terrific winds that they blew the first foot of soil off our lands . . . Our lands in October were like the sand dunes one sees at the coast; the fence which enclosed our plots consisted of six strands of wire and 3 feet wire netting, and all that could be seen after 3 months high winds . . . was the top strand.[49]

Partly for this reason, the station was closed down. Wind erosion was a major problem in the United States and a cause of the Dust Bowl. Deep ploughing on poor soil or sloping land could also cause soil erosion in the absence of careful contouring.

F. B. Smith, the first Union Secretary of Agriculture, was a little sceptical, seeing more enthusiasm than science in the dry-farming movement. Du Toit's station in Lichtenburg shut in 1917. This was not because it was seen as a failure. In a quest to make the station self-sufficient, he expanded operations to the point that farmers complained about competition in local markets.[50] Moreover, the Department was confronted with financial retrenchment during the First World War. Perhaps most important, a policy decision was made to the effect that the Agronomy Division should work with the farmers' co-operatives, which were being established in some number: experimental work on the farms would be less expensive and carry greater exemplary power.[51] The government had also decided to establish or enlarge agricultural colleges, with their own experimental farms at Elsenburg and Grootfontein in the Cape, Potchefstroom in the Transvaal, Cedara in Natal, and Glen in the Orange Free State. Specialist officials would be concentrated at these institutions.

Dry-farming techniques were abandoned in some places where they had been tried, and the term itself was not widely adopted in South Africa. Elements such as deep ploughing, contour ploughing, and clean fallows (if for shorter periods) were in any case becoming more general. Undoubtedly the slow progress of mechanization in the inter-war years worked against their introduction. After the Second World War, when tractors became a feature of white commercial agriculture, similar techniques were of great importance, especially in the eastern Free State, for wheat production.[52]

Du Toit rapidly assumed wider responsibilities. He succeeded in creating an unusual role for himself in the Department, involving a great deal of public speaking and mobility with limited day-to-day office work. In 1916 he

[49] SAB LDB 33, DL 40/6, H. Melle, Division of Botany, to A. Holm, Under Sec. Ag., 5 Nov. 1917.

[50] PTA LDB 33 DL10/3, du Toit to F. B. Smith, Sec. Ag., 14 Apr. 1915.

[51] *Journal of the Department of Agriculture*, 1: 5 (Aug. 1920), 463–71: 'The Department of Agriculture during the War.'

[52] Keegan, *Rural Transformations*; Beinart and Coates, *Environment and History*, 67.

initiated a congress of wheat growers in Bloemfontein. Smith, the Secretary, emphasized in his opening speech the need for South African farmers to grow sufficient for national consumption, although not at the cost of becoming 'land robbers'. Du Toit gave a paper on 'Wheat Growing without Irrigation' in English and Afrikaans. He had not given up on dry-farming, arguing that 'we have . . . quite enough experimental evidence to prove that there is an enormous acreage of fertile land all over our sub-continent which falls within the zones of possible and profitable dry-farming'.[53]

In 1917 du Toit moved to Pretoria in charge of the small Division of Dry-land Farming, and increasingly became absorbed in extension work. He established a government seed depot and was chair of the Conference of Field Crop Investigators. From 1920 he served as a member of the Board of Control of the Hartebeestpoort Irrigation Scheme, the major settlement scheme in the Transvaal. The greater part of his time was now spent travelling; he visited 145 centres in a year in 1918–19, 'lecturing, demonstrating, selecting and classifying soils and seeds . . . directing and inspecting co-operative experiments'.[54] He was frequently asked to attend and open agricultural shows. He gave a typically vivid self-description in one of his not infrequent requests for a salary rise, as part of an argument that he incurred many incidental expenses for which it was difficult to claim: 'I have to address meetings at one time of the day and then leave the platform the next moment to conduct field demonstrations, handle seeds or soils, creep through barbed wire fences, walk over muddy "vleis" or stoney hills or push motor cars through mud or sand.' Elsewhere he wrote: 'my house is always full and my grocery bills alarmingly large.'

In 1918 du Toit was appointed Vice-Chairman of the Departmental Wheat Committee, and in fact took the major responsibility for it.[55] The inquiry took him to ninety-four centres, especially in the western Cape. It was appointed to investigate the shortfall of production (about 60 per cent of requirements) in South Africa during the 1910s. Imports had become particularly vulnerable during the First World War; as a result, a Wheat Conservation Act was passed. Wheat supplies, import costs, and national self-sufficiency remained sensitive issues. Although the investigation was primarily concerned with production, not conservation, du Toit was interested in soil fertility. The soils of the wetter areas of the western Cape—the

[53] PTA LDB 34, DL 64/3, H. S. du Toit, 'Wheat Growing without Irrigation'.

[54] Union of South Africa, *Department of Agriculture, Report with Appendices for the Year Ended 1919*, U.G.40-1919, 144.

[55] Union of South Africa, *Report of the Committee on the Growing of Wheat*, U.G.42-1919; see also unpublished parliamentary Annexure, 419–1918.

chief wheat-growing zone in the country—tended to be sandy, with a lack of humus; despite some innovation, yields were static. 'Some new, systematized type of farming must be evolved,' the report argued, 'of which a considerable share is to be *permanently* devoted to the needs of the soil.'[56]

Du Toit also returned to the Karoo, where he had been raised, and where it had long been known that high wheat yields could be achieved under irrigation. The area was also relatively free from rust, a scourge in the wetter, eastern districts. In the midlands, around Cradock, Graaff-Reinet, and Middelburg, the decline in ostrich farming diminished the need for lucerne, potentially increasing the availability of irrigated land for wheat. Where possible farmers did grow some wheat for consumption, sometimes in rotation with lucerne. Despite du Toit's belief in dry-farming, the report concluded that there was limited scope for increased wheat production there. The priority areas would be the north-east Cape, East Griqualand, and the eastern Free State. His experience on this committee helped to give du Toit a national picture of environmental and soil conditions, which proved important in his subsequent work.

The Drought Commission

In 1920 du Toit was appointed Chairman of the Drought Investigation Commission, initially convened as a response to the drought losses of 1919–20. In many respects it continued the work of the 1914 Senate Select Committee that had addressed 'the disastrous effects and steadily increasing severity of the annual droughts throughout most of the inland portions of the Union' and 'the soil erosion which inevitably accompanies these droughts'.[57] Simultaneously, the *South African Agricultural Journal*, its circulation up to 30,000, carried letters and reports on the question: 'Is South Africa Drying Up?'[58]

Charles Stewart, Chief Meteorologist, when pressed on rainfall incidence by the 1914 Committee, would only say that past records indicated that rainfall had 'varied enormously', and that it was difficult to see any clear trends 'one way or the other'.[59] This remained the scientific consensus in the early 1920s. Stewart did recognize, however, that small changes in the timing and incidence of rain in the semi-arid interior could have major effects, because

---

[56] U.G.42-1919, 8.   [57] S.C.2-1914, p. ii.

[58] *Agricultural Journal*, 7: 5 (May, 1914), 631, 732–9.

[59] S.C.2-1914, 20; the Meteorology section was in the Irrigation Department, under the Ministry of Lands.

precipitation could be highly localized and was restricted to a few months. The Committee, and the Drought Commission, both took the position that drought had more to do with the incapacity of denuded soil to absorb water than any change in rainfall.[60]

There was some evidence that the summer-rainfall zones of South Africa suffered from relatively regular drought, roughly every seven or eight years, although this was by no means predictable. In the Cape there had been serious droughts in 1862–3, 1872–3, 1877–8, 1895–6, 1903–4, 1912–3, and 1918–9; these were to recur in 1926–7 and 1932–3. The western Cape winter-rainfall zone seemed sometimes to experience inverse precipitation; heavy rains could accompany drought elsewhere. The influence of El Niño was not then known and most specialists were reluctant to detect any clear cycles.

Critiques of livestock farming were strongly evident in the 1914 evidence: 'the sheep farmer especially', one witness affirmed, 'will destroy the whole country for the sake of his sheep.'[61] The long-serving surveyor E. B. Watermeyer, who lived in Calvinia, blamed fires, overstocking, and transhumance for denudation and drought: 'the great offender is the nomadic trekker, who makes his "scherm" in the veld, and destroys all the surrounding bushes and trees and anything he can lay his hands on for firewood . . . The gypsy of this country.'[62] Witnesses supported enforcement of disease regulations and controls on the movement of livestock. The Committee struggled to define strategies through which farmers could be persuaded that their self-interest would be served by a more conservationist approach. The potential decline in the value of degraded land did not seem to be enough in itself. Poorer whites found it too expensive to invest in remedial work; they sold up and moved on. Both poor whites and Africans who rented land were seen to have less interest in conservation. Poor-whiteism, environmental degradation, suspicion of innovation, and unsettled mobility were all again linked. Yet most witnesses believed that too much compulsion would fail: 'I think you do more', an engineer argued, 'by gentle persuasion than by regulations.'[63]

In the 1919 drought the Department of Agriculture tried to estimate both deaths of livestock through 'poverty' and through essential slaughter of offspring.[64] It calculated that over 200,000 large stock and 5.4 million small

---

[60] C. H. Vogel, 'Climatic Change in the Cape Colony, 1820–1900', *South African Journal of Science*, 84 (1988), 11, and '160 Years of Rainfall of the Cape—Has There Been a Change?', ibid. 724–6.

[61] S.C.2-1914, 10.   [62] Ibid. 11, evidence E. B. Watermeyer.   [63] Ibid. 4.

[64] *Journal of the Department of Agriculture*, 1: 2 (May, 1920), 144–8: 'The Drought of 1918–1919: Estimated Loss of Live Stock and Produce.'

stock were lost, with the Karoo and north-western Cape, where the percentage of average rainfall was lowest, hardest hit. Farmers had been building up stock numbers during the 1910s, so that they were particularly vulnerable. Officials estimated that financial costs amounted to £16 million.

Wool was still the country's most important agricultural export, and the Cape midlands remained a significant centre of farming politics. In March 1920 I. P. (Petrus) van Heerden, a Nationalist, who had won the seat for Cradock in place of H. C. van Heerden, asked the new Minister of Agriculture, F. S. Malan, for a Commission of Inquiry.[65] Malan initially refused; he was anxious not to cede political initiative to Hertzog's party.[66] Van Heerden, however, successfully lobbied MPs on cross-party lines, not least those in the Karoo. The Labour Party wanted an inquiry to look at the impact of drought on unemployment.[67] Malan relented; both he and his Secretary were keen for du Toit to act as chair, although he had no particular expertise on pastoral farming.[68]

Arthur Stead, the agricultural chemist working at Grootfontein in the Karoo, was appointed with the backing of Thornton, principal of the agricultural college there (Chapter 8). Thornton, later a key figure in relation to conservation measures in the African reserves and Lesotho, already had clear ideas about the urgency of changes in pastoral farming (Chapter 10). 'This Commission,' he argued, 'if it is to do its work properly, is probably one of the most important that has ever been appointed.'[69] The Department of Irrigation offered an engineer, Reenen J. van Reenen, superintendent of local works in the Free State, who had also visited the United States and had worked on the Smartt dams. Montagu Gadd and G. A. Kolbe were chosen from the nominees of the South African Agricultural Union. Both had been involved in agricultural politics for some years, including the annual vermin conferences.

The Commission's hearings started in Bloemfontein in November 1920. It collected evidence in a wide range of venues throughout the country over the next two years. Although minutes of evidence do not seem to have survived, some of the proceedings can be gleaned from newspaper articles and other

---

[65] R. Bouch, 'Farming and Politics in the Karoo and Eastern Cape, 1910–1924', *South African Historical Journal*, 12 (1980), 48–64.

[66] *Debates of the House of Assembly of the Union of South Africa as reported in the Cape Times*, 1920 (Pretoria, 1968), 14.

[67] Union of South Africa, *Votes and Proceedings of the House of Assembly*, First session, third parliament, 1920, p. 667.

[68] PTA LDB 1063, R1318/12. The archive on the Commission is relatively small.

[69] Ibid., Thornton to Sec. Ag., 7 Sept. 1920.

sources.[70] *The Friend* in Bloemfontein, for example, reported extensively on the first meeting under the head of 'Conservation: Evidence before Drought Commission, Sluiting, Afforestation and Overstocking'. In his opening address, du Toit stressed that drought losses were due to 'artificial' and not natural causes. Drought was having so large an impact because pastures were mismanaged and overstocked. Farming, he argued, was now a scientific profession, 'no longer merely an occupation for peasants . . . [or] even a trade'; only 'the properly trained, the deep thinkers and the active could reasonably hope for success'.[71] He again stressed the need for working with nature through systematic experiment.

Witnesses in Bloemfontein sketched out themes that were to preoccupy the Commission. Gustav Baumann, a surveyor who had also given evidence in 1913, wanted legislation to enforce the resting of pastures, to provide water in every grazing camp, and to compel people to stop soil erosion. A. M. Spies, sheep farmer and formerly wool expert in the Free State government, pointed to steekgras and bitterbos as evidence of 'worked out' farms. 'Chasing flocks long distances to water' resulted in the process whereby sheep 'stamped out' three times more than they ate. The Commission's visit to Grootfontein was clearly influential in the final report. Here the message hammered home by staff members was: 'overstocking is our curse.'[72] Farmers based their calculations on good years rather than bad. The cry, as so often before, was for rotation of pastures in fenced camps, water provision, and fodder, including the development of indigenous fodder crops. Surplus maize, it was suggested, should be used for fodder rather than exported. Throughout the hearings, witnesses emphasized these points.

In July 1921 du Toit drew up an exhaustive list of questions for written responses from 'scientific men'; a number of these were published as appendices to the final report.[73] Du Toit deliberately broadened the remit of his investigation and was deeply conscious of its importance. Ideas such as Agricultural Advisory Boards to co-ordinate between farmers, officials, and parliament, and rural conservation boards, with legally based authority to monitor and act on denudation and soil erosion, were mooted. As in 1892–4, the commissioners saw their goal as exhortatory and educative as well as investigative. The 102 public meetings were an opportunity to express their

---

[70] W. Beinart, 'The Missing Minutes of Evidence to the Drought Investigation Commission (U.G.49-1923), with Notes on Commission Archives', *Archive News* (South Africa), 39: 1 (1996), 11–21. There are a few notes on the Commission in du Toit's own papers but no substantial record.

[71] du T., 280, 43 cutting from *The Friend*, 17 Nov. 1920: 'Fighting Drought: Bloem Evidence.'

[72] du T., 273, 10, Drought Commission notebook, 7 June 1921, interview, Mr Schumann.

[73] PTA LDB 1063, R1318/12, memo from H. S. du Toit to Sec. Ag., July 1921.

ideas about best farming practice as well as to hear from witnesses. This occasionally laid them open to accusations of 'political propaganda work'.[74] Despite his forceful style, du Toit did listen to witnesses and to his fellow commissioners. 'Mr du Toit', one newspaper reported, was 'a past master at drawing all the salient points out of his subjects.'[75]

Gadd, representative of Cape farmers on the Commission, was particularly concerned about elimination of jackals and other predators as the key solution to pastoral ills. As many witnesses had dwelt on this scourge, both Gadd and Stead argued successfully that it should be central in the final report. Du Toit himself was less preoccupied by this long-standing Cape obsession: 'I think quite enough prominence has been given to the Jackal and if we were a "Jackal Commission["] . . . then the Commission's name and its terms of Reference must have been vastly different and we need only have visited Jackal invested [sic] areas.'[76] He suspected that Petrus van Heerden, the MP who had initiated the inquiry, had put strong pressure on Gadd to highlight this issue so that more government money would become available for eradication. 'Petrus and Monty [Gadd]', du Toit noted, 'are (*rightly*) both very bitter enemies of the jackals' and 'van Heerden had . . . *Jackhal* extermination alone on his brain when he applied for State help'.[77] In fact, the Cape Provincial Council had already voted large new funds towards vermin extermination.

Du Toit was deeply committed to the success of the Commission and anxious for its findings to be available and publicized. He was encouraged by Smartt, who had taken over as Minister of Agriculture in Smuts's last cabinet, to draft an interim report early in 1922.[78] Du Toit worked 'some nights up to 3 o'clock in the morning', writing in English, then translating with the help of the Commission secretary into Afrikaans.[79] His language and style is clearly detectable, but he let his witnesses and fellow commissioners speak. Much of the report focused on pastoral farming, rather than on his own areas of expertise. As he explained:

My Commission at the outset, divided the scope of our investigation into 'circles' comprising what we considered to be the most important points falling under our terms of reference. Of these, small stock farming, in our estimation, ranked first in

[74] Ibid., du Toit to Editor, *Farmer's Weekly*, 6 Dec. 1920.

[75] Ibid., cutting from *Diamond Fields Advertiser*, 8 July 1921, report on meeting at Warrenton.

[76] du T., 266, 59, du Toit to Stead, 29 Mar. 1922; 266, 60, du Toit to Smartt, 4 Apr. 1922, explaining the delay in the draft, partly because one member 'wanted the Jackal to figure first and foremost'.

[77] du T., 266, 59, du Toit to Stead, 29 Mar. 1922.

[78] U.G.20-1922, Union of South Africa, *Drought Investigation Commission, Interim Report*.

[79] du T., 266, 59, du Toit to Stead, 29 Mar. 1922.

the order of importance because South Africa is essentially a stock country and we found also the figures for the drought of 1919 shewed a heavy preponderance of loss in small stock—in fact much higher than all the losses in other branches of agricultural taken together.[80]

The key recommendations included the abolition of kraaling and transhumance, together with the introduction of fenced camps. This, it was emphasized, would be in the interests of the farmer. Farmers, the report argued, judged wetness by the results of rain rather than its actual incidence. Consciously redefining the concept of drought in South Africa in a way that farmers would understand, the report argued that dryness was not so much due to a lack a rainfall but to the inability of the ground to absorb it. The issue was 'veld overstocked, tramped out, semi-waterproof, hard-baked by sun and veld fires'. *'The logical outcome of it all'*, it concluded, drawing on and popularizing earlier conservationist discourse, was ' *"the Great South African Desert" uninhabitable by man.'*[81]

Following the interim report, du Toit pursued further material, travelling to the northern and eastern Cape and expanding the scientific support work in areas such as long-range weather forecasts, drought cycles, and the fodder value of drought-resistant plants. By this time the other commissioners had moved on and he worked largely by himself or with van Reenen. He was involved in long-running battles over the expense of the inquiry: they had overspent the £6,000 budget by £2,000. The numerous maps, largely researched and drawn by van Reenen, increased the length and cost of the report; du Toit also insisted on printing the scientific appendices. The practice of publishing long reports, including minutes of evidence, common prior to Union, had largely been abandoned.

Smartt thought that the Commission report 'evoked more public interest than any other Government Blue Book published of recent years'.[82] It was certainly more widely circulated. The interim report of 1922 was published in full in the *Agricultural Journal*, which then had a circulation of about 9,200, and the *Cape Education Gazette*.[83] Grootfontein School of Agriculture

---

[80] PTA LDB 1063, R1318/12, H. S. du Toit to C. A. Celliers, 3 July 1922. The term circles had been used for vermin extermination committees (and in the nineteenth century for Cape elections).

[81] U.G.49-1923, 3. The interim report was largely republished as the first section of the final report.

[82] PTA LDB 1064, R1318, Sec. Ag. to Secretary for Finance, 28 Aug. 1922.

[83] *Journal of the Department of Agriculture*, 5: 2, Aug. 1922: 'The Great Drought Problem of South Africa. An Outline of the Interim Report of the Commission of Inquiry', 118–130. Circulation figures from ibid. 5: 6 (Dec. 1922), 582. The Journal had been suspended during the First World War, when circulation had reached 30,000, and continued as a private publication before it was resurrected.

organized an essay competition for the Commission with a 1 guinea prize.[84] Bernard Huss, the Catholic missionary, was granted permission to translate the report into 'very simple English' for the 'Native press'.[85] (The Department did not see this as urgent.) A Drought Symposium was organized in July 1923 as part of the South African Association for the Advancement of Science meeting.[86] The Transvaal Agricultural Union asked for 2,500 free copies of the impending final report, ten for each of its affiliated associations. 'It will be the most educative publication in the interests of agriculture that has ever appeared in South Africa,' the secretary argued; 'our farmers require to be shewn where they are going wrong'.[87]

Although du Toit could not win approval for the publication of the lengthy final report on the scale he wished, an unusually large number of 1,600 copies in English and 700 in Dutch was printed.[88] In addition to reports in the national papers, *Farmers' Weekly*, the largest-circulation non-governmental agricultural magazine, summarized the report in instalments. Within six months of publication in July 1924 supplies of the report—most distributed free—were exhausted. Rather than reprint, a summary was published in the *Agricultural Journal* through the second half of 1925.[89] In 1926 these summaries were reprinted (3,350 in English and 4,400 in Afrikaans) in a volume called *The Great Drought Problem of South Africa*.[90] One thousand were distributed free to schools, where they were used for teaching, and many others through the extension service.

In 1929 du Toit published a short book on soil conservation, in English and Afrikaans, designed largely for educational institutions: 'the request of a large proportion of the public for *more* information on the matter', he suggested, 'has been so insistent that the writing of this booklet has practically been rendered obligatory'.[91] When *The Great Drought Problem* went out of print van Reenen, who had gone on to chair a drought commission in Namibia, and also the Irrigation Commission in Pretoria, rewrote it in a booklet

[84] PTA LDB 1064, R1318, R. W. Thornton, Principal, Grootfontein, to du Toit, 22 Dec. 1921.

[85] Ibid., Fr B. Huss to Sec. Ag., 18 Aug. 1922 and following correspondence.

[86] PTA LDB 1064, R1318/12, vol. II, Geo. Potts to du Toit, 1 June 1923.

[87] Ibid., J. Kleynhans, Secretary Transvaal Agricultural Union to Chief, Extension Division, Department of Agriculture, 16 July 1923 and 23 July 1923.

[88] U.G.49-1923; see correspondence in SAB TES 5609, F33/142.

[89] *Journal of the Department of Agriculture*, 11: 1 (July 1925), 22–9; 11: 2 (Aug. 1925), 109–12; 11: 3 (Sept. 1925), 209–14; 11: 4 (Oct. 1925), 324–37; 11: 5 (Nov. 1925), 391–5; 12: 1 (Jan. 1926), 33–7; 12: 2 (Feb. 1926), 111–19. Figures from ibid. 11: 6 (Dec. 1925), 629.

[90] Union of South Africa, Department of Agriculture, *The Great Drought Problem of South Africa* (Pretoria, 1926), reprint no. 16 (55 pp.).

[91] Heinrich S. du Toit, *The Conservation of Our Soil* (Government Printer, Pretoria, 1929), 5. Published in Afrikaans as *Grondkonservasie*.

10. Frontispiece: *Resisting Drought*

entitled *Resisting Drought*; 10,000 copies were published by the Department in 1934.[92] Facing its title page was a photograph of a jackal. It is probably not an exaggeration to say that well over 50,000 copies of versions of the report were distributed, excluding newspaper reports.

Although he explicitly sought scientific authority and academic credibility, du Toit wrote in accessible language. He was proud of his work: 'the whole educated world,' he wrote, 'as well as all our enlightened farmers, label the report (*rightly or wrongly*) a masterpiece which will be worth incalculable amounts of money for South Africa as well as the whole southern hemisphere.'[93] What is striking is the constant appeal not only to conservation principles, but to the national interest and the necessity of far-reaching state intervention. This link had already been made in respect of some elements of environmental regulation at the Cape, such as disease control, predator eradication, water management, and forestry. It had been made in connection with increased production and national self-sufficiency in food. Now it was

[92] Reenen J. van Reenen, *Resisting Drought* (Government Printer, Pretoria, 1934).

[93] PTA LDB 1064, R1318/12/2, H. S. du Toit, Hoof, Afdeling Uitbreidings Werk, to Minister van Landbou, 5 Dec. 1924 (my translation). Original reads: 'die hele geleerde wereld, sowel as al ons verligte boere bestempel die rapport (*reg of verkeerd*) as 'n "Meesterstuk"—wat onskatbaar baie geld vir Suidafrika sowel as vir die hele Suidelike Halfrond werd is.'

being extended more securely to conservation of natural resources. 'A better system of veld management', du Toit wrote, 'is as necessary for the welfare of future generations in the Union, as for the saving of the flocks and herds now grazing on our veld.'[94] 'First and foremost,' he continued, 'the State is bound to prevent such waste of its natural resources which, if persisted in, can but lead to national suicide; so it should take action in connection with soil erosion as it has done in other directions.'[95]

The Extension Service and Departmental Politics

In the years following the Commission, du Toit was deeply absorbed in the politics of the Department of Agriculture, and made considerable impact on its structure. He wished to ensure that the state reached out, especially to the more neglected Afrikaner rural population. While the conservationist message was by no means his only preoccupation, restructuring did facilitate its transmission. A popular speaker at a wide range of white gatherings, du Toit was known for his humour and plain speaking. In an address to the Cape Town Chamber of Commerce in 1922, for example, he was quite prepared to challenge them.[96] First, he emphasized the centrality of farmers and farming for the national economy; the wealth of the land, unlike minerals, would not run out. The potential for exhaustion of gold supplies was being widely discussed in the early 1920s in connection with the future of the low-grade mines. Secondly, he took up an old Hertzogite theme about South African identity: 'the great trouble with you commercial people is that the moment you become millionaires you go overseas.' According to the reporter, this was taken in a humorous way.

But he did not restrict his criticism to wealthy English-speakers, and was happy to tease his own constituency: 'it is said the farmer is the backbone of the country; but a backbone has two ends; with the one end you think and the other you sit on and it all depends which end you use.' Du Toit was happier working with well-capitalized, improving farmers. In connection with poor whites, he said once that he was sorry that they were 'going down' but 'those who were weak minded were very prolific'. There is an element here of eugenicist discourse as well as assumptions about the links between science, knowledge, and national progress.[97]

[94] U.G.49-1923, 14.   [95] Ibid. 15.
[96] du T., scrapbook of cuttings, *Cape Times*, 30 Nov. 1922.
[97] S. Dubow, *Scientific Racism in Modern South Africa* (Cambridge University Press, Cambridge, 1995) for these ideas at the time.

Addressing the South African Maize Growers Association at Milner Park in 1926, du Toit worked in an extended, earthy pun on the word tick to make his point about the malign influence of party politics on agricultural progress. Noting that the political party organizations in the country were 'about as perfect as human effort can make them', he called for similarly effective organization in agriculture. This, he said, required the elimination of ticks from agriculture: the tick or credit system at the stores and banks; the east coast fever tick in animals; and party poli-'tics'. 'I have known quite a few good people', he concluded, 'who were so badly infected with the political "tic" that they became real fana-"tics", and ultimately luna-"tics".'[98]

There was a consistency in his approach to the shape of the Department of Agriculture. One of the surprising features of the agricultural bureaucracy in the early twentieth century was that it had little explicit provision for extension work—this despite the initiatives made in the United States, which were well known in South Africa. Certainly, individual officials—from the first vets in the Cape to du Toit himself—worked with farmers, and addressed meetings, in a wide variety of contexts. But this was often incidental to their main work. It is an irony that a formal extension or demonstration scheme was launched in the Transkei for African farmers, based on the Irish model, in 1911 before this was attempted for whites.[99] Although the five agricultural colleges ran courses and developed limited advisory functions, they did not organize systematic work on the farms. Smith, the first Secretary for Agriculture, laid particular emphasis on scientific work, regulation, and formal agricultural education rather than demonstration.

Du Toit's duties and inclinations had led him into practical extension work, and his commitment to this was reinforced as a result of his Commission experiences. The visit to Grootfontein in 1920 revealed that they had few students; farmers complained that the instruction was too theoretical for their sons and Afrikaners resented the use of English.[100] Du Toit argued in 1921 that the system developed by Smith, recently retired, of using the agricultural schools as a base for training and extension was not a 'roaring success'.[101]

At the same time as he was engaged on the Drought Commission, du Toit began a long battle to carve out an extension division, under himself (with a raised salary). He threatened to leave for the private sector if he did not get his way. This was probably not a bluff, in that his extensive connections with farmers and farming organizations made him a potentially valuable asset to

---

[98] du T., scrapbook of cuttings, *Farmer's Weekly*, 14 Apr. 1926.

[99] Beinart, *Political Economy of Pondoland*.

[100] du T., 273, 10, notebook, largely from Drought Commission, Grootfontein, 7 June 1921.

[101] du T., 269/37, du Toit to P. J. du Toit, handwritten letter, 8 Oct. 1921.

companies servicing agriculture. He won the cautious support of P. J. du Toit, the new Secretary of Agriculture (no relative, and an anglicized Cape civil servant) and of Smartt. They agreed that it was 'vitally necessary to secure the services of Mr. H. S. du Toit . . . as he possesses all the qualities which are requisite. His prestige and influence among the farming population of all sections is unique.'[102] Du Toit was one of the few officials who had strong influence in Afrikaner circles. As the *Huisgenoot* noted, not only was he 'alombekende' (known everywhere), but a 'landseun' (son of the soil).[103] The Department needed people like him if it was to be effective amongst the majority of white landowners.

By the time he wrote the drought report, du Toit was Chief of the Division of Extension.[104] It is striking that this was instituted under Smuts's government, and before the more populist Nationalists won power in 1924. There were still battles to win, not only over funding but also against the principals of the agricultural colleges. Du Toit wanted his division to have a monopoly of itinerant work and face-to-face encounters with farmers. He felt that regular, centrally planned, and systematic contact with the rural population, which the schools did not provide, was essential.[105] While he believed that the English-speaking heads of schools would oppose him, not least as an agent of Afrikanerization, the lines of division were not so clear-cut.[106]

Du Toit won the support of Thornton, former head of Grootfontein, who had strongly backed his work on the Drought Commission, and who moved to Pretoria as Director of Field and Animal Husbandry.[107] This post incorporated du Toit's former functions as agronomist. Pole-Evans, Cambridge-trained friend of Smuts, the most English of division heads (Botany), and Arnold Theiler, the leading veterinary scientist, also supported him. The new Minister of Agriculture in Hertzog's Pact government, General Kemp, spent two days at a meeting on the subject in 1924 and came out in favour of du Toit's demand for a monopoly on extension services. One of the most interesting early products of the new division was the demonstration train, drawing on the American model, which made its first tour in 1924 through the Free State and Karoo to the eastern Cape. Staffed by lecturers and demonstrators, it had twelve individual carriages devoted to different branches of agriculture.

---

[102] du T., unnumbered, persoonlike leer, Acting. Sec. Ag. to Sec. Public Service Commission, 21 Aug. 1922.

[103] *Die Huisgenoot*, 7: 82 (Feb. 1923), 411.

[104] PTA LDB 1505, R2278/2, Sec. of Agriculture, circular 41 of 1922, 7 Oct. 1922.

[105] du T., 266, 76, minutes of meetings of Chiefs of Divisions, Pretoria, 7–8 Oct. 1924.

[106] PTA LDB 1505, R2278/2, H. S. du Toit to Sec. Ag., 7 July 1924 and following correspondence.

[107] PTA LDB 1505, R2278/2, H. S. du Toit to R. W. Thornton, 18 Mar. 1925.

Despite his public pleas to keep politics out of agriculture, du Toit seems to have gained strength from Hertzog's victory. He began to write more of his official correspondence in Afrikaans and communicated directly with Kemp. In 1925 he took on another major departmental issue, arguing that the agricultural colleges should be part of an enlarged Division of Extension and Education under himself. Du Toit won in principle, but the Public Service Commission wanted to appoint one of the school heads, with better formal qualifications, to the new position. He again mobilized the Minister, as well as most of the Divisional heads, in his support. He felt sufficiently confident to ask Kemp, perhaps humorously, to 'knock down' any English opposition.[108]

In 1926 du Toit succeeded, this time against the wishes of Thornton, in taking control also of all the experimental stations that were not part of the five schools.[109] Thornton felt that they should fall under his Division, as indeed some had under du Toit when he was Agronomist, because they were primarily 'investigational' institutions. Du Toit argued that they were primarily 'demonstrational' and wished departmental research to cater more directly to the needs of ordinary Afrikaner farmers.[110] Kemp supported him, noting that the schools, which cost £100,000 a year to run, and brought in only £25,000, were now being overtaken in competition for the best students by the universities. The Afrikaans-medium universities of Stellenbosch, Pretoria, and Potchestroom were all developing strong agricultural faculties; Pretoria, with Onderstepoort, trained vets.

In little over a decade du Toit rose from being manager of an experimental farm, within the small Division of Agronomy, to head the most rapidly growing division, including agricultural extension, education, and experimental stations. He was now one of the most senior members of the Department, chairing the annual meeting of Heads of Divisions and Schools, which Kemp attended.[111] By 1928 he supervised 164 officers, 111 at the schools, twenty-four full-time extension officers, and twenty-nine specialists— second only to the Veterinary Division which, up to the mid-1930s, accounted for about half the Departmental budget. Expansion of extension services opened opportunities especially for the employment of Afrikaners. (It is worth noting that by 1930 there were close on 100 African demonstrators employed in the Transkei.)

[108] du T., 283, 104, du Toit to Kemp, 26 Jan. 1926. Original: 'weet Generaal mos hoe om hulle kaf te loop.'
[109] du T., 269, 9, du Toit to Sec. Ag., 8 Feb. 1926.
[110] PTA LDB 2327, R3436, Minutes of Conference of Heads of Division and Agricultural Schools, Pretoria, 26 Sept. 1927.
[111] Ibid.

Du Toit's position gave him an unrivalled opportunity to advance conservationist farming, although special reclamation officers, as recommended by the Drought Commission, were not appointed. He was chair of a committee set up in 1927, following a further serious drought, to see through policy recommendations in connection with drought and soil erosion. Many key initiatives were already partly in place: restrictions on movement to control disease; jackal eradication; locust eradication; control of prickly pear; planting of spineless cactus; irrigation development; and borehole subsidies. Subsidies for jackal-proof fencing were provided under the Fencing Act of 1922, and from 1924 Land Bank loans became available for internal fencing and water development.[112] Between 1913 and 1936 over £2 million was loaned by the bank for fencing. Pole-Evans emphasized the need for exploring the properties of indigenous flora, and he co-ordinated veld experiments with du Toit in this area. The Department investigated the idea of a national fodder bank on the Australian model, but it was not pursued. Policy and extension work focused on encouraging farmers to provide their own drought fodder.

Compulsory policies had been developed in disease and environmental regulation, but the Department shied away from these in more controversial areas such as legislation against overstocking.[113] Officials were well aware, from the annual livestock statistics that were collected in the 1920s, that farmers were driving up their livestock numbers. Du Toit himself was keen on state controls in this area and firmly in favour of stock-reduction nationally: the Department should specify stocking limits in each district and warn farmers when carrying capacities in any district were exceeded.[114] He had great hopes for prickly pear, recalling his own experience of its value on his father's farm, high in the Sneeuberg, where hard frosts and voracious animals ensured that it did not become a pest.[115] But the Department decided that it could best work through integrating other initiatives and a propaganda campaign.[116] In fact, policy was somewhat contradictory. From 1916 increasing amounts of drought aid were available for restocking, as well as for fodder and seed. In 1924 and 1927 new Drought Distress Acts facilitated payments

[112] PTA LDB 1064, R1318/12, vol. II, Sec. Ag. to Secretary, Economic and Wage Commission, 3 Nov. 1925.

[113] My analysis here differs in part from S. Schirmer and P. Delius, 'Soil Conservation in a Racially Divided Society', *JSAS* 26: 4 (2000).

[114] PTA LDB 1064, R1318/12/1, notes by Lamont, 14 Feb. 1928.

[115] du T., 269, 54, du Toit to Sec. Ag., 20 Nov. 1929.

[116] PTA LDB 1064, 1318/12/3, 'Droogte. 'n Bespreking in verband met droogte . . . op 4 Aug. 1927'.

11. 'The Revolution in Farming in the Transvaal: the Disappearance of the
Old-fashioned Modes of Trekking'

that increased from £386,000 in 1924–5 to £720,000 in 1934–5.[117] In this area
the welfare of farmers took precedence, and the pastures had little rest after
droughts.

One key issue for du Toit was in finding clear alternatives to transhumance.
By the 1910s movement of livestock by rail was supplementing that by
trekking.[118] The South African Railways agreed in 1910 to a rebate of half
the cost of carriage of livestock during droughts. In order to ensure that the
concession was not misused for the purposes of marketing, livestock had to be
returned to its place of origin. Prime Minister Botha, an eastern Transvaal
landowner, insisted on this use for the rail network, even when agricultural
officials expressed doubts. Some of his constituents in that area still trekked
seasonally from the highveld to the lowveld. From 1914 other parts of the
Union could participate in the schemes, so that Karoo farmers could rail
sheep cheaply to grassland districts. Technology in the shape of the railways
was being harnessed to prolong and extend old practices. In drought years,
hundreds of thousands of animals crowded onto the railway network.

[117] PTA LDB 1930 R3435, G. B. Laurence and G. v. H. du Plessis, 'The Effects of Drought
on South African Agriculture with Special Reference to Losses Caused', unpublished memo,
6 Dec. 1937, pp. 8–9.
[118] PTA LDB 550, R594/1, Sec. Ag. to General Manager, South African Railways (SARH),
25 Feb. 1910. There had been an earlier rebate in 1905 for this purpose.

In 1921 the system was broadened again, with higher subsidies for districts declared by the Department to be suffering from abnormal drought. Officials preferred movement by rail, in that it reduced losses experienced in long overland treks, saved grazing en route, and limited the spread of scab. But some thought that it still encouraged farmers to overstock and neglect fodder production.[119] In the late 1920s, as practical steps were being discussed to resolve soil erosion and drought losses, du Toit put his considerable weight behind a critique of rail transhumance. He painted what he suggested was a typical scenario:

A stockfarmer . . . has a few good years and makes robust progress. His farm is heavily stocked or overstocked . . . He watches the sky day and night and takes courage from the appearance of a few thunderclouds, but these disappear again . . . The west wind blows them all away. There is a copper sky for a week or more. Again a few clouds, again new courage, again clear heavens, while the pastures and water dwindle. The farmer gains and loses hope until there is eventually no veld or water and the livestock begin to die of poverty; then he makes a dash for the nearest railway station with his emaciated animals. Some die along the road. At the station there are already great troops of sheep waiting for trucks. The water supply and fodder at the station is long finished. There are too few railway officials and loading places . . . Again, a batch of dead animals. Eventually the animals are transported to a place where the farmer has heard, or read, that veld is available. When he arrives, he finds that thousands of sheep are there before him. He offloads and finds that more animals lie dead in the trucks. He still has to trek to pasture and returns with a declining flock . . . He then has to prove to the railways that his animals died [and were not sold] or he does not get his rebate.[120]

When working as Government Agronomist, du Toit had tried to match up farmers in different districts in order to facilitate rail-trekking, but because these decisions were usually contingent and competitive, it was very difficult to resolve the inherent problems. Far better, du Toit vehemently argued, to transport fodder to animals, or grow it on farms, or to rotate grazing. 'The camp system,' he reiterated, 'which was given so prominent a place in the Government Drought Investigation Commission's report has already done wonders in the dry parts of our country, especially in the districts where the jackal has been exterminated.'[121] These were some of the key projects for the extension service.

[119] PTA LDB 550, R594/1, vol. III, R. M. Harrismith to Sec. Ag., 14 Oct. 1914; General Manager, SARH, to Sec. Ag., 18 May 1918.
[120] PTA LDB 2327, R3435, Heinrich S. du Toit to Sec. Ag., 15 May 1927, 'Vervoer van Vee gedurende Droogte Periodes'. The memo, written in Afrikaans, was also published in the press, although without this vivid critique of farmers. My translation; see du T., 269/6 for his.
[121] PTA LDB 2327, R3435, du Toit to Sec. Ag., 15 May 1927.

Du Toit's analysis was underlined when the north-western districts of the Cape were particularly hard hit in 1927–8. The influx of sheep into neigh-bouring districts caused them in turn to be overstocked, because permits were issued to farmers who had no specific place to go. Britstown, the nearest district with reasonable pastures, was 'assailed from all sides'.[122] Disease spread; the trains ran out of water. In view of the costs to the railways, and the blame heaped upon them for livestock losses, they became increasingly uneasy about the system.[123] In 1928 concessions on railway traffic were being restricted. Farmers were, however, reluctant to forego this strategy and their political clout again won out; rail transport of livestock was in any case essen-tial for marketing. During the acute drought of 1933, according to depart-mental research, 8 million head of sheep were transported by rail, perhaps 20 per cent of the total.[124] One major route was from the northern to the eastern Cape. During three years from 1933 to 1936, £1.8 million was spent on transporting livestock by train, 25 per cent each by farmers and the gov-ernment and 50 per cent subsidized by the railways. Officials questioned this system and the wisdom of restocking, but farmers' welfare won out against conservation.

Du Toit's focus was dispersed by the late 1920s. Still energetic, he was also extending his involvement in a range of voluntary activities and in Afrikaner nationalist politics. When he retired from the Department in 1931 he was sufficiently well-established to become organizer of the National Party in the Transvaal, and would have stood for election as a Member of Parliament but for his death in 1933, aged 58. Nevertheless, he maintained a major interest in environmental conservation. In addition to his book published in 1929, he wrote Kemp's address to the National Soil Erosion Conference of that year, and also spoke himself.[125] This was the beginning of a new state initiat-ive, culminating in the 1932 Soil Erosion Act, through which millions of pounds were channelled into conservation works and water provision during the 1930s (Chapter 11). By 1930 he felt, perhaps optimistically, that they had made 'gigantic strides' towards conservationist farming.[126]

When he died du Toit owned a suburban house, a farm in the western Transvaal, and a Studebaker car, but little money.[127] As he sometimes claimed, he devoted much of his life to public service and to championing the

[122] PTA LDB 570, R594/1A, Vet, De Aar, to Senior Vet, 12 Feb. 1928.

[123] Ibid., Ag. Gen. Manager SARH to Minister SARH, 13 Feb. 1928.

[124] PTA LDB 1930 R3435, Laurence and du Plessis, 'The Effects of Drought on South African Agriculture'.

[125] du T., 269, 20.   [126] PTA LDB 1064, R1318, vol. III, notes by du Toit, 10 June 1930.

[127] PTA Estate papers, Transvaal, 82013, H. S. du Toit.

causes so central to his bureaucratic mission. He was deeply committed to modernization and scientific agriculture, although increasingly as an administrator and popularizer rather than an experimental agronomist. An outline of his career begins to fill in some gaps in understanding of the development of a scientifically based agricultural bureaucracy as well as a specifically Afrikaner technocracy. While such approaches had deeply split Afrikaners in earlier years, they became an increasingly key element in the new Afrikaner nationalism as well as in the South African state. Here du Toit's capacity to be simultaneously Boer war hero, practical son of the soil, advocate of science, and powerful senior official was important. His career also facilitates understanding of the power and breadth of conservationist thinking and rhetoric in the Department of Agriculture and in the country at the time.

However, in linking conservationism to white South African and even narrower Afrikaner nationalisms, it is important not to subsume scientific ideas within these ideologies. The enthusiasms which were so attractive to du Toit were developed also in other and very diverse political contexts. While they were tightly linked in South Africa to 'progress' and to agricultural capitalism, elements of these scientific approaches were absorbed by a range of people, including African modernizers (Chapter 10). The adoption of scientific techniques and discourses did not necessarily require adherence to particular ideologies or identities.

8

Prickly Pear in the Cape:
Useful Plants and Invaders in the
Livestock Economy, 1890–1950

The Spread of Prickly Pear

The South African Department of Agriculture was an important site of applied scientific research in the first half of the twentieth century, not least in respect of the pastoral economy. At the same time, scientific understanding shaped approaches to agrarian problems and the conservation of natural resources. The spread of prickly pear presented a particular challenge, and required sophisticated and adaptable policy responses. It was very difficult for the state to organize a consensus on the question, even amongst white landowners. And the scientific resources of the Department, especially its Entomology Division, were tested to the limit. The outcome of intervention had ambiguous and complex implications for conservationist strategies.

Pastoral farming on the scale pursued at the Cape inevitably impacted on the vegetation of the colony. Aside from changes in the established vegetation, colonization in general, and farming in particular, precipitated the introduction of many exotic plant species, with unpredictable results. Some were brought intentionally as food crops; some came by chance, mixed with grain seeds or through other means along the trade routes of empire.[1] Exotic trees, planted at the Cape from the seventeenth century, were seen as useful for timber and firewood. And although the Cape proved rich in plants favoured for gardens, many new species were introduced for aesthetic reasons.

Most exotics remained under human control, or, if they reproduced themselves easily without cultivation, they remained relatively localized. Some

---

[1] Lance van Sittert, '"The Seed Blows about in Every Breeze": Noxious Weed Eradication in the Cape Colony, 1860–1909', *JSAS* 26: 4 (2000), 655–74.

spread as weeds. The khaki bos came from Canada around the turn of the century, took hold in the grainlands of the western Cape, and spread throughout the colony to become ubiquitous in cultivated fields in eastern Cape. While it proved uncontrollable in cleared land, it could not compete on the veld.[2] Exotics such as burrweed, scotch thistle, and hakea have been considered dangerous at particular periods. Burrweed was of primary concern to wool producers because it fixed in the sheep's fleece and spread uncontrollably in this way; it had no discernable benefits. Some became such serious pests that they earned the name noxious weeds, the plant equivalent of vermin. They are now classified as invader species.

However, the boundaries between useful plant, weed, and invader are difficult to define with precision. These are cultural as much as scientific appellations. Australian eucalypts were valued as quick-growing timber and firewood species, also used to hold sand-flats. Some became self-spreaders and displaced indigenous vegetation, but for many years their usefulness was perceived to outweigh their disadvantages. They formed the basis for Natal's commercial timber and, in the case of the black wattle, tanning industries; the latter was also absorbed into African gardens as an all-purpose plant for firewood and construction. Questions were raised about the blue gum in the nineteenth century (Chapter 2). Hakea, an acacia, was regarded as a noxious weed in the forested areas of the Cape from the time it was introduced in the 1890s.[3] But eucalypts are still widely grown in South Africa, despite the growing critique by environmentalists of their impact on water and soil.

Prickly pear species (opuntia) were simultaneously amongst the most successful invaders, and the most useful self-spreaders in South Africa. Travelling through the Karoo and eastern Cape in the 1990s, scattered wild prickly pear plants could still be seen. Many farms have patches of a few hectares of a plant that looks similar to prickly pear—the spineless cactus or cactus pear. But the landscape has changed. In the early decades of the twentieth century it was possible to see large, dense stands of wild prickly pear, covering thousands of hectares. Some of the plants were almost tree-like, growing to a height of 20 feet and guarding impenetrable thickets.

In the late nineteenth century prickly pear became a major issue of public concern in the Cape. Four select committees considered the plant between 1890 and 1906. The Department of Agriculture, established in 1887, soon directed attention to it. MacOwan, the Colonial Botanist, published an

---

[2] *Agricultural Journal* (Jan. 1907): R. W. Thornton, 'The Khaki Bush: Another Noxious Weed', 76–8.
[3] CA PAS, 3/151, N42/2.

article in 1888.[4] After consultation with him, A. C. MacDonald, appointed as one of the first agricultural assistants, conducted an investigation on behalf of the first parliamentary select committee in 1891.[5] These are valuable sources for the history of the plant.

A number of different opuntia species, cactus plants from the semi-arid areas of meso-America, were introduced to South Africa, probably as early as the seventeenth century. MacDonald suggested that the plant had been imported from India—a country to which it was certainly taken. Older Dutch dictionaries identify prickly pear as Indisches Vijg (fig), but the term 'Indies' did not necessarily then imply the East. The Afrikaans name, turksvy, or Turkish fig, suggested a Middle Eastern source, although this may simply have indicated an exotic origin. (The Xhosa name, itolofiya, is an adaption of this word.) As MacDonald was well aware, opuntia species were brought back soon after the European incursions into America and established in the Canary Islands, the Azores, Madeira, and on the Mediterranean coast. Prickly pear hedges can still be seen in southern Spain and Morocco; on Madeira and La Palma islands it has become an invader. Various species may have been introduced directly from one of these sources. Ships bound for the Cape stopped at the Canaries, and Cape species, such as the strelitzia, became established there.

Thunberg recorded opuntia in the western Cape in the 1770s, both in cultivated hedges and growing wild. MacDonald heard a story that a farmer named van der Berg had brought two leaves from Cape Town to his frontier farm in Buffels Hoek around 1750; and that these had been the source for further plantings in the Bruintjieshoogte, between Pearston and Somerset East.[6] Sparrman was told in the 1770s that alcohol was made in the Camdeboo and elsewhere from a '*cactus* of considerable size'.[7] Whatever the precise history, the prickly pear was sufficiently important to accompany trekboers to the furthest reaches of settlement almost immediately. Somerset East, Pearston, and Graaff-Reinet districts became core areas of dense spread in the nineteenth century. When Wylie, the geologist, travelled the road

---

[4] P. MacOwan, 'Prickly Pear in South Africa', *Royal Gardens, Kew, Bulletin of Miscellaneous Information* (London, 1888), 165–73, originally a memorandum to the newly established Department of Agriculture.

[5] A.9-1891, *Report of the Select Committee on the Prickly Pear*, 20 ff.: A. C. MacDonald, 'Prickly Pear in South Africa', repr. in the *Agricultural Journal of the Cape of Good Hope* (30 July 1891).

[6] MacDonald, 'Prickly Pear'. The date of 1750 sounds early, and is probably an approximation. Although hunting parties had reached this area, farms were only laid out in the 1760s. It is possible, but unlikely, that prickly pear was spread by animals in advance of settlement, or that it was planted in anticipation of settlement.

[7] Sparrman, *Voyage*, ii. 260.

from Graaff-Reinet to Somerset East in the 1850s, he found it 'perfectly amazing' to see 'miles upon miles of these valleys are covered with it, in some cases, to the exclusion of almost every other plant'.[8] Prickly pear was so dominant that he wondered whether, contrary to Thunberg, it was 'indigenous'.

Cochineal insects, which fed on some species of the plant in the Americas, converted its juice into a reddish liquid. Native Americans had long used this as dye, catching and drying the insects in large numbers. Under Spanish rule, cochineal dye became a major industry in Mexico. In the nineteenth century production spread to the Canary Islands and elsewhere.[9] One of the plant species suitable for dye, the *Opuntia coccinellifera*, as well as one species of cochineal insect, were established in the western Cape in the nineteenth century, and von Ludwig investigated the possibility of an industry. Unsuccessful attempts were also made in the 1860s to establish cochineal dye production in the southern Cape.[10]

Rather, prickly pear inserted itself into the culture, food supplies, and farming practices of both Africans and whites as an all-purpose plant that required little care. The fruit was peeled carefully, to remove the spiky skin, and eaten. Both fruit and (especially) leaves, suitably treated, were valuable fodder. By retaining moisture in its large fibrous leaves, the plant was highly resistant to drought, even more so than most indigenous karoo bushes. Whatever its value as stock feed, a point much debated, the thirst-quenching quality of its leaves was undeniable. One species in particular, the *Opuntia ficus indica*, called common or sweet prickly pear (turksvy), was the most highly valued for human and stock food. It spread easily where climatic and soil conditions were favourable, notably in the livestock farming districts of the midland and eastern Cape, but also in pockets of the Transvaal and Natal with predominantly African settlement.

Progressive farmers and agricultural experts advocated the use of fodder in order to supplement natural veld, as a vital resource for drought years and dry seasons, and as a means of terminating transhumance. Especially in districts where irrigation was limited, edible exotics that could withstand the rigours of the Cape environment provided an alternative. The three most important for Karoo livestock farmers were opuntia, *Agave americana*, also from meso-America, and Australian salt bush. (Agave—confusingly called aloe in the

---

[8] Cape of Good Hope, 'Appendix of the Report of the Geological Surveyor presented to Parliament in June, 1859', by Andrew Wylie.

[9] *Kew Bulletin* (1888), 169.

[10] G.23-1864, *Report of the Colonial Botanist for the Year 1863*, 26–8: letter from John C. Brown to Mr Titterton, Kracha Kama, on the cultivation of the Prickly Pear, with a view to the preparation of Cochineal, 12 Jan. 1864.

Karoo, although it is not a South African aloe—and salt bush are discussed in Chapter 9.) The great advantage of these plants was that they needed little cultivation and no irrigation. But farmers were deeply divided on prickly pear. A boon for some was a pest for others.

R. P. Botha, MLC, recalled in 1890 that he had lived on a 'prickly pear farm' in the Vogel river valley in 1847; at this time relatively few farms were 'infested'.[11] The farm he mentioned was just north of present-day Pearston, near the source of the Voel river. This watercourse proved to be one important conduit for the pear. There are farms near Pearston called Turks vyg Rivier and Turksvy Laagte, as well as a Turksvykloof in the south of the district.[12] By 1861 Botha claimed that he had lost control of the prickly pear on his farm and was forced to sell it. Similarly, B. J. Keyter, MLA for Oudtshoorn, farmed for some years on the Melk river, immediately to the west of the Voel, between Graaff-Reinet and Pearston in the 1860s. So dense did the pear become that his animals could not be herded and sheep died. As a result he sold up and moved to Oudtshoorn.[13] MacOwan kept a worried eye, during the 1870s and 1880s, on major thickets near the Bruintjieshoogte pass, south-east of Pearston, and also at Cookhouse.[14] In 1891 MacDonald calculated that 478,000 morgen were 'overrun' and much more 'infected', largely in the semi-arid midlands: Jansenville, Graaff-Reinet, Aberdeen, Somerset East, Willowmore, Cradock, and the drier parts of Albany district, especially along the Fish river.[15]

Prickly pear was divided by farmers into two types, the doornblad or thorny leaved and the kaalblad or bare leaved variety. The kaalblad was valued far more highly as a stock feed, because spikes or spines, harmful to stock, were largely absent from its leaves; animals could eat it literally as it stood. A fodder or drought food that needed no water, little effort to plant, and no labour to prepare was a godsend. As a Cradock farmer noted, however:

the *Doornblad* greatly preponderated, not that it grew more readily, or was hardier, but because, on account of its thorny protection, stock could not eat it or destroy it, while the kaalblad was eaten down to the bare stumps in many instances, and almost all animals greedily devoured the fruit. Further, the *Doornblad* nearly always threw true, while the *Kaalblad* always threw a heavy percentage of the *Doornblad*.[16]

[11] A.29-1898, *Report of the Select Committee on Eradication of Prickly Pear*, evidence R. P. Botha, 19.

[12] Information from 1 : 250,000 topocadastral map.

[13] A.9-1891, 13, evidence B. J. Keyter, MLA, Oudtshoorn; MacDonald, 'Prickly Pear'.

[14] *Kew Bulletin* (1888), 166.

[15] C.3-1890, *Eradication of Prickly Pear and Poisonous Melkbosch*, Select Committee of the Legislative Council, 25, evidence, J. O. Norton, MLA.

[16] *Agricultural Journal* (2 July 1891), 246: 'Resumé of Paper on the Prickly Pear (Opuntia Vulgaris) and its Eradication, read by Mr. A. L. Grobbelaar before "The Cradock Farmers' Association", June 6th, 1891.'

For MacOwan this was a sign of Cape carelessness. 'That the kaal-blad has not been spread purposely over the length and breadth of the land in otherwise useless wastes', he wrote, 'is just one of those many things that make one wonder and pity poor Africa'; 'if by touch of a magician's wand the vast thickets of Prickly Pear along the Klyn Visch, Melk and Blyde Rivers could be turned into kaal-blad, there would be small chance of hearing of stock slowly perishing of combined hunger and thirst'.[17]

Debates about the provenance and character of these two varieties, the doornblad and kaalblad, proved important in the 1890s, because they were central to discussions about the wisdom, or otherwise, of eradication. Some thought that kaalblad might be a different species from the doornblad. Those opposed to eradication had an interest in supporting this view in the hope that the doornblad could be eradicated and the kaalblad retained. Others noticed that both seem to grow from seed of the same plant. Some farmers suggested that they might be male and female varieties, and talked of prickly 'mannetjies' and 'wyfies'; this was not unknown in plant species. It was also suggested that the kaalblad produced thorns when it was grazed very heavily as a means of protection.[18]

By the turn of the century the more general view, especially amongst those with botanical knowledge, was that these were varieties of the same species. They believed that the kaalblad originated as a cultivated variety of the *Opuntia ficus indica*. It may have been the only variety of this species originally introduced into South Africa. Farmers in Aberdeen and Graaff-Reinet recalled a time when kaalblad alone was found in their districts. As in the case of other cultivars, it seemed to revert to the wild variety when it grew from seed.[19] MacDonald heard in Aberdeen that an isolated hedge of kaalblad had produced doornblad plants in this way. Charles Rubidge experimented by growing seeds from kaalblad and found that some produced some doornblad. Once the doornblad was established it was likely to spread far more quickly, not only by seeding, but because it was eaten less by animals. Botha believed that the doornblad variety hybridized with the kaalblad.[20]

Prickly pear reproduced by rooting from its leaves (or cladodes) when they came into contact with soil, as well as from the seed contained within its fruit. Rivers were an important conduit of invasion, because cladodes were swept downstream during floods and took root in their favoured alluvial soil. It seemed clear to the committees that the bare-leaved variety could only be reproduced with certainty from leaf sections by cloning—though the term

[17] *Kew Bulletin* (1888), 168.
[18] A.9-1891, *Report of the Select Committee on the Prickly Pear*, 5.
[19] A.8-1906, *Report of the Select Committee on the Prickly Pear*, 16, evidence Dr Rupert Marloth.
[20] C.3-1890, 4.

was not used then. Some farmers used this technique purposely. In fact, farmers who wished to propagate prickly pear, for example to lay a fence, invariably used the leaves—whether thorny or bare—because the seeds did not easily germinate.

Animals did feed off the thorny cladodes. Cattle coped better with it than sheep or goats. The content of the leaf was not very different, although it was suggested that kaalblad leaves tended to be larger and juicier than doorn-blad. Ideally doornblad leaves required preparation in which the spikes were burnt or scraped off before being fed to animals. Despite the labour involved, some farmers did organize such preparation, which was widely done in other parts of the world, from Madagascar to California. Prickly pear was con-sidered valuable in the 1880s and 1890s for ostriches, especially in semi-arid districts such as Jansenville and Graaff-Reinet. They took to the pear easily, perhaps because of their famously undiscriminating approach to food. Arthur Douglass, the ostrich breeder, allowed prickly pear to spread on his Graham-stown farm and chopped leaves for fodder. Ostriches devoured the fresh green tops of young prickly pear and seemed to cope well with the thorns. Pigs thrived on prickly pear: 'we carry the leaves to them in the sty', a farmer told the 1891 committee, 'and we can fatten them on the fruit.'[21]

Nevertheless, the kaalblad was clearly superior as fodder. The only way to ensure its predominance was to protect it, plant it, and to prevent fruiting and seeding. In order to understand why this was not done, we need to explore human priorities, neglect, and ecological relationships. Many rural people did not know that kaalblad could only be ensured by cloning, and many had interests in prickly pear which were not restricted to its fodder potential. Both whites and Africans used the quick-growing, thorny variety for hedges around gardens to keep livestock out, or for hedges around kraals to keep stock in.[22] It was favoured at one time in the Sneeuberg, north of Graaff-Reinet, because it was one of the few large plants that could withstand the climatic extremes.

Prickly pear was taken in the nineteenth century to Natal and the Transvaal, where white farmers used it for hedging. The Pedi in Sekhukhuneland adapted it further for military defence: 'at the time of the Swazi invasion in 1874', one tradition related, 'their villages were so well pro-tected by barricades of prickly pear, that the Swazi warriors had to use their shields as platforms to cross over into them.'[23] In the late 1880s 'most of the

[21] A.9-1891, 16, evidence P. J. du Toit, MLA, Richmond, and 18, evidence A. S. le Roux, MLA for Victoria West.

[22] Ibid. 7, evidence E. R. Hobson; G.3-1877, 84, evidence, W. Eales, Somerset East.

[23] P. J. Quin, *Foods and Feeding Habits of the Pedi* (Witwatersrand University Press, Johannesburg, 1959), 91.

12. Prickly Pear and Ostriches; Graaff-Reinet Farm in the Late
Nineteenth Century

native kraals were defended by hedges of prickly pears'.[24] There is not
evidence of such systematic use by Africans in the Cape. But white farmers
certainly accused Africans of taking advantage of the spreading pear to protect havens for 'squatting' and stolen stock. The first Select Committee on
eradication considered 'that unbroken thickets of this plant furnish shelter
for thieving operations to a very serious extent'.[25] George Palmer, a leading
figure in the campaign against the jackal, was just as determined in his support for eradication of prickly pear. He pinpointed a stand in the north of
Pearston district, near his farm, where it was impossible to see more than
twenty paces, as a 'nest of thieves'.[26] Prickly pear thickets were also seen to
provide cover for jackals, which found 'perfect safety from pursuit'.[27]

Prickly pear's contribution to African subsistence sheltered 'squatters' in
other ways. Wallace, the Scottish agriculturalist, recorded in the 1890s that
Africans avoided work during the three months, February to April, when the
fruit was at its best.[28] The 1898 Committee heard that 'for six months of the

[24] *Transvaal Agricultural Journal* (Jan. 1907): Joseph Burtt-Davy, 'The Prickly Pear in the
Transvaal', 450–2. This article also mentions the story of the Swazi invasion and may be its source.
[25] C.3-1890, p. viii.   [26] Ibid. 7, evidence George Palmer.   [27] Ibid., p. viii.
[28] Chas. F. Juritz, *The Prickly Pear (Opuntia): Possibilities of its Utilization* (Government Printer,
Pretoria, 1920) Industrial Bulletin Series, 65, reprinted from the *South African Journal of Industries*
(Aug., Sept. 1920), 5.

year the fruit provides them with a means of subsistence'.[29] Poor people had little incentive to control the doornblad. Once land had been overrun by prickly pear, owners, reluctant to use it for sheep, sometimes rented it out to Africans.[30] Some white farmers associated the plant with poverty, jackals, African occupation, labour problems, and disorder.

Prickly pear fruit was widely eaten by whites as well as blacks. In Oudtshoorn, 'the blacks wander[ed] about from farm to farm selling the fruits to farmers at sixpence a hundred'; poor whites consumed it and brought it into town for sale.[31] Doornblad overran part of the Graaff-Reinet commonage, and there was a seasonal migration by farm-workers in the fruiting season to pick it; 'fruit was hawked for sale in the town or converted into a concentrated syrup by boiling it in three-legged pots'.[32] Africans with wagons or donkey carts took the fruit from Uitenhage into Port Elizabeth. Railway workers also ate it at work and used their favoured access to transport to carry it long distances, by bag, for sale. Charles Lee, influential MLA, and Secretary of the Zwart Ruggens Farmers Association, whose farm in Jansenville straddled the line of rail, found he had repeatedly to clear pear spreading from this source.[33] Railways as well as rivers became routes for the spread of doornblad.

One of the great rural skills, amongst both whites and blacks in the Cape, was to turn any suitable natural substance into alcohol. Graaff-Reinet was a centre for wine- and brandy-making by smallholders until the late nineteenth century, when the vineyards were wiped out by phylloxera. Peach brandy was legion in Afrikaner stories and folklore. Prickly pear fruit, with its high sugar content, fermented quickly. It was reputed to make a particularly 'intoxicating and maddening liquor'; this could be mixed with Cape brandy to produce 'a most villainous compound'.[34] MacDonald, echoing a constant complaint of employers, wrote that:

the native servants make use of the fruits in the manufacture of pernicious intoxicants which they consume in large quantities, totally unfitting them for their ordinary duties, and in all parts of the country where these liquors are prepared, the

[29] A.29-1898, p. iv.

[30] C.3-1890, 18, evidence, J. H. Smith, MLA, Graaff-Reinet; A.9-1891, 3, evidence E. R. Hobson.

[31] A.9-1891, 13, evidence B. J. Keyter, MLA; C.3-1890, evidence, P. H. du Plessis, MLC, an Oudtshoorn farmer. His use of 'blacks' in interesting, and unusual at the time, although it may have been a translation.

[32] Norah Massey Pitman, 'The Peoples of Graaff-Reinet and District', *Lantern: Journal of Knowledge and Culture*, 35: 2 (1986), 29.

[33] A.29-1898, 41–2.   [34] C.3-1890, 7, evidence George Palmer.

assembling of natives during the night for drunken orgies is carried on to such an extent that the matter is becoming really serious.[35]

There were other uses for this multi-purpose plant. P. J. du Toit, MLA for Richmond, made his opposition to eradication clear by reading a letter from an Afrikaner constituent:

I get on very well with the prickly pear. I feed cattle, horses, and ostriches and all animals therewith in times of drought, and I can send you samples of vinegar, sugar, syrup, and dried prickly pear all made from the fruit; and I am of the opinion that there is nothing better in this country.[36]

In the midlands, some farmers collected the fruit 'in wagon loads' for the manufacture of preserves.[37] Hannah Brown of Glen Avon, a farm close to Somerset East village, wrote enthusiastically on 'The Prickly Pear: A Source of Wealth for the Union' in 1919.[38] She noted that the South African variety was so sweet that it could be used to make jam without sugar, and as a sweetener for preserving other fruits. Africans made a coarse black sugar by boiling down the syrup. During the influenza epidemic of 1918 she had made a 'cough and bronchial medicine', mixing pear syrup, watercress, wild mint, and linseed oil. The yeast, 'karee moer', was one of the best for bread and biscuits; dried fruits served as a coffee extender and crushed seeds as oil. She, with her servants, had recently made 250 pounds of prickly pear soap: 'my factory consisted of a big three-legged iron pot and a wood fire under a willow tree.' A source for sweeteners, treacle, beer, and yeast for 'the most delicious light bread and pastry' seemed a godsend for those without ready access to manufactured products.[39]

Many rural people thus had an interest in allowing the pear to fruit, and the conditions were established for the spread of the doornblad. Here the Cape ecology played a major role. It became clear to the select committees that the seeds would 'germinate more readily after passing through the stomach of any animal'.[40] Multitudes of prickly pear seedlings propagated like a miniature forest on cow dung, a natural fertilizer pack; the plants grew from the 'droppings of cattle as thick as grass'.[41] One witness thought that the seeds

[35] MacDonald, 'Prickly Pear in South Africa'.

[36] A.9-1891, 15, evidence P. J. du Toit, quoting a letter in Dutch from 'Mr Vosloo'.

[37] A.29-1898, 41, evidence Charles George Lee, MLA and secretary of the Zwart Ruggens Farmers Association.

[38] PTA LDB 1250, R1592, Prickly Pear Commercial Value of: Mrs Hannah L. Brown, 'The Prickly Pear: A Source of Wealth for the Union'.

[39] PTA LDB 1250 R1592, E. Cawood, Bulawayo, to R. W. Thornton, 29 June 1926.

[40] A.9-1891, 2.   [41] Ibid. 14: evidence B. J. Keyter.

spread in animal dung produced 'a more injurious plant'; the rapidity of growth may have given him that impression.[42] (The formidable digestive tracts of ostriches were thought, however, to neutralize the seed.)

Prickly pear sprouted under trees where birds perched or nested and spread their droppings.[43] It was said to grow in the vicinity of human consumers who defecated in the open air. The fruit was eaten—and seed spread—by wild animals of many different kinds, notably jackals, monkeys, porcupines, and, it was believed, especially baboons. Birds and babooons spread the pear to the most remote corners of farms, and to high and inaccessible krantzes. In the same way that sheep provided additional food for jackals, and contributed to an increase in their numbers, so prickly pear in some areas may have provided a new food source for the wild species that thrived on it. The combination of growing numbers of livestock and a variety of fruit-eating wild animals provided particularly favourable ecological conditions for prickly pear in the Cape.

Not all livestock favoured the plant, and some farmers suggested that sheep had to be weaned onto it carefully. MacDonald argued that some animals resorted to it first in droughts. As a result, the spread of pear was most notable when droughts were broken and the moisture enabled the seeds planted in dung to burst forth. Damage to livestock was also likely to be worst in drought years. The spikes on the doornblad were bad enough. But the fruit from both kaalblad and doornblad, favoured by livestock, was particularly dangerous. It was covered in small tufts composed of large numbers of spicules that easily detached themselves and stuck in the mouths and lips of animals. (Anyone who has eaten a prickly pear fruit without peeling it thoroughly will recognize this problem).

The spicules caused swelling and sores, diminished an animal's capacity to eat, and sometimes resulted in death, especially for sheep and angora goats. Ostriches could be blinded, and some farmers fenced prickly pear thickets to exclude their birds during fruiting season.[44] The damage caused by the spicules could extend down the gullet to the internal linings of the stomach and digestive organs. Hutcheon, the veterinary surgeon, reported that animals 'will just stand and eat away till they die'.[45] He thought that it took six months for livestock to recover from the severe inflammation caused by the fruit.

---

[42] G.3-1890, 23, evidence J. O. Norton, MLA.
[43] C.3-1890, 6–7, evidence G. M. Palmer.
[44] A.29-1898, 8, 13, evidence M. J. du Plessis, MLA, Cradock.
[45] A.8-1906, 6, evidence Duncan Hutcheon, Acting Director of Agriculture.

Here was the central dilemma. For owners of valuable livestock, the disadvantages of doornblad, and of any prickly pear fruit, increasingly outweighed its advantages. By the 1890s it seemed clear that the plant was spreading quickly, that this spread could not be controlled by most individual landowners, and that the dominant variety was the doornblad. To its opponents the spread of prickly pear resembled that of a virus, as was reflected in their language about infection and infestation. In Charles Lee's view, kaalblad 'degenerated' together with the white families on prickly pear farms.[46]

Yet the plant could be used, and many opposed its outright eradication. Even committed progressive farmers such as G. H. Maasdorp, MLA for Graaff-Reinet, affirmed in 1906 that 'there are many people who look upon it as a good fodder plant, and who during the last droughts have been keeping stock, especially ostriches, alive on it'.[47] To those who argued that the pear was not a particularly good stock food, and produced a purgative effect, proponents responded that it should only be fed as part of a mixed diet.[48] Experiments were conducted in the 1890s to establish the most effective combinations—with lucerne, maize, and veld.[49] Some farmers who kept ostriches in the drier districts, where they were more reliant on Karoo bushes, actually valued the diarrhetic qualities of prickly pear.[50]

For officials and politicians, the idea of killing two birds with one stone was attractive: the costs of partial eradication would be much reduced, and its effectiveness increased, if the pear leaf could be used on a large scale for feed. MacOwan eloquently advanced such a solution in his 1897 'Plea for the Pricklies'.[51] He described Australian methods of preparing the pear by large-scale boiling or steaming in vats. Euphorbia species had also been boiled to render them palatable for stock in droughts. Many burnt off spikes.[52] At the Cookhouse thicket, leaves were placed with water in a revolving barrel to rub off the spikes, and one farmer adopted an American strategy of pulping by machine.[53] A process was developed in Graaff-Reinet for converting prickly pear into dry fodder balls.[54] MacOwan hoped 'that some one down in the Opuntiaries of the Midlands' would evolve an economical machine to do this on a large scale, as in Arizona, Texas, and New Mexico. In this way, it would

[46] A.29-1898, 39, evidence Charles Lee.   [47] A.8-1906, 41.

[48] A.29-1898, 14, evidence G. Wilhelm.   [49] *Agricultural Journal*, 16: 1 (4 Jan. 1900), 52.

[50] A.9-1891, 18.

[51] *Agricultural Journal*, 11: 4 (19 Aug. 1897), P. MacOwan, 'A Plea for the Pricklies', 158–62.

[52] Ibid. 14: 12 (8 June 1899): 'G.M.', 'The Much Abused Prickly Pear', 817.

[53] *Kew Bulletin* (1888), 167.

[54] Chas. F. Juritz, *Prickly Pear as a Fodder for Stock* (Government Printer, Pretoria, 1920), Union of South Africa, Department of Agriculture, Science Bulletin, 16, 7.

THE SOUTH AFRICAN
IMPROVED PATENT WHITEFORD
ALOE LEAF
AND
PRICKLY PEAR CUTTERS
The Only Machine
that will cut American Aloe
Leaves and Prickly Pears for
OSTRICH FEEDING.
IT HAS NO EQUAL.

Ostrich Farmers
should not be without one.

PRICES ON APPLICATION.

Chas. J. Stirk & Son
GRAHAMSTOWN,
Sole Suppliers throughout the World.

13. Prickly Pear Cutters

be possible to 'clear a depreciated, pear-curst piece of land, and raise a mob of cattle at the same time'.

Some progressive farmers felt that they could benefit from the kaalblad and control the doornblad. Richard Rubidge, at Wellwood, planted new stands of kaalblad in 1894, as did his son Sidney in 1910.[55] At the same time, a hedge of doornblad planted in the 1860s was scrubbed up and teams of farmworkers were assigned to systematic eradication of this variety over many years. But those committed to eradication were convinced that it was too expensive to process fodder on any scale. They argued that it would be pointless to eradicate prickly pear in pockets. Kaalblad could not be assured and doornblad in inaccessible areas, or on prickly pear farms, could reinfest land already cleared.[56] Prickly pear, like disease and jackals, seemed to be undermining the pastoral economy as a whole, and they felt that a colony-wide campaign was essential.

The political impetus for the select committees to consider government intervention came partly from the wealthier, progressive, livestock farmers,

[55] PTA LDB 1263, R1688, vol. 8, Sidney Rubidge, Wellwood, to Minister of Agriculture, 8 Nov. 1947, enclosing memo on 'Spineless Cactus on Wellwood'.
[56] A.29-1898, 18 ff., evidence R. P. Botha.

following a petition to parliament from the midland-based Zwart Ruggens Farmers Association, whose office-bearers included Lee and Palmer. As in the case of scab control and jackal eradication, the issue to some extent cut across political divisions. R. P. Botha was a key Bond member, a founder of the movement in Graaff-Reinet, former MLA for Cradock, and chair of the Provincial Executive Committee. Similarly, M. J. du Plessis, Bond MLA for Cradock, was adamant in 1898 that he would 'rather let my birds die than bring prickly pear on my farm'.[57]

Protagonists of eradication emphasized the economic ills as well as the social evils resulting from invasion. Prickly pear diminished the value of farms and could be very expensive to eradicate, up to £3 a morgen for heavy thickets. A single clearing was seldom sufficient. One farmer in Jansenville put six men into clearance for a month every two years—and this on a farm which had been cleared twenty years previously. Teams of African migrant workers were also employed. Land devalued by prickly pear could benefit well-capitalized farmers. Palmer bought a neighbouring prickly pear farm at so low a price that it was worth his while to spend 5 shillings per morgen on clearing it.[58] But personal advantage was outweighed by the risks of reinfection and the losses to the agricultural economy as a whole. Most of all, they argued that a failure to act while the problem was containable would result in far greater costs at a later stage. Douglass, MLA for Grahamstown, changed his mind about the plant to argue in 1893 that prickly pear was spreading so quickly that half the farming population in the Cape would be reduced to poverty if nothing was done[59] (though he wanted proof that the kaalblad could produce the doornblad, before advocating total eradication). While losses, estimated at £200,000 a year, were less than attributed to predators, they were still significant. Progressives argued that the Divisional Councils were too poor, inefficient, and politically divided to take control.[60] They looked to the central government.

It was difficult to mobilize opinion on this issue. MacDonald, the Agricultural Assistant, estimated in 1891 that it would cost £320,000 to eradicate the pear in heavily infested districts. This was a potentially huge commitment in the context of the Cape, where state expenditure on agriculture was still very limited. Support remained uneven. In the words of one observer: 'some farmers would not eradicate it, because they only had a little, others because they had too much, others again actually tried to grow it.'[61] It

---

[57] Ibid. 8.   [58] C.3-1890, 6, evidence G. M. Palmer, and 17, evidence J. H. Smith.

[59] CA AGR 74, F244 ff., cutting including House of Assembly debate, 27 July 1893.

[60] C.3-1890, 13, evidence George Palmer; Davenport, *Afrikaner Bond*, 6–7.

[61] Grobbelaar, 'The Prickly Pear', 246; C.3-1890, 5, evidence R. P. Botha, MLC.

also seemed clear by the late nineteenth century that prickly pear invasion was by no means uniform. The plant could grow in a wide range of conditions—although it thrived in sweetveld areas, and on rich soil in the valley bottoms. But invasion seemed to depend partly on climatic conditions.[62]

Prickly pear was most widespread in districts with a rainfall of between 300 and 500 mm. In Richmond, not far to the north of heavily infested Graaff-Reinet, the pear had to be carefully cultivated and even irrigated.[63] This was the case throughout the dryer western and northern Karoo districts, and the southern Free State. Frosts in the interior at higher altitudes were too hard and regular for opuntia to spread easily. The eastern Cape grasslands were, by contrast, generally too wet and humid. Although this was not reported at the time, prickly pear found it more difficult to compete where there was a denser cover of grass. In Graaff-Reinet, it was less likely to take root on elevated, grassier sourveld. Yet parts of Albany and Uitenhage districts, with a higher rainfall, were susceptible to invasion. Dr Eric Nobbs, a recent recruit to the Department of Agriculture, suggested a preference for dry air and a hot summer, whatever the rainfall.[64]

In sum, state intervention would support farmers in particular geographical zones—more so than in the case of predators. For this reason, key politicians such as Sprigg and Merriman, who were in favour of concerted government action against scab, refused to take full responsibility.[65] The Department of Agriculture compromised in the 1890s by distributing arsenite of soda at half of cost price; MacDonald demonstrated its use in Graaff-Reinet, Pearston, Bedford, and Fort Beaufort.

By this time the consensus was that doornblad succumbed best when chopped down to its roots, piled in stacks, dried, turned so that any sprouting leaves on the outside of the pile would be destroyed, and then burnt as soon as this was feasible, after about one year. This was a time-consuming, labour-intensive, and expensive process that required careful supervision. Eradicators had to be vigilant so that leaves were not dropped on the ground during their transport to stacks. Stacks could become a source of rotting fruit, attractive to birds and animals and hence a new node for spreading the pear.[66] In some cases, the area on which pear was piled had to be cut and treated again.

[62] A.8-1906, 21 ff., evidence Dr Rupert Marloth.

[63] A.9-1891, 16, evidence P. J. du Toit, MLA, Richmond.

[64] *Agricultural Journal* (Nov. 1906): Dr Eric A. Nobbs, 'Notes on the Prickly Pear', 637.

[65] CA AGR 74, F244, cutting including Legislative Council and House of Assembly debates, 27 July 1893.

[66] C.3-1890, 12.

An alternative method of poisoning the plant where it stood, which saved costs and labour, became increasingly popular. Various solutions were tried, including Cooper's Dip, used for dipping livestock, an Australian Scrub Exterminator, arsenite of soda, and sodium arsenate. MacDonald experimented with these on Palmer's farm, Cranemere, near Pearston, and found none worked very well.[67] Arsenite of soda seemed the most promising; it was adopted by the government over the next decade as the cheapest and most successful compound, convenient to distribute in powder form.[68] The rural districts were awash with poison by now: strychnine for jackals, and arsenic compounds for dipping and prickly pear. Concern about their accumulated impact was articulated at the time.[69]

Poison tended to kill only parts of the plant. The result was that live leaves dropped to the ground and sprouted again. Poisoning worked better if the plants were first punctured and injected, especially in the stems and thicker stem joints, before spraying. It worked best on plants cut down and stacked because this hastened decomposition, and reduced the risk of regrowth.[70] MacDonald's experiments suggested that it could reduce the time before burning to six weeks after the materials were piled.[71] Burying pear before poisoning, as done in India, could also be effective, but the labour costs involved, especially in hard, stony Karoo ground, were a disincentive.

Government subsidy significantly reduced the costs of this combined mechanical and chemical technique; 200,000 pounds of exterminator were distributed by 1898. In some districts farmers were highly motivated: 'the traveller by rail through the midlands can see for himself in every direction piles of the extirpated pear.'[72] In one of the worst-affected areas along the Great Fish river near Cookhouse, landowners 'got rid of the pest wholesale; and large agricultural areas are now under the plough and carrying crops which had for fifty years been impenetrable thickets of the Prickly Pear'.[73] Here, access to the most valuable riverine land provided an added incentive.

From 1898 to 1905, following these apparent successes, poison was distributed free. In 1905, during the acute recession, the government charged

---

[67] CA AGR 74, F244 and following, report by A. C. MacDonald, 18 July 1891.

[68] *Agricultural Journal* (Dec. 1907): E. A. Nobbs, 'Experiments upon the Destruction of Prickly Pear, 1907, Final Report', 676–82.

[69] A.9-1891, 42, evidence A. Fischer, Sec. Ag.

[70] *Agricultural Journal* (14 June 1894), 285, extract from A. C. MacDonald's report to the Sec. Ag.

[71] A.29-1898, Appendix, i, memo by W. Hammond Tooke, 25 Nov. 1898.

[72] A.29-1898, p. iv.

[73] *Agricultural Journal*, 15: 8 (12 Oct. 1899), 548: Eustace Pillans, Agricultural Assistant, 'Extirpation of Prickly Pear'.

half cost price again and there was a fall in demand for poison.[74] The 1906 Select Committee was less optimistic: the area heavily infested was still estimated at about half-a-million morgen.[75] For every success there seemed to be counter-evidence of invasion on the farms of poor whites. The total area densely infested was limited to the equivalent of about 300 average-sized midland farms, or one district, but prickly pear was scattered so widely, in such variable concentrations, that the dangers of further spread remained. As Nobbs put it, no other weed 'has become such a characteristic of the landscape'.[76]

After Union, noxious weeds, along with vermin, became a provincial responsibility. Alarms were soon sounded in the Administrator's office about the pear. By this time jointed cactus (*Opuntia aurantiaca*) was identified as an equally important scourge. It probably spread from a farm in Bedford, or a mission station in the Kat river valley, where it had been introduced as an ornamental plant in the 1850s. Jointed cactus had no value either as fodder or fruit and was very difficult to eradicate. Called *injubalani* in Xhosa, for its capacity to stick fast to passing livestock, it was easily spread in this way or by flood-water.[77] Eradication costs were now being estimated at £20 per morgen; commonages and Crown lands were especially susceptible—and this implied government responsibility.

The question was whether, like the jackal, opuntia should be viewed 'as a national danger.'[78] At the Congress of Divisional Councils in 1914 a delegate argued that if the provincial council did not 'eradicate the pest . . . then jointed cactus would eradicate the farmer'.[79] Representatives of infested areas pointed to the assistance given to western Cape farmers over phylloxera. Two members of the Drought Distress Commission (1916), including the President of the Cape Province Agricultural Association, took up the issue with de Waal, the Administrator. 'While at Hankey', they 'were . . . horrified to see the cavalier way in which that terrible scourge "jointed cactus" . . . [was] allowed to grow.'[80] Districts such as Albany and Uitenhage, previously on the peripheries of the problem, were increasingly affected.

[74] A.8-1906, 10: evidence Dr Eric A. Nobbs, Agricultural Assistant.   [75] Ibid., p. iv.

[76] Nobbs, 'Notes on the Prickly Pear', 637.

[77] *Agricultural Journal*, 5: 7 (28 July 1892): A. Fischer (ed.), 'New Cactus. (Prickly Pear.)', 93–4; Ibid. (23 Aug. 1894): John B. Bowker, 'Jointed Cactus (*Opuntia aurantiaca*)', 405. Here the Xhosa word is given as Injubalinie. The Xhosa name came from the root ukujuba, which can mean to hold fast, or rebound and scratch in the manner of a thorn tree (A. Kropf and R. Godfrey, *Kafir–English Dictionary* (Lovedale Mission Press, Lovedale, 1915), 174; there is no direct reference to jointed cactus here).

[78] CA PAS 3/151 N42/2, Noel Janisch, Office of the Adminstrator to Acting Sec. Ag., 29 Apr. 1912.

[79] Ibid. N36, cutting, *Alice Times*, 19 Feb. 1914: speech by 'Mr Coetzee', Cradock.

[80] Ibid. N42/2, O. Evans and P. M. Michau to Administrator, 3 Nov. 1916.

De Waal did not develop the same enthusiasm for opuntia eradication as he had for jackal extermination, but the Provincial Council did continue to subsidize poisons. Following experiments in 1917 with Rademeyer's new Exterminator, its inventor was funded by the Provincial Council to manufacture the product on a large scale to a uniform standard. The province retained an option to purchase the secret of his mixture for £10,000.[81] Basson's Destroyer, analysed as arsenious sulphide in alkaline solution, proved less effective.[82] Rademeyer's mixture was distributed for some years, but the contract was terminated in the 1920s because it was found to be more expensive, yet no more effective, than generic arsenic compounds.[83] By this time, however, expenditure on eradication began to escalate. Following a change in local-authority financing systems, they were permitted to raise loans and this proved to be one of the first priorities of some Divisional Councils. Specific legislation on the jointed cactus was passed in 1928. Local and provincial government employed eradication teams. And new options for control, developed by the central government, were opening up.

Spineless Cactus, Cactoblastis, and Cochineal

Although the eradication of weeds was a provincial responsibility, the national Department of Agriculture did not lose interest in the ubiquitous prickly pear after Union. Four reports were written in the early 1920s: two by Charles Juritz, a leading agricultural chemist; one by Joseph Burtt-Davy, a botanist in the Agriculture Department who had long been interested in the plant; and one by Arthur Stead, the soil chemist, and E. N. S. Warren, lecturer on sheep and wool, both at Grootfontein.[84] Three of these reports were commissioned primarily to examine more fully the old question of prickly pear's fodder potential.

Juritz ranged widely over the international literature and was well aware of prickly pear's importance as a food, 'especially of the poorer classes'.[85] In the

---

[81] CA PAS 3/124 N14/6.

[82] CA PAS 3/150, N26, Government Chemical Laboratory to Provincial Secretary, 8 June 1918.

[83] PTA LDB 11260, R1688, vol. 1, J. B. Grewar to Sec. Ag., 8 May 1925.

[84] Juritz, *The Prickly Pear (Opuntia)*; id., *Prickly Pear as a Fodder for Stock*; Joseph Burtt-Davy, *Utilizing Prickly Pear and Spineless Cactus: Their Value as Fodder for Live Stock* (Government Printer, Pretoria, 1921), Industrial Bulletin Series, 70, repr. from the *South African Journal of Industries* (Nov. 1920); A. Stead and E. N. S. Warren, *Prickly Pear: Its Value as a Fodder for Sheep in Droughts and in Ordinary Times* (Government Printer, Pretoria, 1922), Union of South Africa, Department of Agriculture, Bulletin, no.4 (1922).

[85] Juritz, *The Prickly Pear (Opuntia)*, 4.

Mediterranean it was 'cared for as if it were an orchard plant' and exported to London; its 'cool watery sweetness' was mingled with a 'flavour of cucumber and melon'. In some countries prickly pear was used as green manure, rich in humus, potash, and lime; it was also burnt as ash fertilizer. In addition to rural Cape uses as a source for syrup, a coffee substitute, vinegar, and alcohol, Juritz found reports on experiments with opuntia as a base for industrial alcohol, textiles, paint, paper fibre, and soap. (In the 1940s an Australian firm, which manufactured gramophone needles from the spikes of *Opuntia monacantha*, ran out of supplies because of the success of clearance in that country and tried to find replacements in South Africa.) But the chemical composition of prickly pear meant that it was by no means the best source for any of these products on a commercial scale. Juritz concluded that its advantages in mass industrial use, particularly if the aim was also to eradicate wild pear in rural districts, were 'nebulous'.

The best option still seemed to be mass use for fodder. Doornblad had by now been chemically analysed by a number of scientists. All were agreed that it had a relatively low nutritional value, and was especially deficient in digestible protein; it had to be used alongside other fodder crops or veld. The key problem remained whether it could be processed at sufficiently low cost. Juritz was sceptical and his reports, without coming to any firm conclusions, suggested that although there was evidence of successful use, the disadvantages tended to outweigh the advantages.

Burtt-Davy, by contrast, was keen to emphasize that a weed in one area need not be dangerous in other climatic conditions.[86] He re-examined Texan methods of preparing spiny prickly pear for stock by cutting, boiling, and singeing. New paraffin torches had been developed in the United States that allowed the thorns to be singed on the plant, without cutting. One version, the B&H Pear Burner, sold by Mangold Bros. of Port Elizabeth, was touted in the 1920s as 'Worth It's Weight in Gold'; it competed with the New Mercantile Pear Burner.[87] R. W. Thornton, principal of Grootfontein college, was also initially an advocate of the plant. Before Union he had confirmed in experiments that it was a valuable fodder when properly prepared and mixed with lucerne—a legume with a high protein content—and maize.[88]

Thornton instituted new tests with sheep at Grootfontein in 1921, recorded by Stead and Warren.[89] Ten large 95-pound hamels (wethers/castrated rams) were fed with blocks of cut prickly pear cladodes less than two

---

[86] *Transvaal Agricultural Journal*, 5: 18 (Jan. 1907), 450: J. Burtt-Davy, 'The Prickly Pear in the Transvaal'.

[87] PTA LDB 1250 R1592, copies of advertisements.   [88] Juritz, *Prickly Pear as a Fodder*.

[89] Stead and Warren, *Prickly Pear*.

inches square and not additionally treated. For twenty-five days the sheep ate an average of 10.75 pounds of prickly pear and 0.6 pounds of lucerne per day, and maintained their weight. From then on they received pear only for long periods, averaging over 12 pounds a day. This was supplemented occasionally with lucerne when their condition deteriorated too quickly. They needed no additional water, and in fact urinated more frequently than usual. The sheep gradually lost about a quarter of their weight over nine months. When some weakened too rapidly, they were turned out onto the veld and recovered their weight in three months. The four strongest survived on prickly pear, with occasional supplements, but with no water, for over a year. The experiment showed that sheep would eat pear continuously—at least if they had no other options; that although a pear-only diet did not maintain condition, small additions of lucerne could make a major difference; that sheep could survive for over seventy days at a time with no supplements; that they regained condition when lucerne or natural veld was available; and that little internal damage was done despite frequent purging.

It was known that prickly pear was inadequate in itself as a fodder. What excited the investigators was its value as a drought food for sheep and its role in diminishing the need for transhumance. 'No water supply is so proof against the effects of drought as the prickly pear plantation,' they concluded, 'and no fodder crop makes such perfect use of a scanty and irregular rainfall.'[90] They revived MacOwan's optimistic assessment of opuntia if only farmers could 'condescend now and then to supplement Nature's raw material with a spice of ingenuity and labour'.[91] Experiments were repeated on Graaff-Reinet commonage, densely covered with prickly pear in the late 1920s. This time Arthur Stead kept sheep alive for 250 days on prickly pear, with some veld grazing, alone; although they became emaciated, they recovered condition when returned to a normal diet.[92] In the final report on this experiment, it was argued that freshly pulped prickly pear mixed with lucerne was the most successful feed; that it did not affect the quality of wool; and that purging helped to clear internal parasites.

Opuntia species became all the more valuable at this time because new stable versions of the kaalblad, called spineless cactus, were bred. One from Algeria was imported by Burtt-Davy in 1907 and widely distributed.[93] The most successful were developed in the United States by the innovative plant breeder Luther Burbank of Santa Rosa, California. He would 'rub his face

[90] Ibid. 8.   [91] Ibid. 12.
[92] PTA LDB 1554 R2457/1a., F. C. Smith, Officer in Charge, 'Review of Graaff-Reinet Prickly Pear Experiments, March 1927–March 1928'.
[93] Burtt-Davy, *Utilizing Prickly Pear*.

against the pads to determine whether the spines are really there'.[94] Cuttings were imported in 1909 by a nursery at Grahamstown. They were sold as 'the camels of the vegetable world'; 'they must have water but they can get along for long periods without it'.[95] Individual farmers such as Sydney Rubidge imported their own plants direct from California.[96]

Chemical analysis of spineless cactus showed that it did not differ greatly from the spiny varieties. It would grow in the same areas, and was palatable to most livestock. The leaves grown in nursery conditions were bigger and heavier than the kaalblad. Livestock could eat the plant as it stood. The great innovation, as farmers were assured, was that it would not produce fertile seed, hybridize, or revert to thorny cactus. Experimental plots were instituted at Grootfontein in 1913, soon after its foundation. Despite occasional complaints from commercial nurseries, officials were so enthusiastic that the government engaged directly in the production and marketing of spineless cactus.[97]

Demand could hardly be met. In 1916 Grootfontein distributed 8,000 leaves, in 1918 20,000, and between 1918 and 1930 an average of roughly 25,000 leaves a year. Farmers could reproduce the plant themselves relatively easily by cloning. In the 1920s the Department of Agriculture released circulars in praise of the spineless cactus as 'capable of doing as much for the stock industry of our country as turnips and mangels have done for that of Western Europe'.[98] No crop was 'so easy to grow'. By the 1930s Grootfontein had experimented with thirty-seven varieties. Just how much of this new fodder was planted became a matter of some dispute. It was clearly regarded as very valuable by some of the leading midland sheep farmers (Chapter 9).

At the very moment that a panacea for droughts and transhumance seemed to be on offer, so too new urgency was articulated about the need to control wild pest pear. The perception that it was spreading rapidly was very likely based on accurate observation. No systematic survey was conducted, but returns were received from some local officials in 1931, and F. W. Pettey, a government entomologist, spent two weeks touring pear-infested districts of the Cape in 1932. Given the time constraints, he stuck largely to small towns and farms along the main transport routes. He did, however, travel with

[94] *Transvaal Agricultural Journal*, 5: 18 (Jan. 1907), 309: William MacDonald, 'Agriculture in America'.

[95] *Agricultural Journal of the Union of South Africa*, 3: 2 (Feb. 1912), 227: J. Lewis, 'Note on Burbank's Spineless Prickly Pear'.

[96] PTA LDB 1713, R2846, vol. 6, F. W. Pettey to T. J. Naude, 26 Jan. 1938.

[97] PTA LDB 1040 R1194, Spineless Cactus.

[98] PTA LDB 1260 R1688, vol. 1, Department of Agriculture Weekly Advice service, 3 Aug. 1925.

extension officers and the cactus inspector of the Cape Provincial Council who had been monitoring the plant. Major areas of infestation were identified in Uitenhage, Bedford, southern Graaff-Reinet, and Cookhouse. There he estimated that 50,000 morgen of farmland, some along the Fish river, was 'a dense jungle of prickly pear as far as one could see, right up and over the top of hills and koppies'. Some plants were 20 feet high.

Pettey estimated that 6 million morgen were now affected by prickly pear invasion—ten times the figure at the turn of the century.[99] A figure of 8 million morgen, or 27,000 square miles, 'entirely taken up by cactus' had been published in an article in the Department's journal.[100] This number, amounting to over one-tenth the surface area of the Cape, was attributed to a participant in a 1929 debate on eradication by the South African Agricultural Union. A direct comparison with earlier figures was difficult to make; Pettey and these other sources clearly included areas of light infestation. The incomplete estimates by officials in 1931 were lower. Of four districts for which 1891 figures are available, their returns from Somerset East and Jansenville actually showed a significant reduction, while Uitenhage and Albany showed an increase.[101] Calculations suggested that £20 million would be required to clear the prickly pear with poison. Over 30,000 morgen were estimated to be infested with jointed cactus.[102] This was even more expensive to eradicate, because stumps had to be dug out and frequent follow-up was essential.

Even if Pettey did exaggerate, there were a number of predisposing factors for the spread of doornblad during the first few decades of the twentieth century. The sudden fall in ostrich numbers during the First World War had removed one major consumer. As Pettey commented of Albany district, 'not only was much fed to the birds but they destroyed the young plants by feeding on them. Prickly pear is increasing 100 per cent more rapidly now that ostriches are absent.'[103]

Secondly, although wealthier livestock farmers were reinvesting in sheep, and devoting resources to clearing prickly pear, poor-whiteism and farm subdivision was intensifying simultaneously. Undercapitalized owners could

[99] PTA LDB 1711 R2846, vol. 2 F. W. Pettey to Chief: Division of Plant Industry, 4 July 1932, 'Report of Tour of Inspection of Jointed Cactus and Prickly Pear Areas in the Cape Province Eastern Districts, June 5–19, 1932'.

[100] *Farming in South Africa*, 5: 49 (1930): C. R. van der Merwe, 'The Eradication of the Cactus Pest', 37.

[101] National Archives, Pretoria, Department of Agriculture Entomology Division (PTA CEN) 947, SF15/2, Prickly pear survey, responses to circular, 13 Feb. 1931.

[102] PTA CEN 1004, 65/1, vol. 2, responses to 1931 survey.

[103] PTA LDB 1711 R2846, vol. 2, Pettey, 'Report of Tour of Inspection', 7, Albany district.

do little to manage it effectively. The Depression years, from 1929 to 1933, probably exacerbated such trends. As one farmer in Bedford noted in 1931: 'our country is becoming more and more infested with prickly pear and in these depressed times our farmers are not able to cope with the pest.'[104] The price of wool plummeted during the Depression, and sheep farmers were amongst the major casualties. Tom Murray in Graaff-Reinet told Pettey that, 'in hard times like the present no farmer can afford to spend a penny in preventing prickly pear from increasing in sheep lands'.[105] Pettey saw dense patches on a number of municipal commonages where clearing had not been organized. Middelburg, which observers remembered had no pear thirty years before, was one.

Thirdly, invasion could be an exponential phenomenon; once doornblad had taken hold in a district it was more likely to spread if it was not cleared. Infestation along river valleys had become particularly serious, exacerbated by flooding and inaccessibility. At Uitenhage, Pettey heard that 'prickly pear forms a jungle the whole length of the Sunday's River . . . for a distance of 75 to 100 miles', and had invaded the valley lands on either side for up to 15 miles.[106] Jointed cactus overhung the Keiskamma river, near Middledrift, and 'broken off joints were resting on the rocks waiting for the next storm to bring them down the river to reinfest the lands of private farms lower down'. Pettey found that 'in places the jointed cactus was so thick that no paths existed to allow walking in it'. Jointed cactus was not, however, an invader further north in the sheep-farming districts around Graaff-Reinet, Cradock, and Middelburg.

And fourthly, the rise in the number of sheep, and concomitant denudation, was probably a major factor. Prickly pear leaves were more likely to take root on bare soil than on land covered with grass and other vegetation. Periodic droughts may have hastened the process, both because animals depended more on fruit and because vegetation cover was even sparser. Petty found that the doornblad took hold not least in sweetveld areas, which were favoured for grazing, had less grass cover, and were more quickly denuded. More dung, with pear seeds, was probably deposited on them.

Despite the optimism of Grootfontein officials about processing of doornblad for fodder, this no longer seemed a practical means of controlling spread. Spineless cactus now provided an alternative, safer fodder. Officials faced strong pressure from farmers, associations, MPs, and local councils to take action. At the same time new techniques for controlling the pest pear

[104] Ibid., vol. 1, Editor, *Midland News*, Cradock, to Sec. Ag., 23 Jan. 1931.
[105] LDB 1711 R2846, vol. 2, Pettey to Chief: Division of Plant Industry, 4 July 1932.
[106] PTA LDB 1711 R2846, vol. 2, Pettey, 'Report of Tour of Inspection', 8.

became available. The link between cochineal insects and the prickly pear had long been known, and as early as the 1880s the insects were mentioned as a possible strategy for eradication.[107] Canary Islanders had objected to the introduction of the insect for dye production in the nineteenth century because they felt it might destroy their fruit supply.

In the late nineteenth century economic entomology expanded as a field in the United States, and the strategy of using introduced species to control pests—called biological intervention—was being more systematically canvassed.[108] There, as in the Cape, locust control was a major concern. Lounsbury, the American who became the Cape Government Entomologist in 1895, and later the Union's Chief Entomologist, was interested in these techniques. Aside from his pioneering work on ticks, his early preoccupation was with insects that inhibited commercial fruit-growing. Although chemical spraying became established as the preferred mode of control, he was involved in introducing a species of ladybird to control scale in fruit. There were also unsuccessful attempts to find a Brazilian wasp to attack fruit fly.[109]

A Commission in Queensland, Australia, where prickly pear had become a major pest by the early twentieth century, visited India, South Africa, the United States, and South America in search of possible biological controls. Lounsbury heard of the devastating impact of one cochineal species on the *Opuntia monocantha* in southern India.[110] The Commission sent him a sample in Pretoria in 1913 and it was transferred for experiments to Natal.[111] With little public debate, or even departmental discussion, the insect was then released near Pietermaritzburg. Cochineal did not spread quickly over long distances because the females had no wings. It required a critical mass to have any major impact, otherwise it tended to find a balance with the host plant. But Claude Fuller, Lounsbury's American deputy, felt that by 1921 it was 'rapidly exterminating' a thin-leaved opuntia prevalent in Zululand and Natal.[112]

[107] *Agricultural Journal*, 1: 15 (11 Oct. 1888); A.8-1906, 41.

[108] P. Palladino, *Entomology, Ecology and Agriculture: The Making of Scientific Careers in North America 1885–1985* (Lancaster University Press, Lancaster, 1996).

[109] Karen Brown, 'Political Entomology: The Insectile Challenge to Agricultural Development in the Cape', discusses Lounsbury's earlier Cape work; forthcoming in 'Progressivism, Agriculture and Conservation in the Cape Colony circa 1902–1908', unpublished D.Phil. thesis, University of Oxford.

[110] *Agricultural Journal*, 1: 5 (May 1915): C. P. Lounsbury, 'Plant Killing Insects: The Indian Cochineal', 540.

[111] *Agricultural Journal*, 7: 3 (Mar. 1914), 387–91: Ernest Warren, 'The Prickly Pear Pest'; Lounsbury, 'Plant Killing Insects'.

[112] PTA LDB 1711 R2846, vol. 1, Claude Fuller, Division of Entomology to Sec. Ag., 5 Feb. 1921.

As soon as the Natal experiment was publicized there were calls of alarm about the danger of an uncontrollable insect pest.[113] Some feared that a biological campaign could produce self-spreading insects that might devour other crops, including spineless cactus, and turn invasive themselves. But Lounsbury had great faith in the capacity of science to regulate environments. He had been central in the research for the Cape's great dipping campaign which was, by the 1910s and 1920s, proving a success. The two species of cochineal already known to be in South Africa seemed to attack only specific opuntia species, a general trait suggested by the 1914 Queensland Commission. The old-established western Cape cochineal was introduced to a farm in Graaff-Reinet around 1915 and had been spread further by farmers. It established itself very slowly on the doornblad, and seemed to subsist with rather than destroy the plant.[114]

Lounsbury was convinced that the entomologists could manage a biological campaign. This also implied that the Department of Agriculture in Pretoria, where the specialists were based, would take control of eradication. The Australian Prickly Pear Board was experimenting with suitable insects, and he sent them both kaalblad and doornblad for testing. In 1924 a species of moth borer called *Cactoblastis cactorum* was identified as particularly promising, and the Argentinian government agreed to breed it for export. Lounsbury tried to persuade his department to establish an experiment at Grootfontein. Thornton, the principal, was concerned about the threat to his heavily promoted spineless cactus.[115] Although he was particularly keen to find an enemy for the jointed cactus, he was unprepared to take the risk.

Instead, cactoblastis, procured from the ship carrying them from Argentina to Australia, were bred at the entomological laboratory in Cape Town.[116] First results on jointed cactus were deemed successful. But some agreed with Thornton that the risks were too great. Lounsbury was confronted at the second national conference of South African entomologists in 1925. He was uncompromising: he had 'no intention of destroying the insects'.[117] The cactoblastis had the advantage of feeding on a number of different species, including jointed cactus, and the worst Australian pest pear *O. inermia*. Unlike the surface-grazing cochineal, cactoblastis larvae bored

---

[113] *Agricultural Journal*, 8: 1 (July 1914), 114: Alfred C. Harmsworth, Norval's Pont, 'The Prickly Pear Pest'.

[114] PTA LDB 1711 R2846, vol. 1, I. P. van Heerden to General Kemp, Minister of Agriculture, 21 Nov. 1925.

[115] Ibid., Chief Entomologist to Principal, Grootfontein, 5 Dec. 1924.

[116] PTA LDB R1688, Lounsbury, 'Prickly Pears: Utilization of Natural Checks'.

[117] PTA LDB 1711 R2846, vol. 1, Chief Entomologist to Sec. Ag., 22 Aug. 1925.

into stems and leaves, eating them away from the inside. Australian scientists had shown that cactoblastis had no damaging effect on over seventy economically valuable plants. South African experiments later confirmed that although cactoblastis larvae survived twenty-one days on cultivated fruit, the insect seemed unable to reproduce or complete its life-cycle except on opuntia species.[118]

The great attraction of biological control was that it promised to be relatively inexpensive once the insect was established, and total in its reach. Australia had already shouldered much of the financial burden of procurement and testing. The great problem was its threat to spineless cactus. The prickly pear files in the Department of Agriculture archives contain a cacophony of contradictory letters: some from farmers desperate for the urgent release of cactoblastis; others equally keen to protect their spineless plantations. In 1926 Lounsbury reported that the Australian results were 'phenomenal'.[119] A new testing station was established at Port Elizabeth. Thornton now lined up behind Lounsbury to recommend liberation of cactoblastis, subject to confirmation that it would not attack important indigenous fodder plants such as spekboom.[120] Although he had recently directed the experiments that showed the value of prickly pear as drought fodder, the growing threat of doornblad and jointed cactus helped to change his opinion.[121] Other, non-invasive, drought fodder plants such as agave and saltbush provided an alternative. 'The sheep men' at Grootfontein, Pettey reported, agreed that prickly pear 'caused havoc with small stock'.

While it seemed that a biological campaign was imminent, the momentum ebbed in 1927 when Lounsbury died and Fuller replaced him. Entomology was absorbed briefly by the Botany and Horticulture Division under Pole-Evans, a committed veld conservationist who was concerned about the impact of introduced insects on indigenous species. The cochineal breeding stations were closed, and a misunderstanding resulted in the destruction of the final South African colony. For Fuller it was a 'profound relief'; the discussion had generated strong personal feelings in and outside the Department.[122]

General Kemp, Minister of Agriculture in Hertzog's government from 1924, had initially authorized experiments. He then changed his mind in the

---

[118] Ibid., vol. 3, Sec. Ag. to Port Elizabeth Divisional Council, 11 Sept. 1933.
[119] PTA LDB 1260 R1688, vol. 1, 7 Apr. 1926; PTA LDB 1711 R2846, Lounsbury to Sec. Ag., 16 July 1926.
[120] PTA LDB 1711 R2846, vol. 1, Thornton to Sec. Ag., 8 Oct. 1926.
[121] Ibid., Thornton to Chief, Division of Botany and Entomology, 28 Feb. 1927.
[122] Ibid., Chief Entomologist to Chief, Division of Botany, 7 Mar. 1927.

face of the spineless cactus lobby.[123] There was a clear geographical split on the issue. Spineless cactus growers in the northern Cape and Free State, largely free of the pest pear, were adamantly opposed to biological campaigns, and these areas were generally Nationalist in sympathy. Positions, however, remained fluid and the issue cut across party loyalties. Some of the strongest advocates of cactoblastis in the early 1930s proved to be Nationalist MPs. English-speaking farmers were equally split. Towards the coast, pest pear and jointed cactus were more of a threat; these districts supported the South African Party as well as cactoblastis. Agitation from English-speaking farmers in 1930, especially some sheep farmers around Graaff-Reinet, helped to place biological control back on the political agenda. Yet John G. Collett, Secretary of the Midland Farmers Association, sponsored a resolution against a biological campaign. Sidney Rubidge lined up on this side (Chapter 9). Jack Bowker in Middelburg noted the extensive spineless planting taking place: 'one can hardly place the potential value too high.'[124]

When Pettey visited the districts most affected in 1933, he found majority support for release in eighteen out of twenty-one meetings with farmers and municipalities.[125] (In Willowmore and Somerset East, poorer whites opposed release as a threat to their marketing of prickly pear fruits.) The Department of Native Affairs strongly advocated release because of the difficulties experienced in controlling opuntia in heavily infested districts of the Ciskei, such as Middledrift. White-controlled Divisional Councils bordering such African reserved land in turn placed pressure on Native Affairs officials to take more effective action. Thornton's position in favour of biological control was cemented for these reasons when he became Director of Native Agriculture in 1929.[126]

An underlying issue in the debate was the question of just how much land was overrun by pest pear and how large an area had been planted with spineless cactus. Pettey and others in favour of the biological campaign talked of millions of morgen infested.[127] By contrast, he underestimated spineless cactus plantations in the midlands and eastern districts as 'apparently . . . a few hundred morgen'. In 1930 a farmer estimated the area of plantations as 5,000 morgen.[128] Evidence from Grootfontein and from individual farmers suggests that by the early 1930s far more had been planted. Surprisingly,

---

[123] Ibid., Minister of Agriculture to Minister of Lands, 19 June 1930; D. Gunn, Government Entomologist, Port Elizabeth to Chief Entomologist, 1 Aug. 1930.

[124] Ibid., vol. 3, cutting, *Farmers' Weekly*, no date (1933).

[125] Ibid., Pettey to Sec. Ag., 24 Aug. 1933.

[126] Ibid., vol. 2, Thornton to Sec. Ag., 17 Nov. 1931 and 9 Dec. 1931.

[127] Pettey, 'Report of Tour'.

[128] LDB 8194, 4/345, cutting from *Farmers' Weekly* (Aug. 1930): W. H. Morris, Miller station.

given the political status of spineless cactus growers, the Department did not attempt to quantify their plantations or record them in the agricultural census. In 1947 a survey of losses calculated that in Graaff-Reinet and Aberdeen districts alone over 7,000 morgen had been planted.[129]

The turning-point in the debate was not contingent upon the figures. It came in 1931 as a result of a trip to Australia by the Secretary of Agriculture, Colonel Williams (the last of British background), and Gerard Bekker, Nationalist MP for Steynsburg. They travelled with a South Africa delegation for a wool conference and used the opportunity to examine biological control methods. Both were bowled over by Australian hospitality and their programme. Williams telegrammed home: 'Bekker and I convinced cactoblastis complete solution.'[130] They were intrigued to find that spekboom had been introduced into Queensland and grew 'abundantly' in areas cleared of opuntia by cactoblastis.[131]

Williams's enthusiasm, together with the perceived intensification of the problem in South Africa and the support of Nationalist MPs, shifted Kemp's position. Rumours circulated that some farmers would take the matter into their own hands and introduce cactoblastis. This had always been the entomologists' fear. A chance introduction might have unpredictable results. If South African officials knew of events in southern Madagascar in the late 1920s, these would have shown their concerns to be well founded. An unauthorized introduction of cochineal had a major effect on that region's prickly pear, which had become central to the rural economy. Livestock died and widespread hardship followed.[132]

The Department's hand was forced when Bekker started to raise money for cactoblastis importation. Williams insisted that the Department had to control all insect introductions centrally. So sensitive was the issue that the order for new cactoblastis eggs was sent to Australia in code; the authorities there had great difficulty in interpreting the message. The Department was reasonably open about the possibility that spineless cactus would be lost and South Africa might have to live with any imported insect in the long term.[133] In 1932 the government passed legislation indemnifying itself against financial claims arising from damage to spineless cactus plantations.

[129] LDB 1263 R1688, vol. 8, cutting from *Farmer's Weekly*, 1 Oct. 1947.

[130] PTA LDB 1711 R2846, vol. 1, telegram, Williams to Department of Agriculture, 22 June 1931.

[131] Ibid., R. J. Tillyard, memorandum re Introduction of Insect Enemies of Prickly Pear into South Africa, 19 July 1931.

[132] Karen Middleton, 'Who Killed "Malagasy Cactus"? Science, Environment and Colonialism in Southern Madagascar (1924–1930)', *JSAS* 25: 2 (1999).

[133] PTA LDB 1711 R2846, vol. 1, Sec. Ag. to Editor, *Eastern Province Herald*, Port Elizabeth, 8 Aug. 1930.

Cactoblastis eggs were brought back to Pretoria under quarantine late in
1932. Petty, who visited Australia, was already warning against unrealistic
expectations. South Africa's pest species differed from those in Australia:
they were taller, tended to have harder stems, and were usually less dense.[134]
Cactoblastis had not controlled the giant species in Australia, such as a
20,000-acre patch of *O. streptacantha*, similar to the doornblad, in
Queensland. South Africa also proved to be less hospitable to the cactoblastis.
Within a couple of months a parasite attacked the insects in their Pretoria
cages, causing high mortality.[135] Reproduction rates improved when a station
was opened at Graaff-Reinet in November 1933, although they remained
half those achieved in Australia.[136]

In March 1934 the first eggs were put in the veld in Graaff-Reinet,
Cradock, and Uitenhage. A number of problems beset the South African
campaign. Australian experience suggested that success depended upon a
single rapid release with wide insect distribution, before the enemies of the
cactoblastis gathered their forces. A critical mass was essential in order to
minimize the possibility of balance being reached quickly between the insect
and its host. This was not achieved in South Africa, and it was a year before
the first releases were supplemented with more systematic infestation at
10-mile intervals.[137] When the front was broadened opposition was encountered, notably from Africans in Middledrift: they supported eradication of
jointed cactus but not prickly pear.[138]

A further decision facing the Department was whether to continue the
mechanical eradication and poisoning programmes under the provincial and
local authorities. With additional funding these were now making more
impact. Pettey was concerned that there would not be enough prickly pear
leaf to sustain the cactoblastis, and that the insects themselves might be
poisoned.[139] He wanted a 5-mile gap between biological control areas and
poison areas, with preference given to the cactoblastis campaign. This issue
bred heated disputes between national and provincial officials, and about
techniques of eradication.[140]

[134] Ibid., vol. 2, Report by F. W. Pettey in Chief Entomologist to Chief Division of Plant
Industry, 24 Nov. 1932.
[135] Ibid., T. Naude to Pole-Evans, 23 Jan. 1933; 30 Jan. 1933 and 1 Feb. 1933.
[136] Ibid., vol. 3, Pettey to Pole-Evans, 15 May 1934.
[137] Ibid., Chief Entomologist to Chief Division of Plant Industries, 15 Mar. 1935.
[138] PTA LDB 1712, R2846, vol. 4, Parish memo, 7 June 1935.
[139] PTA CEN 1004, 65/2, Pettey to Chief Entomologist, 10 Sept. 1934; Pettey to E. du Toit,
15 Apr. 1935.
[140] PTA LDB 1712, R2846, vol. 4, Asst. Chief to Chief Division of Plant Industry, 7 June
1935.

It soon transpired that cactoblastis only destroyed the aerial growth of jointed cactus and not the root systems, which could sprout new growth. Even members of the Department now felt that jointed cactus was being given a lease of life by the curtailment of poisoning. A similar problem arose in relation to what were called the 'rondeblaar' varieties of prickly pear, spreading around Stockenstrom and Fort Beaufort.[141] The local MP, Fenner-Solomon, conducted a sustained campaign to persuade the government to take effective action. He had become a large landowner in the area, purchasing properties from Coloured freeholders, sometimes by unscrupulous means.[142] He certainly stood to benefit from state expenditure to clear land that he had obtained cheaply. Pettey found that along the Kat river 'the common prickly pear forms a jungle . . . reaching as much as twenty-five feet in some cases'. He counted five invader species.

In 1934, following the Jointed Cactus Eradication Act, responsibility for this weed shifted from the provincial to the national level. The Department of Agriculture decided to pursue mechanical eradication itself. As in the case of locust control, the work was combined with a scheme to relieve unemployment in these post-Depression years; between 1934 and 1936 750 European and Coloured men worked on eradication gangs in the white-owned farming areas and about 1,000 Africans in the Ciskei. When private farms were cleared, a certificate was issued to the owners and the responsibility for keeping the land clean was transferred to them.[143]

The Department then introduced new species of cochineal tested by Australian researchers working in Mexico and Argentina.[144] By 1937 they seemed very promising. Officials in charge of the Jointed Cactus Eradication Programme agreed that it was a waste of money to continue to subsidize arsenic pentoxide. Mechanical eradication by the government was stopped. Pettey focused his energies south of Graaff-Reinet town, away from the main spineless cactus plantations, and initially declined to meet requests for eggs further north.[145] In 1937 30 million eggs were bred at three stations; 200

[141] PTA CEN 1004, 65/2, E. du Toit, Officer Controlling Jointed Cactus Eradication to Sec. of Agriculture, 24 Dec. 1936.

[142] Jeff Peires, 'The Legend of Fenner-Solomon', in Belinda Bozzoli (ed.), *Class, Community and Conflict: South African Perspectives* (Ravan Press, Johannesburg, 1987), 65–92.

[143] PTA LDB 1261 R1688, vol. 5, E. du Toit to Chief, Division of Soil and Veld Conservation, 23 May 1944.

[144] Ibid., vol. 3, Chief, Division of Entomology, to Chief, Division of Soil and Veld Conservation, 4 Sept. 1940 enclosing J. W. Geyer, 'Report on the Progress of *Dactylopius Confusus* as a Biological Control Method of Jointed Cactus, *Opuntia Aurantiaca*'; PTA CEN 1004, SF65/2, vol. 1, 26 July 1937.

[145] PTA LDB 1712 R2846, vol. 4, Pettey, to Chief, Division of Plant Industry, 15 Nov. 1935.

colonies were distributed in sixteen districts.[146] The *Graaff-Reinet Advertiser* published an upbeat report on the 'Doom of Opuntia' following successes against dense thickets in the south of the district.[147] The new United Party minister, Denys Reitz, threw his support behind the campaign, and at least within government 'nobody' now denied that eradicating prickly pear, rather than salvaging spineless cactus, was 'the larger national issue'.[148]

Yet the South African campaign never ran smoothly. Ants attacked cactoblastis, especially along river beds where opuntia was sometimes at its thickest. So did a disease, probably a parasite of the genus nosema, similar to that identified by Pasteur on silkworms in France.[149] Wasps, monkeys, and baboons fed on the cactoblastis and cochineal.[150] Purple mouse droppings were found, stained with the typical cochineal dye. Ladybirds, introduced in a separate biological campaign in order to control the 'mealiebug' on citrus trees in the Sundays river valley, also ate cochineal. Such unpredictable problems threatened to undermine the whole biological campaign.

The Department did now have more resources for eradication following the huge rise in state revenues after the Depression. Over £1 million had been spent on locust eradication in 1934–5 and over £2.5 on conservation in the eight years following the 1932 Soil Erosion Act (Chapter 11). The Chief Entomologist later calculated that the Provincial Council spent about £120,000 between 1928 and 1934, and the central government a further £180,000 between 1934 and 1944, on jointed cactus eradication alone.[151] Prickly pear expenditure was even greater, and individual farmers had cumulatively spent large sums themselves. Yet compared to Australia's expenditure, South Africa's 'biological engineering' remained unambitious and progress was uneven.[152]

At the end of 1939 a new Division of Soil and Veld Conservation was established in the Department of Agriculture and took shared responsibility for opuntia control. Its weed inspectors made the first systematic survey of opuntia in 1939–41. By this time the Department distinguished formally a

[146] *Farming in South Africa* (Dec. 1937): P. R. Viljoen, 'Annual Report of the Secretary for Agriculture and Forestry for the Year ended 31 August 1937', 484.

[147] PTA LDB 1713, R2846, vol. 6, cutting, 25 June 1937.

[148] Ibid., Naude to Sec. Ag., 21 Jan. 1938.

[149] L. B. Ripley, 'Nosema Disease of Cactoblastis', *Farming in South Africa* (Aug. 1937), 325.

[150] PTA CEN 1004, 65/2, E. du Toit to Chief, Division of Soil and Veld Conservation, 11 Sept. 1940; PTA LDB 1260 R1688, vol. 3, J. C. Ross, Chief: Division of Soil and Veld Conservation, to Sec. Ag. and Forestry, 31 July 1940; ibid., Geyer, 'Report on the Progress of *Dactylopius Confusus*'.

[151] PTA LDB 1261 R1688, vol. 5, E. du Toit to Chief, Division of Soil and Veld Conservation, 23 May 1944.

[152] PTA LDB 1712, R2846, vol. 4, T. J. Naude to Chief, DPI, 23 Mar. 1936.

'biological area' in the eastern and midland Cape where insect releases were concentrated. Here, about 1 million morgen were sufficiently infested to curtail farming activities;[153] 200,000 morgen of dense pear was found in the eight worst districts.[154] Outside of the main biological areas, where no insect releases were allowed, 21,000 morgen were recorded as densely infested and 350,000 lightly.[155] There were pockets of dense infestation in the Transvaal, and widespread light infestation in the Free State and Cape. Officials thought that, while dense stands of pest pear were being reduced, the area penetrated by opuntia was expanding.

It became clear that biological control, which had initially been touted as a cheaper and universal solution, was working only in patches. Entomologists recognized that they had a good deal to learn about the social as well as ecological complexities involved. When the state assumed responsibility, some farmers became less inclined to spend money themselves; entomologists had, after all, been discouraging poisoning. The halting of mechanical eradication was resulting in further spread in some districts. Entomological developments reinforced a change of approach. In 1939 a new cochineal, *Dactylopius opuntiae*, proved effective against the hard stems of the larger doornblad, so resistant to other insects, and they seemed to thrive best of all when the pear was first cut. The Chief Entomologist accepted that systematic felling of the tougher trees should accompany the laying of *D. opuntiae*; eradication would require simultaneous mechanical and biological approaches.

Reinvolving farmers on a more compulsory basis was a necessary part of this strategy, and the recently passed Weeds Acts (1937 and 1939) provided scope for doing so.[156] Ironically, this could not be imposed on farmers in the 'biological area' of dense infestation because it was unenforceable. But the Department felt that it could be extended to areas of light infestation, especially to the north of Graaff-Reinet and Cradock, where spineless cactus plantations were widespread. If doornblad was cleared in such areas, there would be no bridging-points that could serve to spread the insects to spineless plantations. Small-scale chance transfers could be dealt with by manual clearance of eggs or larvae.

Although the Department was prepared to sacrifice spineless cactus, it was still attempting to follow a strategy that might protect these plantations by

[153] *Farming in South Africa* (May 1942), 300–4: R. du Toit, Professional Officer (Weed Control), Division of Soil and Veld Conservation, 'The Spread of Prickly Pear in the Union'.

[154] PTA LDB 1260, R1688, Pettey to Chief, Division of Entomology, 1 Aug. 1941.

[155] du Toit, 'The Spread of Prickly Pear in the Union'.

[156] PTA LDB 1260, R1688, vol. 3, J. S. Taylor, Entomologist, Graaff-Reinet, to Chief, Division of Entomology, 19 Sept. 1940 and following correspondence.

distinguishing between biological and non-biological areas. Ultimately, disagreement amongst farmers themselves made it impossible to do so. Individuals in a wide variety of districts in the Transvaal and Natal, as well as in the non-biological areas of the Cape, called for insects.[157] The Division of Soil and Veld Conservation now emphasized conservationist arguments in favour of total eradication. Prickly pear was an enemy of the natural veld. After much internal debate, the Department sent cochineal and cactoblastis consignments to nearly 200 farms in fourteen districts outside of the biological control area in 1941.[158] Unauthorized transfer continued.

The new cocktail of insects was bringing 'spectacular results' in some districts. On the coast, however, ecological factors and ladybirds produced 'retrogression'.[159] Bulldozers and tractors were tried, but there was little alternative to hard manual labour. Smuts approved the use of Italian prisoners-of-war to fell the plant. They resisted this heavy and unpleasant work, staging sit-down strikes.[160] It was only when Africans, who also reduced the costs, replaced them in 1944 that felling was successful.[161] From 1945 felling teams worked widely through the southern, midland, and eastern Cape, especially from March to June when the cochineal was at its most active and the prickly pear semi-dormant. By mid-1947 they had made sufficient progress for prickly pear to be proclaimed a weed in all cleared areas and the onus transferred to landowners to maintain clearance. Old trouble-spots proved intractible, with constant regrowth reported; the analogy of cancer was used. Yet the pear was driven back across a wide front.

The Department continued to face a spate of complaints by spineless cactus growers. A sceptical entomologist, who visited Sidney Rubidge's plantation at Wellwood in 1940, found no control of insect infestation being attempted: 'there is much talk of the great value of spineless cactus, but very few of the growers are prepared to go to a little expense and trouble in order to save it'.[162] Hofmeyr district, immediately to the north of Cradock, was the centre of political agitation. The secretary of the local Farmers' Association had planted 500 morgen of spineless cactus, grazed by livestock in a systematic rotation.[163] Demonstrators were sent in 1943 to show how plantations

[157] Ibid., Ross to Sec. Ag. and Forestry, 6 Nov. 1940 and following correspondence.
[158] Ibid., Ross to Sec. Ag. and Forestry, 13 May 1941.
[159] Ibid., vol. 4, Naude to Sec. Ag. and Forestry, 3 Sept. 1942; Sec. Ag. and For. to Minister, 8 Jan. 1943.
[160] Ibid., vol. 5, Chief, Division of Soil and Veld Conservation, to Sec. Ag., 26 Jan. 1944.
[161] Ibid., E. du Toit to Sec. Ag., 31 Mar. 1944.
[162] PTA LDB 1260 R1688, memo by J. S. Taylor, Sept. 1940.
[163] PTA LDB 1261, R1688, vol. 4, Geyer to Chief Entomologist, 19 Apr. 1943.

could be kept clear. Cochineal were easy to spot, because the sedentary females produced white waxy filaments which sheltered them; males wove a white cocoon towards the end of their life-cycle. In 1945 an attempt was made to introduce ladybirds on a large scale into Hofmeyr as an inverse biological experiment, and tests were conducted with chemical sprays. These were not effective.[164] *D. opuntiae* had spread more rapidly than they anticipated, given the problem experienced with earlier insect introductions. Flightless females were carried by the wind, and hence their movement was unpredictable.

Scattered doornblad, which farmers had not cleared, provided a bridge for the insects to reach spineless cactus plantations in many districts. The Department could find no effective antidote, and most plantations in the Karoo succumbed. By the late 1940s the area of dense prickly pear infestation was probably reduced by three-quarters.[165] The campaign was less successful against jointed cactus. In 1953 an estimated 750,000 morgen, or three times the 1930s figure, was affected. A hormone weed-killer, 2,4,5T was adopted and the Entomology Division sidelined.[166] Farmers continued to use arsenic pentoxide, injected rather than sprayed. Annual expenditure rose from about £50,000 to close on £200,000 by 1960.

In summary, prickly pear eradication was initially a class issue. It was supported in the early twentieth century largely by the same group of progressive, improving livestock farmers, and state officials, who pushed for veterinary controls and predator eradication. It was not so central an issue for the state, first because the pest pear affected only a limited number of districts, and secondly because many found the plant useful. Some farmers called for coercive and compulsory measures because eradication of the doornblad presented the same problems as disease or jackals. A voluntary system of eradication, even if subsidized, could not resolve the problem of reinfestation from uncleared land.

The social base of support for eradication changed in the 1920s and 1930s because of scientific and technical developments. The first was the availability of spineless cactus, which became particularly popular with well-capitalized livestock farmers in semi-arid and arid districts because of its

[164] Ibid., vol. 5, and 1262, R1688, vol. 6.

[165] F. W. Pettey, 'The Biological Control of Prickly Pears in South Africa', *Union of South Africa, Department of Agriculture and Forestry, Scientific Bulletin*, 271 (Government Printer, Pretoria, 1948), is an extended analysis by the key entomologist involved. D. P. Annecke and V. C. Moran, 'Critical Reviews of Biological Pest Control in South Africa: 2. The Prickly Pear, *Opuntia ficus-indica* (L.) Miller', *Journal of the Entomological Society of South Africa*, 41: 2 (1978), 161–88.

[166] PTA LDB 1264, R1688, vol. 5, memorandum by R. du Toit, 1953.

value as a supplementary fodder and drought food. Secondly, biological control strategies using insects promised a total solution to eradication, but they could not differentiate between spiny prickly pear, kaalblad, and spineless cactus. As a result, some of the well-capitalized farmers, especially in areas less infested with pest pear, turned against a national eradication campaign. They preferred to use mechanical and chemical methods on their own farms, with subsidy if possible.

By contrast, many landowners whose forebears may have earlier valued these multi-purpose plants, or who found their farms overrun, saw in the biological campaign a means to clear their land at very little cost. By the inter-war years farming families were less dependent upon home manufacture of their requirements. Sheep were the Karoo priority. Their support coincided with a more systematic attempt by the South African Department of Agriculture to reach out to Afrikaner farmers and incorporate them in more scientific, and conservationist forms of production (Chapter 7). This policy outcome was not primarily related to party politics. The biological campaign was launched under a Nationalist minister who initially opposed it. And it was pursued most energetically by the United Party governments between 1934 and 1948, despite the fact that some of their rural support came from wealthier, anglophone farmers in the midland Cape, some of whom were very uneasy about the policy.

The eventual losers were both wealthier landowners with large spineless cactus plantations, and poorer rural communities, including Africans, who still used prickly pear fruit. Not all Africans were opposed to the campaigns, especially in respect of the jointed cactus, and the Native Affairs Department strongly supported it. The biological strategies were as successful in the African reserved areas as on farms. In the longer term, the survival of scattered prickly pear in the coastal districts, where African settlement tended to be concentrated, has meant that everyday use of the fruit for consumption and localized sale has continued. In the 1990s it was still possible to buy prickly pear fruit from vendors on the roadsides around Grahamstown and the former Ciskei.

Prickly pear control was a divisive and emotive issue over a long period of time in South Africa. Much of the momentum for the biological campaign, as well as the strategies adopted, was generated within the Department of Agriculture by officials, especially entomologists. To a greater extent than in predator clearance, scientific knowledge and expertise were at the heart of the enterprise. Locust control, which was to some extent coterminous with the prickly pear campaign, although it did not use biological methods, provides a closer parallel. In both cases legislation introduced further elements of compulsion into environmental regulation.

Partly because of the scientific expertise required, the central state effect-ively absorbed functions that had been assigned earlier to provincial and local government. In turn, scientific knowledge and experiment shaped the development of policy. Without the ideas and advances made in Australia, and pursued further in South Africa, biological control would not have been embarked upon. While some of the key early state entomologists, such as Lounsbury, Fuller, and Pettey, were from the United States, South Africans, notably Afrikaners, increasingly took these positions. This reflected the more systematic development of training within the country, as well as political pressures.

Crosby, amongst others, has illustrated the significance of the transfer of new species through the colonized world during the centuries of European expansion; historians have focused less on the way in which species suppres-sion by colonial governments also helped to shape ecological outcomes.[167] The South African state was reasonably successful in suppressing the pest opuntia species over the long term, and there is little doubt that the indige-nous vegetation and South Africa's biodiversity benefited. This was not initially a significant aim of eradication—it was more strongly influenced by the expectation of economic gains, social improvement, and environmental control. Throughout, however, there was some concern articulated about the impact of the prickly pear on the natural pastures. Such ecological concerns came increasingly to the fore from the 1940s, when the new Conservation Division assumed partial responsibility for eradication. Recent eradication campaigns aimed at exotic species have been more strongly influenced by aesthetic and ecological considerations.

Although state officials shaped policy in this sphere, debates about prickly pear, like those about the jackal, water, and pastures, called upon, and enhanced, environmental understanding. Most farmers certainly took their positions on the issue out of self-interest. But the controversy gave rise to fre-quent articles and debates on related botanical and entomological questions. Ecological approaches and ideas were being widely developed in the British empire at this time in the quest for agricultural improvement and conserva-tion.[168] Scientific innovation in turn expanded the field of popular environ-mental knowledge in a number of spheres, at least within the landowning

---

[167] Crosby, *Ecological Imperialism*; Lucile Brockway, *Science and Colonial Expansion: The Role of the British Royal Botanical Garden* (Academic Press, New York, 1979).

[168] P. J. Anker, 'The Ecology of Nations: British Imperial Sciences of Nature, 1895–1945', unpublished Ph.D. dissertation, Harvard University (1999); Helen Tilley, 'Africa as "Living Laboratory": The African Research Survey and the British Colonial Empire: Consolidating Environmental, Medical, and Anthropological Debates, 1920–1940', unpublished D.Phil. thesis, University of Oxford (2001).

groups. Complex ecological interactions became part of everyday rural discourse because so many people were involved in the campaigns.

An assessment of the impact of opuntia on livestock farming is difficult.
Prickly pear undoubtedly enhanced productivity on many farms in the nineteenth and early twentieth centuries. It proved especially valuable for ostrich
farmers. The rural poor benefited from the multiple uses to which the plant
could be put. Some farmers fed treated prickly pear intensively to sheep and
cattle, and Grootfontein officials encouraged this development, although it
does not seem to have been universal. At the same time, the spread of prickly
pear undoubtedly undermined livestock production in some districts.

During the first few decades of the twentieth century farmers in the
semi-arid districts sought fodder plants that could survive without irrigation
and cultivation. This change reflected the demise of ostrich production, a
concentration upon sheep, and the rapid development of borehole water
sources rather than further investment in large farm dams to irrigate lucerne.
The spineless cactus, a cultivated opuntia, became by the 1920s probably
the most important dryland fodder plant. For a significant number of well-
capitalized farmers it was a major asset that facilitated, alongside other
improvements, increased flocks and wool yields.

Spineless cactus plantations were probably not a major factor in expansion
of sheep numbers in the Cape up to their peak in 1930. Ironically, they seem
to have spread more rapidly after the early 1930s, when the biological campaigns were initiated. Many plantations succumbed when the cochineal
finally bit, and there is no doubt that individual farmers lost a good deal, for
which they were not compensated. The loss of spineless cactus in the 1940s
was one factor, together with many others, that prompted wealthier livestock
farmers to expand their landholdings, rather than intensify fodder production, as a way of maximizing production and income (Chapter 9).

In the longer term, a few spineless cactus varieties with harder leaves were
found to withstand insect infestation relatively well, although they were less
palatable for sheep. A survey of forty-one Karoo plantations in 1969 found
that all but one harboured cactoblastis, despite the fact that the oldest of them
was planted only twenty years before.[169] Cactoblastis was clearly very
widespread and had survived well beyond the period of the major biological
campaign. Cochineal was found in eighteen plantations and was then less

---

[169] D. P. Annecke, W. A. Burger, and H. Coetzee, 'Pest Status of *Cactoblastis cactorum* (Berg)
(Lepidoptera: Phycitidae) and *Dactylopius opuntiae* (Cockerell) (Coccoidea: Dactylopiidae) in
Spineless Opuntia Plantations in South Africa', *Journal of the Entomological Society of South Africa*,
39 (1976).

injurious than cactoblastis. Over a two-year experimental period it destroyed about one-third of the leaves of spineless cactus plants and greatly inhibited new cladode formation. Both insects could be controlled with insecticides. Spineless cactus plantations could still be seen throughout the semi-arid Karoo in the 1990s. However, they were no longer a central part of livestock production.

9

'The Farmer as a Conservationist': Sidney Rubidge at Wellwood, Graaff-Reinet, 1913–1952[1]

Wellwood Farm, Production Regimes, and Early Conservation Management

White farmers, or their political representatives, sat on a number of key conservationist commissions, and the progressive elite clearly shared a general concern about soil erosion. Some anglophone landowners in the midlands and eastern Cape had contributed significantly to defining South African environmental problems and elaborating conservationist concerns in respect of pastoral farming. For them, intensifying production was closely linked to environmental management; both were in their own and the national interest. In the inter-war years, however, major reports by the Drought Commission (1923) and of the Native Economic Commission (1932) tended to pin most of the responsibility for environmental degradation on the methods and practices of white and black stock-owners respectively. In more recent years critical, anti-apartheid academic research has also targeted white farmers for their environmental record.

This chapter illustrates the experience of one sheep farmer in Graaff-Reinet district who came from a conservationist background. Especially in the inter-war years, he was increasingly alert to complex ecological interactions and argued for policies that might restore his version of the 'balance of nature'. Sheep farmers were primarily concerned with making a living, often in difficult circumstances, in the early decades of the twentieth century,

[1] Thanks to the Rubidge family, and especially Richard Rubidge, for allowing access to their diaries and papers, and for their willingness to share their knowledge. The title is taken from an essay by Aldo Leopold, 'The Farmer as a Conservationist [1939]', in Susan L. Flader and J. Baird Callicot (eds.), *The River of the Mother of God and Other Essays by Aldo Leopold* (University of Wisconsin Press, Madison, 1991).

and for many of them conservationist concerns were secondary. Sidney Rubidge (1887–1970), who farmed Wellwood from 1913 to 1952, was not typical. Nevertheless, he was not entirely isolated and had wide networks amongst the Karoo farming elite; a number of them were deeply aware of the environmental context of their farming operations.[2] Their concern about depletion of natural resources echoed that of officials. Although farmers did not always see eye-to-eye with officials about the details of environmental management, these issues were publicly debated in reports and commissions, the Department of Agriculture's journal, small-town newspapers, as well as in magazines such as *Farmer's Weekly*.

Wellwood, situated in one of the oldest and most important sheep districts, has been used as an example for a range of historical developments throughout this book. Like its owner, it cannot be seen as typical. It was a larger than average farm (although by no means amongst the largest in the midland Cape) and the site of a leading merino stud. The farm was better capitalized and developed than most. But for these very reasons it is interesting. And it is one of relatively few farms on which it is possible to capture with some specificity the nature of environmental change and farming practices over a long time-span. It has been owned by the same family since 1838, and a daily diary has been kept for most of the period. Farm diaries often record only brief reports of daily routine. To a greater extent than his predecessors, Sidney Rubidge confided his ideas to paper. He also wrote a number of articles on environmental topics and kept files with cuttings and correspondence.[3] Other records survive, and the family has a strong historical sense. Moreover, Wellwood remained stable in size (around 6,700 morgen or 5,700 hectares) for the period covered in this chapter, so that numerical series can be more securely interpreted.

As owners of a model farm, and as educated participants in public life, some members of the Rubidge family are also traceable in the public record. Charles Rubidge sat on the 1877 Commission (Chapter 4); his younger brother Richard (1821–67) wrote on geology, palaeontology, botany, and denudation (Chapter 2). Sidney Rubidge pursued his great-uncle's interests

---

[2] In addition to the many articles cited above, and evidence to committees and commissions, books on the Karoo by farmers evince conservationist concerns: see e.g. Alfred de Jager Jackson, *Manna in the Desert: A Revelation of the Great Karroo* (Christian Literature Depot, Johannesburg, n.d. [c.1910–20]); G. Reilly (ed.), *A Karroo Farmer Looks Back: The Memoirs of A. A. Kingwill* (Futura Press, Pretoria, 1953); Roland Kingwill, *Anchors in the Karoo* (privately published, David Kingwill, 1997).

[3] Sidney Rubidge probably had considerably more papers and subject files. As an old man in the 1960s he sorted through them and discarded some. The surviving material does, however, give an indication as to which issues were close to his heart.

14. Wellwood Homestead

in fossils and became a leading amateur palaeontologist; there was still a fossil museum on the farm in the 1990s.[4] Charles's eldest son, Walter, did not inherit Wellwood, but he farmed elsewhere in Aberdeen, Vryburg, and Graaff-Reinet. He became an MLA, a leading progressive, and gave evidence to a number of Select Committees. Because Wellwood was well known, and situated close to the main road between Graaff-Reinet and Middelburg, it was frequently visited. It is mentioned in connection with anti-erosion works, prickly pear experiments, and in a few popular historical works.[5] Richard Rubidge, son of Sidney, compiled a short history of the stud.[6]

Focusing on a single farm provides a different perspective on conservation to that offered by scientists and officials. It is also possible to chart and con-textualize changes in Sidney Rubidge's views that do not run exactly parallel to official concerns. His understanding of ecological interactions was deeply shaped by his own interests and priorities as a sheep farmer. For this reason, it is imperative to sketch the major economic activities on Wellwood. His

[4] For a study of links between fossil-hunting, natural history, and settler identity, see Tom Griffiths, *Hunters and Collectors: The Antiquarian Imagination in Australia* (Cambridge University Press, Cambridge, 1996).

[5] Southey, *Footprints in the Karoo*.

[6] Rubidge, *The Merino*. The name Richard is, confusingly for the historian, used in alternate generations.

farming income derived largely from sale of wool, livestock, and oranges. Wellwood was primarily a sheep farm. The bulk of animals kept were merinos—between about 1,900 and 3,000 during his time (Table 9.1). Nearly 200 ostriches were kept on Wellwood in 1911. As feather prices collapsed, the numbers dwindled and Rubidge dispensed with them completely in 1927. In the 1930s he also kept a few hundred Black Persian mutton sheep, then Karakuls, and a small dairy herd.

During some years in the 1910s and 1920s, when wool prices were high (especially 1918–20, and 1924–5), this was probably his major income source. By comparison with farms in wetter, grassier districts, where heavier stocking was possible, wool sales from Wellwood were not large. For example, the Barkly East grassland farm owned by Claude Orpen, son of the soldier, administrator, and surveyor Joseph Orpen, produced two to three times more wool annually in the early twentieth century, even though it was smaller and the yield per sheep was slightly lower.[7]

The major earnings of the farm increasingly came from sale of livestock, both stud rams and excess sheep. Select rams were sent annually to the Bloemfontein sales; some were also sold direct off the farm. In the 1930s the income from this source alone exceeded that for wool. In 1931, when wool and orange prices plummeted and sales fetched only a few hundred pounds, ram sales of over £1,000 were of critical importance.[8] Even in 1940, when the flock was much expanded and wool prices were booming again, a successful (and expensive) breeding programme resulted in Rubidge's rams fetching top prices at Bloemfontein and still bringing in more than wool.[9]

Excess sheep were sold off the farm each year. Quantities varied considerably, depending on lambing rates, losses, and the state of the veld. In good years, when stock numbers were high, there were up to 800 lambs, but generally fewer. Occasional figures suggest that about 150–60 sheep were slaughtered annually for consumption on the farm—they were an agreed part of farm-workers' income in kind. Losses from disease, drought, and predators varied from a high of 457 (17 per cent of all stock) in 1924 to a low of 80 (3 per cent) in 1936. When lambing was successful, or losses were low, this would leave at least a few hundred sheep for sale, and they usually fetched about £2–3 each, or up to £1,000 in total.

[7] Avoca diaries and stock books, Barkly East, visited 1995.

[8] Diary, 31 Dec. 1931, summary for year. Numbers have been taken from a variety of references in diaries and other notes. From 1924 Sidney Rubidge usually recorded copies of his returns for the annual agricultural census and for the annual enquiries of small-stock numbers.

[9] Diary, 28 Aug. 1940.

15. Stud Ram, Wellwood, 1900

Numbers sold could also be shaped by Sidney Rubidge's decisions about stocking rates. In 1933, for example, when a searing drought destroyed the pastures, he destocked. Even though he lost about 400 animals, and only 655 merino lambs were born, he nevertheless sold an unusually high number of 940. He may also have been influenced by the need for cash. Thus, in the depths of the Depression, his income was boosted with £1,883 in off-farm stock sales, compared to £805 for wool and £242 for oranges.[10] Sheep numbers declined in 1934, and he sold fewer sheep during the following years when numbers were rebuilt. He also sometimes bought sheep.

Rubidge partly maintained his stud out of tradition and pride: 'I kept on persevering because I felt it my duty to maintain the reputation of my ancestors and of the earliest recorded flock in the Midlands.' But on a farm like Wellwood, where it was very difficult to increase sheep numbers, and at a time when wool was vulnerable to price-swings in the international market, a good stud was particularly valuable.[11] Even the biggest rams ate far less than their value, compared to other sheep. Although risks could be high, because of the price of individual animals, losses were diminished by investment in fodder. Rubidge spent about £6,000 on the stud between 1920, when he visited Australia, and 1930. By chance, he chose the right moment, because Australia banned exports of the best pedigree rams from 1929. While the returns on this investment came slowly, the stud became his mainstay and his access to the best Australian merino strains gave him an advantage. There

[10] Ibid., 1933 summary.   [11] Rubidge, *The Merino*, 39 (diary, 28 Aug. 1940).

were windfall profits from prize rams, and the reputation of his animals enhanced the value of Wellwood wool and non-stud surplus stock.

About 200 orange trees were successfully planted at Wellwood around 1860 and proved to be a very valuable long-term asset, usually producing between 150,000 and 200,000 saleable fruits a year. With an assured local market, the average annual income from oranges for the ten years from 1918 to 1927 was £446. Demand slumped in the Depression, but picked up in the late 1930s; there were some boom years in the Second World War when income exceeded £800. Wellwood had initially been well positioned, because Karoo oranges matured out of season. After the Second World War, improved transport, quality, and lengthening growing seasons in the major centres of production reduced market opportunities and income dwindled.

Overall farm income is difficult to calculate from the records available. Turnover from farm produce was seldom over £4,000 in these years and probably never under £2,000; the average was perhaps between £3,000 and £3,500 annually. Aside from expenditure on imported livestock and heavy investment on upkeep, farm-workers were a significant expenditure. Even on a sheep farm in a semi-arid area, a wide range of tasks required constant attention. The diaries suggest that, with some exceptions such as borehole drilling and shearing, the farm depended mostly on resident waged workers. The 1930 figures are not untypical: two white, eight coloured, and four African men with women, usually their wives and daughters, employed in the house and on piece work, for example, in clearing weeds. In 1919 'servants' owned over 200 animals, but this practice, which never amounted to labour tenancy, was phased out over the next two decades.

The diaries suggest that, compared to his innovative ideas about the environment, Sidney Rubidge had a relatively unquestioning approach to the racial hierarchy and labour questions. He was also a royalist and an economic conservative, generally opposed to state intervention in markets. Although he had close contacts with the moderate, partly anglicized Afrikaner families who were part of the Graaff-Reinet elite—his wife, Anne van Niekerk (married 1922) came from one of them—he could be very hostile to the 'rowdy racialists' of nationalist Afrikanerdom.

While the natural veld was the bedrock of most Karoo sheep farms, they required considerable investment if they were to be productive. Wellwood was unusual, though not exceptional, for the scale and character of early dam building and for the widespread use of fodder plants to enhance its resources. The provision of water on Wellwood (Chapters 1 and 5) is central to the family's own oral history of the farm. When Charles moved to this site an Afrikaner neighbour is said to have commented, 'the Englishman is mad to lay out a farm at so dry a place'.[12] Dam building was emblematic of enterprise and investment by English-speaking settlers, who could fatten this unprom-ising land where Afrikaners could not. The story of dam construction on a farm with no natural dam sites carries powerful images of water being con-jured in a waterless semi-desert.

In the absence of natural run-off channels into the dams, 'arms' or furrows were constructed at the base of an escarpment to collect water washing down the slopes over a large area. Problems were soon experienced with the furrows. In 1869 Walter, Charles eldest son, planted a row of *Agave americana* along the arms to stop water breaching their earth walls.[13] Harvey, the Irish botanist who spent some years at the Cape in the 1830s, noted that this 'Mexican aloe' was already a common hedge plant around Cape Town (Chapter 2).[14] Charles Rubidge had planted it for this purpose in 1862. The Southeys, on the neighbouring farm, Bloemhof, found it particularly effective, when planted around fields, against *voetgangers* (locust hoppers): 'the leaf of the aloe was so smooth that the little pests could not climb it, lots of them made a jump and got between the leaves of the aloe, and died there.'[15]

Agave reproduces quickly by sending out suckers, so that by the late 1860s there were sufficient for larger-scale planting. In addition to protecting the dam furrows, a row was planted on the boundary along the main road, as a barrier. It was not, however, used further for fencing. Charles Rubidge first imported wire in 1861, and from the mid-1870s this was the main fencing material.[16] A wire fence was completed around the external perimeter in 1890. Other uses were soon found for agave. The plant flowered irregularly, after a gap of some years, at the top of a long stem. When this dried, it became a hollow, light, strong tube, not dissimilar to bamboo. Aloe poles, as they were called, were cut on the farm and found to be durable. Timber was always at a premium in the Karoo, and the Rubidges sometimes sold poles to farmers in the area.

---

[12] Original written as 'De Engelsman is geck om op so een drooge pleck een plaats uit te leg', in Richard Rubidge (1853–1927), 'Extracts and Notes from Wellwood Diary 1845–1892', which are collated handwritten diary entries and his reminiscences compiled around 1920. In the 1946 drought SR recorded the story in his diary (5 Mar. 1946) with a wry twist. He wrote of a visit by the 'Stretton party', coming from 'green country' (of Molteno further to the east). In explaining the sit-ing of Wellwood he told them, 'the main explanation was that we were of British settler stock and not of the Voortrekker breed who abandoned (quite wisely) this area because of recurrent droughts 1834–38'.

[13] Richard Rubidge, 'Extracts'; Rubidge, *The Merino*, 12.   [14] *Memoir of W. H. Harvey*, 71.

[15] *Agricultural Journal* (23 Jan. 1890), 304. This story was attributed to 'old Mr Rubidge'.

[16] Richard Rubidge, 'Extracts'.

Agave proved particularly valuable as fodder in droughts, and by the late nineteenth century this was increasingly a major motive for further plantings. The large spiky leaves were inedible as they stood, and an effective bar to live-stock. But their bulbous base stored a great deal of moisture. If these were cut out, and chopped against the grain, they were edible. (The chunks could not be too long, or animals could choke on fibre.) As in the case of prickly pear, the agave was valuable in droughts, and one reason for its spread of in the Karoo was as fodder for ostriches.[17] The Rubidges used it especially for sheep.

By the late nineteenth century the Wellwood farming unit had become smaller. Charles Rubidge had assisted Walter, his oldest son, to purchase another farm in 1872. He then divided his own farm and gave part to another son. The Wellwood owned by Richard Rubidge from 1887, and Sidney from 1913, was reduced to its 5,700-hectares size. Richard had to take a bond of £4,000 in order to ensure a portion of the estate for his mother and younger sisters.[18] Such arrangements were not unusual amongst English-speaking families in order to keep farming units of reasonable size intact and within the family. Richard thus had a far larger bond than his father on a smaller area of land. Moreover, his period in control of the farm coincided with that when the price of wool was particularly low—less than half of the peaks in the 1870s.

Even in Charles Rubidges's time, overstocking of parts of the farm, espe-cially near the house and water sources, had produced noticeable erosion. There was more pressure on his son to stock heavily, and the erosion intensified in the late nineteenth century. Richard Rubidge remarked in 1920 that the vleis which had been so important as a water resource in the early years of the farm 'were unhappily all . . . washed out into deep dongas'; most had been formed within his recollection.[19]

Sluit formation had become a major and much publicized concern in the Cape. From the turn of the century Richard Rubidge began a programme of reclamation and later considered that he had 'always been a pioneer in the vital questions of conserving our limited rain-water supply and stopping ero-sion of the soil'.[20] The techniques of control partly involved stones and weirs to fill in sluits—a system that was promoted in the *Agricultural Journal*. There was little scope on the farm, which had no significant rivers, for reclamation by flood irrigation in the mode of the Southeys. Richard, and subsequently his son Sidney, found that the most effective method of combating erosion was to extend further the agave plantings. They planted rows all over the

[17] *Agricultural Journal* (23 Jan. 1890), reports on its use in the 1880s by farmers in Graaff-Reinet, Middelburg, and Uitenhage where attempts were made to develop agave for a fibre industry.
[18] Rubidge papers, Charles Rubidge's will.   [19] Richard Rubidge, 'Extracts'.
[20] Rubidge files, Sloot dam file, Richard Rubidge to Minister of Agriculture, 19 Aug. 1923.

farm, at intervals along the contour, not as fences but in order to control water run-off.

Eric Nobbs, later Director of Agriculture in Zimbabwe, wrote about the success of this system of erosion control on Wellwood as early as 1907.[21] Considered a model in the district, the farm was visited by various delegations including, in 1917, Graaff-Reinet town councillors who were anxious to address the problem of erosion on the municipal commonage.[22] Government officials came to study and photograph the 'Wellwood works' and lectured on them. The Rubidges had good links with Grootfontein college, which opened in neighbouring Middelburg in 1911, and they provided the experimental farm with some of its sheep.

During the 1920s Sidney Rubidge developed more complex erosion works. In 1927 he drew up a plan for controlling a forty-year-old gulley which had 'defied damming' and had diverted around stone barriers. He placed a series of agave hedges across it, interspersed with rows of prickly pear. 'This method, after my life's attention to the subject, is the only solution to stopping erosion under our conditions.'[23] He used indigenous plants to help reclaim gulleys or bare soil. 'Mimosa' (*Acacia karoo*) had been planted on the farm since the 1850s to provide fuelwood, shade, and extra grazing. Plantings were later interspersed in the agave contour hedges. He saved indigenous 'ganna' seed in 1927, if not before, and by 1930 this was being used with 'gom bosch' amongst the agave anti-erosion hedges.[24]

Sidney Rubidge became a public advocate of *Agave americana* in erosion control—especially when government officials, despite their early interest in the Wellwood system, began to emphasize earth banks in the 1930s. In an article written for the *Farmer's Weekly* in 1937, he argued that earth contours were often disastrous in the dry and stony Karoo, where grass cover was very difficult to establish.[25] Similar objections were raised by black farmers, notably in Herschel in the northern Cape (Chapter 10). Aloe hedges, he suggested, had a number of advantages. They were a 'living barrier', which kept growing and expanding, 'yearly increasing in strength, utility and resilience against storm waters' rather than eroding and decaying like earth banks.[26] They were more effective than banks of soil in catching silt, thus creating

[21] Rubidge papers, American Aloe file, copy of pamphlet by Arthur Stead, 'The Conquest of Drought Agave Americana, its use as emergency fodder and general feed; Farmers Experiences' (1922?).

[22] Rubidge papers, Cutting of Minutes of Mayor, Graaff-Reinet, for year ended Sept. 1917.

[23] Diary, 22 Apr. 1927.   [24] Ibid., 30 Apr. 1927.

[25] Rubidge papers, American Aloe file, *Farmer's Weekly*, (24 Feb. 1937).

[26] He coined or borrowed the phrase in the 1930s; the quote is from Rubidge papers, American Aloe file, *Veld Trust News*, 1, 9 (1945).

level areas behind them, conducive to the growth of a wide range of vegetation, including good grasses. They required less labour and less accurate
alignment along the contour. They were not, however, maintenance-free.
Agaves die after flowering, and if regular lines are to be maintained they have
to be replaced by young sucklings. Rubidge organized a good deal of repair
work in the 1930s. Porcupines were found to eat the roots, and farm-workers
received rewards for killing them. Rubidge later estimated that the plantings
cost him £10,000 over fifty years. But much of the soil erosion on the farm
seems to have been controlled in the inter-war period.

Stock Feed and Stocking Rates: Agave and Cactus

Government officials and progressive farmers had long argued that the
proper care of livestock required fodder crops; these would also reduce pressure on the veld during the dry months and droughts. By the early twentieth
century Wellwood had about 50 hectares of irrigable land. Sidney Rubidge
tried to irrigate fields of lucerne, oats (for hay), rye, and mealies. Results were
uneven. In 1924, for example, 12 morgen of oats failed completely, and a
similar area of lucerne gave no crop. He entered 'no agricultural crops' on
his annual agricultural census return more than once. Perennial lucerne was
the most reliable irrigated crop, but even in good years it made little impact
on the food requirements for the bulk of sheep. Fodder was used largely
for the stud rams, and—after ostriches were dispensed with—a relatively
small number of cattle, horses, and mules. While irrigation remained crucial
for the orange orchard and kitchen gardens, he gradually abandoned crops
except for a few acres of lucerne (Chapter 5).

Instead, Rubidge devoted a great deal of time and energy to perennial dryland and drought-resistant fodder plants. By the inter-war years there was a
vast quantity of agave on the farm—perhaps 30 miles in total. The problem
was not supply but the labour involved in preparing it. The serrated edges
and spiky tops had to be cut away, and the base chopped across the grain.
Workers cut leaves on the spot and deposited them in feeding boxes next to
the aloe hedges so that the difficulties of transport were avoided. There were
no tractors on Wellwood until 1946—the farm was run with little machinery.

When Arthur Stead, the agricultural chemist at Grootfontein and member
of the Drought Investigation Commission, visited Graaff-Reinet in 1922 he
found agave used more there than any other district.[27] Its most enthusiastic

[27] Rubidge papers, American Aloe file, Stead, 'The Conquest of Drought'.

advocates were the Murray brothers, one of whom had bought Bloemhof, across the main road from Wellwood. They fed it regularly to ostriches, sheep, and Friesland dairy cows which consumed up to 40 pounds each a day. Younger plants were most palatable and the flowering heads seemed particularly nutritious. No farmer suggested feeding agave exclusively. As in the case of prickly pear, it was deficient in nutrients and believed to be a purgative; it had to be part of a mixed diet, with veld or other fodder. Some farmers did find that it became a favourite food of animals which ate it regularly.

Although Sidney Rubidge noted in 1921 that agave was 'king of fodder plants' in the Karoo, he used it with caution, largely as a drought supplement rather than as continuous feed. The high water content of the bulbous leaf bases made it particularly suitable for this purpose. It was fed extensively to livestock in 1908, 1912, 1914–15, 1919, 1926–7, 1933, and 1945–6. In 1915, during a severe drought, over 1,000 sheep, including breeding ewes, were saved very largely on an agave diet. Rubidge told Stead that he would not attempt to keep so many expensive breeding animals on the farm if it was not for 'aloe'.

During the 1910s and 1920s Rubidge turned increasingly to two other introduced fodder plants: old man saltbush and spineless cactus. Australian saltbush (atriplex species), similar in character to some karoo bushes, was discussed at least as early as the 1870s Stock Diseases Commission as a potential fodder resource. By 1890 seed was available in the Cape.[28] Peter MacOwan became one of its strongest protagonists. Although it could be difficult to establish, it seemed to flourish under the toughest Cape conditions and did not become an aggressive invader, in the manner of prickly pear. Saltbush was tried on Wellwood in the 1890s.[29] In 1913 Rubidge imported seven varieties of seed direct from Australia.[30] The largest plant, which was called, aboriginal style, old man saltbush (*Atriplex nummularia*), proved most successful and was planted widely, also spreading slowly by self-seeding. When Rubidge made a calculation of the carrying capacity of the farm in 1933, he estimated the saltbush camp to have the highest capacity per morgen.[31] Saltbush plants could be grazed direct, so that labour in preparation was unnecessary.[32]

[28] *Agricultural Journal*, 2: 38 (6 Feb. 1890), 315 and *passim*.

[29] Rubidge papers; C. D. Hobson, 'Environmental and Socio-Economic Effects associated with the Planting of *Atriplex nummularia Lindl.* (Oldman Saltbush) in the Karoo', M.Sc., Rhodes University (1990)—research done partly on Wellwood.

[30] Rubidge, *The Merino*, 22.

[31] Rubidge papers, Spineless cactus file, sheet on 'List of camps on Wellwood and carrying capacity', 12 Aug. 1933.

[32] In the 1990s salt bush was widespread, and naturalized, in the camps on the flats, and around the sparsely vegetated dam area. Hobson, 'Planting of *Atriplex*', suggests that it displaces indigenous species.

Sidney Rubidge's greatest investment was in the spineless cactus. He had extended his father's thornless kaalblad plantations in 1910/11, at the same time as assigning workers to eradicate doornblad in the veld, with reasonable success. In 1915 and 1920, he imported Burbank varieties direct. Both his own experiments, and those done at Grootfontein, suggested that spineless cactus was a better all-round fodder than agave, and it required less preparation. In the 1927 drought Rubidge lost a few hundred merinos, despite having established 20,000 spineless cactus plants on Wellwood. He calculated that he needed 146,000 plants for 2,000 sheep.[33] This was a major operation, achieved with his usual thoroughness by planting teams using slabs from existing plants. By 1946 he estimated that 258,000 cactuses had been planted on 244 morgen (over 200 ha.).[34] The benefits, he reckoned, were reaped in an average 250 extra, and better-fed, lambs between 1930 and 1944. The plantations cost about £1,000 to establish, but he calculated that they were worth about £900 a year: 'the most profitable investment in the recorded history of the farm.' Spineless cactus gave him the confidence to increase his dairy herd with sixteen Jersey cows.

In 1911 there were less than 2,000 small stock on Wellwood and in the 1920s an average of about 2,400 (Table 9.1). In 1933 Rubidge calculated the carrying capacity of Wellwood at 2,253. In view of his clear concern about soil erosion, it is therefore difficult to explain why he had already driven numbers well above this, and continued to stock at much higher levels, reaching a peak of over 3,600 in 1940/1. While he clearly wished to maximize income, his strategy was probably not born out of financial desperation in the Depression. In South Africa generally sheep farmers sharply increased numbers in order to pay debts and maintain income when wool prices collapsed in 1928–31. Similarly, even though prices stabilized in the 1930s, farmers attempted to recover quickly by stocking heavily. Thus the two peaks of small stock holding in the country as a whole were 1931 (the worst year for wool prices) and 1937. In Graaff-Reinet, an early centre of intensification, the peaks were earlier.

Rubidge's holdings did not entirely replicate either of these patterns. Unusually for a sheep farmer, he does not seem to have been in financial difficulty during the Depression. He profited from successful livestock sales in 1931 and 1933. His bond of £8,700 on the farm, at a little over £1 a morgen, was less than half the estimated average in Graaff-Reinet. He certainly feared for his accumulated savings of about £7,000, mostly in local and rather vulnerable financial institutions: 'Oh how can my foolish sin be

---

[33] Diary, note pinned to diary page, 21 Apr. 1927.
[34] Rubidge papers, Spineless cactus file, memo 28 Dec. 1946.

TABLE 9.1. Stock Numbers on Wellwood

Date	Sheep		Goats	Total small stock	Cattle	Ostrich	Staff stock[a]
	Merinos	Other					
1911	1,904	10	42	1,956	65	189	included[b]
1919	1,914	420	118	2,452	81	70	included
1924 (Sept.)	2,424	240	13	2,677	36	39	170
1925 (Sept.)	2,674	188	34	2,876	32	28	90
1926 (Aug.)	2,256	130	20	2,406	32	19	
1927 (Aug.)	2,016	70	29	2,115	29		
1928 (June)	1,930	24	20	1,974	25		
1929 (June)	1,944	32	54	2,030			35
1929 (Sept.)	2,202	26	32	2,260	32		
1930 (Mar.)	2,102	38	57	2,197			
1930 (Sept.)	2,353	44	75	2,472	36	12	
1931 (Feb.)	2,377	44	36	2,457			
1932 (May)	2,690	471	38	3,199			
1933 (June)	2,642	412	16	3,070			
1934 (June)	2,231	358	7	2,596			
1934 (Sept.)	2,360	20	9	2,389	51		
1935 (Sept.)	2,496	156	10	2,662	55		
1936 (June)	2,785	293	3	3,081			
1936 (Sept.)	2,838	no records			63		
1937 (June)	2,557	373	0	2,930			
1937 (Sept.)	2,671	379		3,050	65	20	39
1938 (July)	2,500	251	0	2,751	96		
1938 (Sept.)	2,570	208		2,778	92		
1939 (Sept.)	2,450	275 karakul		2,725	101		
1940 (Oct.)		364 "		4,000			
1941 (July)	3,227	374 "		3,601			
1942	2,904	462 "	+56	3,422			
1946 (July)	1,758	210 "	+40	2,008	70	11	

Notes: [a] This is livestock owned by farmworkers ('staff'), allowed as a perquisite or right; [b] Staff stock numbers only available as part of total for whole farm.

Source: Rubidge papers.

forgiven—the sin of my hoarding up £7,000 made out of this dear old farm and not poured back straight into it again!'[35] Given his investment in Australian rams and fodder crops, he was being a little harsh on himself. And his anxieties proved unfounded.

[35] Diary, 31 Dec. 1931, summary for year.

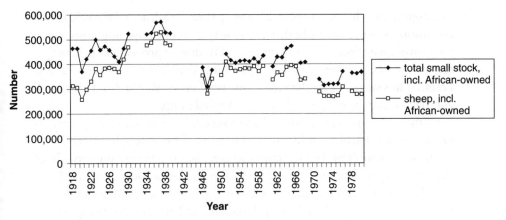

FIG. 9.1. Small Stock in Graaff-Reinet, 1918–1980

Three major factors seem to have influenced him. First, the success with fodder crops, especially spineless cactus, gave him more confidence that the bad years and dry seasons could be seen out. Secondly, he expanded water provision on the farm, especially in the 1930s. He concentrated on small dams for stock, and expended a good deal of money on clearing existing dams of silt. In 1935 alone, four successful new underground water sources were established.[36] Water shortage had been a severe constraint on stock numbers in earlier years, and the new boreholes, coupled with the sequence of relatively wet years from 1933, clearly helped to change his outlook. In 1911 twenty-four dams were recorded, as well as two wells, two boreholes, and five (weak) fountains.[37] By 1946 forty-three dams were fed from rainwater and fourteen water-storage facilities from boreholes.[38]

Thirdly—and this is most difficult factor to trace and explain—Rubidge seems to have boosted sheep numbers because he was increasingly convinced that heavy stocking was to some degree beneficial. This was not always his view. The completion of jackal-proof fencing, and the eradication of jackals on the farm by 1920, allowed him to leave animals in camps to run more freely. Previously the sheep had been kraaled at dispersed sites around the farm. It was powerfully argued at the time that leaving animals in camps for longer periods, together with rotation, would reduce tramping and increase carrying capacity. Rubidge was able to increase sheep numbers around this time in the late 1910s and early 1920s. He noted that sheep grazed more evenly and took themselves to the farthest reaches of the camps. But in 1926,

[36] Rubidge papers, Clearing Irrigation Dams file, cutting of article in *Graaff-Reinet Advertiser*, 11 Dec. 1935 by Sidney Rubidge under pseudonym, 'The Roamer'.
[37] Diary, 6 May 1911.   [38] Ibid., 2 Sept. 1946.

a drought year, when his wool yields were particularly low and the veld in bad condition, he wondered whether the new system of camps might not cause too thorough exploitation of pasturage.[39] His doubts proved justified, in that merino numbers declined from 2,674 to less than 2,000 over the next few years. At this stage, his fodder crops were not fully established and his overall approach was to be cautious, despite his fenced camps.

By the early 1930s the position had changed. During 1934 Karoo farmers experienced particular problems with grasses. An oversupply of grass may seem an unlikely curse in this semi-arid area, especially after the drought of the early 1930s. But towards the end of 1933 Wellwood experienced two months of heavy rainfall, totalling about eight inches.[40] Although the situation in August 1933 had looked desperate, and sheep were being fed on aloe, by the end of the year the veld was in 'superb order'.

Sudden good rains after a long drought were not always an unrelieved blessing, because all kinds of species went into reproductive overdrive. By 1934 unpalatable pioneer grasses, notably steekgras (adropogon species) and klitzgras, were spreading. Steekgras was inedible except when very young, and its seed stuck in the wool, penetrating the skins of sheep, which could lead to infection and death. In 1934 Rubidge was forced to shear some of his sheep early because steekgras threatened to ruin the wool completely.[41] He became convinced that wet years produced too much unpalatable grass and that this also inhibited the growth of good karoo bush. Burning was not possible on the two-thirds of the farm that was largely Karoo flats, because it would destroy the shrubs. Heavier stocking during the summer seemed to offer the best means of controlling steekgras.[42] In 1938 he noticed that the most heavily grazed camp seemed to produce the best lambing rates and best wool. Rubidge explicitly formulated and wrote down an idea which seemed to have been guiding him for some years: '*Verdict*. Karoo veldt must be kept short and tramped.'[43]

This reasoning applied to the flats of the farm, which were the richest grazing areas. About one-quarter of the farm consisted of upland areas with a thicker, sourveld cover. This was less valuable grazing, and Rubidge was keen to find how best to exploit it. Burning to remove less palatable grass and encourage fresh spring growth was one option; the grassier plateau had few Karoo bushes. Rubidge did this occasionally, especially when droughts hardened the sourveld early, as in 1933.[44] Heavy stocking was another. Since the mid-nineteenth century farmers had debated the degree to which sour,

[39] Rubidge, *The Merino*, 31.   [40] Diary, 1933 summary.   [41] Ibid., 1 May 1934.
[42] Ibid., 29 Oct. 1938.   [43] Ibid., 2 Sept. 1938.   [44] Ibid. 1933, summary.

unpalatable veld could be improved into sweeter veld through heavy grazing and dung. This was certainly thought to be the case in some coastal districts. In the 1930s Rubidge 'tried a crash treatment to get it [the sour plateau] mown down' by heavy grazing.[45] He also believed—with some justification— that this upland area with its thicker and continuous grass cover was far less susceptible to erosion than the fragile Karoo flats. This was a further factor encouraging him to increase the number of sheep on the farm.

There is an anomaly here. Whereas Rubidge was to some extent a pioneer of conservation measures, his strategy hardly accorded with some of the points that agricultural officials were trying to drive home, notably cautious stocking rates. Clearly, it was in Rubidge's interests to stock heavily in order to realize the heavy investment he had been making in the farm. Neverthe-less, he was not financially stretched and he did not express this as a motive for his strategy. He saw what he was doing as environmentally safe, and even beneficial in the sense that long-term infestation with steekgras could destroy the productive capacity of parts of the farm.

Rubidge's strategy of investment was successful. The stud improved, live-stock numbers increased, fodder resources expanded, and soil-erosion works were greatly extended. He scribbled in his diary in 1940: 'census of sheep on farm while dipping: 4,000 including 364 karakuls which is a record.'[46] It is less clear, however, whether the veld improved. His comments are uncertain on this score, and before it was clear to him the position changed dramatically.

During the 1940s the biological campaign against prickly pear took hold in Graaff-Reinet; the government considered this 'one of the finest soil con-servation tasks yet undertaken in the Union'.[47] Rubidge had expressed his concerns about cochineal to agricultural officials for nearly a decade. In early 1946, as his Burbank fodder plants were attacked and devoured around him, he wrote to the *Farmer's Weekly*, suggesting that the biological eradication campaigns were a mistake. In this and later letters he emphasized that the areas subject to uncontrollable prickly pear infestation were relatively small, whereas the areas where spineless cactus fodder had been planted were get-ting larger. Furthermore, some farmers, like himself, had organized eradica-tion of prickly pear at considerable cost, while those who had not done so were effectively being subsidized for their neglect and seeing their land increase in value. It particularly infuriated him that the best-organized farmers, who had both kept prickly pear under control and planted large

[45] Interview, Richard Rubidge, 1995.
[46] Diary, 8 Oct. 1940; he also noted on 5 Mar. 1969 that this was twice what he would then con-sider an acceptable limit.
[47] Rubidge papers, Spineless cactus file, cutting from *Graaff-Reinet Advertiser*, 24 Dce. 1945.

areas of spineless cactus, were losing out. Despite a three-year campaign, compensation was not forthcoming.[48]

His predicament was exacerbated by drought in 1946. 'Today I am viewing hungry ewes and dying stud rams', Rubidge wrote in September 1946.[49] It does not seem that he was exaggerating. He had to dispose of his dairy herd. The number of merinos declined to 1,800 and the total of small stock on the farm to about 2,000, probably the lowest since the 1910s.[50] Only 450 lambs survived, rather than the usual number of between 700–800. Boreholes dried and the veld withered: 'an inexplicable bad dream which I cannot realize as really true.'[51]

Reduced OC [Ostrich camp] sheep . . . from 134 to below 100. Used to have 200–250 rams in years 1928–1944 in this once useful camp. Today overstocked with 100 sheep and 60 springbucks [see below] while unable to maintain the last remaining 4 mules from my once-proud span of 12 to 14. Yet possibly the good was too good, so let us not pronounce the bad as too bad.[52]

As if to symbolize his problems, jackals returned to the farm for the first time in twenty-six years—perhaps their movements were related to the drought and the availability of dead and weak sheep. In 1947, for the first and only time, Rubidge had to organize 'trekking' of sheep to Middelburg district, where they spent nine months.[53] Transhumance was anathema to him; he noted with dismay in 1948 that 'for past 18 months my farming deteriorated into a trek boer'.[54]

Pastures, Wildlife, and the Balance of Nature

Sidney Rubidge's thinking about the veld evolved alongside a broadening ecological interest and understanding. One of the most striking examples of this was his recognition of the dassie (rock hyrax, *Procavia capensis*) problem. In 1930, when wool prices had plummeted and his diary is more than usually full of anxiety and disappointment, he walked up the ridge on the farm:

Shocked beyond words at the state of fountain water—now only a pool left at very top—not even 1914–15 nor 1926–27 were things so bad. And mountain sides look like a picture of overstocking whereas only 50 goats and 20 cattle inhabited that

---

[48] Ibid., circular by W. J. J. van Heerden, 25 Jan. 1948.
[49] Ibid., Rubidge to W. J. J. van Heerden, 12 Sept. 1946.   [50] Diary, 3 Sept. 1946.
[51] Ibid., 19 Jan. 1946.   [52] Ibid., 23 July 1946.
[53] Rubidge, *The Merino*, 41 (diary, 3 Mar. 1947).
[54] Rubidge papers, Spineless cactus file, note on drafts for compensation claim, 1948.

1200 morgen camp the past year. Came to the realization of a new and great plague, *Dassies*. Teeming dassies.[55]

At first his concern seems to have focused on dassies in the mountain camps. But he soon recognized that the range of the 'dassie menace' had spread. Later he told a story about how he was sitting in his office at the farmhouse when he heard scratching and scampering outside.[56] On investigation, he saw dassies on the wall near the house. Usually they were shy and timid, and confined themselves to the ridge; here they were brazenly scavenging for food right under his nose.

While I have no evidence that Rubidge heard about excess dassies elsewhere, the danger of animal plagues had been more broadly canvassed for a long period at the Cape. From the late nineteenth century some concern had been evinced about the environmental costs of killing predators (Chapter 6). F. W. Fitzsimons, Director of the Port Elizabeth Museum, wrote and spoke widely about raptor preservation during the 1920s as a means of controlling insects and small mammals; 'the balance of nature', in this respect, he felt, 'was perfect before the advent of man'.[57] Rubidge consulted Fitzsimons on the dassie problem and compared dassies 'to the rabbit pest in Australia'.

The *Farmer's Weekly* published Rubidge's ideas in 1933 alongside another article on baboons, under the headline 'Readjustments of Nature's Balance Enter the Baboon and the Dassie'.[58] That on baboons presented a more typical farmer's view in concentrating on their destructive capacity rather than on the cause of the problem. The author saw baboons as even worse than jackals: 'the jackal attacked only our stock, but "Mr. Kees" attacks our crops and our livestock.' Baboons could not be contained by fences; they were found 'tearing lambs limb from limb' and 'making off with pieces of flesh and skins in their jaws and hands'.

Rubidge was more reflective in examining why dassies had swept down from the mountains to the plains. 'The dassie', he argued, 'is one of the many "substitutional pests" brought about by our successful endeavour to exterminate the once arch-pests of farming, namely the jackal and the red-cat.' The problem was compounded by the farmers' war against the *lammervanger* ('lamb-catcher'; the black eagle). Farmers felt all eagles to be greedy predators of lambs. Dassies were freed from the threat of their predators and in turn

---

[55] Diary, 19 Dec. 1930.   [56] Information from Richard Rubidge, Dec. 1995.
[57] CA PAS 1/113, V4 (F1), including cuttings from *Cape Times*, 28 Mar. 1924, *Argus*, 28 Mar. 1924, and *Graaff-Reinet Advertiser*, 17 Aug. 1925, reprinted as pamphlet; CA PAS 3/251 C22/G, Protection of Natural Enemies of Vermin.
[58] Rubidge papers, Plea for Protection of Lammervanger file, cutting from *Farmer's Weekly* (13 Dec. 1933), articles by Bruce Miller and Sidney Rubidge.

consumed the vegetation that should have sustained sheep. In a manner typical of farmers, Rubidge still sought the remedy in extermination of the dassie by offering a bounty on pelts. In 1933 he paid one African dassie hunter, who used dogs, £3.12s. (430 pelts at 2d. each); 763 pelts in all were collected on Wellwood. He argued strongly for a government bounty as offered for rabbit skins in Australia.

Dassies seem to have been a less urgent concern from the mid-1930s, when, first, farmers were beset by other problems such as steekgras, and secondly, sheep numbers increased. But at the end of 1945, when conditions were again very difficult, Rubidge renewed his campaign against the dassie and expressed annoyance with his earlier approach. He felt that he had failed to emphasize sufficiently protection for the black eagle, which he now recognized as the main predator of dassies.[59] Again, this was not an entirely new insight. In 1920 Peringuey, Director of the South African Museum in Cape Town, had questioned the inclusion of the lammervanger (however that was construed) in the vermin legislation, and asked whether 'any man has even seen the deed' of this eagle taking lambs.[60]

Rubidge also tried to analyse why Wellwood might have been particularly susceptible to dassies. The flats of the farm were flanked by an escarpment that provided a natural habitat and a retreat. The farm also 'unfortunately' had in the past 'more deep soil erosion than average'.[61] Dassies frequented dongas, man-made cliffs, where they lived in extended meerkat holes. Early intensive development on the farm had resulted, he felt, in more than the average length of 'pioneer stone walls' which housed dassies. Widespread agave had produced another ideal new habitat away from the mountains. The long rows sheltered dassies, and by catching water and creating small temporary vleis, nurtured green grass shoots for their consumption. In short, while the dassie problem was quite widespread, Wellwood may have been particularly susceptible because of the nature of human intervention on the farm.

Rubidge was struck in retrospect that the onset of the Depression was accompanied by a more systematic campaign against the lammervanger. A farmer from Somerset East claimed to have killed fifty-seven eagles in five years.[62] Rubidge estimated that 150 eagles had been killed on two

---

[59] Handwritten notes on cutting from *Farmer's Weekly*, 13 Dec. 1933.

[60] CA PAS 1/113, V4 (F1), L. Peringuey, Director, South African Museum, Cape Town, to Provincial Secretary, 23 June 1920.

[61] Rubidge papers, Spineless cactus file, notes for 'protection for the lammervanger' article.

[62] Ibid., Lammervanger file, cutting of letter by H. P. Shone, *Eastern Province Herald*, 2 Apr. 1953.

neighbouring farms in 1929–30.[63] This figure sounds high, as the black eagle is territorial and only one pair breeds in a particular area. Perhaps other raptors were included in the figure. In any event, he was convinced that this episode was a major factor in the onset of the 'dassie menace'. He quoted farmers who had examined eagles' nests and found that dassies were the major prey, rather than lambs; his own dissection of the stomach of a slaughtered eagle suggested the same. In effect, he felt that farmers were perpetuating a myth about lammervangers. At most these took the occasional lamb, not more than domestic dogs.

Rubidge also became convinced, against the opinion of some, that jackals and red-cat (caracal) were insignificant predators of dassies. While arguing powerfully that lammervangers should be protected, he could simultaneously change his mind and accept that extermination of the caracal and jackal was achieved 'without any repercussions in the balance of nature'. This may not have been entirely consistent, in that he had suggested earlier that there were costs to jackal eradication in the spread of carrion and blow-fly infestation as well as dassies (Chapter 6).[64] By 1946 he also questioned the bounty for dassie skins, even though he continued it on his own farm. Dassies could not be caught in sufficient numbers, and hand-outs to farmers would alienate taxpayers. There was no more efficient dassie catcher than the lammervanger.

Rubidge proposed protection of eagles at a Graaff-Reinet Farmers Association meeting in 1945. There was 'jeering' at the suggestion, something that rankled with him for many years. A quiet, punctilious man, he was, by his own admission, not very effective on the political front. Although he had a wide correspondence, maintained the Wellwood reputation for hospitality, and received some support in the press for his campaign, he tended to operate by himself rather than through farmers' or political organizations. He certainly felt very strongly about the issue. Later, in assembling the file of cuttings on the controversy, he drew some striking, naive cartoons that depicted large dassies with ferocious teeth, dripping with blood, over the graves of eagles. A caption was attached: 'monarch of all we survey.'

The Graaff-Reinet Divisional Council agreed to introduce a bounty on dassies, but insisted on maintaining that on eagles. In 1947 it paid rewards on 19,562 dassie skins (at 6d. each), 2,623 baboon skins, and thirty eagles.[65] Rubidge argued that this would have minimal effect because it was a contradictory policy; the dead eagles would probably have caught as many dassies as

---

[63] Ibid., cutting of letter by Sidney Rubidge in *Eastern Province Herald*, 27 Mar. 1953.

[64] Diary, 3 Feb. 1932.

[65] Rubidge papers, Lammervanger file, cutting from *Graaff-Reinet Advertiser*, 8 Jan. 1948.

were brought in for reward. A recent study suggests he was not that far wrong. Nest investigations showed that 76 per cent of the prey of black eagles in the Cape as a whole, and nearly 90 per cent in Karoo districts, consisted of dassies.[66] Less than 4 per cent of total prey was domestic stock. A pair of black eagles was estimated to catch about 350–400 dassies in a year, so that thirty eagles may have caught 6,000 dassies. As important, the absence of eagles is thought to encourage dassies to use areas of veld away from their more secure cliff homes, and therefore facilitates rapid increase and competition with livestock.

At the same time, Rubidge came up with the apparently novel idea of finding a market for dassie skins as a stimulus to their slaughter. In 1945–7 he pressed his wool agents, Coutts of East London, and his karakul agents, the Hudson Bay Company in Windhoek, to find a reliable market for dassie pelts. The idea caught on in Graaff-Reinet, and supplies were not a problem. When he received a cheque for £27.8s. from Coutts for dassie skins in September 1946 he thought it was the beginning of 'a New History in S. African farming'.[67] However, after some interest in the early exports, London and New York dealers could not shift the product. Problems were experienced in dressing and drying the small skins. More important, there was little demand for 'tropical' furs because they tended to consist of top hair only, so that they were flat and lifeless when dressed. Furs from temperate zones had under-wool, which gave them a thicker appearance. Dealers also felt that the rather stiff, quill-like base to the dassie hair would be unattractive to purchasers.[68] Exports failed. Marketing of dassie meat, eaten by farm-workers, was canvassed from time to time, without any commercial outcome.

Rubidge and other advocates of protection for eagles were eventually successful in the 1950s, although many farmers continued to kill them. Species protection and aesthetic priorities rather than dassie control clinched the argument. Even if his view of the 'balance of nature' tended to fit his own particular interests, Rubidge had developed a complex view of ecological control and intervention. The idea that the protection of lammervangers would actually benefit the veld was in direct contradiction to the widely held view that control of predators was essential to veld improvement. Most farmers were hostile to all raptors and predators. His radical view echoed that of Aldo

---

[66] A. Boshoff, 'Black Eagles and Stock Farmers', *Pelea Journal of the Eastern Cape Game Management Association*, 8 (1989), 28–33.

[67] Diary, 15 Sept. 1946.

[68] Rubidge papers, Lammervanger file, correspondence between E. Coutts and Co., East London, Hudson Bay Co., Windhoek and Rubidge, 1945–7; cutting from *Graaff-Reinet Advertiser*, 13 June 1946.

Leopold, the pioneering environmentalist in the United States.[69] As a forest officer in the late 1920s Leopold participated in a predator extermination campaign that led to an explosion, and then crash, in the deer population because of overgrazing. This taught Leopold about the 'value of varmints'.

If Rubidge's views on the black eagle were relatively unorthodox, those which he and some others were exploring on locusts were positively radical in the context of white farming opinion and departmental policies. Up to the mid-1930s Rubidge seems to have shared the general perception that the best approach to locusts, following decades of experiment by the government, was eradication by poison before they swarmed. Farmers had largely backed the government's locust campaigns, although these prompted some opposition in the African reserve areas, where there were fears that stock would also be poisoned.[70] Locust eradication also provided scarce employment during the Depression years; one farmer wryly commented, echoing earlier jibes about jackal bounties, that farming locusts was a profitable activity in his area.

Environmental problems in the mid–1930s raised doubts about the mass poisoning campaigns in the minds of a few Karoo farmers. In 1934 Rubidge privately expressed scepticism about the efficiency of the government's efforts.[71] John G. Collett of Middelburg noted later that the expensive locust eradication campaign in 1933–4 failed to prevent swarms in the Karoo.[72] The locusts swept some areas clean of grass in 1934. But it was this event that caught Karoo farmers' attention, and allowed them to see locusts in an altogether different light. As noted, many species took advantage of good rains after a severe drought. Locust hoppers tended to hatch under these conditions, which had also produced large quantities of steekgras. Some farmers noticed that locusts cleared the dangerous steekgras. Karoo bushes were not consumed.

Drawing from this mid-1930s experience, and from Australian reports, these farmers began to argue that locusts were actually beneficial. In 1938 they actively opposed the locust extermination campaigns, partly on the grounds that they were costly, too free with poison, and inefficient, but largely because they were ecologically mistaken. In the same year, as noted above, Rubidge confided to his diary that sheep were doing best in one

---

[69] There is probably no direct influence. Leopold's ideas were being formulated in the late 1920s, but only became popularized in his posthumous book, *A Sand County Almanac* (1949).

[70] William Beinart, 'The Environmental Origins of the Pondoland Revolt', forthcoming in Stephen Dovers (ed.), *Perspectives on South African Environmental History* (David Philip, Cape Town, 2002).

[71] Diary, 18 June 1934.

[72] Rubidge papers, Locusts file, letter by John G. Collett, *Farmer's Weekly*, 21 June 1939.

heavily grazed camp which was free of steekgras.[73] When his neighbour fetched two bags of government locust poison, following widespread reports of hatchings, he wrote: 'I beg to predict that time will reveal the error of the whole system . . . no pest has ever been eradicated by poisoning.' The campaign would lead to an 'eradication of the true allies of mankind and total upset of the laws of nature'.[74]

The issue was debated in *Farmer's Weekly* during the government locust eradication campaign of 1938–9.[75] Hopper outbreaks occured in semi-arid districts, including Graaff-Reinet, late in 1937 and again from November 1938 to March 1939. Swarms threatened to migrate eastward into more densely inhabited and cultivated districts. These were controlled with some success by the laying of poison bait and its distribution to farmers (ground maize bran with 3 per cent fine arsenite of soda).[76] A government locust officer argued that the expenditure was minimal compared to the scale of losses that might be caused by locusts, and that it was inconsistent to leave locust control to nature. The sheep industry would collapse without chemical control of scab, ticks, keds, and blowfly.

Rubidge responded under the heading 'Hoist with the Petard of Poison Bait'. Farmers were shifting from their pro-poison position, he argued, partly because of the carelessness of government locust gangs, and partly, as in connection with blowfly and fruitfly, because when poison regimes were relaxed, pests returned. In 1933 Rubidge had abandoned the strategy of leaving poisoned carcasses to eradicate blowfly.[77] He continued to use poison for wild cats, an annoyance on the farm, at least until 1934.[78] But he seems subsequently to have reduced use of poison bait and suggested that poison had 'the effect of breeding up an intelligence so remarkable' in jackals that they would no longer succumb.[79] This argument was echoed in van der Merwe's writing on jackals in the 1950s.

Rubidge admitted that 'from earliest records, mankind has regarded locusts as 100 per cent enemy', and that 'it certainly appears like overstepping the mark of sanity to declare in favour of locusts'. But for sheep farmers locusts were at least '60 per cent allies', because they helped control steek-gras. He suggested that locusts did the Karoo 'spring cleaning', rather as

[73] Diary, 2 Sept. 1938.   [74] Ibid., 26 Oct. 1938.
[75] Rubidge papers, Locust file, cuttings from *Farmer's Weekly*.
[76] *Farming in South Africa*, 13 (Dec. 1938), 468; and 14, (Dec. 1939), 476.
[77] Diary, 1933 summary; Rubidge papers, Locust file, cutting from *Farmer's Weekly*, 21 Nov. 1963.
[78] Diary, 16 and 20 May 1934.
[79] Rubidge papers, Locust file, cutting from *Farmer's Weekly*, 7 June 1939. Rubidge did experiment with DDT as an insecticide in 1946.

Fitzsimons had argued that jackals were 'nature's sanitary corps'. While he accepted that crops might be threatened, early summer hatchings, which kept the grass under control, should in some way be permitted. Another correspondent speculated about even more complex relationships between locusts and veld. During wet years caterpillars, the Karoo ruspers, also multiplied. They ate Karoo bush but left the steekgras, allowing the latter, in the absence of locusts, to colonize. (Rubidge had noted in earlier years that caterpillars also devoured his lucerne.)[80]

Collett, writing alongside a picture of the 'curse of steekgras' in wool, bewailed the fact that 1,400 morgen of his 4,000-morgen farm was a 'solid mass of steekgras' while ruspers had swept valuable Karoo bush bare elsewhere.[81] He argued that locusts were not all-devouring, in that they did not eat Karoo bush, lucerne, agave, and prickly pear—the most valuable resources for sheep farmers. What they did eat was all grass, most crops, and insects, including the caterpillars. Farmers should now recognize their mistake: 'locusts are scavengers and were created for a very good purpose by the same all-wise God who created man and the universe.' (Rubidge does not seem to have used this kind of religious language.) Their droppings were even a valuable fertilizer for the veld. Locusts might also help to control the 'rice-ant' or termites—another perennial problem. 'To the veld they did no damage,' one correspondent affirmed, 'as coming only in good seasons they helped greatly to keep the veld short and healthy.'[82] These ideas, which clearly excited the farmers involved in formulating them, appear to be far out of step with the government strategy. The state was committed to protection of crops, which were becoming steadily more important, and the costs of diminished locust protection were too unpredictable.

Rubidge's rethinking of ecological relationships was closely bound up with his desire to maximize environmental resources for his sheep. Yet during his 1940s crisis there are hints that he began to conceive of other forms of farming. A brief history of springbok on the farm is necessary in order to contextualize this point. By the late nineteenth century large hunts had been curtailed on the farm, to be replaced by family hunts around Christmas. In 1881 all six of Charles Rubidge's sons went springbok shooting on New Year's Eve. In 1901 Sidney Rubidge 'shot a springbuck for Christmas'.[83]

In 1902 farmers in Graaff-Reinet had to hand in their rifles to the military authorities so that they would not fall into the hands of Boer commandos. As

---

[80] Diary, 12 Nov. 1911.
[81] Rubidge papers, Locust file, cutting from *Farmer's Weekly*, 21 June 1939.
[82] Ibid., H. H. McCabe in cutting from *Farmer's Weekly*, 9 Aug. 1939.
[83] Diary, 22 Dec. 1901.

a result, springbok numbers rose to an estimated 400 on the farm. This was seen as too many, because they competed with sheep for pasturage, and numbers were subsequently reduced. For the next few decades a rough balance was struck. Springbok were allowed to breed but not to increase rapidly, and numbers were monitored. During the 1930s between twenty and fifty were killed each year.[84] In 1940, however, the declaration by Smuts of martial law in order to control Afrikaner anti-war activists again resulted in farmers having to part with their guns. By 1941 the springbok count on Wellwood rose to 445. Steenbuck, which had been exterminated by traps during the jackal campaign of 1915–20, also re-established themselves.

In view of the high sheep numbers on the farm in these years Sidney Rubidge became perturbed, and in 1943–4, when rifles were regained, over 100 springbok were shot annually. When drought returned in 1945 he not only began his second big anti-dassie drive, but 154 springbok were shot in the biggest slaughter for years.[85] Despite this, 334 were counted in July 1946. As the drought worsened, and the spineless cactus disappeared down the maws of the cochineal, he decided on a further major cull. In two hunts nearly 100 were killed, including thirty-four ewes, most with kids. Rubidge was clearly upset:

Personally I sicken at this big-scale slaughter and have long vowed that it must cease, but today with the cruel prospect of continued drought I gave the reluctant order for the depletion of not more than 45 buck. These buck could be substituted with sheep . . . and provided sustenance for farm and family needs.[86]

Biltong was made and 20 pounds of meat allocated to each farm-worker family.

Rubidge noted with some surprise that the culled springbok seemed to be in good condition, even fat, despite the drought which had so badly affected his sheep. At this stage he did not take the realization further. He did try to sell springbok meat in Port Elizabeth and Bloemfontein, but the costs of railage made it unprofitable. Within a decade farmers such as Walter Murray, across the main road at Bloemhof, were exploring the idea that wildlife, so well adapted to Karoo veld, could be more systematically farmed. By the early 1950s ecologists working in Africa were advocating the same idea in publications.[87] Bloemhof became, from the 1960s, an increasingly sophisticated game-farming operation—a strategy adopted by a number of Karoo farmers.[88]

---

[84] Rubidge papers, stock book.   [85] Diary, 4, 10, and 30 July 1946.
[86] Ibid., 30 July 1946.
[87] Material on game farming from Dawn Nell's forthcoming Oxford D.Phil. thesis.
[88] Interview, Walter Murray, Bloemhof, 1993.

Following the difficulties of the late 1940s, the family's farming strategy changed. They purchased land and relied on increasing the size of their pasturage, rather than focusing primarily on investment in fodder and intensification. Wool prices had been partly stabilized through state intervention in marketing. The wool boom of the early 1950s, driven by the Korean War, meant that successful farmers were, comparatively speaking, awash with cash. By the 1990s Wellwood was at the heart of a very large holding of over 20,000 hectares, including plots in the village of New Bethesda which had water rights. And although it had a wider range of indigenous wild animals than for most of the twentieth century, it remained essentially a sheep farm.

'Conservation', Aldo Leopold argued in his 1939 essay 'The Farmer as a Conservationist', 'is keeping the resource in working order as well as preventing over-use . . . a positive exercise of skill and insight, not merely a negative exercise of abstinence or caution.'[89] Leopold accepted that in using land, farmers necessarily disturb it, and intensive human intervention produces contradictory outcomes. He conjured a hypothetical conservationist farmer who would begin to understand the 'life drama' of different species, so that farming could become a 'subtle self-expression' in a specific landscape rather than 'blind compliance with economic dogma'. Rubidge was, like some of the farmers Leopold discussed, increasingly aware of environmental issues in his 'early fumblings for "conservation"'.

Rubidge was an intensive farmer, in the context of the Karoo, and his capacity to maximize use of the rather limited natural resources on his farm was critical to his income and position. He was not, however, particularly ambitious or speculative in orientation, and it is striking that he did not 'buy on' land during his farming years, even though the opportunity did arise. He took pride in the success with which he had invested in an inhospitable environment. Clearly, his views on the balance of nature were deeply influenced by the pre-eminence he accorded to his sheep. As a rural patriarch with a large amount of private property, he arrogated to himself the right to control and manage nature as well as people. But partly because of the family's sense of history, and his own stability as a landowner, he saw his involvement with the land as a long-term commitment with certain responsibilities. He too was reworking a vernacular approach, which was sometimes at odds with the scientific or modernist vision of the state.

We should not expect Rubidge to hold entirely consistent positions. In the first place, he was spontaneous with his pen, in a way that few farmers are, and

---

[89] Leopold, 'The Farmer as a Conservationist', in *The River of the Mother of God*, 257; further quotes from 265.

the ideas he confided to his diary were sometimes telegraphic, or in embryonic form, and could later be revised. He realized that he made mistakes. Secondly, as illustrated in the chapter on jackals, there were deep inconsistencies in the resource-oriented conservation of the time—so that veld conservationists advocated the slaughter of predators.

Thus Rubidge could defend eagles and locusts while attacking jackals and dassies, porcupines, and meerkats (which damaged dam walls). He could simultaneously stock his farm at its limit in the 1930s, arguing to himself that this was ecologically beneficial, expend considerable amounts on erosion control, and eschew transhumance. He could shoot springboks while also ensuring that they survived in reasonable numbers on the farm. His strategy was not simply self-interested. He felt that jackals and dassies were increasing beyond their 'natural' number while eagles had decreased; that springboks and eagles did have a right to exist. In other words, the fact that his ideas about the 'balance of nature' were influenced by his production regime is not to deny his sensitivity to the ecological effects of sheep farming and other interventions.

Some of the key works in the new environmental history, such as Donald Worster's *Dust Bowl* and William Cronon's *Nature's Metropolis*, address the relationship between agrarian and ecological change. They tend to emphasize environmental destruction and degradation at the hands of capitalist agriculture in the United States—not only in the 1930s but also more recently, when lessons should have been learnt. Worster concludes: 'nowhere is there much sense of living in the presence of nature: of working with and being a part of an organic order that is complex, mysterious, awesome and alive.'[90] Such absence of mind is clearly a possible outcome; carelessness about the natural world has often been a by-product of modernity.

Yet this same society produced far-reaching conservationist ideas. It is intriguing that Aldo Leopold, although himself an official and academic, was able to discern the possibility of conservationist approaches arising from people at the cutting edge of managing nature. Perhaps this is less noteworthy in a British context: for example, Keith Thomas in *Man and the Natural World* clearly sees landowners in England as amongst the early conservationists, admittedly of a far more controlled and stylized version of nature.

Sidney Rubidge cannot be taken as representative of all Karoo farmers. And sheep farming in the semi-arid Karoo may be an inadequate base for generalizations, because it depended so much on managing natural veld

---

[90] Worster, *Dust Bowl*, 238.

rather than introduced crops, which tend to transform the environment more radically. But he was not unique, and there are other specific histories to be found amongst black and white in South Africa, and elsewhere, which might allow us to explore the complexities of what Leopold called sympathetic self-expression in a landscape.

10

Debating Conservation in
the African Areas of the Cape,
1920–1950

Regulating African Livestock

My research for this book as a whole was initially sparked by the issues addressed in the present chapter: what were the origins of the conservation-ist ideas that underpinned environmental regulation in African districts?[1] African opposition to such conservationist intervention, apparently con-ceived in their best interests, is now a richly researched field.[2] In both the settler states of South Africa and Zimbabwe, as well as in British colonies, the most acute phase of rural anti-colonial struggle in the 1940s and 1950s coincided with heightened government commitment to conservation and development. Agricultural schemes, which touched on the arrangement of settlements, and the control of land, labour, and livestock, were sometimes highly effective in mobilizing rural communities against the state.

How did the South African government arrive at schemes which stimu-lated such hostility, and why did officials persist, sometimes with crusading zeal, in trying to implement them? A journey through the labyrinths of official, as much as peasant, minds is called for. A rounded answer would require a multilayered analysis, including discussion of: changing concepts of the state as a social and economic initiator; segregationist policy and political

---

[1] Beinart, 'Soil Erosion, Conservationism'.

[2] For South Africa: Beinart and Bundy, *Hidden Struggles in Rural South Africa*; W. Beinart (ed.), 'The Politics of Conservation in Southern Africa', special issue of *JSAS* 15: 2 (1989); Fred T. Hendricks, *The Pillars of Apartheid: Land Tenure, Rural Planning and Chieftaincy* (Acta Universitatis Upsaliensis, Uppsala, 1990); Peter Delius, *A Lion Amongst the Cattle: Reconstruction and Resistance in the Northern Transvaal* (James Currey, Oxford, 1996); Anne Kelk Mager, *Gender and the Making of a South African Bantustan: A Social History of the Ciskei, 1945–1959* (James Currey, Oxford, 1999); J. Beall, W. Beinart, J. McGregor, D. Potts, and D. Simon (eds.), 'African Environments: Past and Present', special issue of *JSAS* 26: 4 (2000).

control; food supply and land tenure; and the South African commitment to underpinning a migrant, rather than urban, African labour force by shoring up agricultural production in the rural supply areas.[3] This chapter is less ambitious. It illustrates the ideas and convictions of government officials who debated and shaped government intervention.[4] The evidence suggests that their approach was not merely determined by the immediate needs of metropolitan or settler capital, nor by the imperatives of segregation. Their ideas had roots that were sunk more deeply into the colonial encounter, and derived not least from older ideas about improvement and conservation.

A perusal of the major policy documents and archives on agriculture in the African reserve areas of South Africa between the 1930s and 1950s reveals a preoccupation amongst officials with soil erosion, the necessity of combating it, and the control of African livestock. The welfare of the soil often emerges as the cutting edge of justification for intervention in peasant agriculture. Conservationist ideas also deeply affected the way in which agricultural schemes were designed and implemented. Jacks and Whyte, experts in soil science and pastures, perhaps went further than most in their book *The Rape of the Earth* (1939) when they suggested that 'the white man's burden in the future will be to come to terms with the soil and plant world, and for many reasons it promises to be a heavier burden than coming to terms with the natives'.[5] Yet their aphorism captured a sense of anxiety across the anglophone world. Their global survey was concerned also with white farmers in South Africa and relied heavily on the Drought Commission for its material, speaking of the 'Great African Desert' that was in the making.[6] They saw environmental degradation as a process that could be triggered both by white settler and indigenous farmers.

In an earlier attempt to explore 'Soil Erosion, Conservationism and Ideas about Development' (1984), I suggested that conservationist concern did not arise originally out of the relationship between colonial states and African peasantries, but from the perceived difficulties facing settler agriculture.[7] The preceding chapters confirm and strengthen this argument. However, three points made there should be modified. First, too much emphasis was

[3] H. Wolpe, 'Capitalism and Cheap Labour-Power: From Segregation to Apartheid', *Economy and Society*, 1 (1972); William R. Duggan, 'The Native Land Husbandry Act of 1951 and the Rural African Middle Class of Southern Rhodesia', *African Affairs*, 79 (1980); Fred Hendricks, 'Loose Planning and Rapid Resettlement: The Politics of Conservation and Control in Transkei, South Africa, 1950–1970', *JSAS* 15: 2 (1989), 306–25.

[4] John McCracken, 'Experts and Expertise in Colonial Malawi', *African Affairs*, 81: 322 (1982).

[5] G. V. Jacks and R. O. Whyte, *The Rape of the Earth: A World Survey of Soil Erosion* (Faber & Faber, London, 1939), 249.

[6] Ibid. 250.   [7] Beinart, 'Soil Erosion, Conservationism'.

laid on the US experience as a model for intervention. It is true that South African environmental understanding grew from the late eighteenth century within a broader international and imperial context. Particular American influences can be traced, such as dry-farming strategies (Chapter 8), and soil conservation committees (Chapter 11). Especially in the 1930s and 1940s, the American Dust Bowl lent urgency to South African debates. But the preceeding chapters illustrate the depth and specificity of many elements of conservationist concern in the Cape.

Secondly, my earlier article was part of a critique of over-ambitious planning, careless science, and authoritarian intervention in Africa. There is plenty of evidence for overreach and misunderstanding by the state, both in the colonial period and afterwards. However, I suspect that in order to underline this point scholars writing in this vein have underestimated the value and interest of earlier scientific work on African environments. In retrospect, it is striking how quickly scientists and officials began to develop understandings of complex ecologies. Glossing over the growth of knowledge, which was by no means always uniform in its conclusions and prescriptions, can close off important areas for research. Historians and social scientists have to some degree been dependent on the language and concepts developed by scientists to discuss the history of ecology and conservation.

Thirdly, my article, as in the case of others, tended to highlight the increasingly coercive elements of environmental regulation in respect of Africans. Delius and Schirmer have specifically contrasted this muscular approach to soil conservation in African districts with the subsidies and encouragement offered to white farmers.[8] However, the preceding chapters show that many elements of environmental and disease management became compulsory for whites as much as for blacks. State intervention could also imply major social changes for whites, particularly the gradual curtailment of transhumance. The state, supported by scientific officials and progressive landholders, acted differentially in respect of white and African landholders, but it could be coercive towards both. Nor should we ignore a degree of African support for certain measures, such as veterinary controls, that seem to have underpinned an expansion in African livestock holdings, as well as white, in the first few decades of the twentieth century.

Following the completion of conquest in the late nineteenth century, Africans in the Cape were left with significant access to land in four areas. The Transkeian Territories, heart of major pre-colonial chiefdoms such as

---

[8] Delius and Schirmer, 'Soil Conservation'.

the Gcaleka Xhosa, Thembu, and Mpondo, formed the largest block of reserved land in South Africa as a whole. Situated along the well-watered east coast from the Kei to the Umtamvuna and Umzimkulu rivers, it was a potentially rich agricultural zone, sustaining peasant production of crops and livestock. Although Transkeian administration fell under the Secretary of Native Affairs in Cape Town and Pretoria (after Union), a distinctive system had evolved there. The white magistracy worked together with district and regional advisory councils that included African nominees and representatives. The Transkeian Territories General Council (TTGC), or Bunga, which combined with the Pondoland General Council in 1930 to form the United TTGC, developed its own bureaucracy, especially in the agricultural sphere, and ran experimental farms, agricultural schools, and a demonstration scheme.

Secondly, the Ciskei, where conquest had deprived the Xhosa chiefdoms of much of their land, consisted of smaller reserves, mission stations, and African-owned farms, interspersed with white-owned land. It included two large districts occupied by Africans alone: Herschel in the north-east of the colony, bordering Lesotho, and Glen Grey. Administered by a Chief Native Commissioner (CNC), the Ciskei had its own separate council from 1934 but did not achieve so significant a measure of local autonomy as the Transkei. Thirdly, substantial areas were reserved for Tswana-speaking people in the northern Cape. Fourthly, some Africans living on white-owned farms in the eastern Cape had limited access to land and livestock as tenants. This discussion will focus largely on districts that fell within the Transkei and Ciskei.

Many of the regulations designed to control disease and environmental ills in the Cape were extended to the African districts. During rinderpest (1897), attempts had been made to halt the disease in African areas. Scab legislation and dipping were rigorously enforced. East coast fever restrictions made an enormous impact in African areas because they curtailed free movement of cattle. Forest reserves, locust-eradication measures, and noxious weed proclamations all impinged on African lives.[9] While conservationist concerns were most urgently voiced by officials servicing the settler agriculture sector, it would be misleading to suggest that Africans were immune either from criticism or regulation.

Through the nineteenth century missionaries and settlers had commented on the environmental profligacy of African farmers and their apparent

---

[9] Beinart, *Political Economy of Pondoland*, and Beinart and Bundy, *Hidden Struggles*; Andrew Charman, 'Progressive Elites in Bunga Politics: African Farmers in the Transkeian Territories, 1904–1946', unpublished Ph.D. thesis, University of Cambridge (1998).

propensity for cutting down trees.[10] Conservation-minded officials were
attuned to any perceived threat to natural resources, from whatever source.
Some noted the denudation of densely settled and heavily stocked peasant
districts, or that rinderpest and east coast fever, while deadly to cattle, gave
a lease of life to overtaxed pasturages in African reserves.[11] Practices peculiar
to African farmers were occasionally singled out: the ox-drawn sledge, for
example, widely used in place of wagons, was thought to have a particularly
damaging effect because the routes along which it was dragged became bereft
of vegetation and thus incipient dongas.

Lesotho, with its steep slopes, vulnerable pediment soils, and dense population, was a major point of reference for the identification of soil erosion in
African areas. Kate Showers records many reports of denudation by officials
and missionaries dating back to the late nineteenth century. They saw
'numerous, vast and unsightly scars upon the surface of the land'.[12] Overstocking, lack of wood for fuel, careless cultivation, and grass-burning were
all cited as causes. The Resident Commissioner told the Basutoland National
Council in 1917: 'the fact is that your country is being washed away.'

In response to growing national concerns, the South African Secretary
of Native Affairs circularized officials about soil erosion in 1917. Coastal
Transkeian districts, such as Lusikisiki in Pondoland, with their rich grass
cover, seemed to manifest few problems. Inland districts were patently more
vulnerable. Glen Grey district council discussed erosion at some length in
1918; a white official suggested that some locations had been 'absolutely
ruined by dongas'.[13] African councillors welcomed advice, but warned that
expenditure on remedial work was not a priority and that they would not
win popular support for intervention. Alarms bells had already been sounded
in Herschel, which was geologically and ecologically an extension of the
Lesotho lowlands.

The Drought Commission heard a little evidence on African districts,
although it did not examine them systematically. Schonland, a botanist at
Rhodes University, and MacOwan's son-in-law, detailed the spread of the
'Helychrysum weed' in the Amatola range, situated between a number of
Ciskeian settlements. Much of the Crown and forestry land was let out to,
or used by, African communities for pasture. Schonland argued that it had

---

[10] Grove, 'Scottish Missionaries'.

[11] Cape of Good Hope, *Blue Book on Native Affairs*, G.12-1904, 40.

[12] Kate Showers, 'Soil Erosion in the Kingdom of Lesotho: Origins and Colonial Response,
1830s–1950s', *JSAS* 15: 2 (1989), 269.

[13] Union Archives, Pretoria, Secretary of Native Affairs (PTA NTS) 9496, 138/400, Secretary,
Glen Grey District Council, to RM Lady Frere, 15 Jan. 1918 and following correspondence.

been so heavily stocked that a 'large area is now practically useless for grazing purposes'.[14] Helychrysum was an indigenous plant, preferring altitudes over 2,500 feet, with a strong tap root and creeping side branches that blanketed the ground. It colonized bare areas, and in that sense it was useful for erosion control. It could also be attractive: 'the aspect of the plant, covering mile after mile of mountainous land, with its silvery leaves and yellow flower heads, affords an unforgettable sight.' But 'not even a hungry goat' would eat it. The Chief Conservator of Forests added his voice to the long-standing critique of African intrusions into his domain. Areas occupied by Africans in the northern Cape, he reckoned, were a 'wilderness bare of vegetation and the drifting sand a menace to neighbouring farms'.[15] Unusually, for the time, he criticized the 'Communal System' as 'disastrous to the land and to themselves'.[16]

In the 1920s the newly appointed Director of Agriculture in the Transkei turned his attention to soil erosion and, following the Drought Commission, a TTGC Select Committee was appointed to investigate.[17] Transkeian African councillors recognized the problem but resisted the idea that overstocking was a major cause. The magistrate of Glen Grey had been prompting his seniors to focus on the 'Uninhabitable Desert' in the making around him. Action in Glen Grey and Herschel was 'the most urgent in the Union'.[18] Commissions and memos from the late 1920s certainly brought considerable evidence to light, including some photographs, which indicated that erosion was reaching serious proportions.

This was not simply an official or white perception. D. D. T. Jabavu, son of the editor of *Imvo Zabantsundu*, the leading Cape African newspaper, was educated in England and visited the Tuskegee institute in the United States. In 1916 he became a lecturer at Fort Hare, founded as the first African institution of higher education. Although it was not his field of teaching, he became an energetic and articulate advocate of improvement in African agriculture. Together with the Revd East, a black American minister, he founded the Native Farmers Association in the Ciskei in 1918.[19] Jabavu was part of the self-consciously progressive African elite, who espoused modernizing ideas yet could be highly critical of government policy. He was acutely aware of soil erosion. Visiting Herschel in 1923, he saw 'soil damaged by rains which make cliffs and dongas'. Through the Native Farmers Association he attempted to highlight the issue before African audiences, stressing the link between

[14] U.G.49-1923, 104.   [15] Ibid. 122, C. E. Legat, Chief Conservator of Forests.
[16] Ibid.   [17] Charman, 'Progressive Elites', 184.
[18] PTA NTS 9496, 138/400, RM Lady Frere to CNC, Ciskei, 27 Oct. 1928.
[19] Farieda Khan, 'Rewriting South Africa's Conservation History: The Role of the Native Farmers Association', *JSAS* 20: 4 (1994), 499–516.

shortage of land and environmental degradation. W. M. Macmillan, the liberal writer and historian, who researched in Herschel in the 1920s and vehemently attacked segregationist policies, echoed such dismay about rural poverty and degradation.[20] In 1931 an African visitor to eastern Cape talked of 'land that has been carried away by the water' and of kraals abandoned 'owing to the dongas'.[21]

By the late 1920s it was commonplace for officials to view the African reserves as eroded. Established conservationist discourse intertwined with old colonial perceptions and new anthropological analyses. Africans had long been seen as deeply attached to their cattle, and the 'cattle complex', elaborated in anthropological work, helped to define an understanding of the relationship.[22] In this view, Africans valued cattle for status rather than as productive animals, and accumulated for customary payments rather than for sale. They also replicated the worst features of settler livestock farming, such as nightly kraaling. Africans were characterized as practising 'shifting cultivation', which, while it may have been appropriate in conditions of land plenty, was becoming dysfunctional because of land shortage and population increase. The very nature of peasant agriculture seemed destined to precipitate ecological collapse. This led officials to believe that visible erosion was but the tip of a recently sighted iceberg.

Undoubtedly, officials were seeing the reserves with new eyes, but it would be misleading to argue that there was no problem. Through the second half of the nineteenth century, a growing rural population was attempting to farm declining areas of land with more intensive techniques. While most of the African districts were used for pastures, plough cultivation became general, allowing greater areas of land to be more thoroughly turned. In the first few decades of the twentieth century the great majority of African families depended to some degree on wages from migrant workers, and these were often invested in livestock. There is evidence of a considerable increase in the number of cattle and sheep in African hands at this time, and holdings peaked at much the same time as those on white-owned farms, around 1930 (Fig. 10.1). Changes in family structure consequent on colonial rule and wage income compounded the effects of population growth, in that the number of household units seeking an independent base for production tended to increase.[23] The success of veterinary measures contributed in two ways to the

[20] D. D. T. Jabavu, 'Uhambelo eHerschel' [Journey to Herschel], *Imvo Zabantsundu* (1923); Macmillan, *Complex South Africa*.

[21] Charman, 'Progressive Elites', 180.

[22] M. Herskovitz, 'The Cattle Complex in East Africa', *American Anthropology*, 27 (1926); M. Hunter, *Reaction to Conquest* (Oxford University Press, London, 1936), 68 ff.

[23] These arguments are elaborated in Beinart, *Political Economy of Pondoland*.

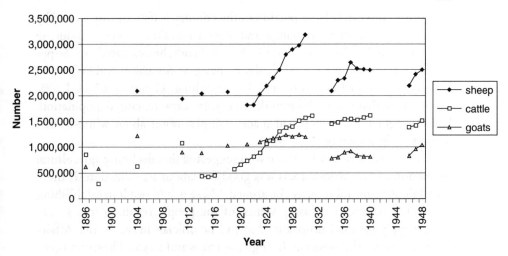

FIG. 10.1. Livestock in the Transkei, 1896–1948

build up of livestock: deaths from disease declined, and controls over the movement of livestock hampered sales. Changes in African agriculture could have profound effects on the environment, and many Africans, like settlers, were experimenting with new methods, new crops, and animals.

Russell Thornton's appointment as the first national Director of Agriculture in the Native Affairs Department in 1929 precipitated intervention.[24] Formerly principal of Grootfontein, and with a few years experience as head of a Departmental division in Pretoria, he was highly attuned to environmental issues on white-owned farms. Thornton was well aware of the large increases in cattle numbers in the country as a whole, not least because he had been trying to deal with the overproduction of beef, and low market prices, in his previous post. He had strongly advocated state provision of breeding bulls for livestock improvement on white-owned farms. For an official of his background, he was also surprisingly sympathetic to African cattle-owners who had largely been blocked from markets by veterinary regulations.

Shortly after his appointment he toured the African reserves and wrote an anxious and forceful memo on 'Denudation, Depopulation and Destruction of Native Areas'.[25] Thornton agreed that some districts, such as parts of Herschel, were 'beyond redemption'. Except for northern Zululand and the

[24] Shaun Milton, ' "The Apocalypse Cow": Russell Thornton and State Policy Towards African Cattle Husbandry in the Union of South Africa 1929–1939', unpublished paper, African History seminar, School of Oriental and African Studies, University of London (1994).

[25] Transkei Archives, Umtata, General Council papers (UTA TTA), 544/44, 'Agricultural Policy', Director of Agriculture for Native Affairs to Secretary for Native Affairs, 25 Oct. 1929.

northern Transvaal, 'a large portion of the country is temporarily ruined by overstocking'. Vegetation change and 'desert conditions' were producing weak scrub cattle. The average cow in African hands, he estimated, was 60 per cent the weight of those in the 'old days'; they gave few calves and little milk. Trek oxen were like rats, too weak for ploughing. Conditions had deteriorated so far that some Ciskeian districts were experiencing depopulation. The Drought Commission had made a similar point about white-owned districts in the midlands.[26]

Thornton took issue with those who suggested that declining agricultural production in the African areas was good for labour mobilization. If there were 'fair agricultural returns', he argued, 'these would result in establishing the wants, and ever increasing wants, of the people resulting in a steady labour supply for the Europeans'. Most Cape officials in the Native Affairs department took this position through the 1930s and 1940s. Thornton's central point was that the 'time for gentle, slowly moving measures has passed'. Despite systematic demonstration work in the Transkei, and expanding agricultural education, the region's agriculture and natural resources were 'going back not forward'.

The primary culprits, he thought, were small stock, growing rapidly in numbers, which grazed the grass shorter. Sheep and goats in African districts should be reduced by 80 per cent. The whole exercise should be done quickly, over three years, and African people should receive all the money from such enforced sales as an incentive. In order to stem the demand for bridewealth payments, cash equivalents had to be established instead. Others argued for rural banks as a necessary precursor to stock limitation.[27] To those who said Africans needed more land, Thornton responded that they could not care for what they had. His was a passionate plea for conservation, insensitive to the priorities of African life, but backed by the belief that short-term social costs would be justified by longer-term benefits: 'Nature, if led and assisted, is kindly and will help; but, if she is flouted, in the end she will punish us.'[28]

Thornton attended the 1929 Soil Erosion conference with a Transkeian official on behalf of Native Affairs, and he was keen to show that his new department could take a lead in combating environmental degradation.

[26] UTA TTA, 544/44, Director of Agriculture for Native Affairs, 'Report of Agricultural Economic Position in Native Areas in relation to Agricultural Segregation and Agricultural Policy', memo., 24 Sept. 1929.

[27] UTA TTA 518/39, Report of Recess Committee on Soil Erosion and Reclamation, District Forest Officer, Umtata, to Conservator of Forests, Umtata, 19 Mar. 1930.

[28] UTA TTA, 544/44, 'Report of Agricultural Economic Position in Native Areas', 24 Sept. 1929.

He immediately came into conflict with the Transkeian Chief Magistrate, W. T. Welsh, who was schooled in an older, liberal-paternalist mode of authority, which placed considerable value on carefully built alliances with African leaders. Welsh felt highly defensive about the Transkeian system of agricultural education and the demonstrator scheme. By 1930 the Bunga agriculture section employed nineteen Europeans and 118 Africans, of whom eighty-six (and soon over 100) were demonstrators in the field—more than the number servicing white farmers.[29] A third agricultural school for Africans was about to open, and Fort Cox, on similar lines, was flourishing in the Ciskei. The Transkei itself had three additional small demonstration farms as well as a ram-breeding centre. The journal *Umcebisi* was distributed to 2,750 people; farmers' associations and shows were being encouraged. £16,500 had been spent on erosion control and 281 stock dams. This was a major operation, not that far behind the Department of Agriculture's extension effort, on a far smaller budget. Thornton seemed to be suggesting that it was pointless.

Welsh was also deeply aware of the necessity of keeping the UTTGC on side in any policy initiative. While magistrates sat on the councils and the senior officials were all white, Africans played a significant role and frequently initiated motions. Welsh was perturbed that Thornton's explosive recommendations about a quick and enforced livestock reduction would leak out. This approach had already been rejected. As for Thornton's proposed conservationist slogans, such as 'Save our Soil and Save our Sons', Welsh suggested that they would 'not be appreciated', and were 'more likely to amuse than instruct the populace'.[30]

Welsh mobilized his own experts, the principals of the Transkeian agricultural schools, in defence. They argued that soil erosion and overstocking were not generalized and they were doing something about both. The UTTGC Director of Agriculture maintained that sheep were actually improving in quality, that there was 'no grain shortage in the Transkeian Territories' and 'no lack of oxen for ploughing'.[31] F. R. B. Thompson, the principal of Teko school (Butterworth) was less optimistic:

[29] UTA TTA 544/44, Director of Agriculture, General Council, to Chief Magistrate, Umtata, 11 Jan. 1931; Beinart, *Political Economy of Pondoland*, 85–8; Charman, 'Progressive Elites in Bunga Politics'.

[30] UTA TTA 544/44, Chief Magistrate, Transkei, to Secretary for Native Affairs, Pretoria, 17 Jan. 1930, 'The Agricultural Economic Position and Agricultural Policy in Native Areas'.

[31] UTA TTA 544/44, J. W. D. Hughes, General Council Agricultural Director, 'Comments on Mr Thornton's Report on the Economic Position', n.d. (late 1929 or early 1930).

Twenty years ago when the wind blew, one noticed the grass waving on ridge and hill in these Territories, and the cattle were in prime condition almost all months in the year. When the wind blows now the dust fills the air, and there is no waving of luxuriant grass, and the cattle are thin and poverty stricken almost all months of the year.[32]

But taxation revenues were up, the flow of labour strong, and immediate agricultural prospects promising. Welsh resented Thornton's readiness, 'after two brief and localised visits', to generalize about the absence of African progress. 'A great many experts have, from time to time, visited these Territories', Welsh grumbled, and 'he is the only one, so far as I am aware, who holds this view.'

The CNC of the Ciskei was consulted and, while he affirmed the alarming soil erosion in his region, agreed that Thornton painted too gloomy a picture, perhaps because he visited after a drought. Depopulation in districts such as Glen Grey was an intentional government policy in that individual tenure, introduced there in 1894, was designed to limit the number of landholders. As to compulsory limitation of stock, the CNC agreed it would be 'extremely unpopular with both rich and poor and would tend to destroy confidence without which no official, Agricultural or otherwise, can hope to effect anything'.[33] The Transkei system, he felt, offered the best way forward, based on 'many years of practical experience in dealing with a backward, conservative and superstitious people who resent sudden changes and whose devotion to their own customs is far more deeply rooted than is generally understood'. Welsh was quick to note that the East London Chamber of Commerce, which represented a wing of white opinion still in favour of expansion of African agriculture, also commented favourably on the work of the Transkeian demonstrators.[34]

Welsh specifically ruled out a conference proposed by Thornton because it might undermine the UTTGC's authority and set off disturbing rumours. Thornton was a persuasive man, and was able to secure backing from the Secretary of Native Affairs for a meeting in the Ciskei in April 1930. African representatives, including a journalist from *Imvo Zabantsundu*, attended and were fully alert to the potential importance of the event. D. D. T. Jabavu requested that proceedings be public so that popular suspicions would not be

---

[32] UTA TTA 544/44, F. R. B. Thompson, Principal Teko School of Agriculture, 'Agricultural Economics and Methods in the Territories', n.d. (late 1929 or early 1930).

[33] UTA TTA 544/44, Chief Native Commissioner, Ciskei, to Secretary for Native Affairs, Pretoria, 22 Jan. 1930.

[34] UTA TTA 544/44, cutting, *Daily Dispatch*, 30 Jan. 1930.

aroused. The press was allowed in only for the first morning, but Thornton was quite explicit, even then, that the Ciskei was carrying more than double the number of livestock that it should. Magistrates were quick to counter publicly that 'compulsion must never be attempted'.

Welsh had nevertheless to respond to Thornton's challenge and the issues were referred to a committee of the TTGC, with African membership, in 1930.[35] Its report accepted that 'unless the evils of overstocking are remedied, it will be impossible to cope with the soil erosion problem'. Key recommendations included voluntary reduction through marketing, which had largely been blocked by veterinary regulations. On this point the African members of the committee were strongly agreed. They had already attempted to secure a relaxation of controls for this purpose. The committee echoed the preoccupation of experts addressing white livestock farming: how to stop non-essential movement of animals in day-to-day herding activities. Cattle dipping was not done by individual owners but at council dipping tanks where large numbers of animals gathered at regular intervals. Sheep and goats were similarly concentrated for veterinary inspection and dipping on stock days. More dipping tanks and dispersed inspection would reduce the journeys backwards and forwards and hence limit trampling around the tanks and along the droving routes.

Dispersed earth dams, already being built at some pace by the UTTGC agriculture department, would diminish daily movement from kraals to water sources. Although a few officials were beginning to imagine rotated, fenced camps, the committee recognized that this was not yet feasible. One problem in leaving animals out in the unfenced communal rangelands was that they often trespassed onto cultivated fields. Fencing around lands might achieve some of the same objects of allowing 'freer ranging of livestock by day or night'.[36] Thompson, who was soon to be appointed as Director of Agriculture in the Transkei, called for this 'progressive step', not so much to allow freer grazing, but to advance crop production.[37] 'In reading the history of Agricultural Development in older countries,' he explained, 'one learns that greater production was obtained from the time the open field system was abolished in favour of fencing cultivated areas.' Progress implied new spatial parameters: 'as the artist revels in the jagged peaks of the mountains

[35] UTA TTA, 544/44, 'Report of a Committee on the Report of the Union Director of Agriculture on the Transkeian Territories', 2–3 July 1929; UTA TTA 518/39, Report of Recess Committee on Soil Erosion and Reclamation, 1930, with memoranda as evidence.

[36] UTA TTA 544/44, F. R. B. Thompson, Principal, Teko School of Agriculture, 'Agricultural Economics and Methods in the Territories', n.d. (late 1929 or early 1930).

[37] UTA TTA 544/44, Thompson, 'Agricultural Economics and Methods in the Territories'.

silhouetted against the sky, so the delight of the Agriculturalist should be "straight lines".[38] This would ensure efficiency, neatness, and higher yields.

Fencing of arable plots, Thompson believed, might also facilitate controls over grazing by livestock on maize stubble after harvest. For most African livestock owners, stubble was a valuable fodder at the height of the dry winter months. By releasing animals onto the fields, dung was also transferred with little labour. Officials, by contrast, thought that cattle 'tramp[ed] the fields as hard as a brick', diminishing their capacity to absorb water and thus reducing yields. In their view, a far better system would be to plough stalks back into soil for humus, and encourage winter fallowing to conserve moisture.

Scanlen Lehana, a progressive chief from East Griqualand, proposed the use of compulsory labour in conservation works and noxious weeds eradication.[39] He had long been a prominent supporter of the councils, and of improving agriculture, including dipping, in an area where east coast fever measures had provoked a rebellion. For him, it was the 'duty of the Natives themselves as communal farmers to work for their own benefit and salvation'. Senior white officials were divided about how much pressure could be applied. They agreed on a propaganda campaign in schools, and through 'adult erosion clubs'.[40] While they concurred that it was 'absolutely essential' to find some means of stock limitation, strategies would have to be devised within the structures of the UTTGC itself. The report did, however, recommend that confiscation of fields should be possible if occupiers failed to plough on the contour, or build protective conservation works. This measure would have constituted a major departure in land administration had it ever been implemented in this way.

Thornton's campaign was continued in his evidence to the influential Native Economic Commission. Its report provided strong and authoritative support, drawing on the rhetoric of science, for a more muscular approach to policy.[41] Ciskeian districts such as Herschel and Middledrift were again placed under the spotlight. In 1930 the Native Affairs Department agreed to make stock limitation and conservation works compulsory on any land

[38] Ibid.

[39] For Scanlen Lehana, see C. Bundy, 'Mr Rhodes and the Poisoned Goods', in Beinart and Bundy, Hidden Struggles.

[40] UTA TTA 518/39, Report of Recess Committee on Soil Erosion and Reclamation, evidence S. G. Butler, Principal, Tsolo School of Agriculture, 8 Sept. 1930.

[41] Delius and Schirmer, 'Soil Conservation', 721; Adam Ashforth, The Politics of Official Discourse in Twentieth Century South Africa (Oxford University Press, Oxford, 1990); Saul Dubow, Racial Segregation and the Origins of Apartheid in South Africa 1919–36 (Macmillan, London, 1989).

bought for African occupation under the 1913 Land Act.[42] Proclamations were passed to legalize intervention. In 1931 Thornton claimed proudly that: 'in this particular instance the black sheep has taken action which is ahead of the white sheep.'[43] Soil erosion surveys were made in forest reserves within the Transkei, and by the early 1930s attempts were made to institute regular donga reports.[44] Thornton secured the adoption of his favoured slogan: by the early 1930s 'Save the Soil' was emblazoned on the Transkei Department of Agriculture's magazine and on memos and circulars.[45]

Thornton did use the argument, in the early 1930s, that environmental regulation in African areas was vital to secure the basis for settler agrarian production.[46] The response to stock diseases provides an analogy. Scab in African-owned sheep could threaten white farmers' flocks; the ticks that carried east coast fever were no respectors of farm boundaries. Thus, diseases in black as well as white-occupied areas had to be eliminated if settler stock was to be protected. Similarly, natural boundaries, watersheds, and forests were not congruent with the division of land between white and black. Erosion in African areas could threaten the water supplies, dams, and pasturages of some settler farmers. Carlson, the Conservator of Forests in the Free State, had earlier called for controls in Lesotho in order to protect the sources of the Gariep and Caledon rivers for the benefit of both Sotho and South African farmers.[47]

Thornton found this argument about watersheds useful in order to win further funds, and garner support from other departments whose resources might prove important in conserving African areas. But it was not a major element in his advocacy of conservation, nor is it adequate as an explanation of intervention in African areas. He clearly prioritized saving the soil, everywhere, and saw this as an essential condition for the progress of black as much as white agriculture. The worst-affected districts demonstrated what were likely to become general conditions of degradation. By the early 1930s more cautious administrative officers were being shouldered aside with respect to environmental policy, and many were adopting the enthusiasms of the conservationists. The soil had to be saved if Africans were to develop.

[42] PTA NTS 9496, 138/400, Secretary, Soil Erosion Council to SNA, 27 Aug. 1930 and following correspondence.
[43] PTA NTS 9496, Thornton to Sandrock, Irrigation Dept. 28 Nov. 1931.
[44] UTA TTA 518/39, Report of Recess Committee on Soil Erosion and Reclamation, District Forest Officer, Umtata, to Conservator of Forests, Umtata, 19 Mar. 1930.
[45] Transkei Department of Agriculture, Umtata, *Umcebisi Womlimi Nomfuyi* (Advisor to the Cultivator and Stock-Keeper), journal begun in 1925.
[46] PTA NTS 9496, 138/400, Director of Native Agriculture to SNA, 2 Nov. 1933.
[47] Carlson, 'Forestry'.

Contour Cultivation and Earthworks in Herschel

Filling in dongas in African areas, or constructing dams and weirs across them, a task begun in the late 1920s, was an art in itself, but it hardly began to address the causes of erosion.[48] Forestry policy was one area where stringent regulation was pioneered: in this case, the state's capacity to reserve land facilitated controls that were far more difficult to impose on areas farmed by Africans.[49] The Bunga ran its own forestry section, and dispersed plantations were developed in order to reduce pressure on natural vegetation for building and firewood. Additional small, forested areas that fell outside of reserves had been placed under the authority of headmen who were supposed to control but not deny access.

Another central policy preoccupation was to encourage the basic principles of conservationist cultivation—farming on the contour, and some system of terracing in sloping land. Much of the land in the Ciskei and Transkei was hilly. It was not unusual for African farmers, as it had been for white, to plough up and down slopes. This method saved the strength of the oxen and was adapted to the heavy ploughs, with fixed shares, such as the American 'seventy-five', that had been in general use. The soil would be cut largely on the down-run, when gravity minimized the need for draught power; oxen would merely drag the plough up the hill. The extension service propagandized heavily in favour of contour ploughing, as well as advocating the distribution of lighter ploughs and hillside ploughs with reversible shares. (If the share was flipped over at the end of each run along the contour, soil could be thrown downhill every time.) These ploughs also reduced the need for large teams of oxen and potentially, officials thought, would diminish the number of the animals considered essential for draught. Such measures were relatively successful and they demanded less labour.

Level or bench terrace construction on sloping land was expensive and highly labour intensive. It was seldom attempted in South Africa. Both the Department of Agriculture and the Native Affairs Department advocated contour banks—usually called bunding, or ridge terracing, in the British empire. These entailed ridges of earth, about two feet high, along the contour, at a regular vertical drop within fields, or at their top and bottom. The

[48] UTA TTA 518, 'Soil Erosion General'.

[49] On Transkeian forestry and conflicts over reservations: Karen Brown, 'The Conservation and Utilisation of the Natural World: Silviculture in the Cape Colony, c.1902–1910', *Environment and History*, 7 (2001), 427–47; Beinart, 'Environmental Origins'; Jacob Tropp, 'Displaced People, Replaced Narratives: Forest Conflicts and Historical Perspectives in the Tsolo District, Transkei', *JSAS* 28 (forthcoming 2003).

16. Contour Ridges on Sloping Land

ground sloped between these terraces, so that water would wash down them. But it was well established that the quantity of soil carried by water increased exponentially in relation to the speed of the water. The scientific basis for ridge terracing was that water running down slopes would be stopped before it picked up too much pace, and before it began to scour out dongas in channels.

Contour banks entailed heavy work, which usually reduced the land area available for cultivation. Planting of crops on them was discouraged because they were supposed to become permanent; they were usually planted with grass or agave to help hold the soil. Sidney Rubidge used agave hedges, without ridges, for much the same purpose. In some areas, such as the wheat-growing districts of the western Cape, broad-based banks were planted, as part of the field, in gently sloping land.[50] But even for white farmers, contour banks often involved moving a good deal of earth without any immediate benefit. For African cultivators with smaller fields, banks could diminish the area available for planting. The technique of ridging, widely deployed in British colonial territories, which involved planting on ridges dug at regular intervals along the contour, was not much pursued in South Africa. It was better suited to hoe-agriculture systems.

[50] J. T. R. Sim, 'Anti-Erosion Measures for the Swartland', *Farming in South Africa*, 2: 250 (Jan. 1947), 17–24.

One of the first bunding campaigns pursued by the Native Affairs Department was in Herschel district, which had become a byword for environmental degradation. Bordered by the Gariep and Telle rivers, along the Free State and Lesotho borders respectively, it was also part of an important watershed.[51] This was a highly vulnerable zone ecologically, and neighbouring white farming districts of Aliwal North, Lady Grey, and Burghersdorp were also seen, a little later, as severely eroded.[52] The project was supervised by Thornton, and executed by his colleague Collett.[53] The majority of people in Herschel had resisted a local council as part of a sustained campaign in the 1920s against taxation, government intervention, and segregation. This had delayed construction of small earthworks, dams, and dipping tanks. By the time they were persuaded to accept this institution in 1930, soil erosion control had emerged as a national priority.

In many respects the early years of the Herschel project were a success. In 1931 the Herschel council, under pressure from the Magistrate, voted over £4,000 from its newly collected local tax to this purpose. A similar additional amount had accumulated from central government, earmarked originally for an experimental farm that was abandoned. Collett started work in 1933, and by the following year over 500 men and 300 women were employed on damming dongas and building contour banks. The government gave further financial assistance in the shape of a contribution to wages, as part of a relief scheme, to tide the district over the severe drought at the end of 1933. Free seed was distributed at the same time. Wages of 1 shilling a day for unskilled workers were less than those available in the major cities, but people could work for short periods locally. This proved of particular value when the harvest failed in 1934, and skilled workers received considerably more.

A sharp reduction of livestock in 1933–4, as well as the local wages available, undoubtedly facilitated the project in Herschel. Thornton was concerned that livestock would build up again if no compulsory limitation was imposed. Given the state of the district, he wanted to restrict numbers to the 'carrying capacity of the veld in years of low and diminished rainfall'.[54] The Department ruled this out and livestock numbers increased, thus averting any confrontation with local communities on this front. Conservation works

[51] PTA NTS 9496 138/400, vol. 1, W. Power Leary, Acting Magistrate, Herschel, to Secretary of Native Affairs (SNA), 20 Nov. 1918.

[52] Union of South Africa, Department of Agriculture and Forestry, *Report of the Departmental Soil Erosion Committee* (Government Printer, Pretoria, 1941).

[53] Material from PTA NTS 9496 138/400; NTS 9502 138/400(6), Soil Erosion in Herschel file; NTS 1688/15/276, Local Administration in Herschel.

[54] PTA NTS 9502 138/400(6), SNA to NC Herschel, 12 Mar. 1935.

brought a significant injection of central funding into the district, which helped to secure support for such measures. From 1934 most of the costs were met directly from the central Native Affairs budget.

Other districts were singled out for attention, including Glen Grey and Whittlesea in the Ciskei, Thaba Nchu in the Free State, Nqutu and Bergville in Natal, and Tzaneen in the Transvaal. But in 1936 over half the Department of Native Affairs's conservation expenditure (excluding Transkei) was spent on the Ciskei and half of this in Herschel.[55] Collett and his teams, working initially with ox-drawn implements, constructed 372 miles of contour banks, as well as 521 small dams and twenty-five weirs to provide water for livestock and control storm water; they planted 71,220 trees and 5,403 spineless cactus.[56] Local white farmers asked the government to halt soil erosion works for a few months in the shearing season because they could not recruit the migrant teams from Herschel who usually sheared their sheep. By the end of the 1930s some £30,000 had been spent on soil erosion works, more than in any other comparable district.

The techniques used in Glen Grey and Herschel districts were a model, viewed and visited, for other areas. Organized government intervention seemed to hold great promise in the African areas. As important, in 1934 Thornton became agricultural advisor to the British High Commissioner in South Africa. He and Collett moved into the employ of the British Colonial Service in Lesotho. They became key figures in developing even more ambitious conservation works in that Protectorate—some of the most extensive, relative to the budget as a whole, in colonial Africa.[57] Collett visited the United States in 1937 to study the latest conservation techniques.

In 1940 work in Herschel was suspended because of wartime financial stringencies and the shortage of officials. By this time over 2 million yards or some 1,200 miles of contour banks had been built. At the beginning of 1941 the Magistrate reported that severe problems were being experienced with the banks.[58] Detailed monthly reports on the project suggest that banks collapsed following heavy storm rainfall. This was not a problem unique to Herschel. In 1934 recently constructed contour banks at the Grootfontein School of Agriculture were washed away in floods.[59] A visit there by officials

[55] PTA NTS 9497 138/400, vol. 3, Thornton to SNA, 4 June 1934.

[56] PTA NTS 9497 138/400, part IV.

[57] Showers, 'Soil Erosion in the Kingdom of Lesotho'.

[58] PTA NTS 1688 15/276 II, Acting Native Commissioner, Herschel, to CNC, Ciskei, 19 Mar. 1941.

[59] PTA SAB NTS 9497 138/400, vol. 3, Telegram, Director of Native Agriculture to SNA, 13 Feb. 1934.

of the Native Affairs Department had to be cancelled. Earth banks were vulnerable to water that welled up behind them and broke through, especially so in the first couple of years before vegetation was established. This weakness was one reason for Sidney Rubidge's preference for agave hedges. Transkeian officials tended to prefer grass strips around fields, which were far easier to form, often by leaving the earth unbroken. Grass strips also diminished weed growth on contour banks. In Herschel, where grass was less dense, this strategy was not seen as sufficiently secure.

Collett attempted to respond to such problems, but in doing so new difficulties arose. The gap between the contour banks was reduced in order to slow the flow of storm rainfall. Tractors were introduced, speeding up the work. Repair teams were assigned to breakages, and by 1937 Herschel's maintenance costs were the highest of any district.[60] In that year the first reports of contour banks being deliberately ploughed out were recorded, and communities refused any fencing of eroded areas on mountain slopes in upland locations.[61] A new agricultural officer had been appointed in 1938 who chose to use prosecution as much as persuasion; those found guilty were fined and made to replace the banks at their own expense. Tractor construction required less involvement by local people and was less sensitive to the layout of existing fields. When work ceased in 1940, and the banks were left in the hands of a small maintenance team, they stood vulnerable to increasingly hostile landholders who began to plough across them. By 1941 sixty-one people had been charged and six taken to court.

Bennett Mlamleli, formerly interpreter at the Supreme Court in Bloemfontein, who had served as government nominee on the Herschel council, advised that the fines were creating great unhappiness, even amongst those who accepted the purpose of the contour banks.[62] Hosea Phooko, a well-established local political activist, who had been dismissed as a headman, launched a campaign against the fines and the methods used to combat soil erosion. Some of his support came from the remnants of the *Amafelandawonye* movement, which had so adamantly opposed all forms of government intervention in the 1920s.[63]

As the conflict came to a head in 1941, the Chief Native Commissioner (CNC) of the Ciskei was called in. A flagship project, in which the

[60] PTA NTS 10208 1/423/1.

[61] PTA NTS 9519 138/400(43), vol. 1, J. S. Murray, report on Herschel Soil Erosion Works, July and Aug. 1937. Reference thanks to Kate Showers.

[62] PTA NTS 1688 15/276 II, Bennett Mlamleli to Col. D. Reitz, Minister of Native Affairs, 24 Mar. 1941.

[63] Beinart and Bundy, *Hidden Struggles*.

Department had invested a great deal, seemed on the brink of collapse. Aside from the punitive fines, protestors explained that the banks had been built with little or no regard to the boundaries of existing agricultural plots and that the area available for cultivation had been much reduced. Recent mechanically constructed banks, spaced more closely together, were particularly unpopular. One man claimed that five lines of contour banks passed through his three lands; he had damaged 900 yards. The Department had considered total reallocation of arable lands at a reclamation conference in 1936 so that contour banks lay between rather than across fields. But there had been no opportunity to pursue this in Herschel. In any case, there were no adequate records of landholding, and intervention on this scale would have met with strong resistance. One of the major triggers for the popular movement in the 1920s was the threat of land registration, precisely because people thought that with such knowledge the government would be empowered to interfere in their holdings.

Spokesmen maintained that while some of the damage may have been 'wilful'—and thus punishable by criminal sanctions—a great deal of the damage was either inadvertent or 'due to natural causes'.[64] People in the district later suggested that the local system of channeling water around fields was ignored.[65] Although the CNC considered Herschel a notoriously difficult district to administer, and its people disposed to make an issue of any state intervention, whatever its intent, he accepted that there was some truth in the case put forward by the protestors. Some of the banks may have been breached by rainwater because of the 'feverish anxiety to complete the construction work' and the lack of maintenance; similar situations had arisen elsewhere in the Ciskei.[66]

Administrative and technical officials were again at odds. A Departmental engineer sent to inspect in 1941 reiterated that it was the people who were largely to blame. The banks were in 'an appalling state of disrepair'—over half, or 600 miles, were damaged.[67] Where sections of banks remained, they could be harmful rather than beneficial because channelled water sought out the breaks and scoured out gulleys in the fields below. 'The Native', as the magistrate explained, 'does not value the work done.' Faced with this powerful mix of engineering expertise and colonial wisdom, the CNC agreed that the people had been led astray by 'reactionary influence'. Those opposed to the works swept the local council elections. The Department did not give up;

[64] PTA NTS 1688 15/276 II, CNC to SNA, 9 June 1941.
[65] Interviews in Herschel district in 1984.
[66] PTA NTS 1688 15/276 II, CNC to SNA, 9 June 1941.
[67] PTA NTS 1688 15/276 II, Engineer, Native Affairs Dept. to CNC, Ciskei, 5 Nov. 1941.

banks were repaired in 1945 when funds again became available, and around 600 labourers were being employed early in that year. Work was only abandoned on the older banks when the more overarching rehabilitation schemes were introduced, which required complete replanning of settlement and fields.

An ecological survey by the Department of Agriculture in 1946 suggested that little had improved. Herschel's soil, once wonderful and easily cultivated, was now 'totally denuded' and two-thirds washed away.[68] Rooigras had been replaced by steekgras. 'I was under the impression that I have seen some bad soil erosion elsewhere in South Africa', the author recorded, 'but this District is just something worse than a nightmare . . . [A] bizarre effect is created with native huts standing on thin strips of soil left, with deep dongas on either side and only one way out'. Boulders were rolling down the mountains from subsidence. One official dreamed of removing the whole population from Herschel for a few years to give nature a chance 'to lick her wounds'.[69]

Conservationist interventions in Herschel promised much and were espoused by officials with great enthusiasm. They were desperate to reverse what they saw as deepening degradation, which local people, unaided, seemed unwilling and unable to address. But, as Showers argues for Lesotho, the techniques of contour bank building at this time left something to be desired. Few experiments were conducted on the effects of particular types of banks in the sensitive terrain of this region. Methods of building changed in response to design failures, or constraints of time or finance. The physical structure of the banks was at times inadequate to cope with storm run-off, and the banks required constant maintenance and protection. When banks were breached, erosion could be compounded.

Such difficulties were not insurmountable. Nor were all government works attended by similar design and maintenance problems. Various forms of contour bank became commonplace in sloping fields in the white-owned farming areas of South Africa. Grass strips in the Transkei were also more successful, as was the network of small dams for stock. But contour banks were vulnerable in Herschel for both environmental and social reasons. The conflict over them was less about conservation techniques and more about how land and natural resources were to be controlled, and who should control and use them. Officials found it difficult to understand the context of African responses. For them, the problem was that rural African people had

<hr>

[68] PTA NTS 10208, 2/423, Secretary of Agriculture to SNA, 27 Aug. 1946, enclosing 'Cross sectional survey of Ciskeian Territory'.
[69] Ibid., Secretary of Agriculture to SNA, 9 Oct. 1946.

little to offer on the technical front. Opposition was expressed as resistance to innovation, and a demand for more land.

Livestock Improvement, Culling, and Betterment

Such systematic and centrally controlled contouring drives were not replicated in the Transkei. Yet by the late 1930s the scene was set, nationally and locally, for a new phase of intervention. In 1936 the Native Trust and Land Act drove South African policy further towards segregation. African political rights were curtailed, notably in the loss of the common roll franchise in the Cape. Africans were forbidden to purchase land in most farming districts. And the terms of tenancy allowed on white-owned farms were also further restricted. As a *quid pro quo*, more land was to be purchased for sole occupation by Africans and the reserve areas extended. The South African Native Trust was funded by central government to make such purchases, and the budget for agricultural and conservation planning was enhanced. In the Transkeian Territories, the agricultural budget increased from about £15,000 in 1910 to £25,000 in 1925, nearly £60,000 in 1931, when the UTTGC was formed, and £80,000 by 1939.[70] Much of the subsequent expenditure on planning came from central funds.

Interventions in pastoral farming initially focused on stock improvement policies, based on the introduction of pedigree bulls and rams, and the elimination of scrub males.[71] These were well-established elements of extension work by the 1930s: improved breeds, providing more draught power, milk, meat, or wool per capita, might encourage rural families to reduce their holdings and thus save the grazing. In 1937 alone, when additional funding became available from the national Native Trust, 16,000 bulls and 5,000 rams were castrated in the Transkei; 1,000 pedigree bulls and 1,200 merino rams were introduced in their place.[72] It was not easy to keep exotic breeds alive in communal grazing areas, nor did they always have the all-round capabilities of locally bred cattle. In later decades the ambiguous results of early improvement programmes led to experiments in cross-breeding and attempts to identify and improve indigenous breeds.

As important were livestock sales. While officials accepted the idea that Africans tended to 'hoard' cattle for bride-wealth, they recognized that some

---

[70] Charman, 'Progressive Elites in Bunga Politics', 228.
[71] UTA TTA 539, 'Livestock general' and 518 'Soil Erosion general'.
[72] Charman, 'Progressive Elites in Bunga Politics', 189.

would be sold if opportunities arose, and they were keen to encourage a more commercial approach to livestock. The great stumbling-block was the veterinary regulations which, while they were applied across the whole country, were construed in such a way as to make export of livestock from the Transkei, where vestiges of east coast fever persisted in some districts, very difficult. Thornton pushed hard for stock sales from the start of his appointment.[73] Reducing livestock was for him the fundamental step, and any method was worth trying: selective sales might improve overall quality and African owners might find an incentive in lower dipping fees, which were charged by the head. He began negotiating for markets with canners, exporters, and mine compound suppliers. It was later suggested that a Bovril factory be established in the Transkei.

Sales were an area of policy where officials, African chiefs, and council members could agree. The latter were amongst the largest livestock owners and felt the prohibition on movement keenly as a blatant example of discrimination. Traders and speculators were equally enthusiastic about a new supply of cheap animals. The Chief Magistrate worked hard to overturn the rigidity of the veterinary regulations.[74] He would not, however, support Thornton's linked recommendation of prohibiting the import of cattle and sheep. This would be difficult to control and an infringement on the rights of both traders and African buyers. Rather, the administration relied on its established policy of castration.

Although some private transactions were possible in the early 1930s, the UTTGC was only able to pursue regular sales from 1934. Purchase for export was restricted to white buyers who could meet veterinary regulations. Significant numbers of cattle were sold, mostly for slaughter in the urban areas, in the early sales. In 1939–40, for example, UTTGC schemes alone accounted for over 25,000 exported cattle in a year, with about half going in the four months from March to June as the dry season set in.[75] Even more were sold at auction for local slaughter. African owners were paid in cash, and the 5 per cent for auctioneers came from the purchasers. Culling, which meant enforced sale rather than slaughter, became bound up with government-sponsored auctions; it was initiated in Glen Grey in 1934. But by the 1940s the response to government livestock sales was less enthusiastic, despite increasing prices during and after the Second World War.

[73] UTA TTA 544/44, Thornton to Dr du Toit, personal, 23 Oct. 1929, 'Export of Slaughter Cattle from the Transkeian Territories'.
[74] Ibid., 'Agricultural Policy', Chief Magistrate, Umtata, to SNA, 13 Aug. 1930.
[75] UTA TTA 545/44/2, 'Cattle Slaughtered and Exported during the Period July 1939 to June, 1940'.

Whereas it was unusual to get over £5 for any animal in the late 1920s, oxen averaged about £12 and cows £7 in the early 1940s.

Two key developments in the debates about livestock management in the Transkei were evident from the late 1930s: a turn against small stock, and advocacy of fenced camps. Africans had long kept goats and Cape sheep. Many adopted woolled merino sheep, especially in the drier Ciskeian and south-western Transkeian districts, in the nineteenth century. In 1930 roughly 15 per cent of the Cape's sheep were in their hands. Between 1900 and 1930, sheep numbers in the Transkei increased from less than 2 million to more than 3 million.

Sheep-farming was strongly encouraged by agricultural officers and demonstrators in the Transkei in the 1920s and 1930s as part of the drive for agricultural improvement. Sheep produced a marketable product in wool, whereas cattle were at this time largely unsaleable outside the Territories. Sheep were also thought to be better adapted to the now shorter grass in the area. As the Chief Magistrate told the Pondoland General Council in 1927, when cattle 'give way in favour of sheep . . . the better it will be for all concerned'.[76] Merino rams were featured enthusiastically in stock improvement programmes.

Influential voices began to question this policy from the late 1930s. Thompson, the Director of Agriculture in the Transkei, raised concerns about 'Agriculture in Relation to Malnutrition' in 1938.[77] He pointed particularly to the shortage of milk in this respect, and reflected on a central dilemma: how to provide sufficient draught power for ploughing, while also reducing the number of oxen. Aside from fodder, he proposed new shoulder harnesses, that might be more efficient than yokes, and community ploughing schemes. (The district council in Herschel bought two tractors for ploughing around this time.) An interesting study, which reflected and helped direct these changes, was commissioned by the Chamber of Mines from two medical doctors, Fox and Back. Their brief was to examine how economic and social conditions in the Transkei and Ciskei impacted on labour supply and the health of migrant workers.

Their report (1938) affirmed that overstocking was a major problem and blamed it largely on merino sheep, which by then greatly outnumbered cattle. Sheep were, in the words of people to whom they spoke, 'driving the

[76] *Pondoland General Council*, Proceedings at Special Session (1927), 13.

[77] Cape Archives, Chief Magistrate's papers (CA CMT) 3/952, 14/1, F. R. B. Thompson, memo., 11 July 1938: 'Agriculture in Relation to Malnutrition', forwarded to Chief Magistrate and Secretary for Native Affairs.

cattle off the land'.[78] Sheep ownership was far more concentrated amongst 'a small minority consisting mostly of Bunga councillors, headmen, and chiefs'. Cattle, they argued, were more important for poor people, in that they provided milk and draught. The accumulation of sheep was therefore pursued at the cost of food supplies for the majority. Moreover, it was sheep, primarily, that caused semi-desert conditions in the Ciskei, now threatening the Transkei, by eating the grass so short.[79] They also criticized the introduction of Afrikander bulls into the Territories; while these were sufficiently hardy to survive on the commonages, and were excellent for beef and draught, their progeny were poor milkers.

Fox and Back agreed with Transkeian officials that improved food supply would enhance both the number and health of migrant workers. In this sense, their recommendations were certainly congruent with the maintenance of the migrant labour system—although they were not specifically advocates of it. They distilled arguments that better cattle and fewer small stock were the key to improved food supplies. Malnutrition in African areas had recently been identified as a major problem, and Fox was one of the pioneers of South African research in this field.[80] The logic of this position was that culling should fall most heavily on non-bovines.

Culling (enforced sales) of any kind became a major political issue, but over the longer term it was not so greatly emphasized in South Africa as the spatial reorganization of grazing into rotatable, fenced camps along the lines specified by the Drought Commission. Thornton was deeply committed to such strategies, and the white agricultural staff in the Transkei and Ciskei were drawn partly from Grootfontein.[81] A camp system implied extensive resettlement and planning of agricultural land. The Xhosa-speaking peoples of the eastern Cape had lived in scattered settlements. Homesteads, comprising a number of huts, were often sited on higher ground, at some distance from one another, with common pastureland in between. Gardens abutted the homesteads, and cattle kraals were traditionally placed within the

[78] F. W. Fox and D. Back, 'A Preliminary Survey of the Agricultural and Nutritional Problems of the Ciskei and Transkeian Territories, with Special Reference to Their Bearing upon the Recruiting of Labourers for the Gold Mining Industry', unpublished report, Johannesburg (1938?), copy from Chamber of Mines library, 24 ff., 47.

[79] Fox and Back, 'A Preliminary Survey', 40.

[80] Randall M. Packard, *White Plague, Black Labor: Tuberculosis and the Political Economy of Health and Disease in South Africa* (University of Natal Press, Pietermaritzburg, 1989); Diana Wylie, 'The Changing Face of Hunger in Southern African History, 1880–1980', *Past and Present*, 122 (1989), 159–99, and *Starving on a Full Stomach: Hunger and the Triumph of Cultural Racism in Modern South Africa* (University Press of Virginia, Charlottesville, 2001).

[81] Fox and Back, 'A Preliminary Survey', 70 ff.

semicircle of huts. Larger fields were sometimes situated together in areas of suitable soil at some distance from the homesteads.

Officials felt that a camp system would require concentrated village settlements so that pastureland could be separated from residential and arable areas. Fenced camps could not, in their view, contain homesteads clusters. Villagization had been attempted on a piecemeal basis in the nineteenth-century Cape by missionaries on their stations, and by officials who supervised the distribution of land after conquest in the Ciskei.[82] The term 'centralization' had been used in the Cape in the 1890s, when the government compressed Tswana communities onto a narrower band of land in the northern Cape to make way for settler farms.[83] In the early decades of the twentieth century various African colonial governments had similarly tried to create denser settlements: for example, in pursuance of tsetse control or ease of administration. The Zimbabwean scheme, also called centralization, and pioneered in the late 1920s by the Native Agriculturalist, Alvord, was probably the first general attempt at villagization designed to be implemented throughout the African areas.[84]

Alvord argued that closer settlement and the rationalization of land use were essential if agricultural improvement was to be achieved. In existing settlements, crops were destroyed by cattle, lands were not in the most suitable place, rotational systems of cultivation could not be implemented, and grazing could not be controlled. Far better if all the homesteads were grouped together and arable plots demarcated in regular sizes together on suitable land. Stock limitation, conservation works, and rotational farming would all be more feasible in this context. Scientific soil surveys and the consolidation of each family's holdings into one plot could all precede spatial reordering. Alvord's ideas were translated into policy by the mid-1930s; some of the Zimbabwean officials had cut their teeth in South Africa.

South African officials elaborated on these approaches in the late 1930s. African communities in the Transkeian areas had used a variety of systems of transhumance, cattle posts, loans, and exchanges to disperse herd and flocks and save pasturage. Some of these, however, were constrained by increasing

---

[82] E.g. Cape of Good Hope, *Government Gazette*, 29 July 1847: Government Notice, 7 July 1847; Crais, *Making of the Colonial Order*; J. B. Peires, *The Dead Will Arise: Nongqawuse and the Great Xhosa Cattle-Killing Movement of 1856–7* (Ravan Press, Johannesburg, 1989), 290–6.

[83] K. Shillington, 'Irrigation, Agriculture and the State: The Harts Valley in Historical Perspective', in Beinart et al. (eds.), *Putting a Plough to the Ground*.

[84] E. D. Alvord, 'Development of Native Agriculture and Land Tenure in Southern Rhodesia', unpublished MS (1958) in the Zimbabwe National Archives, is a revealing autobiographical account of his work; T. Ranger, *Peasant Consciousness and Guerilla War in Zimbabwe* (James Currey, London, 1985).

density of settlement and veterinary restrictions. Proclamations of 1926 and 1931 gave officials and headmen the power to enforce resting of portions of location commonages in the dry winter months when grazing was at a premium.[85] (The relatively well-kept records of stock numbers indicated increasing deaths during the winter.) Earlier policy had also allowed for the allotment of new residential and arable sites in more concentrated areas in order to protect grazing; a 1934 circular provided for sites of an acre.

In 1936 the Native Affairs department initiated a nationwide conservation survey of African locations with the aim of replanning settlement 'to save them from absolute ruin'.[86] New village sites were being developed in the Transvaal: the department preferred long thin settlements along roads for ease of service provision, drainage, and sanitation. By the late 1930s Ciskeian officials were beginning to introduce fenced grazing camps on land purchased for African occupation by the Native Trust.[87] Reineke, the new national Director of Native Agriculture, wished to introduce grassland surveys of the Ciskeian locations, because rotational grazing required 'very highly specialised knowledge'.[88] Such innovations in policy were debated in the Ciskeian and Transkeian councils.

As magistrates became more enthusiastic and persuasive, so some African leaders also responded. In 1938, for example, the magistrate of Qumbu in the Transkei reported that residents of one of the locations 'desire[d] to concentrate their kraals into rough villages and so provide additional grazing for their stock'.[89] He insisted that this emanated 'from the people themselves', encouraged by their progressive Chief Ludidi. They reported that their grazing and arable lands were 'finished' and they were concerned that unless they reorganized, they might face both higher winter losses and government-imposed stock limitation. 'We would rather give up our kraals and gardens', a spokesman maintained, 'than our stock'. The magistrate, reporting on a meeting, argued that grazing would be improved, administrative controls enhanced, crime reduced, and local industry stimulated. Some villagers might even voluntarily relinquish livestock holdings because they would be able to purchase dairy products from others. Africans clearly had their own

---

[85] UTA TTA 539/43, 'Livestock General', 1930–42, proclamations 235 of 1926 and 331 of 1931.

[86] PTA NTS 10204, 1/423, SNA to CNC, Ciskei, 14 Nov. 1936 and following correspondence.

[87] PTA NTS 10208, 1/423, CNC, Ciskei, to SNA, 6 July 1937.

[88] PTA NTS 10204, 507/400 or 1/423, memo., T. G. W. Reinecke, Director of Native Agriculture, 6 June 1939.

[89] Transkei Archives, Umtata, Chief Magistrate's papers (UTA CMT) 1157/64, Resident Magistrate, Qumbu, to Chief Magistrate, 12 Sept. 1938, 'Conservation of Grazing', enclosing 'Meeting at Tsilitwa (Jafta's Trading Site) in Locn 20C on 10.9.1938'. For background, see W. Beinart, 'Conflict in Qumbu', in Beinart and Bundy, *Hidden Struggles in Rural South Africa*.

interests in the scheme and did not necessarily prioritize the same points as officials. But one key argument that emerged around this time—attractive to both parties—was that fenced grazing camps would obviate the need for daily herding and so free the boys, who were mainly responsible, for schooling.

These ideas were incorporated at a national level into the Betterment Proclamation in 1939 and put into practice in Tanga location, Butterworth, Transkei, in a pilot scheme that year. Betterment was voluntary at first and attracted some interest from those involved in farmers' associations as well as Christian communities anxious to expand education. A planning committee was formed including five local residents elected by council taxpayers. The area was fenced into seven camps with eleven stock dams.[90] Goats and donkeys were culled, as well as an estimated 50 per cent of sheep.[91] Less than 20 per cent of the cattle, all old, were sold. In a later cull, in 1944, horses were removed from the location. All of those who had land before received sites again. Tanga was frequently referred to in the next few years as a success, with surprisingly little resistance to stock limitation. Grazing conditions were reported to have improved rapidly.

While betterment was set back during the Second World War, as officials left for military service, its advocates felt no less urgent in their commitment. In 1942 the Young Committee on Overstocking in the Transkei was appointed. As it was initiated by the Department of Native Affairs, and not directly through the UTTGC system, it did not include African members.[92] But evidence was taken from Transkeian officials, African councillors, and some chiefs. Most warned strongly against compulsory stock limitation. A local white Member of Parliament argued that it 'would shake for ever [African] faith in the White Man and the Government' and be 'more than a blunder'.[93] However, a significant group of African witnesses, including the two paramount chiefs of Pondoland, were prepared to go further. Saul Mabude, a leading council member from Pondoland, accepted that 'the magnitude of the evil of overstocking in the Territories is so appalling' that before long, the country would be 'transformed into a wilderness unsuitable

[90] UTA CMT 1157, Director of Agriculture, Transkei, 'Comments on S.N.A's Minute of 16/6/43 to the Chief Magistrate'.
[91] Department of Native Affairs, 'Report of the Departmental Committee regarding the Culling of Livestock in Native Areas' (unpublished, 1953). Copy from former Chief Magistrate, Mr V. Leibbrandt.
[92] 'Report of the Committee appointed to Enquire into Overstocking in the Transkeian Territories', *Transkeian Territories General Council, Reports and Proceedings, 1942* and debates; a further copy and itinerary is at UTA TTA 539/43, 'Livestock General', Acting Chief Magistrate to Magistrates, 23 June 1941.
[93] Ibid. 3, evidence Gordon Hemming, MP.

for both human and animal habitation'. Compulsory limitation and fenced paddocks, he felt, had become 'an essential solution'.

The Young Committee incorporated new ways of thinking about environmental degradation and agricultural decline. A distinction was made between donkeys (eradicable), sheep (where limitation would be acceptable), and cattle. Following medical opinion, milk supply and child malnutrition were cited as issues of major importance. Witnesses reported that, owing largely to the lack of milk, 'nearly 50% of babies born alive in the Umtata district die before reaching the age of two years'.[94] Veterinary controls over livestock movement and sales were sharply criticized; the vet on the committee felt forced to defend himself with a minority report. Dipping was openly blamed for erosion because of the incessant driving of animals to and from tanks: the 'vigorous and relentless battle against East Coast Fever', so the report recorded, 'is one of the biggest agents or factors in aiding the destruction of the veld'. The Forestry Department was also criticized for reservation of mountain areas that used to be available for seasonal grazing. And the committee noted a point frequently reiterated by African witnesses: if only African workers were paid a living wage, 'vast numbers would abandon agriculture and stock raising and go over to a money instead of a cattle economy'.

Considering its context and membership, the Young Committee was highly sensitive to poverty and malnutrition. Smuts's wartime government was more liberal than any of its predecessors since Union, and the Young report came close to admitting how segregation and a low-wage migrant labour system impacted on the African reserves. It prioritized food supplies and the acquisition of land to extend the areas of African settlement under the Natives Land and Trust Act. Yet it was also more aggressive and interventionist with respect to the imperatives of conservation. The whole of the Transkei should be declared a betterment area as soon as possible; there was 'no alternative to drastic action', in the shape of 'regular and systematic reallocation of homestead and arable holdings and grazing areas'. 'Without such fencing,' the report argued, 'any attempt to rehabilitate the country will fail.' An addendum, headed 'Save the Veld' and ending 'Save the Grass', summarized arguments about degradation and added that 'the most serious effect of overstocking is the harmful result on the health of the people and particularly on that of the children'. 'If we are to build up a healthy and prosperous Bantu people in the Transkei,' the report concluded, 'we must treat the veld as our most valuable asset.'

[94] Ibid. 7, evidence Dr Mary McGregor.

In 1943 Thornton was brought back from Lesotho to a follow-up meeting in Pretoria on livestock improvement in the Transkei.[95] He was surprisingly forceful in his views, taking issue with more cautious, senior South African officials. Thornton was adamant that 'peasant farming cannot include the Merino'. He did not rule them out entirely in the Lesotho highlands. But the pastures of the Transkeian Territories, he felt, were naturally better for cattle, at least before sheep destroyed them. Thornton's department in Lesotho had refused to provide angora rams, considered uneconomic and destructive, for stock improvement. He also took up the themes of nutrition and equity. Culling should hit the big owners: they should 'deal gently with the poor and harshly with the rich because it is not right in the first instance, from a social-istic point of view, for one person to possess 100 and the other only 5, on com-mon grazing'.[96] Protection should be given to those who owned 5 head of cattle and less. Reinecke, the Director of Native Agriculture, backed this position in principle: 'there is so much abuse by capitalists in our native Reserves at the expense of other less privileged people. I have therefore come to the conclusion that we have to give everybody a chance to have stock.'

Thornton wanted to translate this approach into a clear policy of eliminat-ing sheep in the Transkei. Reinecke was more cautious. While they could agree in principle that sheep were 'Public Enemy No. 1', African witnesses had emphasized to Young that sheep and goats were used for food and cere-monies.[97] Small stock rather than cattle were slaughtered on a more regular basis. Sheep could be the 'poor man's cattle'. Nor was there any legal mach-inery under the Betterment Proclamation to get rid of sheep. In effect, drastic action was ruled out as a breach of faith in respect of earlier promises about the aims of conservation.

Differential culling according to species would also cut across a key prin-ciple of progressive, conservationist approaches—the need to improve live-stock. Castration had been done largely in order to eliminate animals of poor quality, whoever owned them, and whatever their species. Poorer people probably lost most. A change in policy, after all the propaganda in favour of livestock improvement, would require a great deal of explaining. Thornton maintained that reduction had to come before quality, but others disagreed.

[95] UTA CMT 1157, 'Rehabilitation' file, Livestock Improvement Scheme in the Transkeian Territories', Records of Discussion, Pretoria, 5 Mar. 1943.
[96] UTA CMT 1157, 'Livestock Improvement Scheme in the Transkeian Territories', R. W. Thornton, Agricultural Advisor, Basutoland, 3. Thornton's use of 'socialistic' here seems to imply social fairness, rather than socialism.
[97] UTA CMT 1157, 'Livestock Improvement Scheme in the Transkeian Territories', T. G. W. Reineke, Director of Native Agriculture.

They were more sensitive to pressures from African livestock owners. One compromise position was to cull on the basis of poor quality, then allow owners to use the money to buy back subsidized, high-quality animals.

In the small Free State reserve of Witzieshoek, those with fewer than five animals were allowed to buy back up to that quota. The Department had been 'forced to do this' by the depth of opposition to culling, even though livestock numbers had crept up beyond the specified carrying capacity. Officials in Thaba Nchu, an early target of conservationist intervention, were equally 'afraid of trouble from the prominent leaders of the Natives'. This was an area of African private landowners, some with considerable livestock holdings, including Dr James Moroka, who later became President of the African National Congress (1949–52). He had received assistance from the government in the 1930s under the Soil Erosion Act for the construction of small dams.[98] One of the issues in Thaba Nchu was whether black private landowners were to be treated differently from white, and it did become a site of intense opposition to betterment.[99]

Officials in Pretoria agreed to stop subsidizing stud rams.[100] But this was an unsatisfactory outcome. It failed to satisfy the anti-sheep radicals like Thornton, and failed to prioritize livestock improvement, which had been at the core of the old Bunga projects. Instead, pedigree bulls would be more heavily subsidized. In Lesotho, Thornton had found that the best results came from government-maintained bulls, kept permanently in bull camps, rather than those sold to African owners. They could service more cows—delivered to them in the camps—because they were kept in peak condition. So central was stock improvement, he argued, that the service should be free: 'we must build up the Natives'; 'we must work for milk to save the people'. This, the Secretary of Native Affairs agreed, would be the 'salvation of the reserves'.[101]

Little progress was made in respect of eliminating sheep. Their numbers in the Transkei dropped under 2.5 million in the droughts of the early 1930s, and then stabilized until the 1950s. Government intervention through betterment was not a significant factor in controlling Transkeian livestock numbers as a whole before 1950. However, where culling did take place, donkeys, goats, and sheep bore the brunt of it.[102] In some senses, culling took the line of least resistance in exempting most cattle.[103]

[98] PTA NTS 9497, 138/400, part IV.   [99] Murray, *Black Mountain*.
[100] UTA CMT 1157, 'Livestock Improvement Scheme in the Transkeian Territories', T. G. W. Reineke, Director of Native Agriculture, 18.
[101] UTA CMT 1157, Secretary of Native Affairs to CMT, 27 May 1943.
[102] UTA CMT 1157, Memo., 'Agricultural and Pastoral Rehabilitation in the Transkeian Territories', n.d., attached to 'Livestock Improvement Scheme in the Transkeian Territories'.
[103] W. Beinart, 'Chieftaincy and the Articulation of Modes of Production', *Canadian Journal of African Studies*, 19 (1985); Hendricks, *The Pillars of Apartheid*, 109 ff.

Civil strife in the cities during the Second World War leant extra urgency to rural rehabilitation. The Native Affairs department bulletin 'News of the War', designed to keep Africans informed about the war effort, started to include a home-front supplement on soil erosion in 1944.[104] The Minister promised 'planning on a vast and long-term scale', over twelve years, to save the soil, purchase land, and work 'towards the health and happiness of the Native people'.[105] While the Chief Magistrate advocated devolution of the policy, so that headmen and councils could take more responsibility, Pretoria officials envisaged a centrally directed campaign, uniformly pursued through the country. In 1945 the Secretary of Native Affairs announced 'a new era of reclamation' in a speech to the Ciskeian General Council. Planning committees were set up in four zones, with detailed briefs. The government was now fully committed to the demarcation of residential, arable, and grazing land throughout the African areas of the country: 'if kraals are scattered over the arable and grazing areas there can be no efficient control of livestock.'[106] This implied moving millions of people.

Government would pay for rehabilitation, as it was now called. Compensation would be paid to those moved at a rate of £2 for a hut and £3 for a more substantial building.[107] 'Properly organised and controlled villages' would become sites for essential services, such as schools, clinics, waterpoints, and roads.[108] Village wood lots would provide for timber needs. There was some consultation on spatial reordering, but the state committed itself to 'measured and helpful compulsion'.[109] Transkeians, borrowing from military terminology, came to call the new villages 'dressed'.[110] The government now distinguished two types of village or denser settlement. The rural villages were intended to house those who had previously lived in the same rural location. At the same time, additional villages, for non-landholders, would be constructed. While they would include vegetable plots, irrigated where possible, livestock would be disallowed. In the medium term, these were to be growth points, absorbing Africans pushed off white-owned farms.

---

[104] PTA NTS 10203, 1/423, I, cutting from *Cape Times*, 2 June 1944.

[105] Ibid., Ministerial Statement of Policy, P.G. van der Bijl, 1944.

[106] D. L. Smit, *A New Era of Reclamation: Statement of Policy Made by Mr. D. L. Smit, Secretary for Native Affairs at a Special Session of the Ciskeian General Council at Kingwilliamstown on the 8th January, 1945* (Government Printer, Pretoria, 1945), in UTA TTA 759/114.

[107] Ibid., Chief Magistrate to Magistrates, 24 Sept. 1945, Circular 41 of 1945.

[108] An eloquent argument in favour of serviced, modern villages is in E. Jokl, 'A Labour and Manpower Survey of the Transkeian Territories', unpublished MS (1943), South African Institute of Race Relations Library, Johannesburg.

[109] UTA TTA 759/114, Smit, 'New Era', 3.

[110] 'Dressed' had other connotations, in that it referred to the Christian communities who were generally seen to adopt white or Western ways more readily.

Thus discussions at the most senior level of the Native Affairs Department during the Second World War linked conservation interventions with social planning and nutrition, which implied favouring cattle and discouraging livestock accumulation by a minority. In fact, these proposals had relatively little impact on the ground in the Transkei. Betterment proceeded too slowly, and other forces shaped the distribution of livestock holdings over the long term. Many migrant workers continued to invest some of their wages into cattle, ensuring that cattle holdings were sustained amongst poorer families. The ratio between cattle and sheep was also relatively stable, although recorded goat numbers did decline somewhat.

Similarly, betterment does not seem to have made a significant impact on the distribution of landholdings. Here, officials were divided as to the appropriate policy. Many rural homesteads had more than one agricultural field, and these were often dispersed, either because they had been allocated or inherited at different times, or because families wished to minimize risk. A communal tenure Land Proclamation in 1919 aimed to group family holdings into one plot in the Transkei, but most districts had neither the records nor the staff to begin implementing such a policy. It was only in the seven Transkeian districts surveyed under the Glen Grey Act (1894) into individual tenure holdings that some degree of concentration was achieved. The maximum plot size laid down in land proclamations for the Transkei was 5 morgen, over 10 acres, probably more than that cultivated by the average peasant family.

Consolidation of holdings did become part of the betterment programme. Some officials in the Transkeian Department of Agriculture hoped that this process could be linked to concentration of agricultural resources amongst a 'farmer class'. Liberal intellectuals tended to sympathize with such an approach. They were disturbed by the effects of migrant labour on both rural and urban African society, and envisaged a stabilized urban work force and a secure, non-migrant, peasantry. For the latter to flourish, they would require access to more land. Transkeian officials linked concentration to the imperatives of conservationist agriculture. It was insufficient, so their logic ran, to make isolated conservationist interventions, or even engage in comprehensive planning, without changing the economic base of rural families. Only those with a permanent 'stake in the land', dependent upon it for their income, would look after the soil properly. Some, but by no means all, officials tied this argument to private tenure. A Ciskeian magistrate railed against 'adherence to customs which are relics of more spacious times and concepts which are not only obsolete but which have become a positive menace'.[111] This was not a majority view.

---

[111] PTA NTS 10208, 2/423, W. R. Norton to CNC, Ciskei, 1 Feb. 1946.

The idea of the 'economic unit', borrowed from the United States, was introduced into planning as a basis for calculations about how much land and stock would be necessary to meet the subsistence and cash needs of a rural family. The Tomlinson Commission accepted and developed this approach to rural planning in the 1950s, suggesting economic units rather larger than those proposed by agricultural officers, a solution which implied moving considerable numbers of rural Africans off the land. (The report did also recommend some smaller plot sizes, including half economic units.) It was never really pursued. When the planners moved back into the Transkei after the Second World War they tended to provide land in reorganized villages to all of those who had previously held plots. As in the case of cattle, resources remained quite widely distributed. While the percentage of families holding land and cattle gradually declined, the absolute number did not.

Despite official caution about concentrating resources, this comprehensive approach to spatial reorganization and grazing management was ambitious. It must be seen as part of new confidence born out of post-war optimism in the state's capacity to direct society as a whole, and a new preparedness by the government to make such expenditures. Compared with the sums spent in Herschel, or on Transkeian agricultural improvement, the projected costs of betterment were huge. As early as 1943, costs in the Transkei alone were estimated at about £3.5 million for fencing, livestock improvement, water supplies, and soil reclamation, not including staff and maintenance. In 1944 Reinecke expected that they would need to spend £10 million nationally over twelve years in a 'vast undertaking', 'beset with difficulties'.[112] It was soon apparent that even this was an underestimate. A calculation of fencing costs in the Ciskei came out at £1 million. Transkeian officials suggested in 1949 that at the current rate of progress the whole operation would take over 150 years, not allowing for increases in population and lands.[113]

The realities of planning soon limited the content and ambition of the schemes. Simplified methods of survey were used. Land was distributed through the old channels controlled by headmen; road, afforestation, and social projects were downgraded; culling, grazing control, and resettlement took precedence. Most progress was made in areas newly acquired (at least in legal terms) for African settlement by the Trust. Shortage of staff, planning and survey problems, and the need to purchase land or sink boreholes all delayed implementation, and opposition from rural people mounted. This was evident throughout the country, even on land purchased for Africans by the Trust.[114] The Ciskei General Council rejected the 'New Era of

[112] PTA NTS 10203, 1/423, I, Director of Native Agriculture to Senior Engineer, 16 May 1944.
[113] UTA CMT 1157, Report of the Committee on Rehabilitation, 1949.
[114] Delius, *Lion Amongst the Cattle*, 58–63.

Reclamation' document in 1945. Although the UTTGC accepted it in principle, and a large number of locations were proclaimed as betterment areas, the 'people as a whole [were] still bitterly opposed to the scheme'.[115]

Betterment and rehabilitation required moving large numbers of homesteads, often with very limited compensation, into villages which might not have been perceived as the most suitable places for settlements. Established patterns of social interaction, rural power, and authority were disturbed. Some local chiefs or educated members of the rural elite could see advantages in planning, or at least in co-operating with officials. In the Ciskei, women sometimes welcomed the schools and services promised in the new villages. But when opposition began to surface, aimed as much against local collaborators as the government itself, a heightened level of compulsion became necessary. Comprehensive planning and conservation works began to displace the formerly more varied activities of the extension services in the Transkei. Officials felt that these could hardly bear fruit until land use had been transformed. The diffused demonstration schemes, which had been the cornerstone of the Transkeian department's efforts for thirty years, took a back seat. Two of the three Transkeian schools of agriculture were closed in the late 1940s.

The content of conservationist thinking emphasized the role of the expert and lent itself to unilateral interventions and centralized planning. In the early phases of intervention in African areas, some of the techniques that drew on, and developed, elements in the changing pattern of peasant agriculture met with acceptance, at least in sections of the rural population. But limited and educative intervention tended to be abandoned in favour of total planning. The frame of reference for agricultural officers was the settler farm, where the landowner had the capacity to reshape land use on the whole unit of production. When applied to African-occupied areas, such schemes were insensitive to rural social relationships and often highly disruptive.

---

[115] UTA TTA 759/114, cutting from *Imvo Zabantsundu*, 26 May 1945; see n. 2.

11

Postscript: Debating Degradation Over the Long Term: Animals, Veld, and Conservation

Desert Encroachment?

Awareness of environmental change ran deep in South African society. By the 1930s both white and black rural communities were being confronted with its perceived consequences and with the state's determination to act. At the heart of conservationist concern was the desire to guarantee agricultural production in the long term by protecting and enhancing natural resources, and especially the veld. However, investment and regulation had facilitated more intensive livestock farming before a sufficiently protective regime had been put in place. Veterinary measures contributed to rising stock numbers amongst both white and black owners. Debt and depression helped further to drive animal numbers up in the late 1920s and early 1930s. While it is difficult to make cross-national comparisons because of the variety of ecological conditions, South Africa does appear to have been comparatively heavily stocked at the time. Sheep and cattle numbers in 1930 were more than twice their levels in the first decade of the century.

The developing conservationist critique was sometimes overgeneralized, uncertain in its explanations, alarmist, and infused by racial ideas. But I have argued that it revealed deep-seated agrarian problems. Important elements of environmental change had been identified, if not scientifically tested, despite the fact that ecology as a discipline was in its infancy. The response was not simply an environmental or moral panic by the state and agrarian elite, triggered by the American Dust Bowl or African urbanization. The drought of 1933 resulted in losses, especially of small stock, on a scale that had seldom been experienced before.

While the impact of a century of increasingly intensive stock-farming was uneven, soil erosion was painfully evident, both in districts dominated by

17. Dongas at Vlekpoort, Hofmeyr District

white-owned farms and in African communal areas. Dongas had become a symbol of the countryside, not least in the Karoo.[1] The sensitive soils of north-eastern Cape and Herschel were scarred. Even if the southern Cape coastal belt could still boast forests, they were heavily depleted. Some of the richer eurphorbia bush and grassland districts around Albany, Uitenhage, and Kingwilliamstown were infested with prickly pear and jointed cactus.

What of the longer term—the period from the Great Depression to the late twentieth century? In this concluding chapter I want to suggest four arguments, focusing largely, as in the case of the book as a whole, on white-owned farming districts in what was formerly the midland Cape. First, the concerns about continuing degradation of pastures became an orthodoxy, repeated by government experts and subsequently by academics critical of the apartheid regime. Secondly, however, there is significant evidence that the condition of the veld stabilized or even improved in the second half of the twentieth century; biodiversity in respect of indigenous mammal species probably also increased. Thirdly, stabilization was not primarily a result of cyclical changes in climate or rainfall—as some have argued—but of environmental regulation, changing farming methods, and lower stocking levels, particularly on the white-owned farms. Fourthly, the evidence from the African areas is less certain, partly as a result of the unforeseen impact of betterment and the social devastation of apartheid. The persistence of

---

[1] Union of South Africa, *Report of the Desert Encroachment Committee* (U.G.59-1951), 2.

customary forms of tenure and the relative failure of environmental regulation may also have contributed to their problems.

The idea that soil erosion threatened the future of agriculture and of the
nation persisted in the second half of the twentieth century. A further inquiry
by the ominously named Desert Encroachment Committee (1948–51) aimed
to examine more definitively both the spread of aridity and whether 'man-
made desiccation had altered the natural condition of the veld to such an
extent that the climate itself had in turn been affected'. The relationship
between rainfall and denudation had long been debated in South Africa. As
the Committee reported, 'at all times there appears to have been a fairly
widespread belief that climatic conditions were slowly, but progressively
deteriorating'.[2]

Most of the evidence was taken in and around the Karoo, and Grootfontein
remained an important focus for research.[3] The report was strongly influenced by the work of John Acocks, who served on the Committee. Acocks, an
ecologist employed by the Department of Agriculture since 1935, and partly
based in the Karoo, conducted extensive fieldwork.[4] He had begun to publish
on such topics as indigenous fodder plants and poisonous species, and was
completing a national survey of *Veld Types of South Africa*, first published in
1953. As in the case of the Drought Commission, his formulations helped to
fix the language of debate and were later widely quoted. Although he did not
devote an extensive section of *Veld Types* to pasture history, the authority of his
observations, incorporated in the Desert Encroachment report, was such
that they became commonplace in the literature.

The discipline of ecology, now better established, influenced both British
imperial and South African views of environmental change.[5] Botanists had

---

[2] Ibid. 1.

[3] J. P. H. Acocks, *Veld Types of South Africa: Memoirs of the Botanical Survey of South Africa no. 40*,
2nd edn. (Pretoria, 1975), 8 (first published 1953). See also Meredith (ed.), *Grasses and Pastures*.

[4] C. E. Tidmarsh, 'Veld Management in the Marginal Grassveld Areas', *Farming in South Africa*,
22: 250 (1947), 13–16; J. C. de Klerk, 'Pastures of the Southern O.F.S., A Century Ago and To-day',
ibid. 22: 253 (1947), 347–54; C. E. Tidmarsh, 'Conservation Problems of the Karoo', ibid. 23: 269
(1948), 519–30; H. Klintworth, 'Desert Encroachment over the Karoo', ibid. 23: 272 (1948), 723–8.

[5] Anker, 'The Ecology of Nations'; Tilley, 'Africa as a "Living Laboratory"'; for South Africa at
the time, J. W. Bews, *The Grasses and Grasslands of South Africa* (P. Davis, Pietermaritzburg, 1918);
Bews, 'Plant Succession and Plant Distribution in South Africa', *Annals of Botany*, 34 (1920),
287–97; J. F. V. Philips, 'Succession, Development, the Climax and the Complex Organism: An
Analysis of Concepts', *Journal of Ecology*, 22: 2 (1934), 554–71; 23: 1 (1935), 210–46; 23: 2 (1935),
488–508; Phillips, 'Some Problems Presented by South African Grasses and Grass Communities',
Journal of South African Botany, 1 (1935), 47–63. For application of these ideas, see e.g. L. C. C.
Liebenberg, 'Veld Burning: How it Affects the Farmer as well as the Country', *Farming in South
Africa*, 9: 99 (June 1934), 213–5, and 9: 100 (July 1934), 265–6.

long been interested in vegetation change, and systematic research on grasses and Karoo shrubs, funded by the Department of Agriculture, had begun in the inter-war years. Ecological concepts and concerns were absorbed into this work in order to examine how species related dynamically through time under conditions of heavy grazing. The 'succession' of species in veld that had been disturbed or burnt was being explored, guided by the idea of a climax species that would be dominant in undisturbed or rested pastures. It was increasingly accepted that rooigras (securely named as *Themeda triandra*) was a key climax species, an indicator of well-managed pastures, and valuable for all grazing animals. Acocks and his colleagues developed these ideas in their investigation of pasture management.

As in the case of the Drought Commission thirty years earlier, the Desert Encroachment Committee was sceptical about any long-term decline in rainfall. Rainfall records suggested that there had been a peak around 1890, and a gradual, irregular fall until the droughts of the early 1930s. Subsequently rainfall had been relatively high. They accepted that there might be long-term cycles, although these were difficult to detect with the evidence they had available. On the issue of degradation, however, the Committee, and Acocks's survey, expressed no doubts and they confirmed the general desiccation of the Karoo.

In its dryer western parts, the Karoo had turned into 'near desert in the sense that soil erosion [was] universal and that there [was] no longer a permanent, unbroken vegetation cover, and only rarely a temporary cover'.[6] Most strikingly, Acocks reiterated the points made by Shaw, and others since, that Karoo vegetation had moved eastwards, in parts up to 250 kilometres, to replace sweet grassveld. There was also a slower, but accelerating, northward movement. He was particularly concerned about what he called the False Upper Karoo, covering many of the midland, north-eastern Cape, and southern Free State districts: 'the development of this veld type constitutes the most spectacular of all the changes in the vegetation of South Africa. The conversion of 32,200 square km of grassveld into eroded Karoo can only be regarded as a national disaster.'[7] Elsewhere, sour or rank grasses, less suitable for year-round grazing, had spread at the cost of mixed and sweeter veld, especially the climax grasses, such as rooigras. In short, there was 'widespread deterioration in all veld types over the last 500 years'.

The Desert Encroachment Committee reiterated the view, often expressed in the inter-war years, that the state should take a lead in resolving the crisis: 'it is quite clear that farmers do not know what is best.'[8] Members also

⁶ Acocks, *Veld Types of South Africa*, 8.   ⁷ Ibid. 78.   ⁸ U.G. 59-1951, 7.

examined research done on siltation of dams and on possible depletion of underground water as a result of the rapidly increasing number of boreholes. 'It would not be too much to say,' they concluded, 'that the determination of correct systems of veld management combined with the optimum stocking rate for every veld, soil and climatic zone would be one of the greatest contributions that this generation could make to the future welfare of agriculture in South Africa.' In language reminiscent of the Drought Commission, and of American inter-war commentators, the Committee concluded that 'the very existence of stock farming is at stake because, unless we can succeed in arresting further deterioration of the veld, it is doomed'.

From the late 1940s P. W. Roux and colleagues conducted a series of investigations on and around Grootfontein, using new and more thorough techniques of surveying vegetation cover. In a later summary of findings, they confirmed many of the tendencies highlighted by Acocks, but differed in one important respect.[9] They proposed a five-phase deterioration from pristine veld to desert. Following the first two phases of denudation, when most of the best grass and shrub species were thinned out and erosion set in, they detected a third phase of re-vegetation by less desirable and less palatable species. Much of the Karoo, they thought, was in the third phase and, especially in the 1960s and 1970s, bare patches were often covered in a general 'thickening-up' of vegetation.[10] Woody invader plants were still spreading 'at an alarming rate', and they considered that the loss of soil, and of the best pasturage, was so great that it was 'quite impossible' to revert to the original veld. The early stages of phase four, the domination of a few inedible succulent or woody species, was already present in some areas—a 'disclimax' in vegetation terms. Phase five, the complete destruction of vegetation cover and exposure of soil to unchecked erosion, could be detected in parts of the arid western Karoo, especially around Calvinia district, site of transhumant settler stock-farming for two centuries.

The authors of such analyses were scientists and government officials who worked with white farmers and were not explicitly critical of broader apartheid policies that reserved much of the land for exclusive white ownership. Yet this well-established critique was readily incorporated into anti-apartheid literature on the rural areas. Evidence of environmental degradation provided an argument with which to castigate the greed of white farmers, who were at the core of support for apartheid and, together with the

---

[9] P. W. Roux and M. Vorster, 'Vegetation Change in the Karoo', *Proceedings of the Grassland Society of Southern Africa*, 18 (1983), 25–9; M. Vorster and P. W. Roux, 'Veld of the Karoo Areas', ibid. 18–24; P. W. Roux et al., 'Stock Production in the Karoo Region', ibid. 16 (1981), 29–35.
[10] Roux, 'Vegetation Change', 27.

state, seen as responsible for severe rural dislocation through forced removals of black tenants and farm-workers. It also helped to illustrate the iniquities of the homeland system. Rural black people were restricted, as independent occupiers of land, to a limited proportion of the country, and their freedom of movement was curtailed. Whereas the Native Economic Commission (1932) had blamed African culture and attitudes for the state of the reserves, it was not difficult to invert the argument and pin the responsibility on apartheid.

General publications dealing with apartheid frequently mentioned in passing the way in which environmental ills, along with poverty, were concentrated in the African homelands. Some with a more specific focus also summarized key points in regard to white-owned farms. *Uprooting Poverty* (1989) and *Restoring the Land* (1991), two important books by anti-apartheid social scientists, are good examples.[11] Despite government measures, Francis Wilson argued that 'the rape of the soil has continued'. He reiterated Acocks's view that sweetveld had become scrub and that by 2050 the sheep-farming areas would be desert: 'the combination of soil erosion and deteriorating vegetation is held by some to be far and away the most serious of the many problems facing South Africa.'[12] He reported the estimate that 400 million tonnes of topsoil were being lost annually in the 1960s. Overstocking on sheep farms in the Karoo was around 30 per cent and the desert advancing at about 2.6 kilometres per year. (This would suggest it had spread 100 kilometres further since the Desert Encroachment report.)

Alan Durning's hard-hitting Earthwatch pamphlet, *Apartheid's Environmental Toll* (1990), also recorded some of these points; he conjured the 'south-western deserts . . . marching to Pretoria, expanding across two and a half kilometers of exhausted pastures a year'.[13] Huntley, Siegfried, and Sunter, the former a leading South African environmental scientist, saw the 1980s as 'the decade the environment hit back . . . for over a century of careless environmental management'. They accepted the idea of continuous decline manifest in the unparalleled diversity and seriousness of natural disasters—floods, droughts, urban degradation, hail, fire, locusts—which, they argued, were worse than those in the 1930s. 'We have had to pay the price for over a century of careless environmental management and South Africa's unique experiment in social engineering.'[14] They similarly estimated that annual

[11] F. Wilson and M. Ramphele, *Uprooting Poverty: The South African Challenge* (David Philip, Cape Town, 1989); M. Ramphele (ed.), *Restoring the Land: Environment and Change in Post-Apartheid South Africa* (Panos, London, 1991).

[12] F. Wilson, 'A Land Out of Balance' in Ramphele (ed.), *Restoring the Land*, 30.

[13] A. Durning, *Apartheid's Environmental Toll* (Worldwatch Institute, Washington DC, 1990).

[14] B. Huntley, R. Siegfried, and C. Sunter, *South African Environments into the 21st Century* (Tafelberg, Cape Town, 1989), 37.

losses of soil were 300–400 million tonnes, nearly three tonnes per hectare, that the Karoo was still overstocked by almost 50 per cent, and that 3 million hectares had become unusable because of erosion.

Huntley reflected increasing concern about biodiversity, which became a major new element in debates about environmental degradation. The botanist Richard Cowling noted that a particularly large number of species were at risk because of the unusually diverse and unique nature of Cape plants and animals. He estimated that 60 per cent of the veld was in poor condition.[15] Approaching the issues from an apparently innocent ecological viewpoint, Cowling came up with some very radical suggestions. Because it was wrong, he argued, to confine stock to small areas in semi-arid zones, 'an ecologically appropriate intervention in the Karoo might involve the removal of barriers to stock migration and nationalisation of the herd'.[16] Taken to its logical conclusion, this proposal seemed to favour a reversion to an open range and the abolition of private property.

It is not my intention to dispute the fact that there had been, and remained, serious environmental problems in South Africa. A core argument in this book is that the massive increase in livestock numbers made a fundamental impact on the natural world. But there are difficulties with this view of continuous degradation. Alarming reports were consistently expressed for one-and-a-half centuries, and if some of the estimates of the pace of change were correct, then much of South Africa would be a desert. This is patently not the case. Desert has clearly not marched across the highveld croplands to Pretoria, in an echo of the South African War song. These remained the heartland of intensive cereal production. Moreover, generalized scenarios of the spread of desert conditions ignore the fact that much of the land they describe is private property, and that farms are subject to significantly different management regimes. Eroded land can be contiguous to well-maintained pastures. And there is some evidence to counter the view that the veld continued to deteriorate during the second half of the twentieth century.

Evidence and Reasons for Stabilization

One of the Grootfontein officials serving on the Desert Encroachment Committee, C. E. Tidmarsh, agreed that the Karoo was spreading, but in a 1948 article raised questions about long-term climatic change or cycles as a

---

[15] R. Cowling, 'Options For Rural Land Use in Southern Africa: An Ecological Perspective', in M. de Klerk (ed.), *A Harvest of Discontent: The Land Question in South Africa* (IDASA, Cape Town, 1991), 17.

[16] Ibid. 17.

major cause. To a greater extent than other experts, he was cautious about a linear view of human-induced decline. In a short article written in 1952, Tidmarsh noted:

The results of the past seventeen years of research at the College have shown clearly that the amount of natural vegetation that can be maintained per morgen of land, is controlled more by the available moisture supply than by the grazing treatment to which the veld may be subjected, and that in the extensive flats of the Mixed Karoo, the quantity of vegetation growing at present on the soil is, with the exception of local areas of denuded soil, in approximate equilibrium with the available moisture supply, and that, without increasing the latter, it is virtually impossible to increase the natural cover of the soil by any measure of grazing control, including complete protection.[17]

Even more controversially, Tidmarsh argued that while extremely heavy stocking rates changed the composition and quality of the veld, it was very difficult to produce a lasting impact: 'within limits, the composition of the veld appears, thus, to be more a function of the interaction of the soil type, moisture supply, and climate, than of the grazing treatment.' He was aware of similar research results in the United States, and in some respects his views were similar to those of James C. Malin, who de-emphasized the role of people, and particularly European settlers, in shaping pasture histories over the long term.[18] Tidmarsh could have drawn some support from the findings of an American agricultural economist who reported on South Africa during the 1930s, and calculated that the number of sheep per acre in any district correlated strongly with average rainfall.[19]

In the post-Depression United States, where soil conservation was one major justification for state intervention, Malin's views were associated with an anti-federal and anti-interventionist political standpoint. For Tidmarsh, Acocks, and most other South African experts, the role of the state was less problematic—the question was how to intervene effectively.[20] Tidmarsh did recognize that there were limits to safe stocking. Both he and Acocks argued

[17] Tidmarsh, 'Conservation Problems of the Karoo'; C. E. Tidmarsh, 'Veld Management in the Karoo', Grootfontein College of Agriculture, reprint no. 4 (Government Printer, Pretoria, 1952), from *Farming in South Africa*, 27: 310 (1952), 4.

[18] James C. Malin, *The Grasslands of North America: Prolegomena to Its History* (privately published, Lawrence, 1947); Worster, *Dust Bowl*.

[19] Clifford C. Taylor, *Agriculture in Southern Africa*, US Department of Agriculture, Technical Bulletin no. 466, Washington DC (1935). The report was largely written in order to assess South Africa's capacity to supply international commodity markets and compete with the United States after the Depression.

[20] For a summary of recommended grazing strategies at the time, see Meredith (ed.), *Grasses and Pastures*.

that whatever the long-term effects of livestock, selective grazing of more palatable species could have serious short-term consequences. However, Tidmarsh suggested that production was at its highest when animals were grazed more continuously, at moderate levels of stocking, in large camps with long rests. Acocks experimented more enthusiastically with relatively rapid rotations of animals in smaller camps, in order to avoid the inevitable selective grazing of the best species. Both advocated internal fencing of particular veld types on individual farms.

Echoes of Tidmarsh's approach can be found in recent botanical research by Hoffman and Cowling, who contested the view that Karoo vegetation was extensively altered and was spreading.[21] They assembled a formidable range of historical sources on the appearance of the Karoo before the period of intensive farming of woolled sheep. With reference to the eastern Karoo, they argued that 'although there are some references to a grass-dominated landscape, even the earliest accounts suggest that, at least in places, dwarf karroid shrubs were dominant'. Archaeological research tends to confirm this paucity of grass cover at periods in the past.[22]

Secondly, and more dramatically, they found photographic records taken by botanists concerned about the state of the veld in the early twentieth century. These include a series by Pole-Evans, the Cambridge-trained botanist who became Divisional Head of Botany in the Department of Agriculture and was influential in stimulating research on indigenous flora and pastures.[23] Matched photographs taken in 1989 suggested that the state of the veld had improved considerably since 1917–25. Thirdly, Hoffman and Cowling resurveyed eleven sites in the Karoo and southern Free State, which had previously been investigated by Roux in 1961–3, and concluded that 'all sites showed an increase in total percentage canopy spread cover from 1961–63 to 1989, attributed chiefly to an increase in the cover of grasses'. Some sites showed a decline in shrub cover.

The authors suggested that the evidence for an expanding Karoo was not strong, nor did the photographs and surveys reveal 'desert-like conditions' at any of the varied sites.[24] They did not claim that veld in the Karoo was

[21] M. T. Hoffman and R. Cowling, 'Vegetation Change in the Semi-arid Eastern Karoo Over the Last 200 Years—Fact or Fiction', *South African Journal of Science*, 86 (1990), 289.

[22] M. T. Hoffman, B. Cousins, T. Meyer, A. Petersen, and H. Hendricks, 'Historical and Contemporary Land Use and the Desertification of the Karoo', in W. Richard, J. Dean, and Suzanne Milton, *The Karoo: Ecological Patterns and Processes* (Cambridge University Press, Cambridge, 1999), 257–73.

[23] I. Scoones, 'Politics, Polemics and Pastures: Range Management Science and Policy in Southern Africa', in Leach and Mearns (ed.), *The Lie of the Land*.

[24] Timm Hoffman, 'Is the Karoo Spreading?', *Veld and Flora*, 77: 1 (1991), 5.

necessarily improving, but explained their findings as likely to be related to cyclical change, and especially a period of higher rainfall since the mid-1980s. The prevalence of grass cover recorded in 1989 did not in itself constitute evidence for a longer-term reversal of denudation or that grasses were now invading the Karoo. They were also cautious about the relationship between climatic factors and the impact of livestock. 'Except for a very general understanding,' they concluded, 'we do no know what influence grazing has on these processes'.[25] Hoffman had already raised questions about the rationale for various grazing systems, both the slower rotations favoured by the Department of Agriculture, and the quicker rotations in smaller camps that were being pursued by some farmers.[26] Insufficient was known, he suggested, about the growth and reproduction patterns of the very large variety of grasses and shrubs involved.

Hoffman and Cowling's article helped to stimulate an intense debate on the long-term ecological history of the Karoo. It is very difficult for a historian untrained in science to evaluate these various studies, but it is possible to discuss them in the light of other evidence—notably long-term stocking rates and environmental regulation—which have affected the intensity of veld use. Their findings may well reflect a longer-term stabilization or improvement in at least some Karoo districts and farms over the second half of the twentieth century, and not simply climatic variation or rainfall cycles.

The photographs used for the period 1917 to 1925 were taken during a period of spectacular growth in small stock numbers in the Cape, from about 15 million in 1904 to 28 million in 1926, before they peaked at about 33 million in 1930. Cattle numbers were also increasing rapidly, at least doubling over the same period, though not necessarily in the sheep districts. Perhaps it is unsurprising that the pictures present a denuded landscape. Surveys done in 1962–3 by Roux and his colleagues similarly took place at a time of high small-stock numbers, after more than a decade of sustained increase, and near to their post-Second World War peak (Fig. 11.1). By contrast, 1989 was at the end of a period in which small-stock numbers had been low for over fifteen years—lower than at any time since the first decade of the century. Cattle numbers were also fairly stable in this period. If this evidence about small-stock numbers is put together with the claims about the capacity for veld to recover under more favourable circumstances, it may help to explain why Hoffman and Cowling's pictures and surveys showed improvements.

[25] Hoffman and Cowling, 'Vegetation Change', 292.
[26] M. T. Hoffman, 'The Rationale for Karoo Grazing Systems: Criticisms and Research Implications', *South African Journal of Science*, 84 (1998), 556–9.

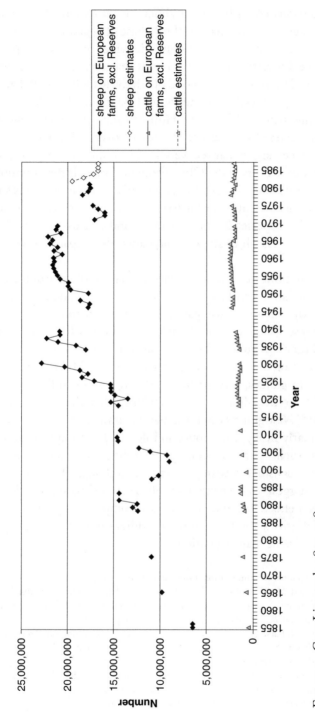

Fig. 11.1. Cape Livestock, 1855–1987

Note: Figures from 1983 are not strictly compatible and may exaggerate the numbers.

Various questions could be raised about this argument. One is Roux's contention, discussed above, that the third phase of degradation consists in a thickening of vegetation. While photographic evidence may show this, more detailed botanical investigation might reveal that unpalatable species were dominant.[27] The late 1980s was a period of relatively high rainfall that could, for example, have produced dense steekgras (Chapter 9). This does not seem to have been the main finding of the Hoffman surveys, which suggest that valuable grass species also experienced some recovery. Hoffman and others would not, however, argue that recovered veld would necessarily reproduce its pre-nineteenth-century state. Older ecological models that attempted to map a regular succession of vegetation, or a particular mix of climax species, are now seen as insufficiently flexible to capture the unpredictable dynamics of the thousands of species in complex rangelands.[28] Loss of topsoil, or its transfer from slopes as silt to streams and dams, also impacts on vegetation patterns.

A second important question concerns the nature of environmental degradation. Denudation can be only one measure. Vegetation may respond relatively quickly when land-use patterns change, but soil erosion is more difficult to reverse. While weirs and small dams can slow the flow of water in gulleys, it is difficult to build sufficient to stop all channels. Recent research in the Sneeuberg, on the borders of Graaff-Reinet and Middelburg districts, suggests that old gulleys, formed before the 1940s, are still active during intense rainfall events, despite the probability that the farmland is less heavily grazed.[29] New gulleys can form many years after original denudation during particularly heavy downpours and floods. Karoo upland headwater environments, such as the Sneeuberg, according to a recent researcher, display 'extreme sensitivity' with respect to erodibility.[30] It is true that the same research suggests that 'channel way obstructions', used to block gulleys, have often been effective and that there is a 'comparatively rapid return to conditions of relative stability'.[31] However, gulleys and topsoil are in general less quickly restorable than vegetation.

[27] P. W. Roux, personal communication, Grootfontein, July 1994.

[28] S. J. Milton and M. T. Hoffman, 'The Application of State-and-Transition Models to Rangeland Research and Management in Arid Succulent and Semi-Arid Grassy Karoo, South Africa', *African Journal of Range and Forestry Science*, 11: 1 (1994), 18–26.

[29] J. Boardman, A. J. Parsons, R. Holland, P. J. Holmes, and R. Washington, 'Development of Badlands and Gullies in the Sneeuberg, Great Karoo, South Africa', unpublished paper presented to workshop on African Environments, University of Oxford (2002).

[30] P. J. Holmes, 'Central Great Karoo Headwater Catchments and Valley Fills: An Overview of Short Term Change', *South African Geographical Journal*, 83: 3 (2001), 274–82.

[31] Holmes, 'Central Great Karoo Headwater Catchments', 280.

A further question about the argument for veld improvement concerns the reasons for the decline in livestock numbers in the later decades of the twentieth century. Did numbers decline because the carrying capacity of veld was deteriorating? This link was made by the Drought Commissioners in 1923, who maintained that both the sheep and human populations (they referred to whites only) of some of the midland Cape districts were declining because pasturage and soil were exhausted. The Commissioners were wrong on both counts. Although sheep numbers fell between 1919 and 1923, they continued to increase up to 1930, and in fact remained higher than the early 1920s figure for much of the next forty years (Fig. 11.1). They were also probably wrong to see environmental factors as the major reason for the fall in the white population; it was more likely due the extrusion of white tenants or bywoners. In this context, reduction of the number of whites on the sheep farms probably facilitated greater productivity and more conservationist farming. Moreover if the black population was included, figures would show an increase in the overall rural population at least for the first half of the twentieth century.

An argument similar to that in the Drought Commission has recently been developed by Dean and Macdonald.[32] They compared stocking rates by district since the agricultural censuses began in 1919 to show an overall reduction, especially marked in the drier districts of the Karoo. By contrast, some grassland districts on the peripheries of the Karoo have experienced growing stock numbers. They cited the negative correlation between increased water provision and decreasing livestock numbers as evidence that veld quality is the major constraint. They also noted the tendency for farmers to switch from wool-bearing merino types to the hardier Dorper mutton sheep, which coped better in poor pastures. Dean and Macdonald examined and rejected various other causes of lower stocking rates, to 'conclude that the current (1994) livestock stocking rate in the semi-arid and arid rangelands of the Cape Province is unrelated to market forces or state policy but is determined by utilizable primary productivity of rangelands'.[33]

Dean and MacDonald's conclusions, however, are by no means the last word. A number of points require far more systematic historical research. We need to look more carefully at the impact of state regulation and changing farming strategies. Nor are numbers the only factor at play. Sheep were, on average, bigger over the last few decades of the twentieth century and gave a

<hr/>

[32] W. R. J. Dean and I. A. W. MacDonald, 'Historical Changes in Stocking Rates of Domestic Livestock as a Measure of Semi-arid and Arid Rangeland Degradation in the Cape Province, South Africa', *Journal of Arid Environments*, 26 (1994), 281–98.

[33] Dean and MacDonald, 'Historical Changes in Stocking Rates', 281.

higher yield of wool and meat. Overall, they may not have been eating less. And, as will be illustrated below, the decline in small-stock numbers on Cape farms has been accompanied by a rise in the number of other animals. The final section expands on these points, and reiterates the argument for a stabilization of the veld.

Environmental Regulation, Conservationist Ideas, and Farming Strategies

At various moments in the twentieth century the South African state enacted far-reaching measures for environmental regulation, and initiated propaganda drives to encourage conservation. Some of the momentum provided by the Drought Commission, a frequent point of reference, was sustained in the Soil Erosion Advisory Council and the 1932 Soil Erosion Act (Chapter 7). By 1945 £2.5 million pounds had been spent under this initiative, largely on the construction of small dams, but also to subsidise contour works. During this period the Department of Agriculture found some support at the highest levels of government. Smuts, Deputy Prime Minister from 1934 to 1939, then Prime Minister to 1948, had a wide botanical knowledge and a well-known appreciation of nature. In 1934 he had given a stirring address to parliament linking patriotism, love of the land, and conservationism; he was reported as saying 'erosion is the biggest problem confronting the country, bigger than any politics'.[34] At the end of 1939 a dedicated Division of Soil and Veld Conservation was established in the Department of Agriculture to co-ordinate such activities as pasture research, weed eradication, and erosion control. It was placed under the energetic leadership of Dr J. C. Ross, a South African-born official who, like du Toit and Thornton before him, brought great conviction to his task.

A Forest and Veld Conservation Act of 1941 provided the state with powers to expropriate land and develop government schemes for erosion control, including the reservation of river catchment areas.[35] One of the priorities was Vlekpoort in Hofmeyr district in the Karoo, where conservation work had already begun on a severely eroded valley of vleis and streams.

---

[34] General J. C. Smuts, 'We are Destroying Our Country', *African Observer*, 1 (1934), 10–14; Jacks and Whyte, *Rape of the Earth*, 21.

[35] These developments are recorded in many memos by Ross and others in the main Departmental file on soil erosion (R4250): e.g. PTA LDB 3573, R4250(4), J. C. Ross, Division of Soil and Veld Conservation, to P. R. Viljoen, Sec. Ag., 15 June 1945, enclosing 'The State and Soil Conservation' forwarded to Minister.

The valley lay in the catchment of Lake Arthur, one of the two major dams irrigating the Fish river valley. Completed in 1925 at considerable cost to the state, its capacity was already reduced by half due to silting from eroded upstream farms. Eighty thousand morgen were proclaimed and Vlekpoort was subsequently cited as a major success in state-sponsored erosion control. The high Drakensberg in Natal, watershed for major rivers flowing to the Indian Ocean, was the site for a more ambitious project of protection. Private land was purchased by the state and the remaining landowners were required to develop conservation plans, with the aid of loans. By the mid-1940s two-thirds of the 1.4 million morgen held by the Department of Forestry was for watershed protection and mountain conservation, rather than for afforestation.

Ross was enthusiastic about propaganda films, which the Department of Agriculture had used in earlier years, claiming audiences of tens of thousands. A conservation film, *South Africa in Danger*, was made and shown by C. J. J. van Rensburg in a mobile cinema.[36] By 1945 the Secretary of Agriculture became worried about its success. In showing the extent of erosion, it seemed to paint too negative a picture of government inaction. In 1944 Hugh Bennett, the head of the United States Soil Conservation Service, visited South Africa on a particularly high-profile and well-publicized tour.[37] The National Veld Trust, founded in 1943, included influential figures, such as Charles te Water, High Commissioner in London, who worked closely with the Department to create public awareness. The urgency of conservation was highlighted in post-war reconstruction plans formulated by the Social and Economic Planning Council, the Committee on Reconstruction of Agriculture, and by the Native Affairs Department.

At the end of war the National Veld Trust and the Department formulated a new Soil Conservation Act, passed in 1946. Borrowing from the American example, it aimed to create district-based Soil Conservation Committees throughout the white farming districts of the country. These, aided by extension workers, would take increasing responsibility for monitoring and enforcing environmental regulation. In some respects this strategy replicated the principles of the vermin extermination campaigns by trying to mobilize farmers themselves. The Act was seen as a means of taking the conservationist message, and subsidies for conservation work, to the furthest reaches of the farmlands.

---

[36] PTA LDB 3588 R4250/9 (1).

[37] Belinda Dodson, 'Dustbowls and Dongas: Hugh Bennett's 1944 Visit to South Africa', unpublished paper presented at the Association of American Geographers' Conference (2000).

The impact of the Act, a major weapon in the state's conservationist armoury for a few decades, was uneven and, in certain respects, weak.[38] Passed in the dying years of United Party rule, it was not so enthusiastically espoused by the Afrikaner National Party after 1948. The Nationalists, with a shaky electoral base in their early years, depended heavily on the rural vote, and their supporters were not generally drawn from the more conservationist sections of the agrarian elite. District committees varied greatly in their effectiveness. Some barely functioned; some provided a further conduit for government aid to white farmers and became an object of control by local Nationalists. Yet, in districts like Graaff-Reinet, where leading farmers were committed to conservationist strategies, the Act provided a framework for more enthusiastic local action and awareness, especially in its earlier years.[39]

High agricultural commodity prices in the post-war era, and the wool bonanza of the early 1950s, facilitated further investment. In co-ordination with the extension service, over 10,000 farms were planned along conservationist lines and advice given on many more. By the 1960s the great majority of farms in the midland and eastern Cape stock-farming districts were fenced, with internal camps and dispersed water sources, and practised some form of rotational grazing. The voluntary principles embedded in the Act were, however, less successful in limiting livestock numbers. After a dip in the 1940s, stocking rates again climbed between 1950 and 1965—although not to their previous heights.

It seems likely that systems of rotation were one factor in diminishing selective grazing and reducing the effects of tramping. Moreover, while the initial decline in small-stock numbers in the mid-1960s was largely due to drought, that trend was probably sustained as the result of government intervention. A stock-reduction scheme ran for a decade from the late 1960s.[40] About 7,000 farmers, including nearly half of those in the Karoo, participated. They were paid compensation for reducing their livestock to one-third less than the carrying capacity recommended by the Department, and resting one-third of their land each year. Yields for the remaining animals did not increase as much as was expected, but small-stock numbers declined dramatically over the first few years of the scheme. It was followed by a National

[38] Delius and Schirmer, 'Soil Conservation'; J. D. Slabber, 'Die Funksioneering van Grondbewaringdistriktkomitees in 7 Geselekteerde voorligtingswyke', unpublished D.Sc. thesis, University of Orange Free State (1969); I. du T. van der Merwe, 'Die Funksioneering van Grondbewaringsdistrikskomitees in Carvarvon-Voorligtingswyk', unpublished M.Agric. thesis, University of Pretoria (1968).

[39] Interview, Walter Kingwill, Graaff-Reinet, 1994.

[40] Timm Hoffman, Simon Todd, Zolile Ntshona, and Stephen Turner, *Land Degradation in South Africa* (Department of Environmental Affairs and Tourism, Cape Town, 1999), 123.

Grazing Strategy, aimed at longer-term voluntary constraint. In 1983 the Conservation of Agricultural Resources Act moved away from some of the self-regulatory principles in the 1946 Act and laid down more stringent rules concerning the exploitation of natural resources on private land. Taken together, over the long term, there is little doubt that government measures made some impact on farming strategies and livestock numbers. The cosy relationship between organized agriculture and the apartheid state may have facilitated conservationist policies on the white rangelands.

Farmers' attitudes also changed. Many of the large-scale livestock farmers inherited their farms and came from wealthier and more educated backgrounds than earlier generations. At least some became aware of environmental issues, and regarded the stocking practices of their predecessors with some dismay. They saw their caution as having paid off in the serious droughts of the early 1990s. Most of those interviewed in the 1990s were of the opinion that the veld had stabilized or improved in their memory. Some noted, for example, that farm dams filled up more slowly because more water was being held in soil by vegetation. White farmers clearly had an interest in transmitting this view. They were aware that political transformations in South Africa could place their property rights in jeopardy. In arguing that they were good stewards of the land, they were also justifying rights to private property, and defending the technical ideas that governed their pattern of land use. At the very least, however, interviews suggest that the views and practices of individual farmers matter, and that pasture history must take into account developments on particular farms. Other factors, such as the elimination of white and black tenants, largely in the first half of the twentieth century, and the increase in farm size, which roughly doubled between the early 1950s and mid-1980s, may also have contributed to veld stabilization. The number of farming units in the Cape declined from 43,500 in 1953 to 23,000 in 1983.[41]

In responding to Dean and MacDonald's argument, we should also explore the social and economic context of falling sheep numbers. In the 1980s, and especially the 1990s, high levels of stock theft in some districts discouraged sheep farming, because they were seen as particularly vulnerable to theft. For the last few decades of the twentieth century gradually falling real prices for agricultural commodities such as wool probably contributed to such trends. I have suggested that the relationship between wool prices and sheep numbers over the century between 1830 and 1930 appears to be weak (Introduction).

---

[41] Figures from Agricultural censuses and World Bank, Agriculture and Environment Division, Southern Africa Department, 'South Africa: Agriculture Sector memorandum', unpublished paper (1993), 30.

Despite short-term fluctuations, numbers expanded through periods of high and low prices. However, there is some evidence that while sheep numbers tended to expand immediately after a fall in wool price, they stabilized during the sustained period of low prices in the last quarter of the nineteenth century. Some farmers diversified into ostriches, angoras, mutton sheep, and cattle.

In the early decades of the twentieth century investment in water, fodder, and fencing clearly played a major role in expanding livestock numbers. However, by the last couple of decades of the twentieth century investment into wool production was no longer seen as economically rewarding by many landowners, and diversification in the pastoral economy was again evident. Low wool prices played some part in the switch to Dorper mutton sheep, and, where there was sufficient water, cattle. Livestock farmers also reintroduced ostriches, for meat rather than feathers, and, in the Karoo, switched to wild-life. In sum, it would be misleading to deduce that declining sheep numbers provided clear evidence for exhausted pasturages.

A national survey of *Land Degradation in South Africa*, published in 1999, lends weight to the argument that some pastures may have improved.[42] Conservation and extension officers no longer considered the northern and eastern Karoo, site of Acock's most alarming observations, to be of particular concern. Veld in many of the key districts on which this study has focused was categorized as slowly improving. Judgements about the nature of environmental risk, and the most vulnerable sites, had changed. Within the country as a whole, the Northern Province and KwaZulu/Natal, both densely occupied by smallholders, were seen to be at highest risk.

The northern Cape was also cited as a hot-spot of environmental degradation, largely because of bush encroachment rather than erosion. The area was subject to invasion by another exotic plant from the semi-arid areas of northern America, mesquite (prosopis species). Mesquite was probably introduced in the late nineteenth century and was planted widely in the arid areas of southern Africa. By the mid-twentieth century it was regarded as 'probably among the most important fodder trees imported into South Africa', and planting was strongly encouraged by the Department of Agriculture.[43] Mesquite pods have a high nutritional value, and the seed was spread partly by grazing animals themselves so that it became naturalized in dry Karoo districts such as Britstown and Carnarvon. The tree could be pollarded to

[42] Hoffman, et al., *Land Degradation in South Africa*, pp. xii, 108; M. T. Hoffman and S. Todd, 'A National Review of Land Degradation in South Africa: The Influence of Biophysical and Socio-economic Factors', *JSAS* 26: 4 (2000), 743–58.

[43] E. E. M. Loock, 'Three Useful Leguminous Fodder Trees', *Farming in South Africa*, 2: 250 (1947), 7–12.

produce a useful wood. In some respects, changing attitudes to mesquite replicate those expressed about prickly pear in the early twentieth century. They also reflect greater concerns about indigenous vegetation and biodiversity.

Any discussion of the overall state of the veld in the Cape should also take into account further changes in land-use over the last few decades of the twentieth century. Significant areas have been taken out of agricultural production and set aside as national and provincial reserves. The area of reserved land in the Cape before 1950 was very limited, compared to the Transvaal and Natal. Aside from the Kalahari Gemsbok park, in a tongue of arid land between Namibia and Botswana, there were only three small national parks in the province. Each was proclaimed around 1930, largely to protect one rare species: the Bontebok park near Swellendam, the Mount Zebra, near Cradock, and Addo, in the Sundays river valley, to safeguard the remnant elephant herd. In the late 1930s a public campaign resulted in the formation of the Cape of Good Hope Nature Reserve at Cape Point. Some of these initiatives involved the purchase of private farmland, especially when they were extended in later decades.

The Cape provincial government established a Department of Nature Conservation in 1952 in order to provide consolidated administration for a range of proclamations and for the natural history museums in the province. As part of its brief, the Department purchased land for nature reserves.[44] The first of these was at De Hoop in the south-western Cape, which eventually included some of the estate put together by the brewing magnate Ohlsson (Chapter 6). From this period both national and provincial parks developed a new strategy, placing less emphasis on particular endangered mammal species and more on protecting typical habitats or biomes. Some municipalities collaborated by redesignating parts of their large and severely degraded commonages. Private farmland and municipal commonage were amalgamated to form the Karoo National Park near Beaufort West from the 1970s. The provincial department worked with the Graaff-Reinet municipality to establish a large reserve on parts of its old commonage.

Major new national and provincial reserves were proclaimed in the Zuurberg, with plans to splice it onto Addo, the Tankwa Karoo and Richtersveld in the arid west, the Cederberg, the Swartberg, and in the Fish river valley at Double Drift. While the Cape had no single reserve to rival the Kruger park, or the Drakensberg in KwaZulu/Natal, the provincial

---

[44] Douglas Hey, *A Nature Conservationist Looks Back* (Cape Nature Conservation, Cape Town, 1995).

authorities alone supervised over 320,000 hectares by the early 1990s. The areas removed from livestock farming had been greatly extended; in some cases, such as the Double Drift reserve, costly reclamation projects were launched to expunge invader species such as the jointed cactus.

From the 1950s a number of landowners, especially in arid and semi-arid districts, gradually switched from livestock to wildlife farming. By the end of the twentieth century wildlife farming was, along with wine, probably the most rapidly growing sector of the South African agrarian economy, and of even greater significance in relation to the area of land involved. Many live-stock farmers with large holdings had retained a limited number of antelope on their land, for hunting or aesthetic reasons. For innovators such as Walter Murray, who farmed across the main road from Wellwood at Bloemhof, an early fascination with hunting, and a trip to central Africa in the 1950s, alerted him to the possibilities of reshaping the family farming operation.[45] Ecologists were suggesting that game farming would be both more efficient and environmentally beneficial, because wildlife, long adapted to African habitats, could best exploit the natural vegetation.[46]

As the turn to game farming became more widespread from the 1970s, economic factors became more central. The provincial authorities and, after a period of uncertainty, national departments assisted in research, breeding, and the distribution of wildlife species. Landowners' legal rights over wildlife on private land were tightened. Wildlife were farmed for fresh venison and dried biltong, sometimes alongside livestock. Farms such as Bloemhof were geared towards the international market for trophy hunting, specializing in valuable antelopes. Others catered more to the considerable domestic demand for hunting. Wildlife viewing expanded on larger game farms in the Cape, which advertised themselves as malaria-free. While wildlife farming generally demanded higher perimeter fences to keep animals in, fewer inter-nal camps and water sources were necessary. Veterinary and labour costs were also probably reduced. By the late twentieth century over 2,000 farms in the Cape, perhaps 20 per cent of units in the Karoo, and 9,000 farms nationally were at least partly utilizing wildlife.[47]

The ecological implications of expanding wildlife farming have almost certainly been beneficial. By the end of the twentieth century there were probably more wild animals in the Cape than there had been for over a cen-tury, and the variety of mammals had increased. It is true that wildlife in part

[45] Interview, Walter Murray, Bloemhof farm, Graaff-Reinet, 1994.

[46] Dawn Nell, 'The Development of Wildlife Utilization in South Africa and Kenya, c.1950–1990', forthcoming University of Oxford D.Phil. thesis (2003?).

[47] Farm figures from Dawn Nell.

displaced livestock and could also be overstocked. Some farms specialized in particular species, and most discouraged predators. Nevertheless, wildlife utilized a wider spectrum of grazing resources. For example, kudu became widespread in the midland and eastern Cape, partly spreading themselves because they could leap all but the highest fences. They prefer to browse bushes that are less favoured by livestock and small antelopes. Wildlife species are not fully domesticated nor are they generally herded, so that tramping diminishes. In sum, wildlife reserves, together with changing farming strategies, have contributed to diminished pressures on the natural vegetation in extensive areas, including some of the large, privately owned farms in the Karoo and eastern Cape. They have, however, probably contributed to the concentration of landholding in the Karoo.

One further change in land use in the last few decades requires attention, because it may prove to be the most important single trend: the transfer of large commercial farms to African occupation, usually under denser settlement. A primary purpose of the 1936 Land Act and subsequent legislation was to segregate landholding by extruding black tenants from white-owned private farms, but to increase areas reserved specifically for African occupation. The process speeded up in the eastern Cape at the height of apartheid, when attempts were made to consolidate scattered blocks of land, designated as the Ciskei, into a single contiguous area. The Transkei was also extended. Hundreds of thousands of hectares, largely private farmland, was purchased by the state for this purpose. It is an irony that apartheid policies resulted in a significant transfer of land from white to black in pursuit of the chimera of independent African homelands.

Much of the land transferred was occupied in forms of customary tenure under the Tribal Authority system on which homeland rule was based.[48] Settlement and land use followed the betterment system (Chapter 10). At this point we should turn to a detailed study of betterment areas in the Ciskei to discover something about their environmental consequences. The picture has not been encouraging. Whatever their conservationist intent, the betterment schemes brought few benefits in this regard.[49] Planning, it has been argued, became increasingly formulaic, with little attention paid to local

---

[48] Luvuyo Wotshela, 'Homeland Consolidation, Resettlement and Local Politics in the Border and the Ciskei Region of the Eastern Cape, South Africa, 1960 to 1996', unpublished D.Phil. thesis, University of Oxford (2001).

[49] Hendricks, 'Loose Planning'; C. de Wet, *Moving Together, Drifting Apart: Betterment Planning and Villagisation in a South African Homeland* (University of Witwatersrand Press, Johannesburg, 1995) and 'Betterment Planning in a Rural Village in Keiskammahoek, Ciskei', *JSAS* 15: 2 (1989), 326–45.

conditions. Villagization took priority over social provision and conservation. A major problem identified in the Ciskei was the failure of fencing and the camp system in rehabilitated villages. Maintenance proved too expensive, some fences were cut, and many African livestock-owners had to, or preferred to, continue kraaling their animals. The result was that large numbers of animals were returned daily to concentrated villages rather than dispersed homesteads. Pastures, environmental conditions, and water sources in the immediate vicinity of the villages suffered.

Other processes, which were not an intended outcome of government policy, may however have produced different environmental results. In the Ciskei particularly, cultivation declined significantly in the 1980s and 1990s. Many African smallholders found that the costs of production and labour on small areas of land were prohibitive and the outcome too uncertain. Protecting crops grown on arable fields some distance from villages could also be difficult. A good deal of this arable land was left fallow, or incorporated into communal pastures. Betterment might have been more effective if it had consolidated landholdings, and secured tenure rights, around existing homesteads rather than pushing people into villages.

Since 1994, when South Africa became a non-racial democracy, the process of land transfer to African communities has continued in a new context, as part of the land reform programme. By and large, private land in the new Eastern Cape province was restituted or sold to trusts as legal owners, rather than to Tribal Authorities operating customary tenure. But in effect, some farms have been occupied by large numbers of poor families and have been recommunalized. Livestock farming has proved the most common form of land use and, with the erosion of fences and infrastructure, the environmental problems that so absorbed conservationists in the first half of the twentieth century threaten to return. It is clear from the evidence presented in this book that private landholding, and large farms, are no guarantee against environmental degradation. Nor do communal forms of tenure always produce soil erosion. Both forms of tenure require regulation, as well as sympathetic occupiers, if they are to be environmentally safe.

Protagonists of new theories of range ecology have inverted much of the earlier conservationist wisdom.[50] They suggest that rotational grazing in

---

[50] Ben Cousins, 'Livestock Production and Common Property Struggles in South Africa's Agrarian Reform', *Journal of Peasant Studies*, 23: 2–3, (1996), 166–208; C. M. Shackleton, 'Are the Communal Grazing Lands in Need of Saving?', *Development Southern Africa*, 10: 1 (1993), 65–78; Theunis D. de Bruyn and Peter F. Scogings (eds.), *Communal Rangelands in Southern Africa: A Synthesis of Knowledge* (Department of Livestock and Pasture Science, University of Fort Hare, Alice, 1998).

fenced camps may have been appropriate in systems of livestock farming where private landowners, formerly well subsidized, managed pedigree animals on large areas of land, but that fences have become too expensive for most African rural communities. Kraaling is, in this view, an inevitable and acceptable practice. Some argue that heavy, continuous grazing on communal rangelands diminishes selective use of pasturage and may not permanently alter or destroy the veld. Stud animals find it difficult to survive in such systems, but heavy stocking of poorer-quality animals can produce an output similar to a smaller number of the well bred. Output is in any event difficult to evaluate where animals have multiple uses.

Such conclusions remain contested. It may be that there is no short-term alternative on land that is being occupied by many poor families. Given the history of racially based exclusion, there is clearly an argument that very widespread access to grazing resources should take precedence over environmental safety. But the recent expansion of African pastoral farming in the eastern Cape has proved difficult to regulate, and improvements in the shape of fencing, water sources, and fodder production difficult to sustain.

The new South African state faces a dilemma in respect of pastoral land at the start of the twenty-first century. On the one hand, it is essential that land-ownership in the rural areas be de-racialized. On the other, transfer of land to communities under forms of communal tenure may result in lower productivity and in environmental costs. Cowling's vision of a recommunalized Karoo with nomads, roving flocks, and wildlife may be an attractive social scenario, but could also reintroduce great unpredictability in an area where there is some evidence of constrained exploitation, under systems of private tenure. Recent government policies of encouraging and assisting purchase by emergent black farmers, holding their land in private tenure, on units big enough to allow significant capital investment, may help to provide a solution. This may not seem the most equitable route, yet it is by no means clear that a proliferation of smallholdings, or densely occupied farms, will, in the longer term, increase overall rural wealth.

Let me conclude by returning to the themes of the Introduction. We still have limited understanding of the long-term interrelationship between animal numbers, land use, forms of tenure, state regulation, economic influences, and environmental change in South Africa. Botanical research is increasingly rich, if strongly contested. The insertion of perspectives from environmental history that systematically build in political economy, the history of ideas, as well as ecological change, has hardly begun. This book has explored some of these interrelationships, particularly the rise of environmental concern, and the strategies evolved by officials and farmers to simultaneously intensify production and combat degradation. My argument has been that conservationist ideas have had a deep history in the Cape and that intensive pastoral farming required systematic environmental understanding and management. Initially, the system of pastoral farming resulted in overexploitation of resources, but in the longer term, forms of regulation made some impact. While environmental outcomes are difficult to assess or predict, especially in the context of rapid social and economic change, the evidence from the Cape suggests that change cannot simply be described as a linear process of degradation.

A larger point emerges from this conclusion. Measuring change in terms of movement away from a pristine environment, and calling all change degradation, is of limited analytical value. Human survival necessitates environmental disturbance, nor is nature in itself static. There is no possibility of restoring a pristine environment in South Africa—or anywhere else—short of the complete abandonment of farming. Even then, earlier balances of species are unlikely to re-emerge, nor is enough known about past conditions to judge when they would be restored. In this context, a concept of environmental transformation should be set beside that of degradation. Ideas about what constitutes desirable environmental transformation inevitably include some cultural and social elements, and are informed by new scientific developments.

Yet there are patently contexts, such as the Karoo and Ciskei in the early decades of the twentieth century, where damage was being done. We require a concept of environmental degradation, and it is important to find ways of making judgements about particular outcomes. My approach has been to study the history of conservationist ideas and policies as a central theme. This can tell us something about their significance in the past, and also enrich our understanding of present dilemmas.

BIBLIOGRAPHICAL NOTE

Government Published Papers

A major source for this book are printed government papers, reports, and commissions, mostly published as annexures to the Debates and Proceedings of the Cape and Union parliaments and the Transkeian general council. There is a huge volume of material that has relevance to environmental themes, and only a limited quantity could be consulted. Government papers are numbered in each year in various series preceded by letters. In the Cape, up to 1910, the main reports and commissions have G. numbers; select committees have S.C. numbers. After Union the letters U.G. precede numbers and dates. The Cape parliament generally published the evidence taken by commissions and committees. This practice stopped soon after Union.

Commissions, manned by officials, politicians, and others considered expert, sometimes travelled widely, taking evidence from a range of people. Substantial landowners and progressive farmers were most prominent in the documents used here, but evidence was on occasion taken from poorer whites, and where it was considered relevant, from black witnesses. Select committees tended to be more limited exercises, sitting in Cape Town, and consulting parliamentarians and experts.

These printed papers were particularly important for Chapters 3–6 and 8. I have not listed government publications in the Select Bibliography. Full references are provided in the first citations and their numbers used for subsequent references.

The figures and other statistical references have been drawn from annual Statistical Registers, the Cape and Union censuses (1855, 1865, 1875, 1891, 1904, 1911, 1921, 1936), various government reports, and the annual Agricultural Census after 1918. The Cape Department of Agriculture, established in 1887, published an *Agricultural Journal* from 1889, and this was continued, in various forms, mostly on a monthly basis, after Union. (There are some gaps.) These volumes are a treasure-trove of material on a vast range of agricultural topics, including environmental questions. While they often present the official view, or research by officials, they also include talks, articles, and letters by farmers, politicians, and non-government experts, including material drawn from other English-speaking countries.

Archives

Archives were used especially for the period after Union when there is less detail in printed material. The records of the Department of Agriculture in the National Archives, Pretoria, especially the PTA LDB (Secretary of Agriculture) and PTA CEN (Division of Entomology) series, proved valuable for Chapters 7 and 8. For Chapter 10 on the Transkei and Ciskei, I used the papers of the Secretary of Native

Affairs in Pretoria (PTA NTS), the Chief Magistrate's series in Cape Town and Umtata (CA CMT and UTA CMT), and especially the Secretary of the Transkeian General Council (UTA TTA) in Umtata. Unpublished minutes of evidence taken by some Commissions are housed in the Pretoria archives, but I was not able to find those of the Drought Investigation Commission (1923), which would have been the most important for this book.[1] A little material was drawn from the pre-Union Cape Departments of Agriculture (CA AGR), and of Forestry (CA FCE), as well as the Cape Provincial Secretary (CA PAS) and Cape Town municipality (CA 4/CT) series after Union (especially for Chapter 6).

A wide range of non-governmental papers have been consulted for particular purposes. The archives of the Royal Botanical Gardens at Kew proved very useful in tracking down nineteenth-century botanical networks (Chapters 2–3). The most important private collections were the Rubidge family papers, kept on the farm Wellwood, in Graaff-Reinet (Chapter 9 and *passim*) and the papers of H. S. du Toit, kept by his son in Pretoria (Chapter 7). Other relevant papers were housed at the Cory Library and Albany Museum in Grahamstown, and the South African Public library in Cape Town.

Published Primary Texts

Many key texts written by travellers in the eighteenth and nineteenth centuries have been published, or republished, in the van Riebeeck Society and similar series. I used Sparrman, Gordon, Thunberg, Burchell, and others for Chapters 1 and 2, with much enjoyment, and was intrigued to find how often they were referred to by later writers. There are published versions of a number of English-speaking settler diaries or reminiscences, although these are uneven in scope and quality. I used especially publications drawing on the Collett (Chapter 1) and Atherstone (Chapter 2) papers, which contain a wealth of information on nineteenth-century settler experiences.

Magazines and Newspapers

Given the time-span covered by this book, it was impossible to consult magazines and newspapers systematically. I explored the *Eastern Province Monthly Magazine* and *Cape Monthly Magazine* for 1856–61 and for the early 1870s, when they included a number of relevant articles. For the rest, most of my references to newspapers and magazines come from cuttings found in various archival series and personal papers. Thorough reading of rural newspapers could provide detailed local material for environmental history and livestock management.[2] The *Farmer's Weekly*, published from 1911, could be an equally valuable source.

---

[1] Beinart, 'Missing Minutes of Evidence'.
[2] Tamarkin's forthcoming study of the scab crisis in the 1890s uses these sources extensively.

Farm Visits and Interviews

It was initially my intention to use some oral material, and interviews were conducted during the 1990s, partly for other purposes. Between 1993 and 1995 I interviewed about fifteen Karoo and eastern Cape farmers on historical topics and talked to officials at Grootfontein and elsewhere. During 1993 I interviewed about twenty-five farmers, as well as officials at Glen College, when researching a project on environmentally safe land reform in the Free State.[3] This gave me a little insight into the history of farming strategies and conservation legislation. Subsequent research (1994–5) on land reform in the new Eastern Cape province took me to a number of farms, and former Ciskeian districts, which greatly increased my familiarity with the terrain, environmental conditions, and history of the area. Earlier interviews in Herschel district (1986) and in Pondoland (1977, 1982, 1989) have informed my approach to Chapter 10. However, as research and writing progressed, starting with Chapter 6 on jackals, and I went back rather than forward in time, it proved difficult to integrate the oral material. For this reason, I decided not to engage in further systematic interviewing for the book and little reference has been made to the interviews.

I hoped, at an early phase of research, to weave in the histories of perhaps three farms in different ecological zones. To this end I visited Pitlochrie (Sephton family) and Avoca (Orpen family) farms in Barkly East district, and Carnarvon (Halse family) in Sterkstroom—all of which have useful written records. However, the Wellwood material (Rubidge family, Chapter 9) proved so rich that I decided to concentrate on this, and the emerging focus and shape of the book, as well as constraints of space, precluded development of other examples.

Secondary Sources

Three main bodies of historiography have provided a backdrop to research: South African agrarian history; comparative material on environmental history, especially in the United States and Australia; and that on colonial science, conservation interventions, and African resistance. I have consulted some recent scientific publications where these were important to my argument, for example, on jackal behaviour (Chapter 6) or on range ecology (Chapter 11), but it would have been difficult to cover a wide range of current scientific interpretations of the many environmental questions explored.

In addition to some classic texts, such as the writings of P. J. van der Merwe on the trekboer (Chapters 1 and 2), and valuable recent research I have found unexpected riches in a wide range of older books and articles on local history in the Cape. These include the work of professional historians, such as K. W. Smith's *History of Graaff-Reinet*, as well as popular histories and reminiscences, such as Eve Palmer's, *Plains of*

[3] W. Beinart, 'Farmers' Strategies and Land Reform in the Orange Free State', *Review of African Political Economy*, 61 (1994), 389–402.

the Camdeboo, Guy Butler's, *Karoo Morning*, Jane Meiring's study of *Sundays River Irrigation*, and Lawrence Green's *Karoo*. Such volumes—and there are a number of others—give considerable insight into the social world of English-speaking farms and rural villages, but they tend to be uncritical, especially in respect of the political and racial order that sustained the agrarian elite.

SELECT BIBLIOGRAPHY OF
SECONDARY SOURCES

ACOCKS, J. P. H., *Veld Types of South Africa Memoirs of the Botanical Survey of South Africa no. 40* (Pretoria, 1975, second edn.).

ANDERSON, D., and R. GROVE (eds.), *Conservation in Africa: People, Policies and Practices* (Cambridge University Press, Cambridge, 1987).

ANDERSON, P. R., 'The Human Clay: An Essay in the Spatial History of the Cape Eastern Frontier 1811–35', unpublished M.Litt. thesis, University of Oxford (1992).

ANNECKE, D. P., and V. C. MORAN, 'Critical Reviews of Biological Pest Control in South Africa: 2. The Prickly Pear, *Opuntia ficus-indica* (L.) Miller', *Journal of the Entomological Society of South Africa*, 41: 2 (1978), 161–88.

Anon., *Memoir of W. H. Harvey, M.D. F.R.S., etc. etc. Late Professor of Botany, Trinity College, Dublin* (Bell & Daldy, London, 1869).

APPEL, A., 'Die Geskiedenis van Houtvoorsiening aan die Kaap, 1652–1795', unpublished MA dissertation, University of Stellenbosch (1966).

ARCHER, SEAN, 'Technology and Ecology in the Karoo: A Century of Windmills, Wire and Changing Farming Practice', *Journal of South African Studies* (*JSAS*) 26: 4 (2000), 675–96.

BEINART, W., *The Political Economy of Pondoland 1860–1930* (Cambridge University Press, Cambridge, 1982).

—— 'Soil Erosion, Conservationism and Ideas about Development: A Southern African Exploration', *JSAS* 11 (1984), 52–83.

—— 'The Missing Minutes of Evidence to the Drought Investigation Commission (U.G.49-1923), with Notes on Commission Archives', *Archive News* (South Africa), 39: 1 (1996), 11–21.

—— 'Men, Science, Travel and Nature in the Eighteenth and Nineteenth Century Cape', *JSAS* 24 (1998), 775–99.

—— 'African History and Environmental History', *African Affairs*, 99 (2000), 269–302.

—— and C. BUNDY, *Hidden Struggles in Rural South Africa* (James Currey, London, 1987).

—— and P. COATES, *Environment and History: The Taming of Nature in the USA and South Africa* (Routledge, London, 1995).

—— P. DELIUS, and S. TRAPIDO (eds.), *Putting a Plough to the Ground: Accumulation and Dispossession in Rural South Africa, 1850–1930* (Ravan Press, Johannesburg, 1986).

BOLTON, GEOFFREY, *Spoils and Spoilers: A History of Australians Shaping their Environment* (Allen & Unwin, Sydney, 1992).

BRADLOW, EDNA and FRANK (eds.), *William Somerville's Narrative of his Journeys to the Eastern Cape Frontier and to Lattakoe 1799–1802* (van Riebeeck Society, Cape Town, 1979).

BROCKWAY, LUCILLE, *Science and Colonial Expansion: The Role of the British Royal Botanic Garden* (Academic Press, New York, 1979).

BROWN, JOHN CROUMBIE, *Reboisement in France* (H. King, London, 1876).

—— *Water Supply of South Africa and Facilities for the Storage of It* (Oliver & Boyd, Edinburgh, 1877).

—— *Management of Crown Forests at the Cape of Good Hope under the Old Regime and under the New* (Edinburgh, Oliver & Boyd, 1887).

BROWN, KAREN, 'The Conservation and Utilisation of the Natural World: Silviculture in the Cape Colony, *c*.1902–1910', *Environment and History*, 7 (2001), 427–47.

BUNDY, COLIN, *The Rise and Fall of the South African Peasantry* (Heinemann, London, 1979).

BURCHELL, WILLIAM J., *Travels in the Interior of Southern Africa* (Batchworth Press, London, 1953); reprint of 1822–4 edn.

BUTLER, GUY (ed.), *The 1820 Settlers: An Illustrated Commentary* (Human & Rousseau, Cape Town, 1974).

BUTLER, G., *Karoo Morning: An Autobiography 1918–35* (David Philip, Cape Town, 1983).

Cape of Good Hope, *Appendix to the Report of the Geological Surveyor presented to Parliament in June, 1859* (Government Printer, Cape Town, 1860).

CARRUTHERS, JANE, 'Game Protection in the Transvaal', unpublished Ph.D. thesis, University of Cape Town (1988).

—— 'Towards an Environmental History of Southern Africa: Some Perspectives', *South African Historical Journal*, 23 (1990).

—— *The Kruger National Park: A Social and Political History* (Natal University Press, Pietermaritzburg, 1995).

CHARMAN, ANDREW, 'Progressive Elites in Bunga Politics: African Farmers in the Transkeian Territories, 1904–1946', unpublished Ph.D. thesis, University of Cambridge (1998).

COHEN, ALAN, 'Mary Elizabeth Barber: South Africa's First Lady Natural Historian', *Archives of Natural History*, 27 (2000), 187–208.

COLLETT, JOAN, *A Time to Plant: Biography of James Lydford Collett, Settler* (Joan Collett, Katkop, Cradock, 1990).

COUSINS, BEN, 'Livestock Production and Common Property Struggles in South Africa's Agrarian Reform', *Journal of Peasant Studies*, 23: 2–3, (1996), 166–208.

CRAIS, CLIFTON, *The Making of the Colonial Order: White Supremacy and Black Resistance in the Eastern Cape, 1770–1865* (Witwatersrand University Press, Johannesburg, 1992).

CRANEFIELD, PAUL F., *Science and Empire: East Coast Fever in Rhodesia and the Transvaal* (Cambridge University Press, Cambridge, 1991).

CROSBY, ALFRED, *Ecological Imperialism: The Biological Expansion of Europe, 900–1900* (Cambridge University Press, New York, 1986).

DAVENPORT, T. R. H., *The Afrikaner Bond, 1880–1911* (Oxford University Press, Cape Town, 1966).

DEAN, W. R. J., and I. A. W. MACDONALD, 'Historical Changes in Stocking Rates of Domestic Livestock as a Measure of Semi-arid and Arid Rangeland Degradation in the Cape Province, South Africa', *Journal of Arid Environments*, 26 (1994), 281–98.

—— and S. MILTON, *The Karoo: Ecological Patterns and Processes* (Cambridge University Press, Cambridge, 1999).

DE KLERK, M. (ed.), *A Harvest of Discontent: The Land Question in South Africa* (IDASA, Cape Town, 1991).

DELIUS, PETER, *A Lion Amongst the Cattle: Reconstruction and Resistance in the Northern Transvaal* (James Currey, Oxford, 1996).

DE WET, C., 'Betterment Planning in a Rural Village in Keiskammahoek, Ciskei', *JSAS* 15: 2 (1989), 326–45.

—— *Moving Together, Drifting Apart: Betterment Planning and Villagisation in a South African Homeland* (University of Witwatersrand Press, Johannesburg, 1995).

DIAMOND, JARED, *Guns, Germs and Steel: A Short History of Everybody for the Last 13,000 years* (Vintage, London, 1998).

DODSON, BELINDA, 'Dustbowls and Dongas: Hugh Bennett's 1944 Visit to South Africa', unpublished paper presented at the Association of American Geographers' Conference (2000).

DOOLING, WAYNE, 'Agricultural Transformations in the Western Districts of the Cape Colony, *c.*1838–1900', unpublished D.Phil. thesis, University of Cambridge (1997).

DOVERS, STEPHEN (ed.), *Perspectives on South African Environmental History* (David Philip, Cape Town, 2002).

DRAYTON, RICHARD, *Nature's Government: Science, Imperial Britain and the 'Improvement' of the World* (Yale University Press, New Haven, 2000).

DUBOW, SAUL, *Scientific Racism in Modern South Africa* (Cambridge University Press, Cambridge, 1995).

—— (ed.), *Science and Society in Southern Africa* (Manchester, Manchester University Press, 2000).

DUNLAP, THOMAS R., *Saving America's Wildlife: Ecology and the American Mind, 1850–1990* (Princeton University Press, Princeton, 1988).

—— *Nature and the English Diaspora: Environment and History in the United States, Canada, Australia, and New Zealand* (Cambridge University Press, Cambridge, 1999).

DU TOIT, HEINRICH S., *Dry-Farming* (Het Westen, Potchefstroom, 1913).

—— *The Conservation of Our Soil* (Government Printer, Pretoria, 1929).

ELPHICK, RICHARD, *Khoikhoi and the Founding of White South Africa* (Ravan Press: Johannesburg, 1985).

FITZSIMONS, F. W., *The Natural History of South African Mammals*, 4 vols. (Longmans, Green, London, 1919–20).

FLADER SUSAN L., and J. BAIRD CALLICOT (eds.), *The River of the Mother of God and Other Essays by Aldo Leopold* (University of Wisconsin Press, Madison, 1991).

GILFOYLE, DAN, 'Veterinary Science and Public Policy at the Cape Colony, 1877–1910', unpublished D.Phil. thesis, University of Oxford (2002).

GREEN, LAWRENCE G., *Karoo* (Howard Timmins, Cape Town, 1955).

GRIFFITHS, TOM, and LIBBY ROBIN (eds.), *Ecology and Empire: Environmental History of Settler Societies* (Keele University Press, Edinburgh, 1997).

GROVE, RICHARD, 'Scottish Missionaries, Evangelical Discourses and the Origins of Conservation Thinking in Southern Africa 1820–1900', *JSAS* 15: 2 (1989), 163–87.

—— *Green Imperialism: Colonial Expansion, Tropical Island Edens and the Origins of Environmentalism, 1600–1860* (Cambridge University Press, Cambridge, 1995).

HALL, HENRY, 'Modern Geographical Nomenclature, From a Colonial Point of View', *Cape Monthly Magazine*, vol. 3 (1858), 359–68.

—— *Manual of South African Geography* (Saul Solomon and Co., Cape Town, 1859).

HALL, THOMAS D., 'South African Pastures: Retrospective and Prospective', *South African Journal of Science*, 31 (1934), 59–97.

—— *Our Veld: A Major National Problem* (Association of Scientific and Technical Societies of South Africa, Johannesburg, 1942).

HARVEY, WILLIAM HENRY, *The Genera of South African Plants arranged according to the Natural System* (Juta, Cape Town, 1868).

HENDRICKS, F., 'Loose Planning and Rapid Resettlement: The Politics of Conservation and Control in Transkei, South Africa, 1950–1970', *JSAS* 15: 2 (1989), 306–25.

—— *The Pillars of Apartheid: Land Tenure, Rural Planning and Chieftaincy* (Acta Universitatis Upsaliensis, Uppsala, 1990).

HEY, DOUGLAS, *A Nature Conservationist Looks Back* (Cape Nature Conservation, Cape Town, 1995).

HOFFMAN, M. T., 'The Rationale for Karoo Grazing Systems: Criticisms and Research Implications', *South African Journal of Science*, 84 (1998), 556–9.

—— and R. COWLING, 'Vegetation Change in the Semi-arid Eastern Karoo over the Last 200 Years—Fact or Fiction', *South African Journal of Science*, 86 (1990).

—— SIMON TODD, ZOLILE NTSHONA, and STEPHEN TURNER, *Land Degradation in South Africa* (Department of Environmental Affairs and Tourism, Cape Town, 1999).

HOWISON, JOHN, *European Colonies in Various Parts of the World Viewed in their Social, Moral, and Physical Condition* (Richard Bentley, London, 1834).

JACKS, G. V., and R. O. WHYTE, *The Rape of the Earth: A World Survey of Soil Erosion* (Faber & Faber, London, 1939).

JEFFREYS, KATHLEEN M. (trans.), *The Memorandum of Commissary J. A. de Mist Containing Recommendations for the Form and Administration of the Government at the Cape of Good Hope 1802* (van Riebeeck Society, Cape Town, 1920).

JURITZ, CHAS. F., *The Prickly Pear (Opuntia): Possibilities of its Utilization* (Government Printer, Pretoria, 1920).

KANTHACK, FRANCIS EDGAR, *The Principles of Irrigation Engineering with Special Reference to South Africa* (Longmans, Green & Co., London, 1924).

KEEGAN, TIMOTHY, *Rural Transformations in Industrialising South Africa: The Southern Highveld to 1914* (Macmillan, London, 1987).

—— *Colonial South Africa and the Origins of the Racial Order* (Leicester University Press, London, 1996).

KHAN, FARIEDA, 'Rewriting South AfricaUs Conservation History: The Role of the Native Farmers Association', *JSAS* 20: 4 (1994), 499–516.

LEOPOLD, ALDO, *A Sand County Almanac* (Oxford University Press, New York, 1949).

LICHTENSTEIN, W. H. C., *Travels in Southern Africa in the Years 1803, 1804, 1805 and 1806* (van Riebeeck Society, Cape Town, 1928; first published 1812, 1815).

LISTER, MARGARET (ed.), *Journal of Andrews Geddes Bain: Trader, Explorer, Soldier, Road Engineer and Geologist* (van Riebeeck Society, Cape Town, 1949).

LIVINGSTONE, DAVID, *Travels and Researches in South Africa* (The Amalgamated Press Ltd., London, 1905).

MABIN, ALAN, 'The Underdevelopment of the Western Cape, 1850–1900' in W. James and M. Simons (eds.), *The Angry Divide* (David Philip, Cape Town, 1989), 82–93.

MCCRACKEN, JOHN, 'Experts and Expertise in Colonial Malawi', *African Affairs*, 81: 322 (1982).

MACKENZIE, JOHN, *The Empire of Nature: Hunting, Conservation and British Imperialism* (Manchester University Press, Manchester, 1988).

MACLEOD, R., 'On Visiting the "Moving Metropolis": Reflections on the Architecture of Imperial Science', *Historical Records of Australian Science*, 5 (1982), 1–16.

MACOWAN, P., 'Prickly Pear in South Africa', *Royal Gardens, Kew, Bulletin of Miscellaneous Information* (London, 1888), 165–73.

MAGER, ANNE KELK, *Gender and the Making of a South African Bantustan: A Social History of the Ciskei, 1945–1959* (James Currey, Oxford, 1999).

MATHIE, NERINA, *Man of Many Facets: Atherstone, Dr. W. G. 1814–1898, Pseudo-Autobiography* (Grocott & Sherry, Grahamstown, 1998).

MEIRING, JANE M., *Sundays River Valley: Its History and Settlement* (A. A. Balkema, Cape Town, 1959).

MELLVILLE, ELINOR, G. K., *A Plague of Sheep: Environmental Consequences of the Conquest of Mexico* (Cambridge University Press, New York, 1994).

MEREDITH, D. (ed.), *The Grasses and Pastures of South Africa* (Central News Agency, Cape Town, 1955).

MIDDLETON, KAREN, 'Who Killed "Malagasy Cactus"? Science, Environment and Colonialism in Southern Madagascar (1924–1930)', *JSAS* 25: 2 (1999).

MIGHETTO, LISA, *Wild Animals and American Environmental Ethics* (University of Arizona Press, Tucson, 1991).

MURRAY, COLIN, *Black Mountain: Land, Class and Power in the Eastern Orange Free State 1880s–1980s* (Edinburgh University Press, Edinburgh, 1992).

NELL, DAWN, 'Wildlife Alternatives: Wildlife Utilization and Approaches to the History of Wildlife in Africa', unpublished chapter for her forthcoming University of Oxford thesis (2003?).

NEVILLE, D. E., 'European Impacts on the Seacow River Valley and its Hunter-Gatherer Inhabitants, AD 1770–1900', unpublished MA thesis, University of Cape Town (1997).

NEWTON-KING, SUSAN, 'The Enemy Within: The Struggle for Ascendency on the Cape Eastern Frontier, 1760–1800', unpublished Ph.D. thesis, University of London (1992).

—— *Masters and Servants on the Cape Eastern Frontier* (Cambridge University Press, Cambridge, 1999).

NOBLE, J., *Descriptive Handbook of the Cape Colony: Its Conditions and Resources* (J. C. Juta, Cape Town, 1875).

NOBLE, RODERICK (ed.), *The Cape and Its People and Other Essays* (J. C. Juta, Cape Town, 1869).

OUDTSHOORN, F. P. VAN, *Gids tot Grasse van Suid-Afrika* (Briza publikasies, Pretoria, 1994).

PALMER, EVE, *The Plains of the Camdeboo* (Fontana, London, 1974).

PAYNE, JILL, 'Re-Creating Home: British Colonialism, Culture and the Zuurveld Environment in the Nineteenth Century', unpublished MA thesis, Rhodes University (1998).

PETTEY, F. W., 'The Biological Control of Prickly Pears in South Africa', *Union of South Africa, Department of Agriculture and Forestry, Scientific Bulletin*, 271 (Government Printer, Pretoria, 1948).

PLAYNE, SOMERSET, *Cape Colony; Its History, Commerce, Industries and Resources* (Foreign and Colonial Compiling and Publishing Co., London, 1910–11).

PLESSIS, JEAN DU, 'Colonial Progress and Countryside Conservatism: An Essay on the Legacy of Van der Lingen', unpublished MA dissertation, University of Stellenbosch (1988).

POWELL, JOSEPH, *Environmental Management in Australia* (Oxford University Press, Melbourne, 1976).

PRINGLE, THOMAS, *Narrative of a Residence in South Africa*, vol. 1 (Empire Book Association, Brentwood, Essex, 1986).

RAMPHELE, MAMPHELA (ed.), *Restoring the Land: Environment and Change in Post-Apartheid South Africa* (Panos, London, 1991).

RAPER, PETER E., and MAURICE BOUCHER (eds.), *Robert Jacob Gordon: Cape Travels, 1777 to 1786* (The Brenthurst Press, London, 1986).

ROUX, P. W., and M. VORSTER, 'Vegetation Change in the Karoo', *Proceedings of the Grassland Society of Southern Africa*, 18 (1983), 25–9.

RUBIDGE, RICHARD, *The Merino on Wellwood: Four Generations* (privately published, Graaff-Reinet, 1979).

SCHIRMER, S., and P. DELIUS, 'Soil Conservation in a Racially Divided Society', *JSAS* 26: 4 (2000), 719–42.

SCHONKEN, J. D., *Dorre Suid-Afrika* (Nasionale Pers, Bloemfontein, 1921?).

SCHUTTE, G. J. (ed.), *Briefwisseling van Hendrik Swellengrebel Jr oor Kaapse Sake 1778–1792* (van Riebeeck Society, Cape Town, 1982).

SHAW, JOHN, 'On the Changes going on in the Vegetation of South Africa through the introduction of the Merino Sheep', *Journal of the Linnean Society*, Botanical 14 (1875), 202–8.

SHOWERS, KATE, 'Soil Erosion in the Kingdom of Lesotho: Origins and Colonial Response, 1830s–1950s', *JSAS* 15: 2 (1989).

SIM, T. R., *The Forests and Forest Flora of the Colony of the Cape of Good Hope* (Taylor and Henderson, Aberdeen, 1907).

SKEAD, C. J., *Historical Mammal Incidence in the Cape Province: The Western and Northern Cape*, vol. 1 (Cape Provincial Council, Cape Town, 1980) and *Historical Mammal Incidence* vol. 2, *The Eastern Half of the Cape Province, including the Ciskei, Transkei and East Griqualand* (Cape Provincial Council, Cape Town, 1987).

SMIT, D. L., *A New Era of Reclamation: Statement of Policy Made by Mr. D. L. Smit, Secretary for Native Affairs at a Special Session of the Ciskeian General Council at Kingwilliamstown on the 8th January, 1945* (Government Printer, Pretoria, 1945).

SMITH, ANDREW B., *Pastoralism in Africa: Origins and Development Ecology* (Hurst, London, 1992).

SMITH, KENNETH W., *From Frontier to Midlands: A History of the Graaff-Reinet District, 1786–1910* (Institute of Social and Economic Research, Grahamstown, 1976).

SOUTHEY, JOAN, *Footprints in the Karoo: A Story of Farming Life* (Jonathan Ball, Johannesburg, 1990).

SPARRMAN, ANDERS, *A Voyage to the Cape of Good Hope towards the Antarctic Polar Circle Round the World and to the Country of the Hottentots and the Caffres from the Year 1772–1776*, ed. V. S. Forbes (van Riebeeck Society, Cape Town, 1977).

STEAD, A., and E. N. S. WARREN, *Prickly Pear: Its Value as a Fodder for Sheep in Droughts and in Ordinary Times*, Union of South Africa, Department of Agriculture, Bulletin no. 4 (Government Printer, Pretoria, 1922).

STEVENSON-HAMILTON, JAMES, *Wild Life in South Africa* (Cassell, London, 1950).

TAMARKIN, M., *Cecil Rhodes and the Cape Afrikaners: The Imperial Colossus and the Colonial Parish Pump* (Frank Cass, London, 1996).

THOM, H. B., *Die Geskiedenis van die Skaapboerdery in Suid-Afrika* (Swets and Zeitlinger, Amsterdam, 1936).

—— (ed.), *Willem Stephanus van Reyneveld se Aanmerkingen over de Verbetering van het Vee aan de Kaap de Goede Hoop 1804* (Van Riebeeck Society, Cape Town, 1942).

THOMAS, KEITH, *Man and the Natural World: Changing Attitudes in England 1500–1800* (Penguin, Harmondsworth, 1985).

THOMPSON, GEORGE, *Travels and Adventures in Southern Africa* vol. 1 (van Riebeeck Society, Cape Town, 1967).

THUNBERG, CARL PETER, *Travels at the Cape of Good Hope 1772–1775*, ed. V. S. Forbes (van Riebeeck Society, Cape Town, 1986).

TODD, JAN, *Colonial Technology: Science and the Transfer of Innovation to Australia* (Cambridge University Press, Cambridge, 1995).

VAN DER MERWE, N. J., 'The Jackal', *Fauna and Flora*, 4 (1953).

VAN DER MERWE, P. J., *Die Noortwaartse Beweging van die Boere voor die Groot Trek (1770–1842)* (W. P. van Stockum, The Hague, 1937).

—— *Trek: Studies oor die Mobiliteit van die Pioneersbevolking aan die Kaap* (Nasionale Pers Beperk, Kaapstad, 1945).

—— *The Migrant Farmer in the History of the Cape Colony 1657–1842*, trans. Roger B. Beck (Ohio University Press, Athens, 1995).

VAN DUIN, P., and R. Ross, *The Economy of the Cape Colony in the Eighteenth Century* (Leiden, Centre for the History of European Expansion, 1987).

VAN SITTERT, LANCE, ' "The Seed Blows about in Every Breeze": Noxious Weed Eradication in the Cape Colony, 1860–1909', *JSAS* 26: 4 (2000), 655–74.

VENTER, P. J., 'An Early Botanist and Conservationist at the Cape: The Reverend John Croumbie Brown, Ll.D., F.R.G.S., F.L.S.', *Archives Year Book for South African History* (1952), vol. II, 279–93.

WALLACE, ROBERT, *Farming Industries of Cape Colony* (P. S. King and Son, London, 1896).

WILLCOCKS, W., *Report on Irrigation in South Africa* (Johannesburg, 1901).

WILSON, F., and M. RAMPHELE, *Uprooting Poverty: The South African Challenge* (David Philip, Cape Town, 1989).

WILSON, M., and L. THOMPSON, *The Oxford History of South Africa*, vol. 1 (Clarendon Press, Oxford, 1969).

WORSTER, DONALD, *Dust Bowl: The Southern Plains in the 1930s* (Cambridge University Press, New York, 1979).

WORSTER, DONALD, *Rivers of Empire: Water, Aridity and the Growth of the American West* (Pantheon, New York, 1985).

WOTSHELA, LUVUYO, 'Homeland Consolidation, Resettlement and Local Politics in the Border and the Ciskei Region of the Eastern Cape, South Africa, 1960 to 1996', unpublished D.Phil thesis, University of Oxford (2001).

INDEX